APR 7 '87	DATE DUE		
MAY 4 1987			
MAR 2 2 1988			
NOV 1 1 1991			
MAR 8 1997			

Under the Cloud

UNDER THE CLOUD

The Decades of Nuclear Testing

Richard L. Miller

THE FREE PRESS
A Division of Macmillan, Inc.
NEW YORK

Collier Macmillan Publishers
LONDON

The Free Press
A Division of Macmillan, Inc.
866 Third Avenue, New York, N.Y. 10022

Collier Macmillan Canada, Inc.

Printed in the United States of America

printing number
1 2 3 4 5 6 7 8 9 10

Library of Congress Cataloging-in-Publication Data

Miller, Richard L. (Richard Lee)
    Under the cloud.

    Bibliography: p.
    Includes index.
    1. Nuclear weapons—Testing.   2. Radioactive
fallout—United States.   3. United States—History—
1945–   I. Title.
U264.M55   1986   363.1'79   86-4651
ISBN 0-02-921620-6

Credits

I acknowledge with thanks permission to include in this volume quotations from: Stanley
Blumberg and Gwinn Owens, *Energy and Conflict: The Life of Edward Teller* (G. P. Putnam's
Sons); Corinne Browne and Robert Munroe, *Time Bomb* (William Morrow and Co.); Citizen's
Call; Leslie J. Freeman, *Nuclear Witnesses* (W. W. Norton Co.), reprinted from *Nuclear Wit-
nesses, Insiders Speak Out*, by Leslie J. Freeman, by permission of W. W. Norton Company,

94153

To my mother, Ruth E. Miller,
and
to the memory of my father, Lee Miller

The first difficult trick in life is to choose the right parents;
after that, everything is easy and anything is possible. My
heartfelt thanks to you both. I shall be eternally grateful to
have known you.

Contents

Acknowledgments

I would like to express my appreciation to:

—Janet Gordon of Citizen's Call, Martha Bordoli Laird, Joe Fallani, Ken Clark, and the director of the National Association of Atomic Veterans, Wanda Kelly. No written account can adequately convey the gravity of their experiences, living in the shadow of nuclear testing.

—G. Sue Ladd of the Defense Nuclear Agency (DNA), David Warriner and Martha DeMarr of Reynolds Electric and Engineering Company (REECO), and Greg Cook, Phil Krey, and Howard Beck of the Department of Energy (DOE), as well as Dr. Belton Burrows and Dr. Ed Martell— without their help and suggestions the book would have been impossible.

—The librarians of Grand Marais, Minnesota; Scottsbluff, Nebraska; Goldsboro, North Carolina; Wheeler, Texas; Danbury, Connecticut; Paris, Missouri; Coeur d'Alene, Idaho; Old Town, Maine; Nashua, New Hampshire; and Longview, Wisconsin.

—Ken Werner and Kenneth Bowman, former technical book editors at Macmillan, who originally reviewed the manuscript.

—Free Press editor Edward Rothstein, who surgically trimmed the initial colossus down to manageable size, no easy task.

—Copyeditor Sarajane Herman, who went through the manuscript word . . . by . . . word. Sarajane, bless your heart, many times did you rescue this writer.

—Editing supervisor Edith Lewis and editorial assistant Norma Fritz, without whose help the publication date would have been 2086.

—Tony Baronowski, who somehow made the maps suitable for printing.

—Dr. Carl Johnson, who reviewed the manuscript for technical accuracy regarding medical matters.

—Oscar Mulhern, radiation specialist–math wizard, who reviewed the manuscript regarding radiation matters.

—John Barrett, Norma Sandowski, Dianne Long, Steve Long, Jerry Hamilton, and Bobbie Bounds, who reviewed the manuscript for readability.

Thanks also to: Jack Rickman of the *Houston Chronicle*, Georgia S. Cohen, William Overgaard (and Rudy), and Paula Wycoff for their encouragement and suggestions.

Special thanks to the best military history professor in the civilized world, Dr. Leslie Anders, both for his careful review of the manuscript and for his encouragement.

Without the trajectory maps there would have been no book. Special thanks to Robert List, Lester Machta, Philip W. Allen, and the personnel of the U.S. Weather Bureau.

A book cannot be written in a vacuum. To those stellar talents who have preceded me in this subject I owe a debt of gratitude: Roger Rappoport, Thomas H. Saffer, Orville Kelly, John Fuller, Peter Wyden, Corinne Browne, Robert Munroe, Peter Pringle, James Spigelman, Harvey Wasserman, Neil Solomon, David Bradley, William Manchester, Ferenc Morton Szasz, Zhores Medvedev, John McPhee, Bernard J. O'Keefe, and, of course, Paul Jacobs. The toughest acts to follow are still the best to follow.

No one on earth is more single-minded, mean-tempered, or impossible than an author in the midst of a manuscript. Heartfelt appreciation to those who, though bored to tears, *still* provided encouragement: Dianne and Steve Long, Connie Marcus, Mike Gaeth, Sharon Miller, Stephanie Wood, and Deborah Jackson.

And, for always, deep appreciation to the girl from Windsor; you know who you are. From January 28 on, you were absolutely essential to both the author and the book, kid.

RICHARD L. MILLER
December 12, 1985

I

PRELUDE

It is called the Teller Light, a flicker of fluorescence lasting no more than a microsecond. The result of gamma rays and neutrons coursing through molecules of air, it is the first visible evidence that nuclear material has achieved supercritical status. At the Nevada Test Site, 63 miles north of Las Vegas, it is a sign that the experiment is going as planned.

A photo taken of the Teller Light on this morning in early spring would show a tall, thin tower bathed in a soft, ethereal glow. Everything would be intact, even the source of the light: a nondescript canister, resembling a 55-gallon oil drum, placed in the middle of a metal shed at the very top of the structure.

Outside the shed a gentle breeze blows in from the northeast at 8 mph. At the base of the tower, 300 feet below, instruments record a barely detectable 6 mph breeze . . . from the northwest.

Two miles from the tower base, a group of soldiers kneel in the hard desert alluvium. They can't see the glow emanating from the tower; their eyes are closed tight.

It is the morning of April 25, 1953. The men are volunteers at the event known as SIMON, a nuclear detonation. Dosimeters are taped inside their shirts, hip pockets, and helmets. Some have cotton in their ears to keep out the dust: Nuclear detonations generate a lot of dust. A total of 3,000 soldiers will take part in maneuvers under SIMON's nuclear cloud. And as with maneuvers at other such events, the troops will be required to attack an objective near ground zero.

Earlier, the troops had been divided up into two Battalion Combat Teams (BCTs) for the exercise. They were to watch the fireball, wait for clearance, then attack an objective placed about 820 yards west of the tower. After capturing the objective, the soldiers were scheduled to tour the display area, which would consist of military hardware, various fortifications, and even sheep, all fitted with film badges.

As with previous shots, observers drawn from all four services observe the detonation from trenches located at what is presumed a safe distance from the tower. In the case of the April 25 burst, the observer trenches had been placed 3.66 kilometers (2.27 miles) from the hypocenter, that area on the ground directly below the blast point.

The volunteer group consists of seven army officers and one navy officer. Earlier, each had been given a pencil, a pad of paper, and some math formulas. They had calculated their expected radiation doses and determined that their location—a scant 1.8 kilometers (a little more than a mile) from the hypocenter—was safe. One officer had been given a "radiac," an instrument to measure radiation levels.[1]

Upon entering the trench earlier that morning, the soldiers had seen the spotlighted target tower glowing across the expanse of sand. Tall and thin, it closely resembled a radio station antenna. At the distance of a mile, it appeared as tall as a one-inch toothpick held at arm's length.

The day before, the 2nd Marine Corps Provisional Atomic Exercise Brigade had flown three helicopters to the Yucca Lake airstrip. According to the plan, two of the choppers would take off just prior to detonation and, hovering 11 kilometers (about 6.83 miles) from ground zero, await the shock wave. Another helicopter would, at the same time, be 17 kilometers (10.2 miles) from the tower and heading toward it.

Immediately after the blast, an unmanned, radio-controlled navy AD-2 Skyraider is scheduled to fly through the thermal updraft into the center of the mushroom. At takeoff, the drone will be controlled by radio commands from the Control Point; once airborne, control will be turned over to engineers flying nearby in a navy F8F aircraft.

No one was sure the experiment would work; therefore, the plane's course was plotted to take it away from the soldier's maneuver area. Although manned planes had flown through mushroom clouds before, none had gone into the stem-cloud junction, supposedly the area of greatest turbulence and radioactivity.

An hour before the shot, meteorologists checking the weather had noticed the beginnings of a slight wind shift. At the "business altitude" of the cloud—20,000 to 50,000 feet—the wind was from the west at a strong 30 to 50 mph.

At precisely 4:30 A.M. Pacific Standard Time, an electrical current is sent from the Control Point to the SIMON device in the tower. The charge ignites a series of detonators that in turn surrounds a shell of high-explosive material. In an instant, a sphere of plutonium placed at the center of the device is crushed to two-thirds its original size, resulting in a cascade of radiation. A picosecond later, the entire tower is bathed in the violet glow of the Teller Light.

Even in the time intervals where seconds seem like days, the Light flares briefly. In the distance, three helicopters hover above the the desert, waiting for the detonation that has already begun. One, 11 miles from the tower, is facing the Light. Higher up, six B-47 Stratojets and B-50 bombers hang in the air, frozen in tight formation at right angles to the glowing tower.

In an instant, the Teller Light is gone, replaced by a stark glare of indescribable brightness, so powerful that it can be seen 240,000 miles away, the distance from the earth to the moon. Ten miles away automatic high-speed cameras furiously record the ball of molten fire as it consumes the shed and tower: 23¼ milliseconds after detonation the brilliant isothermal sphere at the center of the explosion is "masked" by opaque, heated air.

Within seconds, the 300-foot tower is also gone; concealed beneath a huge mushroom cloud, churning upward at 170 mph. At the Control Point, the shock front from the detonation can actually be seen as it races across the ground at 85 mph. As it hits the building, the pressure wave shatters a window and a number of light bulbs.

The wave continues on, expanding in a series of concentric spheres from the hypocenter (the exact point of detonation), trailing visible rings of dust along the earth. Above the test site, a thin layer of warm air acts as a barrier, reflecting the pressure wave back to the ground in a pattern of ricochets that appear almost random. Las Vegas, only 63 miles away, is spared any shock wave at all. A motorist 20 miles east of the city, however, experiences a terrifying "thud" as the wave pounds into his automobile, severely cracking the windshield.

Eight minutes later, the cloud from SIMON hangs suspended 27,000 feet over the Nevada Test Site. Under its dusty umbrella, the troops begin their maneuvers.

After recovering from the glare and vibration, the pilots direct their aircraft toward the roiling column of smoke and dust. On the ground, the maneuvers begin as the men take the first steps of their long walk toward the "objective," now cooking in the radiation from the atomic burst. High above, the drone Skyraider races toward the cloud; seconds after penetrating the swirling mass, it flies out of control and crashes a short distance from the epicenter.

At the volunteer trench, navy captain Robert Hinners is temporarily blinded by the flash. Six seconds later, upon regaining his eyesight, he notices his radiac instrument behaving in a disturbing manner. The needle of the instrument is pegged at 100 roentgens/hour, representing an exceptionally high level of radiation—500 roentgens/hour for one hour is considered lethal.

With a minute, however, the needle drops back to 20 to 25 roentgens/hour. At the same time, some of the volunteers notice something disturbing about the huge dust column now towering above them: It is beginning to lean toward the volunteer trench. Within minutes the area will be under heavy fallout.

Clambering out of the 5-foot-deep trench, Hinners notices the needle of his radiac again twitch to the right: 40 roentgens/hour.

To the east, the Battalion Combat Team has begun experiencing problems of their own. Approaching the 1.8-kilometer line, they notice a distinct rise in the radiation level. At 2.5 roentgens, they decide to retreat to their own trenches a little over a mile south. With any luck, the walk will take only 15 minutes.

At the opposite side of the display, the western Battalion Combat Team makes it to the objective, then begins to tour the area only to be halted at the 1.8-kilometer line. The radiation levels are much too high. The soldiers are noncommittal; what with the dust and all, there isn't much to see anyway.

The volunteers, however, had already been there. Using their radiacs as guides—and finding "hot spots" as high as 50 roentgens/hour or more—the men had walked from their trench to the display area, looked around briefly, and then headed for the nearest road. After walking about 400 yards through the postshot haze, they are met by trucks that take them to the main trench area a mile to the south.[2]

Above them, helicopter pilots trying to avoid the smoke and dust column run into patches of "hot" air where the radiation intensity is 50 roentgens/hour or more. Though it would take an exposure of ten hours at this level to be considered lethal, the pilots still attempt to maneuver away from these zones. Twenty minutes after the detonation, one pilot finally lands his chopper at a point 1.8 kilometers west of the hypocenter. A member of the survey team climbs out, radiac in hand, and begins walking through the haze toward ground zero. At half a mile from the tower base, the instrument registers a relatively cool 10 roentgens/hour.

Monitors, however, had detected much higher radiation levels elsewhere, at altitude: A river of radiation 5 miles long, a mile wide, and 300 roentgens/hour strong had been detected heading east toward the little town of St. George, Utah.

Within minutes of receiving this information, the Civil Aeronautics Administration bans for 3½ hours all flights above 25,000 feet between Las Vegas and Tonopah, Nevada, and between Ogden, Utah, and Grand Junction, Colorado.

In an unprecedented move, Atomic Energy Commission monitors set up roadblocks on U.S. Highway 90 between Alamo, Nevada, and Las Vegas and on U.S. Highway 93 between Las Vegas and St. George, Utah. Two hundred and fifty cars are checked with radiation meters and geiger counters. Forty vehicles, including—as luck would have it—a Greyhound bus, are found to be contaminated with fallout from SIMON.[3]

By the time the wedge of radiation has crossed into Utah and Arizona, it is 80 miles wide with the center located near the three-state junction. Three hours after the shot, radiation levels at St. George, Hurricane, and Zion National Park are recorded at 0.02 roentgen/hour, about thirteen times the ground zero level of a previous detonation, code-named DIXIE.

Monitors will eventually find fallout from SIMON distributed heavily among a number of small farming communities in southern Utah. Other areas in Utah receiving fallout are Monument Valley and Snow's Canyon, the former a favorite site of movie director John Huston, the latter the eventual site of the Howard Hughes movie epic *The Conqueror*, starring John Wayne.[4,5]

While SIMON's mushroom fans out over the south, the lower section—the debris from its lower level, the stem—takes a more northerly course, floating over Salt Lake City, Utah; Casper, Wyoming; Omaha, Nebraska; and Davenport, Iowa. Areas of precipitation push some of the nuclear debris even farther north: On April 28, 1953, Huron, South Dakota, receives fallout. On the ground, the unstable radioactive atoms transform, disintegrating into lighter, slightly more stable elements. With each disintegration comes at least one burst of radiation: X ray, beta, gamma. Instruments on the ground that day in Huron noted that the radioactive material on the ground was disintegrating at a rate of 1,750 atoms per second per square foot. That same day, a hugh section of the Midwest, from Idaho to Ohio, was covered by fallout. Each square foot of that area was covered by fallout that averaged—over one day's time—500 disintegrations per second.

The official report from the Atomic Energy Commission, dated May 6, 1953, stated: ". . . The large amounts of debris associated with [SIMON], coupled with relatively slow-moving trajectories will undoubtedly result in the continued presence of fallout in much of the United States for several days thereafter."[6]

The mushroom from SIMON had been caught in a fast-moving air current moving west to east. The lower level, representing the main stem, drifted along at 10,000 feet and moved northeast over Utah and Wyoming. Then it tracked due east, crossing Nebraska, Iowa, Illinois, Indiana, Ohio, West Virginia, and Virginia, and left the country just north of Norfolk.

The 18,000-foot trajectory, representing the upper stem and lower levels of the mushroom, meandered southeast to Lukfin, Texas, before taking a sharp turn to the northeast. Upon reaching the vicinity of Franklin, Pennsylvania, it took a turn for the southeast, finally exiting the country over Rehoboth Bay in Delaware.

The 30,000-foot trajectory, representing the middle section of the cloud, took a southern route, passing over Beaumont, Texas; New Orleans, Louisiana; and Orlando, Florida.

The topmost section of SIMON's nuclear cloud, entrained in a fast-moving river of air, headed southeast for Vicksburg, Mississippi, where it was caught in a pressure trough, changed course, and began a slow curve to the northeast, passing over Birmingham, Alabama; Roanoke, Virginia; and Harrisburg, Pennsylvania, at a speed of 100 knots.

The thunderstorm was first reported by the weather station at the Albany, New York, airport at 5:54 P.M. Eastern Standard Time. The storm was severe, and cloud tops were expected to tower above 40,000 feet—the same altitude as the incoming packet of air containing the radioactive debris.[7]

The storm continued for three hours, finally ending at 8:15 P.M. on April 27. When it was over, a significant amount of the radioactive debris from SIMON had been washed from the sky and was now on the streets of Albany and Troy, New York.

The next morning, physics students at Rensselaer Polytechnic Institute in Troy, New York, noticed that their Geiger counters were acting strange. Everything outside the building seemed radioactive. The ground, the walls of the building, trees—everything was emitting radiation. The students were astonished to find that exposed surfaces all across their campus were radioactive. Atomic Energy Commission (AEC) scientists examining the area three days later decided that the Albany-Troy area had received a fallout that was transforming at a rate of 16 million disintegrations per minute per square foot . . . or 1,800 disintegrations per second per each square inch.

An area thousands of miles from the epicenter was hotter than some areas of the Nevada Test Site.

Years later, physicist Ernest J. Sternglass would calculate the radiation exposure to Troy to equal "anywhere from a few hundred to a few thousand millirads . . . equivalent to a whole series of pelvic x-rays."[8]

In a confidential report, government meteorologist Robert J. List estimated the Albany-Troy exposure at a *100* million disintegrations per minute per square foot. This would equal almost *twelve thousand* radioactive atoms disintegrating—and releasing radiation—per square inch each second. In the report, List noted that similar hot spots had probably occurred prior to the SIMON test and cautioned that much higher levels were possible, particularly in the Midwest.[9] The report was classified and the testing continued.

Sternglass would go on to analyze the Albany fallout extensively, concentrating on the biological effect of radioactive isotopes brought to the ground on that day in April 1953. One particularly hot radionuclide, iodine-131, was of particular interest: It could theoretically turn up in the thyroids of milk-drinking youngsters in the exposed areas. Sternglass's calculations would eventually show increases in thyroid-associated illnesses in the Albany area. The diseases would eventually be compared with similar problems found in St. George and Cedar City, Utah, towns much closer to the test site. It had become obvious that as far as fallout exposure was concerned, distance from the test site was of small importance. Towns and cities across the entire continent were at risk.

Between 1951 and 1963 over a hundred aboveground atomic tests occurred at the Nevada Test Site. Each burst produced clouds that rose many thousands of feet, then tracked across the country, leaving a path of fallout in its wake. During the 1950s, the Atomic Energy Commission sent out planes and set up fallout monitoring stations to record the levels. Because of this, an official record exists of the paths of many of these clouds and their associated fallout levels, usually given as bursts of radiation per unit of time. Unfortunately, nothing is known of the strength or exact nature of the radiation "events," only their frequency. Thus, actual exposure levels may never be known.

While the record is flawed, the underlying fact remains: The nuclear clouds created in the Nevada desert passed not only over Utah, Nevada, and Arizona, but over the entire continent. The full significance of this fact may not be fully known for years, if ever. What *is* known, however, is that the shadow of the atomic cloud was shared by not only Nevada, but by all states, not only by St. George, Utah, but by *most* cities and towns across the country. Like the soldiers maneuvering in the desert, every person alive during the 1950s and early 1960s lived under the atomic cloud. This book is the story of how it happened and *why*.

II

THE BEGINNING

Pitchblende and Polonium

The Erz mountains in Czechoslovakia had for hundreds of years been known for two things: a high incidence of lung disease among miners; and the ore the mines produced, a dark gray, heavy mineral called pitchblende.[1] In the last five years of the nineteenth century, French scientist Henri Becquerel discovered that pitchblende possessed an unusual quality: It could fog a covered photographic plate. The researcher quickly decided that the mineral was the source of invisible "rays," perhaps similar to X rays, discovered in 1895 by W. C. Roentgen. There was, however, some debate about the source of the radiation emanating from the mineral. Roentgen's rays required an energy source; the radiation from the mineral was being emitted in the absence of any such source, even sunlight.

At first, Becquerel thought the material might somehow be storing the energy from sunlight and releasing it later. He tested his theory by enclosing the ore in a light-tight box. A few months later, the experimenter found the mineral as active as ever. Obviously, the radiation—and thus the energy source—was within the mineral itself. But was it pitchblende?

Some scientists hoped it might be a material mixed in with the pitchblende, something that could be purified through chemical means.

Two French scientists, Pierre and Marie Curie, pursued this search for pitchblende's radiation source with a vengeance. From mines near Joachimsthal, Czechoslovakia, they obtained samples of the mineral and began the slow, arduous task of distillation. Before they had finished, the Curies had processed literally tons of the dark gray material, finally isolating a fraction of a gram of two previously undiscovered substances. Both seemed to be very heavy and metallic, with a brilliant sheen that blackened quickly when exposed to the air. One of the two seemed to be softer, almost volatile. Both were able to fog covered film plates at a great distance.

One of the materials Marie named radium, from the Latin word *radius* meaning "ray." The other she christened *polonium* in honor of her native Poland.

Though the Curies didn't know it at the time, their newfound metals were at the very edge of stability, producing a variety of particles and rays on their transformation to other, more stable elements. Not only were the radiation-producing materials fogging the film, but their particles were causing transformations in the very atomic structure of the celluloid itself.

In 1902, concurrent with the Curies' experimentation, New Zealander Ernest Rutherford, working at Canada's McGill University, began a series of experiments to study the structure of the atom. By the turn of the century, scientists were in agreement on the *existence* of the atom, they just didn't know what it consisted of: Was it, as Joseph J. Thomson had theorized, a nebulous, jellylike ball of positive charge surrounding several "corpuscles" of negative charge? Or was it composed of something different? No one had seen inside the tiny particle. No one knew what, if anything, was inside the impenetrable outer shell.

By 1911, Rutherford had devised a remarkably simple method of determining if there was anything inside the atom at all. The New Zealander aimed radiation—in this case positively charged alpha particles—at a sheet of gold foil. If Thomson's model was correct, the positively charged alpha particles should all be deflected *slightly* as they passed through the diffuse, positively charged cloud of electrons found in the foil's constituent atoms. The experiment began as Rutherford aimed the alphas toward the foil.

Incredibly, the detection equipment on the other side of the gold foil began picking up alphas. The vast majority were passing through the foil as thought it weren't there. Rutherford was dumbfounded. It was as though the dense gold atoms didn't exist.

To complicate things even further, some alphas—a very few—were being scattered at acute angles, some flying off at 90 degrees, others being reflected back. It was as though they were coming into contact with *something* that had a positive charge yet was anything but cloudlike. Whatever the alphas were hitting was definitely solid. And it was found at the very center of the atom. Rutherford hypothesized that instead of being a nebulous cloud of "electricity," the atom had a structure; more specifically, it had a center, a nucleus (from the Latin *nux* meaning "nut" or "kernal") surrounded by an electron shell.[2] Two years later, a student of Rutherford's, Niels Bohr, postulated the structure of the atom, taking into account the various energy states of the electrons surrounding the nucleus. In his model, Bohr postulated electrons circling the central core in clearly defined energy states. When an electron jumps from one energy state to another, lower one, energy is released in discrete packets in the form of light, or photons. It was the beginning of the quantum theory and the first real link between the structure of the atom and the radiation emitted.

Rutherford's experiments continued, and by 1919 he found that at least part of the nucleus was composed of a particle carrying a positive charge. This he dubbed "proton" form the Greek word *protos* meaning "first."

It was not, however, until February 1932 that Englishman James Chadwick discovered that one of the components of the nucleus was an infinitesimally small, electrically chargeless bit of matter, which he called a neutron (from the fact that it carried a "neutral" charge). Since it was chargeless, it could be used by experimenters to penetrate the atom's outer electron shield. Though scientists had correctly discerned the structure of the tiny particles, no one knew what sort of mechanism, energy, or glue bound the neutrons and protons together and kept them from flying apart. There was yet only a suspicion that the radiation discovered by Becquerel was somehow involved. It would be years before the various radiations produced by the pitchblende and radium-rich minerals could be identified and linked to the various substructures of the atom. The first hints at such a connection, however, came surprisingly early, years before the Bohr model. This was in 1905 when a young ex-postal clerk, Albert Einstein, deduced that matter at rest must still "contain" energy. The second hint came eight years later, from a most unlikely source: a science fiction story.

In 1913, the great English historian and novelist H. G. Wells had published a somewhat unusual work of science fiction. Entitled *The World Set Free*, it was a novel of the future, 1930 to be exact. In the book, Wells described a new source of energy obtained through "atomic disintegration." According to the story, politics intervened and the new energy source was used to make weapons of destruction.

Where Wells had gotten his ideas no one knew; his earlier novels, such as *The Time Machine* (1895) and *War of the Worlds* (1898) often involved cataclysmic events taking place in the near future. At the time of publication, the book was received as an interesting and well-written but wholly unrealistic fantasy. Almost twenty years would pass before the fantasy began to become reality.

1932

Hungarian scientist Leo Szilard was enjoying himself at Berlin's Kaiser Wilhelm Institute. His professor was the great Albert Einstein, who had called his pupil a genius "rich in ideas." Together they drew up plans for a variety of inventions, getting their inspiration from, among other places, books of science fiction, one of which was Szilard's favorite: *The World Set Free*.

Szilard was fascinated by Wells's book and the concept of energy from the atom. Soon after reading it, he left Berlin for England and in the fall of 1933 took up residence in London's Strand Palace Hotel. He spent much of his time there soaking in the bathtub, concocting new theories and inventions. Time and again, his thoughts would return to Wells's story.

The energy *was* inside the atom. Einstein had theorized its presence, and by 1932 it was well known that the radiation emitted from certain minerals and elements originated from the various structures of the atom. Roentgen's X rays, for example, originated from within the electron cloud; alpha particles were in reality nothing more than helium atoms stripped of electrons, while gamma rays and neutrons originated from within the nucleus itself.

But could this energy be tapped, released? Perhaps, as H. G. Wells had suggested, it could be done through a process of "atomic disintegration," of somehow "splitting" the atom to free the energy inside.

Szilard thought that Lord Rutherford might be able to suggest something.

By 1932, Ernest Rutherford had taken the post of director of the Cavendish Laboratory at Cambridge. He was still widely regarded for his early work in elucidating the basic nature of the atomic nucleus; if anyone knew about the energy of the nucleus, he did.

Szilard approached the great man with trepidation. Rutherford was a versatile and ingenious experimenter, but he was not particularly strong on speculation. Earlier, he had indicated that the concept of atomic energy was "merest moonshine." After speaking with him a few minutes, Szilard realized that the director's opinions had remained unchanged. The meeting ended with the little Hungarian being "thrown out of Rutherford's office."[3]

Leo Szilard, however, had never much use for authority; Rutherford's negative reaction to his theories was just the push he needed. He *would* come up with a method, a theory that would work.

It happened not long after that. As Szilard was crossing Southampton Row, it came to him: Find an element that could be split, releasing energy—and neutrons—that would then go on to split *other* atoms, which in turn would release energy—and neutrons—and so on.

A chain reaction.

If the energy inside the uranium nucleus were released slowly, it would result in a usable power source. If released suddenly, then an explosion of truly epic proportions would result. In the book, Wells wrote of 200 cities laid waste by the "unquenchable crimson conflagrations of the atomic bombs."[4]

Was it possible?

After a few months of deliberation and refining of his concepts, Szilard took out a patent for the process. The year was 1934.

By 1938, the Nationalist Socialist party was in full control of German politics and Hitler had begun his policy of "liberation." Szilard watched the events in Europe with a deep sense of foreboding. In the five years since his patent was issued, he had refined his theoretical concepts almost to the point of Wells's 1913 science fiction.

The energy, the power, was there. Szilard, however, had never been able to determine which of the known ninety-two elements was the one that would "disintegrate." By the end of the year, someone in Berlin had identified it.

Otto Hahn was a good chemist, familiar with the various reactions expected of elements as they combined with themselves to form new and varied compounds. But in 1938, he and his assistant, Fritz Strassman, were experimenting in completely new territory as they leveled a stream of neutrons at a speck of uranium metal. Hahn had the necessary analysis equipment in place; he wanted to know just what effect such a bombardment would have on the heavy element. Would the neutrons be "absorbed" by the metal, thus making it heavier? Would it somehow corrode the target? Hahn could hardly wait for the results of the analysis.

What he found surprised him. Mixed in with the uranium target were trace amounts of something that shouldn't have been there—the light element barium. Where did it come from? Had the experiment been contaminated somehow?

Hahn checked and rechecked his technique. It had been a "clean" experiment; still the barium remained. In his report in the science journal *Die Naturwissenschaften,* Hahn wrote that "We cannot yet bring ourselves to this conclusion which is at variance with all previous experience in nuclear physics."[5]

While familiar with how atoms reacted with other atoms, Hahn's knowledge of the atom's *interior* was far from complete. This was the realm of such physicists as Dr. Lise Meitner.

Meitner, a Jew, had fled Germany and was living in Göteborg, Sweden, when Hahn's letter arrived. He asked her to "suggest some amazing explanation" for the presence of the barium. After a walk in the winter woods with her physicist nephew, Dr. Otto Frisch, Meitner came up with an answer: The heavy uranium atom had "split," forming a number of lighter elements, including barium.

Frisch took the information to Copenhagen, to the great quantum mechanics theorist, Dr. Niels Bohr, "Oh, what idiots we all have been!" Bohr replied. "But this is wonderful. This is just the way it has to be!"[6]

Finally, Szilard's fissionable element had been found: It was uranium.

Niels Bohr arrived in New York on January 16 with the news of Hahn's experiment. On January 25, 1939, in an impromptu address to the Fifth Annual Conference of Theoretical Physics, Bohr related Hahn's fission experiment, along with Meitner's conclusions. At his side, Russian-born Dr. George Gamow excitedly scratched figures and diagrams across the chalkboard. The audience was soon in an uproar. What had been scheduled was a rather mundane discussion of low-temperature physics; Bohr's unscheduled speech carried news of a major breakthrough. The atom could be split and its energy released.

One of the physicists in the audience, a friend of Szilard's, also wondered about the possibility of sustaining a chain reaction. His name: Edward Teller.

That evening, after the conference, Teller and Bohr, along with physicist Merle Tuve, met at a laboratory at the Carnegie Institute's Department of Terrestrial Magnetism. After meticulously setting up the equipment, the three physicists bombarded a chunk of uranium with neutrons. In the darkness of the lab, the oscilloscope screen recorded the infinitesimal bursts of energy from the shattered atoms and Hahn's findings were confirmed. However, one question was still unanswered: Were neutrons *also* being emitted?

Szilard was worried. All the scientific theories and experiments had begun to indicate that Wells's atomic weapon was possible. The Hungarian scientist knew that Berlin's Kaiser Wilhelm Institute contained formidable minds including Hahn and the brilliant quantum mechanics theorist Werner Heisenberg. And Adolf Hitler had invaded Czechoslovakia and shut down export from the Joachimsthal mines the year of Hahn's discovery, so now only Germany had access to that mine's uranium. Undoubtedly Hitler would put Hahn and Heisenberg to work on a bomb. Still, if neutrons weren't emitted by the fissioned atoms, a bomb would not be possible.

Szilard decided to find out. Borrowing $2,000 from a friend, the energetic little Hungarian made his way into Columbia University's Pupin Laboratory and requested permission to set up shop. The plan, he told Dr. George Pegram, dean of graduate faculties at Columbia, was to devise an experiment to learn if fissioning atoms released neutrons—which could then go on to fission other atoms and release still more neutrons. He wanted to learn if a chain reaction was possible. Pegram, however, thought the idea "too fantastic to be entirely respectable."

Szilard, however, knew what he was looking for and how to find it. Neutrons behaved in a particular manner. Szilard knew that a mixture of radium and beryllium would produce neutrons and beryllium itself would reflect them, much as a mirror reflects light. Moreoever, he knew the electronic detection equipment was sensitive enough to record their passage. He was ready.

By the afternoon of March 2, 1939, Szilard had completed setting up the equipment. Duplicating Hahn's experiments using a uranium "target," Szilard peered into the tiny television tube, waiting for the flash of light that would indicate a "fast neutron" had been emitted. Dr. Walter Zinn, Szilard's assistant in the experiment, threw the switch that energized the detection equipment. The flashes appeared on the screen. Under the onslaught of the neutrons the uranium target was disintegrating; it was releasing neutrons.

Szilard's experiment had produced an abundance of other radiation as well: The "glue" that had been holding the neutrons in place had also disintegrated, resulting in the release of high-energy packets of light and a flurry of electrons from within the nucleus. Two decades later, the terms "gamma rays" and "beta particles" would be familiar to atomic scientists concerned with radiation exposure during weapons testing. In 1939, however, Szilard only knew that the chain reaction was possible. That evening, he phoned Edward Teller with the news.[7]

While all the activity was going on in New York, German chemist Paul Harteck had been keeping a close watch on the new field of atomic physics. Like Szilard, he wondered about the military uses of the atom. In mid-1939, a letter bearing his signature arrived at Hitler's war office. The letter read: "We take the liberty of calling your attention to the newest development in nuclear physics, which in our opinion, will probably make it possible to produce an explosive many orders of magnitude more powerful than conventional ones. . . . That country which first makes use of it has an unsurpassable advantage over the others."[8]

The race to build the atomic bomb was on.

In 1934, Szilard, while living in Great Britain, had tried and failed to interest the British military in the possibility of an atomic weapon. This time he would attempt a more political route. Contact was made with Albert Einstein (who had not even considered chain reactions) and another Hungarian émigré, Dr. Eugene P. Wigner. Together they drafted a letter to President Franklin Roosevelt, stating that a chain reaction could be started artificially, and that "extremely powerful bombs of a new type" were "conceivable." The meaning was clear: Roosevelt should place in motion efforts to make such a weapon.[9]

Roosevelt, preoccupied with the crisis in Europe, was slow to act. He appointed an advisory "Uranium Committee" to study the feasibility of an atomic weapon, but it lacked both direction and any sense of urgency.

Nevertheless, Szilard, Wigner, and Edward Teller soon found themselves face-to-face with sixty-five-year-old Dr. Lyman J. Briggs, chairman of the new Uranium Committee. Their meeting with Briggs was also attended by navy commander Keith C. Hoover, an explosives expert, and army colonel Keith F. Adamson. When asked how much the "chain reactor" project might cost, Szilard guessed $6,000. The government representatives grudgingly agreed to the funding.[10]

Unknown to Szilard, Prime Minister Winston Churchill had received word that German scientists at the Kaiser Wilhelm were hard at work on an atomic weapon. England's politicians, now taking the possibility of atomic weapons very seriously, created the Military Application of Uranium Detonation (MAUD) commission. It was comprised of scientists whose task it was to determine if atomic weapons were feasible.

In the United States, meanwhile, scientists had begun studying the properties of uranium. Researchers at the University of Minnesota had managed to isolate a new isotope of uranium, U-235. Lighter than the commonly found U-238, it was also more unstable, more easily fissioned. Calculations indicated that it would be a perfect weapons material. There was just one problem: It was exceedingly rare and had to be separated from uranium ore. There was very little uranium ore anywhere in the United States, and shipments from Hitler-controlled Czechoslovakia were out of the question.

Uranium, however, was found in other places, most notably the Shinkolobwe mine in the Congo. Owned by Belgium's Union Minière du Haut Katanga, the Shinkolobwe mine produced a very high-grade ore. In August 1940, Union Minière's director, Edgar Sengier, quietly directed the Shinkolobwe mine to ship 1,200 tons of the high-grade uranium, packed in 200 steel drums, to the United States. By October 1940, the ore had left Port Lobito on its way to a Staten Island warehouse. It would remain at the secluded storage facility for two years.

In 1940, scientists in Berkeley, California, under the direction of Glenn Seaborg, isolated a man-made element that would fission even better than

U-235. They named it plutonium, for Pluto, the god of Hades. It would turn out to be the ideal weapons material.

Early that same year, science fiction writer Robert Heinlein wrote a short story entitled "Blowups Happen." In the story, a "uranium bomb" at an energy generating facility is being used to supply power to an America of the future. One of the characters in the story was a Dr. Silard.[11]

Manhattan

In 1941, England's MAUD commission concluded that atomic weapons were indeed feasible. The only problem was all of Great Britain's resources were directed toward fighting the Germans; they couldn't afford the expensive technology to make an atomic bomb. It was up to the Americans.

On December 6, President Roosevelt appointed the S-1 committee to study the feasibility of such a weapon. He asked the group to report back to him in six months. The next day, Japan bombed Pearl Harbor and the United States was at war.

In June 1942, the S-1 committee reported that, indeed, a bomb was feasible, that one could be made—at a cost of $100 million—and it could possibly be ready by July 1944. The committee further recommended the weapon be built. Roosevelt agreed. H. G. Wells's science fiction story was another step closer to reality.

In September 1942, Brigadier General Leslie Groves assumed control of the weapons project code-named Manhattan, later known as the Manhattan Project. Under Groves's direction, a huge facility was constructed at Oak Ridge, Tennessee, for the purpose of separating easily fissionable U-235 from the more commonly found U-238. Also on the plans was a reactor facility amid the lava fields of eastern Washington. Its job would be to take the U-235 and from it produce large quantities of the more fissionable plutonium.

General Groves quickly surveyed the brightest of the country's physicists and soon assigned young Berkeley scientist J. Robert Oppenheimer the task of assembling the weapons team. Together, Groves and Oppenheimer picked out the spot in the New Mexico mountains that would become the Los Alamos Laboratory.

On November 25, 1942, the federal government, for a modest price of $440,000, bought 54,000 acres of desolate land in Sandoval County, New Mexico. The area included two low mountain ranges on either side of a north–south valley named, appropriately, Jornada del Muerto—the Journey of Death. To the north and west, past Fra Cristobal Mountain, lay the towns of San Antonio and Silver City. To the east, past Skillet Knob and Mockingbird Gap, were the towns of Tularosa, Oscura, and Carrizozo.

At the north end of the Jornada del Muerto, amid the sagebrush and cactus, was a small ranch house. Owned by a family named McDonald, the little building nestled securely in the shadow of Little Burrow Peak to the south and Oscura Peak to the northeast. Two and a half years later, the government would begin construction of a 100-foot tower a scant 1,250 yards to the northwest.

In August 1943, Roosevelt met with Churchill and Canadian Prime Minister King to iron out an agreement outlining cooperation in the construction of an atomic bomb. That year, physicists, chemists, and explosives experts from all over the country began showing up at the remote site: Niels Bohr, George B. Kistiakowski, Edward Teller, Hans Bethe, all luminaries in the world of science, all at the top of their chosen field. Some—such as the quiet, nearsighted, meticulous, German-born physicist Klaus Fuchs—came via Birmingham University in Great Britain.

Fuchs, a refugee from the blustery north German city of Kiel, had left his homeland in 1933, not long after he had been thrown into a river by a Nazi gang. After emigrating to Great Britain, he began work with Birmingham University professor Rudolf Peierls. When Peierls began work with Tube Alloys, the British section of the atomic bomb project, Fuchs came along as an assistant. In November 1943, he received an invitation to travel to America to work on the Manhattan Project. Fuchs accepted, and soon found himself in the American Southwest.

Tickling the Dragon's Tail

Seven months earlier, a secret conference had been held at Los Alamos concerning the capabilities of the proposed weapon. One of the speakers was Oppenheimer:

> The destructive effect of the gadget is due to radiative effects and the shock wave generated by the explosion. . . . The shock wave effect seems to extend over the biggest area and would be, therefore, most important. The area devastated by the shock wave is proportional to a ⅔ power of the energy released and may be simply calculated by comparing the energy released with that of TNT. If the reaction would go to completion, then 50 kilograms of 25 [Uranium-235] would be equivalent to 10 tons of TNT. . . .
>
> The second major difficulty facing us is connected with the question of detonation. . . . It is important that no neutron should start a premature chain reaction. . . . Possible sources of neutrons are cosmic ray neutrons and spontaneous fission neutrons.[12]

Though the scientists were reasonably well-acquainted with the physics involved, putting the complex theories into practice was another thing entirely. The slightest miscalculation could create an enormous safety hazard for the scientists. Of particular concern was the problem of criticality.

It was known, for example, that the business end of the bomb, either plutonium or U-235, would spontaneously fission if enough of it was concentrated in one place. The reason for this was based upon the mathematical relationship between volume and surface area. Neutrons emitted from within small spheres of uranium would reach the surface before hitting many nuclei.

Neutrons randomly emitted during normal decay in larger spheres of uranium would encounter a larger number of atomic nuclei before they reached the surface than would neutrons emitted from small spheres. The greater the number of nuclei, the greater the number of neutrons emitted to strike even more nuclei.

The result could be a lethal dose of radiation to anyone standing nearby. As scientists were fond of saying, "First it goes critical, then *you* go critical." No one, however, had the slightest idea what that "critical" amount would be. To make matters worse, the critical amount seemed to vary with the shape of the uranium and whether it was in the dry state or in a water solution. For example, a dry, flat disk of uranium weighing several pounds might not fission, but if someone machined the disk into a sphere, the ratio of volume to surface area would increase, more neutrons would be available to fission, and the sphere might "go crit," suddenly heating up and turning the surrounding air blue with a furious burst of radiation. Take a tenth of that amount dissolved in water and the result might be similar— and equally lethal (because the hydrogen atoms in water slow down neutrons).

In order to make the bomb, the scientists had to know the shapes and amounts of uranium required for criticality. And young Canadian physicist Louis Slotin was given the job of finding out.

As part of his experiments, Slotin, using remote control devices, dropped uranium slugs through holes cut in the centers of other uranium slugs, then measured the radioactivity as the material briefly went supercritical. Slotin termed the procedure "tickling the dragon's tail." Later in the project he would use a screwdriver to bring two hemispheres of uranium together until the Geiger counter indicated disaster was imminent. Then, with a practiced turn of the wrist, Slotin would move the halves apart again, backing away from the brink.

Through such trial and error, Slotin and others had discovered that water slows down neutrons, making them more effective. For this reason, a given mass of uranium in solution is ten times more likely to "go crit" than when dry. Unfortunately, thanks to secrecy orders imposed by General Groves, scientists working on uranium purification at Oak Ridge were not familiar with this arcane bit of information. Their major concern was how to avoid getting burned when handling the highly corrosive uranium hexafluoride gas.

When Los Alamos scientist Richard Feynman visited Oak Ridge, he was horrified to see appreciable quantities of uranium suspended in a water solution. He strongly suggested they divide up their uranium solutions into smaller tanks.

Other problems of criticality were discovered. Very late in the project, scientists found that a sphere of plutonium, if bare, was *just* subcritical at 10½ kilograms. Place uranium or some other neutron reflector around the plutonium and the criticality drops to 6 kilograms. As with uranium, plutonium in a water solution drops the critical mass to slightly over half a kilogram. Scientists found to their dismay that when working with near-critical amounts their own bodies could reflect back neutrons, causing their experiment to run out of control. Their only protection during the hazardous crit experiments were Slotin's notes and the Geiger counters placed nearby.

There was another, more profound question that unfortunately could not be answered until the actual test: Some scientists wondered if the bomb would activate previously undiscovered natural phenomena. Some wondered aloud if the weapon might ignite the atmosphere, causing a worldwide conflagration. While Enrico Fermi jokingly bet that the weapon would set fire to the air, but only over New Mexico, the concern was still real. Very early in the program, Edward Teller, interested in a fusion explosion, had produced calculations concerning heat buildup. The figures seemed to indicate that the heat would be sufficient to set fire to the air's supply of nitrogen—in effect, turning the entire world into a fiery ball. Horrified, Oppenheimer asked Hans Bethe to go over the calculations. Bethe reported that Teller had forgotten to account for the heat absorbed by radiation. The chances of the world catching fire were only three in a million. The work continued.

Barbarossa

In Germany, the bomb project was not doing well. Hitler's military advisors, like many of their American counterparts, simply didn't believe an atomic bomb could be made. Besides, they had more pressing matters with which to contend.

Despite all appearances, the German generals had decided in late 1939 that the war in the west was going to be protracted. It would weaken just about everyone—except the Soviets. Hitler had thought differently, telling everyone that it would be over within weeks. Some generals thought Der Führer was acting like a drunkard. Others, such as Bavarian chief of staff Franz Halder, had suggested a coup d'état.

Meanwhile, Russia was busy signing peace treaties with Latvia, Estonia, and Lithuania and making threatening gestures toward Finland. Stalin sent a note to Helsinki suggesting the Finns move their frontier back to the city of Viipuri. Lake Ladoga, he complained, was only 13 miles from Leiningrad, much too close. In reply, the Finns mobilized their forces. On November 30, Russians streamed across frozen Lake Ladoga on their way toward Helsinki. They never made it.

The Finns responded with 250,000 soldiers ready for battle. The Russians soon found themselves losing heavily. First, they attempted to divide Finland in two—in failing they lost an entire army corps. Stalin assigned a new general, Marshal Semyon Budenny, who finally made it to Viipuri through a war of attrition, man for man. In March 1940, the Finns signed a peace agreement. The few miles of Finnish territory had cost the Soviets an enormous number of men.

Hitler had been fascinated by the proceedings. The Finns had been severely outnumbered yet they had *still* given the Russians a severe trouncing. The Führer decided that the Soviets were vulnerable.

On May 10, the German army marched through the low countries, and by June 5, Paris was made an open city. France was a shambles and the British were in retreat at Dunkirk. Hitler's gamble had apparently paid off. The German military machine was on a roll as the Battle of Britain began. For weeks London endured the roar of the German Ju-87 bombers.

However, Hitler had made an error by sending tactical fighters on a strategic mission. Because the German bombers were too slow, the faster but shorter-ranged fighter planes were sent to bomb England. The combination of heavy bomb payloads and small gas tanks severely compromised the maneuverability of these planes; no one wanted to waste gasoline dodging antiaircraft fire when there might be barely enough to return to friendly territory. As a result, the British antiaircraft batteries made short work of the invaders.

Then, on October 12, 1940, everything went quiet. The German blitz on England ceased. Unknown to the allies, the Führer had something new on his mind; Aufbau Ost, his buildup in the east. Remembering the trouncing the Russians had taken in Finland, Hitler had decided to take them on.

On December 18, 1940, the German High Command finalized plans for Barbarossa, the code-name for the campaign. Hitler knew that Stalin had recently purged his officer corps, knew that the Soviets had outmoded equipment and no air force. To take advantage of good weather, the attack date was set for May 18 and was to last from eight weeks to four months.

What Hitler didn't know was that the Soviets had just completed a major buildup in defense. During the previous decade, they had produced 3,000 tanks a year. By 1941, they outnumbered the Germans six to one in tanks, five to one in aircraft, and two to one in submarines.[13]

By April 1941, British agents noticed that German units were being detached from the Balkans and heading for the Russian border. When told about the movement, the Soviet ambassador to Germany, Vyacheslav Molotov, didn't believe it. In fact, he had heard a rumor that Stalin would visit Berlin. He was wrong.

On June 22, 1941, Molotov read in the Paris Sunday paper that the Panzer army had stormed through the Pripet marshes into Soviet territory. It was the 129th anniversary of Napoleon's attack of the same territory. By

June 28, the Germans had advanced an incredible 250 miles against minimal Russian resistance.

By the summer of 1941, Hitler had plunged the German High Command into a costly, two-front war. It had become clear that the Russian campaign would take much longer than planned. The German generals were aware that the great Napoleon had been defeated not by the Russians but by the terrible Russian winter, where the daily high temperatures were in the negative numbers.

In a race against time, the Germans began bombardment of Leningrad on September 1. On September 30, the Russian capital city of Moscow fell under German seige.

On October 19, the great Soviet marshal Georgi Zhukov took over the defense of Moscow. A month later, winter set in, with its contingent of snow, wind, and howling wolves. For the Germans, the eastern campaign was becoming increasingly difficult.[14]

At the Kaiser Wilhelm Institute, Werner Heisenberg was facing a dilemma. Fully aware of both the implications of a superweapon and the resistance of the German High Command, he decided to take an enormous chance. He would try to get word to his old professor, Niels Bohr, that the Germans would not be able to make the bomb. Knowing that, the Americans might slow their efforts. Perhaps an Allied atomic weapon would never get off the drawing board.

In October 1942, while the German military was bogged down outside Moscow, Heisenberg met with Bohr at the Carlsberg brewery in Copenhagen. Fearful of saying too much to his old teacher, he said too little, implying that he knew the weapons were theoretically possible and might be manufactured, although with great effort. Bohr understood Heisenberg to mean that the Germans were well on the way to actual manufacture.[15] He quickly notified his friends in the United States, and the atomic bomb project picked up steam.

For the German High Command, the military problems continued.

On December 1, Zhukov counterattacked and made short work of General Hoepner's German forces. Seven days later, the German "attack" had begun to turn into a rout as the Soviets launched a second, spirited counterattack. Things were going badly for the Germans: the supply lines were stretched thin; the troops were worn out; and thanks to the German soldiers' steel-shod jackboots, frostbite was common.[16] Back in Berlin, the generals were suggesting a phased withdrawal.

The Führer would hear none of it. Field Marshal Karl Rundstedt, the general in charge of the southern flank, almost came to blows with the Führer and was fired for his trouble. Hoepner, in charge of the aborted attack on Moscow, was busted to private.[17]

It was against this backdrop that Werner Heisenberg, along with Otto

Hahn and other scientists, met with Munitions Minister Albert Speer and Field Marshal Erhard Milch. Also present were a variety of advisors, designers, and manufacturers, including automobile designer Ferdy Porsche.

For several hours Heisenberg described how a city-destroying bomb could be made using a pineapple-sized ball of Joachimsthal uranium. Because Germany was at that point fighting a two-front war—with the Russians to the east and the Allies to the west—it would be very difficult, Heisenberg said, to compete with the Americans in the bomb effort.

Speer listened thoughtfully, then told Heisenberg he would authorize construction of air-raid shelters for the physicists' reactor so they could continue their work in safety. Hitler, however, was not interested. Rockets such as the V-1 and V-2 were the answer, not some theoretical weapon still in the minds of a few physicists. Besides, thanks to the expensive eastern campaign, money for such projects was in extremely short supply.

When no substantial help arrived from the Führer, Heisenberg knew he had been right: The prospects for a German atomic bomb looked dismal indeed.[18]

The General

Kazan is a town built on the only hill in the midst of the rolling plains of northern Russia. Founded in the fifteenth century by the Tatars, it was annexed by Russia in 1552. The slender minarets of the great Mardzhani and Apanayevskaya mosques share the skyline with the seven-story Syumbek Tower, built in the seventeenth century. Also located there is the Spasskaya Bastion, entrance to the Kazan kremlin, the great Russian fortress. To the west, across a marshy meadowland, the great Volga River winds peacefully to the sea. Eight hundred miles due east of Moscow, it was the ideal place to wait out the German attack.

Igor Vasilevich Kurchatov had spent 1941 there. A tall, gregarious physicist with a long, squared-off beard, he had worked at Kazan University, a school whose former students included Tolstoy and Vladimir Illyich Ulyanov, later known as Lenin.

Kurchatov regularly stopped in at the Kazan branch of the Soviet Academy of Sciences on Lenin Street to read the latest available information about nuclear physics. Prior to coming to Kazan, he had spent time at the Crimea State University and at the tender age of twenty-two, was asked to join the Leningrad Physical and Technical Institute. Later, when he moved to Kazan, however, he found the city more to his liking. Kazan had more of an academic flavor, was reasonably free from the troublesome bureaucracy of Moscow, and the weather was better than at Leningrad. Early in 1942, however, Kurchatov received a request from the Central Committee—that is, Stalin himself. It was an assignment that would take him to the Soviet capital: He had been asked to build an atomic bomb.

In the summer of 1942, Kurchatov arrived in Moscow looking for a laboratory. The city had been evacuated the year before, and there were a lot of empty buildings available.

He immediately began looking for scientists who had a familiarity with nuclear physics. He soon found Yulii Khariton and Yakor Zeldovich, two excellent theoretical physicists who had published articles on chain reactions.[19]

By spring of the next year, Kurchatov, along with twenty physicists and one mechanic, set up a laboratory at the Seismological Institute, located on Pyzhevski Lane. Though overflowing with ideas, stamina, and perseverance, they lacked one thing: uranium—and a coherent, mutually-agreed-upon idea of what to do with it should they ever locate any.

Inside, laboratory equipment was in short supply. In fact, throughout Russia, all equipment was scarce. The enormous arsenal that had existed prior to the German attack was gone, ten years of work had been destroyed under the onslaught of the superior German Wahrmacht. Still, the Germans had been held at bay. The Soviets were nothing if not persistent; more than 1,300 war factories along with 10 million Russians were transferred en masse to the safety of the eastern Urals. Moscow was a deserted city and the Germans were trying to starve Leningrad into submission. If Kurchatov was going to build *anything*, he would have his work cut out for him.[20,21]

Kurchatov decided to rely on foreign expertise, at least initially. He spent days poring over articles by Bohr, Szilard, and others, looking for a clue to the nature of the chain reaction. A call was made for laboratory equipment, and soon, Kurchatov expanded the operations of the laboratory on Pyzhevski Lane, Laboratory Number 1, to a deserted building on Big Kaluga Street, in the Institute of Inorganic Chemistry.

The twenty-one scientists spent long hours debating the best possible methods of bomb manufacture. Arguments broke out, which Kurchatov quelled or defused—probably with a mixture of crude language or none-too gentle persuasion, occasionally tinged with humor. He *was*, after all, in charge; the other scientists often referred to him as The General.

The major supplies of uranium were still considered to be found in the Erz mountains, an area controlled by the Germans. With little, if any, hard experimentation possible, the discussions were mostly academic, conducted at a relatively leisurely pace. It was not unlike the relaxed, well-thought-out academic debates Kurchatov had taken part in while at Kazan University. Then suddenly, in the summer of 1943, the scientists were notified that Stalin wanted results.

Military intelligence had received word—originating with a scientist working on the Manhattan Project—that the Americans were well on their way to building a workable bomb. They had the manpower and they had the materials. Curiously, the Americans had said nothing to their allies—at least no one had said anything to Stalin. For a country that had just been subjected to a surprise—and remarkably successful—invasion, the silence of the Americans was indeed ominous. Kurchatov was ordered to get busy.

A new lab site was found, this one was at Khodysenkoe Field, an artillery range half a mile from the Moscow River. Kurchatov and his scientists surveyed the area for a lab, finally deciding on a nondescript, unfinished three-story brick building that was part of the Institute of Traumatic Medicine. From the outside, it looked like anything but a weapons research center; on one side was a grove of pine trees; on the other, a potato field. Nonetheless, Kurchatov christened it with the unimaginative title of Laboratory Number 2 and set to work building the Russian atomic bomb. He was, however, fully three years behind the Americans at Los Alamos. Stalin had indicated that there was a spy hidden somewhere in the Allied bomb project, maybe the informant could send along some clues. Unknown to Kurchatov, however, the Soviets had lost track of their man. He had disappeared; to where, no one knew. In fact, the spy had left Great Britain for the United States: Klaus Fuchs, the Soviet agent, was on his way to join the Los Alamos team.

Trinity

At Los Alamos, things were running smoothly: The scientists were slowly piecing together the jigsaw puzzle of the bomb's design.

Hans Bethe, John von Neumann, Edward Teller, and the others debated the theories associated with the detonation, their chalkboard figures representative of microsecond intervals and velocities approaching the speed of light. With each new configuration design, the theorists retraced the patterns, attempting with mathematics to visualize the model and predict the outcome.

While things were calm at Los Alamos, at the "Chicago Metals Laboratory" scientists assigned the task of securing the first sustained chain reaction were worried. Applying their scientific calculations to the study of politics, Szilard and others had somehow decided that the Germans would bomb Chicago—with atomic weapons—on Christmas Day, 1943. When that didn't happen, they rechecked their calculations and decided it would take place on New Year's Day.

So concerned were the scientists during those last weeks of 1943 that some of them stayed awake until the early morning hours. At their insistence, the military had sent messages to officers in England, warning them of possible radiation emergencies.[1]

In December 1943, Dr. Klaus Fuchs showed up at Los Alamos. He was immediately put to work performing routine calculations. Within a short time, his expertise would earn him the position of liaison between the theorists and the "X" or explosive division, headed by George Bogdon Kistiakowski.[2]

Kistiakowski, an affable Russian immigrant, a member of the Harvard chemistry department, had originally thought the bomb impossible. When Harvard's president, James B. Conant, initially approached him, "Kisty" downplayed the possibilities of the weapon. Conant urged him to research the available material; a few weeks later, Kistiakowski told his boss, "It can be made to work. I'm a hundred percent sold."[3]

Upon arrival at Los Alamos, Kistiakowski's assignment was to design the conventional explosives charge that would push the fissionable materials into criticality. The task initially seemed easy. But midway through requirements changed and the problem appeared nearly unsolvable.

Slotin's criticality experiments had proven beyond a doubt that relatively small amounts of uranium would, when placed together, begin an uncontrolled chain reaction. If the critical mass was joined or "assembled" too slowly, the material would merely heat up and spray radiation for several yards in all directions—lethal to anyone very close by, but hardly a formidable weapon. The scientists had decided the critical assembly, as it was called, would have to take place within microseconds.

Early in the project, the researchers had agreed that a gun device would do the trick. They would place an explosive behind a wedge of uranium—the "bullet"—on a ramp at one end of a barrel; at the other end would be a subcritical mass of uranium—the "target." To detonate the weapon, they would simply discharge the explosive, driving the uranium bullet into the uranium target. If the "critical assembly" occurred fast enough, the weapon would explode. In November 1943, experimenters at Berkeley notified Los Alamos that U-235 released its neutrons within a thousand-millionths of a second. The rifle bomb would work. The uranium rifle bomb seemed well on its way to production.

But not everyone was satisfied with the idea. Thirty-six-year-old Dr. Seth H. Neddermeyer, a former student of Oppenheimer's, thought the rifle idea had some shortcomings. For one thing, it would probably be wasteful and inefficient. The uranium bullet would serve to disintegrate the target. If the bullet and the target were not aligned *perfectly*, the target might disintegrate *before* critical assembly could take place. The result would be a fizzle, a dud. Worse, several pounds of weapons-grade U-235 might wind up in the hands of the enemy.

What the weapon needed was a method of assuring that the target would not disintegrate, some method of keeping all the nuclear material in one place until the heat from the critical assembly drove it apart. Perhaps the material could somehow be compressed.

Implosion—that was it! The uranium could be *surrounded* by the explosive: In that way, the bomb material could be kept in one place long enough—microseconds, really—for the neutrons to do their work. In the room filled with physicists, chemists, and theorists, Neddermeyer raised his hand to speak.

Neddermeyer, unfortunately, was a terrible speaker. After stumbling through a description of a uranium sphere surrounded by a sphere of explosives, someone asked him if he knew anything *about* explosives. No, he replied, but he was sure his idea would work. Only one man in the room thought the idea had even a remote chance of survival, but it was the one who counted: Oppenheimer.

"This," he told Neddermeyer, "will have to be looked into."[4]

Shortly after that, Hans Bethe and math genius John von Neumann were given the enormous task of calculating explosion waves from a spherical charge. Von Neumann confirmed Neddermeyer's guess that implosion *would* be more economical, but he also noted that it would require unbelievable precision. In order to crush the nuclear material into critical density, the shock wave could not vary more than 5 percent. Any more than that and the core would shatter, spewing uranium or plutonium dust over a wide area. Though more economical than the rifle bomb, it required unheard-of precision, both in calculations and in manufacture.

By January 1944, the problems of the uranium rifle bomb had been worked out and forecasts predicted that, though there would be barely enough U-235, enough plutonium would be available for two bombs. Then came ominous news from the plutonium processing facility at Hanford, Washington. Scientists there, busy making fissionable plutonium-239, had detected traces of another form of plutonium, the isotope Pu-240. Experiments indicated the Pu-240 was a weapon "poison," capable of causing a premature detonation if the gun method was used. By July it became obvious: The plutonium would *have* to be used in an implosion bomb.

At Laboratory Number 2 outside Moscow, Kurchatov had received word of Los Alamos's rifle bomb. Uranium had been found on the eastern slope of the Urals near Sverdlovsk, but no method was available for extraction of the U-235. Stalin's spy at Los Alamos had indicated that the Americans were using some sort of gaseous diffusion technique, but the details were unavailable to him. Undaunted, Kurchatov carefully set up two rifles facing each other on the nearby gunnery range and began firing. Perhaps when the extraction information came in, he would have already accomplished the important ballistics studies.

Fears about the German Bomb escalated through the first half of 1944. In Europe, General Dwight Eisenhower's chief surgeon sent out a memo to field units indicating an investigation into "several instances of fogged and blackened photographic film." Another memo asked medics to report any "mild disease of unknown etiology" whose main clinical sign was leukopenia, a reliable indicator of radiation exposure.

The fears were groundless. Thanks in part to Hitler's two-front war, the German bomb project was in terrible straits. Instead of being concentrated in one place, the atomic researchers were scattered from one end of the country to the other. Some, like Baron Manfred von Ardenne and Otto Hahn, worked essentially alone in their own private laboratories.

Werner Heisenberg, Germany's Great Nuclear Hope, had assembled a small group of scientists at the small town of Hechingen, in the Black Forest. Heisenberg's group had been given a small amount of uranium and assigned the onerous task of making a nuclear pile, something that would convert the ton and a half of raw material to weapons-grade plutonium.

By the summer of 1944, Kistiakowski was working full time on the design of the explosives surrounding the nuclear core, the so-called implosion sphere. The high explosive would be in the form of shaped charges. To assure that all the blast waves arrived at exactly the same time, detonators would be arranged so that some sections would fire before others. Since the shock from the earlier explosions would have to travel through other parts of the sphere before reaching the nuclear material at the core, the high explosive was shaped in such a way as to focus the waves. John von Neumann, who worked out the mathematics, called the shaped charges "lenses." Klaus Fuchs was given the task of calculating the time of arrival of the blast waves on the central sphere, a job he performed with meticulous workmanship. Another task he would eventually be involved with would concern the calculation of the optimum height for blast effects.

Other groups were in charge of their own particular parts of the device, or "Gadget" as it came to be called.

One division of physicists worked night and day planning the configuration of the supersecret "urchin," a tiny fission "initiator" at the center of the weapon. Made of a combination of polonium and beryllium, it was designed to release a stream of fission-initiating neutrons into the plutonium immediately upon detonation.

Another group, using data obtained by Slotin's team, fabricated the tamper, a hollow sphere of uranium that would surround the plutonium core. It would act as a kind of superdense hammer, crushing the inner sphere into criticality while at the same time reflecting neutrons back to the surface of the plutonium, thus causing even more fissioning.

Plans for the device slowly took shape, followed by experiments, and, finally, by construction of the actual components.

That same year, Oppenheimer and Technical Director Kenneth Tompkins Bainbridge began scouting the western United States for the proposed blast site. Eight were under consideration: a training area near Rice, California; a remote section of Padre Island south of Corpus Christi, Texas; an army tank-testing range in the Mojave Desert; the San Luis Valley in Colorado; a mesa flat in northwest New Mexico; and last, the nearby Jornada del Muerto in southern New Mexico.

Bainbridge eventually chose the Jornada del Muerto. It was isolated, was already part of an air force bombing base, and was fairly close to Los Alamos.[5]

Bainbridge phoned Oppenehimer to inform him of the choice, then—so the story goes—Bainbridge asked him to suggest a code name for the test. Oppenheimer was said to have been reading from a book of poems by John Donne:

> *Batter my heart, three-person'd God; for, you*
> *As yet but knock, breathe, shine, and seek to mend. . . .*

"We'll call it Trinity," Oppenheimer replied.[6]

(Historian Marjorie Bell Chambers offers another explanation. Noting that Oppenheimer was Jewish but had studied Sanskrit, Chambers suggests he was referring instead to Brahma, the Creator; Vishnu, the Preserver; and Shiva, the Destroyer—the Hindu concept of Trinity. In light of Oppenheimer's subsequent comments on the morning of July 16, 1945, this explanation has the ring of truth.[7])

On April 12, 1944, America received a jolt: President Roosevelt had died of a massive stroke. His vice president—and now the new president—Harry S. Truman, had not even known of the existence of the bomb. Thirteen days later, a letter was delivered to him from Secretary of War Henry Stimson: "Within four months we shall in all probability have completed the most terrible weapon ever known in human history, one bomb of which could destroy a whole city.[8]

Also in the month of April, 1944, Heisenberg's group at Hechingen had somehow managed to scrape together some reasonably pure graphite inside a cave in an attempt to start a chain reaction.

It was too little, too late. Even before the primitive reactor could be assembled, the American 1279th Combat Engineers stormed into town. The scientists hurriedly buried the uranium in a plowed field, then stuffed research papers into a canister that they threw into a cesspool. Their project finished before it had started, the nuclear scientists departed the area on bicycles. Heisenberg headed for his hometown of Urfeld, near Munich, where he was met by Allied representatives. "If American colleagues wish to learn about the uranium problem," he huffed, "I shall be glad to show them the results of our research if they come to my laboratory."[9]

As the Trinity test date neared, rumors about atmospheric ignition spread among the test personnel. When asked, scientists had difficulty refuting them. It would be the first time anything that hot—tens of millions of degrees—would be on the surface of the earth; no one knew for sure just *what* would happen. Perhaps Teller's initial figures were correct. Perhaps the atmosphere *would* catch fire.

The researchers were certain of Klaus Fuchs's blast effects calculations: If the shot were in the kiloton range, the close proximity to the ground would inefficiently reflect much of the blast wave back to the sky. The prototype, Trinity, would be fired from a 100-foot tower; the weapon that would be used on the enemy should probably detonate at a much greater altitude, maybe twenty times that height.

Just prior to the detonation date, scheduled for July 16, Project Manager Leslie Groves ordered press releases to cover all eventualities. One of them read: "A mammoth explosion today resulted in widespread destruction of property and great loss of life."

On July 14, 1945, at eight in the morning, the Gadget began its slow trip to the top of the 100-foot steel tower erected near the Sierra Oscura in the Jornada del Muerto.

July 16, 1945

It was two hours after midnight and the scientists were worried. An hour earlier the silence of the prairie night had been broken by a familiar sound: rain falling on the tin roof of the observation post. To the west could be seen the unmistakable shimmer of heat lightning. There could be no question: After all the elaborate preparation, a thunderstorm was bearing down on the Jornada.[10]

The scientists paced back and forth. Perhaps the storm would end by morning, but one could never be sure. The stakes were high: Washington had wanted the test to coincide with President Truman's visit to Potsdam and his meeting with Churchill and Stalin. The test required good weather; otherwise the rain might "scavange" and concentrate the radioactive particles and bring them to earth over populated areas. The evacuation of northeastern New Mexico was not a pleasant proposition to consider. And now, at 2:00 A.M., a thunderstorm was bearing down on the tower. Directly beneath it, standing guard, was a very nervous Lieutenant Howard Bush.

Rising into the mist 100 feet above him, amid the crackling lightning bolts and rain, was the metal tower. Inside the dark gray cab at the top was the Gadget: 5,000 pounds of explosives surrounding plutonium and wired to precision detonators capable of responding to the slightest variances in electrical charge, all connected to the X-unit, the firing mechanism. Earlier, in a test run during an electrical storm similar to this one, a copy of the X-unit had fired spontaneously. As a result, the tower was wired with lightning arresters designed to bleed off any charge that might ordinarily be expected to accumulate.

But this was no ordinary storm. Bush watched as huge lightning bolts raced across the sky, crashing into clouds or onto the slopes of the Sierra Oscuras to the north. Earlier, Don Hornig had sat with the Gadget, reading a cheap but absorbing novel: *Desert Island Decameron*. Kistiakowski had been in and out, making last-minute checks of the detonators. Now, for the time being, only Bush was left, rifle in hand. Though not particularly familiar with the design of the weapon, he knew that the device was armed and ready to fire, waiting only for the burst of electricity from the X-unit—an X-unit similar to the one that had fired spontaneously.

Monday, July 16, 1945, at 7:00 A.M., New York radio stations WCAF and WQXR featured variety music, WOR featured news and the "Musical Clock," while Ed East and his Variety Show were on WJZ. Arthur Godfrey was opening up the hour on WABC just as WMCA opened with band music.

Two thousand miles away, the final relay switches were thrown that would connect the tower to the control site. With twenty-five minutes to go, Lieutenant Bush, along with Joe McKibbin, climbed into a jeep and drove to safety. Above them, the sky was almost clear.

Five minutes later, Sam Allison of the University of Chicago began the countdown. The test site radio had inadvertantly chosen the same frequency as a nearby station. In the darkness of the New Mexico summer morning, the Voice of America's "Star-Spangled Banner" could be heard, loud and clear.

At sixteen minutes, the first of three rockets was fired, releasing a colored flare. Five minutes until detonation. Over the test site radio, Tchaikovsky's *Serenade for Strings* poured forth as background interference through Allison's steady countdown.[11]

In Houston, at that very instant, the "Skypilot" feature had just ended on KPRC radio and "The Sunrise Serenade" was just beginning.

At 5:29:45 A.M., Allison dropped the microphone and yelled "Zero!" Such was the world in the last instant before TRINITY.

In an instant, the electrical charge raced from the capacitor to the detonators, firing the explosive "shell." Kistiakowski's "lenses" worked perfectly, sending the blast waves toward the core, crushing the uranium "hammer" and, inside it, the plutonium sphere into a tight superdense ball roughly two-thirds its original size. The nuclear material was now supercritical.

At the same instant, the "urchin" at the center of the device caved in, mixing the polonium and beryllium and sending forth into the surrounding—and extremely hot—plutonium a dense spray of neutrons bouncing through the material, fissioning nuclei and releasing still more neutrons that, upon reaching the surface of the incredibly hot sphere, would only be bounced back to it by the dense uranium tamper-reflector. Within a hundred-millionths of a second, a dense neutron cloud formed, fissioning billions of plutonium atoms with each passing picosecond. In a span of time too brief to be seen except by special cameras, a glow flickered around the cab at the top of the tower, the result of gamma and X-radiation roaring through the desert air, briefly ionizing it before heating it to millions of degrees centigrade.

Within a millionth of a second, 99 percent of the neutrons had already passed through the bomb debris and into the air beyond. But they had already done their work: The plutonium had begun its disintegration to 360 lighter isotopes of 36 different elements, releasing at the same time vast quantities of the binding energy that had once held the plutonium atoms together. For a brief instant, the ultraviolet, gamma, and X-radiation inside the shattered device exerted a pressure of several thousand tons per square inch.

The bomb material was now the core of a miniature star eleven times hotter than the surface of the sun. The metal bomb cab—with its various and sundry cables, pulleys, light bulbs, and sheet metal—was instantly engulfed by the atomic furnace and vanished, becoming the star's surface, its corona. The surrounding air, heated by ultraviolet and X-radiation well beyond 8,000 degrees centigrade, quickly formed a dense, opaque shield of glowing vapor around the fiery star that was TRINITY. Milliseconds later, the bomb debris, racing outward at thousands of miles an hour, broke through the curtain of luminous air. At the same time, the oxygen and nitrogen atoms began to cool to transparency, again revealing the turbulent, brilliant inner core of the explosion. Miles away, instruments recorded this event as a second peak of brilliance, the "second maximum."

In an instant, the ball of fire had enveloped the 100-foot tower, simply dissolving it as the pressure wave pounded the earth below with the force of a 100 million atmospheres. Below the tower, the ground literally boiled as the various components of the soil vaporized and were carried aloft in the tremendous updraft created by the atomic furnace. Within eight-tenths of a second, the fireball was as tall as the Empire State Building. Seconds later, it was a half mile wide. Observers such as Bill Caldes, stationed in a trench by a reservoir, began to wonder if it would ever *stop* growing.[12]

There were those who thought the atmosphere actually did catch fire. Santa Fe Railroad engineer Ed Lane, on his way to El Paso through Belen, thought a meteor had fallen. Others, such as Mrs. H. E. Wieselman, living 150 miles away on the Arizona–New Mexico state line, saw "the sun come up and go down again." From Albuquerque, the entire southern horizon glowed a fiery red. From Amarillo, the fire was in the west, glowing with an unearthly, greenish light.[13]

Seventy miles north of the test site, passengers abroad the Union Pacific saw the fireball.[14] Most thought it was an exploding bomber—perhaps one earlier reported lost over North Dakota had taken a wrong turn and crashed in the southwest.

Seven seconds later, the fireball, like a bubble in a pot of boiling water, began its "ballistic rise" through the atmosphere, shooting skyward at a surprising rate. By the time it had reached half a mile in height, it had turned yellow, then red. At an altitude of 4 miles the mushroom had become orange and pink. When the cloud had reached its maximum altitude, almost 7 miles high, it was a mass of roiling gray ash composed of fiercely radioactive bomb debris mixed with equally radioactive remnants of the tower, soil and just about everything the fireball had touched.

Surrounding the cloud was an odd violet glow, the kind the scientists remembered seeing inside vacuum tubes. Technical Director Bainbridge turned to Oppenheimer and remarked, "Now we're all sons of bitches." George Kistiakowski summed up the feelings of many of the observers: "I am sure that at the end of the world, in the last millisecond of the earth's existence, Man will see what we have just seen."[15]

As Oppenheimer watched the unfolding scene, a thought flashed through his mind, a passage from the Hindu Bhagavad Gita: "I am become Death, shatterer of worlds."[16]

All that was left of the tower was a few concrete stumps surrounded by a crater of green, highly radioactive glass.

That afternoon, an explanation for the explosion appeared on the front page of the *Albuquerque Tribune*: "An ammunition magazine, containing high-explosives and pyrotechnics, exploded early today in a remote area of the Alamogordo air base reservation, producing a brilliant flash and blast which were reported to have been observed as far away as Gallup, 235 miles to the north."

The world's first atomic explosion.

Aftermath

As the sun poured over the eastern horizon, the gray underside of TRINITY's ash cloud hung suspended more than a mile above the smoke-filled Jornada. Its top, almost 6 miles high, took on the peculiar orange cast of reflected sunrise as it began to lean toward the northeast, in the direction of Chupadera Mesa and the New Mexican towns of Bingham, Adobe, and Claunch.[17]

Six hours later at Potsdam, Secretary of War Henry Stimson received the news of the successful detonation. The message read: "Operated on this morning. Diagnosis not yet complete. . . ." Later, he received another message: "Doctor has just returned most enthusiastic and confident that the little boy is as husky as his big brother. The light in his eyes discernible from here to Highhold [referring to Stimson's farm near Huntington, Long Island] and I could have heard his screams from here to my farm [the sender of the cable, Stimson's aide George L. Harrison, owned a farm in Upperville, Virginia]."[18]

Truman, worried about his upcoming meeting with "Mr. Russia [Stalin] and Mr. Great Britain [Churchill]" now had the confidence he needed. Once at the conference table, Stalin grew increasingly aggressive. Perhaps remembering the surprise German invasion, the subsequent battle for Moscow, and the 900-day seige of Leningrad, he wanted to make sure nothing like that ever happened again. He wanted Austria as a buffer to the west and to the south; perhaps as a buffer for the Crimea, he wanted bases in Turkey and parts of Italy.

The Potsdam conference was beginning to turn into a poker game, and Truman had a trump card—one he decided not to show just yet. Though Churchill had been informed of the progress of the bomb, Stalin had been kept in the dark. It was late in the conference that Truman decided to make an oblique reference to the weapon. In an offhand comment to Stalin through a Russian interpreter, Truman mentioned that the United States "had a new weapon of unusual destructive force."

Stalin showed no surprise whatsoever. Instead, he replied that he was "glad to hear it" and "hoped the United States would make good use of it against the Japanese."

Truman was startled by Stalin's reply. Later, he told Churchill that Stalin had "never asked a question."

Stalin never had to. In fact, he had known more about the bomb than had Truman, having followed its progress for two years via the dispatches of Klaus Fuchs. However, he had been troubled that Truman had not told him about it in those two years. Now the United States had the weapon, and back home, their scientists were still firing rifles at each other. That evening, Foreign Minister Molotov told a nervous Joe Stalin, "We'll have to talk it over with Kurchatov and get him to speed things up."[19]

Hiroshima

While the Los Alamos scientists were congratulating themselves on the successful experiment, halfway around the world the Allies were busy hammering Japanese cities and military centers with conventional weapons. Though the plans were secret, it was obvious that a major invasion would soon take place. Admiral William Halsey, the officer in charge of softening Japanese resistance, was familiar with the plans for the invasion, code-named Olympic and Coronet. Olympic was scheduled to begin with an invasion of Kyushu by the Sixth Army on November 1, 1945. Operations Coronet would commence four months later, on March 1, 1946. Headed by the First and Eighth Armies, nine infantry divisions would make a direct assault on Tokyo.[1] Resistance was expected to be strong; many American lives would certainly be lost.

Thus, wave after wave of B-24 and B-29 bombers were dispatched to "soften" the targets. Throughout the spring and summer, the huge bombers had visited enormous destruction upon the islands. Still, intelligence reports indicated that the Japanese High Command was in no mood to surrender. Operation Olympic was only three months away. Exasperated, Halsey dispatched more and more bombers to the Japanese coast. Neither he nor any of his men had been told of any change in plans.

Mokusatsu

By August 1945, Japan was on the brink of political chaos: The Japanese navy had suffered terribly at Luzon, Okinawa, and Iwo Jima. In March, the Americans had dropped jellied gasoline on Tokyo, literally burning it to the ground. In July, the remnants of the fleet moored in Kure Harbor had been utterly destroyed. In recent months, public morale had turned from bad to worse. The mere mention of "B-san," the death-dealing B-29, was enough to send shivers of fear through anyone who had undergone the ordeal of incendiary bombing.

On the first day of June the sky over Osaka had been dark with the silver giants—509 of them, each capable of setting fire to 16 acres of the city below.[2] Over a quarter of Kobe was destroyed four days later, and there really had been no way to resist them. Even the huge 105mm cannons in place at Tokyo had resulted in just seven downed planes. What's more, there was an absence of good searchlights. The ones that worked were only effective up to 26,000 feet—good for the B-24s but worthless against B-san. In 1941, Germany had developed a very effective searchlight that was directed by radar. Unfortunately, Japanese radar was marginally reliable. Until the year before, it had been unable to determine altitude and was totally ineffective for planes flying below 9,000 or above 26,000 feet.[3]

Thousands of leaflets listing which cities would be bombed and bombed again had been dropped from planes. As one factory manager said, "[We] figured that if the enemy could announce a raid beforehand, the enemy was superior."[4]

The populace was in such retreat that a government-sponsored recording of a B-29 had been issued to teach people to recognize the sound and be able to take cover when their city's turn came around.[5]

The emperor himself had never liked the war. Thought of by his countrymen as essentially a diety, his exalted position prevented him from making public announcements *or* military decisions. At an Imperial Conference early in 1941, when his generals had proposed to him the attack on Pearl Harbor, he had condemned the mission by reading a poem he had written:

> *When I regard all the world*
> *As my own brothers,*
> *Why is it that its tranquility*
> *Should be so thoughtlessly disturbed?*[6]

Now, on July 18, 1945, Japan was on the brink of disaster. War minister General Anami Korechika, army Chief of Staff Umezu Hoshijiro and navy Chief of Staff Toyoda were clamoring that things were not as bad as they seemed, but even if they *were*, Japan would fight to the death. Intelligence reports indicated invasion was imminent.[7] There was one last chance.

At the Potsdam Conference, Churchill and Truman had sent an ultimatum to Japan calling for "the unconditional surrender of all Japanese forces." Stalin, however, had not signed the demand. Perhaps there was a glimmer of hope.

A Soviet-Japanese Neutrality Pact had been in effect for some time and had almost a year left to run.[8] Stalin had met with Churchill and Truman at Potsdam; would he help to negotiate an end to the hostilities? Hirohito's envoy to Moscow was sure that, as soon as Molotov and Stalin returned from Potsdam, they would do business. The Japanese government, trying to buy time until they could gauge the Soviet position, decided to hold off on an reply to Truman's demands. Hirohito's prime minister, Kantero Suzuki, suggested *mokusatsu*, a word with a vague meaning, close to "ignore" or "reserve a decision until later." Perhaps there would be good news from Naotaki Sato, Japan's ambassador to Moscow.

By August 2, Molotov and Stalin had long since returned from Potsdam, yet Sato wired back that he was still having a terrible time getting through to them. Worried, Foreign Minister Shigenori Togo cabled, "Since the loss of one day relative to this present matter may result in a thousand years of regret, it is requested that you immediately have a talk with Molotov. . . ."

Three day later, Molotov agreed to a conference. It would be scheduled for August 8.

The Japanese *mokusatsu* reply had since reached Washington where experts interpreted the word to mean that the Japanese government—for reasons that were unfathomable—had rejected the ultimatum. The uranium bomb, now at Tinian, would be dropped on Japan.

Scheduled date: August 6, 1945, two days before the Japanese ambassador's meeting with Molotov.

Nineteen years earlier, on the afternoon of October 2, 1926, Kyoto's Miyako Hotel had been visited by two Americans. The courtly, middle-aged diplomat and his charming wife were newcomers to Japan and they blended in with the occasional American tourist. He had recently been assigned duty as governor general of the Philippines by his employer, President Calvin Coolidge.

After checking into Room 18, the couple traveled about the city, marveling at its treasures: the Ninomaru Palace in the beautiful Niijo Castle with its many works of art; the Katsura Imperial Villa with its meticulous gardens; the Sanjusangendo, the "Hall of a Thousand Buddhas," dating from 1249. The couple promised each other they would return to this beautiful, peaceful city and its excellent hotel.

At the end of October they did return, to the same hotel. This time they stayed longer, five days. Yet even five days was not enough time to see everything; there were, after all, over 200 Shinto shrines and more than 1,500 Buddhist temples in Kyoto. The city represented the heart, the very soul of Japan.

Three years later, the American tourist arrived at the Miyako for his final visit. The year was 1929, the economy of the United States had collapsed; Wall Street was in chaos and the United States was undergoing a domestic crisis. The diplomat had just been recalled to Washington by a new employer, President Herbert Hoover, to be the country's new secretary of state. Before returning, Henry L. Stimson had decided to spend one more evening in this peaceful city.

On June 12, 1945, Henry Stimson, now FDR's secretary of war, listened intently as General Groves explained the bombing plans. The Target Committee had spent months going over data, maps, and weather forecasts in making their decision. To help in assessing effects of the nuclear weapon, they had looked for cities free from prior bombing. They had looked for cities that were of military *and* psychological importance.[9]

Their target city was thick with converted lacquer factories making explosives and rayon plants producing cellulose nitrate. The industrial section covered over 26 million square feet, which included an aircraft engine factory and the Umekoji freight yards. In addition, the choice of the target was perfect in terms of morale: With its shrines and temples, it held great religious significance to the Japanese. Destroying it would destroy their will to fight.[10]

Stimson listened to their rationale. Groves, however, had not mentioned the name of the primary target. Suspicious, he decided to ask Groves for the Target Committee report detailing the bombing plan. Groves replied that it was at his office and "it would take time to get it." Stimson was undeterred.

"I have all day. Here's a phone on this desk. You pick it up and call your office and have them bring the report over."

While they waited, Groves tried to lay the groundwork for what the report would say. Stimson finally decided to ask a direct question: What was the primary target?

"The primary is Kyoto."

"I will *not* approve that city!" was Stimson's reply.[11]

Groves was incensed. Kyoto had been his favorite target. He had pushed its bombing through the Target Committee, had a tentative authorization by General Marshall, and now, because this one old man had vacationed there a few times, the plans had to be changed.

After reading the Target Committee report, Stimson stalked over to Chief of Staff General George C. Marshall's office and suggested they talk. Kyoto would *not* be a target for the atomic bomb. Perhaps one of the others: Yokohama, Kokura, Niigata, Hiroshima.

Hiroshima would be a good military target. It hadn't been bombed before: it had several military garrisons there—25,000 troops—its Mitsubishi factory was cranking out aircraft engines and ships. And it wasn't far from Kure Harbor.

Perhaps Hiroshima.

2:00 P.M., August 2, 1945

Major General Curtis LeMay lit his cigar then strolled over to the map table in his office on Guam. With him were two very important guests: Colonel

Paul Tibbets, an excellent B-29 pilot, and his chosen bombardier, Major Thomas Ferebee. The general had some information for them.

"Paul," he said, "the primary's Hiroshima." Kokura, on the northern edge of the island of Kyushu, would be the alternate if clouds obscured the primary.

Basing his decision partly on information from General Groves, LeMay had picked Hiroshima because it was thick with munitions factories. Furthermore, Groves had said there were no POWs in the city. In addition, the scientists wanted information concerning the bomb's effects and Hiroshima had not been bombed before. It was a logical choice.

Now, what should they aim for? Before the three men were aerial photos of the city. They would need a clear target, something that Ferebee could see from 6 miles up. Ferebee leaned over the photos, then put his finger on a tiny T-shaped object in the photograph. It was near the center of the city and seemed to connect two rivers.

"That's it!" Tibbets said. "It's the most perfect AP [aiming point] I've seen in this whole damn war!"

It was the Aioi Bridge.

To help Ferebee in his aim, the bridge was only 900 yards southwest of a hugh squarish structure, Hiroshima Castle. It also held military significance: It was where the Chugoku Regional Military Headquarters was located.

Several days later, on the morning of August 6, at 2:27, Tinian time, Colonel Paul Tibbets started the engines of his B-29, the Enola Gay. As the Wright Cyclone engines came to life, he radioed the tower:

"Dimples eight-two to North Tinian Tower. Taxi-out and takeoff instructions."

Immediately, the voice of the controller crackled in his headset: "Dimples eight-two from North Tinian Tower. Takeoff to the east on Runway A for Able." At 2:45 A.M., Tibbets pushed the throttles forward.

"Let's go," he said.

Inside the plane was the world's first uranium bomb, nicknamed "Little Boy."

In Hiroshima, the mood among the Japanese citizens was not encouraging. Tokyo had predicted an American invasion within a month or two. Almost all of the major cities had been bombed except four: Kyoto, Niigata, Nagasaki, and Hiroshima. The leaflets the American had dropped the day before warned of devastation to a number of other cities: Yawata, Saga, Takayama, Akita. Ominously, Hiroshima was not on that list. It was *never* on the list. Rumors abounded that Hiroshima was being saved for a special form of destruction.

Certainly there had been nearby bombings—Kure Harbor, for instance. Word was that several B-24s had been shot down. Two crewmen were in jail, and one had landed near the Ota River and was immediately killed by fishermen. A fourth American had landed on the roof of the Mitsubishi plant, where he was thrown from the building to his death. Perhaps it was only rumor.

At 3:10 A.M., Tinian time, William "Deke" Parsons, the Los Alamos ordnance expert, kneeling in Enola Gay's bomb bay, removed the armor and rear plate and began to insert the gunpowder plug into the uranium bomb. At 6:30 A.M., Japan time, Parsons' assistant, Lieutenant Norris R. Jeppson, replaced three green "dummy" electrical connection plugs with red "live" ones.

The uranium bomb was now armed.

7:09 A.M. Hiroshima time: The weather reconnaissance plane, Straight Flush, piloted by Major Claude Eatherly, is seen by ground observers. A warning siren is sounded in the city.

Shigeyoshi Morimoto, a kite maker who was in Hiroshima on business, had come to the shopping district early. The military had asked him to design kites that could carry explosives for use against low-flying aircraft. One of the foremost kite makers from a city known for its kites, Morimoto had decided to round up some paint for a prototype he was constructing. Shortly after seven o'clock he had heard an air-raid siren. Someone had sighted American bombers. Would today be Hiroshima's turn for destruction?

For almost half an hour Morimoto and the rest of the city waited. Nothing. No distant explosions, no popping of the antiaircraft. Nothing to disturb the quiet of the morning.[12]

Then came the long siren blast that signaled all-clear. Morimoto's thoughts returned to securing paint for his kites. The time: 7:31 A.M.

7:45 A.M.: Eatherly to Tibbets: "Cloud cover less than three-tenths all altitudes. Advice: bomb primary."

8:09 A.M.: Deke Parsons, standing behind Tibbets in the cockpit, confers with him about the drop. Through the window the clouds part, revealing the center of Hiroshima.

"Do you agree that's the target?" Tibbets asks, almost formally. He knows that all conversations are being recorded.

"Yes," Parsons replies.

Tibbets keys his intercom microphone. "We are about to start the bomb run," he says calmly. "Put on your goggles."

8:13 A.M.: On the ground, a watch station east of Hiroshima sights three B-29s approaching from the east on a course to Hiroshima.

8:13.5 A.M.: At Chugoku Regional Military Headquarters the sighting report is received. The official in charge picks up the phone to call the radio station.

8:13.5 A.M.: Tibbets to bombardier Ferebee: "It's yours."
Ferebee: "I've got it."

8:15 A.M.: Several men sitting in the jail at Chugoku Regional Military Headquarters hear a school bell. It is from the Hiroshima radio station. An alert has just been received from air defense headquarters. Though blind-folded and unable to speak Japanese, the prisoners know the significance of the sound: A bombing run is expected.

Outside, on the West Parade Ground, a group of army inductees are standing with relatives. Some stop talking and glance upward to the sky. Nothing. Nothing except three tiny specks. At a very high altitude.

8:15.17 A.M.: The bomb bay doors of the Enola Gay begin to swing open. In their headsets, the pilot and bombardier hear a steady electronic tone; when the bomb has been released the tone will stop.

Almost directly beneath the plane, American POWs Roland Brissette and Ralph Neal, under guard, are emptying buckets into a cesspool near the Chugoku jail.

Ferebee, now piloting the B-29, feels the cabin shudder slightly as the drag of the bomb bay doors slows the plane's velocity.

Ferebee: "Bomb away."[13]

Then silence.

For an instant, the 4½ ton bomb is weightless, flying parallel beneath the B-29 at 200 mph. Then, almost in slow motion, it begins to drop, first parallel to the ground, then nose down, toward the heart of the city. At the end of its arc is not the Aioi Bridge, but a point on the ground, 800 feet to the southeast, between the courtyard of Shima Hospital and a concrete building housing the Fuel Distribution and Control Cooperative.

Almost directly beneath the hurtling projectile, Eizo Nomura, a clerk in the Fuel Hall Cooperative building, is told by his boss to go downstairs to retrieve a document. He walks to the stairway and begins to descend into the dank, musty, concrete basement.

At the L-shaped, three-story Honkawa Elementary School, Katsuko Horibe prepares for a teachers' meeting. Outside the room she can see the Aioi Bridge. Someone, perhaps another teacher, has stopped in the middle, leaning his bicycle against the rail.[14]

A thousand yards from the courtyard of Shima Clinic, at the Prefectural Daiichi Middle School, 150 teenaged boys and girls are milling about on the lawn, waiting for class to begin. Inside 150 more were carrying books, talking in the hallways, taking their seats in the classrooms. Near the building, at the schools open-air pool, the morning swimming class is beginning.

There must have been some who had actually seen it fall. Fifteen-year-old Misao Nagoya looked up to see an object "like a silver bird" fall toward her. "I'm going to be killed," she thought.[15] From the Hiroshima Castle, where the American POWs were held, the bomb would have been visible as a ⅛-inch-long speck in the morning sky, a dark, almost imperceptible flicker against a blue background.

Forty-three seconds after its release, Little Boy was approximately 1,890 feet over a point 22 yards east of the gate of Shima Hospital. At that point, the radar unit near the tail fins sent its electronic message to the detonators.[16]

At the Japan Broadcasting Corporation in Tokyo, the control operator suddenly noticed that the telephone line to their station in Hiroshima had gone dead. Workers clearing rubble at Kure Harbor, 12 miles away had been listening to NHK, the Japanese Broadcasting Company, announcer Masanobu Furuta: "Chugoku District Army announcement: three large enemy planes proceeding . . ." then nothing.

Hypocenter

Nineteen hundred feet over Hiroshima, a 49-foot diameter star began to form, burning with a heat of over 300,000 degrees centigrade, consuming the bomb casing and turning it into a random cloud of charged atoms. Touching the ground, the tremendous energy first made the targets radioactive, then destroyed them. Shima Clinic, directly below the atomic nova, simply turned to vapor, leaving behind only two concrete pillars. Anything made of carbon—wood, paper . . . human beings—became shadows in the oven of the hypocenter.

The blast wave struck an instant too late for any human eyewitness. The people that had been walking across the Aioi Bridge, or along the streets of Yokomachi Township; the soldiers standing guard in the jails, the prisoners—all were gone. In the chaos of the hypocenter, the atomic hammer pounded the concrete pillars of a now-empty Shima Clinic into the ground like nails into soft wood, then traveled on.

Strangely, near the hypocenter there seemed to be no sound. The chaos that had begun 1,900 feet overhead was somehow *beyond* the meaning of the word. Indeed, those near the detonation reported sensing nothing but a brilliant, blinding bluish light that had replaced the sky.[17]

As the expanding blast sphere touched the ground it flattened out, forming concentric circles of destruction that radiated outward from the hypocenter, past the Honkawa Elementary School, imploding windows, sending lethal shards of glass toward the occupants. The fiery pressure wave moved on over the Fuel Hall Cooperative building, turning the ground floor into an oven, incinerating everything inside.

It radiated outward past the Daiichi Middle School, searing the lawn with unimaginable heat, turning the swimming pool into a boiling cauldron.

Inside the school, the flash was followed by smoky darkness and screams as the building collapsed. The heat was instantaneous and unbearable. Instinctively, the students ran for the pool, only to find it filled with lifeless bodies. Of the 300 students at Daiichi, only 17 would survive.

The pressure wave moved on, knocking askew the stone lanterns on the Motoyasu Bridge. Then it reflected against the surface of the river back to the underside of the bridge, buckling it upward. From there, leaving a charred destruction in its wake, it crossed over to the West Parade Grounds of Hiroshima Castle on a path to the Chugoku Regional Military Headquarters.

A powerful vacuum had formed at the hypocenter—the exact centerpoint of the explosion. Material on the ground—ash, dust, everything—was gripped by an enormous updraft spiraling toward an extreme darkness where the sky had been. The sun had been completely obscured by the churning, roiling stem of the atomic mushroom. The darkness was accented by brief flashes of lightning as the electrical charges shorted across the superheated cloud. And from the darkness above came a dull, deep heart-stopping rumble. A strange odor hung in the air, a mixture of burnt hair and ozone, like an electrical motor that had become hot. And for those who were alive after the first few seconds, there was a strange, sweet *metallic* taste.[18]

At the cesspool beside the brick center building of Hiroshima Castle, where American POWs Brissette and Neal were emptying the jail toilet, there was a sudden blinding glare followed by the shock wave. By then, the wooden wing housing the jail had already been incinerated. Then came the interminable darkness. Struggling to their feet amid the rubble, they found only the gray-brown haze and fire of the base surge that was plunging the city into night, obscuring everything.

Katsuko Horibe, a scant 650 feet from ground zero, woke to a vision of fire and chaos. Severely injured by flying glass, she stumbled to the window. Outside it seemed as though a thundercloud was directly over the Shima Clinic. To the northwest, through the haze she could barely make out the shape of the Aioi Bridge. Seconds earlier, some of her colleagues were coming to school on that bridge. Now it was empty, swept bare. She saw several objects on the ground near the river. To her horror she realized they were children, bleeding and charred. What had happened?

Eizo Nomura, in the basement of the Fuel Hall Cooperative, was thrown to the concrete floor by the concussion. Beyond the stairs, the ground floor office had become a lethal target, first for gamma radiation and neutrons, then for the monstrous pressure wave. The concrete, however, had protected him from all three. Despite his location near the epicenter, he was unscathed.

Brissette and Neal, beside what was left of Hiroshima Castle, encountered only chaos. The area was enveloped in a blast furnace of hot dust and ash. Fires were springing up everywhere. To the west was the river, but debris and flames blocked the way. To avoid incineration, they eased themselves into a cesspool.

In a short time the fires in the immediate area began to subside, and the two POWs climbed out of the cesspool. Almost immediately they were recaptured.

Miraculously, they had not been burned, but the neutrons and gamma radiation had destroyed their bone marrow. Their immune system would not be able to fight off the bacteria they encountered in the cesspool. Within days, both would notice the greenish bruises that seem to come so easily, then the purplish spots signifying ruptured capillaries just beneath the skin. They would, like so many of the people exposed to the bomb's radiation, experience the constant vomiting and bloody diarrhea as their intestinal lining sloughed away. In twelve days they would be dead.[19]

It is known that twenty-four American POWs were at Hiroshima prior to the bombing. Only one survived: Thomas Cartwright, a captured pilot who had irritated his interrogators at Hiroshima, had been transferred to Tokyo.[20]

In Hiroshima, hell had come to earth. Buildings had been vaporized or shattered and the ground beneath them seared of vegetation. Trees had been stripped of limbs. There was the slow movement of those who were dying, first to water, then to the train stations. Within hours a black rain began to fall; the drops were the size of marbles, leaving a gray stain that would not wash away. Near the center of the destruction, a white ash fell that seemed to burn the skin even through clothing. And everywhere, there were the dead; charred, bloated from radiation, disfigured, unrecognizable.

Many of those seemingly untouched by the fire or the blast would eventually sicken and die, their radiation-wracked bodies unable to fight common bacteria. Many who escaped the trauma of the pressure wave would die of radiation-induced hemorrhage. The intricate internal structure of their veins and capillaries obliterated by the gamma pulse, would within days break down, unable to hold blood.

The bomb would eventually claim 130,000 lives. The lingering deaths convinced some that the Americans had dropped a bomb containing a deadly bacteria or virus. The incendiary destruction led others to believe a new type of chemical firebomb had been used against them.[21]

In Tokyo, officials at the Railway Center had discovered the telegraph lines down—the time: approximately 8:20 A.M.

As the reports came in to the police and military, it became obvious that something, perhaps something horrible, had happened to Hiroshima. *All* the lines were down. It would be five hours before the reports trickled in, confirming fears that the worst had indeed happened, that Hiroshima, for all practical purposes, no longer existed.[22]

Nagasaki

4:45 A.M., August 8, 1945, Moscow

Naotaki Sato, Japan's ambassador to Moscow, sat nervously awaiting his meeting with Vyacheslav Molotov. The situation at home had gone from bad to worse. Hiroshima had been bombed by some sort of new bomb—some scientists claimed it contained sulfuric acid or perhaps a deadly bacteria. Whatever its driving force, one bomb had totally demolished a city.[1] The Japanese prime minister had suggested that Molotov—or perhaps Stalin himself—could act as a negotiator with the Americans and British. Perhaps there could be less than total surrender. The Soviets were Japan's last hope. Molotov had, after all, moved the appointment time up from 8:00 P.M. to 5:00 P.M.

Molotov arrived shortly before 5:00, Moscow time. After the Japanese ambassador greeted Molotov in Russian, he quickly brought up the subject of mediation. Would Moscow intervene?

Molotov was brusque. Instead of letting the ambassador finish his plea, he produced a paper: "I have here, in the name of the Soviet Union, a notification to the Japanese government which I wish to communicate to you. After the defeat of Germany, Japan remains the only great power which still stands for continuation of the War. . . . In view of the above [Russia's duties to her allies] the Soviet government declares that from tomorrow, that is, from August 9, the Soviet Union will consider herself in a state of war against Japan."[2]

Sato was stunned. He knew what would happen next: The Soviets would pour across the Mongolian border into Japanese-occupied Manchuria, into Korea, perhaps take back Sakhalin Island, which the Russians had lost to Japan in 1905. Any glimmer of hope was now gone. He must cable the message to the prime minister.

At the close of the meeting, Molotov assured Sato that he still held him in the highest personal regard, and suggested that he could cable any information home, even in code. Sato returned to his office to find his telephones disconnected and his radio equipment gone.

Not quite two hours later, 1.6 million Soviet troops poured into Manchuria.[3] And at approximately the same time, on the tiny island of Tinian in the Philippine Sea, the B-29 Superfortress nicknamed Bock's Car was preparing to take off. Its destination: Kokura, on the island of Kyushu.

Bock's Car

As he taxied the lumbering Superfortress toward the end of the runway, the pilot, Major Charles Sweeney, was concerned. For takeoff under normal circumstances, a B-29 normally required 8,000 feet of runway. Tinian's four airstrips were 8,500 feet long. The round trip to Japan required a full—and heavy—load of fuel. And in the bomb bay, just 20 feet behind him, was an atomic weapon 5 feet thick and 10 feet 8 inches long: Fat Man. Sweeney was afraid Bock's Car was a shade close to being too overloaded for flight.

Other pilots had made the same mistake. The other end of Tinian's runway was littered with the wreckage of B-29s that had been too heavy for takeoff. If Sweeney couldn't get the plane off the ground, it would not be a normal crash: The atomic bomb riding with them was fully armed.

The huge, pear-shaped plutonium bomb was more complex than the uranium device and had required assembly of its sixty-four detonators prior to takeoff. At the tail of the device, near the fins, was a radar proximity fuse. At a predetermined altitude, it would trigger an electrical detonating mechanism that would then send a charge to the detonators—if everything worked well.

In the rear of the plane, just ahead of the tail section, was the radar observer's position. It was occupied this morning by Lieutenant Jacob Besar, who had been with Tibbets on his Hiroshima run. Would Bock's Car's powerful radar affect the armed Fat Man, perhaps detonating it in midair? No one was sure.

Navy commander Frederick Ashworth, on a bench near Fat Man, adjusted his seat belt. From where he sat he could make out the names and signatures of technicians chalked on the tail fins of the device. His job was to escort the bomb to its target. His assistant, Lieutenant Phillip Barnes, sat nearby watching the slowly blinking red light of a console that monitored the bomb's complex electrical devices. As long as the light remained steady, things would be fine.

Once they were airborne, that is.

Within minutes, the pilot received his clearance for the takeoff run and pushed the throttles full forward. The four Wright Cyclone 18-cylinder radial engines screamed to life with a combined thrust of 8,800 horsepower, and the 99-foot-long plane began to pick up speed. Sweeney's technique would be the same as Tibbets's: hold the plane on the ground as long as possible, then, at the last minute, pull back on the yoke, "jumping" it into the air. It would *have* to work. A crash with an armed atomic bomb would vaporize them—and probably Tinian as well.

At 3:49 A.M. local time they were airborne. In the dark, cramped cabin behind the flight deck, Commander Ashworth breathed a sigh of relief. Nearby, Barnes carefully watched the monitor box for any deviation in the rhythm of the blinking red light. By this time, Besar had turned his radar unit on, yet the bomb's detonator was ignoring it. So far, so good. Only 1,400 miles to the target: Kokura.

At 7:00 A.M., inside the rumbling Bock's Car, Lieutenant Barnes saw something that horrified him. "Look!" Barnes shook Commander Ashworth and pointed to the bomb monitor. The blinking red light on the console that was monitoring Fat Man's detonators had changed its rhythm from the steady blink and now, for some reason, was flashing wildly. There was strict radio silence, but the radar was operational. Had the detonators somehow mistakenly picked up Bock's Car's radar signal? If so, it would mean that they were within a minute of detonation.

As Barnes ripped the cover off the monitor, Ashworth clambered forward to tell Sweeney. If there were no wiring defects in the box, then they would have to assume there was a very serious problem with the bomb. To make matters worse, if Sweeney opened the bomb bay doors, Barnes, working with the weapon, might go out with it. How much time they had, no one could guess.

Crouched on the dimly lit mezzanine, Barnes found the trouble. Two wires had been crossed. The fault was in the monitor. When told. Sweeney replied, "Oh, Lord!"[4]

One hour forty minutes later, Sweeney arrived over the tiny island of Yaku-shima off the southern Japanese island of Kyushu. There, Bock's Car was to meet up with two other planes that would photograph the mission and drop recording instruments. In the clear air a dot appeared. Minutes later the instrument plane The Great Artiste pulled alongside. But where was the third B-29?[5] Sweeney circled the area for forty-five minutes searching the sky. Still no photo plane. In the thin air at 31,000 feet, the four Wright Cyclones were drinking gasoline at 1,000 gallons an hour.

Sweeney glanced at the gauges and made his decision. Checking his gyrocompass, he aimed the B-29 for 16 degrees, slightly east of due north.[6] It was a path that would take him over Kokura, a city of 52,000 on the northern tip of Kyushu, guarding the western entrance to the Inland Sea. Weather reports had indicated the sky was clear there.

By 9:50 A.M. Japan time, they could see the northern entrance to the Inland Sea, partially obscured by low clouds. Through the occasional breaks in the layer bombardier Kermit Beahan could see the towns of Ashiya, Hakata, Moji . . . and Kokura. There seemed to be a plume of smoke coming in from the west, covering parts of the area. It was from an incendiary bombing two days before.

"What do you think, Bea?" Sweeney called in over the intercom.

In the nose of the plane Beahan peered into the Norden bombsight searching for his target. "Shouldn't be any trouble, Chuck."

Sweeney held the plane steady, waiting for the signal from his bombardier to begin the run.

"Damn it to hell!" Beahan swore. His target was obscured by smoke from the nearby firebombing target.

"Pilot to crew," Sweeney called over the intercom. "No drop."

Two more runs were made, but still the smoke obscured the target. By now, the ground defenses had seen the plane and were sending flak up to greet it. Sweeney could feel the pressure from the explosions against the plane's control surfaces. Someone said, "Let's get the hell out of here."

Fuel was running low. There was no way to make it back to Tinian. In fact, they may not even make it to Okinawa. Sweeney wheeled the Superfortress around to a heading of 206 degrees, west of south. Judging from the time spent loitering over Kokura, Sweeney knew they might have to ditch.[7] Then he remembered: They had an armed atomic bomb on board.

There *had* to be some potential targets in the area.

Together, Ashworth and Sweeney looked at the map. The southernmost Japanese island of Kyushu was shaped like an inverted fishhook. Their path to Okinawa would take them over the bend in the hook, a cove, and south past its tip. They would fly just east of several small cities in the area, Akune, Ichiku, Kaseda—none were potential targets. Then they saw it.

Nagasaki. One of the original primary targets and just 30 miles out of the way.

But it was almost completely covered by clouds.

Taking a chance with the low fuel, Sweeney veered to the right in a path that would take him over the city. Beahan, riding in the glazed nose of the Superfortress, peered into his bombsight. The docks were visible, but not much else. Thoroughly familiar with the bombing plans, Beahan knew that the target in Nagasaki was the Mitsubishi industrial complex. Unfortunately, it was completed covered by clouds.

Sweeney turned to Ashworth. "We can make only one run, and Beahan doesn't think we can get a visual fix. I suggest we drop by radar. What do you think?"

"I don't know," Ashworth replied. "Let me think about it."

"Anything is better than dumping it in the ocean," the pilot argued. "I have a lot of confidence in my radar and I will take the responsibility."

Suddenly, both men heard Beahan yell into the intercom, "I've got it! I see the city! I'll take it now!" Though the original aiming point was in the center of the city, a hole in the cloud seemed to be opening up 2 miles away, over an industrial area on the Urakami River.

11:01 A.M.: The clamps holding Fat Man are released and the plutonium bomb falls away from the plane, through a hole in the clouds, and toward Nagasaki, 31,000 feet below.[8]

On the ground, an air-raid observer had just reported the sighting of two planes, flying very high. But two planes are little cause for concern. The observer calmly climbs down the ladder, hangs his sword belt on a nail on the side of the wall, and, still watching the sky, begins unbuttoning his jacket.[9]

On the bank of the Urakami River, in the industrialized section of Nagasaki, ten children are playing a game they have invented: find the bell. Eleven-year-old Koichi Nakajima tosses a small trinket—a tiny bell—into the water and counts to three. "Here we go!" All dive in, swim through the cool, murky pool for a moment, then resurface. It's a good game in the 85 degree cloudy summer morning. There is, however, a problem.

They have lost the bell. Directly above them, the sky has cleared momentarily, and the sun begins to shine.

11:02 A.M.: Kite maker Shigeyoshi Morimoto, arriving home from Hiroshima, hurries into his shop in the center of the city. Worried about his wife and child, he is unaware of the importance of the puffy gray blanket of cloud hanging over his downtown shop, obscuring it from above. Morimoto's shop had been part of the bombardier's original aiming point.[10]

Treading water in the sunlight-dappled Urakami River, Koichi begins to worry. The tiny, guided trinket belongs to his sister and she doesn't know he has it. The others sprawl on the bank, showing no interest. If anyone is to find his sister's trinket, it will have to be him. Taking a lungful of air, Koichi makes a surface dive for the murky river bottom. In the darkness his hands probe the cold mud. No bell. Almost a minute passes and his lungs begin to burn for lack of air. Another few seconds of searching and he makes for the surface, several feet above him.

As he nears the surface he can hear the screaming. Opening his eyes, he finds himself in another world. Everything has changed. The sunlight has gone and in its place is an opaque gray haze.

There are no buildings anymore. Clearing the silt-laden water from his eyes, Koichi sees two of his friends writhing on the bank, screaming. The others are dead, charred beyond recognition. Within minutes, Koichi is alone.[11]

Seconds earlier, the air-raid observer had been watching the sky. Standing at the epicenter, he might have actually seen the dark object fall through the cloud cover, wondering for a brief moment what it was. An instant later the sky had been erased by the atomic glare. When the blast wave reached the ground a millisecond later, all that remained of the observer was a shadow burned onto the wall.

At the city's center, 2 miles away, Mr. Morimoto had begun to tell his wife about the horrors of Hiroshima: "A great blue flash. . . ."

Then an intense bluish light filled the room. Quickly, the kite maker reached down, opened a trap door and pushed his wife and baby into the basement. Then he followed them, closing the door behind him. Seconds later, in the darkness, the basement began to shudder as the shock wave roared overhead.[12] Morimoto emerged to see a dark, ominous thunderhead hanging above the north part of the city.

Second Lieutenant Nobukazu Komatsu started the engines of his seaplane and began to taxi to the runway at Sasebo. A member of the Japanese Navy Cadet Corps, he had heard descriptions of the Hiroshima atomic bomb. Now a similar cloud was hanging in the sky directly south of the base. A radio report had confirmed it: A "great bombing" had occurred in Nagasaki. Perhaps the cloud was atomic.

With him were two friends, Lieutenant Tomimura, in the copilot's seat, and Chief Petty Officer Umeda, sitting behind them. Komatsu pushed the throttle forward and the plane lifted into the air, began climbing, then turned to a heading of 180 degrees: directly for the towering mushroom.

At altitude there was a brisk crosswind almost directly from the west. By the time they reached the vicinity of the cloud, the stalk was only tenuously connected to the ground; it resembled a huge thunderhead rising 25,000 feet or so above a thin cloud layer. Komatsu checked his altimeter. They were at 3,067 meters; 10,000 feet. Still the mushroom towered above them.[13]

Northeast of the dark, roiling stem could be seen black dust, ashes, soot, and paper fragments. By the time the plane reached the cloud, it had drifted some distance, to a point just southwest of Tarami village.[14] Peering up through the windshield, they could see the dark, threatening underside of the huge cloud. The stem hung beneath it like a huge streamer. Komatsu throttled forward and climbed to the level of the mushroom itself.

"Let's cut into it!" Komatsu yelled to his friends, then banked the plane straight for the cloud. Ahead of the them the sky became gray, then dark. Inside the cloud it was almost pitch black.

At 10,000 feet, even on a summer day, the air is usually quite cool. Before entering the cloud, the air temperature was probably hovering around 50 degrees Fahrenheit. Once inside, however, the cabin temperature rose alarmingly. Perhaps thinking the plane was somehow heating up, Komatsu slid the window back to check the temperature of the air inside the cloud. What happened next shocked him. Even though his hand had been inside his flying glove, it felt as though someone had blasted it with live steam. Yanking his hand back inside the cabin, he noticed the glove was completely gray with the sticky soot and dust whirling inside the strange cloud.

In the next instant, he noticed that Petty Officer Umeda was vomiting.

Tomimura, in the right-hand seat, opened his window. The incredibly hot, dark, dust-laden air struck him squarely in the face. Komatsu, mindful of his burned hand, yelled to his copilot to close the window.

Then, eight minutes after they had entered the darkness of the atomic cloud, they returned to clear air. Inside the cabin, the temperature returned to normal.

Later, Komatsu landed in Nagasaki harbor. He and Tomimura decided to inspect the city; Umeda was too sick to leave the plane. Walking through the smoking, charred ruins of Nagasaki, they saw masses of injured people, walking as though in a daze, some apparently unmindful of horrible burns and trauma wounds. Tomimura began to cry.

Deciding they could do nothing to help, the three flew back to Sasebo, discussing the horrible injuries they had seen in the ruined city, totally unaware that they, too, had been injured. Inside the cloud, they had been exposed to near-lethal doses of radiation; the three men had inhaled any number of rare and deadly isotopes: plutonium-239, cesium-137, iodine-131. Their actions, even their positions in the plane during those eight minutes, would affect their lives from that point on. It would also determine the way two of them would die.

Inside their bodies, the isotopes would settle in the thyroid, the liver, the intestines, and, of course, the bone marrow, site of blood formation. In two years, Umeda, the petty officer who had ridden in the back seat, exposed to the blast of air from both windows, would be dead of leukemia. Tomimura, the copilot who had opened the window only to receive a blast of contaminated air, would live until 1964, then he, too, would die of leukemia. The pilot, Komatsu, was the lucky one; unlike his passengers, only his left hand had touched the deadly cloud. Years later, however, he would be diagnosed as having chronic anemia.[15]

As Nagasaki burned, a major confrontation was taking place in Tokyo between those wanting peace and those holding out for a final defense of Japan. Prime Minister Suzuki had for some time wanted peace negotiations to begin as had navy Minister Mitsumasa Yonai and Foreign Minister Shigenori Togo. Togo, by virtue of his position, had seen the approaching difficulties with the Soviets. Now, as word of the Soviet invasion of Manchuria reached them, Togo pointed out that there was no way to continue the war.

Despite the Soviet threat, despite the fact that a major city had been leveled, the militants—General Anami, Navy Chief Soemu Toyoda, and Army Chief Yoshijiro Umezu—still believed that Japan would prevail in the war. A plan to repel the invaders was drawn up. Named Ketsu Go (Operation Decision), it was a study in wishful thinking: It called for everyone over seventeen to take up arms to defend the country. The argument between the two groups continued for hours with neither side giving an inch. Prime Min-

ister Suzuki finally left to attend a cabinet meeting that would continue the
debate. As the meeting was being called to order, a messenger arrived with
news of the bombing of Nagasaki.

Two planes, two bombs, two cities. There could now be no reasonable
alternative, yet the militants held on to Ketsu Go. Truman, in his speech after Hiroshima, had promised a "rain of ruin." With Nagasaki, he was making good on his promise. Which city would be next to die?

The debate had continued for six days with no compromise in sight.
Two cities had been destroyed; there would certainly be others. Should they
accede to the Allies' demands? In an extraordinary move, Prime Minister
Suzuki referred the question to Emperor Hirohito himself.

In a break with a tradition that had roots in the seventh century, the
emperor addressed the cabinet on the matter. For 124 generations, the em-
perors of Japan were considered descendants of the sun-goddess Ama-
terasu. Their concerns were not of this world, thus they ruled only figura-
tively. In a practical sense, they actually had very little power over the
day-to-day political matters, even of great import. Hirohito, for example,
had held a thinly veiled contempt for the military action at Pearl Harbor.
Now he was being called upon to state his views on the war: "I have given
serious thought to the situation prevailing at home and abroad and have
concluded that continuing the War means destruction for the nation and a
prolongation of bloodshed and cruelty in the world. . . . The time has come
to bear the unbearable. I swallow my tears and give my sanction to the proposal to accept the Allied proclamation on the basis outlined by the Foreign
Minister."[16]

It was 7:30 on the morning of August 10 when President Truman was
informed that the Japanese had agreed to surrender—with the stipulation
that the surrender "does not compromise any demand which prejudices the
perogatives of His Majesty as a sovereign ruler."[17]

Truman replied that the rule of the emperor and Japanese government
was to be "subject to the Supreme Commander of the Allied powers." Also
included, however, was the clause: ". . . the ultimate form of government
of Japan will be established by the freely expressed will of the Japanese
people."

An agreement was reached. There would be no more bombs. Japan was
no longer at war with the United States.

But there was still a problem with Russia. The Soviets had been at war
with Japan for only two days. Here was their opportunity to take Sakhalin
Island and the Kuriles, perhaps even Korea, and now the war was being
called off. Stalin began to grumble. He wanted his military in occupied Japan alongside American and British forces. He wanted veto power over the
choice of Supreme Commander. The Americans and British saw it as a ploy
to gain more time to win territory. The distrust between the United States
and the Soviets had been building for some time. Now, during the last days

of World War II, the Americans watched with suspicion as the Soviets took control of vast areas of eastern Asia.

By September 1, when the fighting finally stopped, Russian soldiers were in China, Manhuria, Sakhalin Island, and North Korea. Ominously, most of the 600,000 military and civilian prisoners taken in the eighteen-day war were sent to the Soviet Union.[18]

The West viewed the territorial grab by the Soviet Union with great concern. A rift seemed to be forming between the two allies. In fact, it was the beginning of a competition that would continue for at least four more decades.

Fallout

The morning of August 6, 1945, dawned bright and clear in Vincennes, Indiana. Unaware of the conflagration on the other side of the world, residents of the small midwestern city began their daily routines. One of the major industries in the area was the paper mill. That day, workers would begin production of strawboard that was destined for one of the mill's customers, a photographic lab in New York. In the production process, straw and similar materials were finely milled, mixed with water, then formed into thin cardboard sheets. The water for the process was obtained from the nearby Wabash River, a major drainage system for much of north-central Indiana. On that day, mixed in with the fine brown silt of the river was a very unusual, iron-gray metal. It was of a type that had not existed before.

A month later, and 500 miles to the west, workers in the Tama, Iowa, paper mill began production of strawboard destined for the same client. Using a similar process, the Tama mill obtained water for production from the nearby Iowa River. Like most streams in the eastern half of the state, the Iowa flowed from northwest to southeast. It provided drainage for a string of counties that extended almost to the Minnesota border.[1] Somewhere in the 100-mile journey from its source to the Tama paper mill, the Iowa River had taken on the same rare metal that had contaminated the Wabash.

During the autumn of 1945, film inspectors at Eastman-Kodak in Rochester, New York, had noticed an alarming incidence of film imperfections, tiny pinhole-sized dots and thin lines appearing on the green 14-by-17-inch film sheets used for industrial X-rays. As the autumn progressed, the contagion spread. Some of the sheets were contaminated with hundreds of the splotches.

Clyde Carleton, a Kodak inspector with a good track record, was called in. Prior to this, Carleton had established his credentials as an investigator by tracking down contamination caused by an employee's use of medicinal iodine.

The investigator knew that radiation was probably involved; earlier, Kodak had found paper from an eastern mill that had been laced with naturally occurring radium. The cardboard film separators were sent to the lab for analysis.

There was a contaminant in the paper, but it wasn't radium. It was something else, something Kodak had not isolated before.

Further analysis revealed it to be cerium, a rare earth metal named after the asteroid Ceres. The chemists at Kodak knew something about the metal. The most abundant of the rare earths, it was a constituent of minerals normally found in the western United States. But there was a problem: Cerium wasn't radioactive, and this material was releasing all sorts of radiation—beta particles, gamma rays, X rays. What was going on here?

Careful attention to the decay pattern of the cerium showed that it had a half-life of about thirty-two days—that is, after thirty-two days, one-half of it became something else. It was an impossibly short half-life for a naturally occurring radioactive isotope. Moreover, the material that was replacing it was a substance that was even more rare than the cerium. It was promethium, an element that had never been found in the earth's crust. Predicted in 1902 and confirmed in 1914, the element was named after the Titan Prometheus, who, according to Greek mythology, stole fire from the gods to give to man.[2]

Eventually, Kodak's radiation specialists figured it out. The tiny white dots on their film were the footprints of the atomic explosion that had occurred in July in New Mexico. Neutron bombardment from the detonation had transformed the stable cerium-140 found in the soil into radioactive cerium-141. The huge updraft had picked up the new radioactive element and sent it northeast, where it rained down on the Wabash and Iowa watersheds. Later, it found its way to the mills and eventually wound up in Rochester, ruining film with its incessant X-radiation.[3,4]

Kodak was not amused.

The scientists at Los Alamos were discouraged, but not particularly surprised to find the fission products so far from home. Closer to the test site, the atomic radiation had already manifested its presence in a variety of unusual ways. For one thing, livestock had reacted somewhat adversely to the atom bomb. While cerium-141 was falling into the Iowa and Wabash rivers, the Herefords in the immediate vicinity of the Trinity site were losing their hair. When it grew back, it came in white. The "rada calves" were enjoying immense popularity in El Paso and Alamogordo.

One rancher apparently had been exposed to the same thing as the rada calves; soon after the shot, his beard—or rather *half* his beard—turned gray. The same thing happened to a black cat owned by a hand on a nearby ranch:

The atomic blast had allegedly turned it half white. What finally became of the cat is unknown: A tourist bought it for a dollar.[5] Biologists claimed to have seen larks with feet malformations and rodents with eye cataracts.[6] But much of the information gathered was anecdotal and difficult to attribute to radiation.

That something significant occurred at the Trinity site, there could be no doubt: Ground zero had been pounded down into a dish fully 6 feet deep. Toward the center of the depression, the area looked like something from another planet. The ground was covered with an eerie green glass; the heat of the explosion had fused the sand into trinitite, a new radioactive mineral. It was somewhat fragile, not much more than half an inch thick, and covered the ground in thin sheets. Occasionally, the green was interspersed with splotches of red, from iron and copper mixed in with the silica.

At the time of the explosion, observers had seen balls of fire dropping from the atomic cloud. Touring the test site, they discovered irregular-shaped, glass "eggs" inside of which were lumps of dirt.

Scientists decided that the atomic furnace had scooped the dirt clods into the mushroom, coated them with glass, and then dropped them back to earth. The "atomic eggs" were found to be extremely radioactive.[7]

Beneath the surface of ground zero, plutonium particles had been driven to a depth of 13 inches.

Even though radioactivity was turning up in America's photographic film and certainly at the Trinity site, the U.S. military made an effort to show that there had been none at Hiroshima or Nagasaki. Immediately after the war, a governmental investigative committee was formed to determine medical and other effects of the detonations. Officials of the committee were informed by General Thomas Farrell that the purpose of the committee was to prove that the bombs had not left any radioactivity in Hiroshima and Nagasaki.[8]

It was a useless suggestion. Soil taken from the Nishiyama district of Nagasaki revealed such esoteric—and radioactive—isotopes as strontium-89, strontium-90, barium-140, praseodymium-144, zirconium-95, cesium-137, and, of course, unfissioned plutonium-239. Investigators measuring the gamma ray level one meter (3.26 feet) above the ground found one milliroentgen/hour. The scientists concluded that the total radiation dose to a person at this level was something on the order of 24 to 75 rads.[9,10] Each rad, a unit of absorbed dose, represented 100 ergs of energy absorbed by one gram of tissue. An exposure of 600 rads time is considered lethal. Later measurements of residents of the Nishiyama district indicated that they had absorbed into their bodies twice the radioactive cesium-137 of those living elsewhere in Nagasaki.[11]

Clearly, the area *was* radioactive.

Still, General Douglas MacArthur, now in Tokyo, did what he could to squelch adverse information. The Japanese press was warned about "inflammable" headlines and "needling" articles. Two newspapers, *Asahi* and the *Nippon Times*, were ordered to suspend publication. On September 19, MacArthur imposed a ban on *any* articles dealing with reports of atomic bomb damage. There were to be no exceptions. It was as though the bombing had never happened.[12]

Yet everywhere the investigators looked in Hiroshima and Nagasaki they found radiation sickness: bombing victims experiencing nausea, bloody diarrhea, convulsions, delirium. Two to five weeks after the detonations, many bomb survivors began to lose their hair. It was an ominous sign: Hair loss occurred slightly more often in cases associated with lethal doses. Five days after the hair loss began, fever usually set in. Then came the bruises and purple spots—petechiae—that signified capillary rupture beneath the surface of the skin. The spots often merged to form great purple splotches across the skin of the victim.

And everywhere there were the hemorrhages, blood spilling from the nose, mouth, and rectum. In the makeshift hospitals, the investigators found patients blinded after capillaries in their eyes had first ruptured, then clotted.[13]

Even animals were not spared: Many horses in Hiroshima were found to be suffering from leukopenia, fever, and loss of appetite. The number of crows and sparrows decreased for a short time after the explosion. Mosquitos had also vanished for a brief period of time, but they came back in large numbers several days later.

The only animals clearly not affected by the radiation appeared to be earthworms and rats.[14]

As word got back to Los Alamos of the findings, many of the scientists were horrified. They had expected some radiation, but not on the scale that had been seen in Hiroshima and Nagasaki. Their goal had been to use the nuclear material as a driving force behind the blast, not as a lethal agent in and of itself. The findings at the bombing sites, however, were incontrovertable: In the long run, the radiation from the bomb was more significant than the blast or thermal effects.

J. Robert Oppenheimer, the "father of the A-bomb," soon voiced his opinions about his destructive offspring. Four months to the day after the Trinity shot, he accepted an army-navy Award of Excellence for the town of Los Alamos. At the occasion, he surprised a few of those in attendance by saying that the time may come "when mankind will curse the name Los Alamos."[15] At a seminar given in 1948, he said that "physicists have known sin and this is a knowledge which they cannot lose."[16]

The Soviet physicists in charge of their own atom bomb project voiced no such reservations.

The Russian Bomb

In May 1945, while American firebombs were falling on Tokyo, a Russian-speaking military man arrived at the laboratory of German scientist Baron Manfred von Ardenne. With him were several Russian physicists, all from Kurchatov's Moscow laboratory. The military man, a general in the Red Army, made von Ardenne an offer he couldn't refuse: Amid the pleasant surroundings of Sukhumi, a Black Sea resort, the scientist would be provided with a lab in which to pursue isotope separation. Not sure of his fate at the hands of the Americans, von Ardenne accepted.

Kurchatov seriously needed von Ardenne's help; his laboratory had experienced a number of problems trying to separate the fissionable atoms of uranium from the nonfissionable ones. Scientific data and information coming out of Los Alamos seemed to indicate uranium hexafluoride gas was somehow involved; no one knew precisely why or how. Moreover, the material was extremely corrosive. Perhaps von Ardenne might be able to come up with another technique that would make mass production of uranium-235 a reality.[17]

Kurchatov's team had, in fact, worked primarily on the theoretical aspects of the weapon. Aside from work with ballistics, there had been precious little tangible hardware produced. Kurchatov must have realized that Stalin was becoming impatient. After word came from the spy that the Los Alamos team had detonated a successful atomic bomb, Kurchatov waited for his summons to the Kremlin. It came in mid-August, a few days after Nagasaki.

That day, Kurchatov found himself sitting in a room in the Kremlin with a group of engineers that included Boris Vannikov and Avraami Zavenyagin. Vannikov was a short, stout, bald-headed engineer who had worked in such diversified jobs as shipyard fitter and clarinetist at the Kino, the cinema. He was considered simple, honest, and hardworking, and he enjoyed a reputation for getting things done.

Avraami Zavenyagin presented another side of the same coin. A precisely organized man who was always clean shaven and wore smartly pressed business suits, he was perhaps the best-dressed official at the meeting. Though he had a string of successes to his credit, he had one item in his résumé that made him unassailable: He was the protégé of the infamous and feared head of the secret police, Lavrenti Beria.

Kurchatov no doubt wondered what possible good the secret police could bring to the atomic project.

Stalin came into the room and delivered his "request": "A single demand of you, comrades: provide us with atomic weapons in the shortest possible time. You know that Hiroshima has shaken the world. The equilibrium has been destroyed. Provide the bomb—it will remove a great danger from us."[18]

The message was clear. Kurchatov had spent eighteen months on a nuclear device and had not come up with much of anything. Suddenly the Americans had detonated *three* of the infernal things. For the Soviet Union to remain competitive, the engineers and physicists would have to develop an atomic bomb. And with Beria in control—as he assuredly would be—the scientists and administrators knew what awaited them if they failed.[19] Moreover, most of them understood the time limit: Stalin wanted the bomb before the official celebration of his seventieth birthday—in 1949. Four short years away.[20]

Under the watchful eyes of Vannikov and Zavenyagin, Kurchatov expanded his atomic bomb project. Vannikov, more interested in the engineering aspects, was aware of the problems associated with the project. Information from the West was sketchy and Russian industry was still trying to recover from the ruinous German invasion. Caught between Stalin's "single demand" on one side and an information void on the other, the Soviet atomic scientists doubtless spent many sleepless nights during those first few months after the war. Then, when things looked darkest, their luck changed.

The Americans, justifiably proud of their technological achievements, began to write about them. Articles began to crop up in such magazines as *Life* and *Time* speculating upon the technological aspects of the bomb. The most important, however, was published within weeks of the Hiroshima and Nagasaki bombing. Written by Princeton physicist Henry DeWolf Smyth, it was proclaimed the "official" history of the Manhattan Project. In it, Smyth detailed how the Americans had solved the problem of isotope separation by diffusing uranium hexafluoride gas through a series of membranes. One of Kurchatov's thorniest problems—"distillation" of the fissionable U-235—had suddenly been solved.

The Soviets bought as many copies of the "Smyth Report" as they could find, and in January, it was published in Moscow. Of the first printing, 30,000 copies were sold, one for every sixty-six men, women, and children in the city at the time.

The Smyth Report was a shot in the arm for Kurchatov's team. The Soviets were particularly amazed at how the American scientists had transformed esoteric laboratory experiments into a large-scale—and successful—project.[21]

Now that the secret of isotope separation was out, Kurchatov had another problem: There was precious little uranium available in the Soviet Union. Project coordinator Vannikov decided to delegate the responsibility of uranium supply to one Yefim Slavsky, conferring upon him the title of Deputy People's Commissar of Nonferrous Metallurgy.[22] Slavsky had had some experience with mining; at one time he had been the director of some aluminum plants in the Ural mountains. Vannikov might have picked a more knowledgeable man; he certainly couldn't have found one more rancorous.

Slavsky was probably one of the more vengeful, hysterical, and demanding of the atomic project administrators. He refused to listen to reason, believed himself immune to failure, and was totally authoritarian.[23] Apparently, Vannikov believed that Slavsky would bully his men into finding uranium, even if none were there.

Fortunately for Slavsky's subordinates, uranium *was* found in several places: the Joachimsthal mine in Czechoslovakia, of course; the Fergana basin southeast of Tashkent; and a large area near Aue, Saxony, in occupied East Germany. Slavsky's subordinate at the Saxony operation was Major General Mikhail Maltsev, an engineer. Maltsev, perhaps aware of Slavsky's temperament, decided on a crash program: Miners were recruited and an ex-Nazi who was familiar with the mines was released from prison to advise the operation.

Meanwhile, Vannikov authorized construction of a uranium processing facility to be built on the eastern slope of the Urals, among the small *posyoloks* or "workers' settlements," lying between the cities of Sverdlovsk and Chelyabinsk. The area was dotted with them: towns such as Kasli, Novogorodny (a common Soviet town name meaning "new city"), Karabash, Kaslinskoye, Kyshtym, and Maloyaroslavets. Thanks in part to the German invasion of 1941, millions of citizens from the western and southern sections of the Soviet Union had moved to the relative security of this area, displacing the Bashkirs and other natives who were the original inhabitants. When the war was over most of the immigrants stayed, and the *posyoloks* grew to populations ranging from 10,000 to 30,000.

The area was pleasant enough, with rolling foothills; birch, fir, and pine trees; and lakes filled with carp, perch, and pike. After the war, the area had seemed like one sprawling, relatively peaceful suburb. All that changed in 1947.

Residents of many of the villages such as Kopeisk, about 10 miles east of Chelyabinsk, were evacuated to make way for uranium processing plants and reactors, built using prison labor.

A nuclear power research station was set up near the village of Maloyaroslavets and given not a name but a postbox number. Unofficially, it was referred to as "Maloyaroslavets 2" (twenty years after it was founded, in 1968, it received its own name, Obninsk).

All of the unusable waste from the reactors and processing facilities was to be sent to "Chelyabinsk 40," a storage facility near the town of Kyshtym, where it would be buried in a single pit.[24]

The design of the Chelyabinsk 40 storage facility would later prove deadly.

Using data from the Smyth Report and with the aid of German physicist von Ardenne, Vannikov's engineers began construction of a huge isotope separation facility at Maloyaroslavets 2. Nearby, reactors would work to create the plutonium necessary for the heart of the bomb. Early in 1947, Vannikov, perhaps under strain from Stalin's deadline, suffered a heart attack. Nonetheless, by fall of that year, he moved to the reactor site south of Sverdlovsk to oversee the operations. Kurchatov joined him. They shared a cold, drafty railroad car at the construction site during the winter of 1947–48.[25]

By spring of 1948, despite an absolute disregard for miner safety, despite frequent flooding and a disastrous dynamite explosion, the Saxony mining operation was a huge success. Ore production from the area was at a record level: 900 tons. Word from the Kremlin had indicated that the Americans had tested several new atomic weapons and might be working on an even larger device. Time was running out. In desperation, Vannikov authorized the ore to be *flown* to Sverdlovsk from Saxony.[26] That year a new problem cropped up: Thanks to the corrosive nature of the uranium hexafluoride, the isotope separation plant was continually being shut down for repairs. Enraged at the delays, Beria personally fired the plant director. It became obvious that Russia's first atomic bomb would have to be made of plutonium. Unfortunately, it was discovered that the graphite essential for the reactors had been contaminated by, of all things, linoleum.

Kurchatov stepped up his research, assigning the thorniest problems to two physicists, Yulii Khariton and Yakor Zeldovich. By the fall of 1948, Kurchatov began looking for a suitable test site.

Postwar

Death at Los Alamos

Immediately after VJ Day, orders had come to Los Alamos from Washington to design better, smaller, and more efficient bombs. The uranium bomb used on Hiroshima had been terribly inefficient. Because of its gun-type assembly, the weapon had an efficiency of 1.3 percent—that is, only 1.3 percent of the uranium fissioned to produce energy; the rest was dispersed over the city as fallout. The Nagasaki implosion weapon fared better: 17 percent of its plutonium core had fissioned to produce energy.[1] The implication was clear: Implosion plutonium-based weapons were preferable to the expensive U-235 bombs.

For a brief period of time after the war, there had been a production model of the Little Boy uranium bomb. Called the MK-I, it had been designed for use by the air force, but by 1946, it was pulled from service. The MK-II was designed by Los Alamos to be the first production model of the Nagasaki implosion weapon, but it was canceled early on; scientists were unable to reliably predict either efficiency or yield.

Most of the weapons during this era still used pretty much the same components as had the original Trinity Gadget: plutonium, surrounded by a dense metal tamper that was in turn surrounded by a sphere of high explosives. Bomb design had yet to acquire any sense of precision and reliability. In the summer of 1945, researchers were still unsure of the exact point at which plutonium would begin to fission uncontrollably—the so-called point of criticality. It varied, depending on the size and shape of the nuclear material.

Plutonium and U-235 atoms spontaneously fission, releasing neutrons, gamma, and X-radiation. Each time a neutron strikes the center of another atomic nucleus, two more neutrons are released, which may strike two more atoms, and so on. Thus, one neutron can result in the generation of a vast number of other neutrons. This is the essence of a chain reaction. If the resultant neutron reaches the surface before striking other atoms, it is lost to the chain reaction. On the other hand, if the lump or sphere of plutonium or uranium-235 is large enough, there are more atoms to strike and proportionally less surface area available for the neutrons to escape. The size at which the neutrons begin an uncontrolled chain reaction is called the "critical size" or "critical point."

In order to conserve the expensive plutonium and uranium-235, the scientists and technicians of Los Alamos's Omega had to learn—as they did during design of the Trinity device—what those critical points were.

The Omega Site consisted of a row of buildings separate from the main facility. Scientists working there dealt with the very heart of the atom bomb—its nuclear core; but the procedure they used was simple: The crit technicians simply pushed hemispheres of plutonium closer and closer together and waited for the chain reaction to begin. As the neutrons began to multiply and fly from the surface of the hemispheres, the neutron monitor would emit a loud buzz, then quiet down. The technicians would then pull the hemispheres apart, take note of the distances and masses involved, and start over. In essence, they would use their workbench as a testing ground for a miniature atomic bomb.

Many of the other scientists at Los Alamos saw the crit experiments as extremely dangerous. Enrico Fermi, the inventor of the atomic reactor and someone extremely knowledgeable about chain reactions, would take his crew hiking in the Sangre de Cristo mountains during Slotin's assemblies.

Another procedure at the Omega Site involved the fact that neutrons were reflected by tungsten carbide: a heavy, black, and extremely dense metal used as a component of the bomb. The material, called by the scientists "watercress" because of its chemical symbol, WC, was placed around the machined nuclear sphere until enough neutrons were reflected back to the surface to begin a chain reaction. The heavy tungsten carbide had been machined into 2-by-4-inch "bricks" weighing 13 pounds each.

Standing at a waist-high table, the technician would begin by building a thin wall of tungsten carbide around a mass of plutonium. If the neutron counter didn't register a chain reaction, more of the "watercress" bricks were added until the monitor, connected to a wall loudspeaker, began to respond with audible clicks. At that point, "half" and "quarter" bricks of the tungsten carbide were added until it became clear a chain reaction was imminent.

If the neutron monitor didn't respond by the time a cube 14 inches on a side had been made, the sphere was returned to the metal shop for more plutonium.[2]

Thirty-three-year-old physicist Louis Slotin had been involved in criticality experiments for the Trinity Gadget. His job had been to determine the amount of plutonium and uranium necessary for the Little Boy and Fat Man

bombs, and he had wanted to travel in the planes with them to their intended targets. When Washington refused, Slotin had decided to take a few
weeks vacation. His assistant, Harry Daghlian, took over the experiments at
Omega Site while Slotin was away.[3]

A month earlier, Daghlian had helped assemble the nuclear core of the
Trinity Gadget on the dining room table of the McDonald ranch. He enjoyed an easy familiarity with the gray plutonium metal; he knew approximately where the critical points were with a given mass. So instead of slowly
building the surrounding tungsten carbide reflector "cabin" from scratch,
brick by brick, Daghlian would start with a foundation of bricks already in
place.

He took other shortcuts: One procedure called for slowly sliding the
heavy "watercress" bricks across a table toward the plutonium, listening
for an increase in clicks from the loudspeaker that would indicate near-
criticality. Daghlian amended this procedure by holding the bricks over the
"roof" of the tungsten carbide cabin surrounding the nuclear mass. Often,
as he brought his hand nearer the assembly, the rattle of clicks from the neutron monitor would tell him the plutonium was close to criticality.

At this point, the technician could make neutron monitor "music" by
cupping his hands over the roof of the tungsten carbide cabin, reflecting
neutrons from the plutonium sphere back to its surface and causing even
more fissioning.

On the evening of August 21, 1945, Harry Daghlian walked past a
movie line and down toward the canyon, toward the Omega Site. In the line,
another Omega technician, Vernon Kendrick, considered asking Daghlian to
join him for the movie, then changed his mind.

Once at Omega, Daghlian began his experiment by quickly building a
tungsten carbide cabin around the plutonium sphere. Within minutes, the
neutron monitor began its ominous chatter.

An armed guard, standing at the other end of the room, barely paid attention to the buzzing; he had heard it before. It was part of the experiment.
In the background, Harry Daghlian was holding a full brick of 'watercress'
above the plutonium. Suddenly there was a commotion and the neutron
counter began to scream.

Somehow Daghlian had let the 13-pound tungsten carbide brick slip
from his hand. It had fallen on top of the cabin, reflecting neutrons back to
an already critical nuclear mass. Around him the air had begun glowing purple from the ionization. It was the same purple glow that Daghlian had seen
surrounding the Trinity mushroom cloud the month before.

In a panic, the technician reached for the brick laying across the supercritical plutonium, picked it up, then dropped it again. Then, in a frenzied
attempt to bring the thing under control, he began tearing at the pile of
bricks surrounding the hot metal. Still the neutron counter screamed. Next,
he made a vain attempt to turn the table over. Heavy with bricks, it re-

fused to budge. Finally, Daghlian methodically began removing bricks from around the plutonium, allowing the neutrons to escape. Within a minute the reaction stopped.

Daghlian left the Omega Site thinking he had not been seriously injured. Earlier, during the Trinity assembly, Otto Frisch had been exposed for a few seconds to supercritical U-235, and he was still walking around.[4] But Harry Daghlian would not be so lucky. Within hours he became nauseous and checked himself in at the hospital. The health physicists determined his dose by measuring the neutron-induced radioactivity of some coins in his pocket. The prognosis was not good. Louis Slotin returned from vacation to find his friend dying of radiation sickness. Twenty-one days after the accident, Daghlian was dead.

The death shocked the Los Alamos community. Plans were drawn up to tighten safety requirements at the Omega Site. Construction was begun on a device that would allow the technicians to determine criticality by remote control.

By May 1946, the remote control facility had been completed. The nuclear core that Harry Daghlian and Louis Slotin had worked on the previous summer was now part of a bomb that would be detonated at Bikini Island in the Pacific: CROSSROADS shot ABLE. Travel orders had arrived for Slotin; he would be allowed to visit Bikini to see the results of his latest handiwork.

With the ABLE shot little more than a month away, Slotin decided, on May 21, to perform the criticality experiment one last time. With him were six other scientists along with Al Graves, his replacement as head of the Omega Site. Slotin leaned over the table and began pushing the hemispheres of plutonium closer and closer together. Suddenly the air turned blue, just as it had done nine months before. Amid the screams of the neutron monitor, Slotin dived for the fiercely hot hemispheres and pulled them apart with his bare hands. Behind him, someone yelled, "Let's get the hell out of here!"

Slotin knew at once that he had taken a fatal dose of radiation. His fate was sealed. Calculation by health physicists indicated he had taken about 880 rads. It was as though he had been within 4,800 feet of a nuclear detonation.

Within twelve hours Slotin was suffering bouts of nausea with vomiting. His hands had been closest to the supercritical mass; they were beginning to turn red, then blue. As physicians packed his arms in ice to keep down swelling, they noticed his abdomen becoming red. Within days, his white blood cells virtually disappeared. Throughout the ordeal, Slotin tried to maintain consciousness and tell the attending physicians what he was going through.

Nine days after the accident, Louis Slotin was dead.

The others in the room survived. Al Graves, who had been standing nearest Slotin, developed cataracts but otherwise remained healthy.[5]

Joe One

Halfway around the world, Igor Kurchatov's group continued their progress toward the Soviet bomb. Finally, early on the morning of August 29, 1949, four years after the American TRINITY test, Kurchatov and Avraami Zavenyagin rode by military truck through the Kazakh desert toward a tall, illuminated metal tower. In the darkness they could just make out the shapes of the tanks, buildings, and artillery pieces strewn about the area. In a few hours, Soviet military and government officials would be filing into the observation bunkers to see if Kurchatov's project had been worthwhile, if the time and money had been well spent.

The site, in the Ust-Urt desert between the Caspian and Aral seas, was chosen primarily for its remote location, far from prying Western eyes. The potential for fallout might have also been an influencing factor. Should the blast produce any, the winds would surely take it eastward, toward China and away from Soviet territory.[6]

As dawn began to break, the landscape emerged from the shadows and the equipment-littered test site came into sharp relief. Perched inside the bomb cab at the top of the tower, Kurchatov and Zavenyagin inspected the cables leading to the detonators. There are no unclassified photographs of the device available; however, it is fair to assume it strongly resembled the Los Alamos Gadget. Though the Soviets certainly had capable scientists, they had no qualms about copying a good design. Had an American serviceman been at the test site, he might have seen aircraft that looked suspiciously like B-29s. They were the Tupolev-4 bombers and they were in fact carbon copies of a B-29 that had accidentally landed in Siberia during the war.[7,8]

After glancing outside the bomb cab for a view of the desert and surrounding mountains, Kurchatov and Zavenyagin clambered out into the cool morning air. Below, a truck was waiting to take them to the bunker. The two men most responsible for the test had been the last ones off the tower.

The tension in the control bunker during the final countdown was probably much higher than that at Los Alamos four years earlier. Given Stalin's temperament and Beria's unique managerial style, Kurchatov, Zavenyagin, Vannikov, and countless scientists and administrators knew that their careers and most likely their lives were riding on a successful detonation. Even though they already had enough plutonium for two more devices, a test failure would probably preclude Stalin's giving Kurchatov a second chance.

As with the American detonation, electromechanical devices took over within minutes of time zero. Kurchatov and the others adjusted their welder's glasses and peered into the darkness, waiting for the pinpoint of light.

On the evening of August 29, 1949, the crew of an U.S. Air Force B-29 bomber was on a routine "monitoring mission" at 18,000 feet over the Pacific just north of Japan, when suddenly their radiation instruments began to detect something. A year earlier, when the flights had first begun, the instruments had picked up airborne debris from American tests conducted in the Pacific. But no testing had recently taken place, at least by the United States.

The monitoring crew checked the analysis results. Only one sample appeared to be radioactive; the rest were negative. After determining the coordinates, the pilot circled back, looking for the suspicious patch of air. After a short time, they found it, a cloud of radioactivity that was drifting east.

Within hours, a group of B-29s were busy following the radioactive cloud across the Pacific, over the United States, then over the Atlantic. Monitoring planes from Great Britain's Royal Air Force also picked up radioactivity from the cloud. Clearly someone else had the atomic bomb.[9]

The scientific team analyzing the data came to an inescapable conclusion: the airborne radioactivity was from a nuclear test, specifically, a *Soviet* nuclear test. They began to refer to the shot as "Joe One."

President Truman simply didn't believe it.[10] His advisors had told him a Russian bomb was impossible for the next ten years.[11] Perhaps it had been an accident, similar to the Saxony dynamite blast that had killed seventy in 1947. How could the Soviets have matched the know-how of Los Alamos?

After conferring with the five Atomic Energy Commission members, Truman decided to tell the American public. On Friday, September 23, almost a month after the radioactive cloud was detected, President Truman went on the air: "I believe that the American people, to the fullest extent consistent with national security, are entitled to be informed of all developments in the atomic energy field. . . . We have evidence that in recent weeks an atomic explosion occurred in the U.S.S.R."[12]

The atomic monopoly was over.

Military officials, taken by surprise, wondered if other, earlier Soviet tests might have gone undetected. To test the ability of the Air Force to detect radioactive material, the Pentagon authorized a rather unique experiment: on December 3, 1949, one ton of chemically treated, highly radioactive uranium obtained from the Hanford reactor was released into the air over the states of Washington and Oregon. The resulting mass, 5,500 curies hot, quickly fanned out over the area and began drifting east.

The amount of radioactive material injected into the air during this experiment is now estimated to be 100 times that of the reactor accident occurring at Three Mile Island, Pennsylvania, thirty years later.

III

THE TESTING BEGINS

1946

The war was over. Japan and Germany had been soundly defeated and the American public, for the first time in five years, began to relax. The year marked the beginning of a postwar baby boom that would continue until 1964. One of the most popular motion pictures of 1946 was *The Best Years of Our Lives,* based on the MacKinley Kantor novel *Glory for Me.* Starring Frederic March, Dana Andrews, and Myrna Loy, it was the story of three soldiers returning home from war to their small town, a subject with which most Americans could identify.

A new medium, commercial television, was born in 1946. Only two networks were in operation, NBC and Dumont, and the features were sporadically placed. On Friday evenings at 8:15, NBC viewers could see "Let's Rhumba" with its featured dance, The Ranchero. It was followed by "I Love to Eat" with host James Beard and "The World in Your Home" sponsored by RCA Victor. At 10:00 P.M., "The Gillette Cavalcade of Sports" closed out the evening.[1]

After the uncertainties and privations of the war years, it was a time to unwind and forget about military matters. Russia was too backward to make any kind of bomb. Great Britain probably wasn't interested in making a nuclear weapon, and in June 1946, the French declared that the goals their government had assigned their nuclear scientists and technicians were "purely peaceful."[2]

President Truman, however, was under pressure to do something about spies and "internal security." Late in the year, he named a commission to look into the matter. Communists, specifically the rooting out of Communist subversives hiding in the federal government (and everywhere else), would eventually consume a major segment of each evening's newcast.

In the summer of 1946, while the American public was basking in the glow of victory, the military began setting up camp at an atoll in the Marshall Islands. They had two bombs, about ninety outdated battleships, aircraft carriers, some submarines, and a few old navy admirals who needed convincing.

Influential and capable Admiral William D. Leahy, in fact, had opposed the bombing. He later said that "the use of this barbarous weapon at Hiroshima and Nagasaki was of no material assistance in our war against Japan. The Japanese were already defeated and ready to surrender because of the effective sea blockade and the successful bombing with conventional weapons."[3] Admiral Chester W. Nimitz had gone on record suggesting there was no need for the atomic bomb.[4]

Even General Curtis LeMay was less than enthusiastic about the weapon. He had predicted that the war would have been over "in two weeks" without the atomic bomb—*or* the Russian invasion of Manchuria.

A month after the bombing, the outspoken general flatly stated, "The atomic bomb had nothing to do with the end of the war at all."[5]

In an effort to get the doubters to change their minds, the Target Fleet was assembled in the lagoon of the remote and beautiful Bikini Atoll. Lying about 2,700 miles southwest of Hawaii (and just about everywhere else), Bikini was the perfect site for a bomb test. There was only one problem: The 170 inhabitants were not particularly enamored of the idea of fireworks in the middle of their home lagoon. The military responded by moving them en masse 130 miles away to the island of Rongerik. Shortly after the evacuation, Vice Admiral William Blandy, Commodore Ben H. Wyatt, and other officials convened a meeting with the leader of the natives, King Juda: "The President knows the sacrifice you have made and he is deeply grateful to you for that. You have made a true contribution to the progress of mankind all over the world, and the President of the United States extends to you, King Juda, his thanks for all you have done."[6]

The Bikinians were replaced by 42,000 servicemen, who had been chosen for the dubious honor of observing a nuclear detonation over water. The first test was scheduled for July 1, 1946, and as the day approached there was some apprehension among the men.

After the war, it had become general knowledge that the scientists had been concerned over possible ignition of the hydrogen and nitrogen in the atmosphere. That hadn't happened, some believed, because detonation had taken place in the air. This time the tests would involve an underwater detonation. What if the *water* caught fire? In a filmed statement, Admiral Blandy, the project commander, stressed that it would *not* blow a hole in the bottom of the ocean and let the water run out.[7] He was referring to the popularly expressed notion that "a crack might be opened in the ocean floor allowing seawater to rush into the white-hot interior and produce subterranean explosions and earthquakes."[8] Others thought it would kill all the fish for thousands of miles around, that it might cause a tidal wave that would eventually inundate Los Angeles.[9]

In reply to the atmosphere ignition theory, Berkeley, California, nuclear physicist Ernest Orlando Lawrence had suggested the public not worry, because "we're winning greater, not less, control over nature."[10] Still, many of the observers waiting for the July 1 blast remained unconvinced of the safety of the operation.

CROSSROADS: ABLE

On July 1, 1946, ABLE DAY, the submarine U.S.S. *Skate* floated still and empty 300 yards or so west-southwest of the target ship, the U.S.S. *Nevada,* which had been painted red and white for better visibility. Due north was the *Sakawa;* to the southwest, the dark, hulking Japanese battleship *Na-*

gato. Two thousand yards to the northwest the elegant gray German cruiser *Prinz Eugen* bobbed gently in the peaceful blue waters of the lagoon.

Among the American ships within 1,000 yards of the *Skate*—and "surface zero"—were the *Independence,* the *Salt Lake City,* and the *Nevada.*[11]

Inside, the *Skate* did not have the look of an abandoned ship: dishes were still in the galley, and in the officers quarters were popular records, pictures, and books. But, the engines had been switched off. The submarine was deathly quiet.[12] The U.S.S. *Burleson,* on the other hand, was a cacophony of grunts and squeals. As an experiment, several hundred mice, rats, goats, and pigs had been placed on board.[13]

High overhead, the B-29 *Dave's Dream* slowly circled the area. Inside its bay was a single bomb, a dark pear-shaped object with a hinged door on its nose. Thanks to the experiments of Slotin and Daghlian, the weapon was somewhat more efficient than the ones dropped on Japan.

On its side was scrawled the name Gilda, after a Rita Hayworth movie.

As the countdown drew near, the observers on the U.S.S. *Mount Mc-Kinley* crowded against the rail. Ten minutes until detonation. The men squinted at the hazy blue sky for a glimpse of the B-29, but *Dave's Dream* was above the clouds, too high to be visible.

"This is Skylight One, Skylight One," the voice of the bombardier crackled over the speakers. "Two minutes before actual bomb release. Mark: two minutes before actual bomb release. . . ."

The timekeeper set the huge countdown clock in motion as a corpsman from the Signal Corps Pictorial Center took aim with his 16mm camera. The film footage would be seen in countless movie newsreels and, years later, broadcast on a Saturday afternoon television program called "The Big Picture."

". . . Adjust all goggles. Adjust all goggles. Stand by.

"Coming up on actual bomb release. Stand by. . . .

"Bomb away. Bomb away. Bomb away."[14]

Almost a minute later, a pinpoint of brilliant light began to grow in the air 300 yards from the submarine.

Inside the *Skate,* first silence as the environment was sprayed with a lethal hail of neutrons, then chaos as the blast flipped the submarine on its side, spilling papers, books, phonograph records, dishes—*everything* not bolted down. Topside, the pressure wave sheared the gun emplacements away from their mounts, ripped the deck apart, and bent the gun mount around 180 degrees. On the *Burleson,* one of the pigs was blown from the deck into the ocean.[15]

Even while the mushroom cloud hung in the sky, a group of small boats shoved off from the lagoon, their crew wearing overalls, boots, rubber gloves, and gas masks.[16] One of their jobs, in addition to assessing the damage, would be to fish the *Burleson's* pig from the ocean.

Incredibly, most of the ships remained afloat. Examining them, the inspection crew found twisted metal, fused glass, and an odd assortment of radioactive materials: brass, soap, and chemicals from the first-aid supplies.

One crewmember took a piece of twisted—and radioactive—metal as a souvenir, and kept it in his locker near his bed. By the time a radiation monitor caught up with the gamma emissions, the crewman had been exposed to several evenings of constant gamma radiation.[17]

CROSSROADS: BAKER

The second of the shot of the series, BAKER, was scheduled for July 25. Strictly speaking, BAKER was not a bomb, but a device. It was not to be dropped from a plane but lowered beneath a barge halfway to the bottom of the 180-foot-deep lagoon. Though Operation CROSSROADS was labeled an effects test, the second shot was also to be an evaluation of a new bomb design. Scientists had wrapped the nuclear core with an outer shell of U-238, a fissionable material that would provide scientists with slightly more "bang for the buck." It would also increase the amount of fallout.[18]

Because of the underwater detonation, scientists predicted the stem of the BAKER mushroom would be a chimney of water half a mile in diameter.[19] The detonation proved them correct. One witness remembered the event:

> The flash seemed to spring from all parts of the target fleet at once. A gigantic flash—then it was gone. And where it had been now stood a white chimney of water reaching up and up. Then a huge hemispheric mushroom of vapor appeared like a parachute suddenly opening. . . . By this time the great geyser had climbed to several thousand feet. It stood there as if solidifying for many seconds, its head enshrouded in a tumult of steam. Then slowly the pillar began to fall and break up. At its base a tidal wave of spray and steam rose to smother the fleet and move on towards the island. All this took only a few seconds, but the phenomenon was so astounding as to seem to last much longer.[20]

After the flash, a huge hemisphere of pressurized water vapor—the "Wilson cloud"—formed around surface zero, then expanded to touch and bounce off the cloud layer above. Inside, the mushroom coursed upward, followed by the immense stem of saltwater. Not far from the blast, sensors on one of the islands registered 1,000 roentgens/hour—a truly spectacular burst of radiation.[21] Navy ordnance man Commodore William "Deke" Parsons commented that the BAKER cloud "created the most poisonous fog that ever existed in the history of the world."[22]

Observers reported seeing one ship "on its nose." The U.S.S. *Arkansas* was positioned almost over the detonation point; its stern carved a cavity in the mushroom's monstrous stem. The stern of the U.S.S. *Saratoga* was lifted 43 feet into the air.[23]

As monstrous as the shot was, only eight ships were sent to the bottom. Still, the massive radiation had shown that navy ships would be ineffective in protecting their crews during a nuclear attack.

As the operation came to a close, the doubting admirals had become believers. About ninety ships had been made radioactive, and a new bomb design had been tested. To commemorate the event, some of the enlisted personnel at the CROSSROADS tests presented themselves with "The Guinea Pig Award." The design was of a pig lying atop a mushroom cloud.[24]

SANDSTONE

By 1947, the search for Communists in Washington had begun to take on epic proportions. That year, President Truman had issued Executive Order 9835, which established the Federal Employee Loyalty Program. Within a short time, a congressional investigation committee, led by Republican congressman Robert E. Lee, was demanding the State Department hand over its "loyalty files." The files were unscreened and were essentially a compilation of gossip listing every allegation, innuendo, and unsubstantiated charge that had been leveled against an accused. A number of people lost their jobs because their names appeared in these files.

By early 1948, another committee called for an investigation of Dr. Edward U. Condon, the director of the National Bureau of Standards. Suspecting Condon was the victim of malicious gossip, Truman immediately limited congressional access to personnel files of government employees. California congressman Richard M. Nixon claimed a cover-up was in progress and that the Democrats were responsible for "the unimpeded growth of the Communist conspiracy in the United States."[25] Even Democrat John F. Kennedy of Massachusetts chimed in that Roosevelt had "given away the Kuriles" to the Russians. "What our young men saved, our diplomats and our President [Truman] have frittered away."[26]

It would be August 1948 before real evidence—and any real spies—turned up. That was the month *Time* editor Whittaker Chambers accused the Harvard-educated Phi Beta Kappa Washington lawyer Alger Hiss of being a past member of a Soviet espionage ring.[27]

During the spring of 1948, ships began returning to the Pacific Proving Ground for the new round of atomic tests. Code-named Operation SANDSTONE, the new series would consist of three "proof tests"—that is, the scientists were interested in testing newer, more efficient bomb designs.

At the time, the nation's stockpile of nuclear weapons numbered only about fifty bombs. Military planners had suggested that 200 would be required for a war with the Soviets.[28] Thus, to conserve plutonium, it was imperative that more efficient bombs be made.

At great expense, three 200-foot steel towers were constructed on the islands of Enjebi, Aomon, and Runit. The three detonations, X-RAY, YOKE, and ZEBRA, occurred between April and May 15, 1948. Undoubtedly, the tests were of various models of the MK-IV, an implosion design and the first production model nuclear weapon.[29,30] Clearly, the United States had no intention of losing its lead position in the nuclear race.

There was, however, a problem. What with shipping equipment and personnel halfway around the world, the testing at Bikini was incredibly expensive. If each new design required a proof test, then something would have to be done to cut costs. After the SANDSTONE series, it was decided that another, less expensive test site would have to be chosen; a test site much closer to home.

Bombs in Nevada

By the late 1940s both the army and navy brass were beginning to feel left out of the nuclear action. The air force was busy in the Pacific testing bigger and bigger strategic weapons, the kinds that could be loaded into planes and dropped on enemy territory. Bikini was perfect for testing the expensive, high-yield strategic bombs, but the army and navy had no use for these monsters. They wanted smaller *tactical* weapons, the kind that could be loaded into a 13-inch cannon. By 1949, no design existed for a small nuclear device. To start from scratch and then transport the various devices to Eniwetok or Bikini for testing would have been prohibitively expensive. What was needed was a test site closer to the continental United States. Otherwise, the weapons the army and navy brass wanted would never see the light of day.[31]

The AEC finally agreed that a continental test site probably *was* an economic idea, and, together with the Defense Department, organized a task force headed by Lieutenant General Elwood R. ("Pete") Quesada to look into the matter and come up with some potential sites.

Several factors were taken into consideration: The site had to be flat, desolate, and a sufficient distance from populated areas. Also, it would be desirable if the test range was located so fallout would be reduced as much as possible.

The AEC wasn't sure of the location of the site where the Soviets had detonated "Joe One." Intelligence experts had it located either on the Ust-Urt Plateau between the Caspian and Aral seas or in the Kazakh uplands near the city of Semipalatinsk. Both areas were located a reasonable distance from the weapons production center near the towns of Sverdlovsk and Chelyabinsk. The point was, no one knew for sure; the continental location had provided excellent security from prying eyes.

Great Britain's Harwell Atomic Research Center was also close to testing an atomic bomb and had been scouting for convenient locations.

Though they would eventually settle on Monte Bello Island off the western coast of Australia, real consideration would be given a much closer site: the Scottish Highlands near the town of Wick.[32]

Clearly, a continental test site was advantageous to any nation testing nuclear weapons.

Quesada's task force finally narrowed the list to five possibilities: White Sands Proving Grounds in New Mexico; Dugway-Windover Proving Grounds in Utah; Las Vegas—Tonopah Gunnery Range near Las Vegas; an area of central Nevada between Fallon and Eureka; and finally, Pimlico Sound near Camp Lejeune, North Carolina.[33]

Of the five possibilities, Pimlico Sound initially looked very good from the standpoint of fallout; the prevailing high-altitude west winds would carry the nuclear clouds out to sea.[34]

Quesada, however, had another spot in mind. As an air force pilot, he had spent time at the Nellis Air Force Base in North Las Vegas and knew the area well. He decided that the nearby Las Vegas—Tonopah Gunnery Range would be perfect. The area was sufficiently desolate, easily secured, and Quesada thought the unusual series of ridges north of the Gunnery Range would be helpful in cutting blast effects.[35,36,37]

Shortly after Quesada made his recommendations, 1,350 square miles of the Las Vegas–Tonopah Gunnery Range was turned over to the Atomic Energy Commission. The army and navy finally had their tactical weapons testing site.

Ranger

January 26, 1951

January 1951 ended unseasonably warm for much of the United States. On January 26, Kansas City, Missouri, and North Platte, Nebraska, both reached a warm 60 degrees. Usually chilly Denver was a relatively balmy 60 degrees. The late winter thaw had apparently arrived.

Entertainment in January 1951 consisted mostly of motion pictures, and that, at least in the West, meant Westerns. In Houston, the Lindale Theater featured *Trigger Jr.* with Roy Rogers and Dale Evans. The Globe offered a Rex Allen movie, *Arizona Cowboy.* Some theaters offered such popular serials as *Rocky Lane* or *King of the Rocket Men.*

According to the *Houston Chronicle,* Jack Benny was planning to tape his radio show in Hollywood "and then fly back to New York to do his television show." In a sidebar near the article, Houstonians were reminded that it is "only 14 more days to pay your poll tax." Though the weather had been mild, a "norther" was expected to bring a hard freeze by the next day.

On the evening of January 26, 1951, Memphis residents—including one Elvis Aaron Presley—had been listening to disc jockey Rufus Thomas's midnight "Hoot 'n Holler" show. Others might have been tuned to WHBQ's Dewey Phillips as he broadcast from the mezzanine of the "Old Chikasaw Hotel on Main." Dewey's show was brought to Memphis listeners "by the People's Furniture Company at 310 South Main."

Twenty-three-year-old Hugh M. Hefner has just landed a job at the Chicago Carton Company. His plans included becoming a cartoonist and publishing a magazine called *Chi* that would be "For and about the people of Chicago." At night he drews cartoons, made plans, and, like other Chicagoans, listened to WOPA disc jockey Big Bill Hill.

Many Bostonians on January 26 were planning to attend the big March of Dimes Ball that was to be held at the Gardens the following Monday evening where bandleaders Tommy Dorsey and Jimmy Green were scheduled to wage a "battle of music." Other guests scheduled to appear were Boris Karloff, Jean Arthur, Jack Carson, and Burl Ives. Newspaper ads promised an exciting time.

On the morning of January 27, a sixty-five-year-old Pioche, Nevada, resident was just sitting down to breakfast.

"There was a kinda flash lit up the window—a real big flash it was. With it comes a bang—bingo, just like that. I though two cars must have hit into one another on the road outside. This white flash started on the ground and sort of swooshed up into air. . . . I reckoned there wasn't much I could do about it," he told reporters. "So I just sat down and ate my breakfast. What did you want me to do?"[1]

RANGER: ABLE

At the Pacific detonations, the AEC had followed a time-honored military practice of naming the individual shots using the international airman's alphabet: Able, Baker, Charlie . . . X-Ray, Yoke, Zebra. The series, however, perhaps to throw off foreign intelligence, sported more original, and obscure, names: CROSSROADS, SANDSTONE. The new test series scheduled for the continental United States would be arranged in a similar fashion. The series, sporting the name (chosen at random) RANGER, would involve five tests, named with the somewhat pedestrian Able, Baker, Easy, Baker-2 (a departure from the international alphabet), and Fox.

Though the first detonations at the brand-new Nevada Proving Grounds would number only five, they would involve a great variety of scientific projects and experiments. For one thing, some of the shots were scheduled to test trigger devices for weapons to be tested in the GREENHOUSE operation scheduled for the spring.

The series at the new continental provings grounds would be brief, over in only thirteen days. Unlike TRINITY, the last nuclear detonation in the continental U.S., all the shots would involve airdrops. The same planes and personnel from the Special Weapons Command and Air Force Headquarters would be involved in all the tests.

In addition to the airplane actually dropping the bomb, others were needed to analyze weather data and to track the path of the nuclear cloud. For this purpose, the Department of Defense called on the 2059th Air Weather Wing. The job of the 2059th was to continually monitor the wind speed and direction at various levels up to their service altitude. Some would be required to actually penetrate the nuclear cloud for samples. Analysis would be done at Tinker Air Force Base in Oklahoma.

The military was becoming increasingly interested in the A-bomb as a tactical weapon. Toward this end, Project Gamma was conceived for Operation RANGER.

For the project, fourteen fortifications were constructed in the loose, rocky soil between zero and 1.13 miles from the drop site. They consisted of a one-man foxhole, ten two-man foxholes, and three prone shelters.

The foxholes were not large: 6 feet long by 2 feet wide by 4 feet deep—dimensions roughly equivalent to those found in Korea. Considering the military situation at the time, the purpose of the experiment was clear.

At the test site, officials were worried that the loosely packed soil might cave in prior to the shot, spoiling the experiments. It was decided to line the fortifications with something sturdy: sandbags. For some reason, however, in the middle of the Nevada desert, not enough sand—or perhaps bags—could be found, and it was decided to line the holes with something else: plywood.

So, shortly before the detonation, military personnel were greeted with the slightly unusual sight of plywood-lined foxholes. A bit of realism was restored to the experiment through the use of wetted, tamped earth as additional support. At least these foxholes, like the real ones, would be damp and wet. All the sandbags that could be located had been placed around a single foxhole just 404 yards west of ground zero.

If a bomb was to detonate on a battlefield, the military wanted to make sure the clothing *their* soldiers were wearing wouldn't catch fire. To this end, the Thermal Effects Program rounded up 100 samples of textiles, various plastics, and some pieces of wood, then placed them on forty eight panels at various distances from the proposed ground zero.[2]

As part of the Radiation Exposure project, forty-one film badges were placed at 98-yard intervals beginning at ground zero and continuing along both the West Access Road and the South Access Road. In order to measure only neutrons, some of the badges along the West Access Road were placed inside cylinders lined with 4 inches of lead.

One problem with the monitoring was the difficulty in distinguishing between immediate and residual radiation. As the weapon detonated, a variety of rays and particles were produced, the so-called prompt radiation. Soon after that, however, the "hot" fission particles—the fallout—from the blast also produced radiation, usually alpha and beta particles. To distinguish between the two, some badges along the West Access Road were placed inside an ingenious "mousetrap" device that closed before the fallout reached the site, protecting the badge from further radiation.

The pretest operations were conducted with clockwork efficiency: The day before the test, the device, minus the nuclear capsule, was transported from Sandia Corporation's New Mexico facility to Kirtland Air Force Base. From there, ground crews positioned it into the bay of a Boeing B-50. The bomber, with a Los Alamos scientist and crew of eleven from the 4925th

Special Weapons Group, was scheduled to take off very early the next morning for Nevada.

Late that evening, forty-five minutes before takeoff, a truck carrying the nuclear capsule arrived from Los Alamos. The capsule, the "heart" of the weapon, was delivered to the Special Weapons Group. It would be kept separate from the bomb until just before release. That way, should the plane crash somewhere over New Mexico or Arizona, there would be no nuclear explosion.

At 1:15 on the morning of January 27, three airplanes received ground clearance from the Kirtland tower, a C-47 and two B-50s, one carrying the bomb. Radar showed no air traffic in the vicinity; the only flights anywhere near the route would be later in the morning: American Airlines had a Douglas DC-6 flying the Dallas-Phoenix route. Both United and TWA had late night–early morning flights, but they would be far north of the proposed route to Indian Springs, Nevada, a small town at the edge of the test site. As the plane passed through the 10,000-foot altitude level, the pilot reminded everyone to put on their oxygen masks. There would be no other traffic at 14,000 feet, their flight altitude. As the plane rumbled through the clear air over Arizona's Painted Desert, the pilot checked his watch. Plans required him to be over the target two hours before the drop.

In the center section of the plane, weapons personnel carefully checked the bomb's circuits.

The bomb was equipped with a barometer, a timer, and radar units sticking out from the tail fins. Poring over the safety switches, the weapons specialist removed the green plugs from the circuit and inserted red ones in their place. This would disengage the safety switches, putting the bomb on "automatic."

On the side of the weapon was placed a long, thin, metal tube. It represented the sensor of the barometer, a device that would measure changes in air pressure as the bomb fell toward the target. Wires running through the detonation circuitry included this simple device. Until it registered sufficient atmospheric pressure, the circuit would not be completed. This was to assure the pilot and crew that the thing wouldn't go off too close to the plane. Only after a given barometric pressure had been reached would the rest of the firing circuit open.

The weapons specialist, using a spark-proof screwdriver, gently removed a metal plate on the side of the weapon. Inside were the huge batteries, the origin of the electrical charge that would result in the detonation. On the other side of the bomb were the fat, cylindrical capacitors. As the bomb began its fall toward the target, the barometric/radar switches would complete the necessary circuits, and the batteries would release their electricity into the system and to the capacitors, where it would be stored temporarily.

Packed tightly into the tail section were four small radar units. Two of the units would send continuous radar signals to the ground, in effect monitoring the altitude of the bomb. It was to be a backup system for the barometer. Two other units were designed to send radar pulses toward the approaching desert floor. An electronic device added to the circuit "counted" the number of returns. After a given number had been counted, ususally twenty-one, a signal would be sent to the firing circuits causing the capacitors to release their charge to the detonators. The shell would then explode, crushing the nuclear sphere and its polonium-beryllium capsule. A microsecond later, the center of Able would be at a temperature of 1 million degrees centigrade.

At 3:45 A.M. Pacific Standard Time, the planes entered Indian Springs airspace. At that point, the pilot of the drop plane cut his engines and descended to the 10,000-foot indicated altitude. Glancing to his left, beyond the red "running lamps" he could see evidence of the other planes in the sky. Mixed with the stars were any number of green and red lights. Besides the other B-50 and the C-47, there were also meteorogical planes. From the air, it was impossible to know the position or velocity of a dot of light. The only thing a pilot could go by was color. If, looking ahead of him, the pilot saw an aircraft's running lights and the green light was on the left, then he knew they were flying toward each other; if the green light was on the right, the other plane was flying away.

Whoever and wherever *they* were, they probably knew where *he* was, considering what he was carrying.

On the ground, the observers took their places about 437 yards south of the Control Point. The AEC wanted to assure everyone of its ability to safely conduct atomic tests inside the U.S., therefore, a number of influential political figures, including congressmen, were invited to watch the show. Early that day they had been given an orientation lecture at the AEC's Las Vegas office, then driven 70 miles to the test site where they would witness the detonation.

After talking with the Control Point, the pilot banked the plane north toward the barren areas north of the test site. There, 7,000 feet over Railroad Valley, members of the Special Weapons Crew opened the barn-door nose of the MK-V weapon and inserted the nuclear capsule. The insertion procedure began at 3:50 A.M.. It went smoothly, and at 4:34 A.M., in the dim red light of the bomb bay, the nose doors were closed.[3] The weapons specialists were the last persons to look inside the Able device. The pilot then made a 180-degree turn back toward the south and climbed to the planned bombing height of 19,700 feet.

Monitoring teams on the ground could hear the acceleration drone of the plane overhead. Sitting in their trucks just south of Groom Mine, 20 miles from ground zero, their job was half over. During the days prior to Able, the teams had surveyed background radiation levels to a radius of about 200 miles of the test site, in the direction the weathermen had said the cloud would pass. After the shot, they would survey the same areas, noting any change in radioactivity. Information about the cloud's path would be radioed to them from the Control Point or from Nellis Air Force Base, to the northwest.

After a short period of time, the radio compass indicated that ground zero was directly below: 36 degrees 48 minutes north by 115 degrees 57 minutes west—Frenchman's Flat. The sectional indicated that this part of southern Nevada was actually 3,140 above sea level. That would mean they were about 16,560 feet above the desert floor. The pilot asked for a barometric check. After being told by ground control that they were in a zone of high pressure, he reached over to reset his altimeter. Then, cutting power slightly, he adjusted his altitude. Flying from an area of low barometric pressure to one of higher pressure would cause the altimeter to give a false reading. And were it not for the backup systems, it might cause the bomb's detonation circuits to open.

At 5:07 A.M., the pilot began the first of two practice runs, following a racetrack pattern over the drop zone. Crewmembers with cameras crowded to the windows.

The B-50 photography plane had followed the drop plane from Kirtland at an altitude of 16,000 feet. While the drop plane made the practice runs, the photography aircraft followed 3 miles behind.

About 5:20 A.M., the second practice run was completed and the pilot was given approval for the drop. The plane swung into the downwind leg of the pattern. At 5:27 the bomb bay doors were opened. Seven minutes later, the B-50 began its third and final bombing run over the target. At exactly 5:44.30 A.M. Pacific Standard Time, the bomb was released and the plane, suddenly 1,000 pounds lighter, nosed skyward.

In Las Vegas, Ronald Gardner, circulation manager for the *Las Vegas Review-Journal,* was jolted from a deep sleep. Outside his window the sky glowed briefly with an eerie gray cast and then for an instant it was as bright as day.

In Henderson, a small town 50 miles from the test site, Wallace Johnson saw a flash of light and felt the concussion. Rattling across the foothills, the aftershocks resembled the sound of a freight train in the distance.

The capacitors had sent the charge to the detonators and the bomb exploded 1,060 feet above the desert floor. The fireball immediately roared toward 17,000 feet, carrying with it rocks, dust, and the remnants of a hundred or so sandbags from the one-man foxhole below. The tropopause, that imaginary boundary between the troposphere and the stratosphere, the region of the jet stream, was far above at 33,000 feet. Meterologists were somewhat relieved. Had the cloud breached this boundary, the particles would stay above the earth who knows how long. In addition, the rapid jet would transport them east in a dense package at 200 mph or faster.

In Bunkerville, Nevada, about 100 miles from the test site, eleven-year-old Gloria Gregerson was awakened early. She would remember RANGER: ABLE: "I remember the day nuclear testing started in Nevada . . . the first blast came without warning. No one was informed that it was going to happen. The flash was so bright, it awakened us out of a sound sleep. We lived in an old two-story home, and when the blast hit, it not only broke out several windows, it made two large cracks in the full length of the house."[4]

Immediately after the detonation, two B-29s circling in the vicinity began to depressurize in preparation for an excursion into the nuclear cloud. The two planes, from the 374th Recon Squadron Weather Group out of Nellis, each carried a crew of ten. Two impact collectors were mounted in boxes attached to the fuselage, one on top behind the wing, the other on the bottom of the plane just forward of the tail skid. The depressurization would hopefully prevent any of the fission products from entering the cabin.

As the plane neared the huge roiling pink cloud, the crewmembers put on their masks and began breathing oxygen. Soon they were inside the remnants of the mushroom. Those not wearing headsets could hear the sound of sand hitting the windscreen. Some undoubtedly were concerned about being inside an atomic cloud, but their superiors had told them it was reasonably safe, if they didn't stay too long. Air Force Headquarters had decided that manned sampling was safe after studying results obtained at the SANDSTONE series in 1948 when a pilot accidentally penetrated one of the nuclear clouds.

The laboratory at Los Alamos had planned to use an unmanned drone to capture cloud material, but mechanical problems had kept it on the ground. After the air force informed lab scientists that two B-29s were going to penetrate the mushroom, Los Alamos asked for a share of the filters.

The B-29 crew, as part of their orders, had been instructed not to eat, drink, or smoke until after they left the plane.

To determine close-in radioactivity, headquarters directed an aerial survey outside the ground zero area. A C-47 and a B-17 left Nellis at the time of the detonation and circled until about 6:45 A.M.. At that time, they flew a prescribed pattern over roads adjacent to the test site. Radioactivity measurements were relayed to ground monitors stationed nearby. Unfortunately, this was not a very good method. After two shots, the AEC would improve upon this procedure, setting up a grid system for determining residual radioactivity.

An hour after the shot, with the cloud still visible in the sky, monitors cautiously entered ground zero. The majority of the foxholes had been demolished. Sandbags were scorched, broken open, and scattered about. Radiation levels increased from 0.01 roentgen/hour 700 yards from the target to a maximum of 0.75 roentgen/hour at the bull's-eye. It had been an extremely accurate drop.

Vehicles used by the monitors were rounded up and checked for radioactivity. The hottest areas were found to be the running boards, floor-boards, tires, and mudflaps. Any place that had come into contact with the ground.

The aircraft used at the site were moved to a central location and hosed down twice. After washing, the activity levels were 0.045 roentgen/hour, so the process was repeated until the levels dropped to at least 0.017 roentgen/hour. The effluent was allowed to run off onto the ground, to be soaked up by the dry desert sand. This procedure would also be used for the planes still overhead, following ABLE.

Circling a few miles from ABLE was another B-29, the cloud tracker. This crew's job was to fly in close proximity to ABLE but not to come into contact with it. Their job was somewhat easier and less hazardous than that of the samplers: All they had to do was track ABLE visually for four to six hours, then trace its direction using instruments.

By 6:00 P.M. Pacific Standard Time the cloud had passed across the Sangre de Cristo Mountains south of Denver and the original tracking plane was running low on fuel. At that time, another B-29 with a crew of eleven from McClellan Air Force Base took up the pursuit. That plane tracked the cloud for another 600 miles across Kansas and Missouri before returning to base.

By the time the nuclear cloud reached the southern New England coast, sometime after 9:00 A.M. Eastern Standard Time on January 29, it would be at least 300 miles wide. It would also be the first of several to visit the airspace over New England within the next few days.

East Coast wags occasionally refer to Rochester, New York, as The World's Largest Darkroom, not so much because it is the headquarters of Kodak, but because the sky there is often overcast. The moisture from Lake Ontario combines with the west winds to create a climate that is predominantly cool, cloudy, and wet.

George Eastman had chosen Rochester as the site for his photography processing plant for a variety of reasons. At the time, the air was relatively clean, but more important, there was a noticeable lack of natural radioactivity. Soils with a high granite content such as that found in New Hampshire or Massachusetts contained significant quantities of heavier—and radioactive—elements such as uranium and thorium. While the levels might be inconsequential to humans, they were deadly to film. Eastman found that northwestern New York State had negligible quantities of such radioactivity.

So on the the snowy morning of January 29, 1951, it was with some concern that technicians noticed the Geiger counters clicking wildly. It was turning into a replay of 1945, only this time the radioactivity was much closer. In fact, it was falling on top of them.

Top officials at Kodak first called the Association of Photographic Manufacturers, who in turn drafted a simply worded telegram to the AEC:

"What are you doing?" Then, the general manager of Kodak phoned Sumner Pike, the AEC commissioner, and informed him of the problem.[5]

After the Kodak call, Pike called Colonel R. T. Coiner, Division of Military Applications, and asked him to look into the matter. Coiner, on the morning of February 2, phoned the manager of the AEC's New York office and asked him to look into the matter.

At the same time, the director of the University of Rochester's Atomic Energy Project called the director of the AEC's New York Operations Office Health and Safety lab and notified him of the high readings.

By the time everyone knew of the radioactivity there wasn't much time left to do anything. On January 31, the temperature increased and a brief thaw had occurred; it had begun to rain. In addition, the New York lab simply did not have the facilities or personnel to properly attend to the task.

In order to make the best use of manpower, it was decided to send the monitors to areas that would most affect people and businesses—i.e., the photographic plant at Rochester. Other areas would be sampled as time and energy permitted. Despite the fact that no advance notice was given, the AEC's New York lab performed admirably.

Disintegrations per Minute

The Rochester snow had been found to be quite radioactive after all. The scientists measured the activity of the material using the time-honored method of determining disintegration per minute. The atoms comprising radioactive material disintegrates, or changes, from one element to another. In doing so, the atoms release a variety of radiation: gamma rays, beta and alpha particles, and neutrons. Using sensitive instruments, the scientists detect and count the rays and particles emitted to get an idea of the radioactivity of the sample. The more disintegrations per minute, the more radioactive the sample. Unfortunately, the instruments could only detect the number of gamma rays or beta particles per time period, not the corresponding amount of energy released during each burst. Thus, there was no clear way to determine exposure levels to the population in terms of rads or roentgens.

Scientists found that the Rochester snowfall was unusually hot: Their calculations indicated 25,000 disintegrations per minute per liter of melted snow. That is, the liter bottle of melted snow contained radioactive materials that were disintegrating—transforming—at the rate of 25,000 atoms per minute, and with each disintegration, at least one form of radiation was released to the environment.

Using other instruments, the radiochemists determined the half-life of the material to be from seventy-four to eighty-five hours, definitely second-generation fission products. No natural product with a half-life of seventy-four to eight-five hours is normally found in snow. There could be no other source.

Investigation and back-calculations uncovered more information. At the same time the radioactive snow was falling in Rochester, the town of Ithaca, New York, was experiencing dry fallout. Near midnight on Monday, January 29, radioactivity increased to a peak ten times normal (experienced from natural granite and cosmic rays).

In Lexington, Massachusetts, home of the Minutemen, activity about five times normal occurred between 10:00 P.M., also on January 29, and 2:00 A.M. the next day.

In New York City, the weather fluctuated between cold and thaw. It was difficult to determine just what snow was radioactive. Monitors took samples from streams and taps in the city, trying to determine just when—and how much—radioactive precipitation had occurred.

January 29 had seen light snow across New York State. The next day a thaw occurred, and on January 31 snow mixed with rain fell from New York City south to Wilmington, Delaware. Everywhere else it snowed, and the snow was radioactive. By this time, monitors discovered something else: A second nuclear cloud had passed overhead.

The procedures for the BAKER shot were similar to the one before it. The only difference was the BAKER detonation would be at least eight times larger.

At exactly 5:30 Pacific Standard Time on the morning of January 28, the pilot felt the plane drag noticeably as the huge bomb bay doors swung open. Eight minutes later, at 5:38, the plane banked into a shallow right turn. The final bombing run had begun. Fourteen minutes, ten seconds later, the BAKER bomb was released, 16,560 feet over the target.

A person jumping out of an airplane, unless he chooses to use a parachute, will eventually attain a downward velocity that will stabilize at approximately 125 mph. This is the speed at which the force exerted by the viscosity of the air, the drag, is equal to the downward force of gravity. Unless, the object is designed to cut through the air, this final or terminal velocity is as fast as an object can fall, regardless of the height.

Bombs, however, are usually streamlined. It keeps them from tumbling end over end while falling toward the ground. Aesthetics aside, a streamlined projectile is an accurate one. And it arrives at the target more quickly.

The streamline BAKER device probably was moving in excess of 200 mph as it passed through the 1,080-foot level. Three and seven-tenths seconds before impact with the desert floor, the device detonated.

Bob Alexander was asleep in his Las Vegas home when he was awakened by what he thought was carlights shining through his window. Upon realizing what it was he went outside to get a better view.

Wayne Kirch, an auto mechanic, was driving along the Tonopah Highway, looking for a stalled car he was supposed to pick up. Suddenly the sky lit up.

It was a white, shiny sort of light. I got out of the car and stood in the road to watch. It was as light as day. I guess that lasted, say two seconds, then there came an orange glow that covered almost as much sky. You could see it plainly because it was just before dawn.

It seemed like three or four minutes and then came the air shock and the noise. It wasn't like an earthquake. It was more like a concussion.

The noise came three separate times—echoes, I suppose. I know people who heard up to eleven.[6]

Less than 100 miles away, near Bunkerville, Nevada, little Gloria Gregerson was waiting for the explosion. Excited by the explosion of the day before, her father had packed the entire family, still in pajamas, into the family car and had driven to a nearby hill so they could all witness the detonation. She remembered the event: "From atop that hill we could see a bright flash, and then, a little later, the mushroom cloud. [It took] around three to four minutes for the sound to reach us. It [followed] the river and bounced back and fourth between the mountain ranges. It felt and sounded like a strong earthquake. We could see the planes circles as they approached the spot where they were to drop the bomb, then the flash."[7]

Propelled by an 8-kiloton wallop, BAKER's shock wave first jolted the B-50s flying nearby, then, skipping off the slight inversion layer of warmer air, crashed back to the ground miles from ground zero. The mushroom cloud, a bubble of hot gas, soared through 25,000 feet within a mere five minutes. It would eventually climb 3,000 feet into the stratosphere, 35,000 feet above sea level and 31,800 feet above Frenchman's Flat.

Meteorologists reviewing "winds aloft" charts noticed that the wind was from the west-northwest, 290 degrees at about 40 mph. BAKER would, like ABLE, visit the East Coast. But first it would cross over Bunkerville, Nevada.

In Bunkerville, between 9:00 and 10:00 A.M., school officials called the classes out to the football field to see the pinkish-orange cloud pass overhead.[8]

Tracker planes from McClellan Air Force Base followed the huge, pink cloud as it traced its way across Nevada, Utah, and western Colorado. Near Denver, another plane and crew took over and the initial tracking party went home to relax. Some of them didn't want to miss a radio favorite: Edgar Bergen and Charlie McCarthy. That evening the show would feature Bergen and McCarthy getting lost in the newly constructed Pentagon building and meeting a fellow named Earl Twing, who sold compasses and rations to lost tourists.

The BAKER cloud seemed to follow a trajectory not much different from the ABLE shot the day before. Meteorologists at the AEC, crossing their fingers, were hoping the cloud would take a different course, but no such luck. Like ABLE, the BAKER cloud skated across the Midwest, heading for the Northeast. Estimates and reports from the B-29s sent to tail it placed the arrival time on January 31–February 1.

As February came in, a light snow fell all across New York State. The precipitation ended the next day, but the skies remained cloudy. Those walking in Central Park near 66th Street on February 1 may have noticed a light snowfall that barely covered the ground. The thaw of January 30 had melted some of the snow, leaving the light tan of the grass exposed. Now the ground was again turning white as the flurries returned. Soon it was over.

Monitors from AEC's New York lab had heard that BAKER was heading their way, along the same path ABLE had taken. The product of a detonation eight times larger than ABLE, this cloud could possibly be more radioactive. On February 2, as the AEC monitors placed the snow samples into the glass vials, they were more than a little concerned. What would the readings be? Did New York City receive fallout from BAKER also?

The analysis came in and the results looked bad. BAKER had, indeed, followed the same path eastward. The Central Park samples showed radioactivity levels of 340 disintegrations/minute/liter. It was not as high as the Rochester samples had been, but analysis showed it also couldn't have been from ABLE. Was there some sort of "pipeline in the sky" connecting Nevada with New York City?

Snow samples from the little town of Medina, west of Rochester and near Niagara Falls, had been collected on the same day. They showed a disintegration rate of 22,000/minute/liter of snow, in sharp contrast to the low readings found in New York City. Radioactive elements dissolved in a liter bottle of melted snow taken in the small town of Hannibal, New York, produced a remarkable 25,300 disintegrations/minute. Again, only *rate* of disintegration was measured, not the *strength* of the radiation. Information that would have compared the radiation measurements to more commonly known radiation exposures—for example, medical X-rays—was not taken.

Radioactive snow was also found in the appropriately named Deposit, New York (450 disintegrations/minute/liter), as well as in Chateaugay, a village in the northern part of the state.

The two detonations would be the only ones that would cross the state of New York. Later, after other RANGER detonations, Washington, D.C., would also receive radioactivity, but for the time being, New York had already taken its only fallout of the RANGER series.[9]

The February 1 shot in the RANGER series, EASY, was to be similar to the first.

Gladwin Hill, a reporter in the Los Angeles bureau of the *New York Times,* was standing alone at the edge of the Air Force Bombing and Gunnery Range, just off U.S. Highway 95, 25 miles from ground zero. An excerpt from his report reads:

> Dawn was just lighting the eastern horizon, but the moon and stars were still bright overhead. Not a sound stirred the virtually uninhabited coun-

tryside except the crickets, sawing away despite the almost freezing temperature.

As the hands of my watch crept past 5:45, the expected moment of firing, it looked like the third successive morning's vigil was again in vain.

Then suddenly the surrounding mountains and sky were brilliantly illuminated for a fraction of a second by a strange light that seemed almost mystical.

It was strange because, unlike light from the sun, it did not appear to have any central source but to come from everywhere. It flashed almost too quickly to see. Yet the image that persisted for a fraction of a second afterward in the eye was unforgettable.

It was a gray-green light of infinite coldness, apparently completely devoid of any red tones. In its momentary glare, the mountains looked in the silence like the weird and lifeless peaks of a dead planet. There came the fleeting thought that this indeed was the state in which many atomic explosions might leave the earth.

An eerie silence persisted. Mechanically, I started counting. I got to ten and nothing happened. Twenty. Thirty. Forty. At 110 I hesitated, wondering if this could be some new type explosion without sound. Just then a deafening blast, like heavy artillery, shook the ground, followed by several quick repercussions. The pressure bulged my eardrums.

Then the explosion began reverberating, first in many directions among the nearby mountains, then in the distance. Booming like thunder, the echoes started coursing around the horizon in regular clockwise progression, completing the cycle of the compass in about fifteen seconds. No mushroom of smoke or other manifestation of the explosion was visible. The desert returned to silence.

Experiencing it gave one, despite the scientific explanation about atomic fission, a strange feeling of fleeting contact with eternal powers.[10]

Despite Hill's majestic prose, Easy had been a baby bomb, detonating with the force of only one kiloton. Winds pushed the cloud south toward Las Vegas before it split into two trajectories.

One remained level with the mushroom and traveled south-southwest, crossing California's San Bernadino County, then the southwestern edge of Arizona before swinging deep into Mexico. On February 6 it would return, cutting cleanly across the Florida peninsula between Miami and Tampa before heading toward the North Atlantic.

Storm Warning

Fallout was, to most Americans, still a relatively new and obscure term in 1951. The public seemed interested primarily in the tremendous explosive power of their new weapons. Film clips of the Pacific detonations were part of every motion picture newsreel: The audience watched in awe as the huge fireballs boiled into the sky creating huge white thunderheads towering 40,000 feet or more.

Now these explosions were taking place in Nevada, in America's own backyard. Many wondered how the atmosphere would react to such goings-on. Could it affect the weather?

When queried, government meterologists patiently explained that a nuclear detonation was puny compared to even a medium-sized Kansas thunderstorm. The scientists explained that the climate is related to changes in temperature, that the nuclear debris in the huge fluffy mushrooms was the same temperature of the surrounding air, thus there was really no way that the blast could affect weather patterns.

Many, however, remained unconvinced, particularly in light of the weather following the RANGER detonations.

Strong winds and a complex weather pattern had lifted portions of EASY's mushroom cloud to 30,000 feet, then sent it due southwest, toward El Paso. Several days later it would cross north of Houston then move northeast as part of a cold front, dropping freezing—and radioactive—rain from Texas to Pennsylvania. In Tennessee, the ice storm damaged utilities and phone lines, leaving some areas without electricity or communications for up to seven days. After a tour of the southern United States, the nuclear cloud headed north toward the ocean off New England.

In Boston three days before, New York Congresswoman Katherine St. George told guests at the annual luncheon meeting of the Women's National Republican Club that General Douglas MacArthur—and not President Truman—should decide "when and where the atom bomb shall be used." Also on the agenda was California senator Richard M. Nixon.

As the nuclear clouds from Nevada neared the city that evening, moviegoers in Boston visited the Astor on Tremont and Boylston streets to see *The Magnetic Tide*. Others took in the feature at the Paramount-Fenway, one starring Doris Day, Steve Cochran, and Ronald Reagan. Its somewhat ominous title: *Storm Warning*. It was an appropriate name for a movie considering what happened next.

As the BAKER clouds passed to either side of Boston, the weather began acting strangely. Snow-melting warm weather and a torrential rain combined to inundate the city with water. On February 1, as the EASY cloud passed to the east, Boston's sky cleared and the temperature plunged to 3 degrees Fahrenheit. The city, already plagued by electrical blackouts caused by storm-flooded manholes and waterlogged switches, came to a standstill. The suburbs of Savin Hill, Cambridge, Revere, and Wellesley were plunged into darkness for much of the evening. The downtown Hub Hotel was darkened for 2½ hours. That evening, the weather was so bad that only 2,878 Bostonians visited the Boston Garden to watch Holy Cross defeat Chicago's Loyola University, 81–56.

The next day, the *Boston Globe* remarked on the unusual weather: "Topsy-Turvy Weather Buffets New England: Zero temperatures, record-breaking warm weather, snow, sleet, rain, thaw, fog, ice, strong winds—New

England reeled under the two-day onslaught of turbulent weather, but it looked as if it would calm down today.''

It didn't. That same day an unusually warm southwestern wind raced across the city, raising the temperatures again to a balmy 57.4 degrees Fahrenheit matching a record that had been set in 1917. The winds also brought a thick fog. Visibility on Boston Common by 9:30 that evening was only 10 feet. By that time, however, Bostonians had noticed an unusually strong wind racing across their city. In a short time, the wind was roaring along at 40 mph. By midnight, the pea-soup fog was gone.

Elsewhere, snow—probably radioactive—fell as far south as St. Augustine, Florida. In Greenburg, Indiana, the mercury plunged to a record − 35 degrees Fahrenheit. In larger cities across the nation, phones at the local offices of the U.S. Weather Service were ringing constantly as the meteorologists wearily assured the callers that the bombs had nothing to do with the horrible winter weather. By the afternoon of February 2, yet another atomic detonation had occured.

BAKER-2 was to be a replica of the original BAKER shot. It would involve an 8-kiloton device, similar in design characteristics to the one detonated on January 28. The only hitch in this shot came when the documentary aircraft, a B-50 loaded with cameras, sprang fuel leaks. The Department of Defense decided that the photos weren't all that important anyway, so, in the wee hours of February 2, only two planes left Kirtland for Indian Springs.

At 1:23 on the morning of February 2, one minute after the B-50 "drop plane" left the ground, a C-47 "emergency aircraft" took off. It consisted of a crew of four and a "disaster team" of ten. Should the B-50 go down in the rugged mountains between Kirtland and Indian Springs, the disaster team would notify Kirtland and Indian Springs, cordon off the area, retrieve the weapon material, and attend to the injured.

At 5:32 A.M., high above Frenchman's Flat, the bomb bay doors were opened.

Caldwell, Idaho, is a medium-sized community a few miles west of Boise, nestled near Idaho's Owyee Mountains. To many of the residents, Nevada meant "that desert down south," or perhaps Las Vegas. Thoughts of the test site were far or absent from their minds. After all, southern Nevada was over 500 miles away. But early on the morning of February 2, they saw it, clearly visible over the mountains to the south. The brief flash of blue-green light could mean only one thing: An atomic bomb had gone off somewhere down there and it was close enough to be seen.

Clint Mosher, a reporter for the International News Service, was much closer to the detonation. Excerpts from his report:

At 5 A.M. Thursday, the desert air was like wine—chilled to a punishing 29 degrees. As a veteran member of the early bird atom bomb watchers, I taxied out beyond the city to an open spot where the visibility was good. . . .

Nearby my vantage point was a restaurant. The door was locked and inside a blonde waitress was tidying up the place for the six o'clock opening hour. I banged on the window and made the sign of a man dying for a cup of coffee but she shook her head and went on about her business. I faced back toward the dark mountains, buttoned up my overcoat a notch higher and waited.

Somewhere, on the still air, came a cock's crow, followed by several more in nearby barnyards. In the east a ribbon of light lay along the mountaintops. The moon was a still crescent in the sky.

A single plane flew overhead, its green wing light visible. Maybe nothing would happen. That seemed almost preferable at the time. Nerves are bad before coffee and dawn anyway.

The pilot pushed forward on the throttles and the engines strained in an effort to overcome the drag of the open bomb bay. The target was almost below. The crewmember functioning as bombardier began his countdown, and at 5:48.01 BAKER-2 began its fall toward the target.

Mosher's report continues:

An intense white light, pure in color and frightening to behold, rose up from the desert high enough to silhouette the 6,000-foot saw-toothed peaks of the Sheep Mountains, 40 miles from the fringe of Las Vegas.

Five seconds later the tableland and the sky and the mountains were dark again and the early bird bomb watchers braced themselves for the air shock waves which reach this city as an inevitable consequence of these experiments.

At 5:51 o'clock, they came, five long speculative minutes after the light in the sky. . . . In these intervening minutes I backed against the outside of the restaurant. As anyone would, I thought about Korea and Russia and death and the world 20 years from now. One instant there was a deep rumble as if from the artillery of a dozen armies.

And then two seconds later, the great push of air from which there is no escaping shook houses, rattled windows and sent plaster showering over carpets in some parts of the city. Swoosh. It was like standing too near a cannon.

It wasn't as big a show as the third blast last Sunday and Las Vegans are now taking these things in their stride, but nevertheless [this] blast was an awesome reminder that beyond the far mountains, the government's top scientists are tinkering with the deadliest weapon man has ever conceived.

I asked the waitress, "Did you see it?"

"Yes," she said, "what do you want: Black or cream and sugar?"

And that's the way it was.[11]

BAKER-2 had detonated at 1,100 feet above the target with a force of 8 kilotons. Since the second or third shot, reporters had become more interested in the detonations. For some reason, they thought BAKER-2 was "two or three times the intensity of any of its predecessors," and wondered if the power of the detonations might be increased "possibly to the point of severe damage."[12]

In Los Angeles, some residents had risen early, waiting to catch a glimpse of the flashes. A few amateur photographers had set up cameras facing east, set on photoelectric shutter. When the flash came, lighting the sky with its characteristic glare, the shutter tripped automatically, producing an urban scene illuminated by atomic light.

Las Vegas residents had other concerns. They were close enough to BAKER-2 to experience the more pronounced effects. In the first of many such incidents, a large plate glass window in a Las Vegas furniture store was shattered by the force of the shock wave. A resident living in the downtown area said the explosion made his house shake "like a bowl of jello that had been kicked."

In North Las Vegas, a suburb slightly closer to the test site, two homes experienced broken windows.

Meanwhile, as a result of erratic wind patterns, the stem began to lean noticeably, a dark slash across the sky pointing in the direction of Sunrise Mountain, east of Las Vegas.

By 8:00 A.M. Pacific Standard Time, it had mostly disappeared from view. Some Las Vegas residents, however, thought they saw a very suspicious cloud pass overhead. Authorities, simply said it was merely "smoke accumulated by inversion of the normal sequence of cold and warm air layers."[13] Unfortunately, the authorities were wrong. The lower portion of the stem had in fact passed directly over Las Vegas, heading in the direction of Phoenix and Tucson.

In Schenectady, New York, Dr. Kenneth H. Kingdom, technical manager of the Knolls Atomic Power Laboratory, reported "a slight increase in atmospheric radioactivity presumably due to the same sources as that noticed in Rochester [several days before].

"It should always be kept in mind that measuring instruments are thousands of times more sensitive to radioactivity than is the human body and that, therefore, the detection of radioactivity by sensitive instruments is not a cause for alarm."[14]

Steel Pots and Funnels

The TRINITY cloud had been chased only a few hundred miles. Shortly afterward, Atomic Energy Commission officials were astonished to find the fallout had reached as far away as Rochester, New York. RANGER's clouds received only cursory attention also, and again, fallout turned up in Rochester. A decision was made to closely monitor the paths of the clouds—mile by mile, regardless of altitude—all the way from the Nevada Test Site to the points at which they left the continent.

Special air force squadrons dubbed Larks, were assigned the responsibility of tracking the nuclear debris. Their job was to locate a specific segment of the nuclear cloud, determine its activity and size, and note if it encountered any weather that may enhance fallout.

To augment the system, weather stations around the country would be provided with special steel pots equipped with funnels and sticky filters. After a given amount of time, the filters were to be analyzed on scintillation counters to determine if the dust they collected was radioactive.

The scintillation counters would record the number of gamma rays or beta particles from the fallout, thus giving a rough idea of the relative deposition. Since the bursts corresponded to the disintegration of a radioactive atom, as before, the readings would be recorded as disintegrations per minute, hour, or day. To more accurately depict fallout depositions, a unit of surface area was added, so, an area might experience "340 disintegrations per square foot." That meant, each square foot of surface area was (theoretically) covered by radioactive fallout that was disintegrating at a rate of 40 disintegrations/minute.

To give an overall assessment of fallout deposition, the readings were *averaged* over a twenty-four period. In this manner was born the somewhat cumbersome "disintegrations/minute/square foot/day."

Later, the term "disintegrations/minute/square foot" would be replaced with the somewhat less clumsy "millicuries/100 square miles." This conversion was based on the fact that one millicurie (mCi) represented 37 million bursts of radiation per second. So one millicurie/100 square miles would be equal to 37 million disintegrations per second over the 100-square-mile are (2,787,840,000 square feet) and would be equal to 0.0133 disintegrations/second/square foot of surface area. Unfortunately, the *quality* of the radiation—whether it consisted of gamma rays, X rays, alpha particles, beta particles, or neutrons—would not be examined, only the *frequency* of the disintegrations that accompanied such emissions of radiation. For much of the subsequent testing, the records would indicate only how much fallout landed at given areas. As before, there would be nothing recorded regarding the strength of the radiation; population exposures would remain an unanswered question.

February 5, 1951

On February 4, a reporter for the International News Service asked four-star general J. Lawton "Lightning Joe" Collins if the United States would use guided missiles and heavier artillery in the Korean conflict. Collins replied that the American soldier—"the finest soldier in the world"—would soon be assisted by atomic guided missiles and artillery. Changing the subject to conventional warfare, General Collins went on the discuss the problems inherent in training troops to walk, "particularly American youngsters that are wedded to the idea that if they want to go to the movies two blocks away they take the family car."

"Yes, our troops were roadbound at the start. I'm afraid they will always be relatively roadbound, till they learn that if they're going to save casualties they must get off the roads in the forward areas."

Returning to the subject of atomic missiles, General Collins remarked, "The guided missile has great possibilities as a means of delivering the atomic bomb tactically and for use in close support under adverse weather and lighting conditions."[15]

It was not a particularly surprising statement. During this time period a number of military men and politicians—among them, Senator Margaret Chase Smith of Maine—had already clamored for atomic weapons to be used against the North Koreans.

Congressman James E. Van Zandt of Pennsylvania appeared on the television program "Longines Chronograph" to explain his position on Korea: "It's my opinion that we should fight the war to win in Korea, rather than try to settle it at the diplomatic table, which is impossible when you are dealing with Russia."

When asked if he would use the atom bomb in Korea, Van Zandt replied, "Very definitely. I've always been a firm believer that we should use the atomic bomb not only on Korea but north of the Yalu River in Manchuria. . . . I think that there are several targets, uh, in northern Korea that we could use, uh, we could use—that is, we could destroy them with the atomic bomb . . . we could destroy them and contaminate them. And then, of course, there are targets in Manchuria that *should* be destroyed."[16]

Congressman Lloyd Bentsen (D.-Tex.) also proposed to the president that he "advise the commander of the North Korean troops to withdraw his troops beyond the 38th parallel within one week or use that week to evacuate civilians from a specified list of Korean cities that will be subjected to atomic attack by the United States Air Force."[17]

The Cobalt-60 Line

With Hiroshima and Nagasaki still fresh in the minds of the planners, the use of the atomic bomb was not an unrealistic proposition. It had been used once, with remarkable success. Perhaps it should be used again.

Others thought the use of such weapons would bring Russia into the picture. The Soviet Union was a closed box, in the words of Churchill "a mystery wrapped in an enigma.'' No one knew what they would do or what they would use militarily. In this view, use of the Bomb was too great a chance to take. Perhaps something that wasn't so obvious yet was just as deadly? Something radioactive. In lieu of the Bomb, some military planners finally came up with a place to dump atomic waste: North Korea. Scientists countered that the Koreans could mop up the hot material and make an A-bomb. No, it had to be useless for weapons yet quite radioactive. They finally came up with a plan: Low-flying aircraft would lay down a line of intensely radioactive cobalt-60 across the 38th parallel. With a half-life of only five years, cobalt-60 was the perfect choice. Anyone trying to cross the line in the forseeable future would need a lead suit. This idea was a favorite of General Douglas MacArthur; the military took it quite seriously.

Still others took the middle ground. What if the aircraft were shot down? What if the plane sprang a leak back at the base? The cleanup of nuclear waste after such an accident would involve an horrendous expense. Better, they said, to bomb the enemy, but not with huge, 20-kiloton monsters. Something was needed that was atomic in nature but would give the impression that a conventional war was being fought. What was needed was a bomb small enough to be lobbed by the artillery or even bazookas and ''safe'' enough to allow our own troops maneuverability amid the debris. The military needed a tactical atomic weapon. Not as big as a bomb, but something that would defeat the enemy on the conventional battlefield. Something that could be used in Korea.

Actually, there was another reason why the military, and especially the army, wanted tactical atomic weapons. Stated simply, the backbone of the army—and marines—was the infantry, and any use of A-bombs would involve the air force, the only military service with airplanes that could carry the weapons to the targets. Shortly after World War II, the air force had split from the army, taking its planes with them and leaving behind only helicopters. No one seriously thought a helicopter could deliver an A-bomb. The generals wanted to keep the infantry a viable force in military actions. They also wanted to keep their jobs.

So during the early 1950s, army generals could be heard clamoring for smaller, lighter weapons. Ones that could be fired using a "guided missile," artillery, or even hand-delivered as a satchel charge by some courageous GI. In the February 5 interview with General Collins, it is significant that he made no mention of the conventional method of bringing the weapon to the target: airplanes.

It is possible that General Collins and the others saw Korea as an opportunity for the infantry to gain more control of atomic weapons. Under the circumstances, it is no wonder that Korea was not bombed; at the time, only strategic weapons existed, and the air force would have had to deliver them. The other joint chiefs would most likely have balked at that idea. On the other hand, if true tactical weapons—and the necessary rearrangements made in infantry strategy—had been developed during the period of the Korean conflict, bombing North Korea with nuclear weapons might have been a viable option.

The last shot in the series, Fox, would be extremely powerful—that much was known. On Sunday, the Atomic Energy Commission released a statement warning residents of a major blast "scheduled for the near future." Prior to this, in Las Vegas, some large plate glass windows had shattered, and the AEC was concerned about the potential for injuries. The AEC statement to area residents stated:

> As was demonstrated Friday, test explosions at our Indian Springs site created sound waves which can break windows in Las Vegas. The greatest risk is to large windows and the lesser risk to small windows, such as those in homes.
>
> Glass may fall inwards or outwards. Such broken glass can endanger persons in the line of fall. Persons should avoid being close to inside or close to outside windows immediately after our test detonations. We particularly caution those persons who see the initial flash not to crowd to the windows, nor to stand near them outside. Risk from breaking glass will be materially reduced if the shades are drawn.
>
> The risk of window breakage may be reduced by such methods as opening smaller windows, sections of larger windows, or doors to permit equalization of air pressure inside and outside the structure.
>
> There will be another test in the near future and residents of Las Vegas and other nearby areas are advised to take the precautions indicated above.
>
> Beginning now, they should take these precautions at the appropriate time each day and continue them until notice that the current series of tests is completed.[18]

Although the AEC had warned residents living in the vicinity to stay away, on shot day the highways were lined with hundreds of automobiles. Some people sat on the hoods of their cars, drinking hot coffee from thermoses and eating sandwiches.

Leonard Slater, chief of the Los Angeles Bureau of *Newsweek* magazine, was standing along Highway 95 with groups of sightseers. His report:

> The desert was black as pitch . . . and the temperature had fallen to 35 degrees. Knots of photographers and radiomen fussed over their equipment and stamped their feet to keep warm. A girl giggled in a parked car.
>
> A hundred feet up the highway from Jim Wilkinson's tiny café, a lonely outpost shown on the larger maps as Cactus Springs, a police car's red spotlight blinked solemnly. It, and an Army jeep, marked the end of the line for The Uninvited. Beyond this roadblock lay the forbidden territory of the 5,000-square-mile Las Vegas Bombing and Gunnery Range. Two Stetson-hatted pistol-girded Clark County deputy sheriffs, an AEC guard from Los Alamos, and a plainclothes Army intelligence agent

barred the way—just as they had during four previous dawn "test demonstrations."

In the starry sky to the northeast, under the Big Dipper, a light was
moving. "A plane," somebody shouted. The light went out. The time was
5:48 A.M. We held our breaths. The cops put on harlequin-shaped sun
glasses.[19]

Inside the test site facility, AEC commissioners Thomas E. Murray and
Sumner Pike waited for the explosion. Also with them were AEC general
manager Marion W. Boyer and Senator William Knowland, a California Republican and member of the joint congressional Atomic Energy Commission.

High above the four corners area of New Mexico, Arizona, Utah, and
Colorado, 330 miles from ground zero, Captain Edward Boyce guided his
TWA plane toward Los Angeles. The early morning flight was the New
York—Los Angeles shuttle. The lights were out in the passenger section and
most of the travelers were asleep, blankets thrown over them in the chill of
the cabin. Ahead of him, all was dark. He had received a report that the airspace over Nevada would be restricted, as would much of Utah for a brief
period of time. There must be a test scheduled. Glancing at his watch—5:30
A.M. Pacific Standard Time—he wondered if he would be able to see the
blast from this distance. Over the entire Southwest the sky was clear.

At exactly 5:47 A.M., 1,435 feet over the desert, the capacitors wired to
the detonating caps released their charge.

Newsweek's Leonard Slater:

Then the world blew up.

A tremendous flash of eerie white light glared over the horizon from
Frenchman's Flat, inside the bombing range, about 20 miles from where
we stood. Brighter than daylight, it illuminated, for an instant, Wilkin-
son's café, the cameras and microphones, the red coat of a woman nearby,
the Mobil gas pumps, the purple mountains all around us. We were
blinded momentarily.

Then, over the low-lying Spotted Mountain range which stood between us and Frenchman's Flat, a gigantic red ball of fire whirled into
view. Purple gathered at its edges and spread within.[20] Two minutes and
45 seconds after the initial glare, the first thunderous reverberation hit
us—the sound slamming into our eardrums like blows, then echoing
among the hills around us. Several of us leaped involuntarily into the air.
Again, the reverberation thundered out of Frenchman's Flat and rolled
toward us.

Then, silence and a white plume, gradually becoming mushroom
shaped, rose into the sky.[21]

Captain Boyce, 18,000 feet over Durango, Colorado, had a balcony
seat to the show: "I saw the light reflected off the mountains farther east,
then turned to see this huge thing, growing and getting redder until it finally

died out. I think it hung there in the sky for more than ten seconds. It was just like the sun exploding. It was a frightening thing, really terrifying, far worse looking than I had imagined."[22]

Atop 5,710-foot Mount Wilson, Gil Martyn, a television newscaster for Los Angeles station KTLA waited for the shock wave. The afternoon before, crews from both KTLA and another Los Angeles station, KTTV, mounted cameras on the rocky surface of the mountain and aimed the lenses in the direction of southern Nevada. At 5:30 A.M. the flash came, almost searing the image tubes with its intensity. Sleepy television viewers in fog-shrouded Los Angeles watched as their scenes went from black to white and then back to black. Clete Roberts, a veteran newscaster who had covered the Pacific shots, was broadcasting from Cactus Springs, a small settlement near the site. He stayed on the air for fifteen minutes after the detonation, describing the rosy orange flash and the cloud. "This is bigger than Bikini," he said.[23]

Two large plate glass windows at auto showrooms in downtown Las Vegas were shattered by the blast. Windows rattled on the campus of the University of California at Los Angeles, when the shock wave hit at 6:12 A.M.

At Indian Springs, several small windows were broken or blown out. At that site, the shock wave was followed by a blast of warm air rushing across the ground.

The flash was seen in Oakland, California, where one resident called it "terrifying." Among other cities witnessing Fox's glare was Boise, Idaho, 500 miles to the north.

After the detonation, an irregular white cloud appeared above the Frenchman's Flat area. Those who had watched the entire series called it different from any they had seen before.

Newsweek's Slater:

> At about 40,000 feet, the cloud became a great fist—with four knuckles showing clearly—and the first rays of the morning sun caught this ominous cloud and tinted it a delicate pink.
>
> All the way back to Las Vegas, it trailed our car.
>
> On the road back, we met the first American A-bomb refugee, Mrs. Minnie Cobb, 34, of Indian Springs. Mrs. Cobb showed us through her beaverboard house next door. The screen doors had been ripped off; two windows were smashed; five pictures had been swept off the living-room walls, her stockings, which had been lying on a chair, had been blasted into space.
>
> The hundreds of persons who had arisen early ("these A-bombs are Las Vegas's alarm clocks," one man said) and stood outside their homes in their bathrobes to watch the blast, had by now dressed, breakfasted, and begun their normal workday tasks.[24]

Fox had detonated with a force of 22 kilotons, equivalent in strength to the Nagasaki bomb. Also like the Nagasaki bomb, Fox had exploded fairly close to the ground: 1,435 feet (FAT MAN had exploded at 1,640 feet). That morning, the tropopause was located 40,000-feet above sea level; Fox's mushroom passed this border, reaching into the stratosphere 3,000-feet before beginning its journey southeast toward Las Vegas, Phoenix and the McAllen-to-Brownsville area of Texas.[25]

The first nuclear test series at the Nevada Test Site was finally over.

The Race for the Super

The driving force behind the American H-bomb was born on January 15, 1908, in Budapest, Hungary, to Max and Ilona Teller, a solidly middle-class family. His name originally was Ede (pronounced "Edda"), but he would later change it to the German-English form: Edward. He was an unusual child whose first words—at the age of three—consisted of whole sentences. By the age of six, he was showing an interest in mathematics. Instead of counting sheep at night, he would practice computations in his head until he fell asleep. A few weeks before his birth, his mother had told a friend that she expected her second child would be a son and that he would be famous. Even at age six, Ede Teller was giving every indication of living up to his mother's expectations. Then politics intervened.

Prior to the war, those living in Budapest were acutely aware of the impending break up of the Austro-Hungarian empire. Disparate nationalities began to splinter from the country, wanting to take pieces of it with them. Transylvania was lost to Romania. Slovenia and Serbia soon followed. By war's end, the Austro-Hungarian empire was no more. To the east, Lenin's Communist revolution had toppled the czar and was threatening to spread to the rest of Europe.

In the political vacuum following the war, lawyer Béla Kun and the Communist party took over the government of Hungary. Farms and industries were nationalized. As a result, commerce came to an abrupt halt and economic chaos became a new way of life. Kun, determined to bring order, instead added to the confusion by arresting "traitors" to the new "regime of the proletariat." To show that he meant business, Kun ordered the corpses of the "traitors" hung from lampposts. In 1919, Kun finally admitted failure and fled to Austria. Almost immediately, Budapest was occupied by the Romanian army in league with a wealthy Hungarian aristocrat, Admiral Miklós Horthy de Nagybánya. Hungary was no longer Communist.

Unfortunately, with Horthy it would eventually swing in the opposite direction, toward fascism, and eventually into the grip of Hitler's National Socialists in the form of the Arrow Cross party.

Despite all this, Edward Teller somehow went through an essentially normal childhood and schooling that eventually took him through several prestigious European universities. In August 1935, shortly after his marriage to Mici, his childhood sweetheart, Teller arrived in the United States. Eight years later, he would find himself at Los Alamos, working on the atomic bomb.

There was, of course, no word from Budapest about the horrors of the Holocaust. Hungarian historian Emil Lengyel gives a description of what took place in Hungary during the last weeks of the war:

> What the Hungarist-Arrow Cross government did in these months of Hungarian agony belongs in a book on psychiatry. The Soviets were now deep in Hungary, racing toward the capital, held largely by crack German units. The Hungarian government decided that all streets in Budapest which were called after Jews should be renamed. Up to the last minute freight cars badly needed by the government for the prosecution of the war were filled with Jews to be shipped to German extermination camps. Boys of twelve and teen-agers carried rifles and shot down anybody whom they suspected of being Jews. In a frenzy of murder Arrow Cross [government] men lined up Jews—women and children too—along the Danube banks so that their bodies should topple into the river, saving the inconvenience of digging graves.[1]

Though his family in Budapest escaped death, Teller never forgave the Communists—or the Fascists—for the ravages they had inflicted on his homeland.[2,3,4]

The first glimmer of an idea about a thermonuclear bomb came to Edward Teller in the fall of 1941, not at a laboratory, but while in a New York restaurant. Teller had recently arrived in New York from Washington to begin work at Columbia University. One day, while he was having lunch with physicist Enrico Fermi, the subject of nuclear fission and atomic bombs came up. Fermi mentioned that the heat from such a detonation might equal that inside stars, and it might fuse hydrogen to create even more energy. George Gamow and Hans Bethe had already determined that stars produce energy by fusing hydrogen into helium; why couldn't it be done on earth?[5] Certainly the proposed atomic weapon would create temperatures hot enough to do the trick—a *thermo* nuclear reaction.[6]

The only problem was that light hydrogen atoms would probably be bounced out of the way by the pressure. Fermi suggested that the heavier, neutron-rich form (or isotope) of hydrogen might be more easily fused. Normal hydrogen consists of a proton circled by an electron. Deuterium, relatively rare form of hydrogen, consists of an electron circling a proton *and* a neutron.[7]

Teller was impressed. Inexpensive methods were already available for separating the deuterium from normal hydrogen. What Fermi was describing was a relatively inexpensive weapon of tremendous power.[8] From that point on, Teller was hooked on thermonuclear fusion.

Even during the Manhattan Project, when the only goal was a fission bomb, Edward Teller kept dreaming of his fusion weapon. Oppenheimer seemed concerned that Teller was neglecting his work. Rifts developed between Teller and his supervisor, Hans Bethe. Between 1943 and the autumn of 1945, no one besides Edward Teller seemed the slightest bit interested in thermonuclear weapons.

Then in November 1945, unknown to Teller, his old Los Alamos boss took a seat before an open meeting of the Senate Special Committee on Atomic Energy and began explaining the concept of thermonuclear weapons. "How, then can we ignite atomic nuclei?" Hans Bethe asked rhetorically.

"There are only two known methods to obtain such a nuclear chain reaction. One of these is the nuclear fission on which the atomic bomb is based. The other involves the nuclear reactions which we believe take place in the interior of the stars. . . ."

Bethe went on to say that if a thermonuclear weapon were possible, it would take temperatures *in excess* of 20 million degrees centigrade, hotter than the interior of the sun.[9] Still, there was the possibility that it would work, and Bethe and Teller weren't the only ones who thought so.

While Bethe was instructing the congressional committee on the difference between fission and fusion, a Viennese publisher was going over the final proofs for a rather remarkable book, *Des Geschichte der Atombombe* (*The Story of the Atom Bomb*). Written by a somewhat obscure Austrian physicist named Hans Thirring, it gave a detailed review of the theory behind nuclear weapons. Considering the secrecy surrounding the weapons projects at the time, the work was unusually accurate. Chapter 42 was even more remarkable: It described how a thermonuclear bomb might be constructed.

From the start of the chapter, Thirring raised the possibility of starting a nuclear reaction using heat, which would then begin a chain reaction that would release still more heat. He wrote that plutonium or uranium-235 could be used to start the fusion process.

Thirring went so far as to suggest the fissionable material be surrounded with deuterium in the form of heavy water, paraffin, or lithium hydride, a dark gray, powdery material. Borrowing from fission bomb construction techniques, the deuterium could be surrounded by a dense metal tamper to prevent it from flying apart at the moment of explosion. At the point of fission, the author predicted that high energy particles would form on the surface of the plutonium, which would in turn transfer energy to the deuterium and thus initiate the fusion process—and the thermonuclear explosion.[10]

For the next few years, however, no one paid much attention to the concept of the superbomb. Third- and fourth-generation fission weapons were sent to the Pacific for the CROSSROADS and SANDSTONE tests in 1946 and 1948, but the superbomb still existed only in the minds of a very few scientists.

Then, in 1949, the Oak Ridge National Laboratory began a new and interesting project: the investigation of separation of isotopes of lithium by chemical methods.[11]

That same year, a twenty-seven-year-old Russian physicist had been included in a group of Soviet scientists led by the brilliant Igor Tamm. Their goal was to learn the secrets of the thermonuclear reaction.

Andrei Dimitriyevich Sakharov had graduated from Moscow University in 1942, during the darkest hours of the war with Germany. Sent east, he worked at a war plant until 1945, then he returned to Moscow, where he first met up with physicist Tamm. Sakharov spent the next two years doing graduate work for Tamm, and in 1948 was rewarded with a full position on his research staff.

In September 1949, Igor Kurchatov had just returned from his successful bomb test at Semipalatinsk. Sakharov and Tamm would not take part in fission experiments; they were given a much more difficult task: designing a thermonuclear weapon.[12]

Kurchatov, of course, had been helped immeasurably by the Smyth Report, which detailed isotope separation techniques, as well as by the Soviet operative, Klaus Fuchs, a member of the Los Alamos staff. All Sakharov and Tamm had to start off with was Thirring's book and some sketchy information from the west. Operatives indicated that very few people—a select group?—were involved in the thermonuclear research. Edward Teller's name may have come up, but there was little else to go on. Unlike Kurchatov, Sakharov and Tamm would have to do the work themselves.

In 1950, Lavrenti Beria, the dreaded head of Stalin's secret police—and of the bomb projects—apparently was pleased with a report of Tamm's progress. Soon, thousands of prisoners were headed for the atomic weapon "factories" between Chelyabinsk and Sverdlovsk. The physicists had become sufficiently familiar with the theory behind the thermonuclear weapon. Now it was time to build the Russian H-bomb.

On September 23, 1949, a month after Joe One, Truman made his announcement to the world that the Soviets had the bomb. Reaction in the scientific community was mixed. Some thought the Soviet bomb inevitable. Others, like Edward Teller, viewed a Russian H-bomb on the horizon and enlisted help from California physicists Luis Alvarez and Ernest Orlando

Lawrence. After it became known that some Leningrad scientists had suggested fusion of hydrogen as early as 1932, Alvarez and Lawrence joined the fray. The three—Lawrence, Alvarez, and Teller—pushing for development of the superbomb—became known in the scientific community as the Supermen.

Opposing the H-bomb were some of the fission bomb's parents: Oppenheimer, Harvard president James B. Conant, and Albert Einstein. In October, two months after the Soviet detonation, the Atomic Energy Commission met to decide whether to go ahead with the Super. They decided not to. It was too big, too deadly, and too expensive. Someone counted the Soviet cities that were big enough to justify its use—there were only two: Moscow and Leningrad. No, the AEC decided. Fission would do fine.[13]

By January 1950, however, the Supermen had picked up several allies, among them AEC member Lewis Strauss, Secretary of Defense Louis Johnson, and commander of the Joint Chiefs of Staff, General Omar N. Bradley.

On the afternoon of January 31, President Truman announced that the United States would go ahead with the development of the "hydrogen or super bomb."[14]

Oppenheimer responded: "In some crude sense, which no vulgarity, no humor, no overstatement can quite extinguish, the physicists have known sin and this is a knowledge they cannot lose."[15]

A few days later, London newspapers announced that a Scotland Yard inspector at Harwell had obtained the confession of British scientist Klaus Fuchs. The arrest would lead to the uncovering of a spy ring in Canada and the United States and would eventually lead to the arrest of Fuchs's contact, Harry Gold, and his *other* contact, David Greenglass. Greenglass's sister, Ethel Rosenberg, along with her husband, Julius, would also be arrested.[16]

The very same day Fuchs's arrest became public knowledge, Carroll L. Tyler, the manager of AEC operations at Los Alamos received a letter: "We have noted that work has been approved on the hydrogen bomb, and we need not elaborate too much on the fact that this company is the only one, possibly in the world, that has broad industrial experience in connection with lithium, its production and its many applications. As you know, our company has been active in lithium for the past fifteen years. . . ."

It was signed by Harold J. Ness, president of the Lithium Company of Newark, New Jersey.[17] Apparently, even the presidents of private companies knew something about thermonuclear weapon design.

Two weeks later, on February 16, a memo was placed on the desk of Robert LeBaron, deputy secretary of defense for atomic affairs. Signed by an assistant, H. R. Loper, it was titled: "A Basis for Estimating Maximum Soviet Capabilities for Atomic Warfare."

In it, Loper wrote: ". . . if there is conclusive evidence of a Russian shortage of uranium . . . it must be assumed that they have attempted to balance that shortage by the development of weapons of higher efficiency per ton of ore available, e.g., a thermonuclear weapon . . . [the Soviet Union was proceeding with] the same sense of urgency and disregard of costs as impelled our war efforts, [thus] the thermonuclear weapon may be in actual production."[18]

Although he couldn't have known it at the time, Loper had been close to the truth. In Moscow's Lebedev Institute, Sakharov and Tamm had just completed the theoretical work. The Soviets were preparing for actual production.

By October 1950, Los Alamos began considering using lithium for the proposed superbomb. However, there was a problem that the American scientists could not seem to overcome.[19] While in principle the procedure was simple—ignition of the deuterium-tritium using heat from a conventional atomic bomb—in practice it required a very special design. For one thing, unless the deuterium was placed *just so,* the blast from the atomic "trigger" would blow it apart before fusion occurred.

In order to correct this problem, the scientists had to know the type of radiation caused by the fission trigger, its velocity (near light speed), and its *path* as it careened around inside the bomb casing. The time intervals were almost too small to be measured; the calculations required were tremendously difficult and involved. The situation seemed hopeless.

Then, on February 1, 1951, during the RANGER series in Nevada, Stanislaw Ulam visited the office of Edward Teller. The Polish mathematician had asked Teller to discuss with him a possible solution to the Super's assembly problem. Between the two, a design was worked out that would allow the deuterium sufficient time—though it would still be in microseconds—to ignite and fuse to form helium. At last the bomb was possible.[20]

At about this time, however, air force surveillance aircraft were picking up radioactive dust from a Soviet nuclear test. In the laboratory, scientists analyzing the fallout would notice something unusual about its composition, something, in the words of John von Neumann, "chilly and strange,"[21,22] Years later, when the significance of the findings were made public, serious doubt would be cast on America's early lead in the race for the Super. Scientists analyzing the debris had concluded that there was a real possibility the material had been formed as the result of a thermonuclear explosion. It was possible that the Soviets had the H-bomb.

The scientists reported the results to Robert LeBaron, chairman of the Military Liaison Committee (between the Pentagon and the AEC) and a small group of six air force officers. From there, Secretary of State Dean Acheson and President Truman were notified—verbally. No one else was told, not Edward Teller, not Robert Oppenheimer, not the Atomic Energy Commission. No one.[23]

Edward Teller spent most of March and April trying to convince everyone of the feasibility of a thermonuclear bomb. Convinced of the practicality of the new design. Teller couldn't understand the opposition to it from the scientific community.

Not all was lost, however. Perhaps unknown to him, three Princeton physicists—John A. Wheeler, John Toll, and Kenneth Ford—had begun feeding information into a computer. Called Project Matterhorn, it would, using Teller's new design, predict down to the nanosecond the burn rates for the fusion fuel. Not only that, the RANGER series in Nevada had been successful in testing triggers for the upcoming GREENHOUSE series, and two of the shots would test Teller's ideas.

GREENHOUSE

On April 7, 1951, a nondescript metal canister was raised to the top of a tower at Eniwetok and detonated. Shot DOG was the first of four tests at the atoll. Thirteen days later, 47-kiloton EASY was fired. The first two shots were of purely fission devices. Teller was interested in the last two, dubbed GEORGE and ITEM.

His calculations indicated that complete fusion of a given mass of deuterium-tritium would release twenty-five times the number of neutrons as a similar mass of plutonium. Hans Bethe had shown, though, that such a reaction only occurred around 14 million degrees Kelvin, the temperature found at the interior of the sun.[24] Would the fission weapon be hot enough to start the reaction?

The bomb designers had placed the tritium and deuterium fairly close to GEORGE's nuclear core. To ensure ignition of the heavy hydrogen, GEORGE was packed with an enormous amount of fissionable material, almost to the limit the design allowed. Any more and the plutonium would likely have fissioned spontaneously, providing a replay of the Daghlian and Slotin tragedies of 1945–46.

If the heat from the fissioning plutonium core was sufficient to ignite the deuterium and tritium, the results would show up in the debris samples. Not only that, but if a thermonuclear component was present, the shape of the neutron spectrum would change with distance from ground zero.[25]

The GEORGE device was detonated on May 8, 1951, with a truly spectacular yield of 225 kilotons, the largest shot to date.[26] Scientific analysis of the neutron spectrum, yield, and debris confirmed that a thermonuclear reaction had taken place, although it did not contribute significantly to GEORGE's huge yield. The experiment proved that an H-bomb was indeed possible.[27,28]

The fourth shot of the series, ITEM would be a test of a similar concept, but one that had its start in 1949.[29] Bomb designers had long considered the possibility of boosting the efficiency, and thus the yield, of a fission weapon by adding deuterium and tritium *gas* to the bomb's fissile core, often called the "pit."[30] Another additive the bomb designers considered was lithium hydride, a chemical mentioned by Austrian physicist Hans Thirring in 1946. Edward Teller had designed a "booster" as early as 1947, but it had involved liquid deuterium and tritium, making it impractical for use as a weapon. If ITEM was a success using the gas (or lithium hydride), smaller fissile cores could be made, and thus smaller weapons with the same yield.

By October 1950, the weapons designers had finally agreed on the form of the booster, and now, on May 24, 1951, they would see if the concept worked.

It did. The relatively small fissile core yielded a respectable 45.5-kiloton explosion. Though not as spectacular as the GEORGE shot, ITEM demonstrated that boosting was indeed feasible. It also pointed the way for designers to vary the yield of the weapon merely by adding different amounts of booster. In later years this would result in a feature of nuclear weapons called "dial-a-yield."[31,32]

On June 13, after the success of the GREENHOUSE shots, Teller wrote to Darol Froman, a Los Alamos scientist. In the letter, Teller described the advantages of using lithium-6-deuteride and suggested Oak Ridge begin construction of an isotope separation plant that could produce the material. Froman apparently agreed, and soon shipments of lithium-6 began arriving at Los Alamos.[33]

Teller was one of many who saw the advantages of lithium-6, an easily obtained isotope of the world's lightest metal. Tritium, a heavy form of hydrogen containing two neutrons, was difficult to produce and maintain. The hydrogen isotope was so light that it could escape from almost any container. Also, it was quite radioactive and thus fairly toxic, with a half-life of only 12.33 years. He knew, however, that tritium could be produced *inside* a bomb merely by irradiating lithium-6 with neutrons from the fissioning core. The low-energy neutrons from the core would first combine with lithium-6 to form helium and tritium (with a release of energy), then the tritium and deuterium would undergo a series of reactions to release even more energy as the thermonuclear reaction got underway.[34] (In 1954, it would be proven that lithium-7 could provide even more tritium for the nuclear fuel.[35])

Six days after the letter to Froman, a strategy meeting was held at Princeton. Nuclear scientists from all over the nation showed up: Fermi, Oppenheimer, von Neumann, Teller, and Los Alamos director Norris Bradbury as well as anyone and everyone who had a major hand in nuclear weapon design. The host was J. Robert Oppenheimer.

At the meeting, Teller presented his ideas for the design of the hydrogen bomb. The fusion fuel would be ignited by a "spark plug" consisting of a fission device, sort of a bomb within a bomb. The entire unit would be constructed in such a way that the radiation pressure from the fission device would ignite the entire assembly at a single instant. Though based on months of mathematical calculations, the concept was simple, elegant. Even Oppenheimer, who was opposed to the construction of the H-bomb, called Teller's design "technically sweet."[36,37]

Still, the Super project seemed to be stalled in the water. Though Truman had authorized work on both fusion and fission weapons, not much seemed to be going on with the thermonuclear side of things. In October and November 1951, the BUSTER-JANGLE series had proof tested the new tactical weapons and a new series was scheduled for April 1952. A test using liquid deuterium and tritium—cooled cryogenically to near absolute zero—was scheduled for late 1952, but it would clearly not be of a deliverable weapon. Teller, as a consultant to Los Alamos, took an active part in the planning for the shot, dubbed Project PANDA. He felt, however, that the work on his Super—the deliverable bomb—was simply not proceeding fast enough.

In January 1952, Teller met with air force general James A. Doolittle (hero of *Thirty Seconds Over Tokyo*) in an attempt to persuade him of the usefulness of the Super. Doolittle smiled but said nothing.[38]

Shortly after that Teller heard from Ernest Orlando Lawrence, inviting him to visit the University of California's new Livermore Laboratory, 40 miles west of Berkeley. He decided to accept, and on February 2, Teller found himself discussing with Lawrence the possibility of a second weapons lab—at Livermore.

Lawrence seemed to be all for it, but Teller was worried. Lawrence's politics leaned definitely toward the far right, and Teller's experience in Budapest had taught him to be cautious of political extremism. Earlier, Lawrence had imposed a loyalty oath on his faculty members, then threatened to make public anyone who had refused to sign it. He was also known to be close to ultra-right-wing radio commentator Fulton Lewis, Jr., and an apologist for Communist-baiting Senator Joseph McCarthy, two men Teller refused to trust.[39] His friend John von Neumann even cautioned him against joining "those people [Lawrence and his associate Luis Alvarez] . . . they're too reactionary." Even Enrico Fermi was against the move.[40]

But the opportunity was too great to pass up. Behind the scenes, Lawrence, along with AEC commissioners Lewis Strauss and Willard Libby, had put pressure on the air force to fund the second lab. In the summer of 1952, as operation TUMBLER-SNAPPER was coming to a close at the Nevada Test Site, the Livermore Lab became a reality. Under the cool skies of northern California, Teller finally had a chance to work full time on his Super. As for Project PANDA, it was now in other hands. On a remote island in the Pacific, operation IVY MIKE was about to commence.

MIKE

During October 1952, a huge refrigerator began to take shape on the island of Elugelab in Eniwetok Atoll. Its name: MIKE. Weighing in at 62 tons, MIKE's job would be to freeze heavy hydrogen down to liquid form, near absolute zero, fuse it into helium using an atomic bomb as trigger, then become America's first H-bomb.

MIKE's business end was a 22-foot-long, 5-foot-diameter cylinder housing canisters of the liquid deuterium and tritium, which in turn were surrounded by the plutonium of the atomic trigger. Surrounding the fusion fuel with fissionable material was the key to the MIKE device. Prior to this, scientists were unsure if the heat from the fission device would continue long enough for fusion to begin. Teller apparently solved the problem by placing the heavy hydrogen at the *center* of the fission explosion.[41] The heat and pressure would come from all sides simultaneously. Though the design was indeed brilliant, the 21-ton cylinder was still somewhat unwieldy. Counting the refrigeration unit, the whole setup weighed in at 65 tons; one ordnance expert suggested that the only way MIKE could be delivered to an enemy was via an unmanned aircraft carrier.

In the bright sunlight of Elugelab, surrounded by bermuda-shorted technicians, MIKE resembled not so much a weapon as a small oil refinery.

Outside the refrigeration building, a 9,000-foot plastic and plywood chute stretched away into the distance. Called the Krause-Ogle box, it was lined with building paper and aluminum siding and was filled with helium. Its purpose was to provide a transport for the gamma rays from MIKE to a set of instruments on Boken Island. It resembled a train pulling into a station.[42,43]

Everything was on schedule: MIKE was to be detonated on October 31, 1952, two days before the presidential election.

On the day of the shot, personnel retreated to a ship 40 miles away to begin the countdown. Technicians monitored MIKE's coolants via a television hookup to the bomb cab on Elugelab.

When detonation occurred, the television screen went white as MIKE, the cab, the Krause-Ogle box, even Elugelab disappeared. From the ship the scientists could see a mushroom cloud *miles* in width and still growing. Los Alamos director Norris Bradbury was so shaken by the sight that he briefly considered concealing the true power of the blast from his colleagues back at The Ranch.[44]

After the shot, the results of the analysis were equally startling: MIKE's yield equaled an incredible 10.4 *million* tons of TNT. It had not only vaporized Elugelab, but had ripped out a hole in the atoll big enough to fit several buildings the size of the Pentagon—and deeper than the height of the Empire State Building.[45] Interestingly, analysis of the debris revealed two new elements, numbers 99 and 100. Since MIKE had been the result of Teller's Project PANDA, some wanted to call element 99 Pandamonium.[46] Instead, it was named einsteinium while element 100 was named fermium, after Enrico Fermi.[47]

MIKE was followed on November 11, 1952, by KING, the largest fission device ever tested. A product of Los Alamos physicist Ted Taylor, who called it Hamlet and The Super Oralloy bomb, it was a masterpiece of design.[48] Since materials such as plutonium or uranium-235 tend to fission once a given mass is attained, there is a maximum yield limit—approximately 250 kilotons—coventional atomic weapons may attain. If the weapon maker placed any *more* nuclear material together, the thing would go critical before anyone wanted it to—a replay of the Daghlian-Slotin incidents.

Somehow, Taylor designed a fission bomb that produced an extraordinary 500-kiloton yield without using one atom of hydrogen as a fusion boost. Even more remarkable was what Taylor used as fission fuel: "oralloy," the Los Alamos nickname for uranium, a fissionable substance that had fallen into disfavor because of its poor criticality characteristics.

The KING mushroom rose to a spectacular 67,000 feet over the Pacific test site before spreading out to form a thin, high overcast.[49]

While the American scientists were congratulating themselves on the successful MIKE and KING shots, the Soviets were putting the finishing touches on their latest weapon designs. Under the harsh management of Lavrenti Beria, the Soviet scientists had made great strides and were actually ahead of the Americans in the race for the deliverable H-bomb. But then the unexpected happened: Beria suddenly lost favor with Stalin, and for a most unusual reason.

Stalin had long been anti-Semitic, and in his later years was becoming increasingly paranoid about Jewish conspiracies.[50] Electronic eavesdropping equipment appeared everywhere.[51] Beria began devoting less and less time to his responsibilities as chief of the nuclear weapons projects and more toward surveillance. Now Stalin thought *Beria* was a Jew.[52]

Word spread that a new and bloody purge was in the works, not only for Beria but for other top Soviet party members: Marshals Molotov, Anastas Mikoyan, and Klimont Voroshilov.[53]

Beria and the others were saved by Stalin's health, or rather, by the lack of it: On March 2, 1953, in the midst of a meeting with his top advisors, Stalin suddenly tumbled to the floor, victim of a stroke. By March 5, he was dead. The top administrative position in the U.S.S.R. was now up for grabs. The primary contenders for the job, Molotov and Nikolay Bulganin, didn't trust each other and *nobody* trusted Beria.

In late June, the Soviet nuclear team found they had a new boss, Vyacheslav Malyshev, an ex-locomotive driver from the far northern town of Syktyvkar. According to rumors, Malyshev had been at the battle of Stalingrad and had heroically maintained a tank repair line only several hundred yards from the front.[54]

The change in leadership apparently did little to slow the pace of Soviet nuclear weapons development. On August 12, 1953, the Soviets exploded what was probably their second thermonuclear device. It was crude and inefficient, but it was the first to use lithium-6 deuteride. It was also the world's first *deliverable* H-bomb.

In December, word filtered back to the Soviet nuclear scientists that their old boss, Beria, had been executed.[55]

Buster-Jangle

April-June 1951

Two years earlier, concerned with an increasingly aggressive Communist China, American military strategists were considering a nuclear solution to the Korean conflict.

On Tuesday, April 17, 1951, a member of the House of Representatives urged the U.S. Congress to use nuclear plant wastes to spread a belt of contamination across Korea. Many other congressmen were for stronger action: the use of tactical weapons. That same day the Atomic Energy Commission met to discuss the findings from operation RANGER and explore the requirements of the new Nevada Test Site.

RANGER had been moderately successful in determining fission triggers for the thermonuclear weapons in development. However, the logistical problems left much to be desired. For one thing, the monitoring teams weren't able to talk with the base camp because of problems with the communications equipment. When they had tried to phone in their results, they encountered a busy signal. The final operation RANGER report admitted that, at the Control Point, "complete confusion was the order of the day."

The report indicated problems concerning blast effects. Noting that some windows had been blown out in Las Vegas, the authors indicated that "the factors controlling this are poorly understood."[1]

There was, of course, the problem of fallout. All the shots had taken place at Frenchman's Flat, a smooth expanse at the southeastern edge of the test site not far from Las Vegas. Reports indicated that the Fox cloud had traveled southeast and "practically invested Charleston Peak," not far from Las Vegas. On the mountain, readings as high as 14 milliroentgens/hour were recorded immediately after the shot.[2]

To make matters worse, an incident of contamination had occurred. Two members of the Special Weapons Command, on January 30, landed a helicopter at Frenchman's Flat to inspect the dry lake landing strip. It had snowed not long before, and Special Weapons Command was concerned that the lake might be too soft for landing operations. The evaluation of the area revealed the surface to be suitable for landing, but during the inspection two crewmen kicked around in the damper areas of the lakebed. The wet spot turned out to be highly radioactive.[3]

The report concluded that better washing facilities, including hot showers, be provided for the personnel at the site and that "at no time in the future should test operations involve nuclear detonations on successive days." Apparently, the authors of the report thought it would be wise to wait for ground zero to decay to acceptable levels before another shot at the same area increased the radioactivity. In addition, similar weather conditions might exist on successive days, transporting nuclear clouds over the same areas.

At the April 17 meeting, Los Alamos director Norris Bradbury and Carroll Tyler, manager of the AEC's Santa Fe office, made two suggestions to reduce radioactivity: build detonating towers and pave two of the blast areas. They also recommended constructing a permanent camp at the Nevada Test Site.

On Wednesday, April 25, the commissioners, after studying the various reports, made some recommendations. Partially for increased security, the target areas would be moved from Frenchman's Flat to Yucca Flat, a rugged, boxed-in expanse 20 miles to the north.[4]

By early summer, the public's fascination with the great mushroom clouds was increasing. The AEC had been practically silent throughout the entire RANGER series. After operation GREENHOUSE had been completed at Eniwetok, the AEC was talking again. It seemed that everyone had something to say about the bomb. For a while, the news was concerned with whether the United States would use it in Korea. General Eisenhower, still in the military, was silent on the subject; Secretary Marshall said American troops in Korea may get "new weapons."

Various U.S. senators and congressmen vied for newspaper space with bits of "inside information" regarding the testing.

On May 5, Senator Warren Magnusen of Washington stated that either an H-bomb or an A-bomb was to be detonated somewhere in the Aleutian Islands. In the same speech, he said the U.S. planned to detonate an A-bomb underground "to learn the effect of blast in sub-basement or subway."[5]

A week later, not to be outdone, Congressman Henry M. Jackson stated that reports from the Eniwetok testing showed that troops can enter ground zero "without fear of radiation" immediately after the detonation.

The next day, AEC scientists stated that they had known *that* for some time.

On June 15, Congressman F. Edward Hebert rereleased the Jackson information that a blast area was safe to enter immediately after detonation.

By the end of June, the public was ready for some new information.

So, on June 30, the Atomic Energy Commission, without much comment, released a photo of one of the RANGER shots. The only information that came with the photo was: "Atomic explosion, U.S.A.E.C. test program, January-February, 1951." Reporters were left with the formidable task of inferring information from a photograph.[6]

September 1951

September arrived with its characteristic warm—and turbulent—weather across the country. Floods had ravaged much of Kansas and Missouri, and on September 6, President Truman had inspected his home state to assess the damage.

The Labor Day weekend had ended with a record number of fatalities: 659—70 percent of them in traffic accidents. The first transcontinental television network had begun operations on September 4, by broadcasting President Truman's peace address from San Francisco. The price of other forms of communications doubled: postcards jumped from one cent to two cents. In New Jersey, two air force pilots reported seeing a flying saucer speeding along the coast at an unheard-of 900 mph.

In Korea, General Van Fleet, in a statement to the press, said that the Communists were "suffering badly" in the U.N.'s hill-by-hill "killer campaign" in central and eastern Korea.

And in the American west, a convoy of olive drab trucks rolled toward southern Nevada. Part of the army's Third Corps Artillery, they carried equipment, tents, and sheet metal. On September 12, Camp Desert Rock was born.

Constructed near Mercury Base, Camp Desert Rock was to be, essentially, a temporary military base for personnel involved in the Nevada tests. At the time, no one knew just how many soldiers would be involved in the various weapons tests, or in what capacity, so the project got off to a modest start. The dormatories would be tents, at least for the time being. Later they would be replaced with Quonset huts, and still later, with some more permanent structures. The future would see the camp abandoned, reclaimed, then abandoned again. But in September 1951, it was to serve as temporary home to the small contingent of support personnel as well as the estimated 6,500 men scheduled to take part in the BUSTER-JANGLE series of atomic tests during "Exercise Desert Rock I, II, and III."

The first group of soldiers arrived at Desert Rock from Fort Campbell, Kentucky. They, along with a group from Fort Lewis, Washington, would be among the first to participate in atomic war games. A booklet marked *Information and Guide* was distributed to the men. It read, in part: "The officers and men of this operation share with you the hope that your visit to Camp Desert Rock will prove an informative and revealing experience which you will always remember." It was signed by major general W. B. Kean, U. S. Army.

The book also cautioned soldiers against revealing the nature of the work going on at the test site: "To assist you in maintaining the security of Exercise Desert Rock, it is desired that you maintain secrecy discipline regarding classified information observed here. Everyone will want to know what you have seen—officials, friends, and the enemy."[7]

The Second Series

Operation BUSTER-JANGLE was the second series of nuclear tests to be held at the Nevada Test Site. It would consist of four airdrops, one tower shot, one surface shot, and one underground detonation. Scientists from Los Alamos were interested in some new designs involving not only fusion triggers, but smaller tactical weapons for potential use in otherwise-conventional warfare.

On October 3, the White House announced that a second Soviet atom bomb had been detonated. The military quickly sent additional support personnel to staff the makeshift camp and the total number of support troops swelled to 2,500. Conferences were held between the military and the Los Alamos staff on the feasibility of including troops in various maneuvers during the tests. The brass wanted soldiers to be familiar with the weapons. After all, they reasoned, the technical reports from operation RANGER had indicated that troops could be safely positioned less than a mile from the blast. AEC officials were still skeptical and refused to give the okay to positioning human beings at any distance less than 6 miles. After some discussion, it was decided that troops would be included as observers in three events and participate in only one—at 6 miles. The pressure was on.

While the AEC and military were haggling over troop participation, the series began.

BUSTER: ABLE

The first device to be detonated in the series was placed atop a 100-foot steel tower at Station 5, Area 7, of the Nevada Test Site. Initially, the first test was to be on Friday, October 19, but an electrical problem delayed the shot until the following Tuesday.

A number of Las Vegans climbed to their rooftops in hopes of better seeing the characteristic flash of light. They would be disappointed.

At six o'clock sharp on the morning of October 22, 1951, ABLE exploded with a yield of less than 100 tons. Gladwin Hill of the *New York Times,* a jaded veteran of the atomic testing, called it "a minuscule detonation that hardly ruffled the dawn stillness of the Nevada desert." He went on to write that "today's 'blast' appeared as only the briefest and smallest flicker of light to observers on mountainsides overlooking the test site. . . ." It was, he said, "tiny, shapeless and too feeble" to be detected by cameras pointed at it from the reporters' mountainside perch. "Observers who had seen atomic explosions in the Pacific and last winter's here could hardly believe that the 6 A.M. manifestation was indeed atomic."[8]

A reporter for the International News Service saw it differently. A *Houston Chronicle* headline stated "A-Blast Rips Desert, Opens War Games."

> A tiny but powerful atomic explosion ripped the bleak Nevada desert near Las Vegas Monday and opened history's first atomic war games.
>
> The seventh atomic explosion within the continental United States gave every indication of being the long-heralded "baby atom bomb." Observers in Las Vegas and as close as 30 miles from the detonation neither saw nor heard the explosion. Atomic Energy Commission officials told surprised newsmen:
>
> "You didn't hear it because it apparently was too small, and we're too far away."[9]

As a matter of fact, the bomb may well have been a "fizzle." Weapons scientists at Los Alamos had been attempting to shrink the atomic weapons to tactical size by reducing the amount of plutonium needed for the chain reaction. Regardless of the configuration of the weapons material, however, there is a certain minimum limit below which a chain reaction will not take place. A bomb that contains an amount of plutonium below this limit will, upon detonation, only scatter hot plutonium across the test site. There is ample evidence to suggest that BUSTER: ABLE was such a detonation. For one thing, despite sophisticated electronic and photographic equipment, no accurate assessment of the yield had been determined. The official account was 100 tons, preceded by a symbol indicating "less than." Another bit of information concerns an interview with weapons expert Theodore Taylor reported by John McPhee in his book *The Curve of Binding Energy*. Taylor admitted to a miniaturization attempt that resulted in his one and only "fizzle." No other detonation during this time period fits such a description as well as BUSTER: ABLE.

Fizzle or not, ABLE had been a powerful explosion. Immediately after the detonation, scientists were unable to see what had happened to the tower. A 300-foot-high cloud of dust obscured everything in sight. When it had cleared, the steel tower had vanished without a trace; its particles sent 3,831 feet into the air.

The day of the BUSTER: ABLE shot, the White House revealed that the Soviet Union had detonated its third atomic bomb.

BUSTER: BAKER

The next scheduled event in the series, BAKER, was more impressive than the somewhat disappointing ABLE. Reporters saw a "dead-white, split-second flash of light," supplanted by a "huge orange-red ball." The resulting mushroom "turned from purplish-black to pink" as it met the rays of the morning sun.[10]

Among the scientists and Las Vegas sightseers watching the blast were 5,000 troops of the army's III Corps, stationed 35 miles from ground zero. The soldiers could barely see a group of planes flying high above them.

When the pilot of the B-29 tracking plane flying alongside the mushroom cloud, ordered depressurization—to limit the amount of radioactive material that would get inside the aircraft—the temperature inside the plane dropped rapidly, the windshield quickly frosted over and no one inside the B-29 was able to find the cloud. It was, in fact, heading for California.

From the official report: "Most of the debris moved through the area indicated, except the very lowest portion of the cloud, which was carried so slowly that it may have been subjected to a somewhat different wind field before it reached the coast. Although this was the portion of the cloud which offered the greatest hazard to personnel at ground level, it was not tracked."[11]

The BAKER cloud crossed over the California coast and was immediately entrained in a low pressure area over the Pacific. For several days it simply rotated before returning inland.

On October 29, ground radiation levels at Santa Maria, California, were extremely high, probably because this community was practically beneath the path of the uppermost levels of the cloud.

On October 30, during a light rain, BAKER debris was collected at Topeka, Kansas. Radioactive samples were taken farther east, but were considered *at that time* to be from the Russian burst.

In Texas, fast-moving cold fronts are such a common, but occasionally spectacular, occurrence that they have been given a name: Blue Norther. Consisting of a band of arctic air, the cold norther would push frigid air from the plains over the normally warm Texas countryside, dropping temperatures precipitously and bringing cold, damp, miserable weather. By October 30 snow was falling in the panhandle cities of Amarillo, Dalhart, and Childress, and as the front passed through Houston at 9:00 that evening, the temperature had dropped to 49 degrees.

Part of BUSTER: BAKER, traveling across Oklahoma, had been snagged by the norther and pushed south into the state of Texas. By November 1, a mass of radioactive debris floated 10,000-feet over much of the state.

On November 2, an ad in the *Houston Chronicle* read: "ATOMIC SALE! At Blue Seal Autos, Inc., 1946 Buick Fordor Sedan $645!"[12]

Also on November 1, debris from BUSTER: BAKER was above the historic New England town of Lexington, Massachusetts, mixing with the dark, wet clouds and falling to earth as radioactive rain. The night before, at 7:30, television viewers could have seen Perry Como sing "It's Beginning to Look a Lot Like Christmas."

BUSTER: CHARLIE

On October 29, the AEC issued a warning to civilian aircraft to not only watch out for military planes flying in the Kirtland–Indian Springs corridor, but to stay away from the Indian Springs area altogether. The meaning was clear: There would be another nuclear "event."

At Camp Desert Rock, a detachment of 5,000 troops were told they would witness the blast from a distance of several miles. They would be especially interested in this third detonation; the next shot would involve maneuvers.

It was rumored that over 2,000 special guests of the military and AEC had arrived at Mercury, Nevada, to watch the shot. The list included a number of congressmen and senators as well as various other officials. There was every indication that BUSTER: CHARLIE would be a spectacular shot.

And it was. Dropped from a B-50 and exploding at 1,132 feet, the bomb released energy equivalent to 14 kilotons, four times the yield of the shot before it.

Meteorologists at the site tried in vain to guess the direction the cloud would take. Conflicting wind patterns twisted the stem into a spiral shape almost 6 miles high. The mushroom hung over the test site in that configuration for almost two hours before beginning a grand—and rainy—tour of the United States.

At the time of the shot light rain was falling on both Midland and Odessa, Texas. The next day, while the rain turned to snow, the two Texas cities were under the southern edge of the nuclear cloud from BUSTER: CHARLIE. Atomic Energy Commission planes had flown through the cloud; their radiation detection instruments had recorded a whopping 10,000 counts per minute.

There is little doubt that the snow that fell on Midland-Odessa on November 1 was radioactive.

BUSTER: DOG

The fourth shot, code-named DOG, was to be the largest yield event thus far: 21 kilotons. It would also be the first atomic detonation ever to involve troop exercises, a controversial program that would continue for many years.

To determine damage effects of the blast, tanks, artillery, jeeps, and various other pieces of tactical equipment were placed a short distance from ground zero in what would be termed an "equipment display." After the shot, the personnel would tour the area to assess the damage and complete their particular maneuver—sixty of the 883 men participating in the maneuvers were scheduled to participate in this.

The observer program involved initial lectures and briefings to personnel on the effects of the weapons. After viewing the shot, these men were scheduled to tour the display of equipment that had been exposed to the blast. The plans called for 2,796 personnel to take part in this observer phase.

Tactical maneuvers would be conducted at shot time for the purpose of training troops and to develop effective tactics useful on the "atomic battlefield." There would be 883 personnel involved in this, the world's first "atomic warfare maneuver." The army units that would participate were: First Battalion, 188th Airborne Infantry Regiment, 11 Airborne Division; Third Medical Platoon; and Company A, 127th Engineer Battalion, all from Camp Campbell, Kentucky. Joining them from Fort Lewis, Washington, would be the 546th Field Artillery Battalion.[13]

The scenario developed for Desert Rock I, and used with subsequent maneuvers through the decade, was simple, but improbable: An enemy had landed on the West Coast and was attacking inland. In defending the country from attack, a decision had been made to use atomic weapons.

Prior to the detonation, the various army groups formed a Battalion Combat Team (BCT) for the maneuvers. Based upon information from the RANGER series, foxholes were dug and gun emplacements and bunkers were constructed southwest of ground zero. At shot time, the troops would be 6.8 miles away at an observation point. Immediately after the detonation, a convoy would carry the troops to a "tactical defensive position" near the display area. From that point, they could view the effects of the blast on the foxholes, gun emplacements, and bunkers.

Then, with the nuclear cloud still hovering overhead, they would attack the objective, about 500 yards from ground zero.[14] To assure that none of the 883 participants were overexposed to radiation, survey monitors would precede the men in the advance toward the objective.

Upon reaching the objective, the troops were to tour the equipment displays about three-quarter mile south of ground zero. After that, they would be trucked to a position about 4 miles south of the shot site. There, Human Resource Research Office (HumRRO, of George Washington University) psychologists would attempt to determine the soldiers' reactions.

Convoys carrying soldiers began arriving at the observation site early in the morning.

Though high-ranking officials such as Secretary of the Army Frank Pace, Jr., and chief of the army's field forces, General Mark Clark, were present, nonofficial observers such as *New York Times* reporter Gladwin Hill, had to make do with their usual perch, Charleston Mountain, about 50 miles south of the test site.

Closer to ground zero, the troops were told to sit down and face south. The soldiers could hear the countdown over a loudspeaker placed near their position.

About a minute before 7:30 A.M. Pacific Standard Time, the B-50 released the bomb. As the device reached 1,417 feet above the ground, the capacitors released the charge to the detonators and the object exploded in a brilliant flash of light. Seconds later the fireball was enveloped in gas and dust, forming a peach-colored mushroom that would end eight minutes later at 46,000-feet, 8,000 feet into the stratosphere.

Immediately after the detonation, the troops began their maneuver into the bombed area. In the display zone near ground zero, anything that was made of fabric or wood was smouldering or charred; sandbags, rifle stocks, articles of clothing on the various mannequins, all showed scorched areas.

A jeep windshield was located 40 feet from the vehicle. At the edge of the display area closest to ground zero, the foxholes were caved in. The glass headlights on jeeps were either shattered or fused into opacity by the tremendous heat of the detonation. Sheep tethered nearby had scorch marks on their wool, blisters around their faces.

Soldiers approaching ground zero noted the charred circle of vegetation surrounding the hypocenter. Yet oddly the hypocenter showed no apparent scorching whatsoever.

Upon touring ground zero, personnel noted a survivor at 500 yards: a dazed jackrabbit. As the soldiers approached, it hopped away, apparently none the worse for the experience.[15]

Shortly after the blast, officials waiting at the Control Point climbed into jeeps and personnel carriers and drove to the display area. Monitors had indicated the radiation levels at 500 yards from the epicenter to be only 2 roentgens/hour.

Meanwhile, for the reporters perched 50 miles to the southeast, there was big trouble approaching in the form of the mushroom cloud. The winds at H-hour at almost all levels were from 320 degrees, slightly north of northwest, and above the 3,800-foot level, all blowing at or greater than 35 mph, a fairly respectable breeze. The cloud soon began to lean toward the southeast and Mount Charleston. Located 12,000 feet above sea level and 7,717 feet above the Nevada Test Site, Mount Charleston was directly in the path of the shot DOG mushroom, which was traveling at a speed of 70 mph.

According to *New York Times* reporter Gladwin Hill:

> The white ball, roughly a mile in diameter, was almost detached from its dark "stem" and headed rapidly toward Mount Charleston. A dozen reporters and photographers watching from the mountainside quickly concluded that there might be better vantage points. I was among the last to leave, above twenty-five minutes after the explosion. . . .
>
> The white ball by this time had covered nearly half the distance to the mountain, traveling at about a mile a minute. It seemed to be on a level with the top of the 1,910-foot mountain. Presumably it could be avoided by descending the mountain.
>
> I had driven alone about halfway down the twenty-mile mountainside road and rounded a chain of obscuring foothills when I looked over toward the test site to see what was happening to the "stem" of the radioactive cloud.
>
> It was extending right toward me. My eyes followed its zigzag course across the sky to a point just short of the road I was on almost abreast of my car. There, hanging little more than 1,000 feet up, was the bottom of the erstwhile white ball, now stretched out into a thick fleecy cloud. The estimate of the altitude was corroborated by Dexter Alley and Wayne Clegg, Los Angeles television news cameramen, who came down the mountain shortly afterward.[16]
>
> The cloud looked too innocuous to be the lethal blast residue. But the sky was otherwise cloudless. And there was the cloud's dark "stem" trailing right back to the explosion point. And amid its deceptive whiteness lingered turgid dark and peach-colored whorls. I put on speed.
>
> But the cloud swept ahead faster. In a few minutes it hung over the road, directly overhead, emphasizing its presence with a blast of static on my car radio. I decided that if I was going to be radioactivated, I might as well get a good look at what was doing it. I stopped the car and got out and looked at the cloud, feeling nothing.
>
> Then I drove to Indian Springs, where Fred Bartley, a mining and electrical engineer, has a Geiger counter registering up to twenty milliroentgens per hour. It showed no radioactivity in the vicinity at that time. But when he tried it on the soles of my shoes, which had touched the ground under the cloud, it registered ten milliroentgens—not quite a dangerous dose. But when he tested it on some parts of my car, they knocked the indicator needle off the far side of the dial.
>
> Later, the cloud passed over Las Vegas, rising to an altitude of 40,000 feet and disappearing in the direction of Needles, California.[17]

The cloud actually followed a path southwest across the southern states and then curved up—again toward New England.[18]

BUSTER: EASY

On the morning of November 5, Goldfield, Nevada, sheriff E. N. Kitchen heard the jail cell doors rattle. At first he thought the prisoners were trying to get his attention, then he remembered: He was 85 miles from the Nevada Test Site.

In Caliente, Nevada, city officials had asked schoolteachers to herd the children into the street just before the scheduled shot time. Aware of the shock waves Las Vegans experienced, they were worried the school building might collapse. There was no damage, however, and from where the kids stood they could see EASY's mushroom rise into the air, 105 miles to the southwest. The 9-mile-high column of smoke appeared as tall as a 2.3-inch toothpick held at arm's length. The shock wave arrived nine minutes later.

Twenty-five minutes after the detonation, William Warner at Richfield, Utah, station KSVC, heard "two sharp bangs." It was so loud, he said, "that our meter needle bounced all over the dial."

About the same time, residents of Glendale, California, a suburb of Los Angeles, heard and felt the low-frequency concussion from the 31-kiloton detonation.

Like its predecessor, EASY would run into a cold front and eventually pass over the southern section of the country.

The day of the EASY detonation, Houston, Texas, pigeon fancier J. B. Brooks met with the city council asking them to change the law requiring pigeons be caged. "In the event of an atomic bomb attack on Houston, the city's only form of communication might well be homing pigeons. But they won't be much help if they haven't been trained, and you can't train them if they must be locked up all the time," he said.[19]

In late 1951, the public still seemed to be fascinated by the huge weapons. The arcane tinkerings of the Los Alamos scientists were providing some of the most spectacular fireworks the country had seen.

The "Vital Requirement"

Soon after the BUSTER series ended, Colonel K. E. Fields, a member of the AEC's Military Applications Division, received a letter from Brigadier General Herbert Loper, director of the Armed Services Special Weapons Project. Apparently, Loper had liked the idea of troop maneuvers using atomic weapons. While there was some possibility for additional maneuvers in the next series, Loper wanted to hold the option for all future tests. In his letter, Loper stated, "The Army has a vital requirement for participation . . . in all future atomic testing."[20]

The general's letter was the opening salvo in a series of battles between the military and the AEC regarding the placing of personnel near detonations.

Operation WINDSTORM

Early in 1950, during the search for a suitable test site, one of the possibilities was Amchitka, an island in the Aleutian chain near Alaska. Because of the obvious weather conditions at the proposed site, the military dubbed the earliest test series planned there operation WINDSTORM. The shots, including one surface and one underground, were scheduled for sometime between September 15 and November 15, 1951.

The site was approved by the Joint Chiefs of Staff in late September 1950. The responsibility for administration of the testing was given to the chief of naval operations. On November 30, President Truman authorized the plans for operation WINDSTORM, effectively endorsing the use of Amchitka Island as the "continental" test site.

Members of the Armed Forces Special Weapons Project then asked the army, navy, and air force to submit their proposals for the various tests they wanted to conduct during the Amchitka shots.

After receiving the various proposals, the Armed Forces Special Weapons Project Research and Development Board studied the requirements and began planning the program. During this time, plans had been underway to establish a test site within the borders of the continental United States. By then, Nevada had been chosen, so it was decided to scrap Amchitka Island for operation WINDSTORM. Besides, it was too cold, too windy, and too close to Russia. Eniwetok was out; the shots were only about a kiloton each and not big enough to justify the expense.

After some interservice wrangling, the navy relinquished control of WINDSTORM and turned it over to the air force. The operation was promptly renamed JANGLE.

JANGLE: SUGAR

The first detonation of the JANGLE series would also be the first surface detonation. Scientists wanted to determine what would happen to the ground if an atomic blast occurred at a height of only 3½ feet. The shot, sponsored by the Department of Defense, would be used to determine damage effects on military equipment.

On the morning of November 19, 1951, under the glare of spotlights, a crane lowered the device onto a wooden platform placed in Area 9 of the test site. Attachments were made to electrical cables extending back to the Control Point.

As with earlier shots, dogs and sheep were placed at various distances from ground zero. Scientists from the National Institutes of Health were concerned about injury from inhalation of particles produced by the burst. Film badges were clipped to the animals to correlate the internal inhalation exposure with the external radiation amounts.

The soldiers, meanwhile, collected at a site about 5½ miles south of ground zero, a few miles from the newly named fork in the road, the "Buster-Jangle 'Y'." Meteorologists had predicted the winds to be from the southwest; any fallout would be directed north of the epicenter.

At nine o'clock the next day—in broad daylight—the soldiers would witness SUGAR's detonation. If the radiation survey team permitted, they would load into bus convoys and tour the display area. The problem was no one knew what kind of radiation levels a surface burst would produce. Other shots had been from towers or airdrops. Would the fireball, coming into contact with the ground, "spread out" for several miles, perhaps to include the Control Point?

In many old movies of atomic detonations, one may see streams of smoke next to the mushroom cloud. The streams are produced by smoke rockets, fired at the same time as the detonation. Blast waves, racing through the air, distorts the smoke, giving scientists a good idea of the pressures involved in the vicinity of the burst. It was in the SUGAR event that smoke rockets were used for the first time.

Rockets were also used for another purpose: No one knew what variety of isotopes the soil would contain after the blast and no one wanted to risk being lowered into the crater soon after the shot, so ordnance engineers came up with special rockets for the purpose. Coordinated by the National Institutes of Health and the Public Health Service, the rockets would be brought to within 350 yards of the hot crater two days after each JANGLE detonation. From there, a line would be attached and they would be fired into the crater. After impact, personnel would drag the rocket out, collect the hot rocks, and send them to a lab for analysis.

SUGAR was finally fired at nine o'clock on the morning of November 19, 1951. The 1.2-kiloton explosion formed a typical fireball, then a cloud that extended 11,000 feet into the air. There was no sign of the platform; ground zero was covered in a dense haze of radioactive dust.

The official account: "The base of the primary mushroom was 11,000 ft. A second mushroom, composed of surface dust in an air current which was heated by the hot crater, formed and its top reached a level just beneath the base of the first mushroom. In a minute or two diffusion had closed the gap between them, but the rosy-colored upper mushroom remained distinctly separated from the lower, grayish-white mushroom. Directional wind shear carried the rosy top to the north-northeast and the lower part directly northward. The clouds were observed to rise and fall as they drifted over the first ridge of hills.''[21]

An hour after the shot, the initial survey team, riding in a helicopter, encountered radiation levels exceeding 300 roentgens/hour nine-tenths of a mile from the blast site. Four-tenths of a mile from the epicenter, the radio-activity jumped to 500 roentgens/hour. When the dust cleared, the monitors saw no sign of the platform. The blast had gouged out a crater 90 feet across and 21 feet deep. An estimated 50,000 cubic feet of desert had been vaporized and thrown into the sky by SUGAR's heat. Upon checking the crater lip, personnel were astonished. In prior shots, the radiation at the hypocenter had rarely exceeded 100 roentgens/hour. Now, regardless of the scale, the equipment needles kept pegging to the right—the high end of the measure. It was finally determined that the crater was radiating at an unbelievable 7,500 roentgens/hour. To receive a lethal dose, one would have to stand inside the crater for only four minutes.

After returning to the Control Point, other survey teams, riding in quarter-ton trucks, drove toward ground zero. Using the newly developed grid system, a radiation map was constructed, showing a radiation pattern extending to the north. The meteorologists had been right. To the south, in the direction of the troops, the activity level extended only 600 yards.

JANGLE: UNCLE

The last shot of the series, scheduled for noon on November 29, would be the first underground detonation and was to be fired at a depth of 17 feet. Since the device was similar in design to the SUGAR weapon, the yield was expected to be on the same order: 1.2 kilotons.

The morning before the shot, meteorologists studying upper air patterns discovered a steady 29 mph wind at 14,000 feet blowing from the southwest. It was suggested that the observation point be moved to the west. As a result, the straightline distance from the 202 military observers to the UNCLE device was about 6 miles.

Among the scientific measurements to be conducted at this event was an analysis of base surge. In the Pacific underwater tests, an unusual phenomenon had been observed: Water pushed high into the air by the burst had fallen back creating a doughnut-shaped cloud of mist completely surrounding the base of the mushroom. This cloud then moved rapidly outward at over a mile a minute, flowing almost like a homogenous fluid.

High-speed cameras used in tower shots as far back as TRINITY had noted a similar phenomenon. Scientists wondered if base surges would be more pronounced with surface and underground shots. During the Pacific shots, the Naval Ordnance Lab had conducted base surge experiments. As a result of their experience, they were brought to Nevada for the UNCLE shot. The conditions would be quite different from those found at Eniwetok: Prior to the detonation, samples of the soil revealed only a 7-percent water content.[22]

The UNCLE device was detonated at noon on November 29, 1951, blowing a 980,000-cubic-foot hole in the ground.

One hour later, monitors at the 53-foot-deep crater found radiation levels again at 7,500 roentgens/hour. The records indicate the value as approximate; the survey personnel apparently didn't hang around long enough to get a more accurate measurement. For one thing, the stem was still in the vicinity. The evidence, however, was clear: Subsurface shots tended to be extremely hot.

The cloud of radiation extended approximately northeast in the direction of White Horse Pass, about 200 miles from the test site. The lower cloud stayed around the area for a while; the trailing edge remained near the detonation point for several hours before moving northward. But, as night fell, the wind shifted and UNCLE, like a guest who wouldn't leave, began drifting back over the Control Point and camp area.

Farther north, the channeling effect of the north-south ridges had again brought radiation to Elko, Nevada. The community, located 200 miles north of the test site, was at the receiving end of the ridges. Shortly after the two JANGLE blasts, radiation survey teams checked the town and recorded 400,000 disintegrations/minute/square meter.[23]

A long-range detection "filter flight," Lark William 22, was sent out to determine if UNCLE had cleared the Rocky Mountains. When the plane reached Rapid City, South Dakota, it ran into "moderately strong activity" (40,000 counts per minute). The monitors decided that UNCLE had indeed made it over the Continental Divide.

After both the RANGER and BUSTER-JANGLE series had concluded, project weathermen tried to piece together the fallout maps and determine cloud trajectories. It was decided that a potential radiation danger could exist for communities that received heavy precipitation before dilution of the nuclear cloud took place: "Precipitation is the dominant cause of deposition of high concentrations of radioactive debris on the ground away from the test area. A real hazard to personnel might exist as much as several hundred miles from the site of a burst if rain occurred in the region of most concentrated radioactivity."[24]

Inversions, the weather phenomenon that caused the unusual "bouncing shock wave" effects, also gave rise to a more sinister problem. Meteorologists decided that an inversion could effectively trap low-level debris and channel it north through the ridge system toward the small northern Nevada communities: "The channeling of the cloud by the terrain near the Test Site was very effective, as shown by the high counts measured at Elko, Nevada, after both JANGLE bursts. Under certain conditions, even higher concentrations might exist through a layer several thousand feet thick and, with precipitation, could produce a real hazard to personnel on the ground."[25]

No one was able to explain why Rochester, New York, received so much fallout. While it was understood that the area gets a lot of rain, similarly placed communities such as Binghamton, New York, and Cleveland, Ohio, received comparatively little radiation from the two series.

After studying the data, the meteorologists concluded that there was a significant "lack of success of meteorological forecasts of cloud trajectories under some circumstances." They added that "Even over a region with relatively dense, reliable, and promptly available upper-air meteorological data, it is not always possible to accurately forecast the path of the debris."[26]

While meteorologists were concerned about fallout, military officials had another problem. The AEC was resisting any pressure to move the troops closer to the burst. If the scientists wouldn't let the officers determine its effect on real soldiers, it was entirely possible that they would *never* be able to use the weapon tactically. During the early fifties there was continual debate about whether the Bomb should be used on North Korea. In a report on the BUSTER-JANGLE operation, one officer, Lieutenant Colonel Holstrum of the Army Corps of Engineers, had an ingenious solution to both problems: "[We could] drop an atomic bomb in Korea on a suitable tactical target sufficiently close behind the lines for a quick link-up . . . drop parachutists into the area to capture maximum numbers of prisoners . . . [then] interrogate them closely to determine the bomb's effect on the enemy."

In another report, Lieutenant Colonel Brewer of Army Ordnance and Armor, wrote: "There should be as much troop participation as possible in order that unjustified awe in the minds of soldiers about the A-bomb be dispelled. While there's no desire to belittle this weapon, the troops who will fight a war should judge it in its proper perspective."[27]

The next series would begin in April 1952, and the military would want to be very much a part of it, troop maneuvers and all. If they could only convince the AEC to let them get just a little bit closer to the mushroom clouds.

IV

MANEUVERS

Tumbler-Snapper

1952

The second year of the decade witnessed a number of changes. Chlorophyll tablets appeared on the market. According to the ads, they stopped the "Triple O": Breath Odors, Body Odors, and Other Personal Odors. Beech-Nut chlorophyll gum was introduced. Even the Smith Brothers offered a chlorophyll-flavored cough drop. Prince Matchiabelli of Greenwich, Connecticut, introduced Wind Song perfume and Frances Denney of New York debuted Hope with its "citrus-floral scent."[1]

The new, wide-screen Cinerama found its way to "select" theaters across the nations. Theatergoing couples might be seen with the men sporting thinner ties and the women wearing bouffant skirts with crinoline petticoats.

A favorite confection at the movies was the Clark Bar, made by the D. L. Clark Company of Pittsburgh. Another favorite was Milk Duds, manufactured by the M. J. Holloway Company of Evanston, Illinois.

In January 1952, kids could buy their first copy of the comic *Adventures Into Weird Worlds #1*. Elsewhere, moviegoers were prepared to wear cardboard-and-cellophane glasses for the ninety minutes it took to watch the various 3-D motion pictures that would be popular in 1952 and 1953.

Radio programs would include such great soapers as "Ma Perkins" (3:00 P.M. CST), "Dr. Malone" (3:15), and "The Guiding Light" (3:30) on CBS, while NBC offered, in the same respective time slots, "Backstage Wife," "Stella Dallas," and "Widder Brown."

In Hibbing, Minnesota, eleven-year-old Robert Allen Zimmerman (later known as Bob Dylan) began writing poetry, while in New York, thirteen-year-olds Neil Sedaka and Carole Klein (later known as Carole King) met at Andrea's Pizza Parlor and listened to records on the Wurlitzer.

Seven Thousand Yards

During the first quarter of 1952, plans were being readied for a new series of atmospheric tests at the Nevada Test Site. The shots, scheduled for April 1 through June 5, would involve a total of eight detonations in two phases. The first phase, dubbed Tumbler, would be of primary concern to the Department of Defense and would consist of weapons effects tests. The devices used in Tumbler would be true bombs, airdropped over the targets. On the ground, scientists would take readings concerning the relationship with burst height and overpressure (pressure exerted that exceeded normal atmospheric).

Devices included in the Tumbler phase were Able, Baker, Charlie, and Dog. The second phase, called Snapper, concerned a set of experiments organized by the Atomic Energy Commission and Los Alamos scientists to collect data that would help improve nuclear weapon design. Experiments in the Snapper phase would include the tower shots Easy, Fox, George, and How, as well as the last two airdrops, Charlie and Dog.

In November 1951, during the Jangle series, Brigadier General Herbert Loper had made it clear to the AEC that he wanted army participation during further testing. It was no secret that the military was slightly displeased with what they considered their limited role in the Buster-Jangle shots; the AEC had agreed to only one maneuver during the entire series, and that, frankly, had not involved a realistic tactical operation. For one thing, the boys were kept at a considerable distance from ground zero during the detonation, then had to wait until a survey team had pronounced the area safe to charge through. During real warfare, there would be no "waiting" at a safe distance; there would be no "radiation safety monitor team." As they walked through the mess with their little instruments clicking, the enemy would pick them off one by one. Besides, in real war, the bombs would be going off all around. There would be *no* safe distance. What would the boys do then?

The AEC, however, was adamant. The nuclear weapons released an enormous quantity of lethal radiation during the first microseconds of detonation. These gamma rays and high energy neutrons were capable of causing severe damage at a considerable distance. The AEC balked at allowing its own personnel within 7 miles of the detonation; it didn't want to see soldiers any closer either.

After many rounds of discussion among top military officials during the winter of 1951–52, it was decided to make a frontal assault on the 7-mile limit. Loper's letter in November had already made the army position known, now it was the air force's turn.

On March 7, 1952, just a month before Tumbler-Snapper was to begin, Colonel K. E. Fields received another letter, this one was from air force general A. R. Luedecke, the Special Weapons Project officer, asking for a new, shorter limit. Using the shot DOG reports as reference material, Luedecke complained that the maneuver involved "a tactically unrealistic distance of seven miles." Actually, the troops had been somewhat closer (6.8 miles), but apparently Luedecke wasn't sure everyone in the AEC *knew* that.

In his letter, Luedecke boldly proposed positioning the troops at 7,000 yards—3.97 miles—from the burst. It was a long shot, but General Luedecke took it. After all, the tests were less than a month away. Knowing the AEC would scream, he sweetened the deal by saying the military is "prepared and desires to accept full responsibility for the safety of all participating troop units and troop observers."

In a well-planned maneuver, the marines sent a letter to Fields informing him that they wouldn't participate unless the troops could get closer to the burst.

Upon reading the letters, the AEC's medical director, Dr. Shields Warren, was livid. The radiation facts were known: While the gamma and neutrons produced within the first millionths of a second were considered harmful only within about 1.4 miles, the thermal energy could cause problems at a considerably greater distance. Scientists were aware that for every kiloton TNT equivalent of energy released, about 410,000 kilowatt-hours of thermal radiation was released.[2] From information obtained regarding Hiroshima and Nagasaki detonations, it was estimated that materials on the ground below the burst reached between 5,400 and 7,200 degrees Fahrenheit. At little over half a mile, the evidence suggested temperatures as high as 3,270 degrees Fahrenheit. At 2½ miles, a 20-kiloton shot would probably scorch most anything exposed to its heat.[3]

Then there was the problem of blast and base surge. Desert sand was considered a surface that was "thermally nonideal"—that is, the ground absorbed radiation from the fireball, creating an intensely hot "preshock thermal layer" close to the ground. Carrying dust, smoke, and heated air, the base surge races across the ground ahead of the shock wave. No one really knew what its effect would be on troops crouched in foxholes.[4]

There were other problems such as X-rays, immediate fallout, and the danger of particle inhalation. Also, no one knew what would take place until after the shot. There was the real possibility that someone could accidentally come up with a design that would create a 7-mile-wide fireball and take out everything in the vicinity, including the Control Point.

The risks were enormous. The facts that were known about the effects of the detonations implied two things: one, conditions near an atomic explosion precluded the existence of human life; and two, no one had any idea before the shot what distance constituted "near."

The AEC wanted no responsibility for the lives of the soldiers involved in the tests. After reading the request, Dr. Warren replied that no troops should be stationed any closer than 7 miles from the explosion. Instead of debating the problems associated with blast effects and radiation, he indicated that "the explosion is experimental in type and its yield cannot be predicted accurately."

Carroll Tyler, manager of the Atomic Energy Commission's Los Alamos operation, had amassed years of experience in dealing with the military. After studying the Ranger data, he had recommended not firing shots on consecutive days. That suggestion had been ignored during Buster-Jangle. Knowing the eventual outcome of any protracted disagreement with the military, he suggested to the commissioners that they "disclaim all responsibility for injury which might by some remote chance result from their position."

With that door open, the commission's responsibility to the military personnel was all but abdicated. The AEC then presented a report that essentially gave the military carte blanche in determining the placement of the soldiers from ground zero. The rationale: Realistic training is necessary in all fields, including the military use of nuclear weapons, and realistic training is often accompanied by serious injuries.[5]

On April 2, the day after the first Tumbler-Snapper detonation, AEC chairman Gordon Dean wrote a letter to General Loper. In it, he explained that the AEC had decided to go along with the military and allow the officers discretion in deciding troop positions relative to the bursts. Belatedly, he also suggested the military "prepare a safety plan to minimize risk of injury acceptable to the Test Manager, [however] if officials of the Department of Defense . . . still feel that a military requirement justifies the maneuver, the commission would enter no objections."[6]

At shot Charlie, the troops would be only 7,000 yards from the burst, considerably under the AEC's recommended 7 miles.

Tactical vs. Strategic

Actually, the AEC had little choice in the matter. New manufacturing techniques had allowed the bombs to be mass-produced, and without tactical weapons, there would be a lot of bombs available for only one service: the air force. The navy had some control over the Pacific testing, but the tests in Nevada were still air force property.

The strategic, long-range, 100-kiloton weapons were heavy and difficult to transport. No one at the time seriously believed a missile could be made big enough or accurate enough to deliver any kind of payload to a target (it was not until 1957 that Sputnik disproved *that* theory.) The only methods of waging nuclear war seemed to be through the use of the medium-range B-50s or the ultra-long-range B-36s. In 1949, Vannevar Bush, in his book *Modern Arms and Free Men*, stated that he thought a missile would never be made that could be accurate to less than 10 miles of its target.[7]

Unless tactical weapons were available, the army and marines would be left out in the cold with just conventional rifles, tanks, and helicopters.

As early as 1949, army general Omar Bradley, then chairman of the Joint Chiefs of Staff, seeing the handwriting on the wall had urged development of tactical nuclear weapons. His theory was that the nuclear arms would strengthen Western firepower in Europe and effectively balance the larger Russian army.[8] At the time of the article, Bradley allowed that though the Russians might be able to make the bomb, they probably wouldn't be able to mass-produce them. Thus, in his view, a tactical use of nuclear weapons probably wouldn't lead to an all-out conflagration. Bradley even went so far as to say that nuclear weapons were not decisive strategically, that their best use was on the battlefield.

Coming from an army officer, this was an expected view. However, support for tactical nuclear weapons had also come from another, unexpected group: nuclear scientists. Troubled by the drive to develop the H-bomb or Super, many of them tried to persuade the military that the atomic bomb was all they needed to wage war. The scientists assumed that if they could convince the military to concentrate on tactical weapons, they would forget about building the strategic Super.

In April 1950, the National Security Council received secret report NSC-68. It indicated that the Soviet Union and its satellites had the capacity to overrun Western Europe with the possible exception of Spain and the Scandinavian countries. However, it suggested that even a powerful blow to the Soviets might not slow them down. In order to stop such an invasion, the United States had to be able to hold back the Soviet army. The joint chiefs were not keen on the idea of engaging the Soviets in Western Europe, especially since they were having a rough go of it in Korea. General George C. Kenney, commander of the Strategic Air Force, commented that "The United States has no intention of landing mass armies in Europe and slugging it out with the Red Army—manpower aginst manpower. Napoleon and Hitler both made that mistake."[9]

The Americans were in no mood to fight any kind of protracted two-front war. In fact, the problems in Korea were growing by leaps and bounds. If they didn't use atomic weapons there, then where *would* they use them? By November of that year, the Chinese had poured into Korea and were in the process of routing the United Nations forces. On November 30, perhaps more for bluster than anything else, President Truman suggested that the U.S. might use nuclear weapons in the fighting. At the time, the president honestly believed the Soviets did not have the bomb (they did). Truman was regarded as a man of his word. The allies were horrified at the potential Soviet response of thousands of tanks rushing across the Rhine, toward Paris and, eventually, London. Prime Minister Clement Attlee again packed his bags for Washington.

The prime minister was beginning to dread the visits to Washington. During an earlier trip there, Attlee was being shown the new early warning radar by a proud Secretary of State Dean Acheson, when suddenly the radar picked up what appeared to be a flock of Soviet bombers moving southeast toward the nation's capital. The Pentagon immediately placed the services on war alert. Acheson hustled the bewildered Attlee out of the building and into a car. In a minute they were careening down the street toward the White House. By the time they got there, the radar blips had disappeared. The technicians had an explanation: The "bombers" had apparently landed at some lake far to the north. What the radar had taken for enemy planes had been only flocks of migrating geese.

Truman later told the British prime minister that the U.S. probably wouldn't use atomic weapons in Korea. He just wanted to shake the Communists up a bit.[10]

Perhaps another reason the military hesitated using nuclear methods to rectify the Korean conflict involved lack of appropriate hardware and knowledge of appropriate tactics for use with the smaller weapons. The fact was no one knew *how* to use nuclear weapons in a tactical situation. If the Communists called Truman's bluff in Korea, a lot of mistakes might be made—all in the Soviet's favor. The message to the military was clear: Develop procedures that will detail use of atomic weapons on the battlefield.

Thus, by early 1952, tactical weapons were a very big item with everyone but the air force officers. They saw the whole thing as nonsense and an attempt to weaken the strategic arsenal. When a colonel attempted to brief air force general Curtis LeMay on the implications of tactical armaments, the general became angry and told the colonel he didn't want to hear about it.[11]

But to the other services, it was as though they had been given a fantastic new toy to use as they saw fit. And with the AEC safely out of the way, the generals rushed to the chalkboards. There would be war games to end all war games. Troops. Tanks. Artillery. *Paratroopers*. It would be a busy year.

TUMBLER-SNAPPER: ABLE

The TUMBLER series opened at 9:00 on the morning of April Fool's Day, 1952, as device ABLE rolled out of the bomb bay and toward the desert floor. Flying nearby were B-50s carrying over 150 observers. Waiting below were a number of Defense Department scientists monitoring about thirty diagnostic experiments. At ground zero, the desert was a relatively cool 58 degrees Fahrenheit.

One of the experiments involved an analysis of the shock waves produced by the detonation. As in the earlier tests, smoke rockets would be fired at the precise moment of detonation. Photographic analysis of the vapor trails would help scientists determine the pressures existing near the burst.

The bomb detonated at 793 feet above the desert floor with a yield of one kiloton. Photoelectric sensors then tripped the rocket fuses, sending them soaring into the air, trailing streams of dense white smoke. The reporters stationed miles away and left to guess at the meaning of the experiments, would see something entirely different.

New York Times reporter Gladwin Hill was at his post on Mount Charleston:

New Device Shows a "Flaming Curtain" Plus Normal Fireball

The thirteenth nuclear detonation staged at the site since its inauguration fifteenth months ago . . . while of relatively low power, displayed a "double-barrelled" effect. . . . In addition to the usual central fiery ball, which momentarily outshone the midmorning sun, the blast sent up a lateral "curtain" of slender incandescent parallel columns. Through field glasses from a vantage point 7,000 feet up on Mount Charleston overlooking the test site, twenty of these fiery tendrils were counted. Their span was about equal to the width of the central explosion, possibly half a mile. They surged up even higher than the main orange-yellow fireball, but like it changed in a second from fire into white vapor, resembling a section of picket fence. It was as if a huge hose or sprinkler pipe, stretching along the ground, suddenly had sprung a leak in many places, shooting up parallel streams of fire. The effect resembled that of some of the elaborate aerial incendiary bombs used by the Royal Air Force in World War II to raze German cities.

That these vertical "fingers" of fire involved something very unusual was indicated in the fact that they were evidently responsible for a mysterious "fogging" of some photographic film trained on them from distances of as much as forty miles. Seven news photographers, scattered over hundreds of square miles around the test site, all of whom had successfully photographed far brighter previous explosions, found most of their negatives curiously blackened. Some negatives showed the central fireball, but surrounded by blackness.

The only negative immediately reported which showed the "fingers" was from a camera with a focal plane shutter that, instead of exposing all of a film practically simultaneously, exposes it in a series of horizontal bands. In this negative, about half of the vertical "fingers" were caught before their cumulative effect "fogged" a heavy black line across the picture. The obvious inference was that the "fingers" radiated rays of a sort or an intensity not previously encountered in the tests. Many observers agreed that the jets of fire were reminiscent in their behavior of the characteristic "spray" of phosphorous bombs and the diffused fragmentation of antipersonnel projectiles.

This aroused speculation that the atomic scientists, in addition to "harnessing" the awesome force of nuclear explosions down to the size of manageable missiles, were now making them perform in specialized ways, such as detonating in simultaneous tandem or satellite blasts. . . .

Officials of the Atomic Energy Commission said some of the vertical smoke in today's explosion came from "rockets" set off at the time of the blast for an undisclosed purpose. They had no explanation for the "fogging" of the films but agreed after scrutiny of some of the film that the damage was different from what might have been expected from ordinary radioactivity in the vicinity of a nuclear explosion. . . .[12]

The nuclear cloud reached 13,123 feet above the desert floor before moving east-northeast.

Above the desert, the topmost level of ABLE had become entrained in a rapidly moving mass of air that would, within two days, bring it to the East Coast. The lower, "stem," levels, however, were trapped in a rotating low-pressure "cyclone" that would keep the cloud over the Great Lakes area for an extended period of time; while the 16,000-foot trajectory crossed Memphis at midnight on April 2, forty-eight hours later, the 10,000-foot section of the nuclear cloud was still hovering over Detroit. It finally left the U.S. over New York City at 7:00 A.M. Eastern Standard Time on April 6, five days after the detonation.

The day before, Saturday, April 5, snow began to fall in the town of Bad Axe, Michigan. By the end of the day, it had accumulated to slightly over 2 inches, and by the end of the weekend, there would be over 6 inches of snow on the ground. Despite the snowfall, Ozak's Second Hand Store held a grand opening and St. Paul's Episcopal Church held its annual spring bazaar.

The Bad Axe Theater featured *The Son of Dr. Jekyll*, and in nearby Port Austin, the movie feature was *On Dangerous Ground*.

By April 4, the fallout had become "spotty," and by the next day, had virtually ceased except for the Great Plains region. Meterologists theorized the surface winds were picking up and redepositing the debris, from as far away as the Nevada Test Site. As an indication that they were right, high activity was found at Grand Junction, Colorado, on April 7. Surface dust, apparently, could travel quite a distance.

TUMBLER-SNAPPER: BAKER

BAKER, the second device in the series, was also to be a low-yield device, similar to ABLE. The bomb was released from the B-50 at approximately

9:30 Pacific Standard Time on the morning of April 15, 1952. The BAKER detonation was odd from the start. An observer on Mount Charleston recalled that "the fireball had an unusually brilliant glow in the instant it stood on the horizon before breaking in two like two tails and then becoming obscured in a brownish cloud."

After a minute, the tails "looped together and formed a giant ring. Then the ring became a pinkish mass at an elevation of slightly below 15,000 feet."[13]

In Las Vegas, the detonation was neither felt nor heard, to the consternation and disappointment of hundreds of tourists standing on the roofs of hotels.[14] Just east of the test site, a cyclonic disturbance had unexpectedly cropped up. As a result, the cloud began slowly moving toward the west, then back east again. Because of the unusual weather pattern, the BAKER cloud hovered within a 100 miles of the test site for several days.

TUMBLER-SNAPPER: CHARLIE

For the third shot in the TUMBLER-SNAPPER series, the AEC and the military had decided to finally allow newsmen access to the test site. It would be the test site's first media event; not only would the newsmen be allowed on-site, they would have their own observation post, a hill located halfway between the Control Point and the Yucca Lake airstrip. From its position 7½ miles south of the BUSTER-JANGLE "Y," it offered considerably better viewing of the shots than had Mount Charleston; though most of the shots would take place slightly north of the "Y," shot GEORGE was scheduled for an area slightly south of that location.

Not only would newspapermen be admitted to the site, there would be "live" national television coverage. New York channels 2, 4, and 9 planned coverage of the event "some time between noon and 1 PM" with "a special film showing the blast" scheduled for 11:15 Eastern Standard Time that evening on channel 4.

Carroll L. Tyler, test site manager, explained to the newsmen present that the shot would be a "device" that would be detonated somewhere between 3,000 and 3,500 feet above the desert.

AEC chairman Gordon Dean also addressed the newsmen:

> What you will see tomorrow will be a bomb. It will be a bomb dropped from an airplane. The energy release of that bomb will be considerable. For example, it is planned to give a slightly larger energy release than the bombs exploded at Hiroshima, Nagasaki or Bikini.
>
> But it will not be the largest bomb that we have exploded. If it were, we would not be exploding it here within the continental limits of the United States. We would, instead, be exploding at Eniwetok.

In viewing the explosion of these bombs tomorrow you will not—unfortunately—be able to detect the important improvements in design, in efficiency, and in variety of uses that have been incorporated in our atomic weapons during the past six years, and for which the Los Alamos scientific laboratory—which does a truly outstanding job—has been largely responsible.

But there is one thing that you will be aware of tomorrow—indeed, if you are not aware of it already—and that is the changing concepts, in connection with atomic weapons, which have taken place in the six years since Bikini. In 1946, atomic weapons were thought of by most people as strategic weapons. That is—they were considered to be weapons that could be used only by a strategic air force carrying an attack against the industrial heartland of an enemy. In those days it was fashionable to assume that a dozen or so such weapons, judiciously placed, could knock out any of the major powers of the world.

Since then, this concept has been rather radically revised. Today, atomic weapons are thought of as tactical as well as strategic weapons—that is, they are thought of as weapons that can be employed by military forces in the field against other military forces in the field. In other words, they are thought of as weapons which tactical air force and armies and navies—as well as strategic air forces—have a legitimate interest in and a legitimate need for.

This, quite naturally, vastly increases the quantity and variety in which atomic weapons are needed. It means, among other things, that the assumption that there is an early saturation point in the development and the manufacture of atomic weapons is no longer valid. This explains why we are undertaking a very large expansion of the national atomic energy program, and why we are holding so many of these weapon's tests.[15]

Unlike the first two shots, CHARLIE would involve troops. The Desert Rock IV exercise was scheduled with 535 observers and 1,675 other personnel, including a contingent of paratroopers. Most would be involved in tactical maneuvers beneath the mushroom cloud.[16]

By zero minus ten minutes, the trenches were full. At zero minus two minutes, in the cool 66-degree Fahrenheit morning air, a voice over a loudspeaker boomed out, instructing the soldiers to kneel, cover their faces with their hands, and lean against the trench wall nearest ground zero.

"Minus one minute! Minus one minute!" The voice on the loudspeaker belonged to Dr. Gaelen L. Felt, a test liaison scientist. "Put on goggles. All face away from the target area!"

At exactly 9:30 A.M. Pacific Standard Time, CHARLIE began its plunge toward the detonation altitude, 3,447 feet, while below, the voice on the loudspeaker announced "Bombs away!"

New York Times reporter William L. Laurence was watching from News Nob, the unofficially named area inside the test site where the military now allowed reporters to observe the shots:

We counted a long three seconds, slowly as we watched, and to make sure that we did not remove our goggles too soon, and thus risk serious damage to our eyes, the three seconds were counted as "1001, 1002, 1003."

We stripped off the goggles, and there before us was the great ball of fire, rising and expanding quickly, changing color at breathtaking speed from a dazzling white to an iridescent sphere of many colors, a giant rainbow with the shape of a globe. . . . After about ten seconds, the luminosity of the ball has practically died away, to give way to a series of awe-inspiring and breathtaking phenomena that challenges the imagination and leaves the onlooker incredulous. Watching the fantastic metamorphosis of the great fireball into a giant mushroom, seething and boiling at first like a many-colored geyser and then slowly transforming itself into a flower-like pattern, one becomes aware of the fact that, no matter how many atomic explosions one has seen, the last one is still the first. While the general characteristics of each may be similar, each one has its own personality.

The mushroom in today's blast, which rose in five minutes to an altitude of 35,000 feet, was, from the point of view of symmetry and proportion, the most perfect of all five this correspondent has seen. It was a sculptor's dream, a gigantic hemisphere of white marble streaked with many colors of delicate hue, suspended in space like a giant dome that kept changing in form at a breathless pace. It was like watching a planet in the act of being born in space, being molded by invisible hands. The top of the mushroom, the diameter of which stretched for several miles, was a white foaming fountain glistening in the sun, the rays of which caught its many facets and shone through it, giving its interior a rose-colored tint.

Slowly, imperceptibly, in a sort of a dream sequence, the hemisphere has changed into a flower-like face of many petals that grow out of the mass. At first the flower is just a head without a stem. Then suddenly a great body materializes directly beneath, gradually becoming a huge pillar of white fire rising to attach itself to the main body above it. In a few minutes the hemisphere began to flatten out and to separate itself from the white pillar below. As it flattened, it assumed the appearance of a great cloud, its turbulence ended, and it moved slowly away to the east over the white sands of Yucca Flat. The "stem" also died away in the still, almost motionless air.[17]

Meanwhile, another correspondent, on the ground with the soldiers, offered a somewhat less poetic report:

The soldiers crouched double in their entrenchments, their backs to the sky. The flash heat of the great detonation, which was clearly felt at News Nob where newspapermen observed the explosion ten to eleven miles from ground zero, was far greater in the trenches. If the men had not been protected, they might have suffered light sunburn.

Immediately after the great fireball filled the sky with blinding light the soldiers climbed out of their trenches and stood in the open as the shock wave, driving great clouds of dust, swept toward them. The soldiers said the blast hit them with a perceptible "whoompf."[18]

Another observer at News Nob recalled the explosion: "The noise hurt my ears and of course the dust carried by the blast blotted out everything beyond a yard for a minute or so. The Desert Rock Master of Ceremonies had repeatedly warned the observers of the dust storm which would follow the blast, yet many individuals were so impressed by the first sight of the fireball that they were standing with their mouths wide open. Consequently when the blast wave arrived these persons received a mouth full of dust as their second impression of the atomic detonation. Some observers stated that they could see the dust from the blast rolling towards their position."[19]

An hour later, the troops were trucked to the display area to view what was left of the seven tanks, twenty machine guns, and a few heavy artillery pieces. Hovering above them in a helicopter was Brigadier General Harry P. Storke, commander of Camp Desert Rock. Shortly after 11:00 A.M., the planes began dumping parachutists over ground zero.[20] Unfortunately, their timing was a bit off and some landed 8 miles from their target and were injured.[21] Those who found their target were greeting with smouldering Joshua trees and wrecked and scorched pieces of equipment. Some of the parachutists had walked to within 175 yards of ground zero.

In an interview, General Storke said, "[F]rom our experience here at Camp Desert Rock we have learned that the tactical doctrine of the Army is so sound that an assault supported by atomic weapons will involve the same general tactics as an assault supported by conventional high explosives shelling or aerial bombardment. The attack will, of course, have to be modified as required by the factors of radiological safety, but this will tend to slow down slightly the speed of the advance rather than to change our tactical concepts."[22]

Lieutenant-General Joseph M. Swing, commanding the Sixth Army, also helicoptered to News Nob to discuss the maneuvers with reporters. He told them that troop reaction had been "good" and noted that the men had been half again as close to the detonation as in the previous fall's tests. He said that he had talked to about forty soldiers just after the shot. He claimed they all laughed and joked in a "relief reaction," and told him that the field fortifications (foxholes, trenches) offered sufficient protection from the blast.[23]

Shot CHARLIE had been one of the largest explosions detonated at the test site; the 31-kiloton explosion had sent a cloud of radioactive dust 4,000 feet into the stratosphere. As was the case with many of the shots, the wind direction varied with altitude: At the base of the mushroom the wind was from the northwest at 33 mph, while at the top of the nuclear cloud it was from the west at a steady 25 mph.

As a result, the upper part of the cloud moved eastward, the main part reaching the East Coast within three days. The lower portion moved northward along the Pacific Coast and into Canada, then east and south through the Mississippi Valley. According to the official report, fallout from the lower part of CHARLIE was found in southern California on April 23 and "northward to southern Oregon on the 24th."[24]

On April 25, the New York City area was included in a fallout zone that registered radioactivity measurements of 1,000 disintegrations/minute/square foot/day.[25] That is, radioactive fallout particles deposited over a square foot disintegrated—transformed to more stable atoms—at a rate of 1,000 atoms per minute, averaged over a day's time. And with each disintegration, there was at least one emission of radiation. Readings taken prior to testing indicated that the highest average level determined from the gummed paper filters at *any* of the 116 monitoring stations was 10 disintegrations/minute/square foot/day.[26]

TUMBLER-SNAPPER: DOG

Tactical maneuvers were being developed and tested at shot CHARLIE under rigorous conditions, yet there had been few accidents and no loss of life. The army and air force officials involved in shot CHARLIE were very pleased with the results. Now, it was the marines' turn.

Just after the CHARLIE detonation, General Swing had alluded, however obliquely, to a problem with tactical nuclear weapons: They slowed down an advance. The "perfect" tactical nuclear weapon would "selectively" destroy an enemy position while causing little harm to advancing friendly forces. Not only that, there should be no radioactive fallout to pose problems and cause delays.[27]

The generals had been clamoring for the perfect tactical weapon and the designers were trying to give it to them. The shots in the early 1950s were a time of great experimentation as the Los Alamos scientists attempted to "tailor" their shots to emit specific radiation: neutrons, gamma, X rays, anything. In the early 1970s, during an interview with author John McPhee (*The Curve of Binding Energy*), nuclear scientist Ted Taylor said: "A great variety of things, many forms of energy, come out of a nuclear explosion—gamma rays, alpha particles, neutrons, X rays, visible light, radio frequencies. To some extent—and in all cases, to an important extent—you can select what to enhance and what to suppress. The relative amounts and directions can be controlled over very wide ranges. There are so many things you can do—through conceptual design. If you want a bomb that spews out nothing but green paint, you can do that.[28]

After the high-altitude DOG shot, the marines loaded into trucks and began the drive toward ground zero.[29] The tour of the display area was cut short, however, when monitors discovered high levels of radiation about 900 yards from ground zero. Had they continued on to a third of that distance, they would have encountered radiation levels of 10 roentgens/hour.

Despite their inability to complete the tour, the officers were delighted. Some even asked Los Alamos for a small one-kiloton bomb to detonate at their El Toro (San Diego) base "for training purposes." Los Alamos denied the request.[30]

On May 5, Dog's 18,000-foot trajectory crossed Philadelphia at 10:00 A.M. local time. On the same day, while much of the rest of the nuclear cloud was hovering north of Lake Superior, the western states again began to record increased fallout. But Dog was not the culprit. The radioactivity was from shot Charlie, which had circled the globe and now returned to drizzle activity onto the West Coast.

TUMBLER-SNAPPER: EASY

The next shot, Easy, was scheduled for May 7. Technically, it was part of the Snapper series and would involve weapons development tests. No troop maneuvers were scheduled; however, over 1,000 support personnel from Camp Desert Rock were invited to the Control Point to watch the detonation.

Unlike its predecessors, Easy would be a tower shot. The evening before the event, the Easy device was placed into an elevator, raised 300 feet, then placed in the center of an 8-by-8-foot corrugated iron cab. A millisecond or so after the detonation, very little would be left of the iron cab—or tower. The very atoms themselves would be changed, made "heavy" by neutron bombardment or perhaps even changed to another element entirely.

Miles away, photographers for the Cambridge, Massachusetts, firm of Edgerton, Germehausen and Greer (EG&G), readied their cameras for the next day's shot. Using a special electromagnetic shutter, the cameras would record the blast in terms of milliseconds. On some of the tower shots, the cameras would take the photo too late, showing only a white glare. Other times, the shutter would trip too soon. The result would show the bomb cab glowing, surrounded by intense radiation, with pockets of ionized air popping through the corrugated metal a microsecond before it is consumed by the fireball.

At 4:15 A.M. Pacific Standard Time, Easy was detonated with a force of 12 kilotons. The cloud shot up 29,671 feet above the desert floor. At the other end of the dirty gray stem was a small stump where the 100-ton tower had been.

While the wind at the surface had been calm at the time of detonation, a mile above the surface it was blowing from due south at a respectable 41 mph. At 30,000 feet, the height of the mushroom cap, the wind was from the southwest at a fierce 107 mph, carrying tons of vaporized iron oxide, cobalt, and silica toward the northeast, where rain was falling.

When the monitors finally were able to sample the outlying areas, they were astonished at the radioactivity they encountered. From the official report: "Almost eight million disintegrations per minute per square foot were observed at Salt Lake City in the observations started on 8 May; activities of several hundred thousand disintegrations per minute per square foot were observed as far away as western Nebraska and South Dakota, all associated with rain.''[31]

As for the rest of the country: "Deposited activity of several hundred disintegrations/minute/square foot was observed at various stations throughout the country for at least fifteen days following the fifth [EASY] burst.''[32]

On May 8, between 3:00 and 4:00 P.M. local time, EASY's cloud crossed over Cleveland, Ohio, at 24,000 feet. Four days after the burst, radioactive hot spots were found over the entire East Coast. Nine days after EASY, a "Wasatch Canyon wind" blew in from the mountains at 82 mph, causing extensive damage to areas east and north of the Great Salt Lake. According to the surveys taken at the time, the wind was radioactive with fallout from the EASY detonation.[33] On May 19, at 4:00 A.M., part of EASY's cloud passed 18,000 feet over Bad Axe, Michigan, home of St. Paul's Episcopal Church and Ozak's Second Hand Store.

TUMBLER-SNAPPER: FOX

The sixth shot of the series, code-named FOX, was scheduled as a weapons development event. Even so, it would involve a large contingent of observers, 950 in all. The troops would be from the army's 701st Armored Infantry Battalion, First Armored Division, Fort Hood, Texas. They would witness FOX's 11-kiloton blast from trenches 7,000 yards away (about 4 miles).

The May 25 detonation would be an initiation of sorts of the army's radiation monitor trainees: They would be on their own to judge the radiation levels at areas through which the Battalion Combat Team would have to move.

Several days prior to the shot, tanks, jeeps, and other military equipment were moved into position a short distance southwest of the 300-foot tower. No one really expected the equipment to sustain much damage. In most of the small shots prior to FOX, only minor damage had been noted: scorched canvas, cracked and blistered paint, headlamps made opaque by the heat. Of course, the lighter equipment—machine guns, rifles, and small artillery—would be scattered across the desert, that was to be expected. Placed at a respectable distance from the tower was a tank. The bomb might jar it a bit, but nothing more.

At 3:50 A.M. on May 25, the desert was characteristically cool, 57 degrees Fahrenheit. The troops huddled in the trenches, shivering; army field jackets are notoriously useless against even moderate temperatures. The relative humidity just prior to shot time—41 percent—made the trenches slightly damp. There was absolutely no wind.

At the Control Point, the countdown had begun. Systems were double-checked to ensure that each of the twenty-seven scientific tests would measure data properly. The meteorologists indicated that the height of the tropopause was about 32,691 feet above the desert floor. Above this level the air would be relatively stable; any fallout would be suspended there for quite some time, an undesirable situation.

Calculations were made taking into consideration air temperature, air density values, and yield *range* of the device (the yield could never be accurately predicted). If the fireball was to be nominal, about 45 feet in diameter at 300,000 degrees centigrade, then its rise would be "ballistic"—that is, it would shoot up through the atmosphere like a solid projectile.

Bets were taken. It was a cool morning; most agreed Fox would make it to the stratosphere.

Almost incidentally, the weathermen noted the presence of an inversion, a layer of slightly warmer air floating some distance above the desert. Since sound waves travel up and down rather than follow the earth's surface, and since a warm air layer has the peculiar ability to "skip" or reflect sound waves, no one was sure where the weapon's blast would be heard.

At 4:00 A.M. Pacific Standard Time, Fox was detonated, propelling its mushroom almost a mile into the stratosphere. In passing through the inversion layers, with the attendant moisture, the cloud had picked up three successive ice caps. As the cloud climbed higher, the ice caps "slid" down over the side of the mushroom to form an "ice skirt." Six and nine-tenths miles below, the tower had simply vanished.

Shortly afterward, members of the 701st, along with Desert Rock commander Harry P. Storke, visited the display area. They were astonished to find much of the equipment demolished. Jeeps were smashed flat. Almost unbelievably, the weapons' shock wave had picked up the tank and thrown it a short distance where the fireball then engulfed and melted it.

In Las Vegas, thanks to the atmospheric inversion, residents heard nothing. Upon questioning, an AEC official admitted that "they haven't developed a silent bomb yet."[34]

Radiation monitors riding in heliocopters were astonished to see levels within 400 yards of ground zero reaching 2,000 roentgens/hour. As with the previous nuclear cloud, Fox headed east, toward an area of showers, where it sprinkled the Great Lakes area with radioactive rain.

On May 26 at 7:00 P.M. local time, the cloud crossed Paris, Missouri, at 40,000 feet, while the 30,000-foot trajectory passed over Grand Rapids, Michigan, the next day at 6:00 P.M. At 11:00 Eastern Standard Time on the morning of May 28, 1952, the nuclear cloud drifted over the town of Lexington, Massachusetts.

The official report indicated "fairly strong activity from the burst was general over most of the United States at least until 1 June, undoubtedly the result of the great amount of debris from a tower burst as compared with an air burst."[35]

TUMBLER-SNAPPER: GEORGE

Often, when a device was detonated at the Nevada Test Site, among the dignitaries chosen to watch the shot were the scientists responsible for its design. Should the gadget fizzle, some claimed, the person most responsible would then have the first opportunity to explain.

The designer most responsible for the seventh shot of the TUMBLER-SNAPPER series was a shy, brilliant Los Alamos scientist named Ted Taylor. Following his blueprints, technicians had replaced the heavy uranium reflector surrounding the plutonium core with beryllium, a much lighter metal. The addition of the beryllium would prove to be a very important step in the miniaturization of the devices.

Beryllium, a light, brittle, and extremely toxic metal, had some interesting characteristics. For one thing, like most light elements, when mixed with an alpha emitter such as plutonium, it would release a neutron. Deep inside most weapons, located at the very center of the plutonium spheres, lay the "initiators" or neutron sources. It was the job of these tiny hickory-nut-sized capsules to release neutrons into the surrounding plutonium a microsecond after implosion. The initiators were usually made of beryllium and polonium. They worked quite well.

Taylor had wondered if the metal had other uses. Among beryllium's other qualities was the extremely high "neutron scattering cross-section"—that is, if a beam of neutrons were directed at a piece of beryllium, most would be deflected. A beryllium sphere surrounding a fissioning plutonium object might reflect a large number of neutrons back into the nuclear material. The result might mean a significant increase in the efficiency of the device—that is, the percentage of nuclear material undergoing fission prior to breakup.

While the detonation event scheduled for the test site was to be code-named GEORGE, the Los Alamos scientists called the device itself Scorpion. It had been assembled to Taylor's specifications at Los Alamos, then transported to Albuquerque where the detonator cables were attached. When it finally arrived at the test site, its appearance matched most of the other tower devices: a dark mass of wires surrounding a central mass of dull metal.

The day before the shot, Scorpion was checked for observable defects. It was then placed in a canister and transported to the corrugated metal cab perched atop the 300-foot tower in Area 3. There, even more wires were attached, including the thick cables leading back to the power source. At the other side of the connection, deep inside Scorpion, the electrodes were connected to the detonators.

Other, smaller cables went from the device via pipes to instruments located at the tower's base and nearer the Control Point. The day before the test, Taylor rode the elevator to the top of the tower to view his device and to catch a glimpse of the equipment display scattered across the desert below. Nearby, a technician worked to clear a conduit pipe; a rat had somehow managed to wedge itself inside, threatening to ruin the shot. A break in even one circuit, regardless of how minor, would scuttle the detonation.

While Taylor was waiting, he managed to locate a concave, parabolic mirror. After determining the point at which the light would converge, he attached a small wire. The next day, June 1, 1952, he would conduct an experiment of his own.

At 3:50 on June 1, the troops in the trenches were told to kneel and lean against the side of the trench nearest the tower.[36] Five minutes later Scorpion/GEORGE ignited with a force of 15 kilotons.

At the Control Point, Ted Taylor aimed his parabolic mirror at the intensely bright, fissioning mass. At the end of the wire he had attached a Pall Mall. In a second or so the concentrated, focused light from the weapon ignited the tip of the cigarette. He had made the world's first atomic cigarette lighter.[37]

The explosion had hurled a mushroom cloud 37,308 feet into the sky and into the path of a 41-mph south wind. Fallout quickly began to fall on the northern Nevada town of Elko.[38] The nuclear cloud then passed over northern Nevada and curved east in a tight trajectory that took it across the northern plains states before fanning out over the East Coast.

On June 5, at 5:30 P.M. local time, while children in Chicago might have been reading the very first issue of *Archie's Joke Book Magazine* or perhaps the more appropriate *Atom-Age Combat* detailing "The Exploits of Buck Vinson in the War of Wars," parts of Scorpion/GEORGE were drifting 35,000 feet overhead.

The highest fallout from GEORGE occurred in Illinois, Indiana, Michigan, and Wisconsin, where several hundred thousand counts per minute were recorded for each square foot of land area. As usual, the instruments recorded the number of disintegrations per second, not the strength. It could be likened to placing an instrument at a firing range that would record only the number of strikes on a target, and nothing about the caliber or speed of the bullets that produced the strikes.[39]

TUMBLER-SNAPPER: HOW

Shot How, the last of the series, was scheduled for June 5, 1952. Originally, there had been a ninth shot scheduled, but by the time GEORGE had been fired, scientists agreed they had the data they needed. The ninth shot was canceled.

How, a weapons development test, exploded with the force of 14 kilotons, hurling a mushroom cloud 37,308 feet into the air, 1,800 feet into the stratosphere.

The cloud crossed over Warm Springs, Nevada, then fanned out due north in a band approximately 80 miles wide. Light rain falling to the north of the test site the day after the shot resulted in high radioactivity being measured in Great Falls, Montana, and Boise, Idaho (both several million disintegrations/minute/square foot). At Elko, Nevada, a radioactivity value of 130,000 disintegrations/minute/square foot was recorded.

As with GEORGE, How traveled across the continent in a relatively tight band, finally crossing New York City at 1:30 P.M. local time June 7, 1952.

Even though shot How was rather small in comparison to some of the others in the series, its debris was tracked across the Atlantic to Europe, specifically to Prestwick, Scotland, and Rhein-Mainz, West Germany.

On the same day shot How was leaving the continental United States for European airspace, an advisory committee in the AEC's Division of Biology and Medicine met in St. Louis, Missouri. They had been asked to discuss the problem of radiation protection for pilots flying sampling missions through the nuclear clouds. It seemed that some of the pilots had received heavy radiation doses while skimming the mushroom clouds.

The meeting lasted two days and three things were decided:

1. A successful sampling mission probably meant an exposure to the pilots of about 20 roentgens;
2. Any excessive protective clothing to reduce such an exposure would "hamper the success of the mission," and
3. The pilots should "be permitted to receive a dose of 20 roentgens with an upper limit of 25 roentgens."[40]

This, however, posed a problem: two standards. The ground personnel were still limited to only a 3-roentgen exposure. So, on September 19, 1952, Dr. John C. Bugher, chairman of the AEC's Division of Biology and Medicine received a letter from Captain John T. Hayward, chief of the navy's Weapons Research Branch. It read, in part: "20 roentgens has been allowed crews of sampling aircraft without apparent ill effect while the limit for ground personnel has been maintained at 3 roentgens . . . some people in the Department of Defense have felt the AEC was not realistic in setting present exposure limits."[41]

The AEC had not expected such a letter from the navy. Judging by Hayward's phrasing, it was obvious that a concerted military effort was underway to relax radiation standards for military personnel involved in the testing.

The AEC, aware that it was up against tough opposition, bounced the letter around for about two weeks. Finally, George P. Kraker, deputy manager of the AEC's Santa Fe Operations Office was selected to write the reply.

There was little question who was in charge of the military campaign to reduce the standard; Kraker ignored Captain Hayward and addressed the letter directly to Brigadier General K. E. Fields, director of the AEC's Division of Military Applications. The reply was in essence a surrender coupled with a weak warning: "Exposure problems at the Test Site have not been completely solved. . . . Our position is that we probably cannot dictate exposure limits to the military, but we do have the responsibility of informing them of the hazards in order that they may be fully aware of the responsibility which they assume."[42]

Less than a week later, a letter from a familiar name arrived on the desk of Brigadier General Fields. On October 15, 1952, none other than Major General Herbert Loper wrote that the military was ready "to accept full responsibility for the physical and radiological safety of troops while in the Nevada Proving Grounds."[43]

In December 1952, General Fields wrote a report entitled *Troop Participation in Continental Tests* in which he stated that "The Department of Defense has assumed responsibility for the safety of troops participating in military exercises at the United States' AEC's Nevada Proving Grounds. . . . Military monitoring teams trained by AEC radiation safety monitors at previous tests will govern the movement of troops in the test areas to prevent exposure to harmful radiation. The maximum permissible level of radiation for troops who will participate will be slightly higher than the AEC's standard industrial level . . . [but] is far below that at which any detectable radiation effects have been found in the human body."[44]

The course had been set.

Upshot-Knothole

1953

The year 1953 would be an interesting one, particularly for the entertainment industry: 3-D would make its debut in motion picture theaters. The fad spread to comic books and, for a very short time, even to the fashion industry. One ad in the *New York Times* described 3-D clothes:

> Everything is 3-D. It all began with Cinerama. Now everything is three dimensional. Even men's clothes . . . Contrasting touches of color stand out from subdued backgrounds of tans, grays or blues, giving a third-dimensional effect to the appearance of the fabric.
>
> What happens is that special weaving techniques cause short lengths of yarns of contrasting color to appear and disappear. They add interest and give an impression of depth. It's what the trade calls a splash weave and is one of the numerous surface effects that is setting a whole new style trend this year.[2]

At almost any corner drugstore a 3-D *Batman* comic could be found "featuring a Penguin and Tommy Tomorrow story." In March, *Atomic Attack* and *Atomic War* comics also appeared.

It was a year that would bring liquid rouge, stereo-realist cameras, and Dacron. Estee Lauder introduces Youth Dew, and women would be seen wearing blanket ponchos and dresses with hoods. For men, wash-wear Dacron suits were beginning to catch on.

In Newport, Rhode Island, Massachusetts senator John F. Kennedy would marry twenty-four-year-old *Washington Times–Herald* photographer Jacqueline Bouvier.

In Chicago, in December, the first issue of *Playboy* would be published; the cover photo would be of Marilyn Monroe.

In 1953, among those showing interest in the atomic detonations were the officials of the Southern Chemical Cotton Company of Chattanooga,

Tennessee. As the prime supplier of cotton film base to Kodak, Southern Chemical was very concerned with the problem of radioactive contamination. In 1951, and occasionally thereafter, radioactive particles had become mixed with the cotton and had subsequently ruined a substantial amount of film for their client.

Subsequently, the AEC had agreed to tell Kodak of impending shots, no matter how secret. Once the detonation had taken place, Southern Chemical would have about twelve hours before the air and water around Chattanooga became so radioactive it would preclude manufacture of the film.

Any nuclear test series meant loss of revenue to Southern; it would take a week for the air to clear of any radioactivity, twice that long for the water. During the 1952 tests, no sooner had the air cleared than Southern would receive word another shot had taken place.

Radiation-sensitive industries, such as Kodak and Southern Chemical, would be granted advance notice of the shots, but for the most part, the average American would be unaware of the composition or the special nature of the clouds drifting overhead.

And the spring of 1953 would prove to be the most radioactive to date.

The Atomic Cannon and Used Cars

In March, the military announced that, at the upcoming atomic tests, a new weapon would be used: an atomic cannon. Since its unveiling on October 15, 1952, the huge artillery piece had been photographed firing nonatomic shells. Now, the huge, 280mm gun would finally get a chance to become the world's first atomic artillery piece.

The specifications of the cannon were striking: Weighing 85 tons, it was still relatively mobile. Carried between two tractors, it could roll across highways and negotiate fields, then fire a shell to hit a target 20 miles away. Whether it would—or could—be used in hilly Korea, however, was an open question.

On the same day, the Federal Civil Defense Administration announced that the National Auto Dealers Association and the major manufacturers had graciously loaned the AEC both new and used cars for use in atomic tests. The cars would contain dummies and be placed at various locations from the shot towers. The manufacturers supplied sixteen new cars. The auto dealers provided fifty used ones, mostly 1946–49 vintage. The AEC told the dealers they could have the cars back after the tests.

In Baltimore, Mrs. William F. Melville, Sr., a civil defense worker, was selected as a representative of the state's official party to watch one of the shots. The fifty-one-year-old grandmother said she "still can't come down to earth."[2]

Near Las Vegas, television technicians using helicopters, trucks, ski lifts, and "snow weasels" lugged 12,000 pounds of microwave relay equipment to the tops of four mountain peaks between the test site and Los Angeles. The equipment would relay scenes of the detonations across 277 miles and into the broadcast studios of ABC, NBC, and CBS. The technicians manning the equipment were given camp stoves and pup tents to use during the coverage of the blasts.[3]

Upshot-Knothole: Annie

The fourth series of Nevada tests, called Upshot-Knothole, would consist of eleven atmospheric detonations. There would be three airdrops, seven tower shots, and one warhead fired from an atomic cannon. About 21,000 military personnel would participate as observers or take part in scientific experiments and/or maneuvers as part of Desert Rock V.

During this exercise, soldiers (usually officers) would be allowed to decide for themselves how close to the detonation they could be without being harmed.[4]

The very first detonation of the series, Annie, would be an "open" shot—that is, reporters would be allowed on site to view the event from News Nob, which was not far from the Control Point and 7½ miles from the tower. As a first, a group of reporters who dubbed themselves "the trembling twenty" were selected to accompany the 1,700 troops scheduled to participate to the trenches, located only 2 miles southwest of where Annie would explode in Area 3 of the test site.

The morning of the detonation, Brigadier General William C. Bullock prepared to direct the army contingent during the maneuvers. Bullock had been given his star the night before. In the trenches, with the troops, was the new Federal Civil Defense administrator, Val Peterson.

Closer to the tower was "Doom Town," a pair of houses complete with automobiles and dummies. One house was situated 1.4 miles from the tower; the other, a scant ⅔ mile. After the blast, Peterson would walk through the area to survey the damage. According to International News reporter Bob Considine, this test was to "determine what kind of cars and clothes we should have in a world menaced by atomic warfare."[5]

Inside one of the $20,000 suburban-style homes a light was left on. Except for the tower spotlamps, it was the only light in the desert.

New York Times reporter Hansen Baldwin was one of the "trembling twenty" allowed into the tar-paper-and-chicken-wire-revetted trenches. Also calling themselves the "men of extinction," they awaited Annie's blast.

From Hansen Baldwin's report:

The trench positions were two miles closer to "ground zero" than they had been in any of last year's Nevada tests. But as they stood at the lips of their assigned trenches, warming themselves, and staring again and again toward the bright white light two miles away at the top of the 300-foot tower where "The Thing" was awaiting, [the soldiers] received still another foxhole briefing by loudspeaker. The recorded voice of Captain Harold Kinne, an Army expert on atomic energy, started cheerily:

"Good morning, gentlemen; welcome to Yucca Flat, the valley where the tall mushrooms grow. You will see exactly what the survivors of Hiroshima saw in 1945. You will be closer to an atomic burst than any American troops have ever been in history. You may be hurt if you do not obey orders. . . ."

The voice rolled on staccato and sharp from the loudspeakers as the observers stamped their feet and swung their arms to keep warm.

At H-hour, the time of detonation, minus ten minutes, troops and observers would enter the trenches, Captain Kinne said. At H minus two minutes, there would be the scream of a siren and all men in the trenches were to "face left, kneel down, look down and stay down," bracing themselves against the forward wall of the trench. It did not quite work out as the briefings had predicted.

The loudspeakers tolled out the passing time, H minus one hour; H minus thirty minutes.

Light grayed the sky in the east and slowly spread over the vast natural bowl where man in recent years has been vying with nature. The camp fires were put out: the troops and observers hunched closer to their trenches, four parallel lines extending across a mile of desert fronting toward the atomic device.

"H minus ten—H minus ten—get into your trenches, gentlemen."

The long files of dark and helmeted figures went down the steps and squeezed into the narrow trench, head and shoulders still above the ground. It was warmer in the trench and the men were packed closely together, but it was hard to keep still. At H minus two minutes the siren wailed, and we kneeled, faces down away from the "terrible bright light" that was to come, and waited. We heard the drone of a plane across the sky as the dawn brightened over our heads, but we dared not look up.

"Ten seconds, gentlemen, nine, eight, seven—" the countdown started. I instinctively held my breath and braced my shoulder against the forward wall of the trench—"four, three, two, one—zero."

At 5:20 A.M. Pacific Standard Time, ANNIE was detonated, sending a cloud of debris 36,974 feet above the desert floor.

Baldwin continued:

The great white light flared and beneath my eyes the grains of sand and dirt on the trench floor assumed a bold individuality etched in sharp relief by an illumination akin to that of a photoflash bulb set off in front of your face. But there was no heat; the trench and distance protected us from that. Then the trench and the whole surface of the desert seemed caught in quick little subterranean convulsions; the trench appeared to wave and shake; the earth shock, little mentioned in the briefing, was unexpectedly strong.

Still we crouched. The sound came at last—like a heavy distant thunder, neither painful to the ears nor terrifying to the senses. In the trench there were no airborne shock waves; I bowed my head and back and felt no pebbles, stones or sand, which, it had been thought, might have been blown into the trench by the blast. And there was no appreciable "flashback" or sucking back of the air following the violent outward blast.

At last we stood up—relieved and yet disappointed. Above us the atomic cloud was rising with striking speed to enormous heights. It was dun-colored, cloaked by dust sucked up from the desert floor by the low level burst, and the only hint of the raging inferno within was the orange tinge of the upper cloud, which yielded in seconds to the white color of the icecap.[6]

Samuel W. Matthews, a reporter with *National Geographic* magazine, wrote:

Through closed eyelids the world turned orange and, a split second later, crimson. There was no sound; the flash had come and gone in utter silence. I opened my eyes and saw the sergeant huddled in a ball, his face lifted in startled wonder. . . .

Thick brown dust covered the desert like churning fog. Beyond and above, the atomic fireball rose in the sky, a giant sphere of orange and black, tongues of fire amid billowing soot. . . . Higher and higher the cloud boiled against the bright blue-green dawn. On the very summit ice crystals formed, cascading over the rim like pure-white surf in the sky.[7]

Across the nation, television viewers up early to watch the blast were a bit disappointed. As reported in the *Houston Chronicle*, on March 18, 1953, local set owners said that at the instant of the blast, the screen lost the picture leaving "a mass of jumbled designs." It was speculated that the shock wave from the blast upset the synchronization devices located 7 miles from the blast.

When the picture returned, viewers were treated to the sight of a narrow cloud shaped like an upside down letter *L*.

About fifteen minutes after the detonation, the troops and observers moved forward, toward the tower. Nearby, they witnessed blackened wood, scorched sandbags, and an old army truck with a broken windshield and a flat tire. At Doom Town, a two-story frame dwelling placed 3,500 feet from ground zero had been demolished. Incredibly, not only was ANNIE's steel shot tower gone, but one that had been standing next to it had also vanished.

Seeing this, Hansen wrote: "It was clear to all observers that the good earth was the soldier's good friend in the atomic age."

Samuel W. Matthews: "A mile or less from [the explosion] blackened sandbags and blistered paint on vehicles and weapons told of searing heat. . . . Here the landscape had a strange look. I realized suddenly that all vegetation had vanished—greasewood and creosote bush, cactus and yucca. Only bare sand remained. Ahead, where the tower had been, a disk of black scarred the earth. In the first split second when the steel tower itself had vaporized, the fireball had left its grim tattoo."[8]

A short distance east of the vaporized tower, observers found that automobiles had been tossed around "like kiddy cars." Three had been transformed into masses of twisted metal. One of the two-story houses had collapsed onto a tan sedan that had been parked behind it. A green-shuttered house "at the corner of Elm and Main" had come apart at the seams. Inside, the mannequin inhabitants had been crushed under the flying furniture.

Monitors cautioned the troops and observers not to get closer than 700 yards south of ground zero.[9]

That evening, in Paris, Missouri, the Main Street Theater featured *Something for the Birds* with Victor Mature, Edmund Gwenn, and Patricia Neal. The cartoon was *Cruise Cat*. Those staying home could have seen Darren McGavin star in NBC's "Short Short Drama" episode entitled "The Double Cross."

Paris had been having a problem with mud showers in the spring of 1953. One had occurred just the week before over much of the area, coating windshields and everything else a murky brown. High school students washed and washed their cars in preparation for the Future Homemakers of America Confetti Ball that would be held on Friday, March 20, at the Paris High School gymnasium. A promlike affair, it was a once-a-year dance that everyone looked forward to.

At midnight on the night of March 17, the nuclear cloud from ANNIE passed 30,000 feet over Paris. Three nights later, while Paris high school students danced to records by Joni James and Frankie Laine, ANNIE's fallout was showering the Midwest with radioactivity.[10]

Interestingly, on Thursday, March 19, some unexpected fallout was indicated on the monitoring instruments at Oak Ridge, Tennessee, the site of the first uranium isotope separation plant.[11] That same evening was the first coast-to-coast telecast of the Academy Awards.

The next day, March 20, another phenomenon occurred: The first issue of *Atomic Mouse* comics appeared, detailing the origin of the superhero and the significance of his U-235 pill, which gives him his strength.

Almost 3,000 troops were scheduled to participate in the second shot, NANCY. More than 2,000 would take part in maneuvers beneath the nuclear cloud. The soldiers were asked to attack and secure objectives located slightly over half a mile from ground zero.[12]

Positioned less than 1½ miles from the tower, in the display area, was a single trench. It would be manned by nine officer volunteers from the army, navy, marines, and air force.[13] After calculating exposure pressures and thermal effects, they had decided they could weather the firestorm at 2,500 yards.[14] Prior to walking to the trench site, the officers were required to fill out a form:

CERTIFICATE

I hereby certify that I have personally and individually computed the effects expected in an open trench located as far forward as _____ yards from Ground Zero of Atomic Detonation Desert Rock V No. 2.

The validity of these computations is attested to by virtue of having attended

_____.

I volunteer to participate in this exercise by positioning myself in the above mentioned trench.

Prior to the shot, the military closed off the air corridors around the test site. Plans called for fifty-three ultra-long-range B-36 bombers to maneuver over the desert after the event. The B-36 was the plane the U.S. said they would use for targets "elsewhere" in the world. Perhaps because of the involvement of the bombers, the NANCY event was closed to reporters.

NANCY was detonated at 5:10 A.M. Pacific Standard Time. The explosion produced a 37,000-foot-tall mushroom cloud.[15]

Ten seconds after the detonation, three helicopters lifted off the ground; one carried a crewmember who had been blinded for about a minute and a half by the flash.

After the shock wave passed, the helicopters moved on toward ground zero. One was to attempt a landing a short distance west of the epicenter, while the other helicopters circled overhead, ready to render assistance if necessary. Upon reaching ground zero, the column of swirling dust and base cloud had reduced visibility to nearly zero. The survey chopper tried to land several times but failed. Inside, the needles of the radiac radiation meters bounced against the right peg, indicating extremely high radiation intensities. Had they actually landed, they would have found radiation intensities near 2,000 roentgens/hour at ground zero.

In the trenches, the volunteers apparently were unscathed. One of the officers, Commander Robert E. Thomas, Jr., later commented, "It was damn reassuring to get in that hole, have the bomb roll over my head, and still know that an adequate trench was complete protection." Another said that "we felt a definite heat surge like someone had opened and then closed a giant oven door. Things burned around us, but we felt only a minimum of heat."[16]

In the back areas, the BCT troops poured from their trenches and began charging toward their objective to the west of ground zero. Meanwhile, meteorologists began to see something that disturbed them: a shift in the wind. It began to look as though the stem of the nuclear cloud would be carried smack down the middle of the display area—and toward the volunteers.

In the trenches, the officers watched in disbelief as the stem approached. The needles on the radiacs began to climb. They decided at once to evacuate through the swirling dust.

Two sheepherders from Cedar City, Utah, Kern and Mac Bulloch, had been driving their sheep through a canyon near the test site when the burst occurred:

> We were over at Coyote Pass right next to the bomb site just herding our sheep. One morning we were sitting in the saddle there, and some airplanes come up and one of them dropped a bomb. Jesus, it was bright! I put my hands up like that and you could doggone near see your bones. And then that cloud come right over top of us, it mushroomed right over our camp and our herd. And we were sitting there—course we didn't know a thing about radiation or bombs or anything else. Pretty soon, here comes some jeeps with Army personnel [actually AEC monitors], and they said to us, "My golly, you fellas are in a hot spot!" We didn't even know what they were talking about.[17]

The nuclear cloud initially moved north, then northeast, passing almost over Salt Lake City. After the results had been tabulated, it was discovered that on March 24, 1953, each square foot of Salt Lake City earth produced 15 million disintegrations/minute. Ely, Nevada, came in second with 2 million disintegrations/minute.

The third burst of the series, RUTH, was to be detonated on March 31. The first weapon designed by a lab other than Los Alamos, the detonation would be carefully examined to determine yield. RUTH's design team worked at Edward Teller's laboratory, the University of California Radiation Laboratory at Livermore.

After opening in September 1952 under the direction of physicist Herbert York, the lab had immediately begun designing weapons. With a staff of 200 physicists and support personnel, the UCRL lab would eventually provide the Los Alamos scientists with heavy competition in the mass-yield sweepstakes, but not in 1953.

On the evening of March 30, the UCRL device was taken to the top of a 300-foot tower in Area 7–5a and placed in the center of the cab on a 4-foot-high pedestal. RUTH apparently was an extremely small device, a prototype of the nuclear "satchel charges" that would be tested two years later. As a result of its size, the yield was expected to be on the low side. No troop maneuvers were planned.

The detonation occurred at 5:00 Pacific Standard Time on the morning of March 31, sending a cloud 9,600 feet above the desert floor. The explosion, though relatively small, produced a double shock wave felt at the Control Point.[18]

The only off-site station detecting radiation was Phoenix.[19]

The April 6 shot would not involve a tower. Instead, like the bombs in the RANGER series, it would be airdropped over the target.

At 7:30 the bomb was released. Detonation occurred 6,022 feet above the desert floor, sending a cloud 40,975 feet high, almost 3,000 feet into the stratosphere.[20] The yield was estimated to be around 11 kilotons, very similar to that of the Hiroshima uranium bomb. DIXIE, however, had been a much lighter and more efficient weapon. Apparently, the tamper for the device, the metal shell that holds the plutonium core together during initial fission, had been slightly altered. The designers had separated the tamper from the core by a small space, allowing momentum to build before it hit the fissioning plutonium. As weapons designer Ted Taylor once asked, "When you hammer a nail, what do you do? Do you put the hammer on the nail and push?"[21]

The bombardier had been extremely accurate; the detonation had occurred within 50 feet of the assigned ground zero. As usual, windows were broken in Las Vegas.[22]

The mushroom, floating between 25,000 and 37,000 feet, was immediately entrained in the jet stream. This fast-moving river of wind carried the upper portion of the cloud southeast across the country, taking it out over the North Carolina coast twenty-eight hours later. The cloud moved so fast that the tracking planes had considerable difficulty keeping up with it.[23]

On April 7, southern New England was buffeted by a storm off the Atlantic Coast that had arrived from northern Alabama. By 7:00 P.M. on the night of April 8, the trajectory of DIXIE's nuclear cloud was 200 miles southsoutheast of this storm area. By 11:00 that evening, fallout from DIXIE began showing up on Long Island, New York. Shortly after that, radioactive fallout occurred in Boston, Massachusetts; Providence, Rhode Island; and Hartford, Connecticut. Since little rain was involved at the time the fallout began, meteorologists assumed the debris had been brought down by the strong downdrafts associated with the storm.

One source indicates that the Lexington-Boston area received a total of 1,900 milliroentgens from DIXIE, nineteen times the amount of radiation Bostonians normally receive in a year's time.[24,25] While the medical significance of such a dose would eventually be a topic of intense debate, it would be decades before Bostonians became aware of their exposures.

Back on the West Coast, the scientists at Livermore were nervously awaiting the next shot of the series, RAY. This was their second attempt at weapon design and they sincerely hoped it would be better than their first, the rather unspectacular March 31 shot. As an indication of the expectations they held for their second attempt, a decision was made to fire the device from a tower only a third as high as RUTH's had been.

Even these expectations were not met. RAY's cloud shot up to a less-than-awe-inspiring 8,774 feet—826 feet *lower* than the March 31 detonation.[26] To make matters worse, the shot did not even *look* nuclear: Rather, it resembled a stack of burning tires.

An eyewitness account: "The cloud at top level did not mushroom and hold together as ordinarily happens but spread out in streamers with the appearance, even as to color, of coal smoke from a stack.[27] At Los Alamos, scientists joked about the secret neutron reflector material used in RAY: rubber, with a coal tamper.

In addition to being small and ugly, RAY was also contrary: For a while the black cloud leaned back toward the Control Point, then disappeared over a ridge to the west. Concerned, the scientists placed survey meters near the doors, but there was no indication of increased radioactivity. Later, an hour-long air sample taken at the doorway showed radioactivity.[28]

RAY had been such a puny shot that the cloud tracking planes had considerable difficulty locating it, despite the abundance of black smoke.[29,30]

Even before the black smoke from RAY had cleared, the marines were gearing up for a massive operation scheduled to coincide with the next detonation.

UPSHOT-KNOTHOLE: BADGER

The sixth shot of the series, BADGER was scheduled for April 18, 1953, at Area 2 of the Nevada Test Site. Present would be a total of 2,800 Department of Defense personnel, including 2,167 marines who would take part in a huge maneuver under an umbrella of ninety aircraft, including twelve B-50 bombers and thirty-nine helicopters. As part of the test, military officials wanted to know if helicopters could be used successfully to transport troops in a nuclear battleground environment. Four major marine units would be involved in the maneuver: Brigade Headquarters; 1st Battalion, 8th Marine Regiment, 2nd Marine Division; 2nd Battalion, 3rd Marine Regiment, 3rd Marine Division; Marine Helicopter Transport Group 16, also called "MAG-HR-16." Altogether the four units would be known as the 2nd Marine Corps Provisional Atomic Exercise Brigade. Before the maneuver was over, some of the marines in this group would have exceeded the allowable limit of 6.0 roentgens of radiation.

The plan called for the troops to assemble at a trench area 3,660 meters (2.27 miles) south-southwest of ground zero. After the shock wave, the troops were to begin the maneuver that would involve attacking objectives located a little over a mile south-southwest of the hypocenter. Radiological teams would precede the combat teams. After securing the objective the marines would then tour the display area in which foxholes, concrete bunkers, amphibious landing craft, rifles, machine guns, food, and even animals were located. Also found in the display area were dummies in marine clothing.

The helicopters were to begin the airlift about ten minutes postshot. Two "pathfinder" choppers would fly ahead of the others to measure radiation levels near the objectives.

In a replay of shot NANCY, six army and six marine corps officers volunteered to wait out the detonation in a trench close to the tower. This time the officers calculated the safe distance to be 1,830 meters, or 1.14 miles from the tower.

On the evening of April 17, the thirty-nine helicopters were taken to a staging area at a Yucca airstrip 12½ miles from the tower. Early the next morning, the troops, including the twelve volunteers, were brought to their respective trenches.[31]

BADGER was detonated at 4:35 A.M. Pacific Standard Time.[32] Within eight minutes the bottom of the mushroom hung suspended 3½ miles above the troops maneuvering below.[33] After the shock wave rolled over the trenches, the marines climbed out and began their advance toward the cloud. But then something happened: A change in the wind was transporting the tornadolike stem down through the display area, toward the marines—and the officers in the volunteer trench a mile closer to ground zero.

Colonel W. F. Lantz, a marine volunteer in the trench, remembered the BADGER shot:

> I was leaning against the forward wall of the trench holding an AN/PDR 32 dose rate meter with both hands for the purpose of observing the intensity of the initial radiation. The white light was so intense that I was blinded by absolute whiteness. This apparently lasted for several seconds. There was a vague recollection of a slight crackling sound at this time. It is believed that this sound may have been the result of intense ionization which takes place in the atmosphere. I felt no rise in temperature nor any thermal effects, but it is noted that the only part of my body not covered was my hands.
>
> The next sensation was that of earth shock which was very pronounced. The earth seemed to shift back and forth very strongly a number of times. . . . Again regaining my sight, estimated to be about three or four seconds after the detonation, I noticed that the indicator of my meter was off the dial on the high side which read to 500 roentgens/hour. [This lasted for fifteen to twenty seconds.]

The blast wave then hit with a high-pitched crack and general increase in the ambient pressure was noticed. I was enveloped in dust and had the sensation of a heavy windstorm blowing over my head. I was not tossed about in the trench. The wind subsided and I climbed from the trench to observe the atomic cloud. This was not seen due to the very heavy dust which enveloped the position.[34]

The volunteers, only little more than a mile from the explosion, had noticed continued high radiation levels on their radiac instruments as the needles hovered between 30 and 50 roentgens/hour. Looking up to see the huge stem bearing down on them, they decided to take immediate action: a hasty evacuation to safer areas. The officers climbed out of their trenches and hurried to a road about 200 yards to the west of the trenches, walking as fast as they could through the dust, smoke, and burning scrub brush. At the time, no one knew if it was the right direction; BADGER's radioactive "footprint" was detectable only by the instruments that indicated a steady 50 roentgens/hour. As it turned out, the road was still within the 50-roentgens/hour area, but luckily, trucks soon arrived, their headlights barely visible in the swirling dust. From there, the volunteers were taken to the back trenches where the radiation intensity was somewhat lower.

To the rear of the volunteer trench, the 1st Battalion had advanced only 500 yards before their dosimeters read 3.0 roentgens, the exposure limit. The commanders immediately ordered the marines back to their positions.[35]

The 2nd Battalion fared considerably worse. Amid the swirling dust they somehow managed to make it to the display area, as did 500 observers and another marine company flown there by thirty-seven helicopters. Here the soldiers were only about 1,000 yards from ground zero, where the radiation intensity was an unhealthy 50 roentgens/hour. At the hypocenter, the radiation level was 1,200 roentgens/hour. Twenty-five minutes' exposure to such a level was considered lethal.

There were also problems in the sky. The blast had kicked up an enormous quantity of dust; the pilots simply couldn't see where they were going. To compound the problem, the radiac instruments seemed to show radiation intensities greater than 50 roentgens/hour *everywhere*.[36]

Meteorologists at the test site analyzed information obtained from the tracker planes and then called Washington. As a result, the Civil Aeronautics Administration quickly issued a notice barring all flights until 5:00 P.M. Pacific Standard Time above 20,000 feet over an 800,000-square-mile area bounded by Las Vegas; Denver, Colorado; and El Paso and Dallas, Texas.[37]

The BADGER nuclear cloud traveled southeast from the test site, passing 10 miles north of Las Vegas 2½ hours after the detonation—in the direction of the Grand Canyon.[38]

According to the Weather Bureau report, BADGER "accounted for the highest dry fallout observed at stations 1,000–1,400 nautical miles from the test site.[39]

U*PSHOT*-K*NOTHOLE:* S*IMON*

The shot scheduled for April 25, designated S*IMON*, was to have a projected yield of 35 kilotons. Like before, the event would involve troop maneuvers. A total of 3,000 soldiers were scheduled to maneuver beneath the mushroom cloud. And as at the other nuclear events, the troops would be required to attack an objective near ground zero.

As H-hour drew near on the morning of April 25, 1953, seven volunteers found themselves huddled in a trench a little over a mile from the 300-foot tower. Each man had been given a steel helmet, a respirator, canteen, and a flashlight. The device was to be fired at 4:30 A.M. Pacific Standard Time; after the fireball cooled to ambient temperature, the area would be enveloped in a thick, dark haze. The flashlights would be necessary for the men to find their way back to the equipment display and *away* from the intensely radioactive epicenter.

All of the volunteers were fitted with dosimeters and one, navy captain Robert Hinners, had been given a radiac, which measures gamma radiation.

As with other shots, the men were ordered to kneel on one knee and cover their eyes with one arm. In the darkness the voice over the loudspeaker slowly ticked off the seconds, all the way back to zero.

Then silence.

Then the brilliant, soundless glare, followed a second later by the incredible concussion of the atomic blast. The fireball was already churning upward toward the stratosphere.

High above, a navy drone Skyraider was flying straight for the junction of the stem and the mushroom. Within seconds, the powerful pressure wave, coupled with the intense heat destroyed the planes wing panels, sending it out of control. Through breaks in the ground haze six B-47 Stratojets, flying in tight formation, could be seen circling the S*IMON* mushroom.

Placed near the Control Point, instruments had recorded the extremely brief time intervals between the peaks of brightness in the fireball. The information would be used to help determine S*IMON*'s actual yield: 43 kilotons. It would be the most powerful continental shot to date.

As the pressure wave skipped across the countryside, the volunteers were cautiously picking their way through the ground haze. Minutes earlier they had noticed that the huge swirling stem had seemed to be leaning toward them, like a tornado or a huge thick smokestack that was about to fall. In addition, the radiac was registering hot spots as high as 50 roentgens/hour or more.

Overhead, they could hear the sound of helicopters. The chopper pilots were slowly maneuvering their aircraft toward objectives near the roiling stem. Monitoring instruments in the cockpits were recording surprisingly high radiation levels. Pockets of hot air seemed to be everywhere.

Not far from the test site, off-site monitors watched nervously as their instruments began responding to the SIMON cloud: A stream of nuclear debris—300 roentgens/hour hot—was taking aim on southwestern Utah. According to the best information, the band of debris was about 80 miles in width. There was no telling what altitude it reached; the best estimates placed SIMON's cloudtop at 44,000 feet above sea level. The Civil Aeronautics Board immediately banned all commercial and private aviation in a zone extending from Tonopah to Las Vegas and from Ogden, Utah, all the way to Grand Junction, Colorado.

Roadblocks were immediately set up. All vehicles were stopped and checked for radiation, even a Greyhound bus loaded with thirty persons on their way to Las Vegas.[40]

As monitoring teams hurried to southwestern Utah, the SIMON cloud was being entrained in a variety of air currents that would carry it far to the east.

Hot Rain

On the morning of April 26, some students at the Rensselaer Polytechnic Institute, in Troy, New York, noticed something odd: Their Geiger counters were responding to something. It had rained the night before, and when the students took the instruments to the window, the levels went up. They contacted radiochemistry professor Herbert Clark, who then called the AEC. The official told Clark there must be a mistake.

There was no mistake. Several instruments were responding to radioactivity from *somewhere*. Where was all the radioactivity coming from?

Clark and his students turned the event into a radiochemistry project: Puddles were measured for radioactivity. The result: 270,000 times as radioactive as water approved for drinking. Tap water showed a radiation level 2,630 higher than normal. Interestingly, because of either its chemical makeup or electrical charge, the radioactive material stuck like glue to the roof and walls. Scrubbing wouldn't remove it.[41]

After investigating, the AEC meteorologists discovered that each square foot of Albany, New York, was covered by a light layer of fallout transforming—and emitting radiation—at a rate of 16 *million* disintegrations/minute. The source had to be atomic debris. They concluded that the fallout dropped on the Albany, New York, area was from an unfortunate encounter between the SIMON cloud and a thunderstorm. The eventual dose was variously estimated to be between a few hundred to a few thousand millirads.[42]

Oddly, San Diego, only 300 miles from the Nevada Test Site, experienced practically no fallout at all.[43]

A few days after the shot, Brigadier General Harry P. Storke, Camp Desert Rock commander, sent the troops a message: "In this exercise, for the first time in known history, troops successfully attacked directly toward ground zero immediately following the atomic explosion. You can remember, with a sense of pleasure and accomplishment, that you were one of those troops, a real pioneer in experimentation of the most vital importance to the security of the United States.[44]

Four days after the SIMON shot, a special study was made to determine residual radioactivity levels in the Nevada–Utah area. Water samples were taken for analysis from surface streams and community supplies. Radiation levels were determined at a number of areas on Highways 91 and 93 and at all communities between the hours of 9:50 A.M. and 3:45 P.M. local time on April 28.

At a site 29 miles north of Glendale, Nevada, a maximum reading of 21 milliroentgens was found. The monitors said they saw "no people or livestock along the highway in the area of significant fallout."

From the report: "Proceeding eastward from the Glendale Junction on Highway 91 the heavy fallout pattern was observed to cross the highway at a point 13 miles east of Glendale where a maximum level of 13.2 milliroentgens/hour was observed."

Other areas of relatively high radiation included Riverside (15.6 milliroentgens/hour), Bunkerville (10.9 milliroentgens/hour), one mile east of Bunkerville (16.2 milliroentgens/hour), and Mesquite (3.5 milliroentgens/hour). At the time, the monitoring team found 550 dairy cattle in the area, with 280 cows located in Mesquite (with a human population of 600).[45] There is no notation in the report as to whether the monitoring teams contacted the population to discourage the drinking of milk from these areas.

UPSHOT-KNOTHOLE: ENCORE

On May 7, a steam locomotive was seen slowly moving west on a stretch of tracks just outside Camp Mercury, Nevada. This engine was special: Along with its boxcars and tank cars, it would be trucked to the middle of the desert to be part of an atomic event. Eight days earlier, a train had left Fort Sill, Oklahoma, carrying two 85-ton cannons on eight railroad flatcars. One of the cannons would be a spare; the other would fire the world's first atomic artillery shell.

Meanwhile, the test site was gearing up for ENCORE. Scheduled for May 8, the event involved a device to be dropped from a B-50 bomber a mere 2,500 feet over Frenchman's Flat. The bomb was to have a projected yield in the neighborhood of 25 to 30 kilotons.

On the ground, over 3,000 military personnel would take part in troop and helicopter maneuvers and damage effects evaluations. Perhaps to facilitate visibility, the shot was scheduled for midmorning.

Prior to the shot date, personnel from provisional units of the First, Third, and Fourth armies and various air force units combined into two Battalion Combat Teams. For several days, the men attended classes and rehearsed the exercise, which would involve an assault on objectives 3 miles south-southwest and 0.9 south-southeast of the hypocenter. To assure radiological safety, a "pathfinder" team composed of a thirty-men platoon would be airlifted to the nearer objective. At that point, the rad-safe monitors would check the area for radiation.

Other observers would watch the shot from trenches 5.8 miles from ground zero. After the shot, they would be transported to the equipment display area.

For the damage effects test, the 412th Engineer Construction Battalion had dug trenches, bunkers, and foxholes in the hard desert alluvium. The day before the shot, the 3623rd Ordnance Company entered the display area to place equipment consisting of jeeps, rifles, mortars, and other light and medium artillery. On the same day, medical teams trucked in sheep. The combination of artillery and farm animals made for an arresting sight.[46]

To make the scene even more surreal, trees were brought down from Mount Charleston and planted in concrete near ground zero. Twenty-five automobiles that had survived previous blasts were also brought in for the occasion.

Two F-80 drone jets, each carrying a monkey and some mice, would be flown through the mushroom at an altitude of 25,000 feet roughly seven minutes after detonation.

Another project, 8.4.1, "Protection Afforded by Operational Smoke Screens Against Thermal Radiation," which would investigate the possibilities of using white smoke as a thermal "screen," was canceled. The breeze, blowing at 6 to 14 mph, was just too fast.

Detonation occurred 2,423 feet above the desert at 8:30 A.M. Pacific Daylight Time. The explosion sent the cloud 38,923 feet above the desert floor. At Camp Mercury, 10 miles from the burst, windows cracked and light bulbs shattered. At ground zero, the anchored pine trees swayed as they caught fire. Test buildings smouldered briefly, but the fire was doused by the shock wave, which caved in some of the structures closest to the detonation. The rumble from the shot was heard in St. George, Utah, and Bishop, California.

In a change from previous policy, troops and observers were allowed to stand and watch the fireball before the arrival of the pressure front. After the shock wave had passed, the soldiers climbed out onto the desert floor and began the attack. Seven helicopters landed to pick up the pathfinder group and place them at the objective near ground zero. An hour after the shot, radiation monitors recorded levels of only 0.26 roentgens/hour near ground zero.

Other observers were trucked to the display area, where they spent the next five hours and twenty minutes walking through the rubble of damaged equipment.

By 10:45 A.M., both objectives had been taken and the troops returned to Camp Desert Rock.

The only casualties were the monkeys and mice, who, as passengers in the two F-80 drones, had flown through ENCORE's turbulent mushroom. The animals were found to have suffered severe radiation poisoning and were put to death.

Perhaps because ENCORE was an airdropped device, the radiation at ground zero was relatively light, 25 roentgens/hour measured one hour after the detonation. Fallout across the rest of the country, however, would be substantial. The official report indicated that "Although only a relatively thin cloud of debris was observed at the Test Site below the base of the mushroom, it is expected that debris will continue to be found at scattered locations in the United States for several days. . . ."

Most of the debris moved initially to the north, then east, passing over Casper, Wyoming, at 6:00 P.M. on May 8. The cloud encountered rain across the northern plains states, which, according to the report, "resulted in a deposition of considerable activity on the day of the burst as far north as Williston, North Dakota."[47]

When the ENCORE cloud passed over cool and overcast Casper it first drifted over the refineries then to Cypress Street at the western edge of the city. Carried by strong upper-air currents, the center of the debris tracked northeast, parallel to the North Platte River and Railroad Avenue. The wind speed at that altitude was such that perhaps within an hour the trailing edge of the ENCORE cloud had finally moved across Colorado Avenue on the far eastern edge of the city.[48]

On the day of the ENCORE detonation, the Paris, Missouri, Junior-Senior Prom was held, the students' last big dance before graduation on May 15. The theme was "Hitch Your Wagon to a Star."[49]

At the drive-in theater west of town the movie was *Half Angel* with Joseph Cotton and Loretta Young. The motion picture ended at 10:45. As the cars filed out of the drive-in and onto Highway 24, something from Nevada was passing overhead: the debris from ENCORE on its way toward a rendezvous with Chicago airspace at 7:00 the next morning.

Upshot-Knothole: Harry

Western New Mexico in the early 1950s had two good, solid industries: fruit growing and uranium prospecting. The fruit had been there for years, as had the ore, but the increased demand for uranium had turned the latter into a money-making industry. Part-time prospectors combed the area around Gallup, listening for the clicks that meant money.

Early 1953 had brought problems to the area. For one thing, a series of unusually late frosts had damaged the fruit trees, reducing the crop substantially. Growers openly voiced the opinion that atomic testing was to blame for the cold weather. More ominously, several citizens in one small New Mexico town complained of light-headedness and nausea—symptoms, they said, of radiation poisoning.

There was a third allegation, one more easily verified: For days after a nuclear event, prospectors in New Mexico couldn't use their Geiger counters to search for uranium ore. Not being able to distinguish radioactive ore from radioactive air, the instruments would chatter continuously. The prospectors complained that the testing was cutting in on their profits.[50]

Livermore's third attempt, HARRY, was scheduled for detonation on may 19, 1953. Although about 1,000 military observers would be available to watch the shot, there would be no maneuvers.

On the evening of May 18, the device was raised to the top of the 300-foot steel tower placed in Area 3a of the Nevada Test Site. Meteorological projections indicated a wind from the southwest, but at the surface there was a slight, annoying breeze—6 mph—from 20 degrees, the *northeast*. This was mildly distressing to the meteorologists; the observer trenches were southwest of the shot tower.

Detonation occurred at 5:04 A.M. Pacific Daylight Time, with a force of 15 kilotons.

A St. George, Utah, resident, sixty-eight-year-old William Sleight, happened to be driving toward Las Vegas at the time of the shot. He wrote in his diary:

> May 19, 1953: Beautiful morning. We left St. George at 4 a.m. for Las Vegas, Nevada. We were watching for the A-bomb explosion on the desert north of Las Vegas. At 5:00 a.m., just dawn, we saw the flash which lit up the skies, a beautiful red, visible for hundreds of miles away. It was a beautiful sight, a hundred miles or more away from it. I had my car radio on and at 5:01 a.m., the announcer on KFT, Los Angeles, California, said that at 5 a.m., the bomb had been exploded and that it was visible at that station, and also in Idaho. I drove for ten minutes, then stopped the car on the roadside, got out and soon after we heard the report of the blast. It rumbled as thunder, not quite the same as other blasts we have heard. This is the 9th in a series of ten, another next week. It makes me shudder when I think of what misery we may face when men start dropping these terrific bombs on out cities. Some fanatics are now clamoring for their use in Korea.[51]

The fireball was visible for an unusually long period of time, seventeen seconds. Amateur scientists among the reporters suggested that a way had been found to sustain the fission reaction, thus producing a more efficient weapon. There was no confirmation that this had actually been the case with HARRY.

As the cloud boiled skyward, a drone jet succeeded in breaking the "thermal barrier" produced by the fireball. It would later land on the desert floor, radioactive, but more or less intact.

Meteorologists quickly estimated the maximum height of the swirling mass: 38,484 feet, with the base hovering 23,494 feet above the desert floor. At the 16,000-foot altitude, the wind was blowing from the west at a strong 44 mph. The wind's intensity increased with altitude, and at the top of the mushroom the wind roared along at 91 mph—from the northwest.

The weathermen were becoming concerned.

Meanwhile, two congressmen who had witnessed the event were being interviewed by the press. "None of us," one said, "was fully prepared for what we saw, even after three days of intensive preparation and briefings. It was greater than we could have imagined."

The other congressmen was no less effusive in his praise for HARRY: "Today's atomic blast," he said, "made the sunrise a candle by comparison. . . . We were not prepared for what seemed to us an eighth wonder of the world."[52]

As the HARRY cloud passed overhead, some residents of St. George noticed something unusual: A strange metallic taste in their mouths, possibly due to the presence in the air of microscopic iron particles—remnants of the shot tower.[53]

The AEC meteorologists studied the wind patterns and quickly determined that, again, there would be off-site fallout problems.[54] Radiation survey crews set up a roadblock between Las Vegas and St. George, and stopped over a hundred cars for radioactivity checks.

From Mr. Sleight's diary: "After we came back on Highway 91, we were stopped and a young man examined our car with an instrument to see if we had picked up any radioactive dust while traveling on the highway. . . . Found none so we missed a free car wash (which would have been appreciated). . . . Returned to St. George in a high wind which always seems to follow these explosions."[55] Elizabeth Catalan, a school-age child living in St. George at the time, remembered HARRY:

> The news was broadcast on radio that a nuclear device had been detonated, creating a cloud of debris, and although it was headed toward St. George, we were assured there was no danger. People were urged to stay indoors for two hours as a precaution until the cloud had passed. The announcement was repeated, and it closed with the message, "there is no danger."
>
> My family was at home that noon when my father called. He had been told about the cloud's path and wanted my mother to keep us children indoors. Since he had been assured there was no real cause for alarm, he continued his day's business, in and out of doors all afternoon. Looking out the kitchen win-

dow, my mother could see the cloud, looking like a large thunderhead, dark and ominous, spreading across the sky as it approached.

The townspeople were edgy. They had been cautioned about fallout before, but never had they seen such an ugly, thick, darkness overhead. After the two-hour danger period had passed, the AEC issued an "all clear" warning. The cloud had passed over, and residents believed there had been no danger.[56,57]

Agatha Mannering thought otherwise. She had not been near her radio that morning and thus had not heard the reports. As the dark pall from the nuclear cloud hung over St. George, Agatha calmly spent the day weeding her garden.

Toward sundown, she began to feel sick; her throat and lungs began to burn and her scalp began to itch. By morning, she felt as though her skin were on fire, like being stung by red ants. Upon visiting the doctor, she was told that it was only fallout, that there was nothing to worry about, and that "it will go away." In a manner of speaking, it did. Soon after her encounter with the nuclear cloud, Agatha Mannering's hair began to fall out.[58]

Sometime later, Dr. Harold Knapp, an AEC fallout specialist, was asked to evaluate the effect of the fallout to St. George, Utah from the HARRY detonation. His calculations showed that in the twenty-four hours after the burst, the (radioactive) iodine-131 levels in milk may have reached extremely high levels, somewhere between 700,000 to 2.6 million micro-curies/liter. A child who drank a liter of milk a day for the three weeks following HARRY (and not counting the next two shots) would receive from 120 to 440 rads to his or her thyroid, an enormous amount.[59]

In another estimate, Dr. Charles Mays of the University of Utah estimated that 700 infants in St. George received thyroid radiation doses 136 to 500 times higher than the levels permitted at that time.[60]

HARRY's cloud split into three main sections. The upper sections moved south toward El Paso, Texas, while the lower levels followed a more central track. HARRY's 10,000-foot trajectory passed between Ogden, Utah, and Salt Lake City, then curved east, passing just south of Casper, Wyoming. At 8:00 A.M. on Wednesday, May 20, it would cross directly over Scottsbluff, Nebraska.

It was a bad time for a nuclear cloud to pass through. Scottsbluff's weather included clouds and scattered showers with a few locally heavy thunderstorms. The high temperature that day reached only the mid-sixties.

That same afternoon, thunderstorms to the northeast dropped hail-stones an inch in diameter into downtown Alliance, Nebraska. The storm system aparently extended across the entire state; hail was also reported in Norfolk and as far east as Omaha.

The *Scottsbluff Star–Herald* reported that the "AEC Quarantines Utah Town for Radioactivity After Atom Test Jars Parts of Three States: A powerful atomic explosion rocked portions of three states Tuesday and cast a radioactive pall over St. George, Utah, virtually closing the town for three hours. . . . The blast, set off in muggy weather, was felt in Nevada and Utah and gave earthquake-conscious Californians as far as 400 miles away a good jolt before breakfast.''

The official report generated by the Atomic Energy Commission gave a more complete—and classified—account of the event: "Heavy dry fallout from the stem, associated with the 10,000-foot and 18,000-foot trajectories, was observed over Colorado and Kansas, while precipitation over the upper Midwest resulted in the highest values reported in that region for the series . . . on May 21, fallout from this burst covered most of the country east of the Rockies."[61]

The nuclear cloud from HARRY moved on east then north, crossing over Chicago at 10,000 feet at 3:30 A.M. on May 21.

On that same day, Congressman Robert R. Stringfellow asked the AEC to stop the Nevada testing; it was dousing his constituents with fallout. The AEC agreed to send a representative to meet with Stringfellow in St. George on May 25.

On May 22, the AEC held one of its regularly scheduled meetings. Commissioner Henry D. Smythe was a bit concerned about the problem of public relations in the wake of the HARRY incident at St. George. Another commissioner, Eugene M. Zuckert, remarked, "A serious psychological problem has arisen, and the AEC must be prepared to study an alternate to holding future tests at the Nevada test site. In the present frame of mind of the public, it would take only a single illogical and unforeseeable incident to preclude holding any future tests in the United States.[62]

The military would hear none of this. In a joint meeting of the AEC–Military Liaison Committee, MLC chairman Robert LeBaron indicated that the government "must avoid arousing public fears to the point of large-scale public opposition to the continental tests." At the same meeting, the military derided the AEC's practice of setting up roadblocks and washing cars as perfect examples of overreacting.

Gordon Dean, chairman of the AEC, was beginning to grow nervous. The members of the Atomic Energy Commission had fought such a battle with the military just prior to the BUSTER-JANGLE series—and had lost. He was not willing to get into another scrap so soon, especially with a new president who happened to be an ex-general. Though Dean didn't know it at the time, he was correct in his assessment of the situation, as a meeting with Eisenhower just five days later would prove.

UPSHOT-KNOTHOLE: GRABLE

On May 25, 1953, after years of preparation, the army was finally ready to fire an atomic cannon. The shell would be an excellent example of the

weapon designer's art, many thousands of tons of TNT-equivalent firepower packed into a 280mm (11-inch) shell. Because of size constraints, a
gun-type mechanism—similar to the Hiroshima bomb—was incorporated
into the design. The problem with a gun mechanism was its low efficiency.
Nevertheless, it was the tactical weapon the army had been waiting six years
for—and it was something the Soviets didn't have.

The army wanted the north part of the test site, but instead were given
the vast expanse of Frenchman's Flat for their experiment. The cannon
would be fired at a target 6 miles away. Using radio signals from a timer
based at the Control Point, the shell was programmed to explode at 1,500-
foot altitude with 17 kilotons of force. Twenty-five people would witness
the test, including Edgerton, Germehausen and Greer (EG&G) engineer
Bernard J. O'Keefe: "I was disconcerted when I arrived at the gun site. A
280-millimeter gun is an enormous piece of machinery. I had never seen anything that big, even in the Navy."[63]

As with other tests, a large number of troops—2,600 in all—were
scheduled to maneuver under GRABLE's cloud. In addition, over 700 observers would watch the shot. The soldiers were to ride out the burst in trenches
placed 4,570 meters (2.84 miles) from ground zero, then attack due west
across the Short Pole Line Road. The objectives were located 1½ miles
southeast and 1.74 miles east-southeast of ground zero. Combat Team Able
was to take the southernmost objective, number 4, while Team Baker aimed
for objective number 2, located east-southeast of the hypocenter. After that,
the soldiers were scheduled to walk through the display area, where the
3623rd Ordnance Company had placed military equipment, fortifications,
sheep, and the steam locomotive.

As a first, there would be seventy-five military physicians acting as observers just 2,500 yards from ground zero.

Before the shot, scientists and technicians working on Project 8.4.1, the
so-called smokescreen project, placed 175 smoke pots from 33 to 50 yards
from the estimated hypocenter. On the night of May 24, three technicians
visited the area to remove covers from their instruments. They would remain
at ground zero, checking the equipment and remote control relays until 5:30
on the morning of the shot.

Nine F-84Gs from the 4926th Test Squadron would collect cloud samples from GRABLE. The jets would be under the direction of a sampler control crew circling nearby in a B-50. The sampler crew would include a Los
Alamos scientific advisor. As with all the shots, radiochemists would analyze the particles; this information, coupled with analysis of explosion rate,
would help determine the yield, and thus the efficiency of the device.

On the morning of May 25, as several "ranging" shots were fired to determine wind drift, the safety-conscious O'Keefe was having second thoughts
about being on hand for the event. The engineer had taken part in a number

of nuclear tests, and had done so with a high degree of caution. Looking around, he wondered if the firing would be done by remote control.[64]

It would not. The Pentagon wanted tactical conditions for the test, and tactical conditions was what the army would give them: The shell was inserted into the block with its nuclear warhead armed, ready to fire. The question on everyone's mind was: What if there is a muzzle burst?

An artillery shell is a tricky piece of equipment consisting of two explosive charges separated by not much more than a few inches of inert material. Ostensibly, explosive "A" should go off first, propelling explosive "B" through the air to the target. Upon explosive "B"'s reaching the target, a fuze located in the nose of the projectile then detonates explosive "B." It doesn't alway work that way; sometimes the charges go off at almost the same time. This is called a muzzle burst. To protect the artillerymen, even the relatively small howitzers are equipped with thick metal plates called blast shields.

As every artilleryman knows, muzzle bursts occur with depressing frequency.

O'Keefe was astonished. After all his elaborate safety precautions, a soldier was going to fire the atomic cannon the same way one would fire a conventional howitzer: with a lanyard.[65] Resigned to the situation, the engineer nervously huddled in a trench and adjusted his dark glasses, wondering perhaps about the form an atomic muzzle burst would take.

The GRABLE shell, set to explode at 1,500 feet, detonated at a third of that altitude. The yield was 15 kilotons, about 2 kilotons less than expected, yet for a gun-type weapon, the efficiency was still impressive.

GRABLE did not make it to the stratosphere, but still punched a hole in some overlying cirrus clouds. The F-84G sampler jets circled and waited for instructions as the B-50 command plane climbed through the overcast, looking for the rest of the GRABLE mushroom. Minutes later the command was issued: GRABLE was effectively hidden from 28,000 to 35,000 feet; the Los Alamos scientific advisor suggested the F-84s sample the stem instead.

One of the observers at the shot, a Republican congressman from upstate New York, W. Sterling Cole, said that GRABLE added "another major weapon to our atomic stockpile." He also said, "I want to take off my hat to the scientists and engineers in the atomic energy program who spent so many hours and weeks of labor devising this marvelous new gadget, and to the military men who support and assist them."[66]

Congressman Joseph F. Holt, a California Republican, commented that he would like to see the cannon used in Korea.[67]

EG&G engineer O'Keefe expressed a somewhat different sentiment: "I was aghast. I had never really believed in tactical nuclear weapons anyhow. I have always felt that if one were used on a battlefield, the war would escalate. Here was proof! I, of course, knew what was coming. My dark glasses protected my eyes against the first flash. What of the soldiers on a battlefield? The first flash would sear the eyeballs of anyone looking in that direction, friend or foe, for miles around. Its intensity cannot be described; it must be experienced to be appreciated. The electromagnetic pulse would knock out all communication systems, the life blood of a battle plan. In addition to its effect on troops in the vicinity, everyone for fifty miles in any direction who lived through it would realize that it was a nuclear explosion. It would seem like the end of the world, and it probably would be, for any man who had a similar weapon under his control, who had a button to push or a lanyard to pull, would do so instinctively.''[68]

The stem of the GRABLE cloud moved toward Washington and Oregon, while the mushroom headed east, crossing New England within twenty-four hours. Slightly farther south, a violent thunderstorm dropped radioactive hail on Washington, D.C.[69]

In St. George, Utah, that same evening, Frank Butrico, an off-site radsafe monitor for the Nevada Proving Grounds (Nevada Test Site) was busy explaining things to Utah's congressman, Stringfellow. Butrico found that Stringfellow had no intention of closing the test site, but *was* critical of the AEC's security measures.[70]

On May 28, Gordon Dean, chairman of the AEC, was puzzling over a remark President Eisenhower had made the day before. He had been summoned to the president's office, apparently to discuss the weapons program and the problem of fallout. The president, Dean wrote in his diary, ''expressed some concern, not too serious, but made the suggestion that we leave ''thermonuclear'' out of press releases and speeches. Also ''fusion'' and ''hydrogen.'' According to the diary, Eisenhower instructed Dean to keep the public ''confused'' regarding ''fission'' and ''fusion.''[71]

Meanwhile, the 10,000-foot level of GRABLE's cloud was moving northwest, toward the Idaho panhandle and the city of Coeur d'Alene.

Thursday, May 28, 1953, was remarkably clear and sunny at Coeur d'Alene. The annual Ladies Day had been held at the Hayden Lake Golf Club the day before. Girl Scout Troop 5 planned a weiner roast at the lake for Friday and the Camp Fire Girls held their last meeting of the summer on the Monday before. Tickets went on sale at Herbes City Drug for the talent show to be held on Sunday at the Junior College. One of the contestants, Don Luraski, would sing ''Black and Blue'' and ''the Two B's''—Margie Butler and Betty Lewis—''diminutive bundles of personality,'' would sing a revived oldie: ''Afraid.''

Those who didn't attend the talent show could go to the Wilma Theater where the new 3-D motion picture, *Bwana Devil*, was playing. The movie starred Barbara Britton, Robert Stack, and Nigel Bruce.

Ten thousand feet above the town, the debris from GRABLE passed overhead, invisible in the clear mountain air.

In the early morning hours of June 4, 1953, a B-36 bomber from the 4925th Test Group made a practice run over Area 7–3 of the Nevada Test Site. In the hold was CLIMAX, the last device to be detonated during the UPSHOT-KNOTHOLE series. It was also to be one of the largest aboveground bursts *ever* for the continental test site.

A more appropriate name for the device would have been ENCORE; original plans had not called for an eleventh shot. But something very interesting had happened during one of the earlier UPSHOT-KNOTHOLE tests: At HARRY, a protracted flash/fireball had occurred. Prior to that shot, only about 20 percent of the nuclear material in a weapon was expected to fission before the central core exploded and, of course, went subcritical. One of the keys to nuclear efficiency was the design of a system that would allow the tightly compressed nuclear core to *remain* tightly compressed until a greater percentage of the material had fissioned. With HARRY, apparently, the designers had made a major design discovery. Hastily assembled CLIMAX would put the discovery to the test.

At 4:14 A.M. Pacific Daylight Time, the bomb bay doors of the huge strategic bomber opened and the weapon was released.

On the ground, at Mount Charleston, reporters listened to Galen Felt, the "Voice of AEC Control," tick off the seconds: "Five . . . four . . . three . . . two. . . ."

Gladwin Hill: "Just then a row of lights flickered up in the target area—evidently one of the scientists' photographic measuring grids. . . ."

Forty-two seconds after release, at exactly 1,334 feet altitude, the device detonated. Witnesses watched as "acres of Joshua trees, cactus and sagebrush five miles and more away from ground zero . . . burst into flame in a great desert "forest fire.""[72]

A wooden test shack more than 10 miles from the epicenter was leveled by the tremendous pressure wave.

Gladwin Hill:

> The initial, dazzling white flash, normally of only a second's duration, persisted from five to fifteen seconds. Observers disagreed on the time because they had to look away and were momentarily blinded. It illuminated thousands of square miles of darkened desert with noonday brilliance.
>
> The ensuing fireball, which in previous tests had seldom if ever exceeded ten seconds in duration, raged for the better part of a minute, and its ordinary fleeting incandescence did not fade away for more than two minutes.[73]

Oddly, the blast was not heard in Indian Springs, Nevada.

At the time, rough estimates of CLIMAX's yield indicated 40 kilotons. Radiochemical analysis of samples revised the figure upward to 61 kilotons. It had been a very efficient device.[74]

That same month, in Memphis, young Elvis Aaron Presley began work as a $43-a-week truck driver for Crown Electric Company. Later, in the fall, he would begin work for the Precision Tool Company on McLemore and Kansas streets, making 90 and 101mm shells for the army. His job would be to insert three rods and twelve screws into a casing. It is entirely possible that the shells he was to make would be used as part of maneuvers in the desert during the next nuclear operation at the Nevada Test Site: TEAPOT.

In mid-1953, assistants to RKO Studio owner Howard Hughes began searching for locations for his latest epic about the life of Genghis Khan, *The Conqueror*. They finally settled on Snow's Canyon, near the small southwestern town of St. George, Utah. Dusty and desolate, Snow's Canyon reminded them of what the barren hills of Mongolia must look like.

It would be perfect.

Aftermath

The whiteclad men emerging from the haze, Geiger counters in hand, had startled the Bulloch brothers on that dusty day in March, but there was nothing the sheepherders could do. The AEC monitors had told them that an atomic device had been detonated, that they should move the sheep out as quickly as possible. One of the brothers had replied that sheep move about 6 miles a day; there was no way to get them out. The monitors had merely climbed back into their jeep and disappeared in the brown haze. With that, the Bullochs slowly began the trek east, away from the affected area and toward Cedar City, Utah.

Back at AEC headquarters, the reports of sheepherders in the path of NANCY was met with consternation. What could be done? Some suggested airlifting the men out of the affected area, but the monitors refused to reenter the hot spot. Besides, what would they do with the sheep? It would be a public relations nightmare. Officials at the test site decided to do nothing. The sheepherders would be left to make their way out on their own.

The Bullochs crossed into Utah a week after their meeting with the atomic cloud. Many of their ewes were ready to lamb. On the way to Cedar City, Mac Bulloch noticed that one of the ewes was about to give birth. When the lamb was born, the sheepherder knew immediately something was terribly wrong: The lamb had no legs.

The herd arrived in Cedar City in early April and the brothers began preparing the sheds for the birth of the lambs. During this time a sheep died while eating and on examining the animal, Kern Bulloch was startled to have the wool come off in his hand. Looking closer, he saw that the animal had sores on its nose and mouth as well as on its back. Within days, the same thing began happening all through the herd. Sheep would stand still for a moment, then fall to the ground, dead.

Iron County agricultural agent Steven Brower was called for advice, but could offer none. Neither could A. C. Johnson, the Cedar City veterinarian. They had never experienced anything like this before. Though they didn't know what it was, they hoped it would clear up by lambing season, a week or so away.

The nightmare, however, was just beginning. When the ewes began to give birth, the Bullochs were horrified to see lambs looking just like the one on the trail: deformed, missing legs, or strange potbellies. On many, the sheepherders could see the lambs' hearts beating through the pale bare skin. Soon after birth, the misshapen lambs attempted to stand on their tiny legs, then fell over dead.

The scene was repeated in other area ranches. Parawon, Utah, sheepherder Dee Evans had to rent a bulldozer to dispose of his dead sheep, while another rancher, Doug Clark, stacked the dead lambs into piles.

The total losses for the Cedar City ranchers was 4,390 sheep and lambs. It was a biologic—and economic—event of catastrophic proportions. Word quickly spread that the animals had eaten shrubs that had been contaminated with fallout.

The AEC responded by calling in two of their best veterinarians: Dr. Robert Thompsett, from Los Alamos, and Dr. Robert Veenstra, from the U.S. Navy base in San Francisco.

When they finally arrived at Cedar City ten weeks after NANCY, most of the affected sheep had already died. They decided to take a look at the few surviving lambs. Both were familiar with fallout; both knew that strontium-90, a well-known fallout component, probably wouldn't do the sort of damage the ranchers had experienced. There was something else, however, that could. Something with ominous implications for humans living in the area: iodine-131.

One of the many radioactive elements produced during fission, iodine-131 was known to be quite hot. In its decay to a chemically inert gas, xenon-131, it emits relatively high-energy beta particles, gamma rays, and low-energy electrons. With a half-life of eight days, there was more than enough time for the iodine to be transported from ground zero to the grass and on into the sheep.

In both sheep and humans, iodine is stored the thyroid gland. If I-131 was involved, the sheep's thyroid would be highly radioactive. When the AEC vets placed a Geiger counter to the sheeps neck, the site of the thyroid, the needle of the instrument pegged to the right.

"This is hotter than a two-dollar pistol," Thompsett exclaimed. "The needle tried to go past the post." Examining the sores on the mouth of the animal, he told the Iron County agricultural agent that it was "just like the ones at Trinity."

When Thompsett submitted his report to the AEC, he minced no words: "Examination of these lesions leaves little doubt as to their origin . . . a diagnosis of radioactivity damage."

Veenstra was only slightly more subdued: "The location of the lesions and the nature of the sheep to nibble grass short leads one to suspect that the lips and foreface could easily come in contact with material on bushes, grass, etc., that would cause these lesions. . . . It is my opinion that radiation was at least a contributing factor to the loss of these animals.''[75]

Atomic Energy Commission officials were stunned. The SIMON shot had doused upstate New York with an enormous amount of radiation; DIXIE had showered Boston; and HARRY had dusted St. George, Utah, with intensely radioactive fallout. In fact, during the testing program, nuclear material had fallen on just about every square foot of the United States and the public hadn't complained. They had pretty much accepted the AEC's position that fallout was a nuisance but certainly not hazardous.

Now this. What would the public make of thousands of animals dying from exposure to fallout? To make matters worse, the veterinarians had placed the Geiger counter to the animal's thyroid. Thanks to that little experiment, it became obvious that iodine-131 was involved. If the sheep's thyroids absorbed iodine, so would other animals, including humans. The situation was serious.

On May 22, 1953, AEC commissioner Eugene Zuckert complained that ''In the present frame of mind of the public, it would take only a single illogical and unforeseeable incident to preclude holding any future tests in the United States.''[76]

The message was clear.

At Los Alamos, Thompsett was suddenly directed to rewrite his report, ''eliminating any reference to radiation damage or effects.''

On June 10, AEC specialist Paul Pearson arrived in Cedar City. Chief of the Biological and Medical division, Pearson's job apparently, was to investigate other possible causes of the disaster. The real purpose of the visit became clear when he told Agent Brower that the AEC could never let a radiation-damage precedent be established.[77]

On October 15, 1953, Pearson, Lieutenant Colonel Bernard Trum, Dr. John Rust, and the test site operations manager, Joe Sanders, visited with the ranchers. The meeting began with Trum and Rust both stating flatly that radiation was not the cause of the sheep deaths and that the ranchers would get no compensation. The sheep had died of malnutrition and that was that.

This news was almost too much for Doug Clark, who had almost been bankrupted by the losses. The AEC men had brought along a pamphlet describing the effects of radiation on animals. In reply to Rust and Trum, Doug Clark began reading from it. Suddenly Rust interrupted, ''For God's sake, why don't you read the whole thing?''

''I am,'' Clark said.

''You're not,'' Rust replied. He then told Doug Clark that the reason he knew was that he had written the part. When Clark attempted to reply, one of the AEC man yelled, ''You're nothing but a dumb farmer anyway!'' The official went on to say that Clark didn't know anything about radiation and fallout. That was the beginning of a heated exchange that lasted ten minutes. Two hours later, Doug Clark, exhausted and despondent, died of a heart attack.[78,79]

Ten days after Clark's death, a meeting was held at the AEC office at Los Alamos. Present were Trum, Sanders, and Dr. Gordon Dunning of the AEC's Division of Biology and Medicine in Washington. With them were two members of the Public Health Service, Monroe Holmes and Arthur Wolff. The PHS wanted to know what was going on in Utah.

It was an important meeting for the AEC middle managers. The PHS people had not been particularly satisfied with AEC's handling of off-site radiation problems. If the sheep deaths were linked to fallout, the PHS people might reasonably assume that what could sheep could also kill humans. Also, AEC commissioner Eugene Zuckert had displayed a reluctance to spend any more for tests until the sheep matter was cleared up. All Dunning, Trum, and Sanders needed was commissioners like Zuckert and Strauss hearing that fallout killed a lot of animals. Dunning quickly took charge of the meeting.

Gordon Dunning, the technical advisor to the Division of Biology and Medicine, had begun his career as a New York public school system physics teacher. He had also picked up some teaching experience at the New York State Agricultural and Technical Institute and the Pennsylvania State Teachers College. Dunning had been with the AEC only two months when he was appointed technical advisor. Now it was up to him to save the test site (and perhaps, his job).

If Dunning lacked any talent in biology and medicine, he more than made up for it in his ability to properly disseminate information. Diving headfirst into the world of radiation biology, Gordon Dunning displayed slides noting apparent differences between lab-induced radiation burns with those found in Utah.[80] One of the PHS people at the meeting, Monroe Holmes, was impressed with the *similarities* between the two groups. Wolff wasn't impressed one way or the other.

Dunning pleaded with the group to close ranks and come to some sort of conclusion about the sheep deaths. Yes, he would like a report. Yes, it would be for internal use only. The public wouldn't see it.

Without hesitation, the former physics teacher then dived even deeper into the world of radiation biology, drafting a report that flatly concluded that the "preponderance of evidence [supports] the conclusion that the lesions were not produced by radioactive fallout."[81] After some hesitation, the PHS people signed the statement. Dunning and Trum had some difficulty getting one AEC man in the room to sign. He was Bob Thompsett, the vet who had initially seen the sheep.

It soon became clear to Dunning that Veenstra and Thompsett were going to give less than wholehearted support to the malnutrition theory. The two vets were unceremoniously pulled off the case. Reports generated by the two veterinarians were classified, then lost. But it was not the last they would hear from Thompsett.

Back at his office, Trum received a call from Joe Sanders, the deputy chief of the AEC in Nevada. He had bad news: "Thompsett called me last Thursday. He said they had reproduced burns comparable to those found on the Cedar City sheep in the AEC lab at Los Alamos and we are really in trouble."

Soon after the phone call, bone samples taken at Cedar City vanished from AEC labs. Reports by on-site observers were altered to reflect lower values.[82] The task, however, had been formidable. Scientific documents usually are exercises in repetition, with careful step-by-step explanations of how the conclusions are derived. Thus, to alter a report's conclusion requires changing the entire paper. Whoever altered the reports apparently was unaware of this fine point; thus only the conclusions had been changed. One paper later turned up stating the gamma dosage to the sheep failed to exceed 5 rads. The supporting evidence, however, clearly showed the sheep could have received thirty-four times that amount of radiation.

Other information was suppressed, including a study made in 1951 by AEC veterinarian Dr. Leo Bustad at the nuclear facility at Hanford, Washington, Bustad had irradiated fetal lambs and had produced symptoms matching those of the Cedar City lambs. Like those of the Utah sheepherders, Bustad's irradiated lambs were too weak to stand, were lethargic, and smaller than the nonirradiated lambs.[83]

On January 16, 1954, the AEC issued a statement claiming that the Utah sheep deaths had nothing to do with radiation. The case was closed—for the time being.[84]

The Conqueror

The following summer, residents of southwestern Utah had other concerns. For one thing, the Nevada Test Site was silent; the AEC had taken their testing to the Pacific. For another, 220 members of a movie company had come to town, RKO Studio's production of *The Conqueror* starring John Wayne, Susan Hayward, Agnes Moorehead, and Pedro Almendariz. [85,86] Dick Powell would direct the epic.

The filming took place in nearby Snow's Canyon, a hot, dusty, desolate area 12 miles or so west of St. George, Utah, where temperatures regularly climbed to 120 degrees Fahrenheit. To make matters worse, huge fans were brought in to simulate the incessant winds of the Mongolian desert.

At the end of each day, the actors washed off yellow makeup caked with inches of dust. Some actually had to be hosed off. Three hundred Indians hired as extras seemed to spend all their time riding their horses down the sides of the canyon. The movie contained some of the grimiest, dustiest footage ever. Face masks were handed out to those working behind the cameras. The film equipment itself often clogged with the dust, and many scenes had to be reshot.

The only break in the thirteen-week production came on July 6, 1954, when the cast and crew staged a publicity baseball game in St. George. The crowd cheered when Susan Hayward kicked off her shoes and ran the bases to score a run.[87]

Later, after the crew left the location, RKO boss Howard Hughes had 60 tons of Snow's Canyon dirt shipped back to the Hollywood sound stage for retakes.

The movie, released in 1956, was billed as "The Mightiest of All Motion Pictures." It received exceedingly bad reviews and quickly disappeared from the nations theaters. Hughes would go on to sell RKO to a tire and rubber company.

Years later, however, *The Conqueror* would be heard from again as a startling percentage of its cast and crew began to die from cancer. In 1958, co-star Pedro Almendariz was told he had kidney cancer. In 1963, at age fifty-one, the Mexican actor was informed by his doctors that he had developed cancer of the lymphatic system. Hours later, he committed suicide.[88] That same year, Dick Powell, was losing his battle with lung cancer.

In 1974, when Agnes Moorehead was dying of cancer of the uterus, she told a friend, Jeanne Gerson, that "Everybody in that picture [*The Conqueror*] has gotten cancer and died." This was ominous news to Gerson. She herself had played a role in the movie. She also later developed breast cancer.[89]

One year later, Susan Hayward lost her two-year battle with cancer, and in 1979, John Wayne died of cancer of the stomach.

Within thirty years of the filming, ninety-one of the cast and crew of 220 had developed various carcinomas. A radiological expert at the University of Utah commented that "with these numbers, this case could qualify as an epidemic. . . . In a group this size, you'd expect only thirty some cancers to develop. But with ninety-one, I think the tie-in to their exposure on the set of *The Conqueror* would hold up in a court of law.[90,91]

In February 1955, six months after the cast and crew of *The Conqueror* left Utah, a lawsuit *was* filed: *Bulloch et al.* vs. *The United States of America*. The complaint: "Agents of the defendant [the federal government] acting within the scope of their employment, negligently performed, conducted, discharged, and executed such nuclear tests and experiments causing damages to the plaintiffs." The damages: a quarter of a million dollars. At the trial, the judge would, based upon the facts presented, rule in favor of the government: The atomic tests had nothing to do with the sheep deaths. For the sheepherders, it was back to square one.

Castle: Bravo

In late February 1954, technicians carefully placed a heavy canister on a sand spit off Namu Island in the Bikini Atoll.[1] Inside was an array of electrical cables and detonators attached to a conventional atomic device. At the other end of the canister was a layered flask containing two chemicals, the exceedingly scarce tritium, or "heavy water," and lithium-6-deuteride. The canister represented the first real test of the "Teller-Ulam configuration," an ingenious design that was calculated to hold the device together an extra hundred-millionth of a second after the atomic detonation, allowing fusion to take place within the tritium and lithium-6-deuteride.[2]

Central to the configuration was a blanket of special material that would reflect X- and gamma radiation from the exploding fission trigger *back* toward the fusion canister. The radiation would thus reach the canister *before* the expanding debris from the A-bomb trigger had a chance to destroy it. The difference would be only a hundred-millionth of a second, but it would be sufficient time for fusion to occur.

By the morning of February 28, the scientists were almost ready. Like many of its predecessors, the BRAVO device was placed inside a protective building and attached to radiation measuring instruments by a complex array of pipes and tubes. Nearing shot-day, the BRAVO cab resembled a large square fishing shack at the end of the dock. Inside the shack, a leak had developed in a helium tank necessary to an experiment. Studying the matter, the scientists decided that if arming was delayed until 11:00 that night, there would be enough helium left by shot-hour to save the experiment. That evening, while waiting to arm the device, engineer Bernard O'Keefe pulled up a cot next to the bomb and took a short nap.

Shortly after eleven, the men were evacuated by helicopter. Flying toward the control island of Enyu, they could see the luminous glow of the waves breaking on the white sandy beach below.

At Enyu, the men entered a bunker loaded with electronic equipment while the helicopters headed for the safety of ships located another 20 miles away. The bunker was made of 3-foot-thick concrete and covered with 10 feet of sand and dirt; still, its inhabitants would be closer than anyone had ever been to a hydrogen bomb: only 20 miles.[3] The Control Point for MIKE had been twice that distance.

Once inside the damp bunker, the nine men in the control group sat down to their instruments. Surrounding them in a circle of ships and observation aircraft were 10,000 others: scientists, engineers, officers, and enlisted men, all waiting for the dawn.

At 6:45 A.M. local time, a sequence timer was activated; the last fifteen minutes of the countdown went automatic. Fourteen minutes later, engineer O'Keefe spoke into the public address system microphone: "All observers having high density goggles put them on. . . . All observers having high density goggles put them on. . . . All others face away from the blast. . . . Do not face blast until fireball dissipates. . . . Do not face blast until fireball dissipates."[4]

Eighty-five miles east-northeast of the Bikini test site, the crewmen of the Japanese fishing trawler *Fukuryu Maru* (Fortunate Dragon) were getting ready to cast their nets for the last time before heading home. Fishing Master Yoshio Misaki relaxed on the bridge, surveying the expanse of ocean and waiting for the sunrise.

Dawn comes quickly in the central Pacific. With the darkness fading only a few minutes before the sunrise, the transition from dark blue-gray to the full color of daylight seems to take only the briefest amount of time.

At 7:00 A.M., however, Misaki was startled to see the darkness simply vanish. It was replaced by a brilliant whitish-yellow glare that seemed to take up most of the horizon. Dawn had never happened *this* quickly. In the instant that followed, the Fishing Master was astonished to see the orange-red sun rising in the *west*.

On deck, the crew stopped what they were doing and simply stared. Someone guessed that it was a *pika-don*—a nuclear bomb.

By the time Captain Hisakichi Tsutsui could be roused from his bunk, the sun was gone and twilight had again returned, bathing the deck in shades of gray. It had been seven minutes since the flash had appeared.

Suddenly a low roar began, more felt than heard. The Pacific was usually calm this time of morning; the engines had been turned off and the 93-foot vessel was drifting slowly with the current. Still, the vibrations continued. It was as though the *Fukuryu Maru* was somehow in the middle of an earthquake at sea.

Misaki conferred with the captain and soon the order was given: "Start the engines and haul in the lines." The message was clear: These waters were *not* safe.

As the engines came to life, Radioman Aikichi Kuboyama reached for his technical books. *Something* had happened to the west of them. Whatever it was had also sent a wave of low-frequency noise that had traveled at the speed of sound—1087 feet per second. Kuboyama calculated that sound travels about 87 miles in seven minutes; they were 87 miles from whatever had happened. Reaching for a map, the radioman compared the ships coordinates against a circle with an 87-mile radius. The explosion had come from the Bikini Atoll.[5]

Inside the control bunker on Enyu Island, the scientists waited nervously for the shock wave. About ten seconds earlier the firing light had flickered red, indicating that the detonation had occurred. Now the only sound inside the concrete room was the barely audible clattering of relay switches at the rear of the electronics instrument rack. On the control panel itself, lights were behaving like a decorated Christmas tree, flickering on and off at random. Clearly, there was some sort of violent electrical storm over the entire area. Watching the activity on the panel, the men realized—with mounting apprehension—that the center of the disturbance was only 20 miles away.[6]

Suddenly, less than a minute after the shot, one of the engineers, Herb Grier, asked "Is this building moving or am I getting dizzy?"

The others had noticed it, too. The blockhouse on Enyu was behaving like a ship in rough seas. Electrical tools began to slide across the workbench. Small objects that had been resting near the edge clattered to the floor. O'Keefe felt a tinge of nausea and began to worry that BRAVO had "gone big" and had sheared off the entire top of the atoll, sending it toward the bottom of the Pacific. Within fifteen seconds, the rolling motion had stopped.

Then the shock wave hit: a sharp, deafening *crack* followed by the sound of wind as the pressure began to return to normal. Then silence. Enyu had survived. O'Keefe and fellow engineers Grier and Jack Clark decided to step outside and take a look around.

The sight that greeted them gave no hint of the violence only moments before: The island was deathly still under a subdued light. Above their heads, the blue sky had been replaced by a gray and ominous overcast. Grier checked his Geiger counter.

"Any radiation?" O'Keefe asked.

"Yeah," Grier replied. "Too low for fallout; must be 'shine' from the cloud."[7]

On the *Fortunate Dragon* the men had begun to pull in their lines. Two hours had passed since the false sunrise; now the sky was again acting strange: a gray fog of some sort was beginning to descend on their ship and something was starting to fall through the air.

Tiny, white particles that looked for all the world like snowflakes had begun to fill the air. But this was the middle of the Pacific, not far from the equator.

The flakes tasted of salt and seemed to burn the eyes. After landing on a surface, the flakes seemed to stick tight; only with hard scrubbing were the crewmen able to dislodge it from the deck. After the fishing lines had been hauled in, the crew noticed that the rope seemed to have absorbed a large amount of the dust. Since there was no way to remove the unusual material from the rope, the crew packed the fishing gear and stored it away for the trip home.[8]

On Enyu, O'Keefe, Grier, and the rest were becoming concerned. Calculations had predicted the huge gray mushroom cloud to first rise to about 25 miles, then carry its load of fallout to dissipate safely over a wide area hundreds of miles downwind. Under these conditions, Enyu would be reasonably safe; any material picked up by the fireball would take hours to fall from that great a height.

Apparently the calculations were wrong. Herb Grier had noticed it first: His Geiger counter had begun recording a rise in radiation from the moment they stepped outside. At first, the radiation had barely been enough to deflect the needle on the instrument. Now it was recording 5 milliroentgens/hour. The engineers were aware that the radiation was still far less than a typical chest X-ray.[9] Yet the level seemed to be rising. Within minutes it was up to 10 milliroentgens.

"Let's round everyone up," Clark suggested.

Within four minutes the level had gone to an alarming 20 milliroentgens. They were now nearing chest X-ray territory. By this time the air had taken on a whitish haze. It was as though a fog had descended on the island. O'Keefe looked at his hand. It was covered with a strange white ash.

Then someone shouted, "Hey, it's one hundred milliroentgens!" Within seconds the ash had been replaced by dust, sand, and gravel. The men ran toward the blockhouse and slammed the steel door shut. From inside, it sounded as though Enyu was going through a hailstorm. O'Keefe checked his instruments: one milliroentgen/hour. Another engineer, Doug Cochrane, carried his Geiger counter down the corridor toward the door and was astonished to see the needle climb to 1,000 milliroentgens. "It must be a good five roentgens per hour outside," he said. If correct, it meant that one hour after Bravo, the island of Enyu was already ten times hotter than ground zero had been for the Ranger: Able shot.

Inside the blockhouse the instruments began to record a rise in the radiation. Within minutes it was up to 10 milliroentgens. Shaken, the engineers called headquarters. The blockhouse was shielded by a factor of 10,000, meaning that if it was 10 milliroentgens inside, it must be 100 roentgens on

Enyu—an absurdly high figure. There had to be a leak somewhere, allowing contaminated air into the control room.

"The air conditioner, it's still running!"

"For God's sake, shut it off!"[10]

Within a minute the reading inside dropped to one milliroentgen. Outside, however, the level had risen to an alarming 25 roentgens, or 25,000 milliroentgens. O'Keefe made some mental calculations: Two hours at such a level might be lethal to humans. The island was too hot for a rescue party. The men were trapped.

Outside, the level climbed to 65 roentgens/hour, higher than ground zero at *any* of the RANGER series. Then slowly it began to decline.

Jack Clark, in radio contact with headquarters, informed the engineers that the ships were picking up 10 milliroentgens/hour and that measurements had indicated the BRAVO yield had been twice as large as expected: a truly spectacular 15-megaton explosion.

At the task force command ship, the rescue plan began to take shape. Two helicopters would be sent. But there were problems: The radio antennas and poles around the blockhouse would make a landing impossible. Also, the rotors would stir up an enormous amount of radioactive dust and sand. The engineers would have to leave the blockhouse and *drive* half a mile to a paved landing strip where the helicopters would be waiting. On Enyu, Clark had reported 30 roentgens, and that was an *average* reading. What if other parts of the island were hotter? Also, what if the jeeps and trucks outside the blockhouse refused to start?

At 3:30 P.M., a helicopter circled Enyu, making final preparations for the rescue. The pilot stayed over the lagoon; if the copter's engine failed it would have been safer to ditch over the less-contaminated water than on Enyu. Below, the water was littered with scraps of palm leaves.[11]

A half hour later, the engineers were ready for their race to the airstrip. Bedsheets secured with masking tape had been used to cover any exposed skin. Grier and O'Keefe cautioned the others to "trot, not run" during the rescue. A fall in the radioactive sand could be hazardous.[12]

At 4:35 P.M., Clark and the others were instructed to open the door. Five minutes later, the sound of the helicopters could be heard in the distance. Grier's Geiger counter showed a still-uncomfortable 21 roentgens/hour. After two passes, the copters retreated to the safety of the lagoon and hovered. Two men who had volunteered as drivers then ran into the glaring sunlight toward the trucks.

Within minutes the two trucks were edging down the road toward the landing strip. The drivers stayed in first gear for maximum traction and to avoid stirring up the radioactive dust. In the distance, the helicopters slowly hovered closer toward the ground.

The drivers parked the trucks at the edge of the landing strip and the men jogged the 20 yards to the helicopters. Nine hours after it had begun, their ordeal was over.[13]

They had been extraordinarily fortunate. The control blockhouse had actually received upward of 800 roentgens, and islands closer to ground zero had absorbed over 5,000 roentgens, hotter than the ground zero of the dirtiest of the Nevada shots.[14] One hundred and twenty miles east of the shot, fallout had descended on the island of Rongelap where eighty-two Marshallese lived. The radiation intensity there had approached over 100 roentgens/hour, causing vomiting, burning skin, and other radiation-induced illnesses. The uninhabited northern tip of Rongelap island received a whopping—and lethal—1,000 roentgens/hour.

As a result of BRAVO, the islands of the Bikini chain would be uninhabitable during remaining detonations in the CASTLE series. Shots ROMEO, KOON, UNION, YANKEE, and NECTAR were to be set up by scientists wearing heavy radiation protection and respirators.[15]

The day after the "snowstorm," the crew of the *Fortunate Dragon* awoke sluggish, tired, and, in some cases, nauseous. One crewmember, winchman Sanjiro Masuda found his eyes crusted over with a dry yellow film. Later he complained of feeling feverish. Some who had handled the fishing lines noticed that their hands burned and itched. The worst, however, was yet to come. As the days passed, more cases of nausea occurred. Boatswain Masayoshi Kawashima noticed that his hair was falling out in clumps.

Two weeks later, the *Fortunate Dragon* reached Yaizu. By this time it was apparent that the crew had been exposed to something. For one thing, they had taken on an unusual, dark appearance. Some of the men, particularly Masuda, had clearly been burned. The owner of the *Fortunate Dragon* decided that the men should all check into the hospital. Shortly after that, many of the crewmen were found to have low white blood cell counts.

Within a few days the pieces of the puzzle began to fall into place. Lewis Strauss of the United States's Atomic Energy Commission had announced earlier that a test had taken place at Bikini. Now, three weeks later, the clinical picture was emerging from Yaizu Hospital: The men were suffering from radiation sickness. One crewmember was even found to be radioactive.

Soon afterward, the ship itself was checked with a Geiger counter and found to be exceedingly hot. On a hunch, a biophysics professor at Osaka City University decided to monitor the radioactivity of fish at the city market. Ominously, the tuna made the instrument fairly buzz. The repercussions were swift and sure. For the first time in centuries, Japanese consumers stopped eating fish.

Meanwhile, the *shi no hai*, the "ashes of death," were being examined by Tokyo University radiochemist Kenjiro Kimura. He and an associate,

Yoshio Nishina, had, in 1939, produced a rare isotope of uranium, U-237. In sifting through the ash from BRAVO, Kimura was certain he had located more of his unusual isotope. Within weeks, details of the BRAVO device had been pieced together: It was a fission trigger firing a fusion device that had been wrapped in U-238. Thus, the bomb was a fission-fusion-fission device. Most of the fallout had been from the U-238 "blanket."[16]

The case was apparently solved, but the incident was far from over. On September 23, Radioman Kuboyama, who had first calculated the distance to the detonation, died. The cause of death was officially listed as hepatitis, picked up from one of his many blood transfusions. The U.S. government sent Mrs. Kuboyama checks totaling 2.5 million yen "as a token of sympathy of the American government and people."[17]

Eight months later, on May 20, 1955, the remaining twenty-two crewmen of the *Fortunate Dragon* were finally discharged from the hospital. The next tests in the Pacific would not take place for another year.[18] Development of thermonuclear weapons, however, would continue concurrent with testing of the smaller, tactical weapons, and there would be speculation that the H-bombs would eventually find their way to the Nevada Test Site.

V

WATCHING THE BOMBS
GO OFF

The Silence Is Broken

March 7, 1955, seemed to mark a watershed in public opinion about radioactive fallout. Prior to that time, only a few scientists had warned of its adverse effects. Most of the news concerned fanciful predictions for the future, such as atomic powered flying boats as airliners.[1]

Some, like Japan's Dr. Yamazaki, had reported prenatal effects of the nuclear blast.[2] A Professor Nishiwaki had reported radioactive horses in New Zealand, and radioactive rain had been reported in Sydney, Australia.[3,4] There was concern over the unfortunate Japanese fishermen exposed to the CASTLE: BRAVO fallout, but it was relatively short-lived. When Radioman Kuboyama died several months after being exposed to the H-bomb fallout AEC officials were quick to point out that it was in fact hepatitis that killed him, not radiation.[5] In November 1954, AEC chairman Strauss proclaimed that atomic war would not make the world a radioactive cinder, and a month later pledged to support a study of the fallout phenomenon.[6]

Most of the concerns seemed to focus on the possibility of a war involving larger and more lethal weapons. On January 12, 1955, Strauss admitted that the Soviets had the H-bomb and two weeks later, U.S. Civil Defense chief Val Peterson claimed the U.S. had an H-bomb that was three times as powerful as the 15-megaton BRAVO.[7]

Later, rumor spread about the cobalt bomb, a weapon even more powerful than an H-bomb. In February, Peterson claimed it would "destroy everyone" and doubted such a weapon would ever be used.[8]

On February 16, the AEC reported that lethal fallout from the BRAVO shot covered an impressive 7,000-square-mile area of the Pacific.[9] This was two days before the one-kiloton WASP shot at Nevada, which, "to overcome adverse weather," would be airdropped rather than fired from a tower.[10] (The day after the detonation, the AEC stated that the bomb was airdropped "to minimize radioactive fallout."[11])

After the TURK detonation (known to the public as "Big Shot"), the Weather Bureau reported that a "harmless radioactive cloud" was hovering over the eastern United States and that radioactivity in Chicago had been reported.[12] Just as a New York professor was confirming a radiation rise in his city, another atomic blast was set off in Nevada.[13]

The next day Drs. Ray R. Lanier and Theodore Puck of the University of Colorado Medical Center publicly stated their opposition to the Nevada testing. In a statement to the Associated Press, Lanier, head of the university's radiology department, said: "For the first time in the history of the Nevada tests, the upsurge in radioactivity measured here within a matter of hours after the tests has become appreciable."

Puck, head of the biophysics department, added: "The trouble with airborne radioactive dust is that we breathe it into the lungs where it may lodge in direct contact with living tissues."

A spokesman for the AEC replied to the scientists' statements: "On the basis of the readings on which their statements are based, the commission is of the opinion there is no concern for the public and that the radioactivity is inconsequential."

Colorado governor Edwin C. Johnson, upon hearing the scientists' position, took stronger exception: "The two scientists should be arrested. This is a phony report. It will only alarm people. Someone has a screw loose someplace and I intend to find out about it. The statements are part of an organized fright campaign."[14]

Jack Lotto, a writer for the International News Service, immediately jumped into the fray. In a *Los Angeles Examiner* column he claimed that the "Reds" were launching a "Scare Drive" against U.S. atomic tests: "A big Communist fear campaign to force Washington to stop all American atomic hydrogen bomb tests erupted this past week."[15]

David Lawrence, a nationally syndicated commentator, claimed that the Nevada testing was actually for humanitarian purposes, to "determine the best ways to help civilian defense" and that "the Communist drive is to stop all tests."

"Many persons," Lawrence continued, "are being duped by the campaign into thinking all the tests held in Nevada are injurious and will hurt future generations. There isn't a word of truth in that propaganda."

On the day after their comments, Puck and Lanier were called into the office of Dr. Ward Darley, president of the university. They also met with Dr. Leo Szilard, now a biophysicist at the University of Chicago. After the meeting, they restated their position, that there was no "safe" minimum below which radiation had been proved harmless. Though somewhat less inflammatory, and probably the result of bureaucratic compromise, it would nonetheless be a significant statement. It would mark the public's introduction to the "no safe level" theory of radiation.

A March 20 story in the *New York Daily News* quoted Merrill Eisenbud, chief of the New York Health and Safety Lab, as saying that "The total fallout to date from all tests would have to be multiplied by a million to produce visible deleterious effects in areas close to the explosion itself."

The exact nature of the deleterious effects to which Eisenbud referred became evident two years later at the Joint Committee on Atomic Energy Hearings. That day, fallout expert Ralph Lapp multiplied by a million the dose received by the Troy—Albany residents after shot Simon. Senator Clinton Anderson then asked Eisenbud if this dose would "kill everybody in sight." Eisenbud answered, "Yes."[16]

The silence, however, had been broken. It was now acceptable to discuss radioactive fallout and other adverse health effects attributable to nuclear testing. Reports surfaced describing a variety of injuries suffered by "atomic victims." The *Harrisburg* (Pennsylvania) *Sunday Patriot-News* reported that, contrary to AEC statements, there *had* been several injuries during atomic testing. After initially denying it, the AEC grudgingly admitted that *eye injuries* had occurred during the *Pacific* operations.[17]

To the AEC, things were getting out of hand. What was needed was a "friendly" article on the subject of fallout. The March 25 issue of *U.S. News & World Report* filled the bill admirably. In an article entitled "The Facts About A-Bomb 'Fall-Out': Not a Word of Truth in Scare Stories Over Tests," the unlisted author concentrated on the effects of the March 7 TURK shot.

It was a remarkable piece of journalism: a map was included that accurately showed the trajectory of the TURK nuclear cloud. Its source was raw data that would remain classified until April 10, 1956. Among the conclusions reached:

- From the "Big Shot" [TURK] test, a radioactive "cloud" crossed the U.S. but harmed no one.
- Effect of its "fall-out" on anyone in U.S. equalled that of a luminous-dial watch.
- Total "fall-out" on any one place for a year will be a fourth of "normal" allowance.
- New experiments show present "fall-out" level cannot harm future generations.
- Even fish contaminated in Pacific H-bomb "fall-out" could have been eaten, if skinned.

To get the facts, of what really is going on, *U.S. News & World Report* went to official sources. Extensive tests of every conceivable reaction from A-bomb and H-bomb tests have been studied. Results of those tests are facts. . . .

The simple conclusion is this: There isn't a word of truth in scare stories about this country's atomic tests that are getting the nation and the world in a dither.

The article went on to quote AEC commissioner Willard Libby, not exactly an unbiased judge of radiation hazards: "The world is radioactive. It always has been and always will be. Its natural radioactivities evidently are not dangerous and we can conclude from this fact that contamination from atomic bombs small in magnitude or even of the same order of magnitude as these natural radiations is not likely to be at all dangerous."[18]

Regarding TURK, the article said:

The most intense radioactivity to fall from this test burst, on a community outside the controlled bomb range, hit a nearby town in Nevada. It measured just one-fifth of a roentgen. The roentgen is a unit of radioactivity. You get 15 roentgens concentrated on one spot when you have an ordinary set of dental X-rays. . . .

At Hiroshima, exposure to 400 roentgens radioactivity was fatal for some, but not for others, while 500 roentgens was fatal in most cases. . . . At Salt Lake City, rain increased the amount of radioactivity measured on the ground, but even so it amounted to only 0.006 of a single roentgen, a perfectly safe exposure. . . .

Nowhere was the effect of "fall-out" on an individual greater than the effect of wearing a luminous-dial wristwatch with its tiny amount of radioactivity. . . .

In a separate section entitled "What U.S. Has Learned From Atomic Tests," the article claimed that the AEC tests showed:

- Fish from the deck of the *Fortunate Dragon*—heavily contaminated after the big H-bomb test in the Pacific—could have been eaten safely, if skinned with reasonable care.
- Cattle grazing in an area of heavy "fall-out" may be contaminated by radioactivity on their hides and in their intestines, but when slaughtered "removal of those parts would leave the edible part quite safe for food."
- Particles of "strontium-90" in the air form the greatest long-range danger to humans from the A-bomb tests. Yet, after all these tests to date, the amount of this substance in the air in the U.S. is only one one-millionth of the level that would produce harmful effects on people.
- H-bomb tests could be held every week for an indefinite period without raising the amount of "strontium-90" to a dangerous level.

In a separate section, "What They Are Saying About Dangers in A-Tests," the author included the statement by Drs. Lanier and Puck: "For the first time in the history of the Nevada tests, the upsurge in radioactivity measured here within a matter of hours after the tests has become appreciable. It is not our desire to alarm the public mind needlessly, but we feel it is our duty to say so."

In a third section that asked "Will H-Bomb Tests Affect Future Generations?" the author was even more encouraging, indicating that the AEC tests showed: "Fruit flies, raised for 128 generations in highly radioactive surroundings, did not degenerate, as expected. Instead, they ended up a better race of fruit flies—hardier, more vigorous, more reproductive, with better resistance to disease."[19,20]

The article, however, failed to reassure the public. On April 26, eleven days after the MET shot, newspapers carried the story of a Hiroshima victim dying of "blood disease."[21] On May 11, three days before the WIGWAM shot, fishermen on the West Coast organized a protest against the operation.[22]

In June, both Commissioner Libby and Chairman Strauss made statements to the press discounting hazards from testing.[23] On June 11, a scientist claimed that households would have atom-powered vacuum cleaners by

1965.[24] Three days later, a physician from India reported finding an herb that "when rubbed on the body protects from radiation."[25]

All to no avail. Nuclear testing was beginning to be viewed as *the* hazard of the atomic age. Soon, in the mind of the public, the hazard would have a more specific name: strontium-90.

Strontium-90

Nuclear physicists and weapons specialists had long known that the detonation of an atomic bomb produces about 300 isotopes, all radioactive. Mixed in with the bomb debris and other materials taken up by the mushroom cloud, the isotopes were the ingredient that made the fallout radioactive. What the nuclear physicists *didn't* know was how these fission particles affected human beings.

Actually, the scientists had long displayed a cavalier attitude toward the effects of radiation. French physicists Pierre Curie and Henri Becquerel both purposely exposed themselves to radioactive materials in order to determine the effects of radiation on tissues.[26] In 1935, long before he started his own lab at Livermore, Ernest Lawrence gave demonstrations on radioactivity at the Berkeley auditorium. During one show, he produced a bottle containing a solution of sodium-24, an extremely hot radionuclide with a half-life of fifteen hours. As part of the performance, he called a colleague, J. Robert Oppenheimer, onstage and asked him to place his hand around a Geiger counter. Oppenheimer did so, then proceeded to drink a glass of water containing the radionuclide. Within fifty seconds the Geiger counter began chattering, proving to the audience that the material had entered Oppenheimer's bloodstream.[27]

Biology and, particularly, genetics held too many variables, too many shades of gray; the scientists were simply more comfortable with the black-and-white world of physics.

They knew that when a 20-kiloton bomb was detonated, only about one gram of matter, or one-third the weight of a penny, is converted to energy. As this happens, much of the plutonium or uranium-235 fractions into 300 isotopes of thirty six elements, from zinc to terbium. While some of these new isotopes are stable, most carry an extra neutron that makes them radioactive.

The scientists knew that for each kiloton of yield about 2 ounces of radioactive isotopes are formed. In addition, about 1,000 tons of material is vaporized, much of it made radioactive by a process called "neutron capture." The problem was that chance played a significant role in what material would capture the neutrons. And, based on their varying half-lives, each of the 300 isotopes would immediately begin to decay to something else entirely.

As a bomb explodes, for example, vast quantities of sand are usually scooped up and vaporized to varying degrees. The elements making up the sand—silicon, sodium, oxygen, magnesium, and aluminum—"capture" neutrons resulting from the initial fission reaction and thus become radioactive. They may become different elements altogether. In the soil, manganese-55 (the normal, nonradioactive form of the element) may capture a free-flying neutron to become radioactive manganese-56. This unstable atom would decay within a few hours by releasing an electronlike object called a beta particle to become another element entirely: iron-56, which is stable and nonradioactive.

In order to know what isotopes would be found in the fallout, the scientists would have to know the makeup of the soil and the exact makeup of the bomb. Fission bombs, to varying degrees based on efficiency, produce plutonium-laden fallout. Fusion bombs (depending on the trigger) will also produce plutonium fallout, but will spread radioactive tritium, too. Not only that, the fusion process, in supplying a vastly greater supply of neutrons, will change the resultant isotope "spectrum" substantially. Two new man-made elements, einsteinium and fermium, were first found in the debris of fusion shot MIKE.

To predict fallout levels, the scientists would even have to know the relative weight of the fallout particles: It was discovered that some materials vaporized more easily than others. They tended to travel farther; the more heat-resistant compounds seemed to fall out of the sky more readily.

Since all isotopes eventually decay to one stable compound or another, the "fallout specialists" in the AEC initially decided to concentrate on the compounds that would be radioactive for a significant period of time. Some elements, such as those resembling calcium, tend to accumulate in humans; therefore the scientists wanted to find a fallout isotope that was likely to be stored or "sequestered" by the body.

Strontium-90 filled the bill.

For every 1,000 uranium atoms undergoing fission in an atomic device, there will be, among the radioactive isotopes formed, about fifteen atoms of the radioactive gas krypton-90. Almost immediately after formation in the nuclear cloud, krypton loses a beta particle and changes to rubidium-90, a silvery-white metallic element that will ignite spontaneously in air.

Rubidium-90 has a half-life of only 4.28 minutes—that is, half of the rubidium-90 formed from the krypton will, after 4.28 minutes, transform itself into something else: strontium-90, which is the radioactive form of an element that chemically resembles calcium. The body has trouble distinguishing between the two and so absorbs both equally well. Strontium-90 thus easily finds its way to bones and even arterial plaque, emitting beta radiation throughout its half-life of 28.9 years.

After this time, one-half of the strontium-90 will have changed to yet another element, yttrium-90. It, too, is silvery in appearance; it, too, can ignite in air. It, too, is considered carcinogenic. Then, after about three hours, half of the yttrium-90 will make one final change to still another element, nonradioactive zirconium-90.

While the scientists knew how strontium-90 was formed, they still weren't sture how *well* the human body would absorb it. And in 1955, no one had *any* real idea of what the long-term medical effects would be.

But there were strong and ominous clues.

Two years before, the Public Health Service in an "Official Use Only" memo reported that the radioactive contamination in parts of Nevada and Utah far exceeded limits suggested by the National Committee on Radiation Protection. It had stated, in part: "In future tests, within such areas, blood changes in man might be demonstrable if systematic observations are made. It is possible also that the immunities of the population might be sufficiently reduced that measurable increased incidences of selected communicable diseases would be discerned by epidemiological investigations. The long-term implications of yearly exposure of a cross-section of the population to levels in excess of those considered to be maximum permissable for occupational workers certainly justify continued observation and maintainance of radiation health records, even though specific consequences cannot be foreseen at this moment."[28]

The Public Health Service had been concerned particularly about the HARRY shot. HARRY had spread radioactive material far and wide over parts of the southwest and had seriously contaminated an entire town of 5,000 people—St. George, Utah. The AEC had responded to concerns about HARRY by planning to check for radioactive contaminants in milk. The study, however, was never performed for fear of alarming the public.

Instead, on May 24, 1953, AEC officials announced that their scientists could find "no hazardous radiation in any part of the U.S. resulting from tests." In addition, they claimed that a survey of areas near the test site showed "no anxiety."[29] It was not reported if the survey included the Cedar City ranchers who had lost over 4,000 sheep to fallout shortly after the NANCY test.

The Utah sheep deaths in 1953 had thoroughly rattled officials in the Atomic Energy Commission. There was little scientific doubt that the sheep had been killed by ingesting fission particles. Yet the AEC officials charged with dealing with the ranchers had stonewalled, refusing to own up to the scientific facts. Haranguing and misleading the locals, even belittling their intelligence in matters of science, they had performed miserably and had generated a mistrust that would continue for decades. Even though the catastrophe was a regional event, it was only a matter of time before a complete account of the animal deaths—and the AEC's mishandling of the affair—would reach the general public.

Inside the AEC, officials searched for ways to defuse the subject of fallout and strontium-90. One result was the tentative reclassification of fallout levels in terms of "sunshine units." Friendly magazines (such as

U.S. News & World Report) were given "inside stories" that depicted fall-out as nothing more than a nuisance. Though there had been no reports that conclusively linked a human death with exposure to radioactive fallout, the AEC decided to learn more about what was falling from the skies.

Since the beginning of nuclear testing, the AEC had tracked the nuclear clouds in their journeys across the country. Ground stations had monitored fallout levels by counting the bursts emitted from the fallout particles. The effort had been hampered by the fact that the scientists were unaware of the nature of the rays they were counting; they only knew the particles were giving off bursts of radiation at a given rate. The levels were recorded as disintegrations per minute (or second) per square foot, and later as millicuries per hundred square miles. The scientists studying the phenomenon were in disagreement as to what level was dangerous: The bursts of radiation that signaled the fissioning (disintegration) of radioactive atoms might vary in energy by millions of electron volts. It was clear that simple counting would not be sufficient to determine population exposures. The scientists would have to know something about the chemical nature of the fallout itself, with particular attention paid to strontium and other body-sequestered fission products.

So, in 1955, in conjunction with the U.S. Weather Bureau, the AEC added sophisticated chemical analysis equipment to its steel pot and funnel network. For the first time, the scientists would know the precise chemical makeup of the material drifting down from the sky. And since strontium-90 was an obvious bone-seeker, it would be a primary target.

The Soviets I:
Bombs in the Kremlin

Soviet military policy had long held that while huge strategic weapons were excellent for long-range defense applications, a huge explosion on the battlefield was more of a hindrance than a help. Trees blown down by a fission bomb would probably get in the way of any armored force trying to make its way through the battle area. Their strategists later indicated that, in fighting a war in Europe, it would be advisable to limit as far as possible the economic damage.

In an article delivered in 1966 in an official Soviet military journal, the author claimed that "the objective is not to turn the large economic and industrial regions into a heap of ruins . . . but to deliver strikes which will destroy strategic combat means, paralyze enemy military production, making it incapable of satisfying the priority needs of the front and rear areas and sharply reduce the enemy capability to conduct strikes."[1]

To this end, Soviet nuclear physicists, such as L. A. Artismovich, had been working since 1952 to tailor their thermonuclear devices down to size, attempting to design a bomb that would produce more radiation than blast through the use of a TNT, rather than a fission, trigger. In other words, a neutron bomb.[2]

The neutron bomb experiments apparently did not go well: In the beginning of 1955, the Soviets suddenly found themselves with a few strategic thermonuclear weapons and no effective tactical nuclear bombs. It was possible for them to wage a strategic war, but not a limited battle using conventional fission weapons.

Having an army that had always relied heavily on artillery, they were also particularly interested in the small shells similar to the one fired during the 1953 GRABLE shot. Thus, some time later, the Russians were delighted when a U.S. Army major walked into the Soviet residency in West Germany offering to *rent* them the latest model of a nuclear artillery shell.

The embassy immediately turned the matter over to the GRU, the supersecret Office of Military Intelligence. The officer in charge was suspicious; the major wanted a *lot* of money for the shell. And it had to be *returned* in two months so his superiors wouldn't miss it.

It was an unusual request, but two months would give the Soviet weapons specialists ample time to determine how Los Alamos had miniaturized its fission weapons. As proof of his intentions, the major had even turned over some documents detailing operation procedures for use with atomic equipment. Specialists in the GRU confirmed that the documents were genuine. To the Soviets, the deal began to look better and better.

They decided to rent the shell.

Key embassy personnel immediately boarded an Aeroflot plane for Moscow. There they were given a week-long crash course detailing what was known about American atomic weapon technology. Upon their return, they made plans to meet with the major and receive the merchandise.

Shortly afterward, the Soviets waited in a forest clearing on a dark rainy night, bank note–laden briefcase in hand, waiting for the their shell. The major finally pulled up in the car and handed the GRU officers the weapon. Pulling out a Geiger counter, the GRU weapons specialist quickly determined that it was indeed radioactive. The size, weight, and markings matched perfectly. After turning over the bank notes to the major, the agents headed straight for their embassy with their new American bomb.

Within hours, the atomic weapon was on its way via armed diplomatic courier to GRU headquarters in Moscow.

The headquarters of Soviet military intelligence was (and still is) located in a drab, windowless brick building complex at one side of Kodinka airfield in the center of Moscow. Surrounded by armed police, guard dogs, and electrified barbed wire, it is a masterwork of security. Inside the fence is a wall-like, two-story building enclosing a central courtyard in which still another building is located: the nine-story head office.

Cars are not allowed inside the courtyard. All coming into the area are scrutinized thoroughly, their clothing checked for any bit of metal that may be a weapon or spy device. Briefcases, cigarette lighters, and "outside" fountain pens are forbidden.[3] Even belt buckles are frowned upon; many of the operatchiks inside the GRU wear suspenders. Surveillance is complete and absolute. No object is too small or insignificant-appearing to be dismissed as a potential weapon.

Into this fortress of security the GRU chief carried an American atomic bomb. As soon as it was safe in the headquarters building, a call was made to the Soviet Central Committee at the Kremlin, not far away.

"Where is the bomb?" someone at the Kremlin asked.

"We have it in GRU headquarters!"

"In Moscow?"

"Yes!"

"And what happens if there is a little spring inside this shell and it explodes right in the middle of the Soviet capital and turns Moscow into Hiroshima?"

Silence. The GRU chief hadn't thought of that.

The chief was soon on his way to the Kremlin to do some explaining. The shell, meanwhile, was heading for the island of Novaya Zemlya, the Soviet atomic testing site in the wilds of the arctic. Scientists there were ordered to tear the weapon apart.

Fearful of "the spring," or some other booby trap, the scientists initially refused. After explaining the situation to them, the military officers finally persuaded the scientists that it was in their best interests to open the atomic shell. At first, the technicians were puzzled by the radioactivity level; it was higher than expected. Perhaps the Americans were using the uranium or plutonium in a new configuration, one that was more radioactive.

When they finally opened the shell, the scientists had their answer: The weapon was a mockup, a "standard weight equivalent" that had been skillfully painted to look like the real thing. As for the question of radioactivity, looking inside the scientists found the answer. For an exhorbitant fee, the Soviet government had purchased several pounds of American nuclear waste.

Furious, the GRU chief tried to locate the American major, but he was too late. He—and the bank notes—had been transferred back to the States. After receiving his "service incompetence note," the chief then petitioned the Soviet Central Committee for authorization to track down the major and have him killed. Permission was denied. In effect, the chief was told that the major had outsmarted him once, he could probably do it again.[4]

Soviet Sleight of Hand

In the spring of 1955, the Soviets were faced with a problem: They didn't have any good long-range bombers. Although they had successfully beaten the Americans in developing a thermonuclear weapon, they still had no reliable means of carrying it to a target.

In 1953, Stalin had directed aircraft designer Vladimir Myasishchev to build a bomber that could fly to the United States, drop a substantial payload (the H-bombs at the time weighed over a ton), and return. Stalin died before the plane was in production, which perhaps was just as well: The Mya-4 was a turkey that barely had the range to make it to the United States, much less return.

The Soviet Central Committee decided to call Myasishchev on the carpet. In his memoirs Nikita Khrushchev tells what happened: "This plane failed to satisfy our requirements. It could reach the United States, but it couldn't come back. Myasishchev said it could bomb the United States and then land in Mexico.

"We replied to the idea with a joke: 'What do you think Mexico is—our mother-in-law? You think we can go calling any time we want? The Mexicans would never let us have the plane back.' "[5]

To make matters worse, Myasishchev's company had been notoriously slow in turning out planes. There were barely enough for a few good formations.

So here it was, nearing May Day, 1955. The Soviets wanted to show off their new Mya-4s at the Tushino air show, and not only did they have bad planes, they didn't have many of them. Then, the generals came up with an idea.

When the U.S. air attaché visited the air show, he was startled to see the sky fairly covered with Mya-4 bombers, or Bisons as NATO called them. He quickly phoned his superiors in Washington telling them that the Soviets had enormous numbers of the new Bisons.

A short time after that, CIA director Allen W. Dulles reported that "every indication pointed to [the Soviets] having adopted [the Bison] as a major element of their offensive strength and to an intention to produce these planes more or less as fast as they could."[6]

Andrew Cockburn, in his book *The Threat: Inside the Soviet Military Machine,* explains what had happened: "In fact, the Soviets had had their limited force of Bisons fly over the Tushino airfield and then, out of sight of the reviewing stand and the watching air attaché, circle around to make another pass. In terms of effect, it was the most successful air show ever."[7]

Though the only real Soviet strategic bomber of the 1950s was the Tu-95 "Bear," the sight of a sky filled with the medium-range Bisons was enough to give the entire United States a case of bomber attack jitters. Civil Defense was stepped up, CONELRAD (CONtrol of ELectromagnetic RADiations) stations began test-beeping more often, and comic books appeared with stories of Russian sneak attacks over the North Pole.[8]

Hot Spots

As in earlier test series, Robert J. List of the U.S. Weather Bureau's Special Project Section had been assigned the task of compiling a report detailing fallout depositions across the United States from the recent detonations.

Under the direction of Dr. Lester Machta, chief of the Special Projects Section, List would bring together the reams of fallout data obtained from the Atomic Energy Commission's Health and Safety Laboratory (HASL) and attempt to make sense of the numbers.

Under the direction of Merrill Eisenbud, the HASL had meticulously obtained fallout data from over 100 stations across the United States. From information obtained by the air force's Special Weapons Command and the 1009th Special Weapons Squadron, List and his associates drew up detailed trajectory maps of the cloud paths across the continent. These, in turn, would be matched up with the appropriate weather maps indicting areas of precipitation.

List and his associates were always on the lookout for thunderstorms and rain squalls in the path of the fallout. It was well-known that precipitation could bring large amounts of the nuclear debris to earth. Called "scavenging," this process had resulted in extremely high levels of fallout in cities far removed from the test site. Rochester, New York, for example, seemed to be a prime target. On November 1, 1951, that city received 360,000 disintegrations/minute/square foot/day. In an earlier report, "The Transport of Radioactive Debris from Operations Buster and Jangle," List noted that Rochester had "the greatest cumulative amount of any station."[1] The meteorologist saw the combination of precipitation and fallout as a potentially serious problem.

In the BUSTER-JANGLE report, List had noted:

The maximum possible deposition of radioactivity at the ground is a function of the quantity and nature of radioactivity in the cloud, the vertical distribution of the debris, the amount of diffusion, and the effectiveness of the mode of downward transport. It has been shown that rain is exceedingly effective as a means of producing the downward transport. One may, therefore, conceive of a combination of conditions which would readily create dangerous activity at the ground. For example, rain which occurs in and over a newly formed atomic cloud might wash down a very large fraction of the debris to the ground and produce a major hazard. . . .

While the tests carried out at Nevada have not produced any serious hazard at places removed from the Site area, these bursts have occurred under conditions selected to prevent such hazard. It is felt that such caution should continue to be exercised in the future since evidence collected during BUSTER and JANGLE indicates a potential danger.[2]

Now, in late 1953, while compiling information for the UPSHOT-KNOTHOLE report, List saw something about the seventh burst that caught his attention.

It was known that the 40,000-foot trajectory from SIMON had crossed the path of a thunderstorm. Scavenging had taken place and considerable amounts of nuclear debris were forced to earth near Albany and Troy, New York. Atomic Energy Commission monitors had traveled to the two cities, took readings, and estimated a fallout intensity level of 16 million disintegrations/minute/square foot in the area.

While this was an extraordinary and somewhat unexpected level so far from the test site, List thought it might be in error. The problem centered on the extrapolation models that AEC had used in arriving at the figure. It appeared that the monitors had failed to take into consideration that the fallout at Albany-Troy was three days old.

Back-calculating, List came up with a much larger number: 100 million disintegrations/minute/square foot. This amounted to an incredible 11,574 disintegrations/*second*/square *inch*.

Looking back over the data, List saw that these conditions occurred in the New York and New England area at least three other times. Since these areas were quite some distance from Nevada, and presumably had less fallout to drop, rain scavenging occurring closer to ground zero might logically produce hot spots of even higher intensity. Examining the records further, List found at least one instance where scavenging had occurred exceptionally close to the test site: in Wyoming, shortly after the 12-kiloton TUMBLER-SNAPPER: EASY detonation on May 7, 1952.

In his report, List expressed his concerns about the Albany levels and, particularly, the 1952 Wyoming incident:

If the activity at Albany is taken to be 10^7 d/m/ft²/day (this value is more nearly the activity at the actual time of fallout, since the debris was 36 hours old rather than one day old as is assumed in the simplified routine extrapolation procedure used), it is possible to estimate the effect of a similar situation in, say, western Kansas, where both diffusion and decay would have had less time to operate. If the fallout occurred within 5 or 6 hours of burst time, the increase in concentration of deposited activity due to the shorter decay time alone would be by a factor of 10. The increase due to the shorter time available for diffusion (and shear) to act would be at least a factor of 6 and could be more than a factor of 100 under certain reasonable assumptions, resulting in activities of the order of 10^9 to 10^{11} d/m/ft^2 at the time of deposition.

It is also of interest to examine the trajectories and precipitation accompanying bursts of this and previous Nevada tests series to see if potentially serious cases of intense localized fallout could have occurred which were undetected by the monitoring network. Several such situations were found. They are: New York and New England on November 1, 1951, November 3, 1951, and April 7, 1953; Nebraska on May 26, 1952; and Wyoming on May 8, 1952. The latter case appears to be the one most likely to have produced intense local fallout. . . .

The last two continental test series, the only continental tests involving high-yield tower shots, have both been in the spring, and the question arises as to whether this is the best season from a meteorological point of view. Of the factors to be considered, the most important is the probability of favorable weather at the test site. However, other factors should also be considered. These include the probability of avoiding intense local fallout at some distance from the test site, the possibility of reducing total fallout in the United States, and the possibility of minimizing adverse public reaction due to the widespread belief that the atomic tests, in some fashion, cause unusual weather. . . .[3]

The occurrence of intense local fallout at distances greater than 600 miles from the test site is dependent on the occurrence of showers or thundershowers in a region having a high concentration of debris aloft. The high concentration of debris aloft is, in turn, the result of a high-yield tower shot which injects large amounts of debris into a fast-moving wind stream that seres to carry the debris to great distance before much dilution can occur[4]. . . .

The efficacy of precipitation in bringing debris to the ground is well-established, and it follows that the most likely method of reducing total fallout in the United States is to schedule tests for periods when precipitation is least likely.[5]

Bad Weather

In the UPSHOT-KNOTHOLE report, under the heading "Minimizing Adverse Public Reaction," List also addressed the subject of nuclear testing and climate:

The spring of 1953 was characterized in several regions of the country by unusual weather conditions: a large number of tornadoes; cool, excessively dry weather in the southwest; and greater than normal precipitation in the east. The theory that these events were in some way related to the Upshot-Knothole tests, which took place in the same period, gained widespread public acceptance, although there is as yet, despite intensive study by the Weather Bureau, no scientific evidence to support this contention.

According to F. W. Reichelderfer, Chief of the Weather Bureau, "The usual thing about weather is that it is unusual in some place or other. The strange thing to us is that the public never remembers this. Year after year, there is very unusual weather someplace—heavy rainfall, tornadoes, freezes, frosts. . . .'' It follows, therefore, that adverse public reaction can be minimized by scheduling test series for periods when weather is of least importance in everyday activities, if such periods exist, and when catastrophic storms are less likely to occur. . . .

From the point of view of suitable weather, both at the test site and throughout the country, it appears that the months of October and November would be most satisfactory for test operations.[6]

The report, released on June 25, 1954, was immediately classified and would remain so for eight more years. In the meantime, the testing at Nevada would continue. The next series would be operation TEAPOT, scheduled for 1955. It would take place in the spring.

Teapot

1955

The year 1955 saw the introduction of Walt Disney's Davy Crockett and coonskin caps. It was also the year that fast food was born. It happened in Des Plaines, Illinois, with the opening of the first McDonald's restaurant. At the Woolworth stores nearby, people could buy roll-on deodorants and filter cigarettes.

Men would greet spring wearing pink shirts and narrow ties. Hatbands were "in." Women shopped for hooded sweaters. In the larger department stores, women tried new colognes: Balenciaga's Quadrille, a roselike perfume; Dana's Ambush with its "modern floral fragrance"; or Faberge's Flambeau, another rose-jasmine combination.

Moviegoers would enjoy such Warner Brothers cartoons as *Beanstalk Bunny* starring Bugs Bunny, Daffy Duck, and Elmer Fudd. Released February 12, it was a variation on the Jack and the Beanstalk tale with Elmer as the Giant.

During March and April, two more Bugs Bunny cartoons would be unveiled: *Captain Hareblower* and *Sahara Hare*—both co-starring Yosemite Sam.

At the Nevada Test Site, the AEC was ready to unveil TEAPOT.

TEAPOT, the fifth in the series of nuclear tests, would include fifteen events of which only one was nonnuclear. The scientific group at the Los Alamos Laboratory figured heavily in this series of shots. For in it they would try newer, lighter, and more efficient bombs.

Beryllium reflectors had been found to be effective in increasing yield in several of the shots in the UPSHOT-KNOTHOLE series. Now the designers had been asked to make the bombs smaller yet even more powerful.[1] What

the military needed for their pentomic army (i.e., one composed of five battle groups) was a lightweight device, something a single soldier could carry
to the target.

The lightweight beryllium reflector helped.[2] To decrease weight even
further, the plutonium sphere was made smaller, almost to the size where it
would not become critical regardless of its shape or configuration. Judging
from the size of the weapons and the effects, some of the plutonium capsules
to be used during TEAPOT would be no bigger than oranges. The Los Alamos
scientists were becoming experts at miniaturization.

The troops were still skittish about tactical weapons. Many just didn't like
sharing a battlefield with a nuclear cloud. Some were frightened by the obvious power involved; anything that could *melt* a tank was something to be
wary of. Most were awed by the fearsome sight of a cloud boiling high into
the stratosphere where minutes before had been a 300-foot steel tower.

The military brass, however, thought the problem could be corrected by
proper training. A report concluded that "the realism engendered by coming face-to-face with an actual nuclear detonation adds a great deal to the
benefits derived, and augments the total fund of training and experience of
the Marine Corps."[3]

Still, all the training in the world couldn't prepare a soldier for the unusual sights that awaited him in the Nevada desert.

To gain some perspective, the reader is invited to take a toothpick and
stand about 9 inches away from a wall with a 10-foot ceiling.[4] First, turn
away from the wall and hold the toothpick at arm's length until only about
half is showing: that represents the view of a 300-foot tower from 6,000 feet,
the distance from which some officer observers viewed the various shots.
Now, having done that, imagine something slightly larger than a basketball
where the top of the toothpick had been. This would represent the atomic
fireball.

This happens so fast—less than a millisecond—that if one second
equaled one day, the transformation time would equal something less than a
minute and a half.

Now, having imagined the basketball sitting atop the toothpick, turn
and face the wall. Now look up to the junction of the wall and ceiling. This
is the angle one would have to tilt one's head to see the mushroom of many
of the nuclear clouds—for example, UPSHOT-KNOTHOLE: BADGER, which immediately after detonation climbed to 36,000 feet.

In addition to determining the psychological effects of nuclear weapons on
the ground soldiers, scientists and military also wanted to learn the effects
of the detonations on different types of military equipment and structures.
Experiments were set up for this purpose at shots WASP, MOTH, TESLA,
TURK, BEE, ESS (for subsurface), APPLE-1, WASP PRIME, MET (for Military

Effects Test), and APPLE-2. One test, APPLE-2, involved a specially constructed Doom Town similar to shot ANNIE in 1953, complete with houses,
automobiles, paved streets, and mannequins, all to be blown to bits.

Prior to TEAPOT, the AEC released a statement briefly outlining the test
plans. Fallout was mentioned only briefly.

The AEC had hoped to counter some of the public concern by publishing a booklet entitled *Atomic Test Effects in the Nevada Test Site Region*
and distributing it to the area residents. It read, in part:

A Message to People Who Live Near Nevada Test Site

*You are in a very real sense active participants in the Nation's atomic test pro-
gram. You have been close observers of tests which have contributed greatly to
building the defenses of our own country and of the free world. Nevada tests
have helped us come a long way in a few short years and have been a vital factor
in maintaining the peace of the world. They also provide important data for use
in planning civil defense measures to protect our people in event of enemy attack.*

*Some of you have been inconvenienced by our test operations. At times
some of you have been exposed to potential risk from flash, blast, or fallout.
You have accepted the inconvenience or the risk without fuss, without alarm,
and without panic. Your cooperation has helped achieve an unusual record of
safety.*

*In a world in which free people have no atomic monopoly, we must keep
out atomic strength at peak level. Time is a key factor in this task and Nevada
tests help us "buy" precious time.*

That is why we must hold new tests in Nevada.

*I want you to know that in the forthcoming series, as has been true in the
past, each shot is justified by national and international security need and that
none will be fired unless there is adequate assurance of public safety.*

We are grateful for your continued cooperation and your understanding.

James E. Reeves
Test Manager
Joint Test Organization
Camp Mercury, Nevada
[January 1955]

During the UPSHOT-KNOTHOLE series, the Atomic Energy Commission
had been particularly embarrassed by the SIMON and dirty HARRY shots. SI-
MON had dosed Albany, New York, with an unbelievable 16 million
disintegrations/minute. HARRY had floated over St. George, Utah, chasing
the residents into their homes and causing some alarm. The rain at Dixie
College, on the outskirts of the Utah town, had no doubt been radioactive.
The AEC did not want such a thing to happen again. The concern, and the
attitudes, are reflected in the oft-quoted minutes of an AEC meeting held in
Washington, D.C., just after Operation TEAPOT had begun.

Senator Clinton Anderson, chairman of the Joint Committee on Atomic Energy, had written a letter to Lewis Strauss complaining that, due to fallout on populated areas, the Nevada Test Site might not be such a good place to detonate the atomic devices. "Your report," he wrote, "should consider whether only very small-yield devices should be tested there, leaving all substantial shots for the Pacific where they can be precisely scheduled."

Commissioner Thomas Murray asked Strauss if Anderson was referring to the recent tests, both quite small.

"Presumably," Strauss replied.

"Is he taking action now?" Murray asked.

"He was out there [at the test site]," Strauss replied. "But he didn't see anything because he left before it was shot."

After some conversation, Commissioner Libby commented, "I am pretty disturbed about this." Then, turning to Strauss, "I noted, Lewis, that you had cooled off about the Nevada site."

"I had been cool before," Strauss told him. "My coolness started in the spring of 1953. But I never discussed this with Anderson. This is spontaneous."

> Libby: "I think this will set the weapons program back a lot if we have to go to the Pacific."
>
> Strauss: "I have gone along with the majority of the commission that this is the thing to do."
>
> Murray: "You wouldn't consider pulling back anything in the present series of tests?"

Strauss replied with startling candor: "If I were asked whether the two large Teapot shots should be made, and it were left to my sole decision, I would say load them on a ship and go out to Eniwetok and put them on a raft and set them off."

After some discussion, Strauss mentioned a Nevada legislator who had introduced a bill in the state legislature asking for the removal of the test site. "Both of the Las Vegas papers, who seldom agree on anything, published editorials agreeing this was nonsense, that we brought a lot of prosperity to the state, that this was a fine thing for national defense. They rather laughed the legislator out of the court."

"That is a sensible view," Libby said. "People have got to learn to live with the facts of life. And part of the facts of life are fallout."

"It's certainly all right, they say," Strauss replied, "if you don't live next door to it."

"Or live under it," K. D. Nichols added.

At one point in the discussion, Strauss again brought up the subject of St. George: "I have forgotten the number of people living there. [He was then told the population was 4,500 persons.] So you can't evacuate them." (The military occasionally evacuated Groom Mine, a tiny community located just 20–30 miles from the blasts.)

Dr. John C. Bugher (AEC fallout expert): "St. George is hypertensified. It is not a question of health or safety with St. George but a question of public relations."

Murray: "Get on with the test . . . we must not let anything interfere with this series of tests—nothing."[5]

Libby: "I don't want radioactivity falling on people's necks, but more delays create an awfully serious problem."

Strauss then discussed the "optimum areas" for fallout: "One is more or less west of north. Ten degrees east of that they got into more settled areas. And there is another apparently optimum direction almost due south."

"Isn't that east?" asked Nichols.

"No," Strauss replied. "East they go over Pioche and over St. George, which they apparently always plaster . . . south of these two places is a very narrow corridor where if the wind shifts ten degrees in either direction, then they are in trouble again. Of course, they really never paid much attention to that before." It was an oblique, if telling, reference to the amount of control the commissioners felt they actually exerted over the test site managers: very little.

Not only that, a reading of the transcript of the meeting indicates that the commissioners themselves were kept in the dark about certain important—and negative—features of the testing. Later in the meeting, for example, Chairman Strauss asked another commissioner what a hot spot was. Libby told him that hot spots were "a fluke of the weather or winds causing local precipitation."

He was wrong. Hot spots were areas on the ground of high radioactivity caused by variances in fallout patterns. Occasionally they were associated with rainfall, but often they were not.

Getting back to the Anderson letter, Murray displayed his mastery of bureaucratese by suggesting, "Just say we are glad to get his letter. That we are taking more precautions and more than we have in the past. It may take longer time to run the series. We will look into it. We recognize the difficulties and we will look for another site."

Strauss was apparently troubled by the problems of St. George and was seriously pushing for a Pacific site. He broke in to summarize, "We were talking, no decision made, about conducting future tests of anything except little ones in the Pacific. It is so easy to do things out there because you can do them one a day, practically. . . . I have always been frightened that something would happen which would set us back with the public for a long period of time."

Murray was candid: "I am interested in the public all right, but if we are not going to have a test for another year, and we don't go out to Nevada again, and we take another year to think of another test place—this Pacific idea you can talk all you want, Lewis, put them on a ship and get them out in thirty or sixty days, it will not be done."

"Fly them out," Strauss replied stubbornly.

"You cannot put troops on a plane and so forth." Libby said, joining in.

Commissioners Murray and Libby then suggested a letter be drafted telling Senator Anderson that the AEC was looking for a new test site and one possibility was Point Barrow, Alaska.[6]

Meanwhile, the tests in Nevada would continue.

But by this time, the Public Health Service was involved in the off-site monitoring, and more samples were taken than previously. Water and milk would be checked regularly for fallout particles that included iodine-131. Public Health Service personnel would visit communities in the area "to facilitate good public relations."[7]

Before the TEAPOT series began, test organization representatives visited the small Nevada and Utah communities. In speeches to schools and civic groups, they explained the value of continental testing and spelled out what precautions they intended to take to assure public safety.

An unclassified report of the program concluded with: "While it may not have altered completely basic public opinion regarding the tests, it at least made the explanations of zone personnel [area monitors] more acceptable."[8]

Although there would be grudging acceptance throughout the area, the AEC would have a definite problem with a Tonopah, Nevada, newspaper editor, Robert A. Crandall. In his weekly editorial in the *Times-Bonanza*, Crandall would be critical of the AEC, especially after the fourth shot of the TEAPOT series.

Back at the site, knowing that over 11,000 military personnel would be involved in this series, additional exposure limits were set. The participants were limited to 5 pounds per square inch of overpressure and one calorie per square centimeter of thermal radiation. The 3.9 roentgen gamma radiation exposure was maintained. Since TEAPOT was planned to last thirteen weeks, this would precisely match the 0.3 roentgen/week occupational exposure recommended by the National Council on Radiation Protection.

There was, however, some leeway allowed. The test manager could authorize higher exposure limits for selected individuals and conditions. For example, a special exposure limit of 10 roentgens was allowed for the volunteer officer observers who would witness the APPLE-2 shot from 1½ miles (about half a mile closer than the other observers).

On February 17, 600 soldiers readied themselves for the first detonation of the series, code-named WASP.

TEAPOT: WASP

The troops had originally been scheduled to watch WASP from trenches about 2.7 miles south of ground zero. At the last minute, the meteorologists discovered that this area would be directly in the path of fallout, so the observers were moved to News Nob, approximately 9 miles south the shot area. The equipment display was also in the path of predicted fallout, so the damaged-equipment tour near ground zero was canceled.

The Wasp device was fired at noon, Pacific Standard Time, on February 18, 1955, opening the Teapot series.

The yield had been measured at one kiloton. Had Wasp been dropped on a city, it would have vaporized about 1,000 tons of concrete, metal, *anything*. The troops, however, accustomed to stories of such giants at Badger and Climax, were disappointed.

The wind at the surface was blowing from the northwest at a steady 26 mph. At 21,500 feet, the altitude of cloud top, the wind speed was a healthy 110 mph. The nuclear cloud was pushed southeast, toward Phoenix, Arizona, and an area of precipitation.

In fact, on February 18, rain areas moved in a giant cartwheel from Nevada to Michigan. Another part of Wasp's nuclear cloud circled around northern Minnesota between 6:00 A.M. and 6:00 P.M. on February 21, 1955.

Teapot: Moth

February 22, Washington's birthday, was set for the next detonation, Moth—another low-yield device, the prototype for an atomic missile warhead. This time, instead of airdropping the device, the scientists placed it atop a 300-foot tower in Area 3, the former home of Upshot-Knothole shots Annie and Harry two years earlier.

As the device was placed in the corrugated metal cab at the top of the tower, troops were given a brief indoctrination regarding the hazards of radiation. Among other things, they were warned not to breathe or ingest any radioactive particles. The soldiers would be placed in trenches 2⅓ miles from the tower. They learned, to their relief, that there would be no maneuvers at Moth.

At 3:00 Pacific Standard Time, on the morning of February 22, the troops filed into the trenches. They could see the searchlights 4,000 yards away illuminating the shot tower. As usual, the tower was lit in part to prevent any unauthorized persons from tampering with the device. As an added precaution, after final arming, the elevator was removed from the structure. Anyone wanting to steal Moth would have to climb down with it.

Immediately prior to the shot, all Desert Rock support personnel were evacuated from the area. One group, the Wire Team B, was responsible for communications. After the detonation, it would be up to this group to assure communications would remain intact.

Seconds before the Moth detonation, the wind was calm. At 5:45 A.M. the switch at the Control Point was thrown and a surge of electricity headed for the shot tower.

The orange flash was seen as far as 400 miles away, in San Francisco. In Los Angeles, 250 miles to the southwest, the glare lit the heavens, briefly creating a false dawn. Windows rattled in Las Vegas, 75 miles southeast of the test site. Residents of St. George, Utah, 135 miles to the east, were wakened by the jolt.

The fireball glowed a brief two seconds before beginning the ascent that would take it to a 24,200-foot altitude. Despite the calm conditions on the ground, the wind at that height was a brisk 62 mph, blowing toward the southeast. MOTH would, like WASP had done several days before, cross over Phoenix.

As the troops stood to watch the cloud and the icecap form on its top, they were sprayed with dirt from the shock wave. According to the official account, there were no casualties.

MOTH had been a very hot detonation: 900 feet north of ground zero the radioactivity indicated a 500-roentgen/hour contour, spreading first to the northeast, then back southeast.

Later, Senator Russell B. Long of Louisiana commented about MOTH: "We had an opportunity to foresee the definite possibility of these small-sized nuclear weapons, launched either from the ground or from an aircraft against invading forces. Yet they are small enough to minimize the danger to our own people."

MOTH toured the southern United States and then moved up the East Coast to New England. Its 24,000-foot trajectory took it 50 miles south of Lubbock, Texas, at 7:30 P.M. and then it moved on to Memphis, crossing there at 1:30 A.M. the next day. By 10:00 A.M. February 23, this part of the cloud crossed over Hershey, Pennsylvania, home of the Hershey Candy Company. One hour later, it passed 25 miles west of New York City on its way toward Lexington, Massachusetts. It crossed that city at 1:00 on the afternoon of February 23. There was precipitation all along the East Coast at the time.[9] As the radioactive rain fell that Wednesday evening, many with both television sets and children watched Walt Disney's "Davy Crockett at the Alamo."

TEAPOT: TESLA

Named for the inventor of alternating current, shot TESLA was readied atop a 300-foot tower in Area 9b early on the morning of March 1.[10]

At 3:30 A.M., 1.4 miles southwest of the tower, 600 army personnel and 25 marines filed into the narrow, dusty foxholes to await the blast. After the detonation, and preceded by radiation safety monitors, they would maneuver through the display areas.

Jim O'Connor, a specialist with Wire Team B, remembered the event:

TESLA was one of those little shots. We were told it was expected to yield slightly more than one kiloton. It was originally planned to go off on February 25 but was postponed.

My team's location was 2,500 yards, or about a mile and a half from the tower.

My position was eight feet to the rear of the switchboard bunker. The bunker was eight feet long and five feet wide. It was covered by planks of wood with a double layer of sandbags on top. I drove a three-quarter-ton truck that carried wire and other equipment. During the shots, I parked the truck in a sloping depression. I knelt next to the vehicle when the device was fired. I [was to use] the truck as an emergency vehicle if there was a call for it.

The night of February 28, a Marine Corps captain, sergeant, and twenty-four men arrived at our location. The officer told my first sergeant his contingent had permission to proceed two hundred yards foward of us. I thought those guys were crazy, but who the hell was I to question the captain. I told them that if there were any problems I'd come down to their position in my truck and help out. The captain then took his men forward and stopped the group about two hundred yards away. Those guys started digging their own trenches. You could hear the sergeant barking out orders telling his men what to do. I had seen two atomic explosions, and I felt those marines had no idea what was in store for them. I couldn't believe people would come out to the site and dig their own trenches. Our trenches were dug by the army engineers who used trench diggers and the trenches were six feet deep. We spent the night out there awaiting word that the shot would be fired.

At 5:20 A.M. the countdown began. The observers were asked to kneel and cover their eyes.

Ten minutes later TESLA was detonated.:
O'Connor's account continues:

I was blown into the side of [my] truck. I was stunned and had a nosebleed, but managed to get to my feet and stagger out of the trench. The first thing I saw was that the vehicle had been knocked over and was leaning against one of the sides of the depression. The canvas top covering the cab was on fire. The bed of the truck was covered with sand and partially buried. The bags on top of the switchboard bunker were even burning. . . .

As I approached the marines' position, I feared the worst. I didn't see any movement. All I saw was mass confusion and some people who were partially buried. . . . All of the marines were trapped. Lots of sand had been thrown into their holes on top of them. They must have been lying down facing the bomb when the thing exploded.

I had to pull one marine from his hole. He was obviously in shock, as he just looked at me with a blank stare and moved his head from side to side, not saying a word. His helmet had been knocked off. We started pulling the others out. Some of them freed themselves, but there was mass confusion. They were disoriented and in a state of shock. Some of the marines began walking back toward the switchboard bunker, while others moved in the direction of ground zero and the service road [Rainer Mesa Road]. Several sat in their holes and didn't move.[11]

Scientists had predicted a low yield for the small device, only 2 kilotons. As soon as the detonation occurred, they know their calculations had been wrong. For a contact surface burst, a 2-kiloton weapon would have produced a fireball only 382 feet across. TESLA's fireball was measured to be almost twice that: 735 feet. The flash was seen over a radius of nearly 500 miles. Persons living in Pocatello, Idaho, to the north, San Francisco and Los Angeles to the west, and Phoenix to the south witnessed TESLA's glare. After the information was collected, the yield was slightly over 7 kilotons, an extremely efficient device.

(Later, at AEC meeting number 1063, Commissioner Murray asked Chairman Strauss: "Lewis, do you have any more information on TESLA?"

Strauss replied, "We say flash results which appeared to be six times larger than estimated. I hope there will not be anything like that in connection with TURK [the next shot]."

"The point is," Murray said, "that it was four or six times larger than Livermore thought it would be, though Bradbury at Los Alamos guessed it higher."[12,13])

On the ground, the personnel began their assault toward ground zero.

The Radiological Safety Support monitors, riding in half-ton pickups, drove ahead of the troops across the sand, toward the tower. Later analysis of the film badges indicated two of the Rad/Safe monitors had been overexposed to the radiation. The official report:

> At 7:38 A.M. the above-named men entered the 1 R/h contaminated area of shot TESLA, approximately 1,270 yards from ground zero . . . to recover some glazed material for an alpha inspection. Approximately 350 yards from ground zero the AN/PDR-39 survey instrument carried in the cab of the pickup and set on the 50,000 scale, went off scale. However, as there was no glazed material apparent at this point, the party proceeded to within 50 yards of ground zero before it was apparent there was no heavily glazed area. [One man] dismounted the vehicle . . . and quickly collected some surface material. The driver of the vehicle . . . did not get out of the cab. . . . The total elapsed time within the 1 R/hr area was approximately three minutes. The total time [the man] was out of the cab . . . was about 30 seconds.[14]

In the air, five cloud trackers in a B-25 Mitchel bomber were into a steep climb on their way to meet up with the TESLA mushroom. By the time the Mitchell had climbed to its sampling altitude of 10,000 feet, TULSA's cloud had already been pulled by wind shear into the characteristic zigzag "lightning bolt" shape, perhaps 30 miles in length, glowing orange in the chill dawn.

Pilot Alden Thompson guided the B-25 as close to the nuclear cloud as his copilot, Bobbie Bagshaw, deemed safe. Bagshaw held a standard-issue Geiger-Mueller counter on his lap. When it began to chatter from the influx of gamma radiation, Thompson knew he had better head for clear air.

The pilot followed the cloud over St. George, Mt. Carmel, and Kanab Utah, circling and banking, attempting to locate TESLA's invisible aura of radioactivity. Each nuclear cloud had one and Thompson headed his plane closer and closer toward the vaporous material until Bagshaw's Geiger counter began to chatter. At that point he pulled back on the stick, cutting sharply away from the area, circled, and moved in again.

Thompson's job was to detect first the leading of edge of TESLA, then its north-south borders. When it was located, the coordinates were relayed to ground stations along the route. By the time the clouds had crossed two state lines, many of them had lost their moisture and were thus invisible. Often, the only way the pilot could tell the location of such a cloud was by the chatter of the Geiger counter. TESLA was no different. At one point in the chase the Geiger indicated a count of 600 milliroentgens, a substantial dose. Thompson immediately veered the Mitchell away from the hot area.

Thompson and his crew chased TESLA for three hours and fifteen minutes, taking "nips" from its side every quarter hour or so. By this time the winds had fanned it into three "spears" heading in different directions. From the plane, the cloud had begun to look like a smudge against the sky.

Flying beneath the cloud over the Bryce Canyon area, monitors noted no radioactivity below about 17,000 feet. After returning to the base, Thompson's plane was washed down and the flight crew checked for radiation. One of the crew was found to have high radioactivity on his hands.[15]

Though invisible, TESLA proceeded on across the continent. On March 2, the cloud inexplicably dumped dry fallout on some small areas of the plains states. The intense fallout that day extended from McCoy, Colorado, just west of Denver to Collyer, Kansas. Other areas experienced the fallout during rainstorms.

The nuclear cloud finally crossed the East Coast on Thursday, March 3.[16] On the same day, Chicago experienced a radioactive rain and hailstorm: Walter C. McCrone, a research chemist at Armour Labs, had noticed increased radioactivity that day; his Geiger counter had registered 2,200 counts a minute, more than 700 counts higher than that from any other atomic test.[17]

Interestingly, TESLA's cloud had not gone near Chicago. It had stayed on an orderly track nearly 300 miles south, crossing Colorado, Kansas, Missouri, Illinois, and points east. Rainstorms, however, had scavanged the material and transported it across the Midwest and then north.

The first four detonations in the TEAPOT series had displayed the separate directions taken by the two weapons laboratories. Los Alamos had designed the WASP and MOTH devices; each small, lightweight, and designed to be used by the infantry or artillery in close-in, tactical combat. TESLA, on the other hand, designed by Livermore, packed a stronger punch and TURK was another matter entirely.

TEAPOT: TURK

Obstensibly, TURK was to be another tactical weapon, as were all the devices tested in TEAPOT. At Area 2 in the northwest, hilly corner of the test site, trenches were dug slightly less than 2 miles from the shot tower, at the very end of the display area. Troops would be asked to leave the trenches subsequent to the burst and walk across the hot ground through the blast-damaged equipment.

The first indication that TURK would not be like its predecessors was in the preparation of ground zero. For one thing, the shot tower would be 500 feet tall, 200 feet taller than any previous test. It would stand above the desert only 55 feet shorter than the Washington Monument. Prior to this, any device with an expected yield of over 20 kilotons or so was airdropped. SIMON, two years before, had been a tower shot of enormous yield, but the fireball had been too close to the ground; tons of dirt had been sucked up and later deposited across the country. SIMON had been a 43-kiloton monster. Watching the activity surrounding the 500-foot tower, observers wondered what kind of a fireball TURK would become.

As if the 500-foot tower weren't precaution enough, the ground surrounding it was being coated with asphalt, something else that had never been done before. Clearly, TURK would be one of the more spectacular shots.

The device had been designed at Livermore under the direction of Edward Teller. Since Livermore was known to be the center for H-bomb studies, there was some speculation that the device would have a thermonuclear component. Information leaked to the press indicated the weapon would eventually be used as a warhead for a "trans-Atlantic rocket." It began to appear that this device was not designed for tactical combat, but for long-range strategic destruction, a "city-buster" to be attached to the nose of an ICBM.[18]

The night before the shot, approximately 600 troops rode toward the site from Camp Desert Rock, turning left at the BUSTER: JANGLE "Y" on to Rainer Mesa Road. The spotlighted tower could be seen to the northwest, glowing faintly against the backdrop of the Belted Range.

At 5:10 A.M., Pacific Standard Time, on March 7, as the first traces of light were beginning to appear in the east, the loudspeakers near the trenches signaled the troops to take cover. No one on the ground knew what to expect.

At 5:20 A.M. the charge was sent to the detonators surrounding the device. An instant later, TURK's tower vanished in a flash of light that was seen as far away as Bellingham, Washington, 1,080 miles to the north. Reporters on Mount Charleston who had been squinting in the darkness, trying to make out the tower, were momentarily blinded by the detonation.

In Salt Lake City, 370 miles away, houses rattled. TURK had indeed been a monster. The fireball had grown so quickly that no record exists of the radius at second maximum, a figure that indicates approximate yield. Other measurements indicated TURK had packed a 43-kiloton wallop. In effect, the device could have vaporized 43,000 tons of anything and then carried the particles aloft to the top of its 40,209-foot mushroom cloud.

Prior to the shot, the troops had been moved to emplacements used for the TELSA shot. In the haze following the blast, the troops saw the reason for the change in plans: The base cloud and TURK's 6-mile-high stem were both drifting right over the site of the original trenches, engulfing the display area in highly radioactive fallout. Measurements, taken later indicated the radioactivity at the original site would have exceeded 100 roentgens/hour. At ground zero one hour after the shot, the radiation level reached 1,000 roentgens/hour.

Rather than face the radiation, the officers postponed the display tour until the next day.

Early March is usually a troublesome time for meteorologists. This time of year the wind seems to have a mind of its own, shifting and changing constantly at every level. At ground level a breeze from the northwest at 12 mph might have no relation to the wind speed and direction aloft. On the morning of the shot, for example, at the height of the vaporized tower, the wind was blowing out of the north at 22 mph. Another thousand feet and the wind came from the north*east* at 24 mph. At 7,000 feet over the test site, however, there was only a slight breeze drifting in from the southeast.

TURK's stem, pushing up through these various crosscurrents of wind, soon began to look like a spiral, or perhaps a black lightning bolt. At the point where it connected with the bottom of the mushroom, the wind was blowing from due west at 13 mph, pushing the business part of the nuclear cloud toward the Utah-Arizona border.

People in towns close to the test site were worried. The three prior shots had produced little fallout, but this one seemed to be different. The wind was shifting constantly, spreading the cloud into a huge gray blanket over the sky west of the test site. The cloud was spreading in every direction except south. Robert A. Crandall, the editor of the *Tonopah Times-Bonanza,* was quoted in *The Reporter* as saying, "As the cloud crept slowly northward, anxious AEC monitoring teams followed its progress. They now admit the cloud wasn't supposed to be there but a last-minute switch in wind direction sent it billowing and weaving across parts of Nye and Esmeralda counties."

Crandall tried to contact AEC monitors but was unsuccessful. Later, a state game warden came to the newspaper office and reported that "the mud on his pickup ran the Geiger counter off Scale II" and the region around Warm Springs, from which he had just come, was so hot one could hardly use a Geiger. Later, an AEC monitor assured the game warden that Geiger counters are not the proper instruments to use in determining personal radiation exposure.

At Twin Springs, Nevada, a small community near Tonopah, Joanne Davis, a schoolteacher, brought the kids to watch the cloud. Joe Fallini, living nearby, took photos of the cloud as it drifted overhead. At the time, Fallini noticed a peculiar "acid-like" taste in his throat. Years later, he said that some of the film had been fogged by the radiation.

Official Interpretations

After Crandall's editorial, he received a phone call from the AEC. In an interview with Paul Jacobs of *The Reporter*, Crandall recalled his exchanges with the government officials:

> Every time we've had an adverse comment in the paper, or what might be interpreted as adverse by the AEC, I've had a couple of boys—or three or four—come in to see me. They come into the office and their tactic has always been along these lines—"Well, you don't believe that the AEC for a moment thinks that there is any possible harm in the tests or that any civilian could possibly be injured in any way?"
>
> Then they go on to talk about all the precautions they take. I recall one time when one of the AEC men said, "Suppose there was some woman living around here who had a weak heart and you were to run a story to the effect that this radiation fallout was harmful. And suppose that she had a daughter or small child that was out there. Do you realize that this woman might suffer a heart attack because of the fact that you were spreading alarming stories?"

A year later, after a particularly scathing article quoting Dr. Linus Pauling on the subject of radiation, Crandall received a letter from an AEC official, Richard G. Elliott:

> As you know, we have tried consistently since January, 1951, to keep you and the people of the general Tonopah area advised of the facts concerning our operations at Nevada Test Site. This has been particularly true with regard to radiation fallout.
>
> Your article "Local Citizens 'Give Up' 1000 years," presented a statement as to radiation fallout experienced in Nye and Esmeralda counties which is inaccurate. We feel that it should be corrected and that you will want to correct it.
>
> The accompanying letter, addressed to the Editor, *Times-Bonanza,* is submitted to you for publication in your newspaper. We believe it merits publication and hope you will also.
>
> Radiation levels and exposures remain a complex subject, Mr. Crandall, and lay interpretation can result in printed reports which are misleading and thereby cause unnecessary concern to the public. We remain ready to help you with official interpretations whenever you give us an opportunity.[19]

TURK's long-range fallout path was first west-southwest, then northeast, crossing the Utah border near Gandy. While the lower levels of the cloud were spreading over southwestern Nevada, the top of the mushroom had become entrained in a fast-moving jet stream heading east. That evening, while the rest of the nation was watching Steve Allen host the "Seventh Annual Emmy Awards" on NBC, TURK's mushroom was crossing the four corners' area of Utah, Colorado, Arizona, and New Mexico. An hour later, while Mary Martin was starring in a "Producer's Showcase" version of "Peter Pan," TURK's radioactive cloud crossed into New Mexico northwest of Santa Fe. On March 10, 1955, the radioactive fallout from TURK blanketed much of the Midwest from Colorado to Ohio.

After TURK, Los Alamos scientists continued their quest for the perfect tactical weapon. HORNET was to be another small blast, perhaps intended for use with artillery weapons. Among the scientific studies to be conducted at the HORNET shot was an experiment to determine if smog would help protect a city against the heat of a nuclear fireball. No troops would be needed for HORNET, only mice. The animals were placed in cages surrounding the 300-foot tower and in the vicinity of a number of smoke pots.

A test at UPSHOT-KNOTHOLE had indicated that a smoke barrier could be an effective shield against some of the thermal effects of a nuclear detonation. The scientists wanted to repeat the experiment using more accurate measuring devices. Even the smog droplets generated in this test were to be of a specific size: 30-millionths of an inch in diameter. By carefully positioning the smoke generators, they knew that the black, sooty cloud would probably extend 50 feet into the air, well within reach of the fireball.

Early on the morning of March 12, the HORNET device, about the size of a small suitcase, was transported to the top of the 300-foot tower.

At 5:20 A.M. Pacific Standard Time, the device detonated, producing a flash that was seen as far away as Los Angeles and Sacramento. Because of a low-level air inversion, the shock "skipped" across the countryside. Residents of Inyokern, California, 130 miles to the west, felt the shock wave, while the rumble of the detonation was heard in a 100-mile radius.[20]

An hour after the shot, monitors found ground zero to be unusually hot for such a small device: 2,500 roentgens/hour within 100 yards of ground zero. Apparently, the oil mist had somehow added to the radioactivity. The off-site radiation contour displayed a wide wedge that extended toward the Utah border, then south and east toward Littlefield, Arizona. Two days later, while the nation was watching the "Hedda Hopper" episode of "I Love Lucy," radioactive fallout from HORNET was detected in a small area near Amarillo-Lubbock, Texas, and in a very large area completely encircling the state of Illinois and much of Indiana and Michigan.

While the HORNET cloud was touring the nation, including the town of Hornet, Missouri, U.S. troops were getting ready for the fifth shot in the series, BEE.

TEAPOT: BEE

Unlike HORNET, the BEE detonation would involve troops, 3,000 in all. In one planned activity, 1,972 enlisted men and 299 officers of the Third Marine Corps Provisional Atomic Exercise Brigade would storm an objective near ground zero. Marine Helicopter Transport Group 36 as well as Air Support Squadron 363 would provide air support.

The exercise required the participants to wait out the blast in trenches about 2 miles from the tower. Immediately after the shot, the troops were to be marched and airlifted to the objectives—"William," "Nan," and "Sugar"—all located 15 kilometers or a little over 9 miles west of ground zero. After taking the objectives, the marines would visit the display area located adjacent to the detonation site.

At 5:05 A.M. Pacific Standard Time, BEE was detonated, spewing molten pieces of the tower back toward the ground. The flash, as usual, lit up the skies in Los Angeles, San Francisco, and Phoenix. Eight minutes later, the mushroom cloud towered 35,455 feet above the desert floor, an ice cap forming on its surface. Several minutes after the detonation, residents of Las Vegas and St. George, Utah, felt the ground shake.[21]

After leaving the test site, the nuclear cloud immediately turned to the southeast, directly toward Las Vegas. For the first time in five years, the city of 51,000 experienced direct fallout from a nuclear blast. Radiation levels of between 0.008 and 0.02 roentgen/hour were recorded there.[22,23]

On March 22, the *Las Vegas Review–Journal* carried this statement: "Fallout on Las Vegas and vicinity following this morning's detonation was very low and without any effects on health."

TEAPOT: ESS

Early on the morning of March 23, the 271st Engineer Combat Battalion excavated a 67-foot shaft in the Nevada soil in the northern section of the test site. In this shaft was placed a small atomic device. ESS, perhaps meaning "subsurface," was the only underground shot scheduled for the TEAPOT series. It was designed by the Los Alamos Lab and, like most of their other creations, it was small. The projected yield would be not much over a kiloton.

The Department of Defense had asked Los Alamos to come up with an atomic demolition "satchel" charge small enough to be carried by one man. ESS was probably a test of their first prototype. Eventually, the experimentation would result in the 58.6-pound Special Atomic Demolition Munition (SADM) charge also called "the suitcase bomb."[24]

ESS was placed at the end of what would eventually become Circle Road, a short distance and almost parallel to Rainer Mesa Road. About 800 troops were stationed across Rainer Mesa Road, 5 miles southwest of ground zero. Since ESS was considered a shallow underground shot, scientists knew there would be an enormous amount of fallout. One rule of thumb is that a nuclear weapon, placed inside a concrete structure, will vaporize its weight in kilotons. ESS would probably vaporize about 1,000 tons of rock and sand, then send it skyward. No one wanted to be anywhere near it.

The ESS detonation left a 96-foot deep, very hot crater.[25,26]

The lowest levels of the cloud moved south over Mexico while the upper, 10,000-foot level crossed Lubbock and Dallas–Fort Worth, Texas, Knoxville, Tennessee, and Richmond, Virginia, before crossing the East Coast. Hot areas on the days of March 23 and 24 included Las Vegas, Dallas–Fort Worth and Houston.

APPLE-1, WASP PRIME

March 29 would be a very busy day for the Nevada Test Site personnel. Not one, but two shots were scheduled, both in the morning. Only the larger of the two would involve troops. Plans called for about 600 troops of Exercise Desert Rock VI to observe the burst from trenches located at the southwestern end of the display area, 3,200 meters (1.98 miles) from the tower. After the detonation, troops would tour the area, noting the condition of the tanks, jeeps, mortars, and other equipment. There were no plans for placing any of the 600 personnel closer than half a mile of ground zero.

On the other hand, twenty-four members of the Sixth Army Passive Defense Training Unit would be required to conduct surveys of the actual ground zero area one day after the shot. Their purpose: to establish the 1- and 5-roentgen/hour lines to within 328 feet of the blast site.

Among the programs associated with APPLE-1 were Projects 6.3 and 40.18, tests of equipment that would, hopefully, locate the detonation of atomic bursts during close-in tactical warfare. In case anyone on the ground missed the mushroom cloud, it was up to the equipment and personnel of Battery C, 532nd Field Artillery Observation Battalion to detect the burst by its telltale radiation.

Projects 5.1 and 8.1 involved aircraft flying about 18 miles southeast of the tower. Among the 112 planes to take part in APPLE-1, three would be used to measure heat from the burst. The military was interested not only in the amount of direct heat a nuclear bomb could produce, but the amount of thermal radiation reflected from the desert sand.

Somewhere beneath the heat-detecting plane, on Lookout Mountain, cameras were set up to record the fireball growth rate and take other photographs of the detonation. An analysis of the rate at which a fireball grows is one method of determining the yield of the device. As usual, the engineering firm of Edgerton, Germehausen and Greer was involved in the photography.

At 4:55 A.M., Pacific Standard Time, APPLE-1 was detonated with a force of 14,000 tons of TNT. Although it was smaller than some of the other shots at the test site, its blast effect was enormous. It managed to crack a ceiling and set off burglar alarms in Las Vegas, 75 miles away.

Just prior to the shot the wind had been from the west at a barely detectable 3 mph. At mushroom-altitude, however, the breeze whipped along at a respectable 53 mph—once again in the direction of St. George, Utah.

To complicate matters, the wind at 5,700 feet was from the southwest at 22 mph. The entire nuclear cloud headed straight for Alamo, Nevada, a town of 400 people.[27] Radiation at Alamo would eventually be measured at 1.4 roentgens.

Alamo residents had never cared for the testing. Rumors circulated about horses receiving radiation burns, and the people wondered what the effect would be of the black clouds that continually—or so it seemed—drifted in over them from the test site. The community attitude was expressed in a *New York Times* interview with Deputy Sheriff A. J. Sharp: "We don't like 'em. Nobody's been hurt so far. But we don't know what they may do to our children and grandchildren."

One Alamo child had asked an AEC monitor, "How long do these rays last, mister?" He was told the radiation largely disappears in a few hours.[28]

Five hours after APPLE-1, a small device was released from a B-50 bomber high over the test site. At precisely 10:00 A.M., WASP PRIME exploded 739 feet above the desert floor, with a force of 3 kilotons, creating a doughnut-shaped cloud that eventually rose 28,000 feet into the sky. Forty planes flew in tight patterns around the cloud as it moved off-site in roughly the same direction as had APPLE-1, except that the 18,000-foot trajectory made a meandering journey through the central plains states, finally arriving on the East Coast on April 2 at about 6:00 A.M. Eastern Standard Time.

The next day, Lewis Strauss, chairman of the AEC finally replied to the Lanier-Puck charges that fallout could be damaging to the population. In a *New York Times* interview he called the charges "irresponsible."

"Fallout from the Nevada tests had brought no injuries to anyone," Strauss said. The only damage he was aware of was some eye injury suffered by military personnel in the 1952 and 1953 tests.

In the same report, an agricultural official, Theodore S. Gold, declared that fallout following an enemy attack would not seriously threaten grain stored in elevators and warehouses. The buildings would offer "some protection" from the radioactive dust, and besides, he said, it would be removed through "normal milling operations."[29]

That same day, April 3, 1955, radioactive rain fell over much of central Iowa.[30] Another hot spot occurred on the East Coast, where Boston received radioactive fallout from both the APPLE-1 and WASP PRIME shots.[31]

The next test in the TEAPOT series would involve the first atomic antiaircraft device.[32]

Plans for shot HA (acronym for High Altitude) had actually begun on February 25, when a nonnuclear device, HADR, (High Altitude Dry Run) was detonated. Studies made at this time indicated the feasibility of the high-altitude shot.

One concern of the meteorologists was the location of the tropopause, the boundary between the troposphere and the stratosphere. Below that level, sufficient turbulence would disperse the nuclear cloud. Above that level, however, the air is generally stable. Radioactive particles might stay in such a region for weeks or months. The scientists, therefore, did not particularly want a nuclear cloud to climb past this level. One TEAPOT event, TURK, had breached this boundary by almost a mile.

Calculations indicated that the HA detonation would actually occur about 1,000 feet *above* the tropopause. Another problem: The wind speed at that height, 32,000 feet, wasn't particularly rapid. In fact, it coasted along at only 36 mph. The debris from the 3-kiloton HA might remain over the country for several days.

Shot HA produced a doughnut-shaped cloud that quickly began to dissipate. Five miles below, at ground zero, no induced radioactivity could be detected. This interesting revelation would lead, two years later, to six people standing at ground zero during a nuclear detonation.

HA's radioactive clouds traveled toward the country's midsection. The 45,000-foot trajectory passed just south of Lamar, Missouri, birthplace of former president Harry Truman. Interestingly, the 55,000-foot trajectory crossed just north of Dennison, Texas, birthplace of the current president, Dwight D. Eisenhower.[33]

POST, an unusually small device for one designed by Livermore, was detonated at 4:30 on the morning of April 9. With a yield of 2 kilotons, the cloud reached to only 11,000 feet.[34] At the time of the shot, the weather was calm practically all the way to the base of the mushroom. The cloud hung in the air for what seemed like hours.

The only air movement occurred at the 10,000-foot level, where the air moved along at a leisurely 8 mph—from the north. The cloud slowly moved toward Camp Mercury. Soon, Geiger counters there began picking up radioactivity. Before it slowly drifted to the east, POST stayed around long enough to drop a significant amount of fallout over the entire test site.[35]

The cloud eventually separated into two segments. The 10,000-foot level moved northeast and finally broke up in the Rocky Mountains near Estes Park.

The 14,000-foot trajectory headed due east. After locking on to the same heading as the shot before it, the cloud passed *directly* over Lamar, Missouri, beating HA's aim by a good 20 miles.[36]

MET

The next scheduled shot, MET (Military Effects Test) would involve a 500-foot tower, thirty-eight scientific projects, and 260 troops stationed in trenches about 6 miles from ground zero.

Among some of the more arcane experiments at MET, scientists would be measuring radiation effects on the winter and summer uniforms of Chinese Communist and Russian soldiers.[37]

Despite a relatively modest yield, within seven minutes of detonation MET's cloud stem extended 5 miles into the sky.[38]

MET broke into four trajectories as it crossed the United States. The 18,000-foot trajectory, remnants of the stem, followed the southermost route, moving across Utah, Colorado, Kansas, and Missouri.

At 6:30 on the evening of April 16, the nuclear cloud crossed the small Missouri town of Paris. At the Main Street Theater the featured movie was *Gunfighters* with Randolph Scott and Barbara Britton.[39]

Though it was only April, the night was quite warm and the outdoor drive-in theater west of town had opened. The movie that evening was *Wyoming Renegade* in Technicolor. Those sitting in their cars couldn't know about the tiny, radioactive particles of silica, iron, and cobalt—microscopic remnants of the top of MET's tower—that were slowly falling from the sky.[40]

The debris from MET hovered above the continental United States for an unusually long time. The next day, most the central Atlantic states and New England received significant fallout. A trace of radioactive rain fell in Boston that day, and the city received 600 millicuries/100 square miles. Twenty days later, MET's particles were still showering large sections of the United States.

Three days after MET, a convoy of M-48 tanks, dubbed Task Force Razor, left Camp Irwin, California, and began a four-day trek across the Mojave Desert. Their destination: the Nevada Test Site.

APPLE-2

In early May, while the American air attaché was being entertained at the Tushino air show, a number of things were taking place around the United States. In Midland, Texas, the Fiesta Drive-In Theater featured *Woman's World* while those visiting the Tower Theater ("Always a Good Show") enjoyed a western. Though the area was experiencing a terrible drought, business was on the upswing. A local car dealer was offering good deals on his DeSotos: "Pick from the power pack—55 color combinations—22 interiors!" The newspaper offered such comics as "Martha Wayne," "Lil' Abner" and "Freckles and His Friends." "Ozark Ike," a recent entry, was about baseball. The new television station, KMID-TV, came on the air at 3:00 P.M. offering a movie. At 4:55 P.M., the kids watched the five-minute "Crusader Rabbit," featuring "Rags" the Tiger.

In Paris, Missouri, country doctors were preparing to administer the new Salk polio vaccine at $3.00 a shot. At the hardware store, homeowners could buy a lawnmower for $12.95 or a wire leaf rake for just 74 cents—"Perfect for spring lawn work." The next day, April 22, the drive-in would feature *A Bullet Is Waiting,* and on Saturday, the Main Street Theater would unveil its "new panoramic giant-size screen" with a Roy Rogers–Dale Evans movie.

Those with television sets no doubt watched the "I Love Lucy" episode in which Lucy was trapped on a terrace and had to climb down the side of a building using bedsheets.

Children with an extra 10 cents might have bought a copy of *After Dark* comics at the nearby Rexall Drugstore. On April 29, a Friday, television viewers watched "Science Fiction Theater's" host Truman Bradley as he introduced "Out of Nowhere," an episode starring Richard Arlen.

In Lubbock, Texas, singer-guitarist Buddy Holly could be found in the studios of radio station KDAV practicing for his weekly show, while in Brooklyn, high school junior Neil Sedaka was still dating Carole Klein and listening to "Peter Tripps' Top 40 Hits" on the local radio station.

Within three weeks all of these people and places would again have something in common.

The detonation scheduled for May 5 was to be a media event, military exercise, and public relations gamble to end them all. One of the major projects at the APPLE-2 shot would involve Civil Defense. Another specially constructed Doom Town—this one complete with two-story frame houses, paved streets, kitchen appliances, and mannequins—was placed within close range of the 500-foot detonation tower. As the weapon detonated, remote cameras would record the effects on the structures and the "residents" inside.

Civil Defense officials from across the country had been invited to view the May 5 shot. As a result, civilians—"just plain folks"—would be allowed in the trenches at position Baker about 2 miles from ground zero. One of them, Miss Helen Leininger of Jackson Heights, New York, was a representative of the Paper Cup and Container Institute. Another civilian at the site was Arthur Landstreet, a community Civil Defense official.

At the same distance but in a different location, military observers would watch the detonation. Among the people to file into the 5-foot-deep trenches that day included Lieutenant Colonel Frances Gunn, chief nurse of the Sixth Army. Also in the trench would be Reva Cullen, a Denver reporter.

Task Force Razor had arrived, somewhat intact, on April 21, and had bivouacked in Yucca Flat, 9 miles from the tower.[41] From the campsite, the tower was a speck in the distance. Troops not accustomed to nuclear detonations wondered if they would be able to see the blast from this distance.

To feed the hundreds of observers, caterers from as far away as Chicago arrived to set up grills on the sands of the test site. Many of the grills were within a short distance of the melted and twisted MET tower.

Originally, the shot had been set for April 26, but the unusual weather conditions that had plagued the MET cloud had postponed APPLE-2. Still, meteorologists were not completely satisfied with the conditions in the upper atmosphere.[42] Scientists were hopeful the nuclear cloud would drift north, away from the test site—and the civilians—but, as TURK had proven, there was no certainty of anything.

The day before the shot, 800 personnel of Desert Rock VI began preparing for the shot. The men attended an indoctrination course that briefly explained the hazards of radiation. Rumors abounded that President Eisenhower would make a special visit to the test site to watch the shot. NBC camera crews from the "Today" show were at the site to record—by remote cameras, of course—the destruction of Doom Town.

About 2 to 3 miles south of the tower, the 1,000 men of Task Force Razor began checking the tanks, positioning them northbound.[43] The drive across the desert had caused a few problems with the engines and treads and no one wanted to be stranded in a radiation area with a dead tank. Since arriving at the test site, the task force had rehearsed the planned maneuver over and over again.

The scheduled maneuver was simple. From Tank Assembly Position in midvalley, the task force had driven north, parallel to Mercury Highway, and had taken up positions due south of the shot tower. Farthest back, southeast of Mine Mountain and 4 miles from ground zero, was the armored artillery. About 2 miles further north, one M-75 and twenty M-59 armored personnel carriers took up positions, while still closer, only 1.8 miles from ground zero, two M-41 tanks and fifty-five M-48 tanks waited.

After the detonation, upon signal from the commander, the task force would charge ground zero, driving parallel to the equipment display. At another signal, the entire group would turn to the northwest, intersect Tippipah Road, then drive through a narrow valley cutting through 1,100-foot-high Syncline Ridge, northwest of the APPLE-2 tower. Leaving the valley, they would take "Objective A." A few miles to the southwest, helicopters from the First Combat Aviation Company would airlift troops over 1,200-foot-high Mine Mountain to "Objective B."

The entire operation would take only ninety minutes from time of detonation. However, three times since they had arrived, the task force had been at this ready position, and three times the shot was delayed because of bad weather. In the hot, dusty desert the men were growing impatient. Was there or wasn't there going to be an atomic explosion?

On instructions, the men rotated the tank turrets to the rear. All sight apertures were sealed with duct tape and hatch seals were tested. The insides of the tanks were to be absolutely light-tight.

In the distance, the tower looked small, a thin dark line of metal against blue sky. The men found it difficult to comprehend the energy that would emanate from the top of that line at five o'clock the next morning.[44]

Desert Rock personnel, awaiting the shot exchanged rumors. Asphalt had been laid down in order to curb fallout—this had been done only once before, at the monster shot TURK. Most agreed the May 5 shot would be spectacular.

At 3:30 on the morning of May 5, two hours before shot-time, Anthony Leviero, a reporter from the *New York Times*, arrived by jeep at the tank site closest to the tower. Excerpts from his account of the detonation:

> This reporter jeeped across the desert to tank 21, Second Platoon, Baker Company at 3:00 A.M.. The thermometer read 50 degrees and there was a full moon. Joshua and yucca trees silhouetted above the sage.
>
> Lieutenant Ralph S. Howard of Albany, Georgia, stuck his head out of the tank command turret and greeted his visitor. Lieutenant Howard is 23 years old, a pre-medical student. The massive breech of the 90-mm cannon dominated the interior of the turret. On its left was Corporal Herbert R. Spector of Brooklyn.
>
> The tanks were deployed in a typical wedge formation. A [Able] Company was on the right flank and, because some of its tanks would come closer to the point of explosion, it had radiological safety officers aboard to steer the force away if it got near a danger line. The atomic explosion was scheduled for 5:10 A.M. [Pacific Daylight Time].
>
> Suddenly Corporal Spector, listening to his earphones, raised his finger and said, "It's thirty seconds to zero. I think that's what he said." But he had heard wrong. It was only three seconds to zero.
>
> Eerie light flooded into the tank. It poured through the two slits and seemed to come through other apertures, even though all the other openings were baffled in one way or another. The unearthly light seemed to last a long time, but it was about twenty seconds. Before anyone could figure out just what was going on, the earth shook. The tank, with its front of four-inch armor facing the atomic blast, rocked upwards slightly, then settled. Dust billowed and darkened the inside of the turret.[45]

Gladwin Hill, another reporter for the *New York Times,* witnessed the event from News Nob:

> From an initial pinpoint of light, the explosion burgeoned in a fraction of a second into an awesome, rolling, orange-red fireball of dazzling brilliance, more than 1,000 feet in diameter. It continued to churn viciously for twenty seconds. Meanwhile, it became enveloped in an iridescent gaseous purple sheath, the result of ionization, or electrification of surrounding air.
>
> Observers eight miles away had to wear almost opaque goggles for the first three seconds of the explosion, and it appeared clearly even through them. People without goggles had to turn their backs for the initial flash.
>
> Surging upward as its incandescence faded into a turgid black-brown shaft, the explosion sucked up dust from the ground and billowed out into

the characteristic "mushroom" about 15,000 feet high. A white "icecap" formed on top as it hit the cold upper air. Within a few minutes the mushroom reached 40,000 feet. The winds were light and it hung over Yucca Flat. Breezes hit its still-turbulent stalk and distorted the lower part into a second mushroom underneath the first, as the cloud was attenuated for miles to the northeast.

As the mushroom grew, another gray-white cloud developed at its base and spread out along the ground. It was dust, kicked up by the explosion's shock wave. Steadily it grew in both width and height, rolling across the desert like a smoke screen or curtain, until it hung over the whole eight-by-twenty-mile expanse of Yucca Flat. It stayed for hours.[46]

Leviero again:

It was like being at the center of the explosion itself. . . . The interior teemed with choking dust, and it seemed as if the tank itself was ripping apart. [Then] at a signal from Lieutenant Howard the turret swung around and the tank's engines roared. The first 90-mm shell (a blank) was on its way, filling the tank with a chemical smell. Gun bursts roared all along the line. Hatches were now opened. Outside, above the tank force, hung the great mushroom cloud of the atomic blast.

Roaring northward across Yucca Flat, the task force charged toward Ground Zero, which was now occupied by a cloud instead of a tower. Then it veered west, to its objective, Syncline Ridge, about seven miles away.[47]

In the trenches closest to the blast, ten instructors from various army schools had tacked a playing card on a stick above the trench. Though the white parts of the card were intact, the black were faintly scorched. The instructors said they found the experience "interesting."[48]

Arthur Landstreet, in the civilian trenches 2 miles from the blast, remembered it differently: "The flash was so terrific that even with closed eyes it seemed as bright as looking into a flashbulb from a camera only a few feet away. Seismic shock followed immediately. The trench seemed to rock back and forth for several seconds, then the noise and blast, ten times the thunderclap of lightning within a hundred yards. The blast was sudden and sharp. It felt like someone had taken a sandbag and struck me in the middle of the back . . . tons of dirt were whirling and there was dust everywhere. We had nothing but a brown, drab sight as our only reward."[49]

Soon after the shot, helicopters began transporting soldiers over Mine Mountain, where two glass searchlight lenses had been fused and blackened by the heat from APPLE-2.

After the detonation, Lieutenant Colonel John G. Whelock III, commander of Task Force Razor, told reporter Leviero that he believed his tanks and armored personnel could have been within 2,000 yards instead of 3,200 yards of the blast. He went on to say that two of his personnel carriers "had got to within about 900 yards of ground zero."

What had happened was that two of the twenty-five M-59 armored personnel carriers at the rear of the formation had temporarily lost contact with the rest of the group. Instead of turning left, they had continued on toward the epicenter. Apparently, they discovered their mistake when they realized they were the only ones there.

The operation proved, among other things, that civilians could be coaxed into trenches to witness an atomic explosion.[50]

The APPLE-2 detonation had been huge, 29 kilotons. The cloud had reached over 10,000 feet into the stratosphere. Four hundred yards from ground zero (at half the distance of the errant personnel carriers) the radiation monitors discovered 500 roentgens/hour. Initially, the cloud had moved north until about 12:00 P.M., when it abruptly turned east, toward Utah.[51]

The nuclear cloud itself remained in a tight pattern as it crossed the central part of the country, meeting up with a series of very strong thunderstorms. On May 6, just east of Denver, down drafts on the lee side of the Rockies forced an enormous amount of fallout to the ground. Monitors found intensites there as high as 5,500 millicuries/100 square miles, or 73 disintegrations/second for every square foot of surface area.

Residents were greeting a drab, rainy dawn in Paris, Missouri, at 6:00 on May 6. Forty thousand feet above them, the remnants of APPLE-2's mushroom cloud was passing by, moving east-southeast. While there had been a light rain at the time, the area received only a slight amount of radiation.[52]

The next day, the entire central plains states was receiving radiation from the sky. Monitors in Missouri recorded 1,400 millicuries/100 square miles, while west Texas received between 380 and 1,600.

As the cloud moved over central Illinois, viewers might have been watching James Dean's last performance on television, "The Unlighted Road" on CBS's "Schlitz Playhouse of Stars."

By May 8, most of the cloud had cleared the United States, leaving the country over the states of North and South Carolina. That same day, hot spots were found in the West Virginia area over Charleston, the birthplace of AEC chairman Strauss. New York City monitors recorded 160 millicuries/100 square miles—that is, the fallout on each square foot disintegrated at a rate of two atoms per second.[53]

But it was not over. During the next six days, the debris continued to pour from the storm clouds. More hot spots appeared along the Ohio River valley, eastern and central Texas, Missouri, and much of the south.

By May 14, while radioactivity from the 29-kiloton APPLE-2 was still being detected over much of the mountain states as well as the Deep South, plans were being made for the May 15 detonation of a device equally as large as APPLE-2.

In the wake of the APPLE-2 event, the entertainment media was flooded with a new group of characters, all suffering various radiation exposures, all benefiting from the experience. Long before Stan Lee's *Spiderman* was bitten by a radioactive spider, cartoonists were involved in the creation of any number of atomic mice, bunnies, and other animals who required constant doses of radioactivity or "U-235 pills" to keep them going in their war against evil.

During the last of the TEAPOT series, cartoonists in New York City were putting the finishing touches on their new creation "Atomic Rabbit" that would debut in August. Somewhere on the back lots of Hollywood, filming was scheduled to begin on a new B-movie, *The Atomic Man*. It was about a scientist who, after being exposed to radiation, finds he is out of synchronization with time. Being able to react to things before they happen gives the lead character a decided advantage over others. It was reminiscent of the 1954 Mickey Rooney film *The Atomic Kid*, in which a poor desert prospector finds, after being exposed to an A-bomb, that he is able to beat the slot machines at Las Vegas.

In 1955, there were probably any number of children who imagined that exposure to radiation could turn them superhuman. To cartoonists and Hollywood scriptwriters, there were no bad effects from radiation exposure.

And on May 15, while radios across the nation played "The Ballad of Davy Crockett" and "Cherry Pink and Apple Blossom White," the countdown had begun on ZUCCHINI, the final shot of the TEAPOT series.[54]

ZUCCHINI was detonated at 5:00 A.M. Pacific Daylight Time.[55]

A band of radiation 60 miles wide crossed into Arizona and Utah. The center of the band was located about 10 miles south of the three-state junction.[56]

The wind direction and speed varied considerably. At the surface, the slight breeze from the northwest was barely noticeable. As a result, the base cloud hovered in the area for hours, creating a brown haze over the test site. At the cloud top the wind was from the west-southwest at 80 mph.

Meteorologists had predicted the cloud would move to the west-southwest. They were wrong. To their consternation, the atomic cloud moved east across Utah and then became entrained in a low-pressure cyclone, looping back up over Montana before splitting into two equal segments. One segment traveled west crossing over Coeur d'Alene, Idaho to Tacoma, Washington, then south over Portland and Sacramento before turning east again to intercept the Texas-Oklahoma border. The other segment crossed high into Canada, then turned southwest, cutting across the north central states, the eastern Midwest, and finally leaving the continent along the border between the Carolinas.

That same night, May 15, only two hot spots were found in the continental U.S.: Salt Lake City and along the eastern border of Colorado and Wyoming. The next day, the hot spots merged to include large portions of Utah, northern Colorado, Montana, and most of Wyoming.

On May 17, heavy rain falling in the Denver–Boulder–Colorado Springs area had deposited a considerable amount of fallout, up to 19 disintegrations/second/square foot. At the same time, Kalispell, and Libby, Montana, just east of the Bitterroot Mountains, received dry fallout producing 5 disintegrations/second/square foot.

By the evening of May 20, ZUCCHINI's fallout had blanketed the entire United States west of Ohio with measurable radioactive fallout. In addition, a hot spot included an area from central Oklahoma–northern Texas to eastern Alabama. Fort Smith, Arkansas, that evening, received an unusually high dose of 3,700 millicuries/100 square miles, or 49 disintegrations/second/square foot. ZUCCHINI had been the last in the TEAPOT series, but it was by no means the least.[57]

WIGWAM

In the sixties, when assessments were finally made on fallout levels, it was discovered that one city was relatively clean. Oddly, this city was also located near the Nevada Test Site, but the fact that it was upwind of the detonations made San Diego, California, a town relatively fallout-free—that is, until May 14, 1955, when it found itself located *downwind* of a 30-kiloton shot.

While the AEC at the Nevada Test Site was busy preparing for the MET shot, the navy was making final preparations for a nuclear test of its own, shot WIGWAM.[58] The only detonation in a series of the same name, this event was scheduled to take place at north 29 degrees, west 126 degrees—a spot in the ocean about 500 miles southwest of San Diego.

The navy, envisioning a war in which atomic depth charges would be used, wanted to learn how much of a nuclear punch a well-built submarine could take. During the CROSSROADS test, the submarine *Skate* had not done so well; perhaps the new test model would be more bomb-proof.

So on May 14, a model submarine named *Squaw-13* was submerged beneath a floating barge, stationed at an undisclosed distance from the "Zero Barge" carrying the atomic device. Surrounding the Zero Barge, presumably at a safe distance, were twenty-four ships and 6,097 personnel.

At detonation, an intensely hot gas bubble formed, then shot to the surface, 2,000 feet away. From above, the first sign of the detonation looked like an ever-widening circle of dark water, a "slick." Forming a concentric circle inside the slick was a ring of white water, the "crack," caused by a reflection of the shock wave off the surface.

As with the larger Eniwetok shots, a plume immediately formed, traveling upward at 200 mph.[59]

Analysis of the explosion revealed the hot bubble had vibrated beneath the surface for about three seconds. Observers didn't see the plume until fully ten seconds after detonation. Ninety seconds after the shot, the plume began to fall back to create a roaring, mist-enshrouded waterfall 1,900 feet high and 4,600 feet across. This was the base surge, and scientists knew from the Eniwetok tests that it was extremely radioactive.

Thirteen minutes after the detonation, all that was left in the area was a ring of foam about 2 miles across. At the same time, radiation monitors aboard a monitoring barge 5 miles downwind from point zero recorded a radiation level of 400 roentgens/hour. Eight minutes later, the radiation level dropped to 140 roentgens/hour. The explosion had formed a cloud 2 miles long with a volume of about half a cubic mile. Scientists sampling the cloud found a variety of hot particles; most of them were irregularly shaped and opaque (41.4 percent). A little over a fourth contained transparent and opaque areas while a fifth of the cloud was represented by microscopic marine creatures. Two percent consisted of microscopic radioactive threads from an unknown source.

The model sub was completely destroyed by the burst. Two ships, the YAG-39 and the YAG-40, had been in part of the nuclear cloud as it drifted south over the water. When these ships reached San Francisco, they were both quite hot; analysis of most of the exposed areas revealed a level of 50,000 counts per minute.

Apparently no weather analysis was performed to determine the ultimate destination of the radioactive cloud.[60]

The year 1955 had been a busy one for the men at the Nevada Test Site. The test series there had been the most complex ever. While the fallout produced during TEAPOT had been somewhat less than in the series preceding it, the AEC began to sense growing public concern with the touchy subject of fallout, particularly bomb debris from Nevada. Perhaps 1956 would offer a brief respite of sorts. The only bona fide nuclear tests would take place in the Pacific, far away from St. George, Cedar City, and the irate sheep ranchers.[61] However, 1956 would be an election year, and the AEC commissioners sincerely hoped that nuclear testing, fallout, and strontium-90 wouldn't be an issue in the Democratic campaign.

Unfortunately for the AEC, it would be one of the *main* issues.

In the mid-1950s the atomic bomb carried with it a certain mystique, an aura of terrible energy and danger that instilled in most Americans a sense of excitement, fear, and curiousity. This attitude is exemplified in an article by reporter Gladwin Hill appearing in the June 9, 1957, issue of the *New York Times*: "Watching the Bombs Go Off."

> *Las Vegas, Nevada*: This is the best time in history for the non-ancient but none the less honorable pastime of atom-bomb watching. For the first time, the Atomic Energy Commission's Nevada test program will extend

through the summer tourist season, into September. It will be the most extensive test series ever held, with upward of fifteen detonations. And for the first time, the AEC has released a partial schedule, so that tourists interested in seeing a nuclear explosion can adjust their itineraries accordingly.

Several of the explosions will be larger than the ones detonated on Japan in World War II, and at least one will be three to four times as large. The detonation point is remote enough from normally traveled areas so that there is no danger of anyone's being blown up. A major precaution for outside observers, however, which should be noted immediately, is: don't look in the direction of the explosions through field glasses. More on this later. Dates for the eight forthcoming detonations which have been announced are June 25 and 27, July 9, 15 and 25, Aug. 8 and 19 and Sept. 1. These are all subject to minor change if weather is unfavorable. But summer weather prospects are stable enough, and the shots are likely to go off with no more than a day or two's delay at most.

The tests on June 27, July 25 and Aug. 19 will be more powerful than the Japan bombs, which had the explosive force of 20,000 tons of TNT. There may be other big ones. There will be a half dozen or more additional detonations, probably interspersed in this schedule. They probably will be announced at least a day or two before they go off. The scheduled shots are those for which special observers will be admitted to the test site. The general public will not be admitted. But there are many vantage points from which anyone can get an impressive view of the explosions.

The AEC proving ground starts 65 miles north of Las Vegas, just off U.S. 95, which runs to Tonopah. The proving ground itself is a rectangle only forty miles long and sixteen miles wide, but it is in the midst of a 4,000-square-mile Air Force bombing and gunnery range from which the public is excluded. If one is interested simply in proximity, the closest approachable points to the blasts are along U.S. 95 in the vicinity of Indian Springs, 45 miles north of Las Vegas. A couple of low ranges of mountains lie between this section and the Yucca Flat test area, barring a direct view of the focus of the explosions. But they are huge enough for plenty of light and noise to be perceptible.

Another close approach, on the eastern side of the whole business, is along U.S. 93, which runs north from Glendale, Utah. (Both U.S. 95 and U.S. 93 branch off U.S. 91, the main east-west thoroughfare from Salt Lake City to Los Angeles.) On U.S. 93, the best vantage points are in the vicinity of Alamo, Nevada, 61 miles north of Glendale. Alamo is only about 55 miles east of Yucca Flat, but here too there are intervening low mountains. The best view of the detonations can be obtained from 12,000-foot Mount Charleston, which lies just east of U.S. 95, only an hour's ride from Las Vegas, over good roads. This is only about 50 miles from the detonation point. From here, the bulk of most of the explosions is visible above the distant low mountains bordering Yucca Flat.

There is an Army radar installation on top of the mountain, and only accredited press representatives will be allowed up to its highest eminence, Angel's Peak. But there are a number of comparable viewing points at slightly lower levels. These can be approached by either of two roads branching off of U.S. 95—State Route 39 branches off 15 miles north of Las Vegas and Route 52 branches off 13 miles farther. Both wind up the mountain. The point is to keep one's orientation to the test area during these convolutions. Most of the firings will be just before dawn, to facilitate test photography, but some will be in daylight. The times of the various tests have not been specified, but will be indicated sometime beforehand. This information is available in Las Vegas a day or two before the tests from such sources as hotels, the chamber of commerce, and the State Highway Patrol.

In most of the explosions, the light is brighter than the sun. Off the test site, they can be viewed safely with the naked eye. But binoculars act as magnifiers and can cause eye burns. With camera lenses, the short length of exposure makes the concentrations of light innocuous. Cameras can be set at the smallest aperture possible, with the fastest exposures. The light from most detonations is bright enough even at 50 miles to trigger photoelectric cell shutter actuators. With pre-dawn detonations, it is dark enough to open shutters a moment before detonation time. The fireballs from the explosions sometimes roll as long as a minute, providing plenty of time for a series of pictures.

In the dawn's early light in the wake of a detonation, the atomic cloud can be seen attentuating across the sky. It may come over an observer's head. There is virtually no danger from radioactive fallout. But anyone who is worried about having been exposed to it can go to the nearest town and inquire about the nearest AEC radiation monitoring team. These teams cover virtually all communities within a 200-mile radius of the test site, and check people and vehicles which have been exposed to fallout.

Aside from the danger of looking at explosions through field glasses, the chief hazard in atom-bomb watching is the omnipresent danger of automobile accidents. With detonations which might momentarily blind drivers near by, the AEC issues warnings and sometimes highway patrolmen establish momentary roadblocks. A worse danger than the light is that in the excitement of the moment, people get careless in their driving. The best base for bomb-viewing expeditions is Las Vegas, which has a couple of hundred motels and hotels of all types, with fairly standard rates.

A perennial question from people who do not like pre-dawn expeditions is whether the explosions can be seen from Las Vegas, 65 miles away. The answer is that sometimes enough of a flash is visible to permit a person to say that he has "seen an atomic bomb." But it is not the same as viewing one from relatively close range, which generally is a breathtaking experience.

1956: The Year of Fallout

On July 29, 1955, at a White House breakfast, President Eisenhower was in a jovial, confident mood. Things were going so well, he told a group of Republicans meeting with him, that the GOP, "properly unified," could keep control of the presidency "forever."[1] This, of course, did not sit well with the Democrats. The following week, at a meeting of Democratic governors in Chicago, several in attendance voiced their support for a familiar name, Adlai Stevenson. He had been picked by Truman in 1952 "to save the world from Dwight Eisenhower" and had subsequently given Ike a tough race.[2] Perhaps he could do it again in 1956.

To be sure, the times had changed considerably. McCarthyism, a liability to Republicans in 1952, was now only a memory. Vice President Richard M. Nixon had quieted down somewhat from the days of Whittaker Chambers and Alger Hiss.[3] Gone, too, were the charges that Stevenson was an "egghead" who spoke only to the intellectuals.[4]

In addition, there had been problems with Ike's cabinet. On July 13, HEW secretary Oveta Culp Hobby resigned reportedly because of her remark that free Salk polio vaccine to the country's children would be "socialized medicine" by "the back door."[5] On May 16, 1955, Hobby had issued a "voluntary" plan to distribute the vaccine. The next day, Oregon's Democratic senator, Wayne Morse, called for her dismissal citing "gross incompetence."[6]

On the balance, maybe the Illinois Democrat would win this time around. Stevenson, however, wasn't so sure. Still smarting from the loss four years ago, he didn't relish the idea of mixing it up with Eisenhower again. He told the governors that he would postpone his decision.[7]

With the election a year away, a Gallup Poll indicated that 51 percent of the Democrats polled favored Stevenson, followed by Tennessee senator Estes Kefauver at 16 percent.[8] Kefauver had made a name for himself in the summer of 1950 during his investigation of organized crime. The networks, not having much else to offer viewers at the time, televised the hearings. Thousands of people watched as Kefauver's committee skillfully trapped alleged crime boss Frank Costello into admitting various acts of wrongdoing.[9] Kefauver was tough, smart, and likeable.

In November, both Stevenson and Kefauver gave perfunctory speeches claiming that what America needs is "moderation" in government. The performance seemed to lack a certain fire: Eisenhower had just suffered a heart attack and currently enjoyed the nation's sympathy. A "new," moderate Nixon was emerging, one that had disavowed the extremism of McCarthy. The economy was in relatively good shape. What the Democrats needed were good campaign issues. One they settled on was, they thought, sure to arouse public debate: Citing fallout as a health hazard, the Democratic candidate would call for a test ban on nuclear weapons.

Privately, many inside the Democratic campaign were worried. They knew that the ethnic and blue-collar voters generally approved of a strong defense, and that meant nuclear testing.[10] And if that meant fallout, that was okay with them, particularly if the scientists *said* it was safe.

Stevenson, however, had made up his mind. On December 14, 1955, he said that he would enter the primaries in California, Florida, Pennsylvania, and his home state of Illinois. Two days later, Estes Kefauver announced his intentions for the office of president.

On Thursday, January 19, AEC commissioner Libby, in a speech at Northwestern University, took issue with allegations that fallout was harmful, saying that the radioactive fallout from the testing was insignificant. He went on to discount the adverse genetic effects of strontium-90.[11]

A month later, AEC chairman Lewis Strauss, in an interview, admitted that there is a "calculated risk" in weapons tests, but that the danger is "greatly exaggerated."[12] In April, Commissioner Libby reiterated his position that there were no health hazards of strontium "so far" from bomb tests.[13]

During the spring, the only voices against the testing seemed to be coming from the Democratic presidential hopefuls. Operation REDWING had begun with hardly a ripple of dissention. It looked as though the testing was dead in the water. Democratic campaign strategists concentrated on other issues, such as the "old-age security" program and national health care.

Then, on May 29, air force general Starbird casually let it slip that not only would there be additional testing in the U.S. in October (he was wrong), but that a new test range was under consideration. It would be located near Albuquerque, New Mexico.[14] Almost exactly two weeks later, a flurry of scientists descended on the problem of radiation. On June 12, the prestigious National Academy of Sciences issued conflicting reports warning that though even tiny amounts of radiation were harmful, the radiation from fallout was less than from natural sources. The six scientists on the National Academy of Sciences Genetics Commission claimed no effect on the weather was found, but one commissioner warned of problems associated with strontium-90.[15]

On June 21, an atomic scientist who had once worked at Los Alamos, Ralph Lapp, gave a speech in Metuchen, New Jersey, warning of the cumulative effects from strontium, and not long after that, a newspaper report claimed that a United Nations commission may study effects of radioactive fallout on the world's milk supply.[16,17]

On August 16, after almost a year of campaigning, Adlai Stevenson won the Democratic presidential nomination. The next day, Estes Kefauver was nominated as the vice presidential candidate.[18]

Both the AEC commissioners and the military brass had been monitoring the campaign closely. They feared that if the Democrats won, the government would close down the nuclear testing. Strategically, most agreed with Edward Teller's assessment that such a ban would be suicidal. Teller had for years distrusted the Soviets in the extreme and felt that any weapons testing ban would give them the opportunity to race past the United States in weapons design and production. Quietly, Teller and other scientists began considering ways of limiting fallout, among them a plan that would involve limiting radioactive nuclear debris to a specified amount based upon what was already disappearing as a result of decay.[19]

Things, however, remained relatively quiet on the nuclear question for almost two months. On September 22, Stevenson outlined his "New America" plan, which included an "old-age security" program "guaranteeing training for citizens over 45 years of age." A week later he called for a massive increase in expenditures for education. On October 8, the Democrats unveiled their "comprehensive national health care plan."

Throughout it all, the public seemed unimpressed. As election day approached, polls indicated the president held to a narrow but definite lead.

Sixteen Degrees of Tilt

Then, on October 15, Stevenson came out with guns blazing, citing strontium-90 as a cause of bone cancer and calling for an "international curb on H-bomb tests."[20] His scientific advisors had informed him that strontium, like its chemical "cousin" calcium, is a bone-seeker. If the radioactive material found its way into the bone, cancer was a possibility. Many inside the Republican campaign conceded, privately, that Stevenson had scored a point. The subject of cancer was emotionally charged. Linking the disease to the Bomb was potentially a political masterstroke. The Eisenhower campaign strategists wondered what the Democrats would say next about nuclear weapons.

They found out the following day. On October 16, at a news conference at the Biltmore Hotel in New York City, Stevenson's running mate, Estes Kefauver, announced that blasts from H-bombs "right now" could blow the planet Earth off its axis. Reporters listened in astonishment as Kefauver even pinpointed the angle of tilt: 16 degrees.

When told of Kefauver's statement, AEC officials were dumbfounded. There was simply no way to answer the charge. Fallout they could handle, but a tilted earth? Quried on the matter, even pro–test ban scientists expressed skepticism.[21] Most knew that even a typical Gulf Coast hurricane packs a wallop approaching megaton range and that an earthquake or a volcanic eruption could release energy equal to hundreds of megatons.[22] A hydrogen bomb could certainly move things around a bit, but *tilt the earth*?

On October 17, while appearing in Springfield, Missouri, Kefauver was pressed for details about the earth tilt. Who had told him? Well, he wouldn't say, exactly. He told the reporters that he had gotten his information from "persons who had information to that effect." Were they atomic scientists? Well, they were people Kefauver "had some confidence in." Well, who *were* they?

"I can't say right now," came the reply.

In the short space of two days, Adlai Stevenson had watched the test ban issue be taken first into the realm of science fiction, then into low comedy.[23] Soon weather experts, astrophysicists, geologists, scientists—anyone who even had a basic familiarity with the earth and its propensity to tilt—came out against Kefauver's theory. The vice presidential candidate gamely replied that the Eisenhower administration "misleads" the public by discounting the dangers from the H-bombs.[24]

Luckily for the Democrats, on October 19, a group of scientists from the prestigious Brookhaven Laboratory stated that strontium-90 was a hazard not only to future generations, but to the present ones: It could cause bone tumors and affect the blood cells.[25] The statement jarred the AEC; Chairman Strauss felt compelled to answer the charge at a speech in Battle Creek, Michigan, denying that atomic weapons "poison" the atmosphere.[26] Several days later, a defensive president issued an Executive Department memo stating that the testing is not a hazard; that strontium-90 is a fission, not a fusion, product.[27] Then next day, nineteen Rochester University scientists, aware of the three-stage (fission-fusion-fission) nature of H-bombs, disputed Ike's contention that strontium-90 came only from fission weapons.

For a while it seemed as though the Democratic candidates were on a roll. They had somehow succeeded in provoking a dispute between the academics and the president. Even Eisenhower himself had been put on the defensive. It was a perfect opportunity for the Democrats to leave science fiction behind and return to the plausible hazards of fallout and strontium-90. But no.

On October 26, just days away from the national election, Adlai Stevenson, in a burst of rhetoric during a Rock Island, Illinois, speech, asked whether Eisenhower would continue the arms race to the point of developing "a force that can shake the earth's axis."[28] In the last week of the campaign, Stevenson raised the possibility of strontium-90 contamination of the milk supply and claimed that children, since they consumed the most milk, would be the principal victims of fallout.[29]

Eisenhower's lead in the polls, however, continued all the way through to election day. With 58 percent of the popular vote and 457 electoral votes, the Republicans handily won the presidential election of 1956.[30]

The Channeling Effect

Alfred and Martha Bordoli heard the election results over the radio. In their ranch near Railroad Valley, they were only 70 miles northeast of the bombs and had been very interested in the possibility of a test ban. The nuclear clouds from the explosions seemed to follow the ridges right up past their home, turning the air hazy and brown, and making life miserable.

During the 1953 and 1955 test series, a young neighbor, Joe Fallani, had taken snapshots of the clouds as they roared north through the mountain passes. Fallini's technique was to snap the picture, place the camera first in a lead case, then put it inside a deep freeze until the film was ready to process. Otherwise the film would be fogged. And if the clouds could fog film, the Bordolis wondered what it could do to people.[31]

They had a special interest in the matter: One day in September 1955, their son had come home from school at lunchtime feeling unusually tired. That evening he began running a fever. Thirteen months later, on October 24, 1956, nine-year-old Martin Bordoli was dead of severe gastrointestinal hemorrhage caused by stem cell leukemia.[32] Remembering the ominous dust clouds moving north toward Elko, they couldn't help but wonder if there was a connection.

There were others interested in the paths of the low-level debris. As early as 1952, Weather Service meteorologists Robert List and Lester Machta had been aware of the channeling effect of the mountain ranges north of the test site. Time and again, often in direct contradiction to the weather patterns, low-level debris would track north, following the ridges to the northern Nevada town of Elko. AEC monitors there repeatedly recorded high levels of radioactivity.

Using data gathered from one particularly dusty underground burst, Uncle, List and Machta found that a low-level cloud moved north along the Belted, Reveille, and Pancake mountain ranges—and over Railroad Valley—at a velocity *greater* than the ambient wind speed. A cloud from an earlier detonation followed a similar path to Elko where it produced fallout levels of 380,000 bursts of radiation per square foot per minute. In their report, submitted to the AEC on March 15, 1952, List and Machta state:

> It must be concluded that the channeling effect of the north-south ridges and valley was such that the debris was carried northward through the valleys at levels below 10,000 feet. . . .
>
> This requires movement at the rate of approximately 20 knots, a speed somewhat greater than the wind speeds measured at the stations nearest to the most likely path of the debris. It is probable that, accompanying the channeling effect of the mountains, there was an acceleration of the wind through the valleys, just as in the period when the Surface [JANGLE] debris moved northward.[33]

The evidence seemed to suggest that two different weather systems seemed to be working north of the test site. While the upper sections of the nuclear cloud, the upper stem and mushroom, climbed to 30,000 and 40,000 feet and moved east across the country, the extreme lower levels, the debris representing the highly radioactive base surge and lower stem, were following their own paths north to Elko and directly over the clutch of farmhouses located north of the test site.

VI

HOT DUST, HARD RAIN

Plumbbob

1957

With the year 1957 came portable electric typewriters, Frisbees, and the chemise, a.k.a. the "sack" dress. Flattops were still popular, as were crewcuts, but some of the more adventurous youths began wearing "D.A." flattops, hair short on the top and long on the sides.

In Hibbing, Minnesota, sixteen-year-old Robert Zimmerman makes a habit of dropping into Crippa's Music on Howard Street to listen to records. Young Zimmerman would soon move east and change his name to Bob Dylan, after Welsh poet Dylan Thomas. In Port Arthur, Texas, eleventh-grader and Future Teachers Association member Janis Joplin climbs water towers and the 300-foot-high rainbow bridge above the Neches River.

In 1957, Lynn Easton and friends at David Douglas High School in Portland, Oregon, are putting together the first "frat band," the Kingsmen, while in San Francisco, Bob Shane, Nick Reynolds, and Dave Guard begin singing together as the Kingston Trio.

On the radio, the songs being played at the beginning of May 1957 are "My Dream" (the Platters), "Bye Bye Love" (the Everly Brothers), and "Bernardine" and "Love Letters in the Sand" (both by Pat Boone). By the end of the month, "Love Letters in the Sand" is at fourth place on the charts, "Little Darlin'" (the Diamonds) is at third place, Gail Storm's "Dark Moon" is number 2, and the top position is held by Elvis with "All Shook Up."

The nuclear tests scheduled for the summer of 1957 would be the biggest, longest, and most controversial in the history of the Nevada testing. Included would be the tallest tower shots to date as well as devices fired while suspended from balloons. There would be misfires; technicians would be required to disarm a "live" nuclear device. One test would involve the largest troop maneuver ever associated with U.S. atomic testing. There is some evidence that the PLUMBBOB series was also associated with the aboveground detonation of a thermonuclear device within the continental United States.

The shot schedule for the operation, originally named Project Pilgrim, had been planned the year before. On December 21, 1956, AEC chairman Lewis Strauss had sent a letter to Eisenhower requesting approval for the tests.

According to the letter, the AEC wanted to: "(1) Proof test a weapon for desired military characteristics before it enters the national stockpile; (2) Provide a firm basis for undertaking the extensive engineering and fabrication efforts which must be expended to carry a 'breadboard' model to a version satisfactory for stockpile purposes; (3) To demonstrate the adequacy, inadequacy, or limitations of current theoretical approaches; and (4) To explore phenomena which can vitally affect the efficiency and performance of weapons but which are not susceptible to prior theoretical analysis of sufficient certainty."[1]

There would be, according to Strauss, twenty-five shots, along with five safety tests. The letter stressed that the shots would be limited in yield "to avoid hazard to participants or the public."

Not mentioned in the letter were a variety of military and civil defense objectives. For one thing, the army was interested in testing its system for detecting underground shots. For this purpose, RAINER, an underground (and, hopefully, low-fallout) shot was planned.

As during the other series, weapons effects on military equipment was planned that would include blast and shock measurements, protection of underground missile-launching structures, and nuclear radiation effects. The military was also interested in knowing how the average foot-solider would stand up, physically and psychologically, to the rigors of the tactical nuclear battlefield.

President Eisenhower signed the approval for PLUMBBOB on December 29, 1956, and on February 23, 1957, the expenditure of plutonium for the test was authorized. The Nevada Test Site manager marked off the areas for the detonations: Most would be in the northern part of the proving grounds, an area of hills and valleys. One event, PRISCILLA, would be located in the southeast corner of the test site, at Frenchman's Flat.[2]

Scientists studying results from previous tests had decided that fallout could be reduced by suspending the devices from huge weather balloons 1,500 feet above the desert. A support group arrived from New Mexico's Sandia Labs to be in charge of that phase of the operations.

Plans were made to provide a total of 18,000 military personnel for exercises in Desert Rock VII and VIII. Many of the troops taking part in the detonations would have only thirty days of military service remaining until release.[3,4]

As a result of fallout problems associated with TEAPOT two years earlier, the military had decided to pay close attention to the problem of off-site radiation. Prior to the blasts, pilots in Beechcraft Bonanzas would fly over the area of suspected fallout. Anyone seen in these danger zones—ranchers, cowboys, sightseers—would be immediately escorted to a safer area.

Within forty-eight hours of shot-time, a perimeter would be established around ground zero. The only personnel allowed inside this zone would be the assembly and firing teams, accompanied by armed security guards. Because the sites were contaminated by previous blasts, those entering frequently would be assigned radiation exposure—"radex" cards. Once the exposure reached 2 roentgens, the entry privileges would be revoked.

After the shot, radiation safety teams would be required to enter the contaminated areas in helicopters and ground vehicles as soon as possible to determine alpha, beta, and gamma intensities. Information concerning levels would be radioed back to the Control Point, where maps would be drawn up showing radiation levels.

Any equipment or personnel found to emit more than 7 roentgens/hour would be tagged and taken to a remote site for decontamination.

PLUMBBOB: BOLTZMANN

Early on the morning of May 28, 1957, thirty-eight reporters, along with Japanese newsman Chugo Koito, assembled on a hill 11 miles from Nevada Test Site Area 7. Koito had been sent by the Kyoto News Agency to cover the first blast in the new series of atomic testing in Nevada. In the distance, the 500-foot tower was barely visible.

Along with Koito were reporters from the Netherlands, Canada, Denmark, Norway, Italy, West Germany, France, Britain, and Turkey, all member countries of the North Atlantic Treaty Organization (NATO). All were nervously anticipating the glare of event BOLTZMANN, named after Ludwig Boltzmann, the nineteenth-century Austrian physicist.

The permanent personnel knew that Los Alamos had designed the BOLTZMANN device. They therefore didn't expect any surprises: The fireball would be small and fission-generated; a routine nuclear shot. This calm, relaxed atmosphere was in sharp contrast to the tension produced by the arrival of one of the UCRL devices. Weapon prototypes produced by the Livermore Labs seemed to be more unpredictable. No one could forget that Livermore was a primary designer of the American H-bomb; some scientists half-expected the UCRL group to throw in a fusion weapon or, at the very least, a pinch or two of lithium-6-deuteride to give the detonation a "boost."[5]

Just prior to shot-time, about 200 Desert Rock servicemen readied equipment for the various projects associated with the blast. As with previous shots, helicopters and jets would be in the air during the blast.

As part of Project 5.4, a navy A4D-1 jet took off from Indian Springs thirty minutes before shot time. For the test, the pilot was given rather harrowing instructions: He was to fly directly toward ground zero until detonation. If everything went well, he could fly to one side of the cloud then return to Indian Springs for decontamination. Other planes in the air included three B-57s and six F-84Gs from the 4926th Test Squadron. Their job was to sample the nuclear cloud before it traveled too far.

Detonation occurred at 4:55 A.M. Pacific Daylight Time, producing a fireball approximately 900 feet in diameter and lasting ten seconds. Observers watched the familiar gray-black mushroom form, then rise to 28,765 feet above the desert floor. The ground dust kicked up by the explosion made the mushroom initially appear to be in the shape of a dumbbell.

Caught by unusually light upper air currents, the mushroom traveled northwest over Tonopah, Nevada. Most photographers in the area tried to take pictures of the nuclear debris but failed. Radiation from the cloud and from the fallout easily fogged the film. Joe Fallani, however, was an expert. Experience with earlier shots had taught him to take the picture, then place the camera in a lead box. From there he would transfer it to a deep freeze until the film could be removed for developing. As BOLTZMANN's cloud rolled overhead, Joe aimed his camera and took the picture.

The cloud soon divided into three separate and distinct parcels, each at different levels. After lingering over the test site, it unexpectedly began traveling west toward California. In the words of a Las Vegas merchant, the first nuclear cloud in the series had "goofed and taken a walk."[6]

The major portion of BOLTZMANN's nuclear cloud crossed the city of San Francisco at 8:00 on the morning of May 29 and brushed the outskirts of Los Angeles twelve hours later. It then doubled back to the east, crossing Salt Lake City, El Paso, Topeka, Muncie, Philadelphia, and Trenton.

The 20,000-foot trajectory took the lower part of the mushroom north into Idaho where it finally dissipated just west of Boise.

The nuclear material in the lowest trajectory, 10,000-feet moved due west south of Carson City, Nevada, then into California, crossing over the small mountain town of Quincy, before veering north toward Portland, Oregon, and the towns of Longview and Kelso, lying just across the Columbia River in the state of Washington.

Paul Larios, an amateur prospector living in Quincy, first noticed trouble when his Geiger counter began registering radioactivity. It had been sitting on a table inside his home. Later, he contacted the county nurse and began checking the sidewalks of Quincy for radioactivity. Everywhere he went, the Geiger counter registered radiation. It didn't take him long to figure out that his town had been visited by a nuclear cloud from Nevada.[7]

At 8:00 A.M. on June 1, the nuclear cloud crossed the Columbia River near Longview, Washington. That same day, the *Longview Daily News* ran a story on the front page, "Farmers Advised on Radioactivity." It read, in part:

> The nation's farmers were advised by the government Saturday on steps they make take to protect themselves, their families, livestock and crops from radioactive fallout from nuclear weapons. A farmers' bulletin entitled "Defense Against Radioactive Fallout on the Farm" said radioactive particles produced by atomic and hydrogen bombs may give off destructive rays which, in certain situations, can injure—or kill—human beings and animals, and can make farm lands and crops dangerous to use. . . .
>   Radioactive strontium—a long-lived material—could affect soils and plants for decades. Since it is chemically similar to calcium, it would be absorbed by plants that require calcium. Plants growing in soils deficient in calcium would absorb more radioactive strontium than those growing in soils abundant in calcium, other things being equal." . . .
>   The department said that if the fallout should be heavy on pasture lands, it probably would be advisable to plow the soil deep, add lime and reseed.

Three days earlier, the *New York Times* had reported a sharp rise in the strontium-90 levels in New York City. The article noted that the strontium-90 level had increased from 2 millicuries/square mile in March 1954 to almost 28 millicuries/square mile in January 1957.

FRANKLIN

The second event of the series, code-named FRANKLIN, was scheduled "to evaluate the effects of a nuclear detonation on civilian structures, products, and food supplies and to evaluate Civil Defense emergency preparedness plans." Among the military equipment to be exposed to the blast were unmanned tanks and trucks parked only 1,804 feet from ground zero.

As part of a test to determine neutron radiation, neutron detectors were placed at various distances from ground zero and attached to a cable. After the shot, one end of the cable would be attached to a truck and the entire assembly dragged out of the zone of high radiation.

On June 1, 1957, at 7:30 the evening before the test, personnel somehow began the task of placing 264 pigs in cylinders at various distances around the shot tower. Two hours later, the job finished, the men returned to base camp.

In one of the more interesting experiments, the navy donated four ASG-3 airships from its Lakehurst, New Jersey, station in order to determine how well they could take the blast wave from a nuclear explosion. As luck would have it, prior to the shot, two of the blimps were torn apart not by an atomic weapon, but by a Nevada windstorm roaring across Yucca lake. Two others, K-40 and K-77, were available for the test and were moored to metal pylons about 3½ miles from the shot tower.

Just prior to zero hour, Airship K-77, nudged by an errant desert breeze, slowly turned tail to the shot tower.

At 4:55 A.M. Pacific Daylight Time, FRANKLIN was detonated, producing only a small "puffball" of a nuclear cloud that eventually ascended to just 12,674 feet. The shock wave rippled across the desert and caused Airship K-77 to break free from its mast. Rather than chase the unmanned balloon across the desert, the scientists decided to deflate the envelope and recover the instruments. Airship K-40 made it through the blast and plans were made for its use in a subsequent shot.

FRANKLIN, a product of Los Alamos Labs, had been unexpectedly puny: Equivalent to only 140 tons of TNT. An hour after the blast, radiation readings at the tower base reached only 35 roentgens/hour, less that what O'Keefe and others had been exposed to 20 miles from the CASTLE: BRAVO shot.

The flash was seen but not heard in Las Vegas, 80 miles southeast of the test site. Rumbles shook the morning air in the California towns of Bishop and Inyokern.

Later that day, Mr. and Mrs. Willis Amidon packed their car for a short trip from Bishop to Barstow, California, unaware that 16,000 feet above them would be the remnants of the FRANKLIN cloud.

The AEC seemed to take great pains not to set off a detonation when the wind was in the east; this would send atomic material toward California, particularly Los Angeles and San Francisco. Morgan Rollo, editor of the *Iron County Record* remembered that a shot was canceled fifteen seconds before detonation because of a wind shift that would have sent the cloud over California. The area to the east, however, was not so fortunate. Called by the AEC a zone "virtually uninhabited," the shots seemed to be timed so as to send most of the fallout over this area. Southeastern Utah soon became known in the press as "The Fallout Triangle."

Areas immediately west of the test site, however, did not fare much better. Jim Deitch, a reporter for the *Las Vegas Sun* gave this description of the atomic detonations from the perspectives of citizens of the southern Nevada villages of Twin Springs, Warm Springs, and Cherry Creek: "The mushroom strings out, and sometimes it passes directly overhead, blotting out the sun and covering the valley with a dense fog. This passes over, but something unseen is left behind that makes their Geiger counters go crazy. Their eyes burn and sometimes the air had a chemical taste. Their cattle are afflicted with a horrible, cancerous eye infection; and one of their dogs went stone blind and another developed an ugly malignant sore.

"A woman went completely bald and a young boy died of leukemia."[8] The boy Deitch referred to was Martin Bordoli, who had died of stem cell leukemia the year before. He had lived on his parents' ranch near Tonopah, just 25 miles from where Joe Fallini was taking pictures of the atomic clouds.

The nuclear cloud from FRANKLIN climbed to 16,000 feet, moved first northeast, then due south, then northwest toward Barstow, California. Before long, it had curled around the state of Nevada, crossed over Boise and the northwestern corner of Wyoming, where thousands were visiting Yellowstone Park. Eventually, the FRANKLIN cloud crossed parts of Nebraska, Missouri, Illinois, Indiana, Ohio, West Virginia, Pennsylvania, Virginia, and Delaware before reaching the Atlantic Ocean on June 9.

When the Amidons arrived in Barstow, a city a hundred miles from Los Angeles, they noticed that their Geiger counter was registering 10,000 clicks per minute on their clothing and 7,000 clicks per minute on their bodies. When advised of the findings, the AEC replied that ten thousand clicks per minute was "a reading far below the level of harmful radioactivity" and that the Amidons should take a bath and change their clothing.

The Public Health Service later noted that because of FRANKLIN, "noticeably higher radioactive readings were reported in samples taken at Boise and Salt Lake City." It also stated that "slightly radioactive fallout was recorded in some . . . Southern California towns."

By June 1957, several prominent scientists were making their views on fallout known. The day of the FRANKLIN shot, Linus Pauling said in an interview in Los Angeles that "a million persons throughout the world would lose five to ten years of life expectancy each if the tests were not stopped."[9]

Fallout was also becoming a popular news item. The cover story of *Life* magazine's June 10 issue concerned the adventures of Arthur Godfrey and air force general Curtis LeMay hunting big game in Africa. In the article, Godfrey told how he cried after shooting an elephant for the trophy. The opening article of that issue, however, was on fallout. The lead photo was indeed eerie: rows of bronze mannequins wearing mass-produced plastic gas masks, designed for the population in the event of nuclear war. On page 26, a photo showed a young scientist, Dr. E. B. Lewis of Cal Tech, leaning back in a chair against a blackboard. The caption "Warning of Danger," had Lewis predicting a 5 to 10 percent increase in leukemia if strontium-90 levels reached a level that the AEC considered harmless.[10]

LASSEN

Up until June 5, 1957, the devices had been detonated a variety of places, from towers to midair to underground. The third blast in the series, named for a nearby mountain peak, would be different. The Nevada Test Site crew would fire LASSEN, a Livermore device, from a wooden platform hanging beneath a huge striped balloon.

Partly because of the disastrous fallout levels experienced during TEA-POT, the AEC was interested in controlling residual off-site radiation. The towers had kept the weapon some distance from the earth, but they had an unfortunate tendency to vaporize, sending hundreds of tons of radioactive metal fume eastward on the winds. Hopefully, a balloon would solve the problem.

Sandia Corporation was responsible for assuring the balloon was tethered properly; the image of a loose balloon carrying a nuclear device bouncing its way eastward toward Las Vegas was particularly unpleasant and would have resulted in terrible public relations. To make sure this wouldn't happen, Sandia designers tethered the balloon with four steel cables, which were in turn attached to electric winches. The winch motors were controlled at the Control Point by a technician who kept the 67-foot-diameter balloon and its "device platform" under close watch via remote television cameras. Should the balloon develop problems, the technician could "reel it in."

As an additional precaution, an incendiary charge was attached near the top of the tiny plastic blimp. Should the bomb platform break free, a radio signal from Control would cause a hole to be burned in the balloon's skin, bringing it down. Should *this* fail, a pressure device attached to a safety valve was designed to release the helium if the platform attained a certain altitude.

As if these precautions weren't enough, Sandia designers constructed the balloon so that, at 5,000 feet, the seams would split from decreased atmospheric pressure.

On the evening of June 4, 1957, in the very center of Area 9, the prototype weapon was loaded onto the balloon's wooden platform.

Early the next morning, the arming and salvage parties, along with security inspectors, removed the AC generator and crane from the balloon. Directly beneath the balloon cab were two television cameras pointing upward. Within hours they would be vaporized by the explosion.

At 4:45 A.M. sharp Pacific Daylight Time, the Control Point manager threw the switch on LASSEN, sending a surge of electricity toward the balloon, suspended 500 feet above the ground. The Sandia technician, watching the balloon on the television monitors, suddenly saw the screen go white.

From Mount Charleston, the detonation looked strangely like an exclamation mark. The yield had been an unspectacular 0.5 ton TNT equivalent, sending the mushroom only to a altitude of 2,370 feet. From all indications, LASSEN was a fizzle. No off-site fallout was recorded.[11]

The same day as the LASSEN shot, President Eisenhower gave a press conference regarding atomic testing. During the conference, Ike made references to an "organized" opposition to the nuclear testing. Some excerpts of that conference:

> *Marvin L. Arrowsmith (Associated Press):* "Mr. President, in the last few days some top geneticists and other scientists have testified that fallout radiation

from nuclear-weapons tests will damage hundreds of thousands, and perhaps millions, of the yet unborn in terms of physical deformities and shortened life spans. Could you, as the man who must make the final decision on these tests for our country, tell us what your scientist advisors tell you on this matter?''

The President: ''Well, first of all, last October, we published a very long report from the National Academy of Sciences which gave a very full discussion of this whole matter, bringing up the amount of radiation you get from natural sources, the sun and X-ray pictures and all the rest of it—I believe down even to include phosphorous on the dial of your watch—and things of that kind.

"That is the authoritative document by which I act up to this moment because there has been no change that I know of. Now, on the other hand, here is a field where scientists disagree.

"Incidentally, I noticed that—many instances—scientists that seem to be out of their own field of competence are getting into this argument, and it looks like almost an organized affair. . . .

"Our tests in recent years, the last couple of years, have been largely of the . . . in the defensive type of armanent to defend against attack from the air and, particularly, to make bombs cleaner so there isn't so much fallout.

"We have reduced the fallout from bombs by nine-tenths. So that our tests of the smaller weapons have been in that direction, to see how clean we can make them.''

Merriman Smith (United Press): ''Mr. President, could you elaborate a little for us, sir, on your saying that among the disagreeing scientists on the question of fallout that some of them are out of their field of competence, and it looks like an organized affair?

"Why do you say that, sir? Who is organizing it, in your opinion?''

The President: ''I don't know. I haven't any idea, but I just say it seems to come up in so many places and so many different speeches, and you find scientists of various kinds other than geneticists and physicists in this particular field that have something to say about it.''

After Ike fielded questions about Soviet premier Khrushchev's motives on disarmament, James Reston of the *New York Times* returned to the subject of the ''organized campaign'':

Reston: ''Mr. President, the comments here this morning, sir, about the fallout are, I think, open to the inference that this is just an organized campaign, and that the scientists who are—''

The President: ''Oh, no.''

Reston: ''—disturbed about it—''

The President: ''Oh, no, I didn't say that at all. I said there does seem to be some organization behind it. I didn't say a wicked organization.''

Reston: ''I think it is, the way it is left right now—this is merely an opinion—is open to that inference.''

The President: ''Well, I don't mean that at all. There are as many of these people just as honest as they can be, there is no question about that. But, as I say, when they begin to talk a little bit out of their field, then I would rather go myself to the Academy of Sciences, which has no ax to grind of any kind, is not looking for publicity, and say, 'Now, what do you people think?' ''[12]

What the Academy thought was: "Thus far, except for some tragic accidents affecting small numbers of people, the biological damage from peacetime activities—including the testing of atomic weapons—has been essentially negligible. Furthermore, it appears that radiation problems, if they are met intelligently and vigilantly, need not stand in the way of the large-scale development of atomic energy. The continuing need for intelligence and vigilance cannot be too strongly emphasized, however."[13]

As for the "organized" opposition the president was speaking of, it was actually the result of a grass-roots letter-writing campaign organized by Dr. Linus Pauling and his wife on a budget of $250.

WILSON

Early on the morning of June 18, more than 850 Desert Rock troops filed out into Area 9 of the Nevada Test Site to await the detonation of yet another University of California device. From their position at the Control Point, the eighty-two army, marine, and air force troops assigned there could see the spotlighted balloon, hovering like an inverted pear above the desert floor. Another 164 troops, not assigned to any particular project, watched from the BUSTER-JANGLE "Y," about 4 miles south of ground zero.

Ominously, just prior to the shot, surface instruments had detected a slight 5 mph breeze from the northwest. Just 1,000 feet up, the windspeed was double that and from the north*east*. The balloon, and the center of the explosion, was at 500 feet.

The day before, a huge D-8 bulldozer had been moved to the primary decontamination station south of the shot site. As part of a new campaign to keep the test site clean of excess radioactivity, the military had planned to use the bulldozer to scrape the hot topsoil from ground zero shortly after the detonation. The military scientists had gone to great lengths to provide protection for the operators during this bit of hazardous duty. For one thing, the entire cab was shielded by a veneer of lead. Fresh air under positive pressure reached the cab through thick air filters. The designers hoped there would be little chance of contaminated air leaking in.

Some personnel, however, while loading the bulldozer onto the trailer, noticed holes visible around the top of the cab. To make matters worse, the gearshift was located slightly *outside* the cab's general configuration, and a peculiar little side door had been built to accommodate it. In order to shift the D-8, the driver would have to open the little side door and expose himself to the dusty—and contaminated—air.

In the early hours before the shot, the ex-farm boys among the personnel could hear a familiar sound: pigs. Over 200 of the animals had been placed in cylinders about 3,500 feet northwest and 2,500 feet southeast of the WILSON balloon.[14]

In the spotlighted sky around the WILSON balloon, the men could barely make out a smaller balloon. In fact, there were four of them, supplied by General Mills with assistance from Sandia, each carrying instruments to measure gamma-ray and neutron doses. The lowest was at 3,200 feet; the highest, 9,000. One would be missing before the detonation, and WILSON would destroy the rest.

At 4:45 A.M. Pacific Daylight Time, the countdown reached zero and WILSON detonated with the force of 10 kilotons. The mushroom quickly climbed to 30,770 feet where the wind blew at a steady 22 mph from the southwest. Unfortunately, the stem, pushed by slight breezes from the north and east, began to drift toward the Control Point and over trenches that would be used for the forthcoming shot DIABLO. Five minutes after the shot, the order was given to evacuate. While the rest of the cloud drifted leisurely toward the northeast, the wayward stem was causing radiation intensities on the ground to reach one roentgen/hour.

The stem continued across the test site and on into California, then doubled back to the northeast, crossing Ogden, and Salt Lake City, Utah; Caspar, Wyoming; and Rapid City, South Dakota. The larger portion of the WILSON cloud began a track that would take it across the heartland of America.

On Thursday, June 13, 1957, the Paris, Missouri, newspaper carried an article about the planned Yampa-Lodore Recreation Area dam in the Nevada-Utah area. The writer said it would "provide a new source of power much needed in the expanding mountain empire and will permit the development of . . . the country's richest deposits of uranium, so important in the atom age."

On Wednesday, June 19, at 2:00 P.M., debris from WILSON passed 35,000 feet over Paris, followed by a mass of unsettled air. The next morning, a tornado touched down west of town, picking up a 7-by-14-foot hoghouse, and dropping it behind a hill 200 feet away.

PRISCILLA

The fifth detonation in the PLUMBBOB series, and the third balloon shot, PRISCILLA, was to be used to test bomb shelter designs. And as with the other tests, pigs were to be transported to the site to determine radiation and blast effects. The army had wanted to test various fabrics for protection against thermal radiation, so a select few of the porkers were chosen to wear army uniform. Unfortunately, the pigs' weight changed so drastically during the waiting period that few actually got to dress for the occasion.

In order to make the devastation produced by the blast wave as realistic as possible, the military placed some of the pigs in foxholes, some behind huge panes of glass. They then trained a television camera on the unfortunate animals.

Farther back, but only slightly more fortunate, were the soldiers awaiting the detonation.

Scientists inside the blockhouse at the Control Point braced themselves for the detonation. Those who had become acquainted with the PRISCILLA device knew it would produce a giant fireball. As the minutes ticked away on the automatic countdown, some of the scientists, wearing dark glasses, walked to the window to watch the shot.

Because of the sensitive nature of the shot—one of PRISCILLA's parents was the Department of Defense—reporters had not been admitted to the test site for the event. Instead, they took up their usual position atop Mount Charleston, about 50 miles to the south. Sitting in their cars, some listened to the Los Angeles radio stations. One of the songs they heard was by someone named Jerry Lee Lewis, "Whole Lotta Shakin' Goin' On."

High above the desert, Captain John Adler, a member of the 4926 Test Squadron, directed his F-84 jet fighter into a holding pattern. Plans called for him to sample the mushroom cloud, a job he had done before over the past three years of testing. His procedure would be simple: He would switch to pure oxygen, then maneuver his jet into a path leading directly toward the huge cloud. Then, when it was only a mile or so away, he would pull back on the stick and accelerate into a loop, penetrating the cloud at the intersection between the stem and the mushroom base. Seconds later, after shooting out through the top of the cloud at perhaps 30,000 feet, he would check his radioactivity survey meter and return for another pass.

Adler expected radiation; his suit was lead-lined and in full view were monitors indicating particulate (code-named dog) and prompt gamma radiation (rascal). He was required to radio the results of the monitors to the base plane, a C-47 flying a few miles away. If the readings were within normal limits, he would radio "red, white and blue"; if the cloud was hotter than expected, the code words were "chili pepper."[15]

"H-minus thirty seconds and counting."

At zero, marine lieutenant Thomas Saffer, crouched in a trench 2 miles from ground zero, heard a loud click.

Atop Mount Charleston, the reporters immediately saw a brilliant flash, blinding even at a distance of 50 miles. It lasted only five seconds before being enveloped by the churning mushroom cloud. Desert soil 700 feet below the detonation point immediately rushed up into the maw of the mushroom to form first a thick stem, then another mushroom. PRISCILLA would form a rare, double-tiered mushroom cloud, surrounded by a halo of fire.

In his foxhole, Saffer felt an intense heat, accompanied by pure white light.

> I was shocked when, with my eyes tightly closed, I could see the bones in my forearm as though I were examining a red X-ray.

Within seconds, a thunderous rumble like the sound of thousands of stampeding cattle passed directly overhead, pounding the trench line. Accompanying the roar was an intense pressure that pushed me downward. The shock wave was traveling at nearly four hundred miles per hour, pushed toward us by the immense energy of the explosion. The sound and the pressure were both frightening and deafening. The earth began to gyrate violently, and I could not control my body. I was thrown repeatedly from side to side and bounced helplessly off one trench wall and then off the other.

Overcome by fear, I opened my eyes. I saw that I was being showered with dust, dirt, rocks, and debris so thick that I could not see four feet in front of me. . . . A light many times brighter than the sun penetrated the thick dust, and I imagined that some evil force was attempting to swallow my body and soul. . . .

I was immediately conscious of an offensively strong smell and taste. The odor reminded me of that of an overheated electrical unit and the metallic taste in my mouth was foul and would not go away.[16]

At the Control Point, the scientists were impressed by the colors of PRISCILLA, and she had been huge: the initial guess was that the yield had exceeded 35 kilotons (it was actually 37 kilotons). Then they saw it: The shock wave that had long since crossed the foxholes was now bearing down on the four-story Control blockhouse, kicking up a wall of dust in its path. The scientists backed away from the window just as the shock wave hit. They heard a loud "bang!" from below. The lower level of the blockhouse had four heavy steel doors. Unfortunately, someone had forgotten to close one of them, and it was blown off its hinges by the shock wave.

Ten minutes after detonation PRISCILLA climbed to 40,000 feet. Captain John Adler maneuvered his F-84 toward the churning mushroom. According to prior estimates, the cloud would produce no more than 50 roentgens. The estimates were wrong. Inside the dark cloud, Adler glanced at the radiation monitor: 500 roentgens.

"Chili pepper, chili pepper!" Adler heard himself yell into the microphone, then, almost reflexively, he headed away from the radioactive mass, back to Indian Springs.

Upon landing, Adler was requested to stop at the end of the runway, climb out of the hot jet and strip down. The ground crew had thoughtfully left a portable shower for him near the tarmac. For five weeks no one would come near the radioactive airplane.

Meanwhile, Lieutenant Saffer and the others were waiting to be transported even closer to ground zero. A brown ash had begun to fall from the sky. A major standing nearby commented, "We're receiving fallout, and I'm worried." By the time the personnel carriers had arrived, everything was covered in light beige. Shortly thereafter, the men found themselves only 300 yards from ground zero. Saffer looked around to see the remains of tanks and trucks, now tossed about for hundreds of yards or simply vaporized. As he walked past the swirling dust devils he felt the hot ground through his combat boots.[17]

Though Saffer didn't know it at the time, ground zero was intensely radioactive, radiating perhaps 500 roentgens/hour. They mistakenly had been allowed into an extremely contaminated area. Before long, an AEC technician wearing protective clothing and a respirator arrived and ordered the soldiers out of the area.

PRISCILLA's nuclear cloud first drifted east, then south, the lower levels crossing into Mexico at El Paso. The upper part of PRISCILLA's mushroom took a more northerly track. It crossed 50 miles north of Clovis, New Mexico, at 2:00 A.M. on June 25 before moving into Texas.[18] In a Clovis recording studio, Texas songwriter Buddy Holly was busy recording "Peggy Sue" and "Oh Boy."

HOOD

On July 1, a surface safety experiment, COULOMB A, was performed. At that shot, an explosive charge was fired near a nuclear weapon containing an undisclosed amount of plutonium. As a result, an amount of alpha particle–producing radioactive material was scattered across the test site. Scientists recorded no yield—that is, no fission took place.[19]

The sixth real weapon test of the series, HOOD, was originally scheduled for July 4, but weather had forced a one-day delay.

The device was to be suspended from a round, striped balloon hanging 1,500 feet above Area 9a of the test site. Below, and 5,500 yards from ground zero, were a series of trenches that would be occupied by a select group of marines.

HOOD's designers had been the University of California Radiation Lab at Livermore, the home of the American H-bomb. Though a gentleman's agreement between the federal government and the military had precluded the use of fusion weapons on American soil, there was some quiet speculation among scientists and officers that HOOD may be more than a standard fission device. Their suspicions had been heightened by the June 24 meeting between President Eisenhower and three Livermore scientists: Ernest Orlando Lawrence, Mark M. Mills, and Edward Teller.[20] At the meeting, they had reported they could eliminate 95 percent of the fallout from the H-bomb, that the radioactivity spread could be made "essentially negligible."

More ominously, they had also informed the president that it was "possible to reduce the hydrogen bomb to the size of a 'nominal' atomic bomb" and that the hydrogen bomb might be a useful weapon on the tactical battlefield.[21]

Then there was the problem of the yield of shot six. As the time drew closer to the event, HOOD's projected yield figure increased dramatically.

On June 24, the AEC issued a press release stating that HOOD would "have an explosive force of less than 20,000 tons of TNT."[22] By July 2, the AEC had upped the figure to "the largest atomic blast ever recorded in the United States."[23] This would make it bigger than even the huge CLIMAX blast of June 4, 1953, which unofficial AEC reports estimated at 40 kilotons. This was particularly worrisome to some scientists on the project who knew the actual yield of event CLIMAX: 61 kilotons. HOOD would be huge indeed.

At 1:30 on the morning of July 5, 1957, a group of marine volunteers, including Second Lieutenant Thomas Saffer, arrived at the trenches. Ahead of them they could see the lighted balloon suspended above the desert floor. Behind them, the taillights of the departing trucks.

While Lieutenant Saffer and others were awaiting the detonation, reporters congregated on a knoll about 13 miles from ground zero. From there they would view the blast, then watch 900 marines advance to an objective near ground zero. Two miles to the south, and 15 miles from the balloon, troop helicopters awaited the dawn invasion of ground zero.

In his personal account of the blast, Saffer wrote:

> I shall never forget my feelings and sensations during the countdown . . . when the last ten seconds of the countdown began and we assumed the kneeling position, I wondered, "Why is my very own government intent on killing me?" My body shook uncontrollably. Perspiration streamed down my palms and my eyes filled with tears. I began to hyperventilate and was convinced I would die of a heart attack if not as a result of the bomb's devastation. I could neither control nor conceal my body's bizarre behavior, and I feared the men nearest me in the trench would notice it. I felt we were there to be sacrificed and was certain we would all perish. I wanted to stand and yell, "Stop!, Stop! You must not explode that bomb! We don't deserve to die this way!" Instead, I prayed harder than I had at any other time in my life and asked to be spared.

As the countdown reached "one," Saffer heard the familiar "click."[24]

At exactly that same instant, 4:40 A.M., the circuits were closed at the Control Point, sending a current of electricity racing to the detonators in the HOOD device suspended 1,500 feet over the desert.

Eight hundred miles to the west, an airline pilot flying to California from Hawaii thought he saw the sun rise. For the first time, Canadian residents living due north of the Nevada Test Site witnessed the eerie greenish glare of an atomic detonation.

At News Nob, the reporters saw an incredibly bright flash of light that began as a pinpoint and seemed to grow and grow. Those watching the trench area, where the marines were huddled, saw other, much dimmer flashes of light: Joshua trees, burning from the intense thermal radiation. Almost instantly, the infrared radiation from the burst made the observers feel as though someone had opened the door of a huge blast furnace.

At Kiko, a small town 100 miles south of Las Vegas, two windows shattered in the home of seventy-three-year-old W. U. Schofield.[25]

In the trench near ground zero, Saffer was again enveloped in the unbearable heat, brightness, and vibration of the nuclear detonation. Within seconds a second shock wave hit and the area was again quiet. Ahead of them, through the brown haze, the men saw an immense mushroom cloud beginning to form. Some of the soldiers began to shake and vomit.[26]

Back at Control Point, technicians took their initial readings; the data indicated the July 5 detonation was indeed a monster. When all the data had been collected, Hood's yield would be placed at an incredible 74 kilotons. It would be the largest aboveground detonation to take place at the Nevada Test Site.

The Hood cloud quickly climbed to 43,770 feet, just a mile below the tropopause. Thirty-six-mph winds from the southwest gently pushed the mushroom toward the northeast. The 10,000-foot trajectory, representing the base and lower stem, traveled across the northern Midwest, crossing near Rapid City and Sioux Falls, South Dakota. By 2:00 P.M. on July 8, the nuclear cloud had reached Grand Rapids, Michigan. From there, it went on to Detroit, crossing over that city four hours later.

The rest of the cloud was caught in a low pressure area and managed to circle over Texas and New Mexico[27] before turning to the southeast, crossing Colorado, Kansas, Missouri, Illinois, Indiana, Kentucky, Tennessee, Virginia, and both North and South Carolina.

The city of Vandalia, Illinois, was visited twice by Hood, at 1:00 P.M. on July 8 (20,000 feet) and again at 1:00 A.M. on July 10 (10,000 feet). One day after the Hood detonation, Decca records released a new Brenda Lee song, "Dynamite."

Years later, it was discovered that Hood had not been a clean (that is, low-fallout) device after all: On January 24, 1978, Frank Putnam of the National Academy of Sciences admitted during questioning by Congressman Tim Lee Carter at a meeting of the Subcommittee on Health and Environment (part of the U.S. House of Representatives International and Foreign Commerce Committee) that Hood had been the "dirtiest [nuclear] explosion in the United States." Moreover, in a letter to Thomas Saffer dated July 7, 1980, Colonel William J. McGee of the Defense Nuclear Agency admitted that the Nevada test of July 5, 1957, had indeed been more than a mere atomic bomb.

"Hood was the largest device detonated in the United States. It was a thermonuclear device and a prototype of some thermonuclear weapons currently in the national stockpile. The neutron output was comparable to that produced in some other tests. . . ."[28]

Saffer and the other volunteers had been only 2 miles from the detonation of an H-bomb.

DIABLO

The DIABLO device would be much smaller than the one preceding it, only 17 kilotons. On June 27, the device was transported to the top of a 500-foot tower in Area 2b of the test site. Engineers checked out the firing mechanisms, then rode the elevator to the ground.

Just after midnight, 2,500 marines filed into their trenches located only 3,500 yards from ground zero. Two thousand yards from the tower, a civil defense test group of seventeen men huddled on the mattress-covered floors of buried shelters. At fifteen seconds before detonation, they were to switch off the electric motor supplying ventilation to the enclosures.

At the Control Point, the arming signal was routed to the capacitors adjacent to the DIABLO device. At firing, the needle would quickly drop to zero, indicating the electricity had successfully made the jump from the charged capacitors to the detonators. The seasoned engineers at the Control Point normally associated this quick needle deflection with an unbelievably bright light pouring through the blockhouse window and on to the control panel.

The countdown had been continuing automatically for some time, but became audible only during the last minute or so. The metallic voice from the loudspeaker counted down the seconds: "Five . . . four . . . three . . . two . . . one . . . Zero!"

Nothing.

At the Control Point, the needle slowly returned to zero. The firing charge was leaking away. Something had gone wrong. Someone in the room said, "It's not gonna go; it's not gonna go."

The desert remained cold, pitch black, and very, very quiet.

Then, a voice on the loudspeaker screamed: "Misfire! Misfire! Hold your positions!"

For some reason the device had failed to perform. Perhaps an electrical circuit had malfunctioned.[29] It would have to be disarmed manually. To make matters worse, since the elevator winch had been removed, whoever disarmed DIABLO would first have to climb the 500-foot tower.

It was decided that those who had worked on the weapon last would have to be the ones to disarm it. The group consisted of a five-man team: Livermore Lab engineers Walt Arnold and Forrest Fairbrother; Livermore chemist Bernard Rubin; EG&G engineer Ed Tucker; and a Sandia electrical engineer, Bob Burton.

Burton's company had been responsible for the trigger mechanism; he had been one of the last men on the tower, manually plugging two electrical cables from the capacitor into the DIABLO canister. Fairbrother and Rubin had been the last to inspect the electrical assembly for the device. Test Director Dr. Gerald Johnson thought about the problem for a moment, then decided that Fairbrother, Burton, and Rubin would climb the tower.

Tucker and Arnold agreed to stay at the bottom of the tower to assist in communications.

Prior to leaving for ground zero, the disarming party cut all power to the tower. At the site, Ed Tucker noticed a jackrabbit bouncing around behind an electrical panel at the tower's base. "There," he said, "is the luckiest rabbit in the world."

After a few minutes to assemble the gear and slip on radiation boots, the three men began the slow climb to the 22-by-22-foot cab, 500 feet straight up. It was 7:30 A.M.

A small landing was stationed every twenty-five rungs; there the men could catch their breath before continuing. The tower was as tall as a forty-story building—it would be a long, difficult climb.

By eight o'clock, the men had reached the 450-foot level, where a variety of recording instruments had been placed. Fifty feet above their heads was the square floor of the cab, and resting on it was the armed nuclear device. Two more ladder sections later, the men found themselves resting on a landing 7 feet below the cab. It was decided that Rubin would be the first to enter the cab.

Climbing the last seven rungs, Rubin climbed onto the landing and opened the door of the bomb room. One side had been left open to allow photographs of the first instant of detonation: "zero time." Nothing looked amiss. Upon reaching the cab, Fairbrother phoned Johnson back at the Control Point: "Gerry, we're at the top. Barney is completing his function and Burton's at the patch cables." After unfastening the locking rings, Burton slowly pulled the electrical cable free of the DIABLO canister. A moment later, DIABLO was unarmed.

"Call for the winch," Burton said into the phone, "we'd like to ride the elevator down."[30]

As it turned out, DIABLO's electrical problem had occurred when the elevator winch was removed; an important electrical cable was damaged, shutting down the entire firing sequence. The problem was corrected and DIABLO was rescheduled for two weeks later.

In the early morning hours of July 15, the Civil Defense test group was again jeeped to the underground shelter, 2,000 yards from the tower. Once inside, the men switched on the ventilation fans and waited for morning.

At 4:29 A.M. Pacific Daylight Time, the electrical charge was sent to the capacitors. One minute later the needle indicating capacitor charge quickly deflected to zero. At the same time, an almost solid beam of intense white light poured through the window and onto the electrical panels: DIABLO had fired.

In an instant the fireball had vaporized the 500-foot tower in a blaze of red and orange fire. Almost immediately, the air surrounding the top of the fireball began to take on a purplish ionization glow. Reporters called the DIABLO shot the most beautiful they had seen.

At 4:50 A.M. windows cracked in the Carson City, Nevada, home of police inspector E. K. Butner. Residents of Bridgeport, California, 350 miles from ground zero, saw the flash and felt the shock wave.

A few hours after the shot, the Civil Defense volunteers emerged from the shelter apparently unscathed. Plans called for the military to remove the entire shelter for study, but this was postponed for several days: The area was too radioactive.

Pushed by 17 kilotons of yield, the DIABLO cloud climbed to 27,531 feet, then it was pushed by a light breeze and began drifting toward St. George, Utah. Atomic Energy Commission spokesmen said they expected the trajectory to shift toward Wyoming.

Even though the cloud had apparently missed Salt Lake City entirely, radiation monitors there reported the radioactivity to be ten times greater than any prior atomic detonation.[31]

While the lower levels of the cloud had traveled due northeast, the mushroom became entrained in a 14-mph breeze from the northwest, causing it to track just north of Las Vegas before turning northwest toward Casper, Wyoming, and Rapid City, South Dakota. Then, over southern Minnesota, the 30,000-foot trajectory suddenly veered due south, passing through central Missouri, eastern Oklahoma, and east Texas. Several days after the shot, the cloud passed neatly between Fort Worth and Dallas before heading toward Waco and Austin.

DIABLO's 30,000-foot trajectory passed over Springfield, Missouri, near Harry Truman's boyhood home, about an hour before sunrise on July 18.[32]

The ninth blast of the series, code-named JOHN, would not involve towers, airdrops, *or* balloons; it was an air-to-air missile. The detonation would involve the air force's new MB-1 Genie missile and would take place at high altitude, perhaps 20,000 feet.

The air force was especially proud of the Genie; for one thing, it carried a small but powerful 2-kiloton warhead. Originally called the Ding Dong and High Card, the rocket had been manufactured by the Douglas Aircraft Company in connection with Los Alamos. The weapons designers had somehow managed to pack an enormous wallop into a small space. Essentially, the warhead was a cross between the 280mm, 15-kiloton UPSHOT-KNOTHOLE: GRABLE device and the 3 kiloton TEAPOT: HA unit. GRABLE had proven that a device could be armed after firing and HA had shown what to expect from shots in the upper atmosphere.

During the 1950s, the Pentagon had assumed that any attacks from the Soviets would involve heavy bombers flying in from Siberia. The Genie was designed to intercept such a flotilla and explode in their midst.[33]

The missile was the result of years of hard work and the military wanted to make the most of the event. Radiation readings taken during the 3-kiloton HA event in 1955 indicated that the prompt gamma and neutron doses at ground zero should be negligible; therefore, it wasn't long before a number of volunteers turned up to stand at ground zero—directly below the detonation.

Five were eventually chosen: Colonel Sidney Bruce; Lieutenant Colonel Frank Ball; and Majors Norman Bodinger, John Hughes, and Don Luttrel. An air force photographer, George Yoshitake, rounded out the group.

While at the Baghdad Hotel in Las Vegas, Continental Air Defense Command public affairs officer Colonel Barney Oldfield, in an inspired bit of promotion, removed the cardboard from a shirt insert and wrote across it in black ink: "Ground Zero—Population 5" (Oldfield didn't count the photographer). Yoshitake took it to the test site with him the morning of the shot.

The group arrived at ground zero shortly before the test. They could hear the roar of the Air Force's F-89D Scorpion jet fighter not quite 4 miles above them.

In the jet, Captain Eric Hutchinson, awaiting the go-ahead signal, made the required practice maneuvers. The procedure called for Hutchinson to accelerate to 600 mph and release the Genie. Then, in order to avoid the 2-kiloton nuclear fire, the pilot would have to pull the Scorpion into an abrupt "backflip" to the left and out of harm's way—all in the space of three seconds. The maneuver would involve enormous positive "g" forces; Hutchinson would need the pressure suit to keep the blood pumping to his brain, keeping him awake through this.

6:59 A.M., July 19, 1957.

On the ground, Major Bodinger picked up a microphone and prepared to give a running commentary on the scene. Ground zero "mayor" Sidney Bruce looked up to see the tiny figure of the jet.

At 7:00 sharp, Hutchinson triggered the Genie to life. There was an immediate jolt as the missile roared toward its detonation point just three seconds away. Hutchinson quickly pulled back on the stick and kicked the right rudder. The horizon slipped from view somewhere below the nose of the plane. One second.

On the ground, the men were silent. The missile, streaming vapor, closed in on a point directly above their heads.

Two seconds. Pilot Hutchinson watched the horizon reappear, this time from the other direction. He had the Scorpion almost on its back, racing away from the detonation point.

Three seconds.

Detonation.

Hutchinson noticed a brightness coming from behind the jet. Later, he would learn that the detonation had occurred 2 miles behind him and slightly to his right.

On the ground, the men watched as the intense pinpoint of light grew into a huge fireball.

At Control Point, the engineers listened as Bodinger reported from ground zero. "The colors are brilliant . . . swirling and changing . . .and now we're getting the shock waves." Over the loudspeaker came a distinct "whump" then nothing. Silence.

A few seconds later, the connection was restored and the sound of laughter and shouts filled the room. The citizens of ground zero had survived event JOHN.

Unfortunately, because of a bureaucratic foul-up, the helicopter that was to take them back to Desert Rock was never sent. As a result, the citizens of ground zero had to endure their hot town for an additional two hours. Eventually, a truck was sent to retrieve them.[34,35]

Above the desert, a flat, plate-shaped pink cloud had formed; the shot had taken place much too high for a stem. Although the detonation occurred at 20,000 feet, the cloud would reach twice that altitude. There, southwesterly winds at 55 mph began to send the cloud to the northeast, eventually taking it over Utah, Idaho, Wyoming's Yellowstone Park, and Montana.[36]

KEPLER

The next blast of the PLUMBBOB series was scheduled for July 24. Named for sixteenth-century German astronomer and mathematician Johannes Kepler, the tenth detonation would involve a number of scientific experiments as well as military maneuvers.

The 500-foot-tall KEPLER tower was constructed in Area 4, the same location of the 1955 TEAPOT: APPLE-I shot. Observation trenches, located 2 miles southwest of the tower, were the same ones originally used at APPLE-I. After determining that the trenches were safe for the KEPLER shot, the military ordered them cleaned out for reuse. By July 23, the trenches were again 5 feet deep; this height offered a kneeling soldier a minimum of 2 feet of overhead protection.

In the early morning hours of July 24, 1957, the military observers were trucked to the trenches, and at 4:50 A.M. Pacific Daylight Time, the 10-kiloton KEPLER was detonated.

Almost immediately, dust and gravel-sized debris began falling onto the observation trenches. Monitors began to register radiation as high as one roentgen/hour. Calls were made for evacuation vehicles.

The last bus finally arrived to pick up the men forty-five minutes after the shot. By this time, the radiation level had climbed to 3 roentgens/hour. At Desert Rock, plans were made to decontaminate the entire contingent of KEPLER observers. Immediately after stepping off the buses, the men were brushed with brooms until the radiation intensity measured 0.007 roentgens/hour or less.

For the military observers, KEPLER had ben an extremely radioactive shot. Two Desert Rock Rad-Safe personnel had accumulated 5.5 and 5.7 roentgens. Three individuals manning a radar station about 3 miles from ground zero accumulated doses exceeding 3 roentgens, while of the seven survey personnel exceeding 3 roentgens, three exceeded the 5-roentgen limit and were subsequently barred from the forward area. One military man received a total of 8.64 roentgens, among the highest in the PLUMBBOB series.

The KEPLER mushroom had climbed to 23,691 feet before fanning out west and north of the test site. The 10,000-foot trajectory moved first northwest and into the mountains of California before turning due north, later dissipating north of Carson City and Reno, Nevada.[37]

One of the basic tenets of atomic detonation scheduling was formulated during the early years of the RANGER and BUSTER-JANGLE series: Never fire when there is the possibility of rain nearby. Mountains of meteorological evidence compiled over the years showed that the rain clouds could, and often did, entrain radioactive debris, creating localized hot spots over various parts of the United States. A corollary was: If there *is* precipitation, the further away it is, the less radioactive it will be. While there were notable exceptions to this rule, the meteorologists paid special attention to the areas of precipitation near the test site. If rain could occur nearby, the shot was usually canceled.

Usually. But exceptions occurred during a few of the shots in the UPSHOT-KNOTHOLE series when radioactive rain fell in southwestern Utah. An exception also occurred in the planning of OWENS. Meteorologists predicted widely scattered showers throughout Nevada for July 25, the day of the scheduled shot.

OWENS was to be essentially similar in strength to the KEPLER, even though they had been made by different labs. Unlike KEPLER, the OWENS device had been designed by Livermore. Because of its projected small yield (9.7 kilotons) and the fact that it was scheduled regardless of the weather outlook, it was speculated that the device was a so-called clean bomb.

Early on the morning of July 25, a Sandia balloon carrying the canister was allowed to rise to 500 feet above the surface of test site Area 9b. At 6:30 A.M. Pacific Daylight Time, the charge was sent to the capacitors and the device was detonated, sending a boiling radioactive cloud 30,000 feet above the test site. Because of the moisture in the air, an ice cap formed as the mushroom roared into the upper troposphere. At 6 miles altitude, the cap cleanly separated from the stem, then, pushed by 35 mph winds, began a steady trek toward the northeast.[38]

True to the predictions of the meteorologists, the OWENS radioactive cloud passed over or through a number of rain clouds on its way across Nevada. July 25 and 26 were very rainy days across the entire state.[39]

STOKES

As the eleventh shot of the series, STOKES, was being readied at Area 7 of the test site, other events were taking place just outside the main gates. Lawrence Scott, a fifty-one-year-old Quaker from Chicago, had organized "a peaceful demonstration against the senseless folly" of the nuclear tests. The group had failed in an attempt to enter the test site, and Scott was making plans for a prayer vigil to take place just as Stokes detonated.[40]

Inside the test site, two unmanned navy ZSG-3 airships from Lakehurst, New Jersey, were to be moored at varying distances from ground zero. The experiment originally called for one blimp to remain moored during the shot while the other would be released about twenty seconds before the arrival of the blast wave; the military wanted to test the free-body response of the airship to the nuclear weapons shock front. Unfortunately, nature supplied a shock front of her own just prior to the test date: a dust storm blew in unexpectedly and totally destroyed one of the blimps.

On August 6, the day before the test, technicians readied the remaining blimp at its mooring and loaded the cab with magnesium flares that were timed to go off with the nuclear detonation. The airship would act as a gigantic flashbulb. At ground zero, Sandia technicians checked the 65-foot-diameter balloon that would carry the nuclear device to 1,500 feet, the detonation altitude.

The same day, eleven of the pacifists were found inside a restricted area of the test site. They were placed under arrest and charged with trespassing.

Early the next morning, while the pacifist group made plans for their peace demonstration 30 miles from ground zero, 499 troops from Task Force Warrior were bussed in from Desert Rock to watch the nuclear event. The August 7 shot would not involve troop maneuvers. Rather, it was to condition the personnel for the main event that would take place later in the month: SMOKY.

At 5:25 A.M., while Scott's group knelt in prayer, STOKES was fired, quickly growing from a tiny pinpoint of light into a roiling ball of fire. Members of the First Battle Group from Fort Lewis, Washington, which had also been present for the smaller KEPLER and OWENS shots, were startled by glare from the 19-kiloton explosion.

With the fireball roaring into the sky, technicians released the ZSG-3 airship from its mooring. The shock wave arrived with characteristic force, rupturing the airship envelope just forward of the cab. The blimp responded by slowly settling to the ground, nose first. From this experiment it was decided that blimps would not provide a high degree of protection from a nuclear detonation.

The STOKES cloud, carried by a 76-mph wind, moved almost due north, toward Ely, Nevada, then turned northeast, crossing the northern tier of states before spreading out over the mid-Atlantic states and New England.

SHASTA

Back in Nevada, the eleven peace demonstrators arrested would eventually be given one-year suspended sentences and warnings against further violations of state laws.

On August 17, personnel prepared instruments for the sixth Livermore event in the PLUMBBOB series. Like most other University of California Radiation Lab shots, this one was named after a California mountain, SHASTA. It was to have a nominal yield, perhaps something slightly less than 20 kilotons, and was to be detonated in Area 2a of the test site.

Members of the Human Resources Research Office (HumRRO) team, all civilians, planned to watch the blast from a hill at the south end of Yucca Flat, about 12 miles from ground zero. The observation area consisted of twelve rows of wooden benches. In preparation of the shot, the civilians were issued steel helmets and protective field masks.[41]

SHASTA was detonated at 5:00 Pacific Daylight Time on the morning of August 18, 1957; the 17-kiloton yield sent up a mushroom almost 28,000 feet into the Nevada sky. An eyewitness on the HumRRO team described the scene: "Dimly visible in the first morning light the golden fireball boiled and churned like a genie from a bottle, cooled to orange splotched with deep dirty brown, cooled to heavy violet and as it cooled, its shimmering blue corona contracted and glowed around it. . . . I didn't know whether to expect [a shock wave,] a crack, or a roar, or what. Then I heard what sounded exactly like a long line of freight cars 'bumping' in the distance, a low quickly punctuated rumble that lasted three or four seconds and faded away."[42]

Early on, various winds had pushed the stem into a zigzag pattern: As sluggish, 7-mph breezes pushed the mushroom east, the middle section of the cloud moved northwest while the lower section tracked northeast.

Just six hours after the SHASTA detonation, radioactive rain fell in eastern Nevada, on the community of Lincoln Mine and in the towns of Hiko and Alamo.

Just a few months earlier, the waitress at Alamo's Alko Cafe had asked Jess Brown, an AEC man why, if the bombs weren't dangerous, couldn't they set them off at any time, why did they have to wait until the wind was right.

"It's this way, Mrs. Graff," he replied. "There are two kinds of radiation effects: physical and biological—immediate effects and long range effects. Physically, there's no danger in these tests. Biologically, it's assumed radiation doesn't do anybody any good—although at the levels we're dealing with it isn't believed to do any harm. But we try to keep it at a minimum.

Apparently, Brown had not completely convinced the owner of the Alko, Mrs. Emma Foremaster. She said that though she thought the tests were "a necessary evil," they should be held "somewhere else."[43]

Doppler

In the early 1840s, physicist Christian Doppler began a series of experiments involving both musicians and railway cars. He wanted to know why there is an increase in pitch as a sound-producing object comes near and a decrease as the object moves away. By 1842, Doppler had his answer: sound waves are, in effect, either "stacked up" or "stretched out" depending upon the direction of travel to or from the listener, resulting in the apparent change in pitch. For this bit of work, Doppler's name became a common one in physics books, and in the summer of 1957, the Los Alamos Lab named an 11-kiloton atomic device after him.

Suspended by a balloon 1,500 feet above Area 7a, DOPPLER was detonated at 5:30 A.M. on the morning of August 23. The mushroom cloud climbed toward its maximum height of 33,770 feet. A member of the Human Resources Research Office team described the shot:

> At H minus three minutes we put on our gas masks and helmets, faced half-right in the trenches and crouched, eyes closed, arm tightly against the goggles of the mask. The three minutes seemed interminable, breathless in every sense; then came the silent, brilliant white flash.
>
> I could feel the heat of the fireball reflecting from the wall of the trench about me. I peeked, but quickly shielded my eyes again. It was still furnace bright. The ground wave caught me unaware, three distinct shocks, seeming to raise me about a foot each time, with the terrible sensation of being detached from anything solid or reliable and thoroughly shaken, as in an earthquake.[44,45]

Strong 60-mph winds at 33,000 feet quickly pushed the cloud to the northeast, over central Utah. Later it fanned out over much of the southeastern United States from Baton Rouge, Louisiana, to Durham, North Carolina.

Although the cloud crossed a number of communities, the town of Covington, Tennessee, was particularly unlucky. DOPPLER's nuclear cloud crossed overhead three times: once on August 24 at two in the afternoon, again on August 27 at two in the morning, and a third time on August 29 at four in the afternoon.[46]

By August 30, the DOPPLER cloud had cleared the continent. But then another atomic detonation had occurred at the test site.

Reporters for the eighth balloon shot of the series, FRANKLIN PRIME, were not allowed on-site; as with many other tests, they had to settle for the observation post on Mount Charleston, 70 miles south of ground zero.

At 5:30 A.M. Pacific Daylight Time, on August 30, 1957, the device exploded, creating, in the words of one reporter, a "vivid red fireball" that lasted for thirty seconds then faded to orange. "The familiar mushroom cloud puffed up to about 20,000 feet within a minute after the blast. The top of the cloud appeared like a ball of cotton."[47]

Eight miles from ground zero, army private William H. Hodsden witnessed the shot. Several soldiers had been taken out to the desert and left off behind some sand dunes. An information officer stepped up and told them that they were about to witness an atomic bomb and wanted to know how they felt. Hodsden replied that he felt "pretty good."

The range officer told them that "When I give the word, 'go,' I want you guys to run up the side of this sand dune and stand on top and watch it."

Hodsden and the others ran to the dune and looked.

> And we saw a little flash, and a little trail of smoke in the air. I had to squint. I said, "What the hell is that?" It was eight miles away and looked like a little campfire. Some of the guys started laughing. "Where's the ball?"
>
> So when the guys start laughing in the group, the range officer froze up a bit. "That's an atomic bomb . . . that was an *atomic bomb*."
>
> One of the guys said, "Aw, man, that ain't nothin'."
>
> Then the range officer said, "That's all right. You guys are going to get yours tomorrow."[48]

The atomic cloud from FRANKLIN PRIME rose to 27,814 feet, then began to move northeast at 51 mph. By the next day, a Saturday, it would be over Montana.

Late Summer in America

That Saturday in late August was a busy one in Wolf Point, Montana.

At 3:00 P.M. the day before, children from the Fort Peck Reservation had hopped the bus at the Sherman Hotel in Wolf Point to attend school in Pierre, South Dakota.

Newscasters on station KVCK reminded the residents that entries to the rodeo at State Line Arena closed that day at 6:00 P.M. Those not interested could visit the Sundown Drive-In to see a 1954 Gary Cooper–Susan Hayward western, *Garden of Evil*. In the movie, two cowboys heading west to California stop to help a woman rescue her husband from a mine, but are then trapped by Indians.

The movie showing at the Liberty Theater was the current release, *China Gate*, with Gene Barry, Angie Dickinson, and Nat King Cole. The Saturday matinee began at 2:30 P.M.

Down the street, Davies Menswear hosted their annual summer clearance sale, selling western shirts for a dollar each.

And on that Saturday in late August, exactly at noon, debris from a nuclear cloud was passing 20,000 feet over the town of Wolf Point.[49] As in other communities across the country, most of the residents of Wolf Point, Montana, were unaware a detonation had even occurred.

The cloud crossed Boston, Massachusetts, and its suburb, Lexington, at 9:00 P.M. on September 1. That night, the Capitol Theater in Lexington offered *The Sweet Smell of Success* with Burt Lancaster and Tony Curtis. The evening before the feature was a Bing Crosby–Inger Stevens movie, *Man on Fire*. In downtown Lexington, various stores offered "Live Maine Lobsters: 57 cents a pound"; turkey sold for 37 cents a pound, and ice cream went for just 29 cents a pint. At Howard's Deli a large mushroom pizza could be bought for $1.10.

That evening, Eddie Albert starred in an "Alcoa Hour" television presentation, "No License to Kill."

Late summer in America, 1957.

SMOKY

The shot that was to be code-named SMOKY did not begin in 1957 or 1956, but almost a hundred years earlier and a half a continent away. During the Civil War battle for Petersburg, Virginia, Union troops had tunneled under the Confederate positions; using explosives, they then managed to blow a large hole in the opposition's line. As a result, they won an advantage of about half an hour, a significant bit of leverage over the enemy. Unfortunately, instead of continuing the advance, the Union were so awestruck at their accomplishment that they did nothing.

A century later, military planners wanted to determine if troops in the new tactical army would act the same way. As a memo from the Nevada Test Organization put it:

> Can a highly trained soldier think clearly and perform the duties of his fighting mission efficiently in the shadow of a nuclear bomb's mushroom cloud? Two minutes after a blast with an explosive force of over 20,000 tons of TNT, will his hands tremble as he kneels to field-strip and reassemble his rifle?
>
> Will he obey promptly the orders of his commanding officer, or will he falter as a choking dust cloud whirls around him?
>
> Will he move quickly to clear a mine field, or will he "gawk" at the eerie "snow cap" forming above his head?
>
> For the first time since man learned to split the atom, the United States Army is prepared to find the answers to these and other unknowns concerning human behavior in nuclear warfare, in connection with the shot "Smoky" which will be detonated above Yucca Flat at the Nevada Test Site Wednesday, August 28.[50]

The SMOKY event was more than a test for army psychologists—that major psychological exam would take place during the next shot, GALILEO. SMOKY was a monster 44-kiloton device designed and constructed by the University of California Radiation Lab under the direction of Edward

Teller. After detonation from its 700-foot tower, SMOKY would induce radio-activity at ground zero of such magnitude that technicians would have to flee the area. It would also be the event in which an army officer led his men within 300 feet of ground zero to salute a melted tower.

The First Battle Group from Fort Lewis arrived by plane from nearby Tacoma, Washington. Once at Camp Desert Rock, the military prepared the soldiers for the 44-kiloton SMOKY by offering them the opportunity to observe its smaller predecessors: KEPLER, OWENS, STOKES, and FRANKLIN PRIME. Coupled with the men from Fort Lewis, a contingent of paratroopers from the 82nd Airborne Division arrived to participate in the event. The code-name for the army units to take part in the atomic detonation: Task Force Big Bang.[51]

The military planners had long before developed the concept of the pentomic army. On the tactical battlefield involving nuclear weapons, the troops could be dispersed over a large area, thus limiting the chance that the enemy could take out the entire battalion using one atomic weapon. The officers wanted to know if the troops would perform their duties despite the awe-inspiring sight of a column of smoke rising 40,000 feet into the air. There were, of course, the attendant problems of flash blindness, X and gamma rays, neutrons, heat and blast effects, but if all of these could be mitigated somewhat, the pentomic army would be *the* fighting machine for the atomic age. As General "Jumpin' Jack" Gavin of the 82nd Airborne remarked, "We felt that the combat divisions would have to be far more flexible and responsive to a battlefield that demanded greater mobility in the face of greater firepower [meaning nuclear weapons]."[52]

Prior to coming to Desert Rock, the soldiers chosen for the assignment were given a pre–Desert Rock course in which they witnessed 3,000-pound TNT detonations, huge gasoline explosions, and the like—all designed to simulate a nuclear detonation. As part of the course, they were instructed in digging slit trenches, wearing gas masks, and charging a make-believe ground zero. Those who witnessed both conventional and nuclear explosions say there was no comparison; the blinding flash of an atomic weapon simply could not be simulated.

During the course, the men were told that the major hazard from an atomic weapon was not radiation, but the fireball. Some were told that the reason for the slit trenches was to protect the troops as the fireball rolled past overhead. Upon arrival at the test site, the men were given a booklet warning them to keep their hats on and to stay cool, "The sun, not the bomb, is your worst enemy at Camp Desert Rock."

The "Information and Guide" booklet also carried a greeting signed by Desert Rock commander Major General W. B. Kean, "The officers and men of this operation share with you the hope that your visit to Camp Desert Rock will prove an informative and revealing experience which you will alway remember."

During the orientation, with baseball-capped HumRRO observers looking on, the soldiers listened to an officer as he gave an outdoor lecture on the realities of a nuclear explosion. Also on hand was a motion picture crew from the Army Signal Corps Pictorial Center, ready to film the event for broadcast on Saturday afternoons.

31 August 1957

Paratroopers from the 82nd Airborne who were to participate in the maneuver were awakened at 2:00 A.M., given cold sandwiches, radiation film badges, and thermoses of hot coffee. They were then loaded onto 40-foot olive drab flatbed trailors equipped with benches and towed by diesel tractors. By 4:00 A.M., the convoy had passed Camp Murray and the broad expanse of Yucca Flat, a silver reflection in the light of the full moon. In the distance they could make out the 700-foot detonation tower, located in Area 2c. In the words of one soldier, it was "lit up like a giant Christmas Tree."[53]

Meanwhile, at Camp Murray, other troops were being roused from sleep. At breakfast, they were issued tablets that, presumably, would help protect them from the effects of radiation. They were told the tablets were sulfa drugs.[54]

The men of the First Battle Group were taken west of the tower to a series of trenches, while most of the personnel of the 82nd Airborne were transported to Lookout Point, a hill just 3 miles from the 700-foot tower. From this position, the detonation tower looked like an inch-long toothpick held at arm's length. Nearby, the Army Corps Pictorial Center set up their generators and began filming.

Some members of the 82nd were given the opportunity of seeing the shot from an even closer position. First they were taken to a trench position 4,000 yards from ground zero, then picked up and transported even closer, 3,000 yards from the shot tower. From this distance, the brightly lit metal structure looked fully twice as tall as from Lookout Point.

From their position west of ground zero, the men could see the elevator going to the top of the tower. Presumably, it was carrying technicians who could complete the arming procedure.

The air was absolutely calm.

Seven miles from the tower, AEC scientist and test site safety specialist John Auxier and technician P. N. "Barney" Hensley waited in the cab of their six-wheel-drive truck. Under orders, they were not to start the engine until after the shot; electromagnetic radiation might interfere with scientific instruments. It might also detonate the weapon prematurely. So tight was this particular restriction, men were not allowed to use electric shavers the day of the test.

The day before, technicians had strung neutron and gamma detectors along a 2,000-foot steel cable stretching almost to ground zero. At the near end the cable formed a loop; Auxier and Hensley's job would be to rush to within 2,000 yards of ground zero, attached the cable loop to the truck, and drag the entire instrument array into a safe zone.

Both Auxier and Hensley were wearing the safety protective equipment used by AEC personnel who were required to venture into the hot zone: cotton coveralls taped at the ankles and wrists; gloves; goggles; and of course, particulate respirators. Thanks to previous "safety" shots, the area was already contaminated with alpha emitters. Should SMOKY be a particularly inefficient shot, then much of its plutonium would be scattered, adding considerably to the area's alpha load.

In addition, there would be the inevitable mixture of fission products emitting alpha and beta particles, gamma and X-rays, and neutrons. Both Auxier and Hensley knew that the cotton coveralls would protect only against the alpha emitters and low-energy betas; gamma rays and neutrons would penetrate the cloth material—and their bodies—like so much vapor.

The men also knew that when SMOKY vaporized the 700-foot tower, there would be an enormous amount of fallout. The journey to ground zero would have to be a quick one. Just *how* quick would depend upon an instrument sitting in Auxier's lap; a radiation monitor. Hensley would drive, Auxier would keep an eye on the needle.

It was almost time for the shot.

In the trenches, the metallic voice of the Control Point "Dragnet" issued from the two-way radios. Unknown to many of the soldiers, a TNT charge would be set off just prior to SMOKY. Its purpose was to calibrate the scientific instruments trained on ground zero.

"This is Dragnet. Stand by for time hack. In one minute the time will be H minus thirty minutes."

A half hour later, as the orange flame leaped into the sky, some of the men thought SMOKY had been detonated. Immediately after the charge, "Dragnet" continued:

> The shot you are about to witness this morning is Smoky. It is expected that the yield will be approximately three times nominal, forty-four kilotons. You are cautioned not to look directly at the fireball until after the initial intensity of the light has faded. Turn and face away from the direction of the shot three to five minutes before zero and shield your eyes with your arms. After the shot you will be told when to turn around and view the fireball. This will be approximately five seconds after zero. In the event of a misfire, remain in position with your eyes shielded until given instructions. That is all.
>
> This is Dragnet. H hour minus three minutes. Take your positions.[55]

At William Hodsden's position, a voice crackled from the loudspeaker, "All right, you guys. Get ready . . . I want everybody lined up in single file."

Hodsden's account:

We all sat down on the ground in single file with our backs to ground zero. There was white powder on the ground and some black stuff. We wait and we wait.

"All right," the corporal says, "stand up." So we stand up. "Everybody turn around and take five steps forward. Okay, you guys on the right, be careful of that wire. Okay, turn around. Everybody down on one knee and cover your eyes."[56]

5:30 A.M.

On the hillside, the men from the 82nd Airborne placed their right arms over their faces. Suddenly, the view changed from black to something else, something strange. It was as if they were looking at a red X-ray of the bones in their arms. At the same instant, residents of Los Angeles and San Francisco saw the early morning sky erupt in a brilliant flash of blue light.

In the trenches, William Hodsden "saw the nerves at the back of his eyes light up," even though his hands were covering his eyes at the time. Seconds later the shock wave hit, a wall of pressure moving at 83 mph. Hodsden thought he felt his heart stop in midcontraction, then felt a warm sensation in a knee he had injured a short time before.

An instant later, the shock wave reached the 82nd Airborne's position. The men on the hill had heard it coming, sounding like a freight train in the distance. The sergeant yelled "Hit It!" and the men dived for the ground, only to feel it vibrate and shake beneath them.

At the instant of detonation, the Joshua trees in the semicircular basin of Area 2c smouldered, then caught fire. In a second, entire hills were aflame.

At Hodsden's position the noise was almost unbearable. "It sounded like about fifteen freight trains going by . . . we became aware of the noise and we felt the pressure on our ears, we grabbed our heads."[57]

Throughout Area 2c, the men felt their eyes sting as the hot air from the detonation permeated the basin with the smell of smoke and burning metal.

At H plus four minutes, Auxier and Hensley received the go ahead signal. As Auxier watched the radiation monitor, Hensley started the engine to begin the race toward SMOKY ground zero. As the 2½ ton truck passed the BUSTER-JANGLE "Y," Auxier watched the needle on the radiation monitor begin to move. Outside, the air seemed permeated with a dense fog. Hensley switched the truck lights to dim. Directly above them, easily visible in the early morning sky, was the unmistakable mushroom formation. It resembled the bottom half of a doughnut-shaped water tower, seen from close up, perhaps just below the catwalk.

Four miles to go.

Hensley had trouble seeing the road through the haze. In 1955, during the Teapot series, he and Auxier had become mired in some loose desert sand and had to leave the contaminated area by foot. He didn't want it to happen again.

Auxier also had some concerns. He had switched the monitor to its highest range, and the needle was still moving steadily toward the far side of the scale: 50 roentgens/hour.

It was too much. Auxier and Hensley decided that the best maneuver under these circumstances would involve a 180-degree turn back to the south. It would be days before the AEC considered the area cool enough to retrieve the instruments.

Years later, Auxier characterized Smoky as the "dirtiest" test he had ever participated in—anywhere.[58]

Smoky was aptly named; the entire fireball seemed to be infused with a dense black smoke; only occasionally would the vapors part to reveal the pink and amber nuclear fires inside. As with the other shots, a blue ionization halo formed around the fiery mass as it began its ascent toward the stratosphere.

After the detonation, the troops on the hillside were loaded into trucks and taken through the smoke and dust to within several hundred yards of ground zero to inspect the damage. What greeted them was a scene from another world: The entire area was bathed in a dense haze extending up several thousand feet. There was no life of any kind: no insects, no plants, nothing. At the hypocenter, surrounded by a glazed area of greenish glass, lay the melted and twisted remnants of the tower.

About 2,000 feet away and to the west, another combat group had begun a steady march toward the hypocenter, the green glass crunching beneath their boots. At 300 feet from the hypocenter, the men stopped and the man leading the group saluted the twisted, smoking tower.

Years later, in testimony before a congressional subcommittee, the man in charge of the group at the time, Lieutenant Colonel Frank W. Keating, acknowledged that "we went right in there [to the hypocenter]."

Overhead, helicopters carrying the Task Force Warrior Pathfinders had considerable difficulty negotiating the haze-shrouded airspace; because of the poor visibility, pilots feared midair collisions.[59]

After the maneuvers, a voice from a loudspeaker blared across the desert: "You have just witnessed one of the most powerful weapons in the world. And it belongs to one of the best damn armies in the world: the United States Army!" The men were then loaded into trucks and sent to decontamination stations. On the trip south, several soldiers looked back to see parachutists descending into the hypocenter.[60]

Forty-four-kiloton Smoky quickly rose 33,521 feet into the air, clearing the stratosphere by 3,000 feet. Though the surface was calm, the wind at altitude was from the west with a velocity that increased with height. At the level of the mushroom, the wind was blowing a steady 43 mph from due west and toward southwestern Utah.

At ground zero, radiation safety monitors recorded activity levels up to 300 roentgens/hour. This extremely hot area formed an elongated pattern that extended due south 2,500 yards. Enclosing this pattern was a similar shaped pattern of 200 roentgens/hour extending over 3,000 yards from ground zero.

The hot area extended a surprising distance; levels of 50 roentgens/hour were recorded as far away as 4 miles southeast of the tower.

The on-site fallout pattern indicated the cloud moved generally east-southeast across the test area. This direction of drift continued until it neared the Nevada-Utah-Arizona junction, where upon it turned northeast, passing over St. George, Cedar City, Hurricane, and Zion National Park. From there the pattern continued on toward Green River, Price, and Wellington, Utah.

At the Bordoli Ranch near Tonopah, Nevada, the sky suddenly grew dark. A pinkish-brown dust storm had come through the mountain pass, reducing visibility to less than a city block. Twenty-five miles away, at Twin Springs, it was so dark that Joe Fallini was unable to take any photos of the cloud.[61]

Across the state line, in the village of Veyo, Utah, little two-year-old Lisa Davis was visiting her grandparents. While the elders canned tomatoes, Lisa stayed in her playpen near the door. Outside, her parents noticed the sky darkening. Ominously, particles of some sort were falling to the ground. By noon, the parents noticed the little girl's skin was bright red, as though she had been badly sunburned.[62]

The upper levels of SMOKY's nuclear cloud fanned out and moved to the northeast, passing into Canada over North Dakota and Minnesota. The 20,000-foot trajectory eventually returned, crossing the northern tip of Maine, over the towns of St. Francis, Winterville, Caribou, and Fort Fairfield.

The 10,000-foot trajectory meandered over the southwest for a time, then moved north and east over Casper, Wyoming; Rapid City, South Dakota; Columbia, Missouri; Paducah, Kentucky; Chattanooga, Tennessee; and Winston-Salem, North Carolina, before leaving the continent near Norfolk, Virginia.

The 30,000- and 40,000-foot levels reentered the United States territory over northern New York and New Hampshire, then headed straight for Boston. Their paths crossed, though at different times, over Nashua, New Hampshire, a city of 37,000.

The 30,000-foot trajectory crossed Nashua at 2:00 A.M. on Sunday, September 1, while the 40,000-foot trajectory moved over the town twenty-seven hours later, at 5:00 A.M. on Monday, September 2, Labor Day. About fourteen hours after the first SMOKY cloud had passed overhead, Nashua experienced a tornado. The storm swept into the western part of the city, near Ninth Street, and damaged a small shed at the Fred Dobens residence. A witness to the disturbance, Mrs. Michael Radziewicz, said the tornado was "funnel-shaped, accompanied by a strong wind . . . and was carrying papers, sticks, wood and other matter when it hit the area."[63]

A few hours after the clouds crossed Nashua, they tracked over Lexington, Massachusetts. At the Lexington Theater that evening, Pat Boone and Bobby Burns starred in the movie *Bernardine*, while the Embassy Theater featured a new motion picture, *The Ten Commandments*.[64]

GALILEO

If the pentomic army was ever to amount to anything, the soldiers would have to become acquainted with the heavy weapons. Problems had surfaced in the past: paratroopers had refused to jump into the mushroom cloud, infantrymen had acted strangely just prior to a detonation, psychological and physiological disturbances of all sorts were displayed by the GI's prior to, during, and subsequent to the bursts.

During prior tests, behavioral scientists from various institutions, notably the Human Resources Research Office of George Washington University (HumRRO), had had to make do with interviews and observations of the troops in action. The HumRRO plans were continually thwarted by changes in scheduling, poor interview techniques, poorly designed tests, and soldiers who said one thing and probably believed something entirely different. One marine from New York told interviewers in 1952 that he would "go in there tomorrow and be a guinea pig and sit in a foxhole right under one of those bombs" *if* they'd give him a discharge.[65]

The research techniques left much to be desired.

Therefore, when the AEC announced plans for a detonation just for the benefit of the behavioral scientists, a swarm of sociologists, psychologists, and physiologists descended upon Camp Desert Rock for the shot. Code-named GALILEO, and scheduled for September 2, it would be their own experiment, an attempt to determine *with precision* how the average GI reacted to a typical tactical nuclear weapon.

GALILEO would be truly tactical-size, about 11 kilotons, and would be detonated from a 500-foot tower in Area 1, a location just 8 miles southwest of the SMOKY ground zero. About 3 miles due east of the tower, engineers had constructed a 60-by-210-foot infiltration course consisting of foxholes, a wall, and grenade pits. The behavioral scientists planned to time the 130 soldiers as they (1) disassembled rifles; (2) walked, crawled, and ran through an obstacle course; and (3) threw grenades over a wall. *All while a mushroom cloud would be developing 4,800 yards to the west.*

To heighten the realism somewhat, there would be no trenches. Rather, the men were to lie face down with their feet toward the blast. One minute later, they were to begin the rifle assembly.

On the morning of September 2, at 5:40 Pacific Daylight Time, GALILEO was detonated, first searing the troop position with a blinding light, then immersing it in thick dust. At 5:41 the scientists blew the whistles and the men began to first take the rifles apart, then put them back together. It was a reasonable, if military, test of memory, motor control, and concentration. In the dust storm and noise of the nuclear event to their west, few bothered with the rifles. Amid the roar, one paratrooper, Charles Newsome, remembered the initial flash: "It was the clearest light I'd ever seen. If there was a lizard on a rock twenty miles away, I think I could have seen him."[66]

Later, a spokesman for the 82nd Airborne reported that "although some paratroopers had their helmets knocked off, none was injured and all were calm."[67] The results of the psychology tests indicated that soldiers could, indeed, perform satisfactorily in the presence of a nuclear explosion.

The GALILEO mushroom, propelled by 11 kilotons of energy, soon reached 32,750 feet into the desert sky.[68] Pushed by southerly winds at the stem level, it then began a slow track first to the north and west, splitting into four distinct trajectories that fanned out over the United States from Rapid City, South Dakota, to Dallas, Texas.

The 40,000-foot trajectory eventually arrived at the East Coast on September 4, crossing the Boston area at 11:00 that morning. It was, coincidentally, the very same day that the first Edsel rolled off the assembly line in Detroit. The 10,000-foot trajectory passed about 100 miles *south* of Detroit at 4:00 A.M. two days later, then went on to cross northern Pennsylvania on September 7. Early *that* day, someone stole an Edsel in North Philadelphia.

On September 5, while GALILEO was hovering over the Iowa-Wisconsin border, Oklahoma, and South Carolina, Dean Martin hosted his first variety show on NBC since splitting up with Jerry Lewis. That day, Elvis Presley was busy recording *Blue Christmas* and *Treat Me Nice* at Radio Recorders in Hollywood. California, incidentally, received no fallout from GALILEO.

Just before midnight on September 6, the Show of Stars was wrapping up its first night in Pittsburgh. The evening's performers included Fats Domino, Chuck Berry, and Buddy Holly. Within the hour, debris from GALILEO would be crossing the countryside 50 miles north of the city on its way toward Manchester, New Hampshire.

WHEELER

The next bursts scheduled for the test site were both scheduled for September 6. The first was a bona fide nuclear device and was set for a morning detonation. Code-named WHEELER, the device was uncharacteristically small for a Livermore design; the yield was expected to be something less than a kiloton.[70]

WHEELER's mushroom cloud was small in comparison to the others, only 3,000 feet thick, suspended a mere 2½ miles above the desert floor. Instruments revealed a yield of just 197 tons.[71]

One segment of the WHEELER cloud passed within a few miles of Wheeler, Texas.[72] The day before, the Wheeler Quarterback Club had held its first regular meeting. The film shown was *Humble Oil Company's Football Highlights of 1956*.

The nuclear cloud continued on north, crossing northern Oklahoma and into Missouri. At 4:40 A.M. on September 12, WHEELER crossed over the small Missouri town of Paris. As in Wheeler, Texas, life in Paris continued on as usual: That afternoon, Mrs. Mary Russel announced that she would reopen the City Cafe on Paris' Main Street. The evening before, the Paris Drive-In Theater west of town offered a Karl Malden–Anthony Perkins motion picture, *Fear Strikes Out*.

COULOMB B

The second test scheduled for September 6, a safety experiment, took place in the afternoon. Safety experiments were designed to determined if a nuclear weapon could be detonated by unconventional means—that is, by fire or an external explosion, such as might occur in a plane crash. The military was very interested in the results of the experiments; great numbers of B-52s were crossing the United States every day, each carrying nuclear weapons. If one of these bombers should crash, they wanted to be sure no nuclear explosion would take place.

Theoretically, the configuration and timing involved in a nuclear detonation was so precise that, unless everything worked exactly right, no fission would occur. All that would happen would be, at worst, a conventional explosion in which several pounds of plutonium would be scattered across the area. Even though plutonium was extremely toxic, this was infinitely preferable to having a major nuclear detonation, with the attendant heat, blast, and radiation.

The safety experiments had begun in November 1955 at Project 56. Four experiments were conducted in which weapons containing various amounts of plutonium were subjected to fires, explosions, and other jostlings. The explosions were carefully analyzed for the telltale radiation indicating fission. All went well until the last test, Project 56 Number 4, on January 18, 1956. A charge was placed near the unarmed device and fired. At Control Point, the instruments measuring neutron and gamma radiation moved slightly. Somehow, detonation—and fission—had occurred. The scientists concluded, to their dismay, that detonation of an unarmed weapon might be possible.

On April 24, 1957, another safety experiment was performed, Project 57 Number 1. The yield was zero. Perhaps the technicians in Project 56 had made a mistake.

One July 1, another safety experiment, code-named Coulomb A, was conducted. An unarmed weapon was placed on the desert floor and detonated using conventional explosives. Again, zero yield.

Twenty-five days later, technicians lowered a weapon 200 feet into an open hole in Area 3j of the test site. On top of that, they placed a 50-foot block of concrete. The hole was then capped with more concrete.

Then, at one in the morning of July 26, the unarmed device, code-named Pascal-A, was subjected to a conventional explosion. A huge cloud, containing, dirt, smoke, and plutonium, shot out of the ground, ascended 1,450 feet, then began to drift northeast. Radiation monitors found heavy plutonium contamination in a strip 200 yards wide by 2,000 yards long. Inside this strip, radiation levels approached 12 roentgens/hour, mostly from alpha particles. But there was something else there, too: beta radiation, apparently from fission products.

Pascal-A had produced a slight yield.

On August 10, the next device, Saturn, was placed in a tunnel and detonated. No yield was detected.

The safety experiment for September 6, code-named Coulomb B, would take place at Area 3g on a platform just 3 feet above the surface. As with all safety experiments, technicians were careful to use respirators; by this time they were well aware of the problems associated with the plutonium cloud. To most of the scientists, the term "safety experiment" was a misnomer; the toxic plutonium scattered across the desert made these shots some of the dirtiest imaginable. It was fortunate that the material was at least confined to the area of the test site.

By noon, the instruments to measure possible neutron and gamma radiation had been calibrated and the countdown began. One difference between a conventional explosion and a nuclear one is the sharp, blinding flash of intensely white light that occurs in the first instant of detonation.

At 1:00 P.M., technicians watching the shot platform adjusted the dark goggles as a precautionary measure.

At 1:05 P.M., the charge was sent to the explosives placed near the unarmed weapon. Even through the dark goggles, the explosion seemed extraordinarily bright. Technicians watched at the radiation meters climbed steadily to the right. There had been a measurable, and totally unexpected, yield. Later analysis of the data revealed a fission yield equivalent to 300 tons of TNT, fully one and a half times the earlier Wheeler shot.

The safety experiment that was COULOMB B produced a cloud 13,965 feet high. Winds from the east at 18 mph carried the radioactive cloud west, reaching the California border at 6:00 that evening.

At ground zero, radiation monitors found levels approaching 100 roentgens/hour, ten times that produced by the conventional nuclear detonation seven hours before.[73]

Following essentially the same path as the earlier shot, a segment of COULOMB B's cloud passed 15 miles northwest of Wheeler, Texas at 5:30 P.M., September 10.

Four days later, September 14, was declared Felt Hat Day in Wheeler. McIlhany's Dry Goods and J. Lee's Department Store both featured a complete line of felt hats for men. As part of Felt Hat Day, it was declared that "the proper head dress for male citizens of Wheeler and the trade area will be some style or type of felt hat."[74,75]

The two events are thought to be unrelated.

Event LAPLACE, like many of the other shots in the PLUMBBOB series, involved "amplified neutron radiation effects"—that is, they were possibly prototype neutron bombs.[76,77] Military scientists wanted to determine the effect these weapons might have on the battlefield; one project involved determination of neutron-induced gamma activity on three types of American soils. The military didn't necessarily want a weapon that would make the entire battleground uniformly radioactive.

LAPLACE was detonated at 6:00 A.M. The one-kiloton yield produced a mushroom 6,000 feet thick, rising to an altitude of 15,814 feet above the desert floor.

An hour after the shot, ground zero radiation levels only reached 50 roentgens/hour. At 15,000 feet, the wind blew from the southeast at a gentle 5 mph; the cloud hung over the general area for most of the day, then slowly began to move south toward Harlingen, Texas.[78]

At 5:24 A.M. on September 14, just six minutes before its scheduled detonation, event WHITNEY was scrubbed because of a faulty circuit. It would have been the nineteenth shot of the series.

Seven and a half miles to the southeast, in Area 3b, Los Alamos scientists had already transported another, somewhat smaller device to the top of a 500-foot tower. Code-named FIZEAU, it was expected to have a yield of about 10 or 11 kilotons. Unlike WHITNEY, the FIZEAU event seemed to be running along without a hitch.

One aspect of the FIZEAU event involved Project 41.2: a weapons vulnerability test. Scientists wanted to know if a nuclear bomb could be set off by a nuclear detonation in the vicinity. They also wanted to know if Sandia Corporation was up to building a "toughened" nuclear device. Several of the Sandia devices had been placed on television towers within a few hundred feet of the FIZEAU tower.

The meteorological information collected several days before the WHITNEY and FIZEAU events had indicated a recurring problem: The wind would carry the nuclear cloud directly over the small mining community of Lincoln Mine. As a precaution, the AEC ordered a temporary evacuation for the sixty residents of that village. Prior to WHITNEY, the Lincoln Mine's location just 35 miles north of the test site, had delayed shots more than twenty times. Finally, the AEC allotted $45,000 to pay the mining company, Wah Chang Mining Corporation, to curtail its operations for three months, until testing was completed.

FIZEAU was detonated at 9:30 A.M. Pacific Daylight Time, sending a "barbell-like, salmon-colored" cloud almost 7 miles into the morning sky.[79]

The cloud immediately moved northwest, toward northern California. After crossing the California coast, FIZEAU's debris became entrained in a circulating area of low pressure. By September 18, much of the cloud had returned to the continent, moving at various velocities toward the north central and eastern United States.[80]

The next day, at 11:00 A.M. local time, amid partly cloudy skies, part of the FIZEAU debris crossed 40,000 feet over Danbury, Connecticut.

That evening, the Danbury Drive-In on Federal Road offered two features, *3:10 to Yuma* with Glenn Ford and *Wicked as They Come* with Arlene Dahl. At the Palace Theater the movies were *The Pajama Game* and *Trooper Hook*. The next day the Palace would feature *Tammy and the Bachelor*.

As FIZEAU moved across the East Coast of the United States, Radio Moscow reported that Soviet scientists were preparing to launch their first artificial satellite. Across the country, newspaper reports of the announcement were usually confined to an inside page.

The twentieth burst in the PLUMBBOB series was scheduled for September 16. A Los Alamos device code-named NEWTON, it was to be suspended from a balloon 1,500 feet over Area 7b, an area that had been witness to events of similar yield.

As a precaution, radio announcements were issued warning spectators away from the area surrounding the test site, and plans were made to order motorists off the road prior to shot time. The week before the shot, meteorologists had predicted the wind to be from the south. As a result, the town of Lincoln Mine was again evacuated. On the morning of September 16, roadblocks were set up on three highways, U.S. 93 and 95 and Nevada 25. At these stations, cars were pulled off to the side and the motorists told to shield their eyes.

At exactly 5:50 A.M. Pacific Daylight Time, the Newton fireball erased the early morning darkness, replacing it with a brilliant orange glow easily visible in Salt Lake City and San Francisco, 350 miles away. The shock wave, traveling at 600 mph, reached reporters at News Nob sixty seconds after detonation.[81]

The 2½-mile-high mushroom ascended to 27,814 feet, where 76-mph winds from the southwest pushed it directly toward Salt Lake City. Upon reaching the northern border of Utah, the lower, 10,000-foot level shifted to a northerly course, traveling over Yellowstone National Park on its way toward Coeur d'Alene, Idaho.

At the same time, the 20,000- and 30,000-foot levels drifted across the north central states before converging on New England. At 11:00 on the morning of Thursday, September 19, NEWTON's debris crossed 20,000 feet over Old Town, Maine, a small industrial community near Bangor that called itself the "Gateway to Northern Maine."

The weather that day was characteristic of autumn in northern New England, clear and slightly cool. The evening before, the Strand Theater on Main Street had featured a Betty Hutton–Dana Andrews film, *Spring Reunion*, about two college classmates who fall in love again at a fifteen-year reunion. Co-billed was the movie *Tomahawk Trail*, a B-western.

On the evening of September 19, Cub Scout Pack No. 78 was planning to meet at the Old Town YMCA, also on Main Street. The next day, a Friday, the high school sophomores had scheduled the annual reception for the new freshmen.

Across the continent, at 11:00 P.M. local time on September 19, the debris from NEWTON's stem crossed at 10,000 feet over the northern Idaho towns of Coeur d'Alene, Hayden Lake, and Harrison.

That day, in Hayden Lake, Mrs. Peter Kellas held a party for her son Tommy on his twelfth birthday, while Kootenai High School in Harrison elected its cheer leaders. The Evergreen Floral and Gift Shop on Coeur d'Alene's Sherman Avenue offered ten roses for just 98 cents: "Take Home a Bouquet for Your Wife."

That night, as the NEWTON cloud moved toward the town, St. Margaret's Guild of St. Luke's Episcopal church held their regular meeting at Parish Hall.

While the Old Town, Maine, sophomores were welcoming the incoming freshmen, a rummage sale was held at the Christian Church at 4th and Garden in Coeur d'Alene, Idaho. Though separated by thousands of miles; both communities were under debris from the same nuclear explosion.

RAINIER

By mid-September, construction and drilling crews had completed excavation of a tunnel beneath a mesa in the far northwestern corner of the test range. The location had been the site of a previous safety experiment, SATURN, which had taken place on August 10. This time, however, the underground detonation would produce a yield.

The AEC and military were particularly interested in underground shots; they wanted to determine how well an underground test could be detected at a great distance. In addition, if the theories proposed by Edward Teller and RAND's David Griggs were correct, an underground shot might release *no* fallout; the intense heat might actually seal the radiation inside a "bubble" of melted rock until the debris decayed to a safe level.

Event RAINIER would test this theory.

Seismologists around the world were notified that an underground American shot would take place in mid-September. Scientists were, however, more than a little concerned about the possibility of the shot generating earthquakes. To impede transmission of shock waves, the scientists picked the spongiest mountain in the area, a mesa in Area 12 rising 3,535 feet above Yucca Flat and composed of volcanic tuff, a very soft, porous, ashlike material.

A tunnel was dug into the side of the mesa. At the far end the engineers fashioned a room 6 by 6 by 7 feet, located 900 feet underground and 790 feet from the side of the hill. At shot-time, the scientists would be in the Control Point, 2½ miles from point zero.

At 10:00 A.M. on September 19, technicians threw the switch, and the nuclear device detonated with a force of 1.7 kilotons. There was a low rumble as the mesa seemed to jump slightly, then settle back in a barely detectable ripple that quickly spread over the face of the mesa. A few rocks fell down the side of the mountain.

The coastal and geodetic seismologists reported the RAINIER blast had corresponded to about 4.6 on the Richter scale.

Vibrations from RAINIER were detected by seismologists as far away as Fairbanks, Alaska. Surveys of Rainier Mesa showed that the puny 1.7-kiloton shot had managed to pulverize half a million tons of tuff, and broken 200,000 tons more. Three months after the shot, instruments detected core temperatures as high as 90 degrees centigrade (194 degrees Fahrenheit).

No radiation was detected, even directly above the epicenter. No fallout was released.

The AEC quickly decided that nuclear weapons almost a thousand times larger than RAINIER could safely be fired underground in the Nevada desert. RAINER, and its two predecessors, JANGLE: UNCLE and TEAPOT: ESS, would be the forerunners of all of the Nevada testing after the early sixties. And thanks to RAINIER's rock-crushing capabilities, it would be the predecessor to Project Plowshare, the ambitious plan to move mountains using nuclear energy.

WHITNEY, CHARLESTON, and MORGAN

By Monday, September 23, the technicians had worked the bugs out of the WHITNEY device and the countdown began at Area 2 for the detonation.

At 5:30 A.M. Pacific Daylight Time, residents of Los Angeles and San Francisco saw a flash in the eastern sky resembling heat lightning. At the test site, WHITNEY's fireball cast a brilliant purple glow across the desert floor. Reporters on Mount Whitney, the event's namesake, clearly saw the 19-kiloton fireball, 120 miles away, as it flashed into the morning sky.

The WHITNEY cloud quickly climbed to 25,514 feet. Pushed by southeasterly winds, the mushroom slowly moved northwest, toward Mount Whitney. By 2:00 P.M., however, it became evident that most of the cloud would not cross into California after all, but rather track just east of the Nevada-California border.

The upper levels crossed over Nevada, Idaho, and Wyoming before splitting up. The 30,000-foot level, captured by a cool front, moved south into Texas. The 20,000-foot "middle" level took a more central route before turning south over southern Illinois, where, inexplicably, it began to follow the Mississippi River to Baton Rouge, then crossed over to Bogalusa, Louisiana, at 10:00 on the evening of September 29.[82]

The shot scheduled for September 28 would be another UCRL-sponsored event, code-named CHARLESTON, apparently for the Nevada mountain located south of the test site. The next-to-last detonation of the series would be a relatively small blast, only 12 kilotons, and would be fired from a balloon over Area 9a, the site of LASSEN, WILSON, OWENS, and WHEELER, as well as the gigantic HOOD.

CHARLESTON was detonated at 6:00 A.M. Pacific Daylight Time from a height of 1,500 feet; it sent a rather unimpressive mushroom 27,779 feet into the sky. [83,84]

The final shot of the series, MORGAN, was scheduled for October 7. The device, supplied by Livermore, was to be suspended from a balloon 500 feet above Area 9a.

Though reporters were told no military tests would be involved in the event, scientists were busy preparing Project 6.5, "Effects of Nuclear Detonations on Nike Hercules." In 1957, the Nike Hercules was the country's chief defense missile for use against enemy bombers. A new transistorized guidance system had recently been implemented, and the designers were interested in determining how well it would withstand radiation and blast effects from an atomic shot. At part of this test, personnel installed both standard (vacuum tube) and the new transistorized versions at stations 590, 1,345, and 2,198 feet from the epicenter.

As part of another military effects experiment, eighteen technicians entered a radar station 6.2 miles from the blast site at 11:30 on the night before the shot. They would remain there to monitor the cloud track until 7:00 A.M. the next day, two hours after the detonation.

Early on the morning of October 7, the device was loaded onto the 75-foot diameter balloon and raised to a height of 500 feet. At 5:00 A.M. Pacific

Standard Time, the charge was sent to the capacitors. The fireball seemed "unusually bright," to reporters stationed on Angel's Peak, while the residents of Los Angeles clearly saw the flash of light in the sky.

The cloud followed the path of many of its predecessors, tracking east and north: The 20,000-foot level moved toward Omaha, Nebraska, crossing just south of that city during late rush hour on Monday, October 7. From there, it moved on into Iowa, crossing the town of Corning two hours later. The debris passed over Chicago at 11:00 A.M., October 9, on its way to a 2:00 P.M. rendezvous with Battle Creek, Michigan, home of Kellogg's Frosted Flakes.

Two days after that, on October 11, the slower-moving debris at the 10,000-foot level also arrived over Corning, crossing from west to east at 4:00 P.M. From there, the nuclear cloud drifted toward Morning Sun, Iowa, just north of Burlington. Eventually, the lower level would also move on to Battle Creek, crossing that city at 5:00 P.M. the next day.

The last debris from the last shot in the PLUMBBOB series finally left the United States over Forest City, Maine, at noon, October 10, 1957.

It would mark the last of the Nevada shots that were documented to have reached entirely across the United States to New England. But the Nevada aboveground tests would resume, one year later, with HARDTACK II.

Hot Dust, Hard Rain

If a person were to look at fallout particles under a microscope, he or she would probably see tiny beige to black colored beads that varied greatly in size. Generally, the closer the site of fallout is to ground zero, the larger the particles will be. After some nuclear tests, soldiers experienced gravel falling on their positions.

The crew of the *Fortunate Dragon*, trapped under the cloud of the CASTLE: BRAVO shot, saw white chaff fall onto their decks.

A thousand miles from ground zero, the fallout particles were so tiny they could be found only as spots on film.

Scientists looking closely at the hot dust made a number of important discoveries. They found that if a weapon is exploded several thousand feet in the air, the *amount* of fallout is reduced considerably. Fallout particles from an air burst were found to be between a hundredth of a micron and 20 microns in diameter, roughly the size of fog droplets. Also, while the mushroom of an air burst is quite radioactive, the stem usually is not.

A land or subsurface burst will send rather large particles into the atmosphere. About 90 percent of the gravel that fell on the soldiers during maneuver was found to be from the mushroom, the rest from the stem, which in the case of a surface burst was quite radioactive.

As for plutonium, present in about every blast, the scientists knew that the metal would combine with oxygen in the air to form an oxide.[1] Close-in fallout often involved plutonium oxide particles about the size of fog droplets.[2] A 1975 study showed that plutonium oxide particles ending up several thousand miles from the test site were usually one-tenth that size or less.[3]

Examined under a microscope, a small percentage of the larger (and hotter) particles were perfectly spherical, tiny magnetic balls of metal slightly less than a millimeter in diameter. It was decided that these beads were part of the tower or bomb casing. Interestingly, the beads were attracted to iron; the blast had somehow made them magnetic. When analyzed chemically, the tiny spheres contained a variety of elements, but one ratio was standard: three parts iron to four parts oxygen—magnetite.[4]

Most of the particles found from the Nevada shots were tiny glass spheres, dark brown or black outside and a transparent, pale yellow-brown inside. Usually, the darker the glass, the more radioactivity was found. The source was obvious: sand. The silicate materials from the soil were first vaporized in the fireball, then cooled into tiny liquid spheres varying in size from as large as raindrops to as small as the aforementioned fog particles.

In addition, the intense heat dissolved fission products from reacted plutonium and uranium in the outer layers of the beads and turned them black—and intensely radioactive. For some reason, many of the "Nevada fallout spheres" contained tiny glass bubbles inside them.

Some of the particles were radioactive throughout; in others, the radioactivity was confined to the surface. Some of the particles were spherical; others were irregular in shape, similar in appearance to common dust.[5]

Researchers found a marked difference in the particles, depending upon whether they resulted from a high air burst or from a detonation closer to the surface. High air bursts, such as TEAPOT: HA, produced mostly spherical-shaped particles that were rarely larger than 20 microns and slightly denser than quartz.[6] Occasionally, two spheres were found to be stuck together. The colors ranged from transparent to gold-yellow, orange, red, brown, green, and black. Radioactivity was present throughout the spheres.

Low air or tower bursts, such as UPSHOT-KNOTHOLE's SIMON, HARRY, etc., produced both spherical and irregular fallout particles that varied greatly in size, from a few microns to the size of gravel (which, of course, fell to earth close to the test site.) The colors were similar to those produced by the high air shots, but the particles were slightly less dense.[7] The distribution of radioactivity varied; some were radioactive throughout, others showed only surface activity. Generally, the darker the particle, the more magnetic it was. In several of the tower bursts, most of the particles were magnetic.

Surface and shallow underground bursts such as TEAPOT: ESS and JANGLE: UNCLE produced irregular-shaped fallout particles. As would be expected, the color of the fallout was related to the color of the soil. Density was about the same as from the tower bursts. Generally, the larger the particle, the greater the radioactivity.[8]

The Wayward Wind

Before the TRINITY shot, the scientists knew that fallout would be picked up by the wind and carried some distance away from ground zero. Most, however, assumed the maximum distance would be about 100 miles or so. In fact, the fallout cloud easily reached as far east as Indiana. Crude attempts at fallout tracking were made during the RANGER series. Better procedures and instrumentation followed during subsequent operations, and by the end of 1952 the meteorologists had assembled a considerable amount of data on wind patterns associated with the transport of fallout. One of the first things the weathermen learned was that the winds were essentially unpredictable.

The northern hemisphere is girdled by rivers of wind flowing generally from west to east; however, different levels may take different directions. The air currents at 10,000 feet altitude may show no relation whatsoever to the currents moving at 20,000 or 30,000 feet. To complicate matters even further, the oceans and the polar and tropical air masses tend to "steer" the wind patterns in unpredictable ways. A packet of air might meander across the continent in a more or less direct west-to-east line, then suddenly, say over Kentucky or Ohio, turn north and head straight for Maine. This "funnel" effect is the result of many complicated meteorological factors, but it explained why New York and New England seemed to receive unusually high doses of fallout from the Nevada tests.[9]

The tropopause is the boundary between the turbulent troposphere where most of our weather occurs and the stable stratosphere. Particles from a nuclear cloud punching up through the tropopause were found to stay in the atmosphere for months or years. Scientists saw fallout from high-altitude shots circle the earth for months before dissipating.[10]

The researchers found that bomb debris tended to remain in the hemisphere in which it was injected. They discovered that it takes about sixty months for half of a given amount of bomb debris in the stratosphere to move from the northern hemisphere to the southern hemisphere.[11]

Hard Rain

Localized weather patterns muddy up the situation even more. Rain or snow clouds, mixing with the fallout mass in its travels across the continent, occasionally brought the fission particles to earth in extremely localized areas. This resulted in hot spots such as occurred in Albany, New York, after the SIMON shot in 1953.

Generally, rain will bring fallout to earth if the nuclear cloud is below the rain cloud. Since the rain or snow clouds average between 10,000 and 30,000 feet altitude, radioactive precipitation was a somewhat common phenomenon in the 1950s. Those living near the test site were particularly affected; the closer the rain to ground zero, the more radioactive it was. In fact, some scientists estimated that if St. George, Utah, had been visited by a thunderstorm while the HARRY cloud passed over, the area would have become a hot spot so intense that half the population of the town would have been killed.[12,13]

Shortly after the PLUMBBOB: BOLTZMANN shot in 1957, scientists found a hot spot about 60 miles north-northwest of the test site. The area, downwind of a mountain range, was seven times more radioactive than its immediate surroundings. As it turned out, rain had fallen at the same time the nuclear cloud had passed by.[14]

Although rain and snow were found to be major influences upon fallout deposition, dry fallout had been reported a number of times, particularly in the plains states. Some researchers believed that a significant amount of this may have been material picked up from the Nevada test site by the winds and deposited at the counting station hundreds of miles to the east.[15]

Hot Enzymes

In the late 1950s, as more and more information came in about fallout, many scientists privately conceded that it *was* probably hazardous. It was just that no one knew *how* hazardous. While strontium-90 enjoyed a certain popularity, knowledgeable researchers knew that it was only one of many potentially toxic substances produced by the fission process. At the crux of the problem was the fact that the body had the unfortunate capacity of storing minerals in various organs. And it didn't seem to care whether they were radioactive or not.

Iodine-131, for example, is a radionuclide produced in the course of atomic fission. With a half-life of just over eight days, it is also a common component of fallout. Of course, unlike "regular" (nonradioactive) iodine-126, the fission product I-131 is quite hot. Wherever it is, the radionuclide spits high-energy beta rays into the surrounding area.

Like many elements, iodine is used by the body, particularly in the thyroid, where control of metabolism occurs. Any iodine entering the body will sooner or later end up in this tiny gland. Since the body can't distinguish between nonradioactive and hot iodine, the I-131 is also stored in the thyroid. As a result, the tiny gland is bombarded by high-energy beta rays from within.

As evidence accumulated, iodine-131 and other hot particles were increasingly suspected of causing the sheep deaths in 1953, mostly by bombarding the animals' insides with damaging beta and gamma rays.

A rad is a unit of absorbed dose roughly equivalent to a roentgen. One rad represents 100 ergs of energy absorbed by one gram of tissue. A dose of 600 rads, taken within an hour's time, is considered lethal to humans. Years after the sheep incident of 1953, Dr. Harold Knapp, an AEC fallout expert, calculated that the sheep's intestines had been exposed to over 5,000 rads, and that their thyroids had taken a dose somewhere between 10,000 and 20,000 rads, certainly enough to kill them.[16]

But iodine was only one of many hot substances produced by fission that the body tended to store. Strontium-90 and cesium-137 seemed to turn up in bones (as did plutonium).[17] The kidneys seemed to have an affinity for uranium, and radioactive zinc often made its way to the prostate.

Some enzymes in the human body were known to depend upon nonprotein structures called co-factors for their activity. Such structures often involved one of the essential trace minerals such as manganese.[18] Unfortunately, the living cell cannot distinguish between stable manganese-55 and the radionuclide manganese-54, produced from decay of radioactive chromium-54. Once in the system, the radionuclide manganese-54 decays to stable iron-54, releasing low-energy electrons to the surrounding cells.[19]

In the same way, radioactive iron-55, a product of neutron capture by stable iron-54 (found in the bomb tower), can enter the hemoglobin in a red blood cell to give off low-level radiation over the life of the cell.[20]

Scientists knew of many elements absorbed by the body that seemed to serve no useful purpose. The average human daily intake of zirconium, for example, was estimated to be about 3.5 milligrams. The daily intake of niobium is somewhere on the order of 600 micrograms.[21] For some reason, these two elements are stored throughout the body and particularly in the lower large intestine.[22] If the elements are radioactive—for example, zirconium-95 or niobium-95 or -96—then whatever cell these materials are stored near will receive radiation from beta particles, gamma rays, and low-energy electrons.

Scientists had known for some time that certain elements, because of their structure, are sufficiently similar chemically that they can actually replace essential minerals in the human body. Under normal circumstances, this would pose no problem. However, when the element is a radionuclide, the potential for a problem exists.

Strontium-90, for example, is absorbed by the bones because it resembles calcium.[23] Manganese, an essential trace element, can be displaced by technetium-99. Rubidium-86 can replace potassium at various locations in the body.[24] Ruthenium-103 is a rather hot radionuclide that was detected in Richmond, California, in the early sixties.[25] Ruthenium-103, after a short period of time, decays to rhodium-103, emitting radiation in the process.[26] Unfortunately, rhodium is a potential carcinogen. Also unfortunately, the body can mistake ruthenium for iron, which, of course, is used in the manufacture of enzymes and hemoglobin.[27]

To many concerned scientists in the late 1950s, the overriding question remained: What would these hot particles do once they were inside the human body?

Fallout: The Questions

In 1956, shortly after nine-year-old Martin Bordoli became ill with leukemia, his parents recalled an event that took place years before.

On November 19, 1951, a brown, hazy cloud had rolled through the pass and over their ranch, depositing a fine layer of particles in its wake. That day, their son, then four years old, had been playing in the yard.[1]

Earlier that day, the AEC had fired a nuclear device in the JANGLE series, code-named SUGAR. It had been a surface shot and had traveled due north of the test site. Was there a link between his leukemia and the many nuclear detonations?

The Bordolis decided there was. After their son's death the couple circulated a petition calling for an end to the testing, citing its possible harmful effects to the local population.

The petition eventually found its way to the desk of Lewis Strauss, chairman of the AEC. Strauss, interestingly, had been "cool" on the idea of the Nevada tests for some time. Nevertheless, as chairman of the AEC it was his responsibility to draft a reply:

Dear Mrs. Bordoli,
　　This letter is in response to the petition regarding nuclear weapons tests on which you were the initial signer. . . .
　　Former President Harry S. Truman put the case for weapons testing at this time in a recent press statement. Mr. Truman said, "Let us keep our sense of proportion in the matter of radioactive fallout. Of course, we want to keep the fallout in our tests to the absolute minimum, and we are learning to do just that. But the dangers that might occur from the fallout involve a small sacrifice when compared to the infinitely greater evil of the use of nuclear bombs in war."

—Lewis L. Strauss, AEC Chairman, Nov 21, 1957[2]

Two months before the Strauss reply, a somewhat more ominous letter had arrived from George Malone, the Republican senator from Nevada:

> *Dear Mr. and Mrs. Bordoli,*
>   *I have received your recent petition regarding the possibility of dangerous atomic fallout and its harmful effects to the people living close to the southern Nevada test site.*
>   *Recently the newspapers in this country have carried stories that make it appear that a large segment of the scientific world is in a disagreement with the government's nuclear testing program in regard to the harmful effect of fallout resulting from atomic explosives. This has resulted in a fallout scare throughout the United States. The President has questioned these reports coming from a minority group of scientists, some admittedly unqualified to comment on nuclear testing, and as he has said, it is not impossible to suppose that some of the "scare" stories are Communist inspired.*
>   —Sen. George Malone, September 12, 1957[3]

The Malone letter also contained the subtle admonition to refrain from starting "scare stories."

The rural population of Nevada and Utah were patriotic Americans; they were also infused with a healthy dose of American skepticism. Even if they didn't know much about fallout, it was apparent that the scientists didn't either.

For one thing, there was an obvious disagreement among scientists on just what was an unhealthy dose of radiation. The National Academy of Sciences admitted that 600 rads—equivalent to an exposure of say, 600 roentgens for one hour—would likely be a lethal dose, but hedged when asked about *accumulated* doses.[4] There seemed to be confusion about rads, rems, and roentgens. One day the fallout monitors would report the radioactivity in roentgens, the next day in rads.[5] Fallout was measured in disintegrations per second for one test, millicuries the next.[6]

Then there was the problem of radiation. One minute the scientists talked about X-ray doses, the next about alpha particles. What kind of radiation, exactly, did fallout produce?[7]

In 1955, the elder Joe Fallini had seen the monitors carrying Geiger counters, checking the area for fallout. He decided to buy one. One day, after a particularly noxious cloud had passed overhead, Fallini took the Geiger counter to the schoolhouse in the tiny community of Twin Springs, Nevada.[8] The radioactivity inside was so high that the needle on the Geiger counter slammed against the right peg.

Later, after describing what he had found to an AEC monitor, the official replied by asking him: "What schoolroom are you talking about?" Incredibly, the AEC had *not* known of the existence of the Twin Springs schoolhouse.[9] Checking around, Fallini found that the AEC had placed film badges in all the neighboring schools *except* Twin Springs. When the AEC finally placed a film badge there on March 30, 1955, nine shots had already taken place.[10]

Clearly, confidence was lacking in the AEC's ability to even adequately monitor the area downwind from the site.

For years the "downwinders" had seen the particles in the air, either as a fine dust or, occasionally, much larger. In May 1952, after shot TUMBLER-SNAPPER: Fox, the Sheahans of Groom Mine saw "bead-like particles, some over a sixteenth inch in diameter" fall out of the sky. Shot Fox had been a tower shot; the beads the Sheahans saw appeared to be composed of iron.[11]

Now they wanted to know what the beads actually were.[12]

By 1957, public sentiment had begun to shift. In 1955, the conservative *U.S. News & World Report* had carried an article stoutly proclaiming the fallout to be harmless. In 1957, it wasn't so sure. In its June 14, 1957, issue, the magazine carried an article by AEC commissioner Willard F. Libby, "Why Nuclear Tests Go On—AEC Gives Officials Reasons."

The next week an uncredited report, "If You're Still Wondering About Fall-Out Danger," cited the views of several "Top Authorities." The tone was far more balanced than in 1955 and was laced with such phrases as "all such radiations are potentially dangerous, their use should be the subject of constant and close scrutiny," and "every endeavor should be made to keep the level of exposure as low as possible." Under the heading "What X-Rays Can Do," the article flatly stated that "Radiologists die five years earlier on the average than physicians having no known contact with radiation." Also quoted was the British Medical Research Council: "It is unlikely that the inhalation of radioactive particles present in the air as a result of fallout would constitute a problem in ordinary civil life. . . . Account must be taken, however, of the *internal* radiation from the radioactive strontium which is beginning to accumulate in bone. . . ."

For those concerned with fallout, it was not a particularly encouraging article.[13]

A week later, the magazine offered reassurances from, of all people, "Folks" from "Fallout City": St. George, Utah.

Jeter C. Snow, mayor of St. George: "I've not noticed any real concern, [though] people here wish it could be some other way."

Dr. M. K. McGregor, physician: "There's a lot of spotty baldness, but it's all due to anxiety—not to any fallout I know of. . . ." (McGregor concluded, however, that it was "important to know more about fallout.")

Wayne Whitehead, of Whitehead's Dairy: "The tests don't worry me. I think that the guys who are doing it are competent. If they weren't they wouldn't be doing it."

Rex Frei, cattleman: "I don't see how that little flash down at Vegas could affect us. I had my wife operated on for cancer and they gave her tremendous doses [of radiation] over two months. She's still alive, so this can't be too bad."

Ellis Everett, physics instructor at Dixie College: "I take the AEC's word on how much people can stand. I'm not worried about it. Our big problem here is finding a physics teacher."

Of those interviewed, only one was identified as opposed to the tests, Mrs. Kate Empey, secretary of the town information office. The article wrote that Kate was once "dead-set against the atom tests," and was ready to circulate a petition to stop the shots, "but never did."[14]

Eighteen years later, Dr. McGregor was more certain about the effects of fallout than he had been in 1957. In a May 1985 interview he flatly said that he feels there's a connection between the fallout and the cancer rate. During the interview he recalled that though most of the others in the *U.S. News & World Report* interview were still alive, Rex Frei had died of prostate cancer in 1976. Frei's brother Newell had died of leukemia in 1980.

Dr. McGregor also recalled the case of a rancher living near the test site, Aaron Leavitt. For some unknown reason, Leavitt's hair had come out during the late 1950s, then grew back. Some time later, both Leavitt and his brother died of pulmonary fibrosis. a disease with a number of causes, one of which is inhalation of plutonium.[15]

Eighteen years later, Ellis Everett also had a different opinion. "I didn't know much about it then," he said. "I didn't know that much about radiation, I thought it was safe. I've changed my mind. . . . There *has* been a lot of cancer here. The president of Dixie College died of it. It was a gradual process, a growing conviction that something was wrong as I saw more and more leukemias and cancers. At one time I though the government knew what they were doing, but I've changed my mind on that score, too."[16]

The month before the *U.S. News & World Report* articles were published, Dr. E. B. Lewis, in an article that appeared in the respected *Science* magazine, flatly claimed that there was no safe level of exposure to radiation and the leukemia risk is in direct proportion to the radiation exposure.[17] A month later, Linus Pauling estimated that 10,000 persons had contracted leukemia from the testing.[18]

Prior to the testing, the residents of St. George and Cedar City had all enjoyed reasonably good health. In an interview years later, mortician Elmer Pickett of St. George recalled the sudden change: "My father and I were both morticians, and when these cancer cases started coming in I had to go into my books to study how to do the embalming, cancers were so rare. In 1956 and 1957, all of a sudden they were coming in all the time. By 1960, it was a regular flood."[19]

In Cedar City, when Blaine Johnson's daughter contracted leukemia, he asked the doctor at the clinic in Salt Lake City if it wasn't unusual that there were seven cases of leukemia within 100 yards of their home.[20]

While the leukemia cases were showing up in Utah and Nevada, another, more celebrated case appeared in the Soviet Union: in 1956, Vyacheslav Alexandrovich Malyshev, who had taken over the Soviet atomic project three years before when Beria was deposed, contracted leukemia. Blood specialists were flown in from Cologne, West Germany, to see Malyshev, to no avail. In February 1957, the head of the Soviet atomic project was dead, quite possibly from an overexposure to radiation.[21]

Hardtack I–II

During the late 1950s, the debate over fallout had heated up considerably. Dr. Edward Condon of Washington University in St. Louis had charged that thousands will die of bone cancer and leukemia from the testing, while Linus Pauling's estimates of deaths from fallout had climbed steadily over the years from "200,000 mentally or physically defective children" to "five million defective children" along with millions of cases of leukemia and bone cancer.[1]

The issue pitted scientist against scientist. A growing cadre of academicians were siding with Pauling and Condon's position that the testing could cause cancer and genetic damage, while pro-AEC scientists couldn't seem to agree on just how much fallout was hazardous. AEC fallout specialists seemed to be unable to agree whether explosions should be limited to 2.5 or 10 megatons a year; while Dr. Charles Dunham, the AEC's director of biology and medicine saw some undesirable fallout as "inevitable."[2]

The issue even pitted laboratory against laboratory. In June 1957, several scientists at Brookhaven Laboratory asserted that *any* amount of radiation would be likely to damage heredity cells. This evoked an acid response from an Argonne scientist who claimed that "fumes from automobiles are a greater hazard than fallout," and questioned the authority of physicians to speak on the danger of fallout.[3]

In addition, there was the problem of secrecy regarding fallout data. Though the AEC had considerable data on fallout, it was almost impossible to obtain, "for security reasons." One person who had difficulty in getting fallout information from the AEC was Dr. Harrison Brown, professor of geochemistry at Cal Tech. Despite the fact that Brown had once worked at Oak Ridge and had a high-order security clearance, he had to make "a special plea" to the AEC for the information. He finally obtained it from the Japanese.[4]

Official response to this barrage of criticism proved somewhat inadequate. Occasionally officials would try to conjure up the Communists one last time by speaking vaguely of "fellow-traveling tendencies."[5] Other times, they would respond by pointing out far worse hazards such as cigarettes. Usually they would say that no one really knew for sure *what* effect fallout had on humans.[6]

And, of course, they were right. No one knew *for sure*. But they had some good suspicions, based upon simple logic.

Specialists familiar with physiology knew that blood is very sensitive to radiation. In fact, one of the first signs of radiation overexposure is a change in the blood picture, a general decrease in the number of cells. They also knew that blood cells are formed in the bone marrow. And if strontium-90 were absorbed by bone—which it is—then the radionuclide would be awfully close to the blood cells at the most critical time: when they were being formed.

In addition, geneticists had known for years that radiation had a nasty habit of breaking apart the tiny threads of DNA inside a cell, damaging that cell's ability to correctly reproduce itself. The result could easily be a cell gone awry, a cancer. And if a blood cell is involved, you have blood cancer, such as leukemia.

One study of particular importance in this area was conducted by Britain's Dr. Alice Stewart. In 1958, Dr. Stewart reported an epidemiological study clearly indicating that women receiving X-rays while pregnant had children with a higher risk of such diseases as cancer and leukemia. For children of women who had been exposed to X-rays during the first three months of pregnancy, the cancer rate had been elevated by ten times.[7]

The evidence was slowly accumulating.

For many of the scientists it was an exceedingly short step between strontium-90 and leukemia, and the AEC's vague assurances of "negligible danger" only angered them further.

Those inside the "atomic establishment" reacted to the furor in a variety of ways. Some felt that fallout was grossly overrated as a hazard. Others, like AEC commissioner Libby, shared the popular administration view that further testing was needed to perfect a "clean" bomb.[8]

The Eisenhower administration, by 1958, was between a rock and a hard place. They wanted weapons, but the problem of fallout was threatening to shut down the testing. A clean bomb was the perfect solution. Unfortunately, it would have to consist of fusion fuel ignited by conventional explosives, not by fission (which caused fallout). It was no easy task, and would require extensive testing that would in turn produce more fallout.

On Monday, April 14, 1958, the radioactivity in the nation's capital was at its highest level for the year.[9] The AEC claimed the fallout was the result of Soviet tests. It was an easy assumption; the Russians had been detonating megaton and near-megaton range devices in the Arctic since February and Operation HARDTACK I, a series of H-bombs scheduled for the Pacific, was still two weeks away.

After HARDTACK I began, the AEC again quieted down about levels of fallout. By examining "tracer elements" found in the debris, the scientists were genuinely able to determine if the fallout had come from a United States test or from a Soviet one. But to the public, fallout was fallout, regardless of its source. The clamor for a test ban continued throughout the summer and on into the fall.

HARDTACK I

HARDTACK I began with event YUCCA, involving a nuclear device attached to a helium balloon and launched from the USS *Boxer* near Eniwetok. The balloon climbed to 7,000 feet in just seven minutes. The device was detonated from almost 100,000 feet altitude, producing a bright star in the afternoon sky that was visible from Eniwetok.

During the summer, thirty-three nuclear devices were detonated at Eniwetok and Bikini, mostly from barges. All of the events were given names of American trees and shrubs: FIR, NUTMEG, SYCAMORE, WALNUT, CEDAR, OAK.

One witness to shot OAK was George Mace, a sailor stationed 15 miles from surface zero on Eniwetok. After the detonation, Mace felt the "unbearable" heat on his back. He then turned and saw a rising column of water ringed by "ragged halos of white waves that seemed to produce some an electrical field." Watching the ascending mushroom, Mace seemed to feel some sort of static electricity in the air as the hair on his body "bristled."

About twenty minutes later, while talking about the shot with his friends, he noticed a slight movement at the shoreline. For some reason, the beach looked different. It seemed larger, somehow.

Then it hit him: The water was receding. In a short time, they could see coral and sea creatures stranded on what was now only damp sand. For a moment he wondered if OAK (which had been an 8.9 megaton explosion) had somehow cracked the bottom of the lagoon, and now the water was rushing out.

Then, suddenly, the water began to return, not in the graceful manner of its exit, but as a tremendous tidal wave bearing down on them.

"For hours," Mace said, "the water in the lagoon continued to slosh like disturbed water in a basin, and for the rest of the day the lagoon water was muddy and treacherous with crosscurrents."[10]

Two very special shots, TEAK and ORANGE were scheduled toward the end of the HARDTACK I series. Army Redstone rockets would be used to lift two H-bombs almost 50 miles over Johnston Island. The scientists admitted that they had no idea how an H-bomb would act at that height.[11]

TEAK was launched thirteen minutes before midnight on August 1, 1958. Three minutes later, the warhead detonated at 250,000 feet. Seven hundred miles away, people walking along Waikiki Beach in Hawaii were astonished to see a bright red ball suddenly appear in the sky near the horizon. Hysterical residents flooded the police with calls.

One resident described the shot: "I stepped out on the lanai and saw what must have been the reflection of the fireball. It turned from light yellow to dark yellow and from orange to red. The red spread in a semi-circular manner until it seemed to engulf a large part of the horizon. A cloud rose in the center of the circle. It was quite large and clearly visible. It remained visible for about a half hour. It looked much closer than Johnston Island. The elevation of the circle was perhaps 20 feet above the horizon."[12]

On August 12, another Redstone rocket was fitted with a hydrogen warhead, fueled with a mixture of alcohol and liquid oxygen, and then fired into the sky. In Hawaii, burglar alarms suddenly began to ring and electric garage doors raised inexplicably.

At the same time, high-frequency radio communication was suddenly cut off all across the Pacific. The blackout lasted two hours in Hawaii and nine hours in Australia. The blast had temporarily destroyed a layer of ionized air high above the earth that, under normal conditions, was used to reflect radio signals around the globe.

The burglar alarms had been triggered by a new and unexpected phenomenon of the high-altitude nuclear shot: the electromagnetic pulse. It was later determined that a high altitude shot produces a flat, saucerlike area below it that generates high-energy electromagnetic waves, or EMP. Twenty years later, scientists discovered that the EMP could fry a variety of devices, including: digital computers, alarm systems, intercom systems, life-support system controls, anything with transistors and communication links.[13]

Eventually, nuclear war strategists would envision the first detonation taking place high above the target zone. The resulting EMP would then shut down communications and traffic in the target zone, preventing retaliation—and escape—before the missiles arrived.

Shot ORANGE was also part of an experiment to determine fallout deposition. Scientists added materials to the bomb casing that would result in the release of "radiotracers" tungsten-185 and rhodium-102. By tracking these two radionuclides, the researchers thought they could learn more about fallout deposition, particularly strontium-90. After the shot, it was learned that the radionuclides were deposited evenly between northern and southern hemispheres. Three years later they discovered that the highest concentrations at or below 70,000 feet were over the *polar* regions. No one knew why.[14]

HARDTACK I was followed by a secret operation—ARGUS I, II, and III—in which three 1-to-2 kiloton bombs were detonated 300 miles above the south Atlantic. Within hours after each shot, a shell of high-energy beta particles 60 miles thick completely encircled the earth and remained for days.[15]

HARDTACK II

As the summer came to a close, it became evident that the public outcry would eventually result in a nuclear test ban of some sort. If the problem was fallout, then perhaps the latest operation might appease the critics somewhat. The PLUMBBOB: RAINIER test the year before had shown that it was possible to detonate a device underground and still contain the debris. Now, over a third of the shots in HARDTACK II would be detonated either in shafts or tunnels. And of the atmospheric shots, none would be larger than 6-kiloton SOCORRO, scheduled for October 22.

On October 28, underground shot EVANS unceremoniously vented radioactive debris onto the test site. The next day, 7.8-ton HUMBOLDT and 1.3-kiloton SANTA FE were detonated; both sent debris southwest and caused a rise in radiation levels in southern California.[16]

The residents of Los Angeles reacted negatively. On October 30, the Los Angeles mayor demanded the tests come to an immediate halt.[17] For the AEC, the timing was perfect. The series had ended the day before with an international agreement to a ban on atomic testing. Yet shot SANTA FE would not be the last aboveground test detonated at the Nevada Test Site.

1959

If the AEC commissioners thought the public concern with fallout would end with the test ban, they were wrong. By March 1959, Senator Clinton Anderson (D-N.M.), an old Strauss foe, was charging that the AEC kept all new fallout data from the public. Minnesota senator Hubert Humphrey also blasted the AEC for "minimizing" the fallout peril.[18] AEC officials countered that they had been busy determining the "extent and amount" of fallout as part of Project Sunshine, begun in 1953. Under questioning, AEC commissioner Libby admitted that only two scientists were working on Project Sunshine full time.

The next day the prestigious National Advisory Committee on Radiation suggested that the "ultimate authority" in protecting the public be shifted from the AEC to the Public Health Service. It was not a good idea, they said, "to assign authority over health aspects" of atomic energy to the same agency interested in promotion of atomic energy.[19]

President Eisenhower agreed, at least in theory. In April, he ordered a study by "high Federal officials to determine which Government body shall be responsible for protecting the public against atomic radiation."

Participating in the study would be John McCone, the new chairman of the AEC, and Arthur S. Fleming, secretary of HEW, parent agency of the Public Health Service. To head the study, Eisenhower appointed Bureau of Budget director Maurice H. Stans.[20] (Thirteen years later, during the Nixon presidential campaign, Stans would be charged with taking contributions from wealthy Texas Democrats, then "laundering" them in Mexico to assure that the contributors would remain anonymous.[21])

While the fallout controversy swept through the scientific world, pitting colleagues and laboratories against one another, one physicist remained adamant in his beliefs. To Edward Teller, radiation just wasn't particularly hazardous. To illustrate his position, he often told a story dealing with the relative hazards of leaning up against a Dresden III reactor versus sleeping with your wife (all humans emit a very slight amount of radiation):

> One young employee of the AEC asked a friend of mine a question: From what do you get more radiation—from leaning up against a reactor for a full year or from sleeping each night with your wife? My friend did not know the answer. The young man from the AEC made some calculations and sent around a notice which said: "I have calculated that, and actually you get a little more radiation if you leaned up for a full year against the Dresden III reactor than from your habit of sleeping each night with your wife. I am not going to initiate a campaign for a regulation that all married couples must sleep in twin beds. However, I must warn, from the point of view of the radiation hazard, that if you sleep each night with *two* girls you will get more radiation than from leaning up for a full year against the Dresden III reactor."[22]

As for Teller's view regarding radiation from fallout:

> It is very small. Its effect on humans is so little that if it exists at all it cannot be measured. Radiation from test fallout might be harmful to humans. It might be slightly beneficial. It might have no effect at all. The smallest doses producing noticeable effects in animal experiments, approximately one-tenth of one roentgen unit per week, are more than a thousand times as great as world-wide fallout. These experiments produced a slight increase in the incidence of animal tumors—and a lengthening of the animals' average life. The living organism is so complicated and the intertwining of cause and effect is so intricate that we may never know the biological effect of so small a cause as world-wide fallout.[23]

Further, Teller believed in the constructive—and peaceful—possibilities of nuclear devices. He believed that, given the opportunity, he could show that clean H-bombs might be used to recover oil, dig canals, and build harbors.

Early in 1957, nuclear scientist I. I. Rabi had visited with Harold Brown and Gerald Johnson at Livermore. Rabi had worked on the Trinity project, but by 1957 he was opposed to the Bomb. During the visit, Brown had tried to reassure him that Livermore's nuclear devices were to be used for peaceful means.

"So," Rabi replied, "you want to beat your old atomic bombs into plowshares." By September 1957, the name was formalized: Project PLOW-SHARE.[24] In December 1958, the magazine *Scientific American* carried an article by Gerald Johnson and Harold Brown entitled "Non-Military Uses of Nuclear Explosives."[25] Two years later, Johnson and Brown would get the chance to put their theories into action.

Plowshare

After the HARDTACK II series, the AEC detonated most of the shots underground. The notable exceptions were those in the PLOWSHARE series, in which scientists attempted to use nuclear detonations for construction purposes.

After their article, "Non-Military Uses of Nuclear Explosions," Johnson and Brown, along with Edward Teller, began planning for the actual shots that would test their theories. By 1960, they were ready.

In the spring of that year, Teller wrote an article in *Popular Mechanics* entitled "We're Going to Work Miracles." In it, he stated his belief that H-bombs could be used to "unlock a treasure chest of arctic oil, dig open an Alaskan harbor, open the spigot for Colorado's shale. . . ."[1]

Johnson, Brown, and Teller believed that deeply buried bombs would fling only the surface material into the air while trapping the radioactive substances in a bubble of molten rock near the detonation point.

To prove their theory, the Livermore scientists persuaded the AEC to undertake Project Chariot, an ambitious plan to create a new harbor in a remote area of Alaska. The plan called for burying five small hydrogen bombs 500 to 700 feet deep at a site about 100 miles north of the Arctic Circle, near Point Hope and Cape Thompson. If everything went well, the detonations would, in a matter of milliseconds, move 20 million tons of earth and rock, creating a channel 800 feet long and 750 feet wide. It would also create a 30-foot-deep inner harbor a quarter of a mile wide by half a mile long.

Project Chariot immediately began having trouble getting off the ground, weighted down by arguments from a coalition of environmentalists and Alaska sportsmen. In an article in the popular magazine *Outdoor Life*, A. W. "Bud" Boddy, executive director of the Alaska Sportsmen's Council, wrote: "Not only sportsmen, but every citizen of the U.S. should be seriously concerned with what effects this planned nuclear explosion might have on game and fish, two of Alaska's most valuable natural resources—to say nothing of their possible effects on our human resources. I think that it is the duty of every citizen to insist that all the facts be made available to the public before the carrying out of Chariot or of any other similar atomic project."[2]

Responding to pressure, the AEC announced that Chariot had been postponed until the spring of 1962, pending environmental studies. It was later unceremoniously dismantled. AEC scientists concluded that "large earth-moving nuclear explosions in the populated areas where they are needed are risky and probably impossible for a long time to come."[3]

In his *Popular Mechanics* article, Teller had mentioned another type of PLOWSHARE experiment, this one involving the use of nuclear weapons to retrieve oil from shale in western Colorado:

> An even more difficult and ambitious problem, one that might be called only a dream, is to extract the hydrocarbons that are trapped in the oil shales of Colorado, Utah and Wyoming. An experiment is being considered for performing an explosion in this area. In this case much more heat is required to liberate the oily substance from the shale. The heat of the nuclear explosion will not suffice. Actually, the explosion is considered only for the purpose of breaking the shale. Once this is done, one might start an underground fire in the shale. The heat of the fire would then drive out some of the valuable hydrocarbons.[4]

The theory of starting a fire to "drive out valuable hydrocarbons" was somewhat flawed, as anyone who has ever seen an underground coal fire can attest. The primary things produced under such conditions are sulfur dioxide, carbon monoxide, and copious amount of noxious smoke. None are considered particularly valuable.

Nevertheless, Teller's "ambitious problem" was finally tackled in the late sixties, with events GASBUGGY, RULISON, and RIO BLANCO. Event GASBUGGY, a 29-kiloton device, was fired near Farmington, New Mexico, on December 10, 1967. The 40-kiloton RULISON device was detonated near Grand Valley, Colorado, on September 10, 1969, while event RIO BLANCO involved the detonation of *three* 33-kiloton devices near the western Colorado town of Rifle on May 17, 1973.

A third Johnson-Brown-Teller dream also ended as something of a failure. The Livermore scientists had envisioned a project that involved firing a nuclear device inside a salt dome. According to their theory, the salt would become molten and remain so for years, becoming a cheap source of heat. Water could even be forced into the molten salt dome to create steam for energy.

The project finally saw the light of day on December 10, 1961, as operation GNOME. A 3-kiloton device was lowered into a salt dome near Carlsbad, New Mexico, and detonated. The ground shook as a 170-foot-diameter, 80-foot-high cavity was formed in the salt dome.

The radioactive cloud emerged from a number of ground fissures and slowly drifted northeast, covering most of the Texas panhandle and western Kansas and extending to the southwestern suburbs of Omaha, Nebraska. Shortly after the shot, scientists examining the area discovered most of the heat had leaked away.

But that was not the end of GNOME. Two years after the shot, Dr. Eric Reiss, during congressional testimony, claimed that GNOME had "delivered sufficient fallout to the vicinity of Carlsbad, New Mexico, to cause thyroid dose levels of from 7 to 55 rads to children."[5]

In a 1981 interview, a Carlsbad pediatrician, Dr. Catherine Armstrong, reported an increase in "congenital heart diseases, bone defects, severely immature livers and jaundice" among the offspring of people who were children when GNOME was detonated.[6]

Despite the problems, twenty-six other PLOWSHARE events took place. Some, like SULKY, produced only a mound of broken rock. Others, like the huge SEDAN blast of July 6, 1962, carved out a 179-million-cubic-foot crater, then sent the dust eastward.

One of the last in the series, 30-kiloton SCHOONER, also sent radioactive particles toward the East Coast. AEC officials were quick to point out, however, that no radiation had been detected east of the Mississippi River. There was, however, a very good reason, as Colonel Raymond E. Brim, a federal officer responsible for monitoring off-site fallout from underground detonations between 1966 and 1975, explained: "It didn't register east of the Mississippi River because the AEC had no monitoring stations east of the Mississippi River."[7]

Unfortunately, PLOWSHARE, begun with the loftiest of ideals, had ended much the same way as had many of the other nuclear projects: under a cloud of suspicion amid charges of AEC cover-up.

TEST SITES

Detonation Tower Used in the TUMBLER-SNAPPER *Series (April–June 1952).* At the top is a small, shedlike structure called the "shot cab." Most of this 310-foot tower will be vaporized by the blast; winds in the upper atmosphere will send its atoms east across the continent. (*Courtesy Defense Nuclear Agency*)

Balloon at Night. PLUMBBOB: CHARLESTON, *September 28, 1957.* Hoping to reduce
fallout levels, scientists placed several nuclear devices on platforms attached to huge
helium balloons. Detonation usually occurred 1,500 feet above the ground. (*Courtesy
Defense Nuclear Agency*)

Bull's-Eye. Aiming point for an air-dropped atomic bomb. Despite the bull's-eye, airdropped bombs usually exploded hundreds of feet above the earth's surface. Air-dropped
devices produced surface radioactivity at levels well below those of tower shots. (*Courtesy
Defense Nuclear Agency*)

DETONATIONS

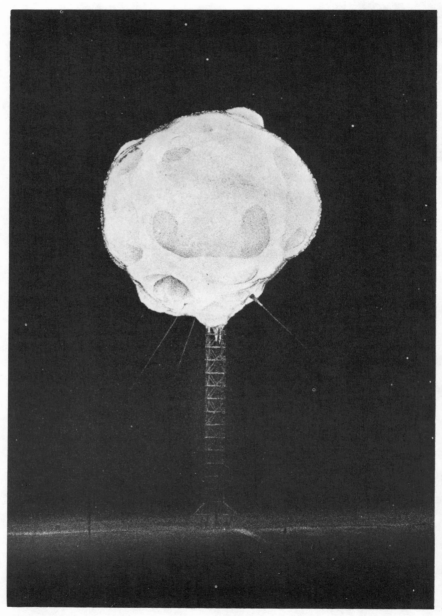

Millisecond Bomb Photo. Atomic fireball milliseconds after detonation. The shot cab already has been vaporized; within an instant, the entire tower also will be destroyed. Seconds later, the fireball will rise like a bubble in the cool morning air, taking with it debris, dust, metal fume, and water vapor to form the familiar atomic mushroom. (*Courtesy Defense Nuclear Agency and EG&G Engineering*)

Bomb Over Desert. Atomic detonation at the Nevada Test Site. The familiar mushroom cloud is actually composed of a mixture of water vapor, metal fume (from the shot towers), desert sand (as microscopic glass beads), dirt, dust, unreacted uranium, plutonium, neptunium, and over 300 different isotopes of 36 elements, from zinc to terbium—mostly all radioactive. As the cloud makes its way to the East Coast, these materials will be deposited in its wake. (*Courtesy Defense Nuclear Agency*)

Airplane Wing. Shot UNCLE, *November 19, 1951.* Dust cloud from shot UNCLE, November 19, 1951. Nevada's first underground shot, UNCLE sent a cloud of highly radioactive debris northeast to Utah, Wyoming, Nebraska, South Dakota, Minnesota, Michigan, and Maine as well as to the Canadian provinces of Ontario, Quebec, and New Brunswick. (*Courtesy Defense Nuclear Agency*)

MANEUVERS

Troops Watching Blast in Distance. Nuclear cloud of shot STOKES, detonated 5:25 A.M. local time, August 7, 1957. One segment of the radioactive debris would leave the U.S. over New York City two days later at 2:00 A.M. Eastern Daylight Time. (*Courtesy Defense Nuclear Agency*)

Soldiers Shielding Eyes.
Shot STOKES at moment of detonation: 5:25 A.M., August 7, 1957. At this early time, the fireball has a radius of about 700 feet and is more than 50 times the brightness of the sun. Soldier observers were asked to face away from the shot and to cover their eyes in order to prevent retinal damage. Many soldiers will be able to see, through their closed eyes, the bones of their hands. (*Courtesy Defense Nuclear Agency*)

Right: *Troops in Trenches During Rehearsal.*
Troops in trenches during rehearsal for shot TUM-BLER-SNAPPER: CHARLIE, April 21, 1952. This 31-kiloton event will involve over 2,000 military personnel and 300 civilian "observers." Days after the CHARLIE shot, high radiation levels will be recorded from Santa Catalina, California, to Savannah, Georgia. (*Courtesy Defense Nuclear Agency*)

WATCHING THE BOMB

Nuclear Cloud, 1953. Photo of nuclear debris over Warm Springs, Nevada, about 100 miles north of ground zero. The photographer, Joe Fallini, protected the film from radiation by placing the camera inside a lead-lined battery case. (*Courtesy Martha Bordoli Laird. Photo by Joe Fallini*)

Nevada Bomb Tests. Locals watching an atomic bomb test in the summer of 1957. Among people living in Nevada, Utah, and California during the 1950s, bomb watching was a major spectator sport. (*By J. R. Eyerman,* Life *magazine* © *1984 Time Inc.*)

Under the Cloud. The Sheahans, standing outside their home at Groom Mine, Nevada, in 1953, watch an atomic detonation 20 miles away. (*Photo by Alan Jarlson for the* Las Vegas Review-Journal)

VII

ACCIDENTS

Bombs Over Mars Bluff

Like much of the south in 1958, eastern South Carolina was mostly rural. The largest city in the area, Florence, was located at the intersections of several highways. The largest, Interstate 301, was the major New York–to–Florida route. Just 5 miles east of town, travelers on the Interstate drove through the small community of Mars Bluff, a quiet suburb nestled amid a thick stand of pine. The tiny suburb was home to fifty residents, mostly farmers.

Thirty-seven-year-old Walter Gregg, along with his wife, his son, and his two daughters, had made their home there. It was, like most of the other houses in the community, a rambling single-story dwelling just 500 yards from the Interstate and within short walking distance of the Mount Mizpah Baptist Church. A conductor for the Atlantic Coast Line Railroad, Gregg enjoyed the peace and quiet of Mars Bluff. The tall pine trees surrounding the Gregg home kept the area shady and cool during the hot Carolina summers and seemed to filter out truck noise from the nearby highway.

It was about 4:30 on the afternoon of March 11, 1958, and Walter Gregg was taking it easy. Spring comes early in South Carolina, and he had been puttering around outside for a few hours, doing odd jobs around the house. On the other of the house, his twin nine-year-old daughters, Helen Elizabeth and Francis Mabel, were playing in the yard with their cousin Ella Davis.

Gregg was standing with his son in the driveway when he heard something. It was three big four-engine jets, B-47s, probably from the air force base in Savannah, Georgia. The Mars Bluff community lay near an "oil burner route"; the big jets flew over the area frequently. After he and his son watched the planes fly overhead, they turned toward the garage. He doesn't remember why.

Fifteen thousand feet above them, one B-47 was having problems. The plane had departed Hunter Air Force Base near Savannah as number three in a flight of four, on its way to an overseas base. The bomb lock on the plane had somehow malfunctioned, allowing one of the weapons to become disengaged from its supports. In an instant, it was gone. A nuclear weapon had been dropped on Florence, South Carolina.

The bomb took less that a minute to reach the ground. In the same amount of time, Walter Gregg and his son had stepped through the door into the garage. Suddenly there came a deafening report as the top and the side of the garage collapsed in a mass of shredded timber.

On the highway, a traveling salesman, J. A. Sanders, was returning to his home in Florence when he heard the explosion. At almost the same instant, a shock wave slammed into his car, turning it completely around on the road.

Gregg opened his eyes to see the air filled with a "green, foggy haze" from the pulverized pine needles. Outside, the sky had gone dark as twilight as a thick cloud of black smoke filled the air.

About thirty seconds later the smoke cleared to reveal a scene of devastation. The top of the house was gone, caved in; one side had been blown completely off. Gregg, a former paratrooper with the Thirteenth Airborne Division, immediately suspected the jet.

Gregg emerged from the garage, shaken and bruised. Although the house had been severely damaged, the bomb had actually landed in the front yard, where, just moments before, the children had been playing. Fearing the worst, Gregg ran to the front yard. The three children were sprawled on the grass, about 100 yards from a huge crater 75 feet wide by 35 feet deep. His niece, Ella Davis, was suffering from a cut on her forehead. Miraculously, his twin daughters were uninjured.

As Walter Gregg and his family were taken by ambulance to the McLeod Hospital in Florence, air force personnel quickly arrived and cordoned off the area. The bomb had been unarmed; a nuclear explosion would have been impossible. However, the high-explosive component of the weapon had detonated, apparently spreading radioactive material over the area. In addition to the Gregg home, the blast had also damaged four other houses and the Mount Mizpah Baptist Church.

In the hospital, Walter Gregg still hadn't been told by the air force what had fallen in his front yard. Initially, he thought it was an artillery shell, or perhaps a conventional bomb. Then a reporter for the *Atlanta Constitution* called and told him his home had been hit by a nuclear weapon.

The Greggs were unable to reenter the home for several days as air force teams completed the decontamination procedures. After the incident, the residents in the neighborhood were troubled with bad coughs, fever, and dysentery. No one, apparently, suffered permanent injuries.[1,2]

The Mars Bluff bombing was not the first accident involving a nuclear weapon; it was, however, the first time an atomic bomb was accidentally dropped on American soil. It would not be the last.

Bombs Over Goldsboro

Shortly after midnight on the morning of January 24, 1960, an eight-jet B-52G Stratofortress bomber began having trouble. The plane, stationed at Seymour Johnson Air Force Base near Goldsboro, North Carolina, had been in the air for eleven hours as part of a Strategic Air Command round-the-clock alert. It had just refueled over the Atlantic and turned inland when the trouble began. To pilot Walt Tulloch, the plane was increasingly hard to control; there seemed to be structural problems. After radioing base, the pilot and flight engineer were put in touch with an official of Boeing aircraft to try to determine exactly what was going wrong. Initially, it was decided to keep the plane over the ocean, then Tulloch was ordered to bring the plane back to its home base.

The pilot received permission to descend to 10,000 feet; in the meantime the flight crew would check the various systems. A B-52G, like most jets, operates best at high altitudes. In denser air, fuel consumption and stress loads increase. When the B-52G reached 10,000 feet, it suddenly began to rattle, then became uncontrollable and went into a spin. Tulloch ordered the crew to bail out.

Just as third navigator Lieutenant Adam Mattocks received the order to exit, he was almost pinned to the side of the cabin from the G-forces. Looking up, he saw Tulloch eject through the top. Mattocks was one of the crewmen *not* assigned to an ejection seat; thinking fast, he dived through an open hatch. Falling through the darkness outside the plane, Mattocks wondered why he had missed being hit by the plane's stabilizer. The reason was that the stabilizer was no longer a part of the disintegrating plane.

The plane passed directly over the home of tenant farmer Marshall Suggs, who had just gone to bed. To Suggs, the plane sounded as though it "was about half running." In a nearby farmhouse, George Howard had also just gone to bed when he thought he heard a plane "whining and sounding like it was about to land." Eight miles away, at Black Creek, night watchman Leland Batts watched something falling through the air trailing sparks. No one had any idea that the plane was carrying two hydrogen bombs.

The plane hit the ground several feet from Bud Tyndall's home, then, trailing a sheet of flame, it skidded across a paved road and into a field. To Tyndall, it seemed as though the "whole world was on fire." Marshall Suggs heard the explosion and thought someone had hit his house with a car. He later told reporters that his "old dog started barking like nobody's business."

George Howard and his wife ran to the window to see the entire field on fire. Their home was just 300 feet from the impact area. Shortly after that some soldiers came to evacuate them from the area because of danger of explosion.

To Aaron Edmundson, who lived a mile from the crash scene, "it was the reddest I have ever seen. It sounded like a bomb going off." The plane had impacted near Musgrave's Crossroads, 12 miles north of Goldsboro.

Within hours of the crash, air force automobiles lined the road, and a lone helicopter circled above, illuminating the surrounding area with a bright beam of light. Two small patches of fire were burning on the road; 100 yards away flames leaped from a huge crater.

Major Tulloch landed in a swamp and was rescued seven hours later. Many of the others landed nearby and were taken either to the crash site or to the base. Three died in the crash, five survived.[1,2]

The B-52G had been carrying two megaton-yield nuclear weapons. One ejected and was parachuted down; the other fell free and disintegrated upon impact, scattering its contents across the waterlogged field. A special weapons crew from the air force arrived to decontaminate the site and search for parts of the weapon. An excavation was made to a depth of 50 feet, but they were unable to find the missing debris. Later, an easement was purchased by the air force that required permission to dig in the area. Subsequent monitoring of the area, now a bean field, has shown no evidence of radioactivity.

An Aside: The 24-Megaton Myth

Two years after the event, scientist-writer Ralph Lapp described the accident as a potential holocaust:

> According to a study of the accident problem made by an independent, non-military group, nuclear weapons have been involved in about a dozen major incidents or accidents, mostly plane crashes, both in the United States and overseas. In one of these incidents, a B-52 bomber had to jettison a 24-megaton bomb over North Carolina. . . . The Defense Department has adopted complex devices and strict rules to prevent the accidental arming or firing of nuclear weapons. In this case the 24-megaton warhead was equipped with six interlocking safety mechanisms, all of which had to be triggered in sequence to

explode the bomb. When Air Force experts rushed to the North Carolina farm to examine the weapon, they found that five of the six interlocks had been set off by the fall! Only a single switch prevented the 24-megaton bomb from detonating and spreading fire and destruction over a wide area.[3]

If Dr. Lapp is correct, Mr. and Mrs. George Howard, Marshall Suggs (and his dog), Aaron Edmundson, and Bud Tyndall would have been at the epicenter of a nuclear explosion almost twice as powerful as the CASTLE: BRAVO blast. It would have totally vaporized the bean fields in the area and created overpressures—pressures in excess of normal atmospheric value—of 12 pounds per square inch for a radius of 6 miles, thus creating winds in excess of 300 miles per hour. The ground shock would have reached Goldsboro within seconds, severing water and gas mains and igniting entire city blocks. The town would have been subjected to overpressures between 2 and 5 pounds per square inch, quickly flattening most woodframe and brick homes in the city.[4,5]

Structures, such as the Odd Fellows Orphanage, would have been leveled, as would much of the downtown area. Anyone surviving the prompt radiation from the detonation would have experienced fallout approaching lethal concentrations. Lethal fallout, in fact, would have likely fanned out to the north in a wide arc between Raleigh and Greenville on its way up the Atlantic Coast.

Estimated accumulated dose contours for the BRAVO shot showed that radiation exceeding 3,000 roentgens reached sites 100 miles away within several hours of the detonation.[6] The lethal 1,000-roentgen level spread 160 miles within twelve hours of the detonation. And this was for a 15-megaton shot. Had the Goldsboro bomb detonated with its force of 24 megatons, the lethal zone would have easily included the nation's capital and possibly New York City.

Had *both* of the devices detonated, the combined megatonnage would have equaled the Mount St. Helens eruption and have undoubtedly contaminated the entire East Coast with lethal fallout.[7]

Fortunately, Dr. Lapp's information was wrong; a 24-megaton detonation could not have taken place. For one thing, the United States had no 24-megaton weapons in its arsenals at the time.[8] The Soviet Union has few targets, most relatively small compared to the United States; strategic planners found no need for weapons larger than 9 megatons. It is also unlikely that the interlocking switches had been "set off by the fall." Though many weapons used in 1960 were protected by only a wire seal, a switch, and a lock, six switches are mentioned in the Lapp article; this would indicate the warheads were fitted with the Permissive Action Link (PAL) safeguard— that is, there had been an electronic "combination lock" inserted in the arming line of the weapon that required the proper combination before the bomb could be armed.[9] It is extremely unlikely that the fall could have randomly produced the proper combination of six digits that would have armed the weapon.[10]

The Soviets II: Chelyabinsk 40

It had been totally unexpected. On April 11, 1958, Soviet ambassador Andrei Gromyko announced that the Soviets had decided to suspend nuclear testing and asked the United States and Great Britain to reciprocate.[1]

On April 13, Senator Hubert Humphrey appeared on a television program claiming that a "catastrophic accident" had occurred in the Soviet Union causing massive radioactive fallout and forcing the Soviets to cancel testing. Claiming his information came from a Danish report, he said that an accident had occurred at the Soviet nuclear weapons manufacturing facility, and that the Russians did not want to test nuclear weapons with defects.

Under questioning, Humphrey guessed that the "accident" had occurred on March 25, when seismographs in Nevada had detected a massive explosion in the Soviet Union. The Russians calmly replied that the March 25 explosion had involved 3,100 tons of conventional explosives and had been used to clear a waterlogged iron mine in the northern Urals.

Humphrey, however, had been right. He just had his dates wrong.

The Accident

Prior to World War II, the two cities of Chelyabinsk and Sverdlovsk had nestled deep amid pine and birch forests at the eastern slopes of the Urals, at the very eastern edge of Europe. Chelyabinsk had enjoyed a long history as a commercial center for travelers between Moscow and the eastern frontier. Founded in the seventeenth century, it was on a major trade route through the Urals.

Both Sverdlovsk and Chelyabinsk were located in picturesque country of rolling hills, thick forests, and lakes and streams. During the harsh winter, the black earth would freeze to a depth of over 3 feet; but in the summer, visitors could fish for carp in the myriad of lakes sprinkled throughout the region.

After the German invasion, industry relocated to the safety of the area, and soon the land between Sverdlovsk and Chelyabinsk was covered with workers' settlements or *posyoloks*, the Soviet equivalent of bedroom communities.[2] Some *posyoloks* sprang up from tiny two- and three-family villages inhabited by Bashkirs and other Asiatic nationalities, hence the names: Karabash, Kasli, Kaslinskoye, Kyshtym, and Kopeisk. Of course, there were the cities that were pure Russian, such as Maloyaroslavets and the ubiquitous Novogorodny, or "New City."

At war's end, some residents of the area returned to Moscow or the Ukraine, others to nearby factory cities such as Magnitogorsk, to the south. Many, however, remained. By 1945, there were workers' settlements every 15 or so kilometers, each with upward of 10,000 inhabitants.[3]

Shortly after the war, rumors circulated that a new military complex would be built somewhere between Sverdlovsk and Chelyabinsk. The rumor became reality as the military descended upon the settlement of Kyshtym, abruptly moving residents out to make way for ten "corrective labor camps." Area residents knew what the new camps were for: The complex would be built with prisoner labor. Still, given the Stalinist paranoia of the time, it is doubtful even local officials initially knew of its purpose.

Suspicions deepened in 1947 with the arrival of a short, bald, fireplug of a man, engineer Boris Vannikov. Those who knew him were aware of his position as an official "facilitator," a "Red Specialist," one who gets things done, usually on an immense scale.[4] Other doubts were erased in the fall of 1947 as Vannikov was joined by a tall man with a square beard, one Igor Kurchatov. The new settlement near Kyshtym would be the home of a nuclear reactor, quite possibly because the hills in the area were laced with a relative abundance of uranium and zirconium ores, both necessary for Soviet nuclear weapon production.[5]

A 2,700-square-kilometer area was chosen as the site of the processing facility.[6] The site included eight small connecting lakes. Soon after construction began, one of the lakes was drained. On its dry bed, the engineers constructed a building of concrete and lead, with an outer coating of rubber. The lake was then refilled.

Adjoining the submerged building, a huge hole was blasted from the slate. In this excavation a factory was built, then covered with earth to a depth of approximately 100 feet. Inside the building, which apparently would be used as a plutonium processing facility, were built eight small shops, all about the same size and separated by concrete walls 15 feet thick, perhaps to protect adjacent areas in the event of an explosion, or critical assembly.[7]

The smaller shops surrounded a large central assembly area approximately 120 feet wide by 300 feet long. Wall cranes were installed to handle heavy materials, perhaps the weapons themselves, moving them from room to room as workers added the various components. At the corners of the central assembly area, four huge concrete pillars supported the weight of the roof and was designed to protect the factory from atomic attack.

Nearby, an atomic reactor was built inside a tunnel that extended into a river. When the reactor was finished, only a smokestack protruding from the ground gave any hint that something unusual was beneath the surface. Nearby, the only sign of the activity beneath the lake was a small tube projecting from the murky water.

By the middle 1950s, several reactors had been built, all surrounding the central underground plutonium processing unit. Waste isotopes—such as radioactive cobalt, barium, cesium, and strontium—were to be placed either in steel storage tanks or directly into a nearby pit.[8]

The new town still had no name; as was the custom of secret facilities, it was known only as a post office box number of the nearest city, in this case, Chelyabinsk 40.[9]

Doubtless, there were rumors of nuclear safety problems at the site. It was known, for example, that from 1946 to 1948 many workers at the Soviet nuclear production sites received radiation cataracts. For this to occur, they would have had to be exposed to 200 rads, a rather enormous dose.[10] Sometime during the mid-1950s, the chief of the Soviet nuclear program, Vyacheslav Malyshev, was reported to have been exposed to a lethal amount of radiation, from which he died in 1957.[11] It could be concluded, therefore, that accidents were common at the weapons production facility. There would be nothing, however, to equal the accident that would take place at Chelyabinsk 40 in the winter of 1957–58.

Little is known in the West of the events leading up to the accident. The Soviets, of course, aren't talking, and what information is known has been compiled by the CIA and by such researchers as Soviet scientist-in-exile Zhores Medvedev. From these sources, a somewhat hazy picture has emerged.

During 1957, the Soviets had been testing both fission and fusion weapons at their various test sites. By the end of the year, production at Chelyabinsk 40 was probably on an extremely tight and rushed schedule. Plutonium from the various reactors was being sent through the tunnels into the processing area for purification and milling, while waste products and "scrap" plutonium were being transported to a nearby disposal site.

It is believed that the facility buried some of the waste in underground steel containers then backfilled with dirt. It is possible that some radioactive waste may have been dumped directly into earthen trenches. Either that or there may have been a long-standing leak in one or several of the tanks, allowing plutonium and other materials to seep into the soil.

Tiny particles, such as those found in clay or other fine soil, have a unique effect upon chemicals percolating through them. Depending upon the molecular weight and other properties of the chemicals, a bed of fine particles will act to separate a mixture into its component parts. In the chemistry laboratory, this property is the basis for column chromatography, a mixture separation procedure. At Chelyabinsk 40, it was an effective method by which, over the years, a thick layer of plutonium gradually formed just beneath the surface of the waste trench.

In 1944, scientists at Oak Ridge were told to be careful when suspending uranium (or plutonium) in water. The water will slow neutrons down, making them roughly ten times more effective at initiating a chain reaction. This means that any fissionable material, such as plutonium, is ten times closer to critical mass when in solution than when dry.

The Chelyabinsk-Sverdlovsk area has a somewhat dry climate; however, in the winter, snowstorms are common. And snow, melting upon the warm surface of the radioactive waste trench, may have been the final ingredient necessary for the catastrophe.

At some time, probably at night, possibly during a winter snowstorm, the radioactive waste trench at Chelyabinsk 40 reached criticality.

The residents of Chelyabinsk, about 30 miles away, reported seeing a red flare to the north, lighting up the sky.[12]

Chelyabinsk 40, for what was probably several agonizing seconds, was bathed in a blue haze of neutron- and gamma-ionized air. Then the trench erupted in a steaming mud volcano composed of hot radioactive wastes. Most of those on the surface at Chelyabinsk 40 were probably killed outright, by direct blast effects or by flooding. Any that had survived near ground zero would doubtless be dead from radiation within days.

The explosion apparently injected an enormous quantity of intensely radioactive materials into the air and in the direction of the nearby settlement of Kyshtym. Reports indicate that "hundreds" died from effects of the fallout.[13]

After a few days, the military arrived to begin evacuation of the injured to hospitals in Sverdlovsk and on the south side of Chelyabinsk, allowing them to bring only the clothes they were wearing. From such places as Muslyumovo, Asamova, Urukul, Kasli, and Kyshtym the victims arrived, all in various stages of radiation poisoning.[14]

Authorities placed the refugees in separate sections of the hospitals, away from the other patients. No one was permitted to visit with them. Entire sections of the hospital ground were cordoned off for use by the radiation victims.

To the east of Kyshtym, soldiers burned houses to the ground to prevent the villagers from returning to the area. Several weeks later, all that remained of some *posyoloks* were acres of stone chimneys, nothing more.[15] Monitors combed the area with Geiger counters. Radiochemists took samples of the soil, only to find incredibly high levels of strontium-90, cesium-137, cerium-144, and zirconium-95.[16]

The military attempted to cordon off the entire area immediately downwind of Chelyabinsk 40. Signs were placed at bridges on the Techa River, which ran through Kyshtym: *Pit strogo vospeshchayetsya, voda zagryaznena* (Drinking strictly prohibited, water polluted).[17] The military even made the *river bank* a prohibited zone.[18]

In the surrounding cities, such as Kamensk-Uralsky, Sverdlovsk, and Chelyabinsk, the sale of food at private as well as collective markets was immediately banned. Weeks after the accident, a system of food distribution was set up through state stores.

Measured radiation levels in the contaminated zone approached 20 roentgens a day, *twice* the radioactivity of RANGER:EASY ground zero one hour after detonation. The radioactive zone itself was probably in the shape of a teardrop or an elongated circle approximately 15 miles across.

By 1959, the pine and birch trees around Kyshtym, exposed to a constant barrage of radiation, had begun to die. The needles and leaves seemed to be affected most on the windward side, the side closest to the site of Chelyabinsk 40. Others seemed to just barely survive, with new shoots surrounding a dry crown. Military bulldozers arrived to remove the dead trees and push them into huge piles. In place of the birch and pine, a thick carpet of bush grass soon began to flourish.

Years later, residents of the area would check the produce with radiometers. Because of the increased risk of genetic damage, women would have to obtain permission to become pregnant. The area between Sverdlovsk and Chelyabinsk would also experience high cancer rates, perhaps as a result of the accident years before.[19,20]

Flight 4154

In the United States, the CIA received word of the disaster at Chelyabinsk 40 about a year after it happened, in March 1959. Undoubtedly, they wanted to take a look at the accident site. The Chelyabinsk-Sverdlovsk area, however, had always been under tight security; admission was tightly controlled. An intelligence agent wouldn't get within 160 kilometers (100 miles) of the place.

However, it was possible they could get a photograph from 12 miles away—straight up. And they knew just how to do it: Operation Overflight.

The CIA had used the high-altitude U-2 spy planes to photograph the Soviet Union since 1956. It was a harrowing piece of business: The pilot would take a thin, black single-engine jet to 65,000 feet, then fly over Soviet territory, taking as many high-resolution photographs as the weather would allow before returning to home base, either in Bodö, Norway, or Peshawar, Pakistan.

Early in the Overflight program, intelligence officials had provided a safeguard to prevent pilots—and information—from falling into Soviet hands: The U-2 pilots were offered the opportunity to carry either cyanide tablets or "The Silver Dollar," a hollowed out coin with a curare-tipped needle inside. Most declined.

As dangerous as the flights were, most involved short sorties over the U.S.S.R., photographing the outlying, lightly patrolled areas—the "fringe" countries of the Soviet Union. The Chelyabinsk-Sverdlovsk complex, however, was in the heart of enemy territory. To send a plane in that far would take careful planning and involve extraordinary risks.

Classified studies of the Soviet defenses indicated that their radar wasn't particularly effective above 50,000 feet; also their missiles weren't accurate enough to hit a target that high. However, intelligence reports had begun to trickle in that newer, more effective radar had been developed and was to be installed at strategic locations. More ominously, word had come in that newer, more powerful SAMs—surface-to-air missiles—were to be installed at the Tyuratam Cosmodrome, and possibly elsewhere. Time was running out. If the CIA was to obtain photos of Chelyabinsk-Sverdlovsk, they would have to do it before the advanced radar and missiles were in place. Plans were drawn up for the most ambitious series of flights of the program.

On April 28, 1960, jet pilot Francis Gary Powers arrived in Peshawar, Pakistan, to prepare for a routine sortie over the southern fringe of western Asia. Reading his directives, he found that it would be a most unusual and hazardous journey: His U-2 plane was to *cross* the Soviet Union, from near Afghanistan to a point over the Barents Sea then east to Bodö, Norway. The flight would take nine hours and cover 3,800 miles, three-quarters of it over Soviet territory.

At 5:30 A.M. local time on May 1, Powers began the preflight check on his plane, U-2 number 360. He was concerned that such a hazardous flight be taken in this particular bird. Number 360 was known among the U-2 pilots as a "lemon," prone to malfunctions. At 6:20 A.M., he was given clearance, and minutes later roared off the runway toward Afghanistan, sortie number 4154.

There was a blanket of solid white cloud over the southern Soviet republics of Tadzhik and Uzbek. The sky cleared over the Aral Sea, however; and as he turned toward the Tyuratam Cosmodrome (the Soviet Cape Canaveral), Powers noticed a condensation trail far below. A jet was flying south, but parallel to his own course.

Coincidence.

To the east, partially obscured by clouds, was the blue Caspian. Somewhere between the Caspian and the Aral lay the Ust-Urt plateau, the site of a number of Soviet nuclear shots. Ahead of him, at the other end of a cloud field, lay the Chelyabinsk-Sverdlovsk industrial complex. Below, Powers noticed another "contrail," this one moving north. Had he been spotted?

Fifty miles south of Chelyabinsk the sky cleared, revealing the rolling foothills of the Urals. To the southwest, in the shadow of Mt. Jalamantau, was the sprawling gray industrial complex of Magnitogorsk. The CIA, however, wanted photos of the Chelyabinsk-Sverdlovsk corridor. Powers turned on his autopilot and began checking his cameras.

Suddenly he noticed something odd: The jet was wanting to nose up. Something was wrong with the autopilot. Here he was, over the very center of the Soviet Union and something had gone wrong with his plane. He would have to fly the thing out of Russia manually. It would be a tedious and difficult five hours.

He was over Sverdlovsk turning north at 65,000 feet when it happened. It first came as a dull thud, and the U-2 jumped forward, as if something had bumped it from behind. Almost immediately, the cockpit was flooded with an orange glare. Powers knew what had happened: "My God," he thought, "I've had it now!" Reaching for the ejection switch, he quickly changed his mind: In a brilliant stroke of planning, the designers of the U-2s had arranged the metal canopy rail to fit snugly over a pilot's legs. Ejection would result in a double amputation 3 inches above the knee.

Instead, Powers decided to get out the hard way, and began struggling with the complex variety of hooks, seat belt fasteners, oxygen hoses, and switches that make for a successful ejection from a damaged U-2. The altitude indicator read 34,000 feet; the vertical speed indicator spun counterclockwise: the plane was in a rapid, spiraling descent. Suddenly he was free of the plane, floating 15,000 feet above the Urals, *1,200 miles* inside Soviet territory. It would be like finding a Soviet airman parachuting into a suburb of Kansas City, Missouri.[21]

Nearing the ground, Powers remembered a conversation with an intelligence officer a few days before:

"All right, say the worst happens. A plane goes down and the pilot is captured. What story does he use? Exactly how much should he tell?"

"You may as well tell them everything," the officer had said, "because they're going to get it out of you anyway."

Powers was captured and sentenced to ten years in a Soviet prison, but released seventeen months later in exchange for Soviet colonel Rudolph Abel, who had been convicted in an American court. No one will ever know what the photos of the Chelyabinsk-Sverdlovsk area showed. U-2 number 360 was destroyed.

Soviet premier Nikita Khrushchev reacted with outrage. A summit conference with President Eisenhower in Paris had been planned. Khrushchev attended, but demanded Eisenhower apologize for the U-2 flights and "punish those responsible." Ike refused. Khrushchev then denounced the United States as "piratical and cowardly."[22] The summit conference would have included a discussion of Berlin. Now Khrushchev announced he would "solve the Berlin problem" by signing a treaty with Communist East Germany.

Tensions were mounting.

VIII

THE ABYSS

Khrushchev

By 1955, the Soviet Union was ruled by essentially three people: Nikolai Bulganin, Marshal Georgi Zhukov, and Nikita Khrushchev. The American people didn't know much about the minister of defense, Marshal Zhukov, but Bulganin had visited the United States. He seemed friendly and resembled an old country doctor, or perhaps a southern colonel. In fact, photos of Bulganin in the mid-fifties bears a striking resemblance to the 1970s fried chicken czar, Colonel Sanders.

Nikita Khrushchev was another matter entirely. Though an expert politician who single-handedly brought the Soviet Union from the dark terror of Stalinism and eliminated many of the notorious *gulags*, Khrushchev was seen by most Americans in the late 1950s as something between a buffoon and an unprincipled thug. He was clearly, as William Manchester described him, "coarse, abusive and intimidating."[1]

Like a later American president, Lyndon Johnson, Khrushchev came from a rural area. In his youth, Khrushchev tended cattle in the village of Kalinovka in Kursk province. Later, he joined the Communist party, becoming an expert at "cloakroom politics." His style, like Johnson's, was a mix of ego, common sense, meanness, intimidation, wit, bluster, and hyperbole.

He gave his adversaries the impression that there was nothing, absolutely nothing, that he couldn't or wouldn't do if he thought he could get away with it. For many Americans, living in the shadow of nuclear war, Khrushchev presented a menacing image.

In 1957, Americans had seen how quickly and firmly the Soviet military had crushed the uprising in Hungary. Though the decision had been the result of weeks of discussions, to the West it was as though the tanks had been sent by Khrushchev without a moment's hesitation, almost as if by reflex. Many Americans wondered what slight provocation might upset the unpredictable Khrushchev; what political gaffe might send him into a final nuclear rage that would result in thousands of bombs careening into America's backyards?

Showdown

To every teenager and adult living in the early sixties, the threat of nuclear war was present and disconcertingly real. The "duck and cover" games played in schools during the mid-fifties were replaced by stern newscasters describing in great detail the military implications of Sputnik and the SS-6, the rocket that put it into orbit. Television film clips featured an enraged, unpredictable Khrushchev in Paris, in Vienna, and at the United Nations.

The relatively quiet 1950s had given way to a new, exciting, and dangerous time. A report by the Mershon National Security Program group at Ohio State University stated that "the chances are of the order of 1 in 100 that a U.S. nuclear weapon will [accidentally] explode at some time in the next ten years." The conclusion was that such an event would probably lead to a "major accidental war" at "some time in the 1960s."[1]

The public was ready to believe it. Early in June 1961, President John F. Kennedy had attempted a summit with the Soviet leader to discuss the touchy subject of Berlin. A treaty had been signed at the end of World War II that had divided the city between East and West. The Soviets now saw the situation as "abnormal" and wanted the U.S. military out of the city entirely.

At the 1961 Vienna summit meeting, Khrushchev pulled out all the stops. Belligerent, boorish, and seemingly on the very edge of physical rage, he had threatened that any agreement that "violated East Germany's frontiers would be an act of aggression" against the Warsaw Pact. In other words, it was either give up Berlin or go to an all-out war with the Soviets.[2]

During the rest of June, both sides made tough, uncompromising speeches detailing their positions on Berlin. Both sides began a military escalation. In late June, Kennedy asked Congress to approve calling up the reserves, increasing draft quotas, and generally preparing the military for war. He stopped just short of declaring a state of emergency.[3]

Kennedy then delivered a televised speech stating that "If war breaks out, it will have been started in Moscow and not Berlin. . . ."

In the divided German city there was chaos. Tens of thousands of refugees flowed across the border to West Berlin. As if to underscore his resolve, Kennedy sent his vice president there. Khrushchev responded by announcing that the Soviets had a *100*-megaton weapon that could be used against any aggressor.

On the evening of July 26, 1961, President Kennedy took the American people with him to the edge of the abyss:

> Good evening.
>
> Seven weeks ago tonight I returned from Europe to report on my meeting with Premier Khrushchev . . . and his grim warnings about the future of the world. In Berlin, as you recall, he intends to bring to an end, through a stroke of the pen, first our legal rights to be in West Berlin and secondly our ability to make good on our commitment to two million people of that city. That we cannot permit.
>
> We do not want to fight—but we have fought before. . . . We cannot and will not permit the Communists to drive us out of Berlin—either gradually or by force.
>
> Tomorrow I am requesting of the Congress new funds for the following immediate objectives: to identify and mark space in existing structures—public and private—that could be used for fallout shelters in case of attack; to stock those shelters with food, water, first-aid kits, and other minimum essentials for our survival; to increase their capacity; to improve our air-raid warning and fallout detection systems; including a new household warning system which is now under development; and to take other measures that will be effective at an early date to save millions of lives, if needed.
>
> In the event of attack, the lives of those families which are not hit in a nuclear blast and fire can still be saved if they can be warned to take shelter, and if that shelter is available. . . .
>
> If war begins, it will have begun in Moscow and not Berlin. . . . For it is the Soviets who have stirred up this crisis. . . . It is they who have rejected the rulings of international law.
>
> And as Americans know from our history, on our old frontier, gun battles are caused by outlaws, and not by officers of the law.
>
> Now in the thermonuclear age, any misjudgments on either side about the intentions of the other could rain more devastation in several hours than has been wrought by all the wars in human history. . . .
>
> Thank you and good night.

Khrushchev answered on August 14 by sending tanks and convoys of East German soldiers to the border between East and West Berlin, closing off the flow of refugees.

Despite the rhetoric, there had been no nuclear testing since 1958, no overt preparations for a *nuclear* war. However, on August 31, 1961, that situation changed as the Soviet news agency TASS made a surprise announcement. Claiming the United States was on the verge of testing anyway, the Soviets had also decided to resume testing.

And what tests they would be: TASS went on to confirm Khrushchev's earlier statement that the Russian scientists had indeed developed a 100-megaton warhead. The very same day, the Kennedy administration answered that the U.S. was now free from the pledge not to resume *its* nuclear tests. Two days earlier, perhaps anticipating the showdown, Khrushchev had stated the United States had adopted a "threatening" attitude. He justified the Soviet decision as a method of persuading the West to negotiate on disarmament.

By September 8, the Berlin wall was completed.

Two days later, Khrushchev notified the West that the Soviets were busy testing the trigger on a 100-megaton bomb. AEC scientists had counted six Soviet detonations in ten days, some at Semipalatinsk, two at Novaya Zemlya, one at an undetermined location east of Stalingrad, probably on the Ust-Urt plateau. Five days later, the Soviets raised the number of shots to eleven, most of them megaton-size blasts. That day, President Kennedy announced the opening of operation NOUGAT, with 2.6-kiloton shot ANTLER.[4]

Three days later U.N. secretary-general Dag Hammarskjold was killed in a plane crash in the Belgian Congo. Early reports indicated the plane had been shot down by Leftists. All the pieces were in place. The world was braced for an all-out nuclear war, Kennedy and Khrushchev in a high-noon standoff, both close to the guns.

Then, amazingly, Khrushchev blinked.

At the beginning of October, he told a visiting Belgian diplomat, Paul-Henri Spaak, "You know, Berlin is not such a big problem for me. What are two million people among a billion Communists?"[5]

From that, Khrushchev continued to back down. Two weeks later, the crisis was over. To millions of Americans, the world had come within a hairsbreadth of a genuine nuclear war.

In fact, it had come even closer.

During the height of tensions, Kennedy had called together a meeting of nuclear strategists and top-level advisors. He wanted them to prepare a report on the possibilities of a "counterforce" nuclear strike against Soviet military targets. The advisors reported that the conditions were excellent for such a strike; that the U.S. had a nuclear advantage over the Soviets and that the United States could expect only token retaliation—perhaps losing only 3 million people in the process, and certainly no more than 15 million. The group's recommendation was for a nuclear strike. Kennedy declined.[6]

He had reached the edge and looked into the abyss. That had been more than enough. And though he couldn't know it, one year later he would be there again.

Novaya Zemlya

The land is intensely cold year around; regardless of the season there always seems to be a harsh wind roaring down from the Arctic's Center, past Franz Josef Land, over the dark, cloud-covered mountains and across the ice desert at the southern edge of the island. South of the island, across the cobalt-gray, unbearably cold water of the Kara Strait, is the flat, drab expanse of the Bolshezmelskaya Tundra. Three hundred miles farther south are the coal mines and labor camps of Vorkuta, at the northern edge of the Urals.

The island: Novaya Zemlya, Russian for "New Land," the site of the Soviet H-bomb tests.

Those arriving by military plane from Moscow rarely are able to glimpse tiny Kolguyev Island lying nearby, a barren rock in the ice-spattered Barents Sea. Undoubtedly, there are radiation and instrument monitors located there, possibly a single, important station in the northern radar net. As the plane approaches Novaya Zemlya itself, one may see through the mist and clouds the northern end of the island, rugged Cape Zhelamiya, jutting like a knife into the Arctic Ocean. Behind it, innumerable drab peaks push through the rugged ice sheets. Except for the occasional polar bear and flocks of Arctic tern, it is uninhabited. Farther south, the mountains decrease in altitude, then give way to a rolling plain. Looking closely, the air passenger might notice that Novaya Zemlya is really composed of two islands, each separated by a narrow, intensely turbulent strait of water.

Once on the ground, the visitor to Novaya Zemlya would discover a drab, barren landscape, punctuated by equally drab buildings. It is early autumn, September 9, 1961. The scientists who live at this permanent settlement have a special and dangerous assignment. The next day they will begin a nuclear test series that will, on October 30, culminate in a nuclear explosion with a projected yield of 50 million tons of TNT.

The next day, September 10, not one but two devices are fired over the Kara Sea. The huge mushroom clouds roar into the stratosphere above

Novaya Zemlya then, pushed by a high altitude southward flow of air, begin to lean toward the mainland. The clouds pass over the large northern Russian cities of Murmansk and Arkhangelsk, where a light rain falls. Both metropolitan areas are undoubtedly dusted with a fine radioactive ash.[1,2]

The western edges of the nuclear debris drift over parts of Finland and Norway, while the eastern edge passes over the prison labor camps at Vorkuta. The camps are located at a rather unpleasant site: on a marsh 50 miles from the northern edge of the Siberian forest and only 300 miles south of the Soviet H-bomb test site. Not only are the prisoners able to see the flashes from the detonations, they are directly in the line of fallout, a captive audience to the displays.

There are other members in the audience even closer to the blasts. By 1961, the United States had abandoned Operation Overflight and had replaced it with a number of spy satellites—such as SAMOS, a photoreconnaissance device; the heat-detecting MIDAS; and two TIROS weatherwatchers equipped with television cameras.[3]

Between September 12 and October 20, fourteen Soviet detonations were detected, two at Semipalatinsk, the rest at Novaya Zemlya. Then, on October 23, while on the nightside of an earth orbit, the satellites pick up an enormous flash. Instruments initially indicate the detonation to be on the order of 35 to 50 megatons. That figure will eventually be revised downward. Still, it is an enormous release of energy.

The mushroom, after climbing to well over 100,000 feet in the air, began to lean south. Within a few hours, the debris was rushing toward the central Soviet mainland at 80 mph.

Upon receiving news of the explosion, Norway, Denmark, Finland, and Sweden began taking emergency precautions, storing dried milk and installing radiation warning sirens. Helsinki's Institute of Radiation Physics examined the rainwater and found that the radioactivity had increased ten times over the past summer.

French nuclear scientist Professor Francis Perrin announced that the radioactivity from a 50-megaton blast "could kill 10,000 persons during the next thirty years and the fallout from bombs already exploded could kill 10,000 to 20,000 others."[4] At the time of Perrin's statement, France had been a member of the nuclear club for twenty months and had exploded four nuclear devices at Reggan in the southwestern Sahara, the largest being a 60- to 70-kiloton shot.

Earlier, *Newsweek* magazine had published an account of the Russian testing, saying "One of the first rules in atmospheric nuclear testing is to check which way the winds are blowing, out of consideration for your neighbor. Seemingly, it does not apply in the Soviet Union."[5]

Newspapers around the world carried varying degrees of protests about the shot. The harshest criticism, however, came from the Japanese, who accused the Russians of "reckless nuclear testing" that would endanger mankind for many future generations. The Japanese public were told that "within a few days the ash of death from the latest explosion will fall on Japan."[6]

Most of the ashes, however, first passed over the Soviet Union itself. Detonation had occurred at 12,000 feet altitude, somewhat low for a 25-megaton shot. The fireball, estimated to have been nearly *11,000 feet* in diameter, had picked up an enormous amount of material and sent it south toward the Vorkuta labor camps and the village of Ust-Usa. Within eighteen hours, most of the heavy particles had fallen from the cloud, covering the western Urals, including Sverdlovsk and Chelyabinsk, in a blanket of radioactive fallout. According to one estimate, the radiation level at Ust-Usa was on the order of 6 roentgens.

In Peking, on October 27, a news broadcast was interrupted midsentence with an announcement calling for "a vigilant alert against a general radioactive fallout from all directions." Although no mention was made of the Soviet tests, the radio said radiation monitors were being sent to China's northern provinces to measure fallout.[7]

That same day, Premier Khrushchev made an announcement to a closed session of the 22nd Party Congress. "Bourgeois propaganda," he said, "has of late raised a clamor around the fact that the Soviet Union has been forced to resume nuclear weapons tests. This clamor assumed a hysterical nature [after the announcement] of the forthcoming fifty-megaton nuclear test explosion." Khrushchev complained that the rest of the world didn't understand the Kremlin's motives in going on with the tests. "Indeed, even fair-minded people expressed concern over the consequences of the nuclear explosions that are being carried out." Nevertheless, he said, the test of the 50-megaton device will take place.

The next day, Saturday, October 28, radioactivity from the 25-megaton shot was detected in the northwestern United States. In New York, twenty-one people were arrested while singing antiwar protest songs at the Soviet Mission to the U.N.

Atomic scientists at Los Alamos and Livermore stated that a hydrogen bomb, unlike an atomic bomb, could be made to any size. A 50- or 100-megaton weapon, they said, just was of less practical use than several kiloton-range bombs.

Speculation was renewed about the physical effects of a large hydrogen detonation. At TRINITY, some scientists had expressed concern that at a certain, unknown size an atomic explosion might "go big": If the explosion was big enough to begin with, the nuclear fireball might become self-sustaining, perhaps burning nitrogen or oxygen in the air as fuel. It would be the world's biggest, hottest—and last—uncontrollable fire on earth.

Still others opposed the test because of the fallout it would produce. One such scientist was the inventor of the Soviet H-bomb, Andrei Sakharov. He was aware of statements opposing the testing made by such scientists as Albert Schweitzer and Linus Pauling and began to feel a responsibility for problems that might be caused by the fallout, including "an increase in the number of illnesses and in the birth of monsters." He felt that "because of the fallout of the radioactive products of a nuclear explosion in the atmosphere, every megaton claims thousands of unknown victims."[8]

During the summer, Khrushchev had called the atomic scientists together to announce his intention of breaking the test-ban treaty. They were told that the testing would support the Soviets policy on "The German Question"—Berlin. Sakharov was upset at Khrushchev's decision and sent him a note "The revival of these tests after the three-year moratorium will be a breach of the test-ban treaty and will check the move toward disarmament: it will lead to a fresh round in the arms race, especially in the sphere of inter-continental missiles and anti-missile defense."[9]

The note was passed to the premier, who put it in the breast pocket of his jacket. Then, after inviting everyone to dine, Khrushchev stood for an impromptu speech: "Sakharov is a good scientist, but he should leave foreign policy to those of us who are specialists in this subtle art. Strength alone can throw our enemy into confusion. We cannot say out loud that we base our policy on strength, but that is how it has to be. I would be a ditherer and not the Chairman of the Council of Ministers if I were to listen to people like Sakharov."[10]

Later, as the testing proceeded, Sakharov became more concerned. To him, the test of a 50-megaton weapon was useless from a scientific point of view. Moreover, he thought that "the number of anticipated victims was colossal."

"Realizing the unjustifiable, criminal nature of this plan," he wrote later, "I made desperate efforts to stop it. This went on for several weeks—weeks that were full of tension."[11]

As the 50-megaton test drew near, the atomic scientist contacted the minister of Medium Machine Building, the tempermental Yefin Slavsky, and threatened to resign.[12] Slavsky told him: "We're not holding you by the throat." Sakharov then tried phoning Khrushchev, who was vacationing in Yalta. It was no use. They would go through with the test.

In his book, *Sakharov Speaks*, he recalled the moment: "The feeling of impotence and fright that seized me on that day has remained in my memory ever since, and it has worked much change in me."[13]

At 3:30 local time on the morning of October 30, 1961, 12,000 feet over Novaya Zemlya there took place an explosion of unimaginable scope. Instruments placed at various locations around the island were unable to record sufficient data on the fireball. It was simply too big: Something well in excess of 2 *miles* across, it reached the earth in a fraction of a second and simply vaporized what was there. For the 100,000 citizens of Murmansk and Arkhangelsk, for the laborors at Vorkuta, for the tribes near Ust-Usa, and for the prisoners at Norilsk, night suddenly became day.

The explosion had clearly taken place too close to the earth. A band of intensely radioactive debris 50 miles wide poured from Novaya Zemlya over the Urals and into Western Siberia. The labor camps at Vorkuta again received 6 roentgens, while for 1,000 miles across the West Siberian Plain the radiation level reached 4 roentgens.[14]

The next day, major cities in the West were under a "fallout alert." Families began stockpiling canned milk and other foods. In St. Louis, the Committee for Nuclear Information stated that the level of iodine-131 in fallout could not be determined quickly enough for preventative measures. The committee recommended that pregnant women, nursing mothers, and small children take small doses of iodine or one drop daily of saturated solution of potassium iodide (SSKI).[15] The report neglected to mention the proper method to drink the dark blue solution: through a straw. As a result, many people in St. Louis greeted Halloween 1961 with blue lips, indicating they were either children, nursing, or pregnant.

After the monster test, Khrushchev appeared at a restricted meeting of the Communist party. Perhaps as a joke, he said that the scientists at Novaya Zemlya had made a mistake. The explosion, he said, "proved somewhat bigger than the fifty megatons that the scientists had calculated . . . we shall not punish them for it." The audience received the comment with laughter and applause.

Operation SUNBEAM

Shortly after the Kremlin announced the resumption of testing, Kennedy had authorized a series of small shots in Nevada: ANTLER, SHREW, BOOMER, and CHENA. While all were fired underground, ANTLER unexpectedly scattered debris to the northeastern coast. The news put the president in an embarrassing position. In the 1960 campaign, he had spoken out against the dangers of fallout; for that reason alone he had opposed atmospheric testing. Now it appeared that even underground shots were hazardous in that respect.

At the same time, it was becoming increasingly obvious that the Soviets had every intention of testing their own "super," a 50-megaton weapon. To stop the testing at Nevada would allow the Kremlin a distinct advantage. On October 12, Kennedy publicly entertained doubts about the feasibility of renewed atmospheric testing. During the next six days, while the Soviets detonated five nuclear devices, most in the megaton range, Kennedy made up his mind.

Three days after the Soviet 50-megaton blast, Kennedy formally ordered a resumption of atmospheric testing "to maintain arms superiority," and promised to keep the fallout to "an absolute minimum."[16,17]

Early in December, the AEC reported on the 13.4-kiloton FISHER, the fifth blast of the NOUGAT series. It had been fired from a depth of over a

1,000 feet and had released visible quantities of radioactive steam from the drill hole. TASS responded by saying that the Soviet Union would continue testing if the United States continued its underground shots. On December 9, Khrushchev rumbled that weapons even more powerful than the 100-megaton bomb "hung over the heads of the imperialist aggressors like the sword of Damocles."[18] Two days later, project PLOWSHARE's GNOME was fired underground near Carlsbad, New Mexico. The explosion rippled the water of an underground lake in nearby Carlsbad Caverns and sent a cloud of radioactive debris northeast toward Omaha, Nebraska.

The first half of 1962 saw furious activity both at the Nevada Test Site and the Pacific Range near Christmas Island. One series followed another with nary a break: NOUGAT followed by DOMINIC I followed by DOMINIC II. Some shots, such as DANNY BOY and PLATTE, released a mixture of radio-isotopes into the atmosphere that were carried away by the winds.[19]

Just before the DOMINIC series ended on June 30, 1962, the Kennedy administration had authorized a third series: STORAX. The first shot in the series, 104-kiloton SEDAN, was set for July 6, 1962. A 36-inch-diameter hole was drilled in the desert alluvium to a depth of 635 feet. After the device was lowered into the hole, it was backfilled with dry sand. The explosion ripped a 1,200-foot-diameter, 600-foot deep hole in the desert floor. Radioactive dirt quickly fell back into the crater, cutting its depth by half. A radioactive cloud quickly formed and tracked toward the midwestern United States. It carried with it a potpourri of fission products, notably tungsten-187 and sodium-24.[20]

SEDAN was quickly followed by operation SUNBEAM's LITTLE FELLER II. On July 7, the device was suspended 3 feet off the ground from a cable strung between two posts. The yield, which was listed officially as "low," produced an intensely hot ground zero (1,000 roentgens/hour) and a cloud that tracked north, then northeast. AEC monitors chose not to follow it beyond southwestern Colorado.

Two days after LITTLE FELLER II, a Redstone rocket carried a 1.4-megaton device 277 miles over Johnson Island. As had occurred in the ARGUS series, the explosion created a shell of radioactivity around the earth. On July 11, 0.5-kiloton JOHNNIE BOY was fired, sending two clouds of debris off-site, one toward Idaho, the other toward California. The shot, officially listed as an underground detonation, actually took place at a depth of only 23 inches.

Shot SMALL BOY, a "low-yield" device, was fired on July 14 from a tower. Its radioactive cloud traveled northeast in a smooth arc that took it over Provo and Vernal, Utah; Craig, Colorado; Cheyenne, Wyoming; and North Platte, Nebraska.[21]

Three days later, weapons specialists converged on Area 18 of the Nevada Test Site with a new and deadly piece of equipment: the 30-inch-long Davy Crockett Battlefield Missile. Only 11 inches in diameter and weighing in at just 51 pounds, the missile was reported to pack a quarter-kiloton wallop.[22] The test was dubbed LITTLE FELLER I and it would be an operations test of a tactical battlefield weapon.

The rocket was test-fired at 9:00 in the morning by army weapons specialists wearing dark goggles. The target was instantly consumed in the familiar glare that could only mean the explosion had been nuclear. The cloud rose over a mile high, then bent toward the north; the AEC chose not to track the debris from LITTLE FELLER I off-site.

LITTLE FELLER I was followed by other underground shots, in a continuation of operation STORAX that took up most of the summer. Meanwhile, at the Johnston Island area, all sorts of high altitude events were taking place. Devices attached to rockets were being sent into the ionosphere to create spectacular explosions and shell after shell of globe-circling debris. Tactical weapons were being studied in Nevada while missiles and warheads were being tested in the Pacific.

All during the Nevada and Pacific tests, Novaya Zemlya had remained strangely quiet. A small underground shot had been detected at Semipalatinsk on February 2, but there had been nothing else—until August 5, 1962.

On that day, the Soviets detonated a 30-megaton device at their Arctic test site. It was followed by fifteen more during August and September. The Soviets were again flexing their nuclear muscles; something was in the wind. Within a month the American public would know the reason why, and the world would be closer to nuclear war than at any time in its history.

Deadly October

It all started on July 2, 1962. That day, a delegation of Cubans headed by Raul Castro arrived at the Kremlin for important discussions. Raul's brother Fidel had been concerned for some time about a possible invasion by the United States. Could the Kremlin furnish him with some defensive missiles? The answer, of course, was "yes." And there was more.

For years Khrushchev had been rankled by the presence of American military bases—and missile sites—in Japan, West Germany, Iran, Turkey, Italy, and Norway. To him, this "ring of containment" had placed the Soviet Union at a great disadvantage vis-á-vis the United States: The Soviet missiles would take fifteen or twenty minutes to reach their targets, while those fired from Turkey, say, would give the Kremlin only about eight or ten minutes. The generals had continually reminded Khrushchev that "in any nuclear war advantage would be calculated in minutes rather than hours."[1] He desperately wanted to even the score; Raul Castro was giving him the opportunity to do it.

Possibly, too, Khrushchev was still smarting from the defeat at Berlin the year before and thought this would be an excellent opportunity to even the score with Kennedy. Whatever the motives, the plans were drawn up: in addition to the surface-to-air missiles (SAMs), the Cubans would also be given thirty to forty medium-range (1,000 miles) and intermediate-range (2,200 miles) surface-to-surface *strategic* ICBMs.[2]

After meeting with the Cubans on July 3 and 8, Khrushchev left Moscow for a lengthy tour of the western Soviet Union. Ever the master of distraction, he was hopeful that the West would concentrate on his activities and ignore the deadly cargo being loaded onto Soviet ships.[3] Khrushchev hoped that, by the time he returned to Moscow in mid-October, the missiles would be in place.

Oddly, the trick had every chance of working. For some reason, the United States had lately ignored activities in Cuba, even after discovering

5,000 Russian technicians were working there. And while there had been mild interest in refugees' stories about long tubular objects arriving at Mariel, the analysts figured—correctly—that they were probably SAM missiles; certainly not a threat to the mainland. It was known that Castro was not held in particularly high regard by the Kremlin; his country had been bleeding the Soviets the equivalent of a million dollars a day. Besides, in the past, the Kremlin had kept their missiles to themselves. Why would they risk sending them to Cuba? Most agreed there was nothing to worry about.

Senator Kenneth Keating of New York had also been keeping up with the stories, and he was skeptical of the analyses. What were all those Russian technicians *doing* there?[4] Under pressure from Keating, the CIA began to pursue the matter. At the end of September, agents uncovered a disturbing but possibly unreliable bit of information: Castro's personal pilot had been overheard in a Havana bar bragging about the nuclear missiles being set up in Cuba. In October, Keating began a series of speeches that warned of Soviet activity on the island to the south. No one particularly believed him. The CIA had concluded that Castro's pilot had been referring to the SAMs; the alcohol, not the Russians, had expanded them to SS-6 size.

Central Intelligence Agency director John A. McCone was not so sure. He happened to learn that no U-2 planes had overflown western Cuba in a month: The Cubans had installed the deadly accurate surface-to-air missiles and none of the pilots wanted to chance getting shot down. McCone ordered the flights anyway. Unfortunately, the weather was on the side of the Cubans: The island remained under a thick cloud cover for several days. Eventually the sky cleared, and on October 14 a thin, black U-2 tracked over the western coast of Cuba, snapping hundred of high-resolution photos. Keating had been right. A flat area near San Cristobal was dotted with partially finished launched pads, each field ringed by surface-to-air missile launchers.

Within hours, the photos had been examined by half a dozen officials, from Depty Secretary of Defense Roswell Gilpatrick to Secretary of State Dean Rusk.

On the morning of October 16, John F. Kennedy saw them. He quickly called together a group of key administration officials to discuss strategy. Among those present were Robert F. Kennedy, Lyndon Johnson, Adlai Stevenson, General Maxwell Taylor, Deputy Secretary of State George Ball, Secretary of State Dean Rusk, and CIA director John McCone. They were known as the Executive Committee of the National Security Council, or Ex Comm. It was up to them to decide what to do about the missiles.[5]

Initially, the committee wanted to bomb Cuba off the map. That would, however, take innocent lives in addition to a quantity of Russians. The United States had never before engaged in a first strike; Kennedy didn't want to tarnish that record.

On October 17, photos came back indicating that thirty-two sites were nearing completion. Intelligence analysts estimated that the Soviets would be able to take out targets as far away as Montana. Asked for the expected completion date, the analysts replied that the Soviet technicians were working furiously. They would be ready within a week.[6]

On the other side of the world, Khrushchev had just returned from his tour of the U.S.S.R. Word reached him that the construction of the launch pads had been proceeding apace; things were going well. Earlier, he had instructed TASS to issue a communiqué: "The government of the Soviet Union has authorized TASS to state that there is no need for the Soviet Union to site defensive weapons—weapons designed to administer retaliatory blows—in any other country [Cuba, for instance]. Our nuclear weapons are so devastating, and the rockets that would carry our warheads so powerful, that we do not need to search for suitable sites for them outside the Soviet Union."[7]

It was, of course, a lie. The Soviets did possess devastating nuclear weapons, including extremely effective 30- and 50-megaton monsters, but their rockets were something else entirely, which was perhaps a third reason why Khrushchev wanted them in Cuba: They weren't particularly accurate.

Sergei Korolev had designed the SS-6 not as an ICBM but as a vehicle to launch satellites. The immense rocket was a virtual symphony of problems. For one thing, it was so heavy that some occassionally cracked their launch pads, which in turn played havoc with accuracy.[8]

In the communiqué, Khrushchev had carefully withheld comment on the response time of these "defensive weapons" and with good reason. The missiles had to be topped off with a volatile mixture of nitric acid and alcohol before flight and the embarrassing truth was that the SS-6 (and many of its descendants) fueled up at a rather leisurely rate: twenty hours from empty to full.[9] The reddish brown nitrogen dioxide clouds generated by these monsters could probably be seen by the tourists in Key West, to say nothing of the more discerning U-2 pilots.

Even worse, both the first- and second-generation Soviet ICBMs were fitted with conical warheads. Not the most streamlined of shapes, they presented an enormous amount of drag and thus slowed the rocket down. Reentering the earth's atmosphere at a reduced speed made the rocket susceptible to wind effects, blowing the vehicle even further off target. Though few people knew it at the time, this was precisely the reason the Soviets had such heavy-yield nuclear warheads: Their rockets couldn't be trusted to hit the target.[10,11]

In Washington, several options were discussed: (a) ignore it, (b) try to quietly reason with Khrushchev, (c) call the Soviets before the U.N. Security Council (d) set up a blockade preventing any more missiles from arriving, (e) descend on the missile bases in a "surgical strike," or (f) mount a total invasion of Cuba.[12]

On October 18, Kennedy meets with Soviet deputy foreign minister Andrei Gromyko. Oddly, the Russian fails to bring up the subject. Kennedy wonders if any of the Soviet delegation in the United States is aware of the missiles. Back at the Ex Comm, General Curtis LeMay pushes for an air strike on Cuba. Kennedy replies: "They, no more than we, can let these things go by without doing something. They can't after all their statements, permit us to take out their missiles, kill a lot of Russians, and then do nothing. If they don't take action in Cuba, they certainly will in Berlin."[13]

On October 20, after two days of debate, the decision is made: There will be a naval blockade of Soviet ships heading for Cuba. The navy is ordered to send 180 ships to the Caribbean. That evening the First Armored Division leaves Texas for Georgia.[14]

In Moscow, the Kremlin is made aware of the upswing in military activity. Early on, Khrushchev and Castro had hoped that the missiles would be in place before the activity was discovered. They had almost made it. Later, Khrushchev would write: "By then we had installed enough missiles to destroy New York, Chicago and other huge industrial cities—let along a little village like Washington."[15]

On Monday afternoon, October 22, 1962, a bulletin flashed on television screens across the nation: "Presidential press secretary Pierre Salinger has announced that the president will speak on television tonight at 7:00 P.M. Eastern Standard Time. Salinger said the topic will be 'of the greatest urgency.'"[16]

That afternoon, Secretary of State Dean Rusk meets for twenty-five minutes with Soviet Ambassador Anatoly Dobrynin. Amazingly, Khrushchev has kept his ambassador in the dark about the missiles. The Americans are incredulous: Khrushchev has left absolutely no lines of communication open in order to defuse the crisis.

7:00 P.M., Monday, October 22, 1962

"Good evening, my fellow citizens. The government, as promised, has maintained the closest surveillance of the Soviet military buildup on the island of Cuba. Within the past week, unmistakable evidence has established the fact that a series of offensive missile sites is now in preparation on that imprisoned island. The purpose of these bases can be none other than to provide a nuclear strike capability against the Western Hemisphere. . . ."[17]

In Moscow, Khrushchev monitors the speech. It is tough. There will be a blockade. Any missiles launched from Cuba will be considered an attack by the Soviet Union requiring a "full retaliatory response." The navy has been instructed to sink any Soviet vessels attempting to run the blockade.

Shaken, Khrushchev confers with his advisors. Are the missiles ready? He is told they are not. Several hours pass in conference. That afternoon, the Kremlin calls the Soviet armed forces to full alert: leaves are canceled, older soldiers are called back. A communiqué is issued: "The United States is demanding that military equipment that Cuba needs for the purposes of self-defense should be removed from Cuban territory—a requirement that, naturally, no state that values its independence can meet."[18]

The Kennedy administration quickly rounds up the Organization of American States to vote on the "quarantine," as it is now called, of Cuba. The vote is an astonishing 18-0. Kennedy receives a telegram from pacifist Bertrand Russell: "Your action desperate. . . . No conceivable justification. . . . We will not have mass murder . . . end this madness." Kennedy's testy reply: "I think your attention might well be directed to the burglars rather than to those who have caught the burglars." He is unaware that Khrushchev has received a similar telegram.[19]

Wednesday, October 24, two Soviet ships, the *Gagarin* and the *Komiles*, approach the blockade. Ominously, they are accompanied by a Soviet submarine.[20] Across the United States, people await word of the impending conflict. If the ships try to run the blockade, they will surely be fired upon. This would in turn be met by torpedoes from the Soviet submarine. Americans brace for war; few know that they would have, at best, fifteen minutes to seek shelter.

In Moscow, the Soviet premier is in a state of exhaustion. A visiting American industrialist, William Knox, stops by; he sees an almost incoherent Khrushchev.[21] On the other side of the world, John Kennedy tells his brother Robert, "It looks really mean, doesn't it?"[22]

Suddenly, at 10:32 A.M., twenty Soviet vessels pull to a halt, then turn around.[23] The news is flashed across the country: The crisis is over. The news is premature. The crisis has in fact begun to escalate.

Thursday, October 25.

Interception occurs. Two ships, the *Bucharest* and *Volkerfreund*, are stopped and questioned. Neither are carrying missiles and are allowed to pass.

Later that evening, television cameras have been set up in the chambers of the U.N. Security Council. Soviet ambassador to the U.N. Valerian Zorin challenges the American representative to the U.N. Adlai Stevenson to produce proof of the missiles. Stevenson is taken aback by the challenge; it is almost too good to be true. He quickly answers that he has the proof, but first, a request. He then asks the Soviet representative to *deny* there are missiles in Cuba. Stunned, Zorin has no immediate reply.

"Yes or no?" Stevenson asks.

Still no reply.

"Don't wait for the translation!" Stevenson demands, honing in on his target, "Yes or No?!" Zorin replies lamely that he is "not in an American courtroom. . . ."

"You are in the courtroom of world opinion right now and you can answer yes or no!" Stevenson says, heatedly.

Zorin, clearly on the defensive, says, "You will have your answer in due course."

"I am prepared to wait for my answer," Stevenson replies, "until
hell freezes over, if that's your decision. And I am also prepared to present
the evidence in this room." Turning, he presents easels mounted with en-
larged photos of the missile sites.[24] It is a one-two punch seen live across the
country, Stevenson's finest hour.

The Soviet press recorded the event: "The representative to the
U.S.S.R., V. Zorin exposed the fiction of the so-called 'discovery of Soviet
rocket bases' in Cuba concocted by State Department officials."[25]

Friday, October 26. The Soviet-bloc ship *Marcula* is stopped and
boarded. No weapons are on board and she is allowed to pass. In Washington, the committee breathes a collective sigh of relief. Khrushchev has apparently ordered the captains to allow searches.[26] The Soviet ambassador in
Washington is consulted, but Kennedy suspects they are still out in the cold.
The strings are clearly being pulled in Moscow, probably by an exhausted
and angry Khrushchev. The next step is crucial and fraught with hazards.
The blockade has been effective; now Kennedy must get the missiles out of
Cuba. Robert Kennedy gives Dobrynin just forty-eight hours to begin dis-
mantling the rockets. After that time, "further action will be justified."[27]

At 1:40 P.M., ABC television commentator John Scali walks into the
Occidental Restaurant on Pennsylvania Avenue in Washington, D.C. Ten
minutes earlier he had received a phone call from one Alexander Fomin, a
counselor at the Soviet embassy, requesting an "important" meeting. Scali
is tense; Fomin is reputed to be a colonel in either the KGB or the GRU, Soviet Military Intelligence. Over coffee, Fomin discusses with Scali three pro-
visions for ending the crisis: (1) Castro will accept no more missiles, (2) the
missiles already there will be removed under U.N. supervision, and (3) a
promise by Kennedy never to invade Cuba.

Scali tells the Russian that he will take the message to the proper officials. Six hours later, Scali tells Fomin that the administration is interested.
Fomin leaves.[28]

An hour and a half earlier, however, the committee had received a long,
rambling message over the teletype from the American embassy in Moscow.
It was from Khrushchev:

> You can be confident that we are quite sane and understand clearly that if we
> attack you, you will retaliate. But we will match you, blow for blow. And I be-
> lieve that you are fully aware of this, which indicates that we are normal people,
> that we understand the position and can assess the situation accurately. Why,
> then, should we court disaster, as you seem to imagine we are doing? Only a lu-
> natic or suicide would do that, someone bent on his own destruction and that of
> the world before he dies. . . .
>
> We must not tug at the ends of the rope in which you have tied the knot of
> war, because the harder we both pull, the tighter the knot will become. And a
> time may come when the knot is so tight that even he who tied it will not have

the strength to undo it—and then the rope itself will have to be cut. Let us not simply slacken the rope; let us also take measures to undo the knot. We are ready for that.[29]

Interestingly, the message went on to spell out the same terms as had Fomin. Those on the Executive Committee feel that the crisis may be coming to a close. They are wrong.

Saturday, October 27. Kennedy awakens to find that a second, much harsher letter has been broadcast by Radio Moscow, demanding that the United States remove its missiles from Turkey. Analysts pounce on the second letter, dissecting it for content and meaning. Something is wrong: the style is unlike Khrushchev's earlier note. There is real concern among the Executive Committee. If Khrushchev is no longer in command, all bets are off. The situation could become explosive. After hours of discussion, it is decided to assume the Soviet premier is still in command and, for some unfathomable reason, has issued two separate letters. Now the question is: which one shall they answer?

In the confusion, the Joint Chiefs of Staff speak up. All are solidly for an invasion of Cuba. The Executive Committee agrees. The lone holdout is the president, saying, "It isn't the first step that concerns me . . . but both sides escalating to the fourth and fifth step—and we don't go to the sixth because there is no one around to do so. We must remind ourselves we are embarking on a very hazardous course."[30] On the other side of the world, Khrushchev is involved in similar debates with his military advisors, who argue against withdrawing the missiles.[31] At this moment, on a bright Saturday in the fall of 1962, the world is as close to nuclear war as it has ever been.

After rejecting the invasion, the committee settles down to other options. First, the question of the bases in Turkey. There had been plans all along to dismantle the bases, yet it couldn't be made to seem that Khrushchev had forced the Americans out of the area.

Robert Kennedy makes a unique suggestion: take the best parts of each letter and draft a reply "accepting the Soviet Union's conditions."[32] If the Soviet's balk, the president will order a strike on Cuba. It will be up to Khrushchev—or whoever is in command.

In Moscow, the Soviet premier, though tense and exhausted, is still in charge. Later, he will write of that time as "when the smell of burning hung in the air."[33] He feels he has scored a major victory: Through other channels Kennedy has assured him that, despite the rhetoric, the bases in Turkey *will* be dismantled. Now the problem is Castro. Anastas Mikoyan, in Havana, had not informed the Cuban leader of the negotiations. Castro still thinks he has a nuclear arsenal. Would he try to fire the operational missiles? Mikoyan is directed to persuade Castro to accept the compromises.[34]

On October 28, Khrushchev sends a message to Kennedy:

I have every sympathy with your concern and that of the American people about the weapons that you describe as offensive, which are formidable weapons indeed. Both of us understand what kind of weapons they are. . . .[35]

　　In order to eliminate as rapidly as possible the conflict which endangers the cause of peace . . . the Soviet government . . . has given a new order to dismantle the arms which you described as offensive, and to crate and return them to the Soviet Union. . . .[36]

In Washington, Kennedy tells the Executive Committee that it must be very difficult for Khrushchev to back down; he cautions against claims of an American "victory." Invoking the oldest rule in politics, the compromise has allowed both sides a graceful exit. In a letter to the Soviet premier, Kennedy writes, "I think we should give priority to questions relating to the proliferation of nuclear weapons, on earth and outer space, and to the great effort for a nuclear test ban."[37]

It was time. The crisis of October 1962 had brought the potential for nuclear war into sharp focus. As Soviet historian Roy Medvedev wrote, "Never before had the post-war world been so close to the brink of catastrophe."[38]

The Hot Years

November 1962: The year was coming to a close. It was a period of relative quiet: The Cuban missile crisis was now a faint memory and Vietnam was not yet a regular feature on the evening news.

The venerable Ed Sullivan was still in command of Sunday evenings, his show followed by Walter Brennan and a young Richard Crenna in "The Real McCoys." On NBC, their competition was "Walt Disney's Wonderful World of Color" and "Car 54, Where Are You?" On Mondays, "The Andy Griffith Show" was into its second year, with a young Ron Howard as "Opie" and Don Knotts as "Deputy Barney Fife." Jim Nabors as gas station attendant "Gomer Pyle" had yet to arrive on the scene—that would take place the following spring. Red Skelton still owned Tuesday evenings, while "Wagon Train," "The Many Loves of Dobie Gillis," and the new "Beverly Hillbillies" stayed high in the ratings among Wednesday night viewers.

Thursday, ABC offered a quadruple helping of suburban schmaltz with "Ozzie and Harriet," "Donna Reed," "Leave It to Beaver," and "My Three Sons." "Mr. Ed" had jumped from the CBS Sunday night lineup to Thursday in September 1962. The popular comedy was followed by the dour "Perry Mason," "The Nurses," and "Alfred Hitchcock Presents." On NBC, the popular Andy Williams, after years of filling in as a summer replacement, finally had his own show. On December 20, 1962, Williams would feature a "youthful barbershop harmony group from Ogden, Utah," the Osmond Brothers.[1] The theme music for the show, beginning in 1962, was "Moon River."

The Columbia Broadcasting Company had Fridays locked up with "Rawhide," starring a young Clint Eastwood as "Rowdy Yates," followed by the immensely popular "Route 66." The situation was the same for Saturdays: The CBS lineup included "The Jackie Gleason Show," "The Defenders," "Have Gun, Will Travel," and finally "Gunsmoke," now expanded to a full hour.[2] A new addition to the "Gunsmoke" cast that year was town blacksmith "Quint Asper," played by Burt Reynolds. Two years before, Reynolds had played "Ben Frazier" in the 1959–60 series "Riverboat."

Pat Boone talked about his role as a bad guy in *The Main Attraction*: "In my first six movies I played myself. From now on I don't care if I play a derelict or a drug addict, just so long as the movie has a worthwhile message."[3] Other movies at the time included the war epic *The Longest Day* and the more modern if bizarre *Manchurian Candidate*, starring Frank Sinatra.

Ford had just introduced a transistorized ignition for its heavy trucks and predicted an electronic ignition for the 406-cc high-performance engine. In November 1962, the new automobile models were unveiled at the 44th National Auto Show. The Chrysler "300" was styled, according to one writer, like "an elongated Rolls-Royce," while the new Ford Thunderbird had a "pseudo-sports car line." The Buick Riveria, designed to rival the T-Bird, had bucket seats and an adjustable steering wheel, while Pontiac's Grand Prix, another T-Bird rival that looked more like a boat than a sports car, sported hidden taillights. The General Motors designers had given the 1963 Chevrolet Impalas spear-shaped rear fenders and the Corvettes retractable headlamps.[4]

At the end of 1962, Sony had just placed its "micro-TV" on the market: 8 pounds and a screen "smaller than a postcard" (4 1/2 by 3 1/2 inches)—for only $229.95. In the fall of 1962, the New York Giants still had thirty-six-year-old quarterback Yelberton Abraham Tittle, Jr., and Desi Arnaz gave up Desilu Productions, Inc., to his ex-wife in exchange for $2 million.

On November 2, a writer for *Time* magazine assessed the Southeast Asia situation: "South Viet Nam, where the U.S. is deeply committed in a bitter guerrilla war against the Reds, looks far more hopeful than it did a year ago."[5]

At the end of the month, the *Time* cover featured singer Joan Baez. On page 54, cover story author John McPhee wrote: "Anything called a hootenanny ought to be shot on sight, but the whole country is having one."[6]

The hottest album in the fall of 1962 was by Boston-born Kennedy impressionist Vaughn Meador: "The First Family." Five months after its release it had sold 5 million copies. Despite the sales, it would be abruptly withdrawn from the stores one year later.

The year 1963 arrived clear and cold for much of the Midwest. Radio station KAAY in Little Rock, Arkansas, began the new year with the new hit "Hey Paula" by Paula and Paula, while Chicago's WLS opened with "Some Kinda Fun" by Chris Montez followed by "Wild Weekend" by the Rockin' Rebels. Here a premonition of music to come: The guitar line for this song would reappear twenty-two years later in the John Fogarty single "Rock and Roll Girl."[7]

January 1963 would also mark the beginning of the hottest year for fallout in the history of the United States. The intense testing activity of the previous two years, in which literally tons of radioactive material were hurled into the stratosphere, were now beginning to drift back to earth in an invisible but steady drizzle of radioactivity.

In 1958 and 1959, the AEC had begun analyzing fallout samples for both strontium-89 and 90. By studying the decay pattern of the element, the chemists could determine the source of the fallout. After the test ban in 1958, fallout had dropped steadily, and by 1960, it was decided to combine samples on a two-month basis. However, after the Soviets began firing their huge multimegaton weapons at Novaya Zemlya, it was decided to go back to monthly reports.

Depending on lab facilities, some reports included analyses not only of strontium-90 but of the more esoteric bomb products: zirconium-95, ruthenium-103 and -106, cesium-137, barium-140, cerium-141 and -144, and the ubiquitous plutonium-239. After 1963, other fission products were included: manganese-54, iron-55, and antimony-124. Thus, a detailed fallout picture of the entire United States had been constructed. What it showed, in retrospect, was alarming: The continent had been constantly showered with a fine dust composed of the highly radioactive products of nuclear fission. And beginning in September 1961, the amount had increased precipitously with each passing month.[8] That month, the average New Yorker's daily intake of strontium-90 was 2.6 picocuries. A year later it had risen to 5.6 picocuries, and by February 1963, the level had increased to 18.4 picocuries. This rise was reflected at the two other cities analyzed, Chicago and San Francisco. Yet for all practical purposes, atmospheric testing had ended. The last U.S. aboveground shot had been TIGHTROPE, a high-altitude detonation fired tens of kilometers above the Johnston Island Test Site on November 4, 1962, while the last aboveground Soviet detonation had taken place at Novaya Zemlya on Christmas Day, 1962. All of these shots, however, had injected massive amounts of debris high into the stratosphere. By late 1962 and early 1963, it had begun to fall back to earth. In analyzing the collected data, scientists began to piece together a picture of fallout deposition in the United States in 1962–63. It was not reassuring.

For the East Coast in particular, July 1963 was the most radioactive month in the history of the United States.[9]

The Summer of Fallout

The strontium-90 intake level for Chicagoans peaked at 21 picocuries in July 1963, compared with 14.6 in March. Those living in San Francisco took in an average of 18.6 picocuries, while the level for New Yorkers two months before had reached an astonishing 37 picocuries.[10] Though the fallout levels were uniformly high, they were not evenly distributed across the country: Despite its relative proximity to the Soviet test site, the coastal area of the Northwest seemed to fare better than the East. In July 1963, Seattle, Washington, received only one-tenth the amount of strontium-90 that fell on Westwood, New Jersey.[11]

Radioactive manganese and antimony fell from the sky over Pittsburgh, Pennsylvania, in April 1963, while the month before, monitors in Westwood, New Jersey, found relatively high levels of radioactive tellurium-204.[12,13] Tellurium is absorbed by many plants and, as dimethyl telluride, helps provide the distinctive taste to onions and garlic; no doubt a number of hamburgers in the New Jersey area contained minute traces of radioactive tellurium during the spring and summer of 1963.[14]

Radioactive iron fell on Richmond, California, particularly between March 13 and 15.[15] Scientists analyzing these "tracer" compounds concluded that much of the radioactive fallout reaching these American cities was from Soviet rather than American tests.

Scientists also found that the radioactivity seemed to concentrate in a band around the midsection of the country. Analyzing various grains, they discovered the Iowa wheat crop in 1962 had received a whopping 536 picocuries/kilogram of cesium-137 and 138 picocuries/kilogram of strontium-90. Missouri wheat was next in line with 332 picocuries/kilogram cesium-137 and 128 picocuries/kilogram strontium-90.[16] Though this equaled only one gram of radioactive cesium in 6.7 billion tons of Iowa wheat, it perhaps was the reason for relatively high radioactivity in bakery products and flour found in New York City, San Francisco, and Chicago the following summer.[17]

Many of the fallout monitoring stations also collected plutonium. Theoretically, this particular element should be found in minute quantities, since its source is unfissioned core material; in a typical nuclear device that uses plutonium, the core usually accounts for no more than 10 or 15 kilograms per weapon. But plutonium was falling to earth in measurable amounts, and plutonium was one of the most carcinogenic substances known.

The Test Ban

President Kennedy found the road to the test ban difficult. Lobbying for the treaty were those who thought the world was getting closer and closer to nuclear war. Others were concerned about the effects of fallout, arguing that not much was known about how radiation damaged the body.

Opposing the ban were conservatives, such as Arizona senator Barry Goldwater, who believed that any testing ban would allow Russia to keep its lead in high-yield weapons.[18] Lewis Strauss, former head of the AEC, had also opposed the ban, saying, "I am not sure that the reduction of tensions is necessarily a good thing." Livermore's Edward Teller was also for a continuation of the testing. At the test-ban hearings, he had warned Kennedy, "If you ratify this treaty . . . you will have given away the future safety of this country."[19]

Despite formidable opposition, the nuclear test-ban treaty was signed on August 5, 1963, and ratified by the Senate the following month. American and Soviet tests had gone underground, but the questions about the effects of fallout remained.[20,21] Soon there would be some disturbing answers.

IX

CONFRONTATION

Windscale

The accident happened during the fall of 1957, inside Windscale, a huge British uranium-reprocessing plant on the edge of the Irish Sea. A uranium fire had begun inside one of the piles and soon the air inside the shell was filled with radioactive fission products. Upon release, the radioactive cloud drifted inland, blanketing the countryside with a broth of radioisotopes, including the extremely hot iodine-131.

British officials quickly studied a map of the area: within 200 miles of Windscale there lived over 80,000 people. To make matters worse, there were twelve dairy farms scattered around the reactor; the farthest being only 2 miles away. British public safety officials quickly concluded that the dairy cattle would have to be kept off the contaminated fields. Further, the milk already produced since the accident would have to be destroyed. Several days later, thousands of gallons of milk were dumped into the Irish Sea. Well over 100 farms had been contaminated by the fission products. For years, the Windscale accident would stand as the worst case of environmental contamination of the countryside by a nuclear reactor.[1]

A report of the accident, published in Great Britain, finally made its way to the United States and into the hands of Gordon Dunning, of the AEC's Division of Biology and Medicine. Years before, Dunning had fought strenuously against the Utah ranchers who had lost thousands of sheep in 1953. Now Dunning was confronted with a report that dredged up old problems: The report flatly stated that 40 rads external gamma dose could result in tens of thousands of rads dose to the thyroid. The British scientists were saying that the tiny gland in the neck somehow managed to absorb and *concentrate* the fission products. It was disturbing news: In the 1953 sheep case, two of the AEC's veterinarians had commented that the underside of the animals' necks had been intensely radioactive.[2,3]

Partially wrapped around every human windpipe, the small, reddish bit of flesh, the thyroid usually weighs no more than 40 grams. Manufactured in this tiny organ is a chemical system absolutely essential to growth and metabolism: a group of chemicals loosely called the thyroid hormones. Running along either side of the thyroid are the four large, elastic conveyances carrying blood to and from the head, the carotid arteries and jugular veins. Like limbs from a tree trunk, arteries branch off from the carotids to supply the thyroid with blood. Once circulated, the blood returns to the body via three other branches: two to the jugular veins, and one directly to the superior vena cava, the main thoroughfare to the heart.

Whether in fish, sheep, or man, the thyroid has the same main responsibility: regulation of the metabolic rate—that is, how *fast* the body burns its fuel. If the metabolic rate goes too low, oxygen consumption goes down and the person may be lethargic; thinking and memory may be impaired. The pulse may slow down; the person may take on weight. If the metabolic rate becomes too fast, just the opposite occurs: oxygen consumption—and metabolism—increases; the person may become nervous and excitable; the pulse is rapid; and there may be a noticeable weight loss.[4]

Manufacture of thyroid hormone begins when the individual eats vegetables or seafood containing iodine, a black, crystalline element chemically related to chlorine. After the element enters the bloodstream, the thyroid scavenges the iodine, concentrating it inside tiny sacs called follicles. The ability of the thyroid to concentrate iodine is considerable: The amount of iodine in the gland may be *fifty times* that found in the blood.[5] It is also done quickly; within fifteen minutes after iodine enters the bloodstream, 90 percent is absorbed by the thyroid.

Inside the gland, iodine is chemically joined to tyrosine, an amino acid found in milk, to form diiodotyrosine. Two diiodotyrosine molecules are then coupled to form the primary circulating thyroid hormone, thyroxine. If the thyroid is unable to form diiodotyrosine molecules, mental impairment and other ailments may result.[6]

Exactly how thyroxine works to regulate cell metabolism is not known, but it is suspected that the kidneys somehow activate the hormone.[7] As thyroxine is passed through the kidneys and liver it is broken down, and free iodine is released back into the bloodstream where it is reabsorbed by the thyroid gland. Thanks to the thyroid, the body tends to retain most of its iodine.

The thyroid is not the only gland found on the windpipe. Located on the rear surface of the thyroid are four tiny, plate-shaped glands, the parathyroids.[8] While situated next to the thyroid (and occasionally embedded *in* it), these glands perform an entirely different function: the regulation, through the parathyroid hormone (PTH), of calcium in the body.

Calcium is important to a variety of mechanisms in the body, from neuromuscular activity to blood clotting. Since the level of calcium in the blood is usually very low, extremely small changes in blood concentration can affect mechanisms dependent on calcium. A low level of calcium in the blood can cause tremors, twitchings, and even death. A high level may result in wasting away of bone, and occasionally, bone tumors and cysts.[9]

In sum, the small bit of flesh surrounding the windpipe amounts to an intricate, complex system of immense importance to the entire body. And in 1960, it became the central point in a controversy that would shake the AEC to its foundations and cast grave doubt on the safety of nuclear testing.

All things considered, 1960 was not a particularly good year for the AEC. On January 27, Dr. Edward Teller, a chief proponent of the nuclear weapons program, came out favoring underground testing.[10] On March 4, the commission bowed to pressure from environmentalists and canceled plans to blast a new harbor near Cape Thompson, Alaska.[11] And worst of all, in the summer of 1960, the AEC asked Harold Knapp to research radiation hot spots across the United States.

Radioactive fallout, and particularly strontium-90, had been a debate topic among scientists for quite some time. Some, Nobel prize winner Linus Pauling for example, claimed that upward of 2 million deaths would result from the fallout; others, primarily those employed by the AEC, countered that the fallout was essentially harmless.[12,13] Some academics in the Midwest were claiming that an enormous amount of radiation—2.5 rads—had been absorbed by the thyroids of some infants in St. Louis.[14] The lack of exposure information had made it impossible to determine the rate at which the rads had been absorbed; still, the implications were worrisome.

In order to clear the matter up once and for all, the Joint Congressional Committee asked the AEC to do a thorough study of localized areas of fallout that had occurred in the United States as a result of the nuclear testing. Of particular interest was the St. Louis area. If dangerously high levels of radiation from fallout were occurring that far from the test site, they could occur anywhere. The AEC had to formulate some sort of response.

The assignment was bounced around upper management until it landed on the desk of one Harold Knapp, an overworked Ph.D. toiling among the catacombs in the obscure Fallout Studies Branch of the AEC's Division of Biology and Medicine.[15]

Knapp was the sort of man who pretty much knew his own mind and had confidence in his abilities. In addition, his academic credentials were impeccable, including a Ph.D. from the Massachusetts Institute of Technology. He had two other attributes: He was honest and he was meticulous.

Knapp settled down to get a good look at the data. He was familiar with physiology and knew the thyroid gland tended to concentrate iodine, radioactive or not.

The transmission route had already been determined: fallout containing iodine-131 had been deposited on grass, ingested by cows, and transmitted to infants via the milk. According to his calculations, children in the St. Louis area received four to five times the radiation to the thyroid that was then considered safe by the Federal Radiation Council.[16] The figures were duly noted in the repor. and submitted to his superiors at the AEC.

Two years passed before Harold Knapp had an occasion to return to the problem of I-131 exposure. Almost by accident he happened upon information detailing the external gamma dose to St. Louis after one of the tests. Having written a report on the subject, he decided to take a closer look. What he saw shocked him: The measured *external* dose to the residents of St. Louis was only several *hundredths* of one rad. Yet the *internal* dose had been *2* rads. What was going on here?

If infants in St. Louis were exposed to 2 rads internally when the external dose was in hundredths of a rad, what of areas exposed to greater levels?

Places like Albany, Troy, Boston? Places like St. George, Utah, which had been exposed to hundreds of millirads of external radiation after only one nuclear detonation?

Having worked in the Fallout Studies Branch, Knapp knew that the AEC measured fallout levels largely in terms of strontium-90, perhaps because the element tended to be stored in the bone. It also had a long half-life, so it stayed in the system for years. But was it as toxic as, say, iodine-131? It was time for some comparisons.

Strontium-90 was formed directly from fission; it had no precursors. Though it stayed radioactive for quite some time (its half-life was twenty-eight years), it emitted no gamma or X rays, only beta particles, and they were low-energy ones at that.[17] Iodine-131 was also a direct product of fission, but there the similarity ended: I-131 had a very short half-life: not much over eight days. In a matter of months it completely decayed to other (radioactive) elements.[18] However, in its decay it emitted not only relatively high-energy beta particles, but a variety of X rays, the majority being also quite hot.[19]

And after the iodine was ingested, the thyroid tended to concentrate it, as much as fifty times over the level found in the blood. Since the material had *already* been concentrated by the lactation system in the cow, the amount of radioactive iodine-131 finally reaching the thyroid was substantial.

As a result of this concentrating effect, the thyroid and parathyroid glands were exposed to surprisingly large amounts of radiation. The radioactive iodine, as part of the thyroid hormone, was carried through the blood to other parts of the body; it had the potential of reaching every cell, particularly those in the kidney and liver. Iodine-131 was turning out to be a major hazard.[20]

Could it be more of a hazard than strontium-90? Was it possible the AEC had been monitoring for the *wrong* things all these years? Knapp decided to dig deeper into the literature.

Among the background information that eventually wound up on Knapp's desk was the report from the WINDSCALE accident. Apparently, the British were less concerned over strontium-90 and cesium-137—the primary targets of AEC monitoring—than they were over iodine-131. The report had concluded that 40 rads external dose could result in many thousands of rads to the thyroid.[21] The similarities to southwestern Utah were beginning to look ominous.

Returning to his data on St. George, Knapp quickly made some calculations. Assuming the milkshed (grazing area) was exposed to fallout, he concluded that children drinking about a quart of milk a day for three weeks would receive an astonishing 120 to 240 rad dose to their thyroids.[22]

There was no question about it. The external gamma doses indicated only one thing: Radiation at far higher levels was reaching internal organs of the populace. In the case of I-131, that populace involved those who drank milk: children.

In 1962, Knapp came across an interesting article about another hot spot, this one in Upstate New York. Dr. Ralph Lapp, a physicist who had once worked on the Manhattan Project, had become interested in the exposures to Troy, New York, resulting from the 1953 UPSHOT-KNOTHOLE: SIMON shot. Also concentrating on radioactive iodine and its effect on the thyroid, Lapp concluded that the SIMON fallout would eventually result in five cases of thyroid cancer.[23]

Harold Knapp continued to concentrate on the St. George area, paying particular attention to the UPSHOT-KNOTHOLE: HARRY shot. The more closely he examined the data—or lack of it—the worse it looked. No monitoring had been done for iodine-131 or -133. After the detonation, AEC monitor Frank Butrico, assigned to gather milk samples from dairies, had only purchased one quart—from a local store.[24,25] Moreover, Knapp found that because of the concentrating effects on internal emitters—that is, fission products that had been ingested—the AEC had underestimated the radiation dose to various areas in the United States by as much as a thousand times.[26,27]

The revised calculations showed that the thyroids of infants in the heavy zones of fallout had been exposed to an astonishing 440 rads.[28]

In 1963, the report was submitted for review to the AEC leadership. The reaction was negative. The report clearly made the Atomic Energy Commission look inept in their monitoring and risk assessment procedures. Almost reflexively, the AEC leadership called the report "of questionable technical validity."[29] After circulating the Knapp report, Gordon Dunning attached a memo: "The Commission has been telling the world for years that it has been conducting its operations safely. Now it appears this may not be so. . . . If a member of the staff says this about the paper, what reaction can we expect from the press and public?"

Knapp, feisty and confident of his work replied: "I expect somebody might want to hang Gordon Dunning from a sour apple tree."

Dunning, clearly angry with the report, attached another memo: "We have spent years of hard, patient effort to establish good and calm relations with the public around the Nevada test site. Such actions as the author's have been harmful."[30,31,32]

The AEC then set out to change Knapp's mind.

Before long, Knapp was presented with a memo requesting his presence at a meeting. A group of scientists from various AEC labs across the country—including an M.D. from the prestigious Livermore Lab—would like to discuss some things with him. Knapp began to feel defensive. The AEC was rolling out the big guns.

Immediately before the meeting, Knapp was asked to take a seat outside the conference room. Inside, behind the closed door, the AEC official was telling the group: "The reason I called you together is we have a problem. We've got a man in the biomedical division in the Washington AEC office by the name of Dr. Harold Knapp who has made some calculations of the true dose that the people of Utah got from the radio-iodine from the bomb tests in 1962. And he says that the doses were something like one hundred times higher than we've publicly announced . . . we must stop that publication. If we don't stop that publication, the credibility of the AEC will just disappear, because it will be stated that we've been lying."

The Livermore physician, however, much to the AEC official's astonishment, decided to argue with him, saying, "If Knapp has that evidence, then he ought to publish it." The AEC official then brought a surly, defiant Harold Knapp into the room.

After the brief meeting, the assembled scientists told the AEC official, "We think Knapp ought to publish his data and you face the music."[33]

The official was stunned. Here were AEC-funded scientists, one from *Livermore*, for heaven's sake, who were recommending that a severely damaging report be published. He couldn't understand it.

The AEC finally released Harold Knapp's report. When Knapp obtained a copy, he immediately noticed something was missing: the section detailing how the HARRY test had exposed the thyroid glands of infants in St. George, Utah, to 120 to 440 rads of radiation. Furious, he subsequently quit the Atomic Energy Commission and submitted the report *with* the deleted information to *Nature* magazine.[34]

Had the official known more about the scientists in the room, and particularly the M.D. from Livermore, one Dr. John Gofman, he might never have chosen them to review the report. John Gofman would eventually show that low-level radiation was more hazardous than even Harold Knapp's report had indicated.

High LET, Low LET

In June 1963, another report appeared concerning radioactive fallout, this one in *Science* magazine. The writer was Ernest J. Sternglass, a Ph.D. working at Westinghouse in Pittsburgh, Pennsylvania. The subject: childhood cancer and X rays, specifically, X rays from fallout.[35]

Sternglass knew his way around X rays. Shortly before he obtained his Ph.D. in engineering physics at Cornell, he had obtained a job in the Westinghouse Research Lab designing low-energy fluoroscope tubes.[36] He knew the effect X- and gamma radiation had on genes and it concerned him greatly. In 1947, his wife had given birth to a son who was afflicted with Tay-Sachs disease. Sternglass's father, a dermatologist, had worked heavily with X-rays. Though a relationship between radiation and Tay-Sachs had never been proven, the physicist wondered if his son's disease was somehow related to his own father's exposure.[37]

For his article, Sternglass closely studied the fallout levels over the entire country and concluded that the previous two years of testing (1961–62) had exposed everyone in the Northern Hemisphere to 200 to 400 millirads, a radiation dose approximately equivalent to a pelvic X-ray.[38]

Scientists working with the AEC were extremely skeptical of Sternglass's findings. They had just begun a close study of the medical effects of the atomic bomb blast at Hiroshima. The AEC physicists had made calculations based on yield and other measurements and had come up with a good approximation of the radiation field that had existed at the time of detonation. The scientists then divided the radiation into two groups: low linear energy transfer (low LET) and high linear energy transfer (high LET).

Low LET radiation loses little energy in its travel. It can pierce wood, metal, brick for quite some distance and keep on going. This group includes high-energy electrons, gamma, and X rays. The scientists believed that low LET radiation imparted relatively little kinetic energy—and thus damage— to the cells as it passed through them.

High LET radiation loses energy more rapidly in its travels through the air or through material, such as a cell. Scientists concluded that high LET radiation, such as neutrons and protons, imparted more kinetic energy to the cell, thus causing more damage.

According to their model, the cancers that eventually showed up were caused by a massive neutron, or high LET, radiation field that had apparently existed at time of detonation. Fallout contained mostly beta and gamma radiation; there was little if any neutron radiation resulting from bomb debris.[39] Most AEC scientists claimed that since fallout produced most low LET radiation, it simply was not carcinogenic.[40]

The year before the Sternglass article appeared, another scientist, radiologist Robert Pendleton, was becoming interested in radioactive fallout. In July 1962, he had taken his class on a field trip to study and measure background radiation. While at a site about 20 miles southeast of Salt Lake City, they happened to see a dust cloud roll overhead. Unknown to them, they were seeing the same kind of thing residents of Tonopah and Warm Springs, Nevada and St. George, Utah, had seen during the 1950s: a cloud of nuclear debris.

The roiling brown dust cloud was the remnants of STORAX: SEDAN; specifically, the segment drifting down from 10,000 feet. It would eventually skirt the southern border of Wyoming, then turn north over the upper Midwest before petering out over the small community of Houston, Minnesota. But Pendleton didn't know that, nor would he have cared. What disturbed him was the reaction of the Geiger counters: The dusty cloud had raised the radiation level to about a hundred times background level, effectively ruining the field trip.[41]

The next day, Pendleton found the air around campus to be hot with beta particles, a sure sign of fallout. The professor quickly organized a new project: the collection of milk samples. All told, milk from thirty-nine dairies turned up contaminated with iodine-131.[42] Apparently familiar with the Windscale debacle, Pendleton persuaded the Utah Department of Health to destroy or store the contaminated dairy products. For the first time in the history of the testing program, reasonable and effective preventive action had taken place. Iodine-131 from SEDAN (and several subsequent shots) was prevented from reaching the thyroids of Utah children. Unfortunately, there is no indication that similar procedures took place for Wyoming, Nebraska, South Dakota, or Minnesota.

The Dilemma

By the mid-1960s, strontium-90 had been replaced by iodine-131 as the primary concern of epidemiologists interested in fallout. Along about that time, Dr. Edward Weiss, a researcher for the Public Health Service, had decided to make a study of the number of thyroid disease patients in Utah from 1948 to 1962. The initial results practically jumped out at him: During the last five years of the study, from 1958 to 1962, thyroid cancer had increased almost four times. Startled, Weiss proposed a broad survey that would include more thyroid exams, visual and dental surveys for strontium, and even an assessment of the leukemia rate.

Again the numbers were surprising. Leukemia deaths were up, particularly in southwestern Utah. That year (1965) there were seventy children in the St. George school who suffered from thyroid nodules. Something serious was taking place and Weiss wanted to know more about it. Then he made his only mistake: He wrote to Gordon Dunning.

After reading the epidemiologist's plans for a project, Dunning called him up and complained about such things as statistical ambiguities and problems in the population samples. While he seemed to want the study, it also became clear that he had some purpose in mind for it. Had Weiss seen Dunning's original letter that purpose would have been revealed: "I agree the study should be done, even in desperation, in the hope of obtaining a better response to the allegations."[43]

The allegations Dunning was referring to were those raised by Knapp years before. The AEC official apparently saw the thyroid project as a tool to battle the Knapp article. An an indication of the AEC official's responsibilities to the public regarding Weiss's leukemia and dental surveys, Gordon Dunning stated that he didn't "know of any compelling public relations need to undertake them."[44]

That didn't stop Weiss; after all, he was employed by the Public Health Service, not the Atomic Energy Commission. The leukemia survey was performed, and sure enough, there *were* excess cases among the populace in southwestern Utah. With yet another cat out of the bag, Dunning was becoming nervous. In a letter to Dwight Ink, the AEC's assistant general manager, Dunning argued that "we should consider the technical staff indicating more formally the fallacies upon which the studies are being based." Then, in a burst of bureaucratese, "Hopefully there might be a chance of averting a potential fallout scare by placing the purpose of the studies in the proper context."[45] The "proper context," presumably, was to be defined by Dunning.

By September 1965, Ink had written AEC chairman Glenn Seaborg about the Weiss leukemia and thyroid findings. The AEC was in a real pinch. The work looked unassailable: Graham County, Arizona, had been used as a "control"—that is, it was a county like St. George's Washington County *except* it was outside the path of fallout. It also had eight cases of thyroid nodules to Washington County's *forty*.

Seaborg didn't know what to do. If Weiss was right, then there was a severe hazard around the test site, and it was the responsibility of the federal government to limit the danger to the public. On the other hand, if Weiss was wrong, the AEC had nothing to worry about. Problem was, no one seemed to be able to find fault with the work.

While Seaborg agonized over the Weiss data, he received another letter from Dwight Ink. Like most federal government in-house memos, it was composed of two distinct parts, the "disclaimer" and the "bottom line." First, the "disclaimer": "Although we do not oppose developing further data in these areas . . . [then, the "bottom line"] . . . performance of the above U.S. Public Health service studies will pose potential problems to the commission." Ink was even kind enough to spell out the problems: "(a) adverse public reaction, (b) lawsuits, and (c) jeopardizing the programs at the Nevada test site."[46]

Thoroughly rattled by the dilemma, Seaborg eventually shuffled the decision to an even higher authority: President Lyndon Baines Johnson. The president wasted no time: The Weiss report vanished without a trace.

Deadly Rain

The article appeared in the late summer of 1969, not in a peer review scientific journal, but from out of left field, a popular men's magazine. In addition, its author wasn't some disaffected former AEC scientist worrying about the finer points of arms control. He was a professor of radiation physics at the Pittsburgh University Medical School. Also, he had a way with words. The article was entitled "The Death of All Children," and it was the lead article on page 1a of *Esquire* magazine. The AEC had been completely blindsided: The initial reaction was shock and outrage. Yet they should have seen it coming. In fact, a condensed version of the *Esquire* article had appeared several months before in, of all places, the *Bulletin of the Atomic Scientists*.

Ernest J. Sternglass was an old and familiar name to many in the field of nuclear energy. His first article had been published years before in the somewhat dry, academic *Science* magazine. In it, he had concluded that people across the United States had been exposed to several hundred millirads. His research was sound, but no one in the AEC said much, preferring to assign cancer deaths to neutrons rather than the ubiquitous gamma rays and beta particles of fallout. Atomic Energy Commission officials ignored the article but remembered the name.

Since the early 1960s, Sternglass had studied disease patterns relating to fallout, paying particular attention to the Troy-Albany-Utica, New York, exposure in April 1953. He had spent literally years tracing and comparing New York's leukemia deaths, stillbirths, and infant mortality figures with other parts of the country.[1] In short, for much of the 1960s, his avocation had been a study of the relationship between fallout and infant mortality.

In late 1968, Sternglass submitted to *Science* magazine an article detailing his latest findings. The article detailed how the infant death rate in New York State had declined steadily *except* after periods of nuclear testing, when the infant death rate leveled off. By way of comparison, in states up-wind of the shots, such as California, no such leveling occurred. What Sternglass was saying, in essence, was that fallout was lethal to a significant number of children. He felt that the rain on Troy-Albany-Utica in April 1953 had indeed been a deadly one.

Like most scientific journals, *Science* screens its articles through a pro-cedure called peer review—that is, prior to acceptance, each manuscript is submitted to three unnamed experts in the field. If the experts like it, the ar-ticle is published. If there is disagreement, then it usually is up to the editors to decide. In January 1969, Sternglass received a manila envelope in the mail. His manuscript had been rejected. One of the reviewers hadn't cared for it.

A similar paper, one linking high leukemia rates in 1954 with the test-ing, was similarly rejected.[2] At this, the physicist was particularly disheart-ened. The data had come from the New York State Department of Health and had showed an obvious pattern: For those born the year after the Troy-Utica fallout episode in 1953, there seemed to be an unusually high number of leukemia cases.

BIRTH YEAR	NUMBER OF CASES
1943–44	4
1945–46	5
1947–48	8
1949–50	5
1951–52	6
1953–54	13

Sternglass read the reason for the rejection. The dissenting reviewer had written: "There has been no increase in the incidence of cancer or leu-kemia over the past ten years in the children of the Albany, Troy and Schenectady areas. . . ." Then, a phrase caught his eye: "as compared with children of this age elsewhere in upstate New York."

Sternglass was incredulous. *Of course* there was no increase if you com-pared it with the rest of upstate New York: The entire northern part of the state had received the fallout—and likely had a cancer rate *just as high* as Troy, Utica, and Schenectady.[3]

A few days later, another letter arrived in the mail. If was from Merry Selk, editorial assistant at the *Bulletin of Atomic Scientists*. Editor Gene Ra-binowitch wanted to publish the article on infant mortality.[4]

In April 1969, the *Bulletin* published the article "Infant Mortality and Nuclear Tests." In a concise three pages, Sternglass explained his thesis: There was a direct correlation between the number of excess fetal deaths per live births and the amount of fallout deposited over New York State.[5] After the article appeared, managing editor Richard Lewis told Sternglass that he had been under pressure "from individuals in Washington" warning him that it would be a "grave mistake" to publish the article.

Interestingly, the April issue also carried an article by respected physicist Freeman Dyson entitled "A Case for Missile Defense." In it, Dyson stated his belief that the country needed an antiballistic missile program. A few months later, the *Bulletin* received a letter from Dyson:

> I welcome this chance to call attention to Ernest Sternglass' article "Infant Mortality and Nuclear Tests" in the April *Bulletin*. I urge everyone to read it. Compared with the issues Sternglass has raised, my arguments about missile defense are quite insignificant. Sternglass displays evidence that the effect of fallout in killing babies is about a hundred times greater than has been generally supposed. The evidence is not sufficient to prove Sternglass is right. The essential point is that Sternglass may be right. The margin of uncertainty in the effects of worldwide fallout is so large that we have no justification for dismissing Sternglass' numbers as fantastic. If Sternglass' numbers are right, as I believe they well may be, then he has a good argument against missile defense. . . .[6]

Shortly after that, Sternglass received a call from Harold Hayes, editor of *Esquire*. Hayes had heard about the *Bulletin* article and wanted to know if the physicist would write a similar story for his magazine. Yes, it was short notice; yes, they would stop the presses. It would be a special insert.[7]

Sternglass, having sensed the silence, had apparently decided that his next publication effort should reach a wider audience. He accepted. "The scientific evidence," he said, "indicates that *already* at least one of three children, who died before their first birthdays in America in the 1960s, may have died as a result of peacetime nuclear testing."[8]

Carefully avoiding scientific jargon, Sternglass patiently explained how he came to his conclusions. Basing his study primarily on the Albany and Troy areas, he followed the cancer rates in the region following the UPSHOT-KNOTHOLE: SIMON overdose and came up with some interesting figures, namely, the number of leukemia cases in the area *doubled* in the eight years following the radioactive downpour of April 26, 1953.

And there was more: The leukemia rate seemed to rise and fall in a delayed cadence with the nuclear testing: "Further examination of the leukemia rate for the state of New York revealed a pattern of increase and decrease following the sequence of individual test series in Nevada between 1951 and 1958, with a characteristic delay of about five years after each detonation. The rise and fall were particularly marked in the age group from five to fourteen years, the group most indicative of radiation-produced cases."

Then Sternglass went for the knockout punch. During the 1950s—the period of atmospheric testing—there had been about 40,000 excess infant deaths, while *after* the tests had ended, the excess infant deaths dropped to

34,000. The physicist had based his conclusions on a careful examination of birth and natal death certificates across the country, particularly comparing California (upwind of the tests) with states directly in the line of fallout.

Sternglass blamed the deaths primarily on strontium-90 and concluded that the bombs "must now be regarded not merely as vastly destructive explosive and incendiary devices, but as the most powerful biological poison weapons that man has ever invented." He went on to warn that close to 400,000 infants in the U,S. may already have died from radiation as a result of nuclear fallout.[9,10]

The article couldn't have come at a worse time for the AEC. The year was 1969 and anti-Vietnam, antigovernment sentiment was at an all-time high. This was no time for the public to become reacquainted with the hazards of fallout.[11]

Shortly after the *Esquire* article hit the newsstands, a copy found its way to the desk of Michael May, director of Livermore Laboratory. It was along about the time the laboratory was involved in designs for the new antiballistic missile system, and there were fears that an adverse public response might dampen enthusiasm for the ABM, which would require additional nuclear testing.

May read the article and sent it along for review to Livermore's medical department and its director, the iconoclastic Dr. John Gofman. Gofman then turned the article over to an associate, Arthur Tamplin.

Earlier, Gofman and Tamplin had aroused the ire of the AEC by reviewing—critically—the cancer statistics prepared by the Atomic Bomb Casualty Commission, the group that had studied latent deaths at Hiroshima and Nagasaki. The two scientists had claimed that there were huge gaps in the Casualty Commission's figures: Several important radiation-related diseases had not been counted. Worse, the AEC started counting the deaths in 1950; since the latency period of some radiation-induced cancers is about ten years, the commission should have made a correction. Gofman had not been charitable in his assessment of the mistake, saying "if you're on a rising curve, you're dishonest to just count how many you have at the bottom of the curve. You should say that when fully mature, this effect or number will be two or three times as big."[12] When the AEC responded that Gofman and Tamplin were "using Hiroshima-Nagasaki material that belonged to other people," Gofman replied with characteristic humor: "that is true. We discussed it, and felt it was not justified for us to go out and drop our bomb and get our own data."[13,14,15]

Regardless of their views, Gofman and Tamplin were still respected among their peers as competent scientists, and Livermore's director was interested in their opinion of the Sternglass figures. After a few weeks, he had his answer. Tamplin had analyzed the data and came to the conclusion that Sternglass was wrong. There would not be 400,000 deaths from fallout. Only 4,000.

"Tamplin was an instant hero of the Livermore lab," Gofman recalled. "They thought it was marvelous because Sternglass's figures would have really hurt the antiballistic missile vote in the Senate. I think if they could have, they would have put up a bronze statue for Tamplin."[16]

A few weeks later, Michael May told Gofman that he couldn't understand the AEC's reaction to the report. It had been good scientific work, yet both Dr. John Totter, head of Biology and Medicine, and his supervisor, Dr. Spofford English, were upset.

Gofman and Tamplin decided to place a conference call to the AEC to find out why. Once on the line, Totter and English told the Livermore scientists that they thought the work was excellent, but why did Tamplin have to go and write that fallout would kill 4,000 children? Gofman patiently explained that it was certainly better than the Sternglass figures, and besides, any intelligent reader would want to know what the correct figures were. And since the article was to be published in *The Bulletin of Atomic Scientists*, Gofman assumed the readership would certainly include those of a certain high level of intelligence.

Totter and Spofford complained that the figures still seemed high; perhaps they should publish the article in a more esoteric scientific journal.

Gofman exploded: "In other words, you'd like a whitewash. And you can go to hell." After hanging up the phone on the AEC, Gofman walked into Mike May's office and told him what had happened. "Fine," May said.[17] The paper was published, the ABM bill passed the Senate, and things quieted down, but not for long.

Gofman and Tamplin, in an effort to determine minimum radiation damage thresholds, had been looking over stacks of data regarding exposures. They were coming up with startling information: There appeared to be *no* minimum threshold for exposure.

The implications were serious. Up until that time, scientists had assumed that there was a minimum level below which no damage occurred. After all, the cell, even DNA, tended to repair itself after minor damage. Background radiation both from the sky and from the earth had been a part of the environment since time began, and it didn't seem to have caused a problem. The atomic testing had dusted the country with several hundred millirads during the 1950s and early 1960s. And there apparently had been no problem from these "light exposures." There *had* to be a minimum threshold level. The AEC depended on it.

But Gofman's research showed the opposite was the case. In fact, it began to appear that the risk *per unit of radiation* was greater at lower doses than at higher ones.[18] The information indicated that even assuming *no* threshold level, the guidelines established by the International Commission of Radiological Protection were twenty times too *high*; if everyone received what the commission, and the AEC, considered an *allowable* dose, then there would be 16,000 to 32,000 extra cancer deaths per year.[19]

Gofman presented his findings first at an obscure convention of electrical engineers in San Francisco, then before Senator Edmund Muskie's committee on underground nuclear testing. The title of the talk left no doubt about its conclusions: Federal Radiation Counsel Guidelines— Protection or Disaster? Muskie's staff recoiled in horror at the speech, but Muskie himself was interested. His home state, Maine, had been a regular depository of nuclear fallout during the 1950s; now, here was a respected Livermore physician saying that even low level radiation, such as found in fallout, might be lethal.

Shortly after that, Gofman received the request he had been expecting. Chet Holifield, the powerful chairman of the Joint Committee on Atomic Energy, wanted to see him.

"We Got Them and We'll Get You"

The Joint Committee on Atomic Energy (JCAE) was composed of a group of congressmen and senators whose job it was to formulate and present to Congress legislation dealing with nuclear matters. Its responsibilities included both military and civilian uses of atomic energy, and as a result, members of the JCAE enjoyed immense power. Legislation originating in the committee directly affected all enterprises involving nuclear power, from uranium mining to bomb manufacturing. It quite literally controlled the atomic establishment; even the AEC yielded to its demands. Fortunately for the AEC, the members of the Joint Committee were very comfortable with matters atomic.

In 1957, for example, one of the JCAE members, Melvin Price, had co-authored the Price-Anderson Act, which limits the accident liability of any company using nuclear power to just $100 million.[20]

The chairman, California Democrat Chet Holifield, held similar views toward atomic energy. In the early and middle sixties, it became known that uranium miners were being exposed to between 20 and 230 times the acceptable level of radioactive radon gas. Yet JCAE, under the leadership of Chet Holifield, did essentially nothing to correct the hazard. The situation became so bad that a New York firm hired by the Industrial Commission of Colorado predicted that future claims from widows of uranium miners would eventually exceed $8.5 million, effectively bankrupting the commission.

In April 1967, atomic energy consultant Leo Goodman had immortalized Chet Holifield in a speech in Washington detailing the miners' problems: "Over ten thousand underground miners," he said, "have been exposed to one or more 'Holifield units' . . . I define one 'Holifield' as that amount of underground exposure which is sufficient to give the statistical chance of 60 percent of lung cancer development following the latent period of 7 to 27 years.'' Holifield, not a man noted for his sense of humor, was infuriated.[21]

Now, several years later, he was about to confront another scientist who had problems with nuclear safety. The meeting with John Gofman began poorly and went downhill from there.

''Just what the hell do you think you're doing,'' Holifield began, ''saying the amount of radiation we're allowing is causing cancer?'' Gofman replied that he had done the calculations the best way he knew how and that was the conclusion he had reached.

''Listen,'' Holifield said, ''I've been assured by the Atomic Energy Commission people that a dose of a hundred times what they're allowing won't hurt anybody.''

''I don't know where you got that assurance,'' Gofman replied, ''but I don't think it's so. I'll look into it. We stand with our numbers.'' At that point, Holifield apparently lost his temper. Gofman remembered that ''he began to rave about how we were going to get all the little old ladies in tennis shoes up in arms.''

After one of Holifield's aides reminded the senator that he was speaking to reputable scientists from the Livermore Laboratory, Holifield replied, ''I know who they are. I'm not changing anything I say; they're going to cause all kinds of trouble.'' Then, according to Gofman, Holifield leaned over to him and said, ''Listen, there have been others who have tried to cross the AEC before you. We got them and we'll get you.''[22]

X

EVIDENCE

After the encounter with Holifield, John Gofman left the meeting thoroughly shaken. On the trip back to Livermore, Gofman told his associate Arthur Tamplin that they would do well if they "survived personally, let alone professionally."[1]

Back at Livermore, trouble was brewing. In the winter of 1969-70, Tamplin was asked to give a talk on nuclear power at a symposium sponsored by the American Association for the Advancement of Science. Prior to that, the AEC had requested all of Gofman's and Tamplin's manuscripts and speeches be sent to Washington for review prior to publication. Now they were exercising their authority. "Look at this, this is my talk," he told Gofman, throwing the manuscript on his desk, "there's practically nothing left in it but the prepositions and the adverbs!" The manuscript had been edited into gibberish.

Not only that, Tamplin had been instructed not to identify himself as being from the Livermore Laboratory. In addition, the trip was on him; he would have to pay his own expenses *and* would be docked the pay for time spent at the meeting.[2]

Gofman assumed that Livermore and not the AEC was behind the censorship of Tamplin, and told his supervisors that they were "behaving like bastards." Tamplin eventually was allowed to give his speech, but the battle was not over. Shortly after that, Tamplin suddenly found that twelve of the thirteen scientists working with him were going to be relieved of their duties, dismissed.[3]

While this was going on, Gofman received another call from Chet Holifield of the Joint Committee on Atomic Energy. The JCAE wanted Gofman to state his entire case on the hazard of low-level radiation. He would be given fifteen minutes to do so.

Gofman was incredulous. To fully explain his work would take *hours*—four at least. The committee extended his time to an hour. At first, Gofman reacted with rage. The AEC—and, apparently, Livermore—had done everything possible to suppress his work: He had been threatened, and by a United States Senator no less. Tamplin had lost his assistants. Now they wanted him to state his case for the record, but were going to force him to leave out pertinent information through time constraints. Within minutes, the anger was replaced by cold determination. The last time Holifield and Gofman met, the senator had scored heavily. This time, Gofman would be ready for him.

During the next three weeks, Gofman and Tamplin worked furiously, writing, editing, compressing, and distilling their research into a final, coherent, single product consisting of 178 pages of testimony.

On January 28, 1970, the two scientists appeared before Chet Holifield and the JCAE. Gofman and Tamplin calmly and carefully produced and explained the data proving that low levels of radiation caused serious cell injuries. They produced diagrams clearly showing that no threshold of injury actually existed; that previously accepted "safe" levels were, in fact, quite hazardous. In their one-hour talk, John Gofman and Arthur Tamplin presented compelling evidence that three decades of nuclear testing had exposed untold millions of persons to the threat of cancer; heart, lung, and thyroid disease; and leukemia. Not only that, the information indicated that the injuries would also be reflected in generations yet unborn.

At the end of the presentation, Gofman turned from his diagrams and, looking squarely at Holifield, issued a remarkable challenge:

> Chairman Holifield, we urge you to nominate a jury of eminent persons, physicians, chemists, biologists, Nobel prize winners, or National Academy of Science members—none of whom have any atomic energy axe to grind. We urge you to serve as chairman of such a debate. Dr. Tamplin and I will debate each and every facet of the evidence concerning the serious hazard of Federal Radiation Guidelines against the entire AEC staff, plus anyone they can get from their nineteen-odd laboratories, singly, serially, or in any combination.
>
> With their twenty-year background on this problem and their large staff to draw on, they should be razor-sharp at a moment's notice. We are ready now. If there is any valid reason for questioning our submission to peers and for questioning our evidence, this eminent jury of peers will certainly determine so. If the debate before eminent peers is not held, then by default I think the entire country and the world will know the answer without further question.[4]

Holifield was speechless. There could be no answer; no one at the AEC would take the challenge, not John Totter, *certainly* not Gordon Dunning. Not anyone. There would be no debate.[5]

The AEC, however, responded in its own way. Through the controversy, Gofman had continued to work at Livermore Laboratory. In addition to his radiation work, he was involved in basic cancer research, trying to determine if the control mechanism for cell division and differentiation resides in the chromosome. It was important work that would have had tremendous applications in the field of cancer therapy. In 1971, shortly after Gofman's challenge, the AEC contacted Livermore official Roger Batzel in an effort to get them to cut off funding for the cancer program. Batzel refused.

Later in the year, Gofman spoke at a meeting in which he said that "all the major forms of human cancer are produced by radiation." Shortly after that, Livermore officials were again contacted by the AEC. The demand was repeated: Cut Gofman's program or the AEC would simply delete an equivalent amount of funding from the Livermore budget.

After being warned what was taking place, Gofman went to see Frank Grousher, head of the National Cancer Institute. Perhaps the NCI could take over the cost of the project. Grousher was impressed with the work and told Gofman that there should be no problem in getting the money. Several weeks later, Gofman received a perfunctory note saying that the chromosome study was "not of any main-line interest to the institute."

Gofman's chromosome study was soon canceled. Shortly after that, in 1973, both he and Tamplin left Livermore Laboratory.[6] Two years later, John Gofman applied to the National Cancer Institute for $32,000 to continue work on the relationship between low-level radiation and cancer. The request was rejected.[7]

Gofman, and others like him, however, had made telling points against the AEC. Increasingly, the scientific debates had become public knowledge and many citizens were finding it more prudent to side with the likes of Gofman, Knapp, and Sternglass than with faceless bureaucrats who blandly assured them that the radiation was at "acceptable levels."

The End of the AEC

During the late 1960s, people all across the United States had begun to reevaluate nuclear testing. Those living in Nevada and Utah remembered the news stories of "taller towers" at the Nevada Test Site-to "introduce an added angle of safety."[8] They wondered what had happened to the 300 tons of steel vaporized in each explosion; two things were sure: it was radioactive, and it came back to earth. Did it have anything to do with the high leukemia rates in Utah and even as far away as New York? The AEC said "no," but some researchers weren't so sure.

Many scientists and much of the public had long come to view the AEC as an inept bureaucracy, operating under a siege mentality and demonstratively indifferent to the question of radiation safety. The clamor for its removal had begun in the late 1950s; by the early 1970s, the end was in sight.

In 1974, the Atomic Energy, Commission was abolished, its duties divided between the newly formed Energy Research and Development Administration and the Nuclear Regulatory Agency.[9] With the end of the AEC, many scientists, no longer fearful that their funds would be cut, turned to the study of the radiation-cancer link. Others began to reassess the quality of research performed by AEC specialists.

The Leukemia Connection

In 1977, an investigative series on fallout appeared in Salt Lake City's *Deseret News*. The article detailed the 1953 Cedar City sheep deaths. It told of how St. George residents had been exposed to the roiling brown clouds of nuclear debris and how later many of those exposed contracted leukemia, cancer, and thyroid problems. And it told of assurances by the AEC that nothing was amiss.

One of the many people interested in the series was Dr. Joseph Lyon of the University of Utah. Lyon knew his way around statistics and epidemiology and decided that a rigorous, scientific study was in order. First, however, he would look at the AEC work performed by one Gordon Dunning, who, in a 1959 study, had declared the area within acceptable limits.

Upon close examination, Dunning's work appeared to contain serious flaws. For one thing, dosages that formed the basis for conclusions were either inaccurate or lacking altogether. Incredibly, there was no reference to *internal* radiation doses: Dunning had stubbornly assumed that only external doses mattered.[10]

Quietly gathering information for his own study, Lyon decided to concentrate on the leukemia rate in the path of fallout. The *Deseret News* article had claimed there was an abundance of leukemias in St. George and Cedar City, and Sternglass had apparently found a leukemia "spike" in upstate New York.

Physicians had long known the association between X-radiation and leukemia. Linman's *Principles of Hematology*, a popular hematology text written in 1966, flatly stated that ionizing radiation "is clearly leukemogenic in experimental animals and appears to play a role in the pathogenesis of some cases of human leukemia." The same book went on to say that there was a "definite but less marked increase in frequency of leukemia" in patients treated with radioactive iodine.[11] Lyon knew that, thanks to the testing, the area had seen an abundance of radioactive iodine. But had there been an increase in leukemia?

After months of analyzing death certificates, the answer came. For children born before the testing, the leukemia rate had been 2.12 per 100,000 population, while for those born *after* the testing began, the leukemia rate was a surprising 6.02 per 100,000. The leukemia rate was more than *twice*—2.4 times—what would be expected in a normal population. According to Lyon's figures, there were nineteen extra deaths from leukemia in southwestern Utah.[12,13]

In an effort to check the radiation dosages in Utah, the Department of Energy sent senior radiation physicists Harold Beck and Phil Krey to the area. Though it was impossible to determine actual exposures to people living there, Beck and Krey wanted to know where the most fallout had occurred. After meticulously measuring cesium-137 and plutonium-239 and -240 in the soil at 150 sites around the state, they found that the areas highest in plutonium and cesium were indeed in the southwestern corner nearest the test site. Interestingly, their calculations indicated that the residents of Salt Lake City "received greater exposures than most Utah residents who lived far closer to the Nevada Test Site, although only about one-third as much as residents of Washington County [St. George–Cedar City]."[14,15] Unfortunately for the Department of Energy, the Beck-Krey study, regardless of other interpretations, proved that the soil of Utah was permeated with considerable amounts of radioactive cesium-137, plutonium-238, and plutonium-239.

In 1981, Colorado physician Carl Johnson decided to look into the relationship between cancer and fallout. Earlier, he had studied the incidence of brain cancer and skin cancer at a nuclear weapons facility outside of Denver. Now he was going to tackle the cancer rate among the "downwinders," people living in St. George, Parowan, Paragonah, and Kanab, Utah; Fredonia, Arizona; and Bunkerville, Nevada. In his background research, Dr. Johnson turned up some extremely disturbing information: On July 14, 1962, the DOMINIC-II: SMALL BOY detonation had produced a hot spot of 100 rads/hour at a site 333 *miles* (540 kilometers) from the Nevada Test Site. Within a radius of 10 to 15 miles about this hot spot, the radiation dose increased by twenty-five times. Another hot area of 100 rads was found on a highway between St. George and Cedar City shortly after the UPSHOT-KNOTHOLE: HARRY shot.

After a phone call to Harold Knapp, Johnson was told that other, similar, hot areas were found after NANCY, SIMON, and BADGER in the UPSHOT-KNOTHOLE series and PLUMBBOB's BOLTZMANN. Johnson and a group of volunteers then traveled to the target communities in southwestern Utah. They asked questions about what, if anything, the townspeople experienced immediately after the fallout cloud had passed by: did they notice skin or eye burns, did their hair change color or fall out, did they experience nausea or diarrhea? Those who had been diagnosed as having cancer were asked to fill out a supplementary form listing date of diagnosis, name of physician, and other pertinent information. The volunteers asked if any stillbirths and/or malformations had occurred.

When the data came in, skin cancer that was not melanoma was rejected from consideration, as were benign tumors even though there seemed to be an increase in the latter. As a comparison group, Johnson selected rural and small-town Mormon communities.

By late 1981, Johnson had most of his information, and on January 5, 1982, at the annual meeting of the American Association for the Advancement of Science in Washington, D.C., Johnson revealed the results of the study: The cancer rate had definitely increased among residents living in an area downwind of the test site.

Two years later, Johnson's paper appeared in the *Journal of the American Medical Association*. It's conclusions were startling: Johnson had uncovered much more than leukemia.

The downwnders also had significantly higher levels of lymphoma and melanoma as well as cancer of the breast, thyroid, colon, stomach, brain, and bone. Johnson later published the complete study in *JAMA*.

| | TIMES EXPECTED RATE | |
	1958–66	*1972–80*
Leukemia	5.3	3.5
Lymphoma	—	1.9
Thyroid cancer	4.3	8.2
Breast	—	1.9
Colon	—	1.7
Stomach	5.0	1.8
Melanoma	1.6	3.5
Brain	3.1	1.7
Bone and joints	10.0	12.5

Johnson found that leukemia was not even the most prevalent cancer in the area: Apparently, the bone-seeking plutonium, cesium-137, and strontium-90 had wreaked havoc on the bones of those living downwind of the detonations. During the years 1972–80, the incidence of cancer was an astonishing 12.5 times the expected rate.[16] It was beginning to appear that John Gofman had been right when he said that "all the major forms of cancer are produced by radiation." The downwinders were providing the evidence with their lives.

Gamma Rays vs. Neutrons

About the same time that the investigative series was appearing in Salt Lake City's *Deseret News*, research was taking place that would eventually affect the course of nuclear testing—and perhaps the entire future of nuclear power. And it began because no one was sure just how big the Hiroshima and Nagasaki bombs had been.

Although there had been vast amounts of data generated regarding the effects of those bombs—blast effects, genetic damage, and increased cancer risks—no one had ever been able to pinpoint the yield of the two weapons. Estimates of yield from the Hiroshima bomb varied from 12.5 to 15 kilotons while for the Nagasaki weapon estimates ranged from 20 to 24 kilotons.[17,18,19]

This imprecision in estimates, coupled with the fact that subsequent information regarding gamma-ray and neutron fields were derived from other detonations, resulted in a slightly flawed picture of the radiation dose-cancer relationship.

George Kerr of Oak Ridge Laboratory had access to one of the world's most powerful computers. In 1977, he wondered if it could be used to reconstruct the two detonations mathematically, thus giving a more accurate picture of the radiation field that existed near the detonation. The task, however, was a formidable one, and other studies eventually took precedence—and computer time. The project was shelved.

At Livermore, however, two other physicists, William Loewe and Edgar Mendelsohn, had also taken a shot at the computerization problem and were having better luck. A clearer picture began to emerge of the Hiroshima blast's gamma ray–neutron field at a distance of 1,180 meters. It did not resemble the prior estimates.

By 1979, George Kerr had resumed his study in the matter, along with Dean Kaul in Chicago and Jess Marcum in Santa Monica.[20] All were founded by the Defense Nuclear Agency. The results of the three groups essentially matched those of Loewe and Mendelsohn: The neutron radiation field at 1,180 meters (0.73 miles) had been overestimated by six to ten times. Since the human effects—i.e., cancer—were already known, the researchers were faced with a serious dilemma. The cancers were caused by *something*: was it from the gamma rays or from the relatively few neutrons present? If the neutrons caused the cancers, then that type of radiation was from six to ten times as toxic as had been previously thought. If, on the other hand, the gammas caused the cancers, then gamma emitters, such as many of the radionuclides found in fallout, are by definition carcinogenic.

In reporting the story, *Science* magazine commented: "The record serves as a compelling argument for declassifying as much as possible of what is done at government labs, for many of the assumptions in this case might have been challenged sooner had the underlying data been available for scrutiny."[21]

Auger Electrons

It had been almost four decades since atomic fallout was first scattered across the countryside; yet by 1979, scientists were looking more closely at the phenomenon than ever before. In that year, Dr. Belton A. Burrows, a physician at the Boston University School of Medicine, saw a patient with the rare "hairy cell" form of leukemia. Upon examination, Burrows discovered the patient had a slightly elevated concentration of cesium-137 in his body. Investigation revealed the man had not only worked in the nuclear zones of the Portsmouth, New Hampshire, Navy yard, but he was also an avid fisherman. On a hunch, the physician examined specimens of fish taken from the patient's freezer, and found relatively high levels of cesium-137.

Startled, Burrows wondered if fish and game had, in some way, concentrated the radioactive cesium in their bodies. He then obtained specimens of wild ducks and woodcock from areas in New Hampshire. Like the fish, the animals contained high levels of the cesium.

But was cesium-137 toxic, and if so, how did it do its damage? Scientists such as Burrows could acknowledge the circumstantial evidence of an epidemiological study, but they were most comfortable when they could see the "smoking gun" of hard, cold experimental evidence.

One clue to cesium's toxicity, Burrows felt, was the element's ability to replace potassium in living systems, plant or animal. Burrows and his colleagues first tested firplace ashes from New Hampshire and New York to determine the potassium-cesium ratio. They were startled to discover a tenfold variation, depending, apparently, upon differences in fallout.

In order to eliminate surface contamination, the scientists decided to analyze maple syrup for cesium. The results were essentially similar to the fireplace ash results.

After establishing the presence of cesium-137 in the systems, Burrows took a closer look at the decay scheme. Upon detonation, uranium and plutonium fission to produce over 300 isotopes, one of them being iodine-137. This radionuclide has an extremely short half-life; within 22.3 seconds, half of it has decayed to another element, xenon-137, which also has a short half-life. Within minutes, the xenon-137 decays to yet another element, cesium-137.

The half-life of cesium-137 is quite long, thirty years, but when it does decay, it emits beta particles and turns into barium-137m (the "m" designation indicates it is only slightly or "meta" stable). This step in the decay chain has a short half-life, only 2.6 minutes. It then decays to stable barium-137 with the release of gamma rays, an X ray, and low-energy or "Auger" (pronounced "aw-zhay") electrons.

During this transformation, the radionuclide can do great damage to the organism. Burrows theorized that in this metastable state, the barium-137m (already in the cell as a replacement for potassium) is highly charged, and is thus attracted to molecules of DNA, the chemical in the cell that is the basis for heredity and the carrier of genetic information.[22]

Once in the vicinity of the barium-137m, the DNA is showered with electrons, gamma and X-radiation. Though the gamma and X rays produced by the barium-137m is in itself harmful, Burrows focused on the wide spectrum of low-energy Auger electrons as co-culprits in the mutagenic process.

Though most of the energy from these electrons is deposited within 25 nanometers—less than the diameter of most cells—the radiation might impinge on certain intercellular structures that may be associated with carcinogenesis. Current theories generally hold that, for cancer to begin, the nucleus of a cell must be damaged. If areas of the cell other than the nucleus are important to carcinogenesis, then the effect of the Auger electrons are important indeed.

In addition to the radiation involved, Burrows saw another problem in cesium-137's decay to barium. He theorized that once inside the cell, the barium may replace magnesium from DNA during cell division, thus resulting in a cell mutation. According to Burrows's theory, cesium-137 has a *variety* of carcinogenic effects.[23,24]

Unfortunately, thanks to the bomb tests, cesium-137 had been scattered across the entire country.

The Atomic Veterans

On September 9, 1945, photographers from a variety of newspapers and magazines, including *Life*, converged on a huge depression in the middle of the Jornada del Muerto: Trinity ground zero. The desert surrounding the area glistened with a frothy green glass, formed from the heat of the fireball exactly two months before. Leslie Groves, ever the showman, wanted to impress upon the reporters there how safe the site was. He summoned his military driver, one Sergeant Patrick Stout, and asked him to step into the crater and pose for the cameras. For thirty minutes, Sergeant Stout stood inside the crater next to the remains of the tower, smiling for the photographers.

In April 1967, Patrick Stout, now retired from the army, suddenly took ill. The diagnosis: leukemia. Before he died in 1969, he told his wife that the source of his illness was those thirty minutes in the Trinity crater.

By this time, other veterans of the atomic testing were experiencing the same and similar illnesses: leukemia, multiple myelomas, polycythemia vera, and vague nerve and muscle disorders. Many of the treating physicians, however, never linked their patients' illnesses with the bomb: The soldiers simply never told them about their experiences at Desert Rock. Loyal citizens, they were simply following orders.

Prior to each test, the soldiers were warned never to mention to anyone about the maneuvers. Many veterans thought that to disclose the information, even to their physician, would be breaking the law. This feeling persisted even though many of the maneuvers during the tests were covered by the newspapers at the time. Still, most soliders remained quiet about their experience—until the late 1970s.

It was then that navy vet Orville E. Kelly was diagnosed as having lymphoma. He had been present at a number of H-bomb shots in the Pacific in 1958, and he didn't care who knew it. Kelly also felt that his disease was somehow related to the radiation at the bomb tests: He petitioned the Veterans Administration for disability compensation for a service-related illness: radiation-induced lymphoma.

The request set off a detonation of its own in the VA. Kelly didn't know it at the time, but there were over 200,000 soldiers who had been at the bomb tests, either in the Pacific or at the Nevada Test Site. What if *all* of them decided their illness was a result of the testing? The VA refused Kelly's request.

Kelly responded not only by resubmitting his claim, but also by forming a new organization: the National Association of Atomic Veterans (NAAV). The claim was again refused. Orville Kelly died in 1979, but his organization survived and grew. In the early 1980s, under pressure from NAAV, the Public Health Service began an epidemiological survey of veterans who had taken part in nuclear testing. In 1985, preliminary results indicated that the leukemia rate among those who had been at shot PLUMBBOB: SMOKY were twice the norm, while prostate cancer was elevated among soldiers taking part in the REDWING shots. The Veterans Administration, however, taking a stand reminiscent of that adopted by the AEC, refused to admit the deaths were associated with radiation exposure.[25]

No Safe Levels

By February 23, 1979, a groundswell of antinuclear sentiment in Utah and Nevada had produced over 447 lawsuits against the government alleging deaths associated with the nuclear testing. Utah governor Scott Matheson, a former Washington County resident himself, arranged to have congressional hearings held in Salt Lake City in the spring.

At the hearings, F. Peter Libassi, counsel of the Public Health Service, Division of Health, Education and Welfare, made an astonishing statement: The preliminary findings of an interagency task force indicated that there is *no* threshold level; there is *no* safe level of radiation exposure. The counsel for the Public Health Service was agreeing with John Gofman's position that the radiation standards adopted by the AEC had been hopelessly inadequate. There *were no* safe limits.[26] Amid a succession of experts, congressmen, and Utah residents speaking on the hazards of nuclear testing was one Dr. Harold Knapp, who spoke about his 1963 finding that the iodine-131 dose had been underestimated by the AEC by 1,000 times.

The Cedar City sheepmen, remembering their loss in the court case almost thirty years before, decided they wanted to talk to this man. When it was explained to Knapp what had happened with the sheep, he was shocked—and interested. After thirteen months of hard study, he came to his conclusion: The sheep had eaten enough fallout to kill them. Moreover, the government's own documents—suppressed in 1954—supported this conclusion.

Knapp wrote a letter to the House Subcommittee on Oversight and Investigations: "In the course of the final review, technical papers have come to my attention from which it is possible to conclude that the government's case, as presented to the federal court by the government, was prejudiced by critical omissions, distortions, and deceptions concerning experimental data on the effects of ingestion of radioactivity on sheep which was in possession of the AEC at the time it made its investigation into the deaths of the sheep. . . .''[27]

This caught the attention of Dan Bushnell and the Cedar City sheepmen: The government, in concealing information damaging to its case, had perpetrated a fraud on the court. There would be a new trial, with the previously hidden information and documents entered into evidence. And there would be more. For the first time, the inner workings of the AEC were revealed. It reflected the mentality of an agency under siege, concerned not with public safety but with public relations.

In 1963, Harold Knapp's article in *Nature* had raised the hackles of the AEC officials, particularly those in charge of safety at the Nevada Test Site. The director of operation safety reviewed the material and apparently decided that no new safety procedures would be necessary: "We do not recommend any new radiation protection guides for nuclear weapons testing at this time. The present guides have, in general, been adequate to permit the continuance of nuclear weapons testing and at the same time have been accepted by the public principally because of an extensive public information program. . . .''

In the last sentences, the director inadvertently disclosed the primary reason for not tightening the safety standards: "To change the guides would require a reeducation program that would raise questions in the public mind as to the validity of the past guides. . . . We recommend the continuation of the present criteria." The primary concern was not for public safety but for public relations.[28]

This, however, was only the tip of the iceberg. The events of the past thirty years had placed into chilling perspective statements by AEC officials rendered in 1953: as part of the original litigation concerning the sheep deaths, the lawyer for the sheepherders had sent a series of interrogatories to the AEC's defense counsel. One of them asked a seemingly simple question: Who has the responsibility for the safety and welfare of persons and property near areas of possible fallout?

The AEC's answer: "It is the responsibility of the heads of families and owners of property to protect the members of their families and their property from possible radioactive fallout.''[29]

In other words, the public would have to protect itself.

XI

EPILOGUE: THE LAST NUCLEAR WEAPON

In the spring of 1977, geologist Walter Alvarez, son of Livermore lab co-founder Luis Alvarez, was busy analyzing rock strata just outside the small Italian town of Gubbio. The project, part of a study of continental drift, was proceeding routinely. Then he saw it, the mysterious "red layer," a tiny, thin line of clay about half an inch thick resting between two layers of limestone. Alvarez was aware of the red layer—it had been discovered by an Italian paleontologist in 1960—but no one knew what it meant. Where had it come from?

Anyone looking at the red line could see that it represented some sort of boundary: directly beneath it was a layer of limestone rich in fossils—the Cretaceous period. Dinosaurs had lived on the earth at that time, between 65 and 91 million years ago. Above the red line, representing a later time—the Tertiary period—there was another limestone layer. Only this one was practically free of fossils. The red line was the boundary between a living, teeming world and one in which practically no life existed. Beneath the line there were fossils of dinosaurs, above the line, only one-celled animals.

Walter Alvarez decided to send a sample of the red line home to his father at the University of California at Berkeley. The elder Alvarez, a Nobel prize-winning physicist, decided to analyze the material. Within hours the results came back. For some reason, the clay was saturated with the element iridium—thirty times as high as in the surrounding rocks. Luis Alvarez knew that irridum was not normally found on the earth's surface in great quantity; it is thought to be a constituent of the earth's core and of extraterrestial matter such as meteors and comets.

After some calculations, the father and son team arrived at a tentative conclusion: The iridium had come from a huge meteor, some 6 miles in diameter, that had hit the earth with the force of a million H-bombs, ripping a 100-square-mile hole in the atmosphere and filling the sky with a huge, reddish cloud of fine dust. For the dinosaurs, day turned into a cold, endless night. Within months, the giant reptiles, along with most other life on earth, were gone.[1]

Six years before the iridium discovery, astronomer Carl Sagan had been watching the Mars orbiter Mariner 9 with some concern. The National Aeronautics and Space Administration had spent millions of dollars to send a photographic orbiter to Mars. Now, after a successful flight, its cameras saw only a reddish haze. A dust storm covered the surface of the entire planet. For three months, while he waited for the storm to clear, Sagan checked various instruments aboard the spacecraft, such as the infrared interferometric spectrometer. Using this instrument, Sagan was able to determine the temperature of the dust cloud and of the surface of Mars. The instrument showed that the atmosphere during the dust storm was warm while the surface of the planet was quite cool—and dark. When the storm dissipated, the surface warmed up as more sunlight reached it. Though Sagan didn't know it at the time, the calculations he had used in analyzing a dust storm on another planet would eventually have profound implications for his own.

Over the years, Sagan became familiar not only with the dynamics of dust storms, but with the geology work of Walter and Luis Alvarez. He wondered if the calculations could be applied to nuclear explosions and the resulting firestorms. After the bombing of Hamburg, during World War II, the close-in, densely packed houses had ignited creating a firestorm with flames 2 miles high. Hamburg had been densely populated: It was calculated that there was about 32 *pounds* of combustible material per square foot in the German city. Where had that fuel—the soot—gone? Had it blocked out the sun for a time, much as the dust clouds had done on Mars? What would be the effect of nuclear explosions, explosions capable of setting fire to far greater areas of the earth's surface? The resulting smoke and soot clouds could be gigantic in size and catastropic in effect.

In 1981, Sagan and others at the Ames Research Center in Iowa decided to look into the matter.[2] Using their own work and that of the Alvarezes, the Ames group arrived at some tentative, and disturbing, conclusions: each megaton could throw an estimated 150,000 *tons* of fine dust into the stratosphere. A strong counterforce would probably result in 5,000 megatons detonated, thus a nuclear war would result in a darkened sky, followed by an intense cold that would last for up to nine months. When the sky cleared, the ozone layer would be severely depleted; there would be no protection against the deadly ultraviolet rays from the sun. Those who survived the initial cold, dark, and radiation would be subject to vastly increased chances of skin cancer.

Others, such as Edward Teller, questioned Sagan's conclusions. Mars, he said, has no oceans, but the earth does. In Teller's view, the top 2 feet of the world's oceans would act as a "buffer," releasing stored heat back to the atmosphere, keeping the earth relatively warm until the sky cleared. Though persuasive calculations were offered by both sides to support their respective views, the fact still remained that there was no safe way to test the hypotheses.

Early in the TRINITY program, Teller's calculations had indicated another, earlier risk: The new device might ignite the air, thus eventually destroying the world. Teller's friend Hans Bethe went over the figures, found an error, and decided that the risk of such a thing occurring was only three in a million. The work continued and the atomic bomb became a reality.

The risk of a nuclear winter seemed much higher. To many scientists, it approached the realm of certainty.[3] But regardless of the view, regardless of the questions, the risk had become too great.

In 1961, shortly after the Berlin crisis and before the horrors of October 1962, when the world literally was at the brink of atomic war, Robert Lowell wrote:

Our end drifts nearer,
the moon lifts,
radiant with terror.
The state is a diver under
a glass bell
A father's no shield
for his child.
— *"Fall, 1961"*

There are those who say the bomb never should have been invented. A careful study of the history of the weapon shows that, given the level of technology present during the 1940s, its invention was inevitable. In fact, one wonders why it was not invented sooner. Some say the United States should never have been a party to the arms race; should have never invented the H-bomb. Evidence exists indicating the Soviets may have bested the United States in the development of a fusion weapon by at least a year.

Current information clearly shows that testing has caused increases in cancer and other diseases—certainly among those living near the Nevada Test Site and possibly among people living as far away as New York. Sound epidemiological studies indicate that, as a result of the testing, many veterans have a greater chance of contracting leukemia. Did anyone know this at the time?

Was the Pentagon aware that soldiers exposed to radioactive fallout might be adversely affected, that some might eventually die from the exposure? Probably so, but that seemed not to be a major concern. The important thing was the testing of the weapon and the troops in a time when Soviet bombers might cross the northern horizon at any moment. To the military, taking their orders from the elected officials, the tests were like a defensive war, unpleasant but entirely necessary.

Were the members of the Atomic Energy Commission aware of the fallout hazards to the rest of the country? Obviously, to many of them, it was a matter of priorities. In their minds, the bomb came first and the hazards seemed vague and unproven. To many in the AEC, the bomb was big, unruly, unpredictable, and occasionally dangerous, but certainly not evil.

What of the scientists? Were they fully aware of the nature of their creations? At the time, probably not. Like the physicist who used an atomic detonation to light his cigarette, they saw in their devices triumphs of science and technology, the world's biggest firecrackers; an early morning at the Control Point was the ultimate Fourth of July celebration. Some, such as Edward Teller, viewed their "gadgets" as something to help man move mountains, not destroy him in some bright burst of light.

Other scientists, Robert Oppenheimer and Andrei Sakharov, for example, saw the dark side of their creations, but only after the control of the weapons had passed from them.

What of those in public office, the representatives of the people? Did they know? Some undoubtedly did. Some were faced with only unsatisfactory choices. Many were never able to meet their responsibilites; rather, they brought to their position an extraordinary variety of petty and unwholesome human traits. One official suggested the public be kept confused; another suggested dissenting scientists be jailed.[4]

Unquestionably, there were officials who thought only of protecting their respective jobs, who committed a crime on the public health by lying about hazards, hiding or actually destroying documents in exchange for a biweekly paycheck. To them, the truth had undoubtedly become whatever their particular position in life required it to be.

Finally, what of the average person? Did the man on the street know about the harmful effects of the Nevada tests? Some did. Those living near St. George, Utah, for example, who witnessed friends and relatives dying of rare cancers, knew early on that the weapons tests were hazardous. It would take years before official, scientifically sanctioned studies proved them right.

In other parts of the country, people rushed to their television sets early in the morning to watch the atomic blast on the "Today" show. Moviegoers watched Mickey Rooney as the "Atomic Kid," a prospector caught by a nuclear detonation who later found he could control slot machines with his mind. Children read *Spider Man* comics, about a young man who gained superpowers after being bitten by a "radioactive spider." Bars served "Atomic cocktails" and stores featured "atomic sales . . . blasting high prices." Women bought swimsuits named after the now-radioactive Bikini Atoll, an island with the middle gone—vaporized by a fusion device.

To the average person, nuclear weapons were interesting, but vaguely remote. The average person had never seen the silent flash of light that seemed to last for eons, had never experienced heat sufficient to blacken a wristwatch dial or an automobile headlamp. The average person had never witnessed a pressure wave traveling toward him or her at 85 mph or seen *anything* connecting the ground to a cloud hanging 40,000 feet in the air.

If there is blame, we all share it, those who were fascinated by the bomb as well as those who made it. If there was a mistake made, it was a simple one made by everyone associated with the bomb, from the designers to the politicians to the AEC officials to the people: They assumed more than they knew. And those assumptions, carrying the weight of truth, in turn became the basis for more assumptions that were also taken as truth. Simply stated, knowledge about the effects of nuclear weapons, of fallout, was often based on wrong assumptions. Looking back forty years to 1945, we now know that the bomb was simply too big, too technical, too complex for the human species. We could build it and we could destroy with it, yet we understood nothing about it.

Philosopher and scientist Abraham Kaplan, in his book *The Conduct of Inquiry*, wrote:

> Not infrequently . . . we unknowingly treat a situation of considerable statistical ignorance as though it confronted us with determinate risks. . . . Ignorance is being made the occasion for a pretense of knowledge rather than for further inquiry. . . .
> Ignorance is bliss only until we must pay the price for our mistakes.[5]

The testing of nuclear weapons, then and now, involves considerable uncertainties. Real questions exist regarding almost every facet of the detonation: yield, trajectory, venting configurations and amounts, biological effects. Of the two primary factors involving off-site populations, fallout radiation, and meteorological conditions influencing trajectory, almost nothing is known. And that which is known is not subject to control.

In the past, these uncertainties were ignored. Political and even scientific discussion continued as though all facets of the Bomb and its effects were understood. Meanwhile, the fate of millions became an open question.

The use of nuclear weapons carries with it the risk of death regardless of whether this death occurs at the epicenter of an explosion, in a cancer ward of a Utah hospital, or in the freezing cold of a darkened earth. It is a fact we cannot ignore.

The invisible shadow of the nuclear weapon, created in the fury of the most intense explosion on earth and falling from sky with the rain, has *already* touched each and every one of us.

APPENDIX A

The Radiation of Fallout

Roentgen, Rad, Rem

Historically, a roentgen is equal to the radiation emitted by one gram of radium at a distance of one foot. One roentgen produces an electrical charge of 2.58×10^{-4} coulombs per kilogram of dry air. A short-term exposure of 500 roentgens (that is, 10 roentgens/hour for fifty hours continuous) is considered lethal.

A rad is a unit of absorbed dose, and equivalent to an absorption of 100 ergs per gram of material. The rad is approximately equivalent to a roentgen.

A rem is a measure of radiation exposure to human tissue. One rad of X- or gamma radiation results in a dose equivalent of about one rem. Adjustment factors are often entered in, depending upon the type of exposure or the type of radiation. One rad of other radiation (that is, alpha, beta, or neutrons) may equal as much as 20 rems.

Disintegrations/Minute/Square Foot/Day (d/min/ft²/day)

A "disintegration" is a nuclear event in an atom in which radiation is emitted. This disintegration is accompanied by a transformation of the less stable atom into one that is more stable. The radiation from a disintegration event may be alpha, beta, gamma, X ray, or neutron. Each disintegration usually involves the emission of at least one, and often more, forms of the above radiation.

Early measurements of fallout were recorded in terms of disintegrations/minute/square foot averaged over a twenty-four-hour period. Thus, a fallout level recorded as 16 million d/min/ft²/day means that the radioactive debris deposited over a one-ft² area is disintegrating (transforming) at an average rate of 16 million atoms a minute. The per day designation usually means the sample was collected or averaged over a twenty-four-hour period.

It should be understood that for each disintegration, there is at least one emission of radiation.

Counts Per Minute

This term refers to the number of radiation emissions detected by a given instrument. It should be understood that not all of the radiation emitted from disintegrating atoms on a given surface will be recorded by an instrument. Counts per minute (cpm) levels are usually less than disintegrations/minute/square foot/day levels.

Curie

A curie is a measure of activity, or rate of disintegration, of the "hot" radionuclide. One curie (abbreviated "Ci") equals 3.7×10^{10} nuclear transformations per second—that is, one Ci of a radionuclide decays to another radionuclide at a rate of 37 billion atoms per second. One millicurie means a radionuclide decays at the rate of 37 million atoms per second, and one *micro*curie decays at the rate of 37,000 disintegrations per second. One picocurie of a radionuclide decays at the rate of 2.22 disintegrations a minute.

Later measurements of fallout expressed the levels in millicuries per 100 square miles. One millicurie/100 square miles is equivalent to 0.01327 d/sec/ft^2 and 0.7962 d/min/ft^2. Thus, a reading of 1,600 millicurie/100 square miles is equal to 1,274 d/min/ft^2.

Types of Radiation

Alpha Particles

Fallout particles produce several types of radiation. Fission products may release a variety of particles and rays at varying rates. The heavier the element (i.e., uranium, neptunium, americium) the more likely it is to emit an alpha particle. An alpha particle is simply a helium nucleus consisting of two protons and two neutrons. After a short distance, usually 1 to 3 inches in air, it picks up two electrons from its surroundings and becomes a standard, harmless helium atom. An alpha particle cannot penetrate the skin, but if an alpha emitter is ingested, it may have serious medical consequences. A fission product sitting in lung tissue for, say, two years, can bombard the cells with alpha particles, causing damage that could result in cancer.

(Alpha-emitters—such as radon-222 and -226 [from radium in soil]; polonium-210, -212, -214, -218; and bismuth-212—have been found to be absorbed by cigarette tars that then collect at the lung bifurcations in smokers. Dr. Edward A. Martell of the National Center for Atmospheric Research estimates that a smoker receives a carcinogenic alpha-radiation dose of 80 to 100 rads [one rad equals 0.01 Joule/kilograms] to about 1 to 10 million lung cells, thus resulting in bronchocenic cancer. Martell believes that the alpha particles produced by polonium-214, with a relatively high alpha energy of 7.7 million electron volts, penetrate to the basal cells and initiate the cancer process. [E. A. Martell, "Alpha-Radiation dose at bronchial bifurcations of smokers from indoor exposure to radon progeny," *Proc. Natl. Acad. Sci. USA*, vol. 80, March 1983, pp. 1285–1289.])

Beta Particles

Lighter fission nuclides emit beta particles, which are simply electrons of varying energies (depending upon the radionuclide). Beta particles, formed when a neutron splits to become a proton and an electron, are quite energetic; they can travel up to 10 feet before being absorbed. However, since they carry a charge, they are deflected by other electrons and subatomic particles. Thus the net travel distance is somewhat less.

Beta particles can cause serious damage to cells. A beta burn often resembles a severe sunburn externally. Ingested fission products can cause similar damage to internal cells.

Gamma Rays

Radionuclides that emit beta particles usually also emit high-energy parcels of light called gamma rays. This type of radiation is the most penetrating; depending upon its energy, a gamma ray can pass through several inches of steel or a foot of concrete. Gamma (and X rays) passing through material separates electrons from atoms, thus producing positive and negative ions. Gamma and X-radiation is measured in terms of roentgens; one roentgen is defined as that quantity of gamma or X-radiation that will cause the formation of 2.09 billion ion pairs per cubic centimeter of dry air. For mammals, including humans, the unit of exposure is the rad, which is roughly equivalent to the roentgen. Light doses of gamma radiation are not detectable by the human senses.

One gram of dry air exposed to one roentgen of gamma radiation absorbs about 88 ergs of energy. This is about half the energy involved in pronouncing an average syllable of a word. A snowflake falling on a surface expends one erg of energy, while a lethal X-ray dose to the "standard" 150-pound man involves the absorption of about 3 billion ergs of energy. The rad is defined as the deposition of 100 ergs of energy per gram of material. Thus, at or near the surface, a roentgen is about equivalent to the rad.

X rays

X rays are identical to gamma rays. Both are examples of electromagnetic radiation, their only difference is their place of origin. An X ray originates from the electron cloud surrounding an atom; a gamma ray comes from the nucleus.

Neutrons

Neutrons are one of the two major subatomic particles comprising the nucleus of the atom. In addition to alpha, beta, and gamma radiation, some radionuclides emit neutrons. Neutrons, though they are particles, can travel a considerable distance through the air. Because of their mass, they can cause considerable damage to a biological system. Fission product radionuclides emitting neutrons are bromine-89 and iodine-137; however, their extremely short half-lives (4.5 seconds and 24.4 seconds, respectively) make it doubtful that anyone would find these products in delayed fallout.

Protons

Protons constitute the other type of subatomic particle found in the nucleus of the atom. Some radionuclides emit protons. These isotopes are *not* likely to be found in the debris of a nuclear weapon.

Examples of Proton Emitters

Proton Emitters	Half-Life (sec)
Calcium-37	0.173
Argon-33	0.180
Sulfur-29	0.190
Silicon-25	0.230
Magnesium-21	0.121
Oxygen-13	0.0087

References

Crocker, G. R., et al, "Physical and Radiochemical Properties of Fallout Particles," 94135 USNRDL-TR-899, U.S. Naval Radiological Defense Laboratory, San Francisco, Calif., June 15, 1965.

Martell, Edward A., National Center for Atmospheric Research; Boulder, Colo., personal communication.

Radiological Health Handbook, U.S. Department of Health, Education and Welfare, Public Health Service, January 1970, pp. 231–380.

A Conversion

Disintegrations/Minute/Square Foot to Roentgens/Hour

An expression for exposure rate, E, in roentgens/hour, from a point source to a point detector is given as:

$$E = (6Ce)/D^2$$

where:

C = number of curies of material
e = X- or gamma energy in MeV
D = distance from the source in feet

This formula can be used as a basis for other geometries by numerical methods. For example:

- 1 million disintegrations/minute/square foot source deposited everywhere emitting 300 keV (0.3 MeV) X- or gamma rays.
- To find: E at one meter (waist) height.

Solution: Construct concentric circles of one centimeter increasing radius and solve for the $E(n)$ of each ring. Sum the $E(n)$ over the radius out to 10 meters for a good approximation to the exposure rate.

The concentration 10^6 disintegrations/minute/square foot (that is, 1,000,000 disintegrations/minute/square foot) can be converted to curies/square centimeter:

$$\times \ 1/(2.22 \times 10^{12} \text{ d/min/C}_i)$$
$$\times \ 1/(30.48 \text{ cm/ft})^2$$
$$= 4.85 \times 10^{-10} \text{ Ci/cm}^2$$

The activity of the source in the ring is concentration times area of the ring. The ring's area is the area of the outer circle in the ring minus the area of the inner circle.

The distance to the effective center of the ring is determined by the pythagorean theorem $c^2 = a^2 + b^2$: a^2 = (one meter)^2, b^2 = (outer circle radius $-$ ½)^2, so $d_n - [10,000\text{cm}^2 + (N - ⅓)^2]\text{cm}^2$; and the D *in feet* needed by the expression is:

$$D_2 = \frac{\{[10,000 + (N - ⅓)^2]\text{cm}^2\}^{-1/2}}{30.48 \text{ cm/ft}}$$

Some examples of $E(n)$ are tabulated below:

Ring #	Area	Activity	Distance, ft	Exposure Rate, R/hr
1	3.1416 cm^2	1.52×10^{-9}	3.281	2.55×10^{-10}
2	$3.1416(4 - 1)\text{cm}^2$	4.57×10^{-9}	3.281	7.64×10^{-10}
3	$3.1416(9 - 4)\text{cm}^2$	7.62×10^{-9}	3.282	7.07×10^{-10}
4	$3.1416(16 - 9)\text{cm}^2$	1.07×10^{-8}	3.283	1.78×10^{-9}
N	$3.1416(2n - 1)\text{cm}^2$	$(4.85 \times 10^{-10})(\text{area})$		

$$n \text{ distance} = \frac{[10^4 + (n - ⅓)^3]^{-1/2}}{30.48}$$

$$n \text{ exposure rate/hr} = 6 \text{ pi}(2n - 1) \text{ cm}^2(4.85 \times 10^{-10}\text{Ci/cm}^2)0.3 \text{ MeV}$$

$$[10^4 + (N - ⅓)^2]/30.48^2$$

In this example, the $E(n)$ were added up to the $E(n)$ out to 10 meters, or 1,000 iterations. This distance is equal to 30.48 feet.

The equation for exposure rate n was rewritten and summed:

$$E = (30.48^2(6 \text{ pi})[4.85 \times 10^{-10}(0.3)] \sum_{N=1}^{1,000} (2N - 1)/1,000 + (N - \frac{1}{3})^2 \text{R/hr}$$

$$E = 1.2 \times 10^{-5} \text{R/hr}$$
$$= 0.012 \text{ mR/hr}$$
$$= 12 \text{ } \mu\text{R/hr (at 10 meters)}$$

Thus, for a fallout rate of a million disintegrations per minute, the external gamma exposure rate (emitters at 300 keV) from a circle (30.48-ft radius) is equal to 12 microroentgens.

Again, such an exposure rate does *not* take into consideration internal exposures and sequestering effects of organs such as the thyroid and bone.

Reference/Acknowledgment

The author wishes to thank Oscar Mulhearn, radiation specialist for the state of Texas, for his assistance and for the development of the above formula.

APPENDIX B

Tracks of Selected Trajectories

The following is a list of selected trajectories of subsurface and aboveground nuclear detonations that took place between 1951 and 1961. Times are Pacific Standard, height of burst is given in feet above surface, and cloud top height is in feet above sea level (MSL). Radiation at ground level is that measured one hour after detonation.

RANGER: ABLE*

Detonation Date: 27 Jan 1951 • *Detonation Time:* 5:45 A.M. • *Area:* Frenchman's Flat • *Sponsor:* Los Alamos • *Yield:* 1 kt • *Radiation Level at Ground Zero:* 0.5 R/hr • *Height of Burst:* 1,060 ft • *Cloud Top Height:* 17,000 ft

10,000-Foot Trajectory: NEVADA: Lincoln County • UTAH: Orem, Provo, Vernal • COLORADO: Pueblo • KANSAS: (Crossed the border at Greeley, left Kansas near Wallace) • MISSOURI: St. Joseph, Cameron, Chillicothe, Brookfield, Atlanta, Bethel, West Quincy • ILLINOIS: Quincy, Jacksonville, Springfield • INDIANA: Lafayette, Kokomo, Marion, Berne • OHIO: Springfield, Dayton, Columbus, Canton • PENNSYLVANIA: Beaver Falls, Kittanning, Williamsport, Wilkes-Barre • NEW YORK: Port Jervis, Middletown, Poughkeepsie • CONNECTICUT: New Haven, New London • RHODE ISLAND: Newport • MASSACHUSETTS: Fall River.

30,000-Foot Trajectory: NEVADA: Caliente • UTAH: Cedar City, Panguitch, Moab • COLORADO: Crested Butte, Buena Vista, Colorado Springs • KANSAS: (The clouds crossed trajectories over Castle Rock at the border of Gove and Trego counties in Kansas), Topeka, Lawrence • MISSOURI: Kansas City, Harrisonville, Warrensburg, Sedalia, Columbia, St. Louis • ILLINOIS: Alton, Vandalia, Robinson • INDIANA: Bloomington, Columbus, Greensburg • OHIO: Hamilton, Athens, Marietta • PENNSYLVANIA: Uniontown, Lancaster, Reading • NEW JERSEY: New Brunswick.

RANGER: BAKER-1

Detonation Date: 28 Jan 1951 • *Detonation Time:* 5:52 A.M. • *Area:* Frenchman's Flat • *Sponsor:* Los Alamos • *Yield:* 8 kt • *Radiation Level at Ground Zero:* 15 R/hr • *Height of Burst:* 1,080 ft • *Cloud Top Height:* 35,000 ft

*Because of the relatively poor quality of the government trajectory maps for RANGER, all tracks in this series should be considered approximations.

10,000-Foot Trajectory: COLORADO: Boulder • MISSOURI: St. Joseph, Clark • ILLINOIS: Alton, Terre Haute • OHIO: Montgomery, New Philadelphia • PENNSYLVANIA: Kittanning • NEW YORK: Middletown • CONNECTICUT: New Haven • MAINE: Nantucket.

30,000-Foot Trajectory: UTAH: St. George • COLORADO: Fort Carson, Arapahoe (This trajectory crossed over into Kansas above 4,039-foot Mount Sunflower, the highest point in Kansas) • KANSAS: Palmer • NEBRASKA: Falls City • MISSOURI: Coatsville • IOWA: Burlington • INDIANA: South Bend • MICHIGAN: Gibralter • NEW YORK: Auburn, Glens Falls • NEW HAMPSHIRE: Portsmouth.

RANGER: EASY

Detonation Date: 1 Feb 1951 • *Detonation Time:* 5:47 A.M. • *Area:* Frenchman's Flat • *Sponsor:* Los Alamos • *Yield:* 1 kt • *Radiation Level at Ground Zero:* 0.5 R/hr • *Height of Burst: 1,080 ft* • *Cloud Top Height: 12,500 ft*

10,000-Foot Trajectory: Crossed San Bernadino County, California, into Mexico over the Cabeza Prieta National Wildlife Refuge. The nuclear debris came back into the United States at Fort Meyers, Florida, and left the continental airspace over Sebastian, Florida.

30,000-Foot Trajectory: TEXAS: El Paso, Austin, Beaumont • LOUISIANA: Baton Rouge • ALABAMA: Montgomery • NORTH CAROLINA: Durham • VIRGINIA: Nassawadox.

RANGER: BAKER-2

Detonation Date: 2 Feb 1951 • *Detonation Time:* 5:49 A.M. • *Area:* Frenchman's Flat • *Sponsor:* Los Alamos • *Yield:* 8 kt • *Radiation Level at Ground Zero:* 15 R/hr • *Height of Burst:* 1,100 ft • *Cloud Top Height:* 28,000 ft

10,000-Foot Trajectory: The nuclear debris crossed north of Las Vegas and into Arizona, passing north of Phoenix and leaving the state at Paradise. It entered Mexico airspace over the Alamo Hueco Mountains in New Mexico, then crossed back into the United States over Ruidosa, Texas. From there is passed out over Big Bend National Park, then to Carrizo Springs, Texas, and out over the Gulf at Aransas Pass, Texas. It entered Florida airspace at St. Petersburg and left near Melbourne.

30,000-Foot Trajectory: The nuclear debris at 30,000 feet passed over St. George, Utah, crossed the state and entered New Mexico airspace north of Crystal. From there it moved south of Los Alamos, then to Clovis, New Mexico, where it crossed into Texas near Bovina. The cloud passed over Petersburg and Waco and left the coast near Winnie, just north of Houston. Later it crossed the Florida peninsula, passing over Miami.

RANGER: FOX

Detonation Date: 6 Feb 1951 • *Detonation Time:* 5:47 A.M. • *Area:* Frenchman's Flat • *Sponsor:* Los Alamos • *Yield:* 22 kt • *Radiation Level at Ground Zero:* 15 R/hr • *Height of Burst:* 1,435 ft • *Cloud Top Height:* 43,000 ft

10,000-Foot Trajectory: This portion of the nuclear cloud passed over Mohave County, Lake Mead, and Prescott, and left United States airspace east of Pedgregosa, Arizona. It crossed back into the U.S. at Laredo, Texas, and left the state at Corpus Christi.

30,000-Foot Trajectory: This trajectory moved north of the 10,000-foot trajectory, passing over Flagstaff, Arizona. After briefly crossing Mexico airspace, the debris crossed the Texas cities of El Paso, Roma, McAllen, Pharr, Donna, Mercedes, Harlingen, San Benito, and Brownsville.

BUSTER: ABLE

Detonation Date: 22 Oct 1951 • *Detonation Time:* 6:00 A.M. • *Area:* 7–5 • *Sponsor:* Los Alamos • *Yield:* Less than 0.1 kt • *Radiation Level at Ground Zero:* 300 counts per minute alpha radiation • *Height of Burst:* 100 ft • *Cloud Top Height:* 8,000 ft

8,000-Foot Trajectory: The cloud of debris passed north of Las Vegas and traveled on to Flagstaff, Arizona, circling down past the Colcord Mountains and Black Canyon, passing near Prescott then back over Flagstaff. From there, the debris traveled north, crossing into Utah over the Rainbow Plateau. The cloud followed Glen Canyon then drifted north over Roan Cliffs and East Tavaputs Plateau and into Colorado at Dinosaur. The cloud crossed into Wyoming at Power Wash and moved on to Rawlins. It left the state near Redbird and crossed into South Dakota near Parker Peak.

The cloud crossed the Badlands, then moved northeast, leaving South Dakota near Corona and entering Minnesota at Clinton. It then crossed over to Kingsdale, Minnesota, and into Wisconsin at Moose Junction. The BUSTER: ABLE cloud reentered Minnesota at Washburn and finally left United States airspace over Lake Superior.

BUSTER: BAKER

Detonation Date: 28 Oct 1951 • *Detonation Time:* 7:20 A.M. • *Area:* 7–3 • *Sponsor:* Los Alamos • *Yield:* 3.5 kt • *Radiation Level at Ground Zero:* 6 R/hr • *Height of Burst:* 1,118 ft • *Cloud Top Height:* 31,700 ft

All trajectories traveled west over California in a band extending between Mount Whitney–Cape San Martin and Stove Pipe Wells–Guadalupe. The entire cloud crossed over San Luis Obispo County in California, circled, then moved east over the rest of the United States. One component of the 8,000-foot trajectory split off from the rest of the cloud and circled back over the Los Angeles area. The debris was tracked along four trajectories: the 8,000-, 10,000-, 24,000-, and 30,000-foot levels. Interestingly, three of the clouds—the 18,000-, 24,000-, and 30,000-foot levels—all crossed over the same point: Concordia, Kansas.

10,000-Foot Trajectory: This level moved north of Phoenix, Arizona, over Montrose, Colorado, then southeast toward Amarillo, Texas. It followed the Red River and crossed over the towns of Eldorado, Oklahoma, Wichita Falls and Denison, Texas (Dwight D. Eisenhower's boyhood home). it crossed over Hugo, Oklahoma, Ashtown, Texas, the state of Arkansas, and entered Mississippi near Tupelo. Other cities and areas under the 10,000-foot trajectory included: TENNESSEE: Chattanooga, Knoxville • VIRGINIA: Roanoke, Alexandria • Washington, D.C. • DELAWARE: New Castle • PENNSYLVANIA: Philadelphia • NEW YORK: New York • RHODE ISLAND: Providence • MASSACHUSETTS: Lexington, Boston • MAINE: Washington County.

24,000-Foot Trajectory: CALIFORNIA: Barrett • NEVADA: Laughlin, Lake Mead • UTAH: Hilldale, Cisco • COLORADO: Grand Junction, Denver, Hale • KANSAS: Goodland, Dresden, Blair, Concordia • MISSOURI: St. Joseph, Chillicothe, Brookfield, Macon, Hannibal • ILLINOIS: Jacksonville, Champaign, Danville • INDIANA: Logansport • OHIO: Celina, Greensburg, Youngstown • PENNSYLVANIA: Sharon, Tioga City (The 8,000- and 24,000-foot trajectories crossed over Elkland) • NEW YORK: Elmira, Glens Falls • VERMONT: Pawlet, West Hartford • NEW HAMPSHIRE: Hanover, Kearsarge • MAINE: (Near the White Mountain National Forest) Waterville, Bangor, Princeton.

30,000-Foot Trajectory: This followed the debris at the 24,000-foot level, the two crossing paths at Concordia, Kansas. The debris at the 30,000-foot level then crossed over Leavenworth, Kansas, and entered Missouri over Liberty. Traveling east, the cloud passed over Terre Haute, Indiana; Cincinnati, Ohio; and left the U.S. over Atlantic City, New Jersey.

BUSTER: CHARLIE

Detonation Date: 30 Oct 1951 • *Detonation Time:* 7:00 A.M. • *Area:* 7-3 • *Sponsor:* Los Alamos • *Yield:* 14 kt • *Radiation Level at Ground Zero:* 5 R/hr • *Height of Burst: 1,132 ft* • *Cloud Top Height:* 41,000 ft

10,000-Foot Trajectory: This part of the atomic cloud moved east, then south over Lake Mead. It crossed Phoenix, Arizona, then moved south into Mexico. It curved back to reenter the U.S. at Texas near the town of Lajitas. It then met up with the 18,000-foot trajectory over Houston, and crossed it again near Mobile, Alabama. From there, the radioactive cloud moved northeast over Columbus, Georgia and Charlotte and Greensboro, North Carolina. North of Richmond, Virginia, it began to curve east and crossed the East Coast over Atlantic City, New Jersey, but followed the coastline up to New York City. It then moved north crossing Danbury, Connecticut, and Pittsfield, Massachusetts, then followed the Vermont–New Hampshire border north to Canada. The cloud then followed the U.S.–Canada border until it left United States airspace.

18,000-Foot Trajectory: This trajectory crossed Death Valley, California, north of Bakersfield, continued west and left the coast over Point Conception, California. Once over the Pacific, however, it turned back east, crossing Mexico and then reentered United States airspace over Texas's Big Bend area. It crossed over San Antonio, Houston, and Beaumont–Port Arthur, Texas, and then entered Louisiana west of Lake Charles. The cloud crossed Louisiana and Mississippi and entered Alabama just north of Mobile. The debris continued on over Georgia and South Carolina, leaving the coast near Charleston.

24,000-Foot Trajectory: This trajectory crossed Fresno, California, and then, along with the rest of the atomic cloud, moved out over the Pacific. It then doubled back and entered Texas near Esperanza. It tracked just south of Lubbock, crossed Wichita Falls and Denison, Texas, then entered Arkansas airspace. Other cities it crossed included Little Rock, Arkansas; Memphis, Tennessee; Gilbert, West Virginia; Washington, D.C.; and Dover, Delaware.

30,000-Foot Trajectory: This trajectory moved west north of Los Angeles, crossed the coastline, then reentered the United States at Cowlic, Arizona. Later it crossed over Albuquerque and Santa Fe, New Mexico, then moved north, eventually crossing the 40,000-foot trajectory at Sterling, Nebraska. Other cities 30,000 feet below the atomic cloud: Indianola and Iowa City, Iowa; Rockford and Waukegan, Illinois; Lansing and Port Huron, Michigan; Toronto; Montreal; Presque Isle, Maine.

40,000-Foot Trajectory: This trajectory moved northeast over the northern tier of Colorado counties, crossing the cities of Fort Collins and Sterling. It then moved across the *second* southern tier of Nebraska counties, crossing the countryside just south of Lincoln. It followed the Missouri-Iowa border, then moved north over Burlington, Iowa, and Peoria, Illinois. Other cities and areas 40,000 feet under the atomic cloud: Fort Wayne, Indiana; Toledo, Ohio; the southern tier of New York counties from Jamestown to Kingston; and Worcester, Boston, and Lexington, Massachusetts.

BUSTER: DOG

Detonation Date: 1 Nov 1951 • *Detonation Time: 7:30* A.M. • *Area:* 7–3 • *Sponsor:* Los Alamos • *Yield:* 21 kt • *Radiation Level at Ground Zero:* 20 R/hr • *Height of Burst:* 1,416 ft • *Cloud Top Height:* 46,000 ft

The 18,000- 24,000- 30,000- and 40,000-foot levels all moved east in a wide arc, crossing over: Las Vegas, Nevada; Phoenix, Arizona; El Paso, San Angelo, Austin, Waco, Texas; and Shreveport, Louisiana. The band tightened over the north part of Madison County, Mississippi, at Camden (home of the Casey Jones State Museum), then spread in a wide arc over the entire Northeast, from a line from Knoxville, Tennessee–Ottawa, Canada, to a line from Asheville, North Carolina–Atlantic City, New Jersey.

The track of the atomic clouds passed over: NEVADA: Las Vegas, Henderson, Boulder City • ARIZONA: Dolan Springs, Hackberry, Dewey, Humboldt, Tonto Basin, San Carlos, Clifton • NEW MEXICO: Silver City, Tyrone, Bayard, Las Cruces, University Park, Mesquite • TEXAS: (Guadalupe Peak), Dell City, Pecos, Barstow, Royalty, Grandfalls, Big Lake, Sherwood, Vick, Eden, Millersview, Placid, Elm Grove, Bee House, Pearl, McGregor, Waco, Mexia, Red Lake, Palestine, Neches, Turney, New Salem, Gary, Carthage • LOUISIANA: Keatchie, Gloster, Castor, Lucky, Liberty Hill, Quitman, Vernon, Richwood, Raysville, Holly Ridge, Warden, Monticello • MISSISSIPPI: Onward, Valley, Yazoo City, Pickens, Goodman, Kosciusko, High Point, Sessums, Artesia, Columbus • ALABAMA: Fernbank, Belk, Corona, Jasper, Empire, Hayden, Oneonta, Rosa, Hendricks, Altoona, Mountainboro, Collinsville, Ringgold • GEORGIA: Summerville, Echota, Calhoun, Resaca, Ellijay, Cherrylog, Morganton • NORTH CAROLINA: Hayesville, Tusquitee, Kyle, Bryson City, Cherokee, Waterville • TENNESSEE: Johnson City, Elizabethton, Hunter, Carter, Shady Valley • VIRGINIA: Sugar Grove, Wytheville, Pulaski, Radford, McCoy, Newport, Blacksburg, Abbot, New Castle, Barbours Creek, Eagle Rock, Lexington, Greenville, Crimora, Lydia, Haywood, Boston, Rixeyville, New Baltimore, Gainesville, Arlington • Washington, D.C. • MARYLAND: Bethesda, Spencersville, Columbia, Baltimore, Sweet Air • PENNSYLVANIA: Oxford, West Chester, King of Prussia, Norristown, Philadelphia, Warminister, Newtown • NEW JERSEY: Trenton, Hopewell, Princeton, Piscataway, Wesfield, Cranford, Newark, Paterson, Hackensack, Paramus • NEW YORK: Millwood, Katona, Salem Center, White Plains • CONNECTICUT: Wilton, Naugatuck, Meridan, Middletown, Portland, Marlborough, Willimantic, Putnam, Harrisville • RHODE ISLAND: Woonsocket • MASSACHUSETTS: Millville, Bellingham, Holliston, Framingham, Needham, Wellesley, Newton, Brookline, Boston, Cambridge, Somerville, Malden, Lexington, Saugus, Lynn, Wakefield, Peabody, Salem, Gloucester, Pigeon Cove.

The 10,000-foot level moved south, crossing Mexico, then the southern tier of Texas counties: Zapata, Starr, Hidalgo, and Cameron.

BUSTER: EASY

Detonation Date: 5 Nov 1951 • *Detonation Time:* 8:30 A.M. • *Area:* 7 • *Sponsor:* Los Alamos • *Yield:* 31 kt • *Radiation Level at Ground Zero:* 20 R/hr • *Height of Burst:* 1,314 ft • *Cloud Top Height:* 50,000 ft

The 24,000-, 30,000-, 40,000-, and 46,000-foot trajectories all crossed over Las Vegas, then moved southwest in a wide arc across the United States and Gulf. Among cities under the high-altitude nuclear clouds: Phoenix and Tucson, Arizona; Juarez, Mexico–El Paso, Laredo, San Antonio, Corpus Christi, Texas; Jacksonville, Florida.

10,000-Foot Trajectory: This part of the nuclear cloud moved southwest to Santa Barbara, Lompoc, and Santa Maria, California. It then followed the coastline to San Francisco where it crossed the 18,000-foot trajectory. It then moved back over Marysville, California, and into Nevada over the Smoke Creek Desert, where it continued Northeast. Over Dunphy, Nevada, it began to turn back to the south. It was last tracked over northern Milliard County in Utah.

18,000-Foot Trajectory: This part of the nuclear cloud followed essentially the same path as the 10,000-foot level, but after crossing that trajectory over San Francisco, it moved northeast, passing over Nevada, then Idaho. The cloud moved over the Teton Range into Wyoming, then drifted over Jackson and Thermopolis, finally leaving the state north of Kirtley. The cloud at 18,000-feet then moved across the northern tier of Nebraska counties before entering Iowa at Sioux City. Once in Iowa, it crossed over Storm Lake, Fort Dodge, Iowa Falls, and Cedar Falls. Soon after, it entered Illinois airspace at Elizabeth. From there it passed over Rockford, Woodstock, and Waukegan, then crossed into Michigan. Other cities 18,000 feet under the nuclear cloud included: MICHIGAN: Kalamazoo • OHIO: Toledo, Cleveland, and Youngstown • PENNSYLVANIA: Philadelphia • NEW JERSEY: Atlantic City.

JANGLE: SUGAR

Detonation Date: 19 Nov 1951 • *Detonation Time:* 9:00 A.M. • *Area:* 9 • *Sponsor:* Department of Defense • *Yield:* 1.2 kt • *Radiation Level at Ground Zero:* 7,500 R/hr • *Height of Burst:* 3.5 ft • *Cloud Top Height:* 15,000 ft

Low-level debris from Sugar crossed north over Nye County, Nevada, passed along the border of Eureka and White Pine counties, and left Nevada through Elko County. It then crossed over the Duck Valley Indian Reservation and proceeded on toward Caldwell, Rayette, and Weiser, Indiana. From there, it curved west toward Huntington, Oregon, where it followed the track of now-U.S. 84 North across Baker, La Grande, and Pendleton. It then moved into the airspace of Washington State, where it passed over Richland, curled north around the Hanford Atomic Energy Works, and was then deflected south and west by the Saddle Mountains. The lower level was last detected over Yakima, Washington.

10,000-Foot Trajectory: Sugar's 10,000-foot section moved north over the Great Salt Lake, then crossed into the southeastern corner of Idaho at Malad City. It left the state near Irwin and entered Wyoming over the Teton Pass near Jackson. The cloud passed over Cody, Powell, and Lovell, then crossed into Montana airspace over the Crow Indian Reservation. From there it drifted over the villages of Bighorn, Sanders, Angela, and Union before it turned southeast toward Glendive. This section of the atomic cloud finally left the state at Wibaux. From there, the debris at 10,000 feet altitude entered North Dakota at Beach. It crossed Bullion Butte, New England, Elgin, Bismarck, Steele, Jamestown, Valley City, and finally left the state at Fargo. Upon entering Minnesota airspace, it crossed Georgetown, Ogema, (Itasca State Park), Deep River, Hibbing, and Virginia before leaving the state, and the United States, at Grand Portage, Minnesota.

14,000-Foot Trajectory: This trajectory moved northeast over Ogden, Utah and entered Wyoming airspace at Sage. It then crossed over to La Barge and the Wind River Indian Reservation. The cloud entered South Dakota airspace at Spearfish. It left South Dakota at Herreid and entered North Dakota at Ashley. From there, it moved over Jamestown and left the state at Grand Forks. The 14,000-foot cloud then moved into Minnesota airspace, crossing Thief Lake. It finally left the U.S. at Warroad, Minnesota, near Lake of the Woods.

APPENDIX B

JANGLE: UNCLE

Detonation Date: 29 Nov 1951 • *Detonation Time:* 12:00 Noon • *Area:* 10 • *Sponsor:* Los Alamos, Department of Defense • *Yield:* 1.2 kt • *Radiation Level at Ground Zero:* 7,500 R/hr • *Height of Burst:* − 17 ft; underground burst: filled shaft in Nevada soil • *Cloud Top Height:* 11,500 ft

The low, surface-level portion of the Uncle cloud traveled due north over Nye County, Nevada, across the Diamond Mountains and over Huntington, Jiggs, the Te-Moak Indian Reservation, and Elko. It split up into two clouds over North Fork, Nevada. Shortly thereafter, tracking of this portion of the Uncle cloud was terminated.

10,000-Foot Trajectory: This part of the cloud crossed Nye County and moved toward the northeast over Railroad Valley and Lund. It crossed into Utah at Trout Creek, then passed over Salt Lake City. It left the state near the town of Upton. After entering Wyoming airspace, it crossed the towns of Mills, Church Buttes, Farson, Rawlins, Como, Medicine Bow, Garrett, Dwyer, and Guernsey. Other cities under the section of the nuclear cloud at 10,000-foot altitude: NEBRASKA: Agate, Crawford, Chadron, Whiteclay • SOUTH DAKOTA: (Slim Butte Mountain), Oglala, Potato Creek, Norris, White River, Kimball, Mitchell, Sioux Falls • MINNESOTA: Luverne, Wilmot, Windom, Odin, Truman, Matawan, Blooming Prairie, Rochester, Winona • WISCONSIN: Ettrick, Black River Falls, Pray, Arpin, Neopit, Beaver, Wausaukee • MICHIGAN: Banat, Carney, Steuben, Seney, Paradise • MAINE: (Kelly Brook Mountain), (Rocky Mountain), St. John, Fort Kent, Notre Dame.

TUMBLER-SNAPPER: ABLE*

Detonation Date: 1 Apr 1952 • *Detonation Time:* 9:00 A.M. • *Area:* Frenchman's Flat • *Sponsor:* Los Alamos, Department of Defense • *Yield:* 1 kt • *Radiation Level at Ground Zero:* 5 R/hr • *Height of Burst:* 793 ft • *Cloud Top Height:* 16,200 ft

10,000-Foot Trajectory: NEVADA: Alamo, Hiko, Pioche • UTAH: Wah Wah Springs, Oak City, Fountain Green, Milburn, Soldier Summit, Roosevelt, Bridgeport • WYOMING: Rawlins, Wheatland, Hawk Springs • NEBRASKA: Kimball • COLORADO: Sterling, Yuma, Kirk, Stratton, Cheyenne Wells • KANSAS: Syracuse, Ulysses, Arkalon, Hayne, Liberal • OKLAHOMA: Forgan, Beaver, Slapout, Harmon, Taloga, Geary, Seminole, McAlester, Page • ARKANSAS: Mena, Sulphur Springs, Hot Springs, Pine Bluff, Crumrod • MISSISSIPPI: Hillhouse, Batesville, Bonneville, Doskie • TENNESSEE: Lowryville, Topsy, Mount Pleasant, Columbia, Nashville, Portland • KENTUCKY: Glasgow, Campbellsville, Harrodsburg, Stamping Ground • OHIO: Georgetown, Hillsboro, London, Port Clinton • MICHIGAN: Detroit, Pontiac, Flint, Saginaw, Bay City, Clare, Big Rapids, Muskegon • INDIANA: Portage, Francisville, Sitka, Young America, Kokomo, Anderson, Rushville, New Trenton • OHIO: Cincinnati, Bethel, Georgetown, Portsmouth, Buckhorn, Gallipolis • WEST VIRGINIA: Ashton, Left Hand, Sutton, Harper, Martinsburg • MARYLAND: Baltimore • DELAWARE: Wilmington • PENNSYLVANIA: Philadelphia • NEW JERSEY: Trenton, Twin Rivers, Englishtown, Leonardo • NEW YORK: Lindenhurst, Mastic Beach, Southhampton • MASSACHUSETTS: Martha's Vinyard, Hyannis, Barnstable, E. Orleans.

16,000-Foot Trajectory: NEVADA: Rox, Carp • UTAH: St. George, Leeds, Mount Carmel Junction, Mexican Hat, Navajo Indian Reservation • COLORADO: Cortez, Durango,. Summitville, Alamosa, Fort Garland, Trinidad • OKLAHOMA: Black Mesa Summit (highest point in Oklahoma) near Kenton, Castaneda, Keyes, Eva, Guyman, Gray, Catesby, Wood-

*The information on pp. 473–483 includes city-by-city tracks of selected trajectories. Cities listed are current as of 1986; some may not have existed at the time of the detonations.

ward, Seiling, Longdale, Bison, Stillwater, Tulsa, Tahlequa, Stilwell • ARKANSAS: Mountainburg, Mountaintop, Clarksville, Russellville, Beebe, Brinkley, Marianna • MISSISSIPPI: Prichard, Senatobia, Abbeville, Tupelo, Tremont • ALABAMA: Bexar, Hamilton, Jasper, Birmingham, Bemiston, Woodland • GEORGIA: Texas, Hogansville, Topeka Junction, Macon, Irwinton, Wrightsville, Rocky Ford, Springfield • SOUTH CAROLINA: Ridgeland, Burton, Beaufort, Edisto Island.

TUMBLER-SNAPPER: BAKER

Detonation Date: 15 Apr 1952 • *Detonation Time:* 9:30 A.M. • *Area:* 7-3 • *Sponsor:* Los Alamos, Department of Defense • *Yield:* 1 kt • *Radiation Level at Ground Zero:* 4.5 R/hr • *Height of Burst: 1,109 ft* • *Cloud Top Height:* 15,700 ft

10,000-Foot Trajectory: NEVADA: Goodsprings, Sandy • CALIFORNIA: Cima, Ludlow, San Bernadino, Redlands, Ontario, Pomona, Whittier, Buena Park, Long Beach, Redondo Beach, Inglewood • ARIZONA: San Luis, Somerton, Wellton, Growler, Quartzite, Bouse, Signal, Yucca, Kingman, Temple Bar • NEVADA: Overton, Glendale, Galt, Pioche • UTAH: Garrison, Provo, American Fork, Murray, Kerns, Salt Lake City, Syracuse • NEVADA: Shafter, Currie, Cherry Creek, Warm Springs, Alamo, Las Vegas • CALIFORNIA: Goffs, Vidal, Blythe, Palo Verde.

16,000-Foot Trajectory: NEVADA: Las Vegas • ARIZONA: Hualpi Indian Reservation, (Grand Canyon National Monument) • UTAH: Rockville, Springdale, Long Valley Junction, Hatch, Lund, Zane, Beryl, Hamlin Valley • NEVADA: Ursine, Pioche, Adaven, Warm Springs, Tonopah, Arlemont • CALIFORNIA: Benton Station, Benton, (Yosemite National Park), Bridgeport • NEVADA: Sweetwater, Babbitt, Hawthorne, Thorne, (Quartz Mountain), Austin, Winnemucca, Paradise Valley, Rebel Creek • IDAHO: Triangle, Silver City, Murphy, Nampa, Boise, Horsehoe Bend, Crouch, Warm Lake, Yellow Pine • MONTANA: Hamilton, Bearmouth, Helmville, Blackleaf, Conrad, Shelby, Sunburst, Sweetgrass.

TUMBLER-SNAPPER: CHARLIE

Detonation Date: 22 Apr 1952 • *Detonation Time: 9:30 A.M.* • *Area:* 7-3 • *Sponsor:* Los Alamos, Department of Defense • *Yield:* 31 kt • *Radiation Level at Ground Zero:* 0.15 R/hr • *Height of Burst:* 3,447 ft • *Cloud Top Height:* 42,000 ft

10,000-Foot Trajectory: NEVADA: Pahrump • CALIFORNIA: Shoshone, Tecopa, Fort Irwin, Pioneer Point, Little Lake, Kings, (Canyon National Park), June Lake, (Mono Lake), Coleville, Markleeville • NEVADA: Gardnerville, Carson City, Crystal Bay • CALIFORNIA: Truckee, Portola, Susanville, Bieber, White Horse, Tule Lake • OREGON: Malin, Beatty, Silver Lake, Millican, (Stevenson Mountain), Mayville, Condon, Arlington • WASHINGTON: Whitcomb, Horse Heaven Hills, Prosser, Ephrata, Soap Lake, Mansfield, Disautel, Havillah, Chesaw • MICHIGAN: Sault Ste. Marie, Barbeau, Hessel, Freedon, Boyne Fals, Lansing, Battle Creek, Kinderhook • INDIANA: Orland, Fort Wayne, Muncie, Connersville, Batesville, Madison • KENTUCKY: Carrollton, Frankfort, Sunnybrook • TENNESSEE: Chanute, Boatland, Crossville, Chattanooga • GEORGIA: Dalton, Carrollton, LaGrange • ALABAMA: Lafayette, Midway, Dothan • FLORIDA: Campbellton, Marianna, Apalachicola, Tampa, Arcadia, Homestead, Florida City, Key Largo.

18,000-Foot Trajectory: CALIFORNIA: Beacon Station, San Bernadino, Anaheim, Santa Ana, Buena Park, Whittier, San Mateo, San Francisco, Santa Rosa, Ukia, Willits, Blue Lake, Gasquet • OREGON: Remote, Swisshome, Tidewater, Eddyville, Willamina, Blaine, Westport • WASHINGTON: Grays River, Doty, Olympia, Bremerton, Burlington, Mount Baker • MIN-

NESOTA: Laurel, Silverdale, Aurora, Castle Danger • WISCONSIN: Ironwood, Pulaski, Green Bay, Two Creeks • INDIANA: Gary, Hammond • ILLINOIS: Kankakee, Rantoul, Centralia, Carbondale • MISSOURI: Cape Girardeau, Belmont • KENTUCKY: Hickman • TENNESSEE: Nankipoo, Collierville, Rossville • MISSISSIPPI: Byhalia, Eupora, Meridian • ALABAMA: Bogueloosa, St. Stephens, Perdido • FLORIDA: Pensacola, Fort Meyers, Hialeah, Miami.

24,000-Foot Trajectory: This part of the cloud followed the California-Nevada, California-Arizona border, then up through San Diego. The other cities are: CALIFORNIA: El Centro, Victorville, Fresno, Merced, Modesto, Sacramento, Burney, Dorris • OREGON: Klamath Falls, Belknap Springs, Sandy • WASHINGTON: (Mount St. Helens), Puyallup, Auburn, Kent, Bellevue, Everett, Sumas • MINNESOTA: Grand Marais • MICHIGAN: Beacon Hill, Houghton, Negaunee, Garden, Traverse City, Battle Creek • INDIANA: Kendallville, Marion, Indianapolis, Lamar • KENTUCKY: Owensboro, Hopkinsville • TENNESSEE: Clarksville, Fort Campbell, Wayland Springs • ALABAMA: Florence, Birmingham, Montgomery, Dothan • FLORIDA: Chattahoochee, Tallahassee, Williston, Daytona Beach.

30,000-Foot Trajectory: NEVADA: Las Vegas • ARIZONA: Signal, Phoenix, Casa Grande, S. Tucson, Bisbee, Douglas • TEXAS: Eagle Flat, Rankin, Barnhart, San Marcos, Cuero, Victoria, Port O'Connor • FLORIDA: Crystal River, Ocala, Jacksonville • NORTH CAROLINA: Wilmington, Jacksonville, New Bern, Elizabeth City.

40,000-Foot Trajectory: ARIZONA: Grand Canyon, Flagstaff • NEW MEXICO: Zuni Indian Reservation, Grants, Los Alamos, Amistad • TEXAS: Hartley, Dumas, Borger, Canadian • OKLAHOMA: Regdon, Oklahoma City, Muskogee • ARKANSAS: Fayetteville, Mountain Home • MISSOURI: Pontiac, Mountain View, Ellington, Minimum, St. Marys • ILLINOIS: Rockwood, Mount Vernon, Bridgeport • INDIANA: Vincinnes, Indianapolis, Anderson, Muncie, Portland • OHIO: Lima, Lorain • NEW YORK: Buffalo, Rochester, Mexico, Camden, Port Henry • VERMONT: Montpelier, Barre • NEW HAMPSHIRE: Lisbon • MAINE: Augusta, Bar Harbor.

TUMBLER-SNAPPER: DOG

Detonation Date: 1 May 1952 • *Detonation Time:* 8:30 A.M. • *Area:* 7, Target 3 • *Sponsor:* Los Alamos • *Yield:* 19 kt • *Radiation Level at Ground Zero:* 10 R/hr • *Height of Burst:* 1,040 ft • *Cloud Top Height:* 44,000 ft

18,000-Foot Trajectory: UTAH: St. George • ARIZONA: Flagstaff, Prescott, Truxton, Crozier, Valentine • UTAH: St. George, (Zion National Park), Cedar City, Parowan, Thompsonville, Castle Dale, Vernal • COLORADO: Dinosaur, Sunbeam • WYOMING: Hanna, Medicine Bow, Casper, Moorcroft, (Devil's Tower National Monument), Hulett • MONTANA: Alzada, Albion, Capitol • SOUTH DAKOTA: Camp Hook, Ladner, Ludlow • NORTH DAKOTA: Bowman, New England, Antelope, Washburn, McClusky, Devil's Lake, Park River, Cavalier, Pembina • PENNSYLVANIA: Erie, Oil City, DuBois, Clearfield, Carlisle, York, Lancaster • MARYLAND: Taneytown, Eldersburg, Parksville, Pikesville, Baltimore, Edgemore, Centreville, Henderson • DELAWARE: Hartley, Dover, Kilts Hummock • NEW JERSEY: Villas, Rio Grande, Wildwood.

TUMBLER-SNAPPER: EASY

Detonation Date: 7 May 1952 • *Detonation Time:* 4:15 A.M. • *Area:* T-1 • *Sponsor:* Los Alamos • *Yield:* 12 kt • *Radiation Level at Ground Zero:* 500 R/hr • *Height of Burst:* 300 ft • *Cloud Top Height:* 34,000 ft

10,000-Foot Trajectory: NEVADA: (Black Rock Summit), Hobson, Cave Creek, Metropolis, Contact • IDAHO: Amsterdam, Twin Falls, Jerome, Shoshone, Richfield, Arco, Mud Lake, St. Anthony • WYOMING: Bechler, (Yellowstone National Park: Lone Star Geyser, Shoshone Lake, Lewis Lake, West Thumb, Yellowstone Lake, Sylvan Pass, East Entrance, Pahaska, Powell, Elk Basin, Deaver, Frannie, Parkman, Sheridan, Rocky Point, Colony • SOUTH DAKOTA: Arpan, Newell, Creighton, Cottonwood, Long Valley, Tuthill • NEBRASKA: Nenzel, Kennedy, Brownlee, Thedford, Broken Bow, Miller, Kearney, Red Cloud • KANSAS: Webber, Concordia, Manhattan, Burlingame, Prescott • MISSOURI: Hume, Nevada, Hope, Manes, Rector, (Taum Sauk Mountain), Ironton, Lixville, New Wells • ILLINOIS: Aldridge, Carbondale, Carriers Mills, Ridgeway • INDIANA: Mount Vernon, Evansville, Boonville, Lama, Alton, Corydon, New Albany • KENTUCKY: Louisville, New Castle, Corinth, Mount Olivet, Maysville • OHIO: Ripley, Waverly, McArthur, Nelsonville, McConnelsville, Caldwell, Bellaire • WEST VIRGINIA: Benwood, Bethlehem, Wheeling, Valley Grove • PENNSYLVANIA: Washington, Pittsburgh, Punxsutawney, DuBois, Johnsonburg, Betula, Port Allegany, Myrtle • NEW YORK: Ceres, Bolivar, Friendship, Wiscoy, Genesco, Avon, West Rush, Henrietta, Rochester, Rondequoit, Sea Breeze.

TUMBLER-SNAPPER: FOX

Detonation Date: 25 May 1952 • *Detonation Time:* 4:00 A.M. • *Area:* 4 • *Sponsor:* Los Alamos • *Yield:* 11 kt • *Radiation Level at Ground Zero:* 2,000 R/hr • *Height of Burst:* 300 ft • *Cloud Top Height:* 41,000 ft

30,000-Foot Trajectory: NEVADA: Hilco, Ash Springs, Alamo, Caliente • UTAH: Minersville, Bicknell, Nanksville, Moab • COLORADO: Gateway, Orchard City, Bowie, Somerset, Oliver, Marble, Avon, Mount Powell, Heeney, Granby, Berthoud, Johnstown, Millikan, Greeley, Barnesville, Cornish, New Raymer • NEBRASKA: Chappell, Lomoyne, Tryon, Neligh, Hadar, Hoskins, Norfolk, Pender, Bancroft, Decatur • IOWA: Onawa, Dow City, Buck Grove, Manilla, Bagley, Perry, Gardiner, Moran, Elkhart, Baxter, Newburg, Belle Plaine, Cedar Rapids, Springville, Anamosa, Canton, Bellevue • ILLINOIS: Loran, Ridott, Rockford, Machesney Park • WISCONSIN: Beloit, Clinton, Delavan, Waterford, Wind Lake, Milwaukee • MICHIGAN: Muskegon, Ravenna, Sparta, Belding, Matherton, Maple Rapids, Eureka, Elsie, Oakley, Burt, Vassar, Caro, Gagetown, Bad Axe, Filion • NEW YORK: Madrid, Unionville, Potsdam, Parishville, Clear Lake, Saranac Lake, Lake Placid, Keene Valley, Moriah • VERMONT: Chimney Point, Cornwall, Salisbury, Sherburne Center, Windsor, Claremont, Deering, Nashua • MASSACHUSETTS: Lowell, Billerica, Woburn, Lexington, Medford, Arlington, Malden, Somerville, Cambridge, Boston, Hull, North Cohasset, Humarock, Kent Park, Rexhame, Ocean Bluff, Brant Rock, Green Harbor, Denis, South Yarmouth.

40,000-Foot Trajectory: NEVADA: Alamo, Ash Springs, Hiko, Caliente, Panaca, Carp, Elgin • UTAH: Milford, Cove Fort, Fillmore, Richfield, Mount Pleasant, Moroni, Price, East Carbon, Ouray, Bonanza • COLORADO: Massadonia, Blue Mountain, Elk Springs, Maybell, Sunbeam, Clark • WYOMING: Baggs, Dixon, Saven, Mountain Home, Woods Landing, Buford, Cheyenne, Carpenter • NEBRASKA: Kimball, Sidney, Lodgepole, Chappel, Ogallala, North Platte, Maxwell, Brady, Pleasanton, Grand Island, Aurora, York, Milford, Lincoln, Denton, Syracuse • MISSOURI: Tarkio, Maryville, Coffey, Chula, Brookfield, Marceline, College Mound, Duncan's Bridge, Holliday, Paris, Vandalia, Louisville, Auburn, New Hope • ILLINOIS: Alton, Edwardsille, Aviston, Bartelso, New Minden, Spring Garden, Broughton, Texas City, Ridgeway, Old Shawneetown • KENTUCKY: Spring Grove, Grove Center, Wheatcroft, Clay, Madisonville, Nortonville, Apex, Kirkmansville, Fearsville, Allegre, Claumour, Whippoorwill, Olmstead, Adairville • TENNESSEE: Orlinda, Portland, Bethpage, Hartsville, Carthage, Buffalo Valley, Bon Air, Roddy, Loudon, Glendale, Maryville, Townsend, Elkmont, Gatlinburg • NORTH CAROLINA: Asheville, Azalea, Vale, Reepville, Davidson, Concord, Albemarle, Candor, Manchester, Eastover, Clinton, Lyman, Fountain, Catherine Lake, Jacksonville, Camp Lejeune Marine Corps Base, Bear Inlet of Onslow Bay.

Note: Both the 30,000-foot and the 40,000-foot trajectory crossed over Chappel, Nebraska.

TUMBLER-SNAPPER: GEORGE

Detonation Date: 1 Jun 1952 • *Detonation Time:* 3:55 A.M. • *Area:* 3 • *Sponsor:* Los Alamos • *Yield:* 15 kt • *Radiation Level at Ground Zero:* 1,000 R/hr • *Height of Burst:* 300 ft • *Cloud Top Height:* 37,000 ft

35,000-Foot Trajectory: NEVADA: Caselton, Montello • UTAH: Artesian City, Carey, Antelope River, Darlington, Winsper, Humphrey • WYOMING: (Yellowstone National Park, Northern Campgrounds) • MONTANA: Dean, Joliet, Silesia, Castle Rock, Brandenburg, Ekalaka, Mill Iron • SOUTH DAKOTA: Ladner, Ludlow, Lodgepole, Glad Valley, Isabel, Ridgeview, Agar, Miller, Iroquois, Oldham, Elkton • MINNESOTA: Ruthton, Aroca, Dundee, Lakefield, Dunnell • IOWA: Buffalo Center, Forest City, Hanford, Marble Rock, Horton, Sumner, Osborne • WISCONSIN: Cornelia, Seymour Corners, Cadiz Springs • ILLINOIS: Durand, Belvidere, Chicago • INDIANA: Coburg, Hamlet, Argos, Luther, Roanoke, Zanesville, Ossian, Curryville, Salem • OHIO: Celina, New Brennen, Lena, Thackeray, Springfield, Brookwalter, Bloomingburg, Austin, Alma, Beaver, Bloom, Pedro Forrestdale • WEST VIRGINIA: Shoals, Eloise, Holden, Christian, Lincoln, Woolsey, Rock, Ingleside • VIRGINIA: Point Pleasant, Shorts Creek, Fancy Gap, Canal • NORTH CAROLINA: Mount Airy, Pinnacle, Cedar Lodge, Cid, Ophir, Norman • SOUTH CAROLINA: Clio, Dillon, Mulins, Galivants Ferry, Toddville, Burgess, Brookgreen.

TUMBLER-SNAPPER: HOW

Detonation Date: 5 Jun 1952 • *Detonation Time:* 3:55 A.M. • *Area:* 2 • *Sponsor:* Los Alamos • *Yield:* 14 kt • *Radiation Level at Ground Zero:* 1,500 R/hr • *Height of Burst:* 300 ft • *Cloud Top Height:* 41,800 ft

24,000-Foot Trajectory: NEVADA: Warm Springs, Round Mountain, Crescent Valley, Midas, Tuscarora • IDAHO: Riddle, Grasmere, Mayfield, Lowman • MONTANA: Darby, Bearmouth, Helmville, Greenfield, Power, Gildford, Kremlin • SASKATCHEWAN: Regina • NEW YORK: Youngstown, Model City, Niagara Falls, Tonawanda, Buffalo, Lancastor, Aurora, South Wales, Holland, Chaffee, Elton, North Cuba, Nile, Allentown • PENNSYLVANIA: Kinney, Gold, Carter Camp, Haneyville, Avis, Ranchtown, Cowan, New Berlin, Selinsgrove, Red Cross, Sharidan, Dayton, Jonestown, Bunker Hill, Avon, Iona, Clay, Ephrata, Groffdale, Gap, Atglen, Jennersville, Kelton, New London, Kemblesville • DELAWARE: Newark, Brookside, St. Georges, Taylors Bridge, Dupont Manor, Dover, Bowers, Slaughter Beach, Nassau, Cottonpatch Hill.

UPSHOT-KNOTHOLE: ANNIE

Detonation Date: 17 Mar 1953 • *Detonation Time:* 5:20 A.M. • *Area:* 3 • *Sponsor:* Los Alamos • *Yield:* 16 kt • *Radiation Level at Ground Zero:* 2,000 R/hr • *Height of Burst:* 300 ft • *Cloud Top Height:* 41,000 ft

10,000-Foot Trajectory: NEVADA: Alamo, Elgin, Carp • UTAH: Modena, Beryl, Paragonah, Spry, Panguitch • COLORADO: Grand Junction, De Begue, Parachute, Glenwood Springs, Boulder, Longmont, Greeley, New Raymer, Sedgwick, Ovid • NEBRASKA: Julesburg, Ogallala, Keystone, Stapleton, Gandy, Anselmo, Taylor, Neligh, Pierce, Carroll, Concord, Jackson • IOWA: Sioux City, Lawton, Kingsley, Diamond Center, Hanover, Nemaha, Rockwell City, Somers, Slifer, Stratford, Story City, Roland, Marshalltown, Chelsea, Haven, South Amana, Tiffin, Iowa City, Downey, Moscow, Pleasant Prairie, Bettendorf, Davenport • ILLI-NOIS: Rock Island, Moline, Buda, Tiskilwa, McNabb, Kangley, Streator, Dwight, Kankakee • INDIANA: Lake Village, Thayer, Wilders, Brems, Grovertown, Hamlet, Koontz Lake, Teegarden, Lakeville, Woodland, Jimtown, Elkhart, Bristol • MICHIGAN: Vistula, Sturgis, Findley, Coldwater, Litchfield, Pulaski, Vandercook, Grass Lake, Ann Arbor, Plymouth, Livonia, Oak Park, Highland Park, Detroit • NEW YORK: Westfield, Point Chautauqua, Jamestown • PENNSYLVANIA: Westline, Guffey, Mount Jewett, Howard, Castle Garden, Spring Garden, Unityville, Elk Grove, Lopez, Sugar Run, Camptown, Little Meadows. • NEW YORK: Binghamton, Oxford, Norwich, Shelburne, Utica, Grant, Saranac Lake, Redford, Dannemora, Jericho, Champlain • MAINE: Dickey, St. John, Fort Kent, Frenchville.

40,000-Foot Trajectory: NEVADA: Alamo, Ash Springs, Hiko • UTAH: Modena, Beryl, Paragonah, Spry, Panguitch, Mount Ellen • COLORADO: Gateway, Delta, Hotchkiss, Paonia, Crested Butte, Granite, Tarryall, Palmer Lake, Elbert, Hale • KANSAS: St. Francis • NEBRASKA: Danbury, Oxford, Mascot, Ragan, Hildneth, Holstein, Roseland, Hastings, Harvard, Lushton, McCool Junction, Beaver Crossing, Malcolm, Ashland, Smithfield, Bellevue, Omaha • IOWA: Council Bluffs, Hancock, Marne, Lorah, Monteith, Minburn, Alleman, Maxwell, Melbourne, Marshalltown, Dysart, Walker, Troy Mills, Farley, Centralia, Asbury, Dubuque • WISCONSIN: Kieler, Cuba City, Avon, Lamont, Argyle, Monticello, Evansville, Edgerton, Fort Atkinson, Hebron, Palmyra, North Prairie, Genesee, West Allis, Milwaukee • MICHIGAN: Holland, Grand Rapids, Cedar Springs, Trufant, Six Lakes, Wyman, Mount Pleasant, Leaton, Edenville, Estey, Rhodes, Bentley, Omer, Twining, Tawas City, Au Sable • NEW YORK: Waddington, Chase Mills, Norfolk, Dickenson Center, Duane Center, Hawkeye, Clintonville • VERMONT: Huntington Center, Waitsfield, Northfield, Corinth, Bradford • NEW HAMPSHIRE: Wentworth, Stinson Lake, Melvin Village, Wawbeck, Tuttonboro, Wolfeboro Center, Wakefield, Sanbornville • MAINE: Emery Mills, Springvale, Sanford, Kennebunkport.

UPSHOT-KNOTHOLE: NANCY

Detonation Date: 24 Mar 1953 • *Detonation Time:* 5:10 A.M. • *Area:* 4 • *Sponsor:* Los Alamos • *Yield:* 24 kt • *Radiation Level at Ground Zero:* 2,000 R/hr • *Height of Burst:* 300 ft • *Cloud Top Height:* 41,500 ft

10,000-Foot Trajectory: NEVADA: (Summit Mountain), Dunphy, Tuscarora, Mountain City, Owyhee • IDAHO: Riddle, Grasmere, Mayfield, Lowman, Cobalt, Salmon • MONTANA: Butte, Boulder, Winston, Neihart, Windham, Benchland, Danvers, Hilger, Fergus, Roy, Mona, Andes • NORTH DAKOTA: Charleston, New Town, Plaza, Sawyer, Velva, Voltaire, Bergen, Balfour, Drake, Maddock, Oberon, Sheyenne, Warwick, Hamar, Tolna, Pekin, McVille, Kloten, Aneta, Northwood, Reynolds • MINNESOTA: Climax, Fertile, Rindal, Bejou, Naytahwaush, Akeley, Hackensack, Manhattan Beach, Fifty Lakes, Aitkin, Giese, Finlayson, Sandstone • WISCONSIN: Webster, Hertel, Barronett, Rice Lake, Canton, Cameron, Chetek, New Auburn, Cadott, Neillsville, Mather, Shennington, Cutler, New Lisbon, Lyndon Station, Baraboo, Prairie du Sac, Sauk City, Black Earth, Madison, Mount Horeb, Belleville, New Glarus, Monticello, Monroe, Juda • ILLINOIS: Rock Grove, Rock City, Ridott, Seward, Chana, Rockelle, Pawpaw, Earlville, Harding, Wedron, Marseilles, Seneca, Verona, Dwight, Reddick, Cabery, Stelle, Dunforth, Milford • INDIANA: Freeland Park, Pine Village, West Point, Romney, Kirkpatrick, Thorntown, Lebanon, Fayette, Royalton, Trader's Point, Indianapolis, Beech Grove, Acton, London, Fairland, Shelbyville, Waldron, St. Paul, Milford, Greensburg, Millhousen, Osgood, Farmers Retreat, East Enterprise, Quercus Grove, Florence • KENTUCKY: Warsaw, Glencoe, Poplar Grove, Mason, Corinth, Cynthiana, Millersburg, East Union, Sharpsburg, Owingsville, Sudith, Frenchburg, Mizel, Grassy Creek, Caney, Lakeville. Royalton, Blue River, Manton, Boldman, Pikeville, Chloe, Shelbiana • VIRGINIA: Prater, Mount Heron, Lynn Spring, Red Ash, Cedar Bluff, Asberrys, Wytheville, Austinville, Hillsville, Laurel Fork, Vesta, Spencer, Glenwood, Harmony, Mayo, Cluster Springs, Clarksville, Alberta, Dophpin, Stony Creek, Savedge, Williamsburg, Mobjack, Mathews, Diggs, Birdsnest, Nassawadox.

40,000-Foot Trajectory: NEVADA: Alamo, Ash Springs, Hiko • UTAH: Molena, Beryl, Lund, Beaver, Koosharem, Ferron • COLORADO: Palisade, Cedaredge, Rogers Mesa, Lazear, Crawford, Maher, LaGareta, Center, Mosca, Fort Garland • NEW MEXICO: (Laughlin Peak), Sofia, Clapham, Stead • TEXAS: Amarillo (near the Pantex Plant), Pullman, Palo Duro, South Brice, Parnell, Swearingen, Crowell, Thulia, Mabelle, Markley, Wizard Wells, Boonsville, Cottondale, Keeter, Springtown, Forth Worth, Hurst, Arlington, Grand Prairie, Dallas, Duncanville, Bristol, Palmer, Telico, Gun Barrel City, Caney City, Malakoff, Bradford, Nechas, Rusk, Wells, Lufkin, Jasper, Newton, Bon Wier • LOUISIANA: Merryville, Reeves, LeBlanc, Indian Village, Hathaway, Evangeline, Rayne, Crowley, Maurice, Youngsville, New Iberia, Jeanerette, Baldwin, Franklin, Morgan City, Houma, Chauvin, Golden Meadow, Leeville, Grand Isle • FLORIDA: Venice, South Venice, North Port, Port Charlotte, Lakeport, Port Mayaca, Jupiter.

Upshot-Knothole: Ruth

Detonation Date: 31 Mar 1953 • Detonation Time: 5:00 A.M. • Area: 7–5a • Sponsor: Livermore Laboratory • Yield: 0.2 kt • Radiation Level at Ground Zero: 10 R/hr • Height of Burst: 304.69 ft • Cloud Top Height: 13,600 ft

10,000-Foot Trajectory: NEVADA: Indian Springs, Las Vegas, Winchester, Nelson, Cottonwood Cove, Riviera • CALIFORNIA: Needles, Vidal Junction, Rice, (Palen Mountains), (Chocolate Mountains), Glamis, (Sand hills) • ARIZONA: (Copper Mountains), (Sauceda Mountains), Casa Grande, Maricopa, Olberg, Palm Springs, Apache Junction, Tortilla Flat, Roosevelt, (Bear Mountain), Carrizo, Pinetop, Lakeside, (Greens Peak), Eagar, Alpine • NEW MEXICO: Luna, Reserve, (Tularosa Mountains), (Elk Mountain), Kingston, Las Cruces, La Mesa, Chamberino, La Union • TEXAS: El Paso, Horizon City, Clint, Andrews, Tarzan, Big Spring, Lomax, Otis Chalk, Silver, Robert Lee, Bronte, Maverick, Balinger, Voss, Mozelle, Trickham, Brookesmith, Indian Creek, Mullin, Golthwaite, Center City, Evant, Pearl, Arnett, Fort Gates, Flat, Moffatt, Pendelton, Moody, Cego, Mooresville, Perry, Otto, Ben Hur, Groesbeck, Personville, Point Enterprise, Fairfield, Red Lake, Montalba, Jacksonville, Reese, Black Jack, St. Clair City, New London, Kilgore, Easton, Darco, Longview, Karnack, Smithland, Gray • LOUISIANA: Trees, Vivian, Gilliam, Hosston, Mira, Bolinger, Ida • ARKANSAS: Springhill, Welcome, Taylor, Emerson, Plainfield, Atlanta, Wasson, Urbana, Gerdner, Strong, North Crossett, West Crossett, Crossett, Parkdale, Empire, Eudora • MISSISSIPPI: Chaltham, Hollandale, Darioue, Belzoni, Cruger, Acona, West, Beatty, French Camp, Weir, Ackerman, Sturgis, Bradley, Longview, Starkville, Columbus, Mayhew, Caledonia • ALABAMA: Fernbank, Kingville, Covin, Howard, Carbon Hill, Townby, Saragossa, Manchester, Macedonia, Cold Springs, Hanceville, Center Hill, Blountsville, Liberty, Brooksville, Nixons Chapel, Douglas, Horton, Boaz, Sardis City, Keener, Sand Rock, Leesburg, Cedar Bluff, Gaylesville • GEORGIA: Coosa, Garden Lakes, Rome, Halls, Cassville, Pine Log, Rydal, White, Waleska, Nelson, Ball Ground, New Holland, Lula, Raoul, Hollingsworth, Avalon, Martin, Lavonia • SOUTH CAROLINA: Anderson, Williamston, Cheddar, Pelzer, Fork Shoals, Owings, Enoree, Cross Keys, Buffalo, Monarch, Union, Chester, Eureka, Richburg, Fort Lawn, Grace, Lancaster, Pageland, Mount Crogham, Rugby, Chesterfield • NORTH CAROLINA: Gibson, Laurel Hill, Old Hundred, Laurinburg, Wakulla, Red Springs, Shannon,

Rex, St. Pauls, Jerome, Parkerburg, Ingold, Magnolia, Rose Hill, Beulaville, Richlands, Petersburg, New Bern, Arapahoe, Merritt, Pamlico, Whortonville, Oracoke, Hatteras, Frisco, Buxton, Cape Hatteras.

UPSHOT-KNOTHOLE: DIXIE

Detonation Date: 6 Apr 1953 • *Detonation Time:* 7:30 A.M. • *Area:* 7–3 • *Sponsor:* Los Alamos • *Yield:* 11kt • *Radiation Level at Ground Zero:* 1.5 mR/hr • *Height of Burst:* 6,022 ft • *Cloud Top Height:* 45,000 ft

30,000-Foot Trajectory: NEVADA: Moapa, Logandale, Overton • ARIZONA: (Grand Canyon National Park), Flagstaff, Show Low, Nutrioso, Alpine • NEW MEXICO: Horse Springs, Negal, Hondo, Roswell, Caprock • TEXAS: Sundown, Lubbock, Roosevelt, Crosbytown, Croton, Truscott, Thalia, Electra, Wichita Falls, Terral, Illinois Bend, Dexter, Dennison, Ivanhoe, Paris, Reno, Detroit, Clarksville, Whaley, Texarkana • ARKANSAS: Homen, Patmos, Lamartine, Smackover, El Dorado, North Crossett, Crossett, Berlin, Wilmet, Indian, Readland • MISSISSIPPI: Glen Allan, Grace, Yazoo City, Vaughn, Carthage, McAffee, McDonald, Econdale • ALABAMA: Demopolis, Burnsville, Selma, Montgomery, Shorter, Tuskegee • GEORGIA: Fort Benning, Tazewell, Ideal, Montezuma, Elko, Hawkinsville, Gresston, Mount Vernon, Vidalia, Lyons, Santa Claus, Claxton, Pembroke, Bloomingdale • SOUTH CAROLINA: Port Wentworth, Forest Beach.

UPSHOT-KNOTHOLE: RAY

Detonation Date: 11 Apr 1953 • *Detonation Time:* 4:45 A.M. • *Area:* 4a • *Sponsor:* Livermore Laboratory • *Yield:* 0.2 kt • *Radiation Level at Ground Zero:* 20 R/hr • *Height of Burst:* 100 ft • *Cloud Top Height:* 12,800 ft

10,000-Foot Trajectory: NEVADA: Lathrop Wells • CALIFORNIA: Death Valley Junction, (Greenwater Range), (Avawatz Mountains), (Bristol Mountains), Bagdad, Amboy, (Bristol Dry Lake), (Cadiz Dry Lake) (Palen Mountains), Blythe, East Blythe • ARIZONA: Ehrenburg, (Kofa Mountains), (Gila Bend Mountains), (Woolsey Peak), Maricopa Akchin Indian Reservation, Casa Grande, Stanfield, Eloy, Pichacho, Catalina, Mount Lemmon, (Lime Peak), Dragoon, (Chiricahua Peak) • NEW MEXICO: Rodeo, (Animas Mountains) • TEXAS: Socorro, Horizon City, (Hueco Mountains), (San Antonio Mountain) • NEW MEXICO: (Carlsbad Caverns National Park), (Sitting Bull Falls), Whites City, Loving, Carlsbad, Malaga, (Antelope Ridge), Bennett, Jal • TEXAS: Stanton, Greenwood, Sterling City, Water Valley, Carlsbad, Miles, Mereta, Millers View, Doole Fife, Placid, Hall, Algerita, San Saba, Lampasas, Watson, Prairie Dell, Bartlett, Granger, Thorndale, Navasota, Conroe, Moss Hill, Silsbee, Lumberton • LOUISIANA: Vinton, Edgerly, Sulphur, Westlake, Lake Charles, Iowa, Welsh, Jennings, Midland, Morse, Indian Bayou, Maurice, Youngsville, New Iberia, Jeanerette, Labadieville, Thibodaux, Raceland, Lockport, Larose, Lafite, Myrtle Grove, Magnolia, Port Sulphur, Empire, Buras, Triumph, Boothville, (North Pass) • FLORIDA: Marco, Goodland, Everglades City, Ochope, Monroe, Miccosukee Indian Reservation, Sweetwater, Miami, Miami Beach.

UPSHOT-KNOTHOLE: BADGER

Detonation Date: 18 Apr 1953 • *Detonation Time:* 4:35 A.M. • *Area:* 2 • *Sponsor:* Los Alamos • *Yield:* 23 kt • *Radiation Level at Ground Zero:* 1,200 R/hr • *Height of Burst:* 300 ft • *Cloud Top Height:* 36,000 ft

40,000-Foot Trajectory: NEVADA: Indian Springs, North Las Vegas, Henderson • ARIZONA: Hualpai Indian Reservation, Peach Springs, Nelson, Drake, Sedonia, Heber, Overgaard,

Shumway, Vernon, Springerville • NEW MEXICO: Red Hill, Pie Town, Polvadera, Lemitar, Florida, Claunch, Ancho, Haystack Mountain, Elkins, Kenna, Milnesand, Pep, Lingo • TEXAS: Denver City, Higginbotham, Seminole, Three Leagues, Knott, Fairview, Big Spring, Otis Chalk, Edith, Tennyson, Orient, Rowena, Concho, Millersview, Lohn, Fife, Rochelle, Hall, San Saba, Lake Victor, Briggs, Youngsport, Little River, Heidenhelmer, Temple, Westphalia, Durango, Barclay, Rosebud, Travis, Lott, Cedar Springs, Marlin, Oletha, Thronton, Donie, Buffalo, Oakwood, Elkhart, Palestine, Rusk, Gallatin, Ponta, New Salem, Laneville, Concord, Dotson, Gary, Carthage, Deadwood • LOUISIANA: Keatchie, Stonewall, Keithville, Gayles, McDude, Elm Grove, Janestown, Heflin, Arcadia, Bryceland, Grambling, Ruston, Vienna, Sibby, D'Arbonne, Rocky Branch, Monroe, Sterlington, Bastrop, Fairbanks, Collinston, Mer Rouge, Goodwill, Pioneer, Forest, Transylvania, Lake Providence • MISSISSIPPI: Cary, Fitler, Jonestown, Valley, Tinsley, Benton, Way, Vaughn, Camden, Ofahoma, Carthage, Edinburg, McAfee, Williamsville, Deemer, McDonald, Moscow, House, Daleville • ALABAMA: York, Livingston, Coatopa, Belmont, Demopolis, Prairieville, Suttle, Summerfield, Burnsville, Winslow, Independence, Booth, Prattville, Cobbs Ford, Ware, Milstead, Tuskegee, Society Hill, Uchee, Seale, Fort Mitchell • GEORGIA: Cusseta, Buena Vista, Murrays Crossroads, Oglethorpe, Montezuma, Unadilla, Hawkinsville, Hartford, Gresston, Plainfield, Mount Vernon, Ailey, Higgston, Videlia, Lyons, Choopee, Collins, Bellville, Claxton, Pembroke, Blitchton, Eden • SOUTH CAROLINA: Pritchardville, Bluffton, Hilton Head Island, Folly Field Beach.

UPSHOT-KNOTHOLE: SIMON

Detonation Date: 25 Apr 1953 • *Detonation Time:* 4:30 A.M. • *Area:* 1 • *Sponsor:* Los Alamos • *Yield:* 43 kt • *Radiation Level at Ground Zero:* 300 R/hr • *Height of Burst:* 300 ft • *Cloud Top Height:* 44,000 ft

30,000-Foot Trajectory: NEVADA: Moapa Indian Reservation, Logandale, Overton • ARIZONA: Tusayan, Cameron, (Painted Desert), Navajo Indian Reservation, Hopi Indian Reservation, Hotevilla, Orabi, Second Mesa, Polacca, Keams Canyon, Nazlini, Fort Defiance, Window Rock • NEW MEXICO: Mexican Springs, Brimhall, Crown Point, Hospah, San Ysidro, Santo Domingo Pueblo, San Felipe Pueblo, Cerrillos, Madrid, Galisteo, Lamy, El Pueblo, Ribera, Serafina, Los Montoyas, Tucumcati, Porter • TEXAS: Adrian, Vega, Wildorado, Bushland, Amarillo, Pullman, Washburn, Conway, Claude, Goodnight, Howardwick, Samnorwood, Lutie, Aberdeen • OKLAHOMA: Madge, Vinson, Reed, Mangum, Hester, Blair, Warren, Snyder, Cache, Lawton, Hulen, Gas City, Duncan, Sunray, Velma, Countyline, Alma, Loco, Fox, Clemscot, Graham, Woodford, Newport, Springer, Gene Autry, Dickson, Baum, Ravia, Tishomingo, Nida, Armstrong, Caddo, Matoy, Cade, Bokchito, Boswell, Soper, Goodland, Hugo, Sawyer, Swink, Valient, Idabel, Haworth, Harris, Bokhoma, Tom • ARKANSAS: Arkinda, Fomby Homan, Stamps, Buckner, Magnolia, Calhoun, Macedonia, Emerson • LOUISIANA: Summerfield, Lillie, Spearsville, Farmerville, Linville, Spencer, Bastrop, Perryville, Fairbanks, Collinston, Oak Ridge, Epps, Monticello, Sondheimer • MISSISSIPPI: Blakely, Redwood, Bentonia, Ballard, Sharon, Offahoma, Carthage, Edinburg, Stallo, Plattsburg, McLeod, Prairie Point • ALABAMA: Pickensville, Beaver Town, Carrolton, Gordo, Echola, Port Birmingham, Bayview, Adamsville, Graysville, Fultondale, Gardendale, Mount Olive, Majestic, Pinson, Palmerdale, Remlap, Allgood, Whitney, Taits Gap, Gallant, Reece City, Gadsden, Keener, Leesburg, Sand Rock, Gaylesville, Ringgold • GEORGIA: Lyerly, Berryton, Holland, Crystal Springs, Summersville, Calhoun, Echota, Oakman, Whitestone, (Brasstown Bald, highest point in Georgia: 4,784 feet), Pillard • NORTH CAROLINA: Brasstown, Shooting Creek, Franklin, Iotla, Webster, Cullowhee, Sylva, Balsam, Hazelwood, Canton, Asheville, Leicester, Alexander, Jupiter, Barnardsville, Little Switzerland, Celo, Estatoe, Miraville, Spruce, Ingalls, Linville, Montezuma, Boone, Jefferson, Warrensville, Lansing, Grassy Creek • VIRGINIA: Independence, Fries, Sylvatus, Indian Valley, Alum Ridge, Copper Hill, Bent Mountain, Roanoke, Montvale, Big Island, Lowesville, Nellysford, White Hall, Free Union, Nortonsville, Ruckersville, Hood, Wolftown, Haywood, Boston, Viewtown, Amissville, Orlean, Old Tavern, Marshall, Rectorville, Halfway, Aldie, Oatlands, Hamilton, Waterford, Point of Rocks • MARYLAND: Tuscarora, Adamstown, Thurston, Buckeystown, Frederick, Mount Pleasant, Johnsville, Union Bridge, Ladiesburg, Uniontown, Middleburg, Tarrytown, Silver Run • PENNSYLVANIA: Hanover, Mount Royal, Newberrytown, Royalton, Hummelstown, Hershey, Shellsville, East Hanover, Bardnersville, Oak Grove, Ravine, Donaldson, Branch Dale, Buck Run, Gordon, Shenendoah, Fern Glen, Plymouth, Luzerne, Upper Exeter, Dalton, Lewisville, Royal, Winderdale • NEW YORK: Fish's Eddy, Shinhopple, Downsville, Lake Delaware, Bovina Center, Stamford, West Fulton, Schoharie, Schenectady, Rotterdam, Chariton, Factory Village, Saratoga Springs, Fort Howard, Hudson Falls, Kingsburg, Truthville, Poultney, Hampton • VERMONT: West Haven, Benson, Brandon, Forest Dale, Goshen, Alpine Village, Roxbury, Northfield, Berlin, Montpelier, Barre, North Montpelier, Plainfield, East Calais, Marshfield, Cabot, Walden, North Danville, Lyndon, Burke, East Haven, Lemington, Colebrook • NEW HAMPSHIRE: Stewartstown Hollow, Mount Pisgah, Magalloway Mountain • MAINE: Eustis, West Forks, Moosehead, Kokadjo, (Mount Katahdin, highest point in Maine), Patten, Crystal, Island Falls, Shin Pond, Knowles Corner, Bridgewater, Blaine, Mars Hill.

The 40,000-foot trajectory passed over the highest points in the states of Georgia and Maine.

UPSHOT-KNOTHOLE: ENCORE

Detonation Date: 8 May 1953 • *Detonation Time:* 7:30 A.M. • *Area:* Frenchman's Flat • *Sponsor:* Los Alamos, Department of Defense • *Yield:* 27 kt • *Radiation Level at Ground Zero:* 25 R/hr • *Height of Burst:* 2,423 ft • *Cloud Top Height:* 42,000 ft

10,000-Foot Trajectory: NEVADA: Moapa, Logandale, Overton • ARIZONA: (Mount Dellenbaugh), Havasupai Indian Reservation, North Rim, Cedar Ridge, Kaibito • UTAH: (Glen Canyon), (Cataract Canyon), (Canyonland National Park), (La Sal Mountains), Castleton, Mount Tomasaki • COLORADO: Gateway, Whitewater, Skyway, Grand Mesa, (Grand Mesa National Forest), Snowmass, Ruedi, Meredith, Norrie, (Tennessee Pass), Climax, Leadville, (Fremont Pass), Jefferson, Como, Deckers, Greenland, Palmer Lake, Peyton, Rush, Eads • KANSAS: Tennis, Wright, Windthorst, Brenham, Haviland, Wellsford, Coats, Sawyer, Isabel, Duquoin, Harper, Danville, Freeport, Argonia, Corbin, South Haven, Ashton, Arkansas City, Silverdale, Maple City, Cedar Vale, Wauneta, Elk City, Sycamore, Morehead, Galesburg, Erie, St. Paul, Walnut, Hepler, Farlington, Hiattville, Garland • MISSOURI: Deerfield, Richards, Horton, Prairie City, Appleton City, Ohio, Deepwater, Brownington, Tightwad, Coal, Leesville, Branden, Mora, Bahner, Otterville, Beaman, Pilot Grove, Bunceton, Bellair, Lone Elm, Lamine, Boonville, Wooldridge, Rocheport, New Franklin, Midway, Hinton, Harrisburg, Rucker, Sturgeon, Clark, Centralia, Paris, Stoutsville, Monroe City, Hassard, Hunnewell, Withers Mill, Palmyra, West Quincy • ILLINOIS: Quincy, Ursa, Mendon, Loraine, Bigneck, Stillwell, Bowen, Denver, Augusta, Plymouth, Colmar, Fondon, Macomb, Bardolph, New Philadelphia, Bushness, Marietta, Blyton, Ellisville, Fairview, London Mills, Rapatee, Farmington, Yates City, Elmwood, Oak Hill, Brimfield, Dunlap, Princeville, Edelstein, Speer, Camp Grove, Henry, Putnam, McNabb, Granville, Spring Valley, Oglesby, Cedar Point, Peru, LaSalle, Ottawa, Dayton, Wedrun, Norway, Serena, Sheridan, Newark, Sandwich, Plano, Yorkville, Bristol, Oswego, Montgomery, Autota, Batavia, Wheaton, Elmhurst, Bloomingdale, Roselle, Des Plaines, Highland Park, Glencoe, Winnettca, Wilmette • MICHIGAN: Graafschap, Beechwood, Holland, New Holland, Hudsonville, Jenison, Grandville, Wyoming, Walker, Grand Rapids, Cannonsburg, Bostwick Lake, Belding, Fenwick, Butternut, Vickeryville, Crystal, Sumner, Ithoca, Breckenridge, Wheeler, Merrill, Iva, Hemlock, Laporte, Freeland, Midland, Bay City, Essexville, Oakhurst, Bay Park, Sebewaing, Bay Port, Pigeon,

Caseville, Pinnebog, Kinde, Port Austin, Grind Stone City • MAINE: Pittston Farm, Seboomook, North East Carry, (Caribou Lake), (Harrington Lake), (North Brother Mountain), (Mount Katahdin, highest point in Maine), Stacyville, Sherman Station, Sherman Mills, (Otter Lake Mountain), Orient.

Upshot-Knothole: Harry

Detonation Date: 19 May 1953 • *Detonation Time:* 4:05 A.M. • *Area:* 3a • *Sponsor:* Los Alamos • *Yield:* 32 kt • *Radiation Level at Ground Zero:* 10 R/hr • *Height of Burst:* 300 ft • *Cloud Top Height:* 42,500 ft

10,000-Foot Trajectory: NEVADA: Preston, Ely, Tippett • UTAH: Callao, Grantsville, Salt Lake City, Layton, Ogden, Woodruff • WYOMING: Frontier, Diamondville, Kemmerer, Fontenelle, Farson, Yoder • NEBRASKA: Scottsbluff, Gering, McGrew, Bridgeport, Broadwater, Lisco, Oshkosh, Lewellen, Ogallala, Roscoe, Farnam, Kearney, Lowell, Prosser, Hansen, Trumbull, Harvard, Lushton, Cordova, Pleasantdale, Denton, Lincoln, Avoca, Union • IOWA: Shenandoah, Bingam, Yorktown, Clarinda, Sharpsburg, Gravity, Conway, Kellerton, Decatur City, Leon, High Point, Corydon, Promise City, Plano, Centerville, West Grove, Bloomfield, Hillsboro, Salem, Danville • ILLINOIS: Monmouth, Galesburg, Wataga, Victoria, Fayette, Toulon, Wyoming, Putnam, Oglesby, LaSalle, Ottowa, Wedron, Lisle, Chicago • MICHIGAN: Allendale, Wyoming, Grand Rapids, Alpine, Sparta, Sherman City, Farwell, St. Helen, Luzerne, Metz, Hawks, Rogers City.

18,000-Foot Trajectory: NEVADA: Elgin, Carp • UTAH: Santa Clara, St. George, Hurricane, Virgin, Rockville, Springdale, Mt. Carmel, Blanding • COLORADO: Pleasant View, Stoner, Spar City, Masonic Park, Center, Cedarwood, Rocky Ford, Las Animas, McClave, Big Bend, Wiley • KANSAS: Lydia, Rush Center, Timkin, Shaffer, Olmitz, Hoisington, Redwing, Odin, Lorraine, Falun, Mentor, Kipp, Holland, Pearl, Abiline, Junction City, St. Marys, Mayetta, Half Mound, Atchison • MISSOURI: St. Joseph, Rochester, Fairport, McFall, Blue Ridge, Goshen, Princeton, Mercer • IOWA: Seymour, Centerville, Ottumwa, Bladensburg, Abington, Brighton, Cranston, Muscatine, Fairport, Montpelier, Davenport, Bettendorf • ILLINOIS: Rock Island, Moline, Hillsdale, Lyndon, Rock Falls, Sterling, Dixon, Rochelle, Hillcrest, Clare, Genoa, Hampshire, Huntley, Algonquin, Libertyville, Waukeegan, North Chicago • MICHIGAN: Douglas, Saugatuck, Hamilton, Bentheim, Green Lake, Caldeonia, Clarksville, Lake Odessa, Portland, Fowler, St. Johns, Eureka, Bannister, Brant, St. Charles, Saginaw.

Upshot-Knothole: Grable

Detonation Date: 25 May 1953 • *Detonation Time:* 7:30 A.M. • *Area:* Frenchman's Flat • *Sponsor:* Los Alamos • *Yield:* 15 kt • *Radiation Level at Ground Zero:* 10 R/hr • *Height of Burst:* 524 ft • *Cloud Top Height:* 35,000 ft

10,000-Foot Trajectory: NEVADA: (Grant Range), Ruth, Steptoe, Currie, (Snow Water Lake), Thousand Springs • IDAHO: Three Creek, Glenns Ferry, Mountain Home, Mayfield, Boise, Pearl, Montour, Payette, Weiser • OREGON: Pleasant Valley, Baker, Haines, North Powder, (Blue Mountains), Pilot Rock, Echo, Irrigon • WASHINGTON: Paterson, (Horse Heaven Hills), Yakima Indian Reservation, (Lincoln Plateau), (Mount Adams Wilderness Area) (Gifford Peak),(Gifford Pinchot National Forest), North Bonneville, Skamania • OREGON: Gresham, Boring, Eagle Creek, Estacada, (Goat Mountain), (Round Mountain), (Monument Peak), (Tombstone Pass), (Three Sisters Wilderness Area), Bend, (Bear Creek Butte), Post (Spanish Peak), Hamilton, (Meadow Creek Pass), (Blue Mountains), La Grande, Island City, Alicel, Imbler, Minam, Walowa • IDAHO: Waha, Lewiston, Lapwai, Spalding, Julietta,

Southwick, Helmer, Boyill, Avery, Saltese, Mullan • MONTANA: Belknap, (Mount Headley), (Blue Mountain), Tray • IDAHO: Moyie Springs, Meadow Creek, (Moyie Falls), Nordman • WASHINGTON: (Molybdenite Mountain), Lost Creek, Arden, Addy, Cedonia, Hunters, Marlin, Moses Lake, Sunnyside, Grandview, Mabton, (Horse Heaven Hills) • OREGON: Arlington, Blalock, Rock Creek, Mikkalo, Kent, Shaniko, Antelope, Ashwood, (Grizzly Mountain).

Upshot-Knothole: Climax

Detonation Date: 4 Jun 1953 • *Detonation Time:* 3:15A.M. • *Area:* 7–3 • *Sponsor:* Los Alamos • *Yield:* 61 kt • *Radiation Level at Ground Zero:* 10 R/hr • *Height of Burst:* 1,334 ft • *Cloud Top Height:* 42,700 ft

40,000-Foot Trajectory: NEVADA: (Pintwater Range), Carp • UTAH: (Snow Canyon), St. George, Washington, Hurricane, Rockville, Mount Carmel Junction, (Cottonwood Canyon), (White Canyon), (Cataract Canyon), (Angel Arch), La Sal Junction, Caselton • COLORADO: Gateway, Glade Park, Grand Junction, Orchard Mesa, Fruitvale, Clifton, De Beque, Parachute, Rulison, Rio Blanco, Buford, (Williams Fork Mountains), Haydon, Clark, Hahns Peak • WYOMING: (Blackhall Mountain), Riverside, Ryan Park, (Medicine Bow Peak), McFaddin, Rock River, Esterbrook, Douglas, Orin, Newcastle, Four Corners • SOUTH DAKOTA: Cheyenne Crossing, Savoy, Central City, Whitewood, Spearfish, St. Onge, Fruitdale, Nisland, Newell, Zeona, Bison, Meadow, Morristown, Watanga • NORTH DAKOTA: Shields, Breien, Fort Rice, Huff, Moffitt, Sterling, Steele, Dawson, Crystal Springs, Predina, Goldwin, Buchanan, Pingree, Spiritwood Lake, Courtenay, Wimbledon, Hannaford, Dazey, Sibley, Luverne, Blabon, Hope, Clifford, Galesburg, Blanchard, Hillsboro, Kelso • MINNESOTA: Climax, Shelly, Halstad, Lackhart, Gary, Rindal, Bejou, Ebro, Bagley, Shelvin, Solway, Bemidji, Turtle River, Tenstrike, Hines, Blackduck, Bergville, Effie, Craigville, Bois Fort, Nelt Lake, Ash Lake, Cusson, Crane Lake.

Teapot: Wasp

Detonation Date: 18 Feb 1955 • *Detonation Time:* 12:00 noon • *Area:* T-7–4 • *Sponsor:* Los Alamos • *Yield:* 1 kt • *Radiation Level at Ground Zero:* 10 R/hr • *Height of Burst:* 762 ft • *Cloud Top Height:* 21,500 ft

18,000-Foot Trajectory: NEVADA: (Sheep Range), Moapa Indian Reservation, (Valley of Fire State Park), Overton • ARIZONA: (Grand Wash Cliffs), (Poverty Mountain), Havasupai Indian Reservation, (Grant Canyon), Tusayan, Cameron, Gray Mountain, Steamboat Canyon, Sunrise Springs, Cornfield, Ganado, Cross Canyon, Fort Defiance, Sawmill • NEW MEXICO: Mexican Springs, Tohatchi, Brimhall, Standing Rock, Pueblo Pintado, La Jara, Regina, Gallina, Coyote, Vallecitos, Las Tables, Tres Piedras, Cerro, Amalia • COLORADO: La Valley, Stonewall, Gulpare, Aguilar, Timpas, La Junta, Swink, North La Junta, Cheraw, Eads, Cheyenne Wells, Arapahoe • KANSAS: (Mount Sunflower, highest point in Kansas: 4,039 feet), Edson, Brewster, Achilles, Traer, Cedar Bluffs • NEBRASKA: Danbury, Cambridge, Holbrook, Elwood, Lexington, Berwyn, Almeria, Rose, Basselt, Burton.

At this point, the 16,000-foot trajectory split into two sections; one traveled east; the other west.

East Trajectory: SOUTH DAKOTA: Burke, Gregory, Oacoma, Reliance, Lower Brule, Harrold, Gettysburg, Lowry, Java, Artas • NORTH DAKOTA: Hague, Napoleon, Dawson, Lake Williams, Sykeston, Cathay, Sheyenne, Devils Lake, Webster, Hampden, Loma, Langden (into Manitoba).

West Trajectory: SOUTH DAKOTA: Wewela, Winner, Witten, Draper, Hajes, Cherry Creek, Howes, Marcus, Redowl, Stoneville, Fairpoint, (Mud Buttes) • WYOMING: Beulah, Aladdin, Sundance, Moorcroft, (Devils Tower), Rozet, Sussex, Powder River, Natrona, (Rattlesnake Hills), (Ferris Mountains), Rawlins, (Medicine Bow National Forest) • COLORADO: Columbine, Clark, Milner, Toponas, McCoy, Bond, Aron, Golman, Redcliff, Leadville, Texas Creek, Fairview, San Isabel, Green Towers, Walsonburg, Pryor, Aguilar, Ludlow, El Moro, Trinidad, (Raton Pass) • NEW MEXICO: Folsom, Des Moines, Capulin, Sofia, Mount Dora, Clapham, Stoad, Sedan • TEXAS: Perico, Dalhart, Cactus, Gruver, Spearman, Waka, Farnsworth, Perryton, Twitchell, Booker, Darrouzett • OKLAHOMA: Catesby, May, Camp Houston • KANSAS: Hardtner, Sharon, Attica, Harper, Duquoin, Milton Violla, Clonmel, Clearwater, Shulte, Wichita, Andover, Towanda, El Dorado, Thrall, Madison, Hartford, Strawn, Sharpe, Halls Summit, Waverly, Agricola, Williamsburg, Homewood, Ottawa, Le-Loup, Edgerton, Wellsville, Gardner, Lenexa, Overland Park, Shawnee, Edwardsville, Kansas City • MISSOURI: Kansas City, Parkville, Gladstone, Kearney, Holt, Elmira, Mirabile, Kingston, Hamilton, Breckenridge, Lock Springs, Jamesport, Trenton, Dunlap, Galt, Osgood, Harris, Newton, Lucerne, Powersville • IOWA: Numa, Centerville, Brazil, Mystic, Rathbun, Moravia, Avery, Eddyville, Cedar, Wright, Keomah, Rose Hill, What Cheer, Thornburg, Millersburg, Williamsburg, West Ammana, Watkins, Norway, Atkins, Palo, Center Point, Waller, Quasqueton, Winthrop, Manchester, Lamart, Dundee, Strawberry Point, Osborie, Elkader, St. Olaf, Farmersburg, Freelich, Monona, Watson, Valien, Waterville, Lansing. • WISCONSIN: De Soto, Red Mound, Victory, Genoa, Chaseburg, Coon Valley, La Crosse, Middle Ridge, Bangor, Rockland, West Salem, Cataract, Melrose, Shamrock, Black River Falls, Alma Center, Merrillan, Humbird, Willard, Thorp, Lublin, Kennan, Catawba, (Butternut Lake), Mallan, High Bridge, Marengo, Bad River Indian Reservation, Ashland, Washburn, La Pointe, Bayfield, Red Cliff, (York Island), (Bear Island) • MINNESOTA: Little Marais, (Nine Mile Lake), (Snowbank Lake), Orleans, Noyes, Humbolt, Northcote, Bowesmont • NORTH DAKOTA: Joliette, Bowesmont, Auburn, Oakwood, Minto, Warsaw, Ardoch, Johnstown, Manvel, Makinock, Holmes, Reynolds, Buxton, Mayville, Cummings, Kelso, Grandin, Gardiner • MINNESOTA: Georgetown, Moorhead, Dilworth, Lyndon, Rollag, Cormorant, Vergas, Perham, Sebeka, Nimrod, Poplar, Pequot Lakes, Breezy Point, Hassman, McGregor, Tamerack, Wright, Cromwell, Cloquet, Twig, Hermantown, Arnold, Lax Lake, Finland, Little Marais, Taconite Harbor, Schroeder, Tofte, Lutsen, Grand Marais, Grand Portage Indian Reservation.

Teapot: Moth

Detonation Date: 22 Feb 1955 • *Detonation Time:* 5:45 A.M. • *Area:* 3 • *Sponsor:* Los Alamos • *Yield:* 2 kt • *Radiation Level at Ground Zero:* 500 R/hr • *Height of Burst:* 300 ft • *Cloud Top Height:* 24,200 ft

24,000-Foot Trajectory: NEVADA:(Spotted Range), Indian Springs, Las Vegas, Winchester, N. Las Vegas, Henderson, Boulder City • ARIZONA: Willow Beach, Dolan Springs, Chloride, Prescott, Mayer, (Mazatlan Mountains), Tonto Basin, (Rockinstraw Mountain), San Carlos Indian Reservation, Morenci, Clifton, (Macerick Hill) • NEW MEXICO: Mule Creek, Buckhorn, Kingston, Hillsboro, Caballo, (Caballo Mountains), Alamogordo, Sunspot, Sacramento, Weed, Dunken, Hope, Atoka, Loco Hills, Humble City, Hobbs • TEXAS: Seminole, Lamesa, Arvana, Mesquite (in Borden County), Gail, Fluvanna, Dermott, Rotan, Hamlin, Tuxedo, Stamford, Avoca, Woodson, South Bend, Eliasville, Graham, Bryson, Jacksboro, Wizard Wells, Chico, Alvord, Greenwood, Slidell, Pilot Point, Tioga, Dorchester, Sherman, Ambrose, Ivanhoe, Telephone, Elwood, Riverby, Direct, Belk, Chicota, Arthur City, Albion • OKLAHOMA: Ord, Frogville, Valiant, Wright City, Millerton, Garvin, Golden, Glover, Broken Bow, Eagleton, DeQueen • ARKANSAS: Gilham, New Hope, Langley, Salem, Glenwood, Bonnerdale, Hempwallace, Lake Hamilton, Magnet Cove, (Hot Springs National Park), Benton, Little Rock, Shannon, Wrightville, Scott, Lonoke, Carlisle, Des Arc, Cotton Plant, Hunter, Wynne, Colt, Gieseck, Parkin, Turrell, Frenchmans Bayou, Joiner, Pecan Point • TENNESSEE: Millington, Kerrville, Rosemark, Brownsville, Belle Eagle, Alamo, Fruitland, Gibson, Mi-

Ian, Cades, Atwood, Trezevant, McKenzie, Mansfield, Manlyville, Big Sandy, Faxon, Tennessee Ridge, Erin, Shiloh, Marian, Cunningham, Fredonia, Port Royal, Cedar Hill, Springfield, Orlinda, Cross Plains, Mitchellville • KENTUCKY: Rapids, New Roe, Chapel Hill, Scottsville, Maynard, Cedar Springs, Austin, Roseville, Eighty Eight, Edmonton, Gradyville, Milltown, Casy Creek, Creston, Pricetown, Yosemite, Middleburg, King Mountain, Gum Sulphur, Conway, Morrill, Kerby Knob, Drip Rock, Old Landing, Zoe, Vortex, Malaga, Elsie, Leatha, Wheelersburg, Volga, Sitka, Nippa, Lowmansville, Clifford • WEST VIRGINIA: Radnor, Dunlow, Sias, Sumerco, Ruth, Rand, Charleston, Bomant, Maysel, Clay, Tesla, Sutton, Newville, Cleveland, Czar, Cassity, Beverly, Elkins, Red Creek, Maysville, Points, Paw Paw, Great Cacapon • PENNSYLVANIA: Lashley, Big Cove Tannery, Webster Mills, Cito, Cove Gap, Le-Masters, Markes, Fort Loudon, St. Thomas, Chambersburg, Stoufferstown, Fayetteville, Wenksville, Laurel, Bendersville, Goodyear, Latimore, Clear Spring, Franklintown, Maytown, Lewisburg, Middletown, Deodate, Lawn, Mount Wilson, Mount Gretna, Iona, Richland, Mount Pleasant, Dauberville, Windsor Castle, Klinesville, Krumsville, Stony Run, Saegersville, Laurys Station, Pennsville, Bearsville, Wind Gap, Roseto, Bossandville, Slaterford, Delaware, East Stroudsburg • NEW JERSEY: Millbrook, Five Points, Myrtle Grove, Crandon Lakes, Augusta, Branchville, Pettettown, McAfee, Hamburg, Vernon • NEW YORK: Amity, Warwick, Edenville, Bellvale, Sugar Loaf, Central Valley, Arden, Harriman, West Point, Garrison Lake, Carmel, Lake Carmel, Putnam Lake • CONNECTICUT: New Fairfield, Candlewood Shores, Brookfield, Roxbury Falls, Hotchkissville, Minortown, Watertown, Plymouth, Pequabuck, Whigville, Unionville, Bloomfield, Windsor Locks, Kings Corner, Enfield, Hazardville • MASSACHUSETTS: Hampden, Monson, Brimfield, Spencer, Leicester, Worcester, Morningdale, South Berlin, Berlin, Marlborough, Hudson, Maynard, West Concord, Concord, Beford, Pinehurst, North Reading, Middleton, Topsfield, Ipswich, Little Neck, (Plum Island State Park).

TEAPOT: TESLA

Detonation Date: 1 Mar 1955 • *Detonation Time:* 5:30 A.M. • *Area:* 9b • *Sponsor:* Livermore Laboratory • *Yield:* 7 kt • *Radiation Level at Ground Zero:* 750 R/hr • *Height of Burst:* 300 ft • *Cloud Top Height:* 30,000 ft

24,000-Foot Trajectory: NEVADA: (Spotted Range), (Sheep Range), (Morman Peak), Mesquite • ARIZONA: Littlefield, Colorado City, Cane Beds, Moccason, Kaibab Indian Reservation, Kaibab, Fredonia, Page, (Tower Butte), (Monument Valley), Mexican Water • NEW MEXICO: Shiprock, (Shiprock Peak: 7,178 feet), Waterflow, Fruitland, Flora Vista, Aztec, Manero, Rutherton, Brazos, Eusenada, Tierra, Amarilla, (San Juan Mountains), Tres Piedras, Cerro, Questa, Red River, (Wheeler Peak, highest point in New Mexico: 13,161 feet), Maxwell, Grenville, Seneca • OKLAHOMA: Felt, Griggs, Guymon, Hardesty, Rosston, Laverne, Buffalo, Selman, Camp Houston, Capron, Burlington, Driftwood, Amorita, Byron, Wakita, Renfrow • KANSAS: Caldwell, Hunnewell, Ashton, Dexter, Oak Valley, Elk City, Sycamore, Morehead, Parsons, Strauss, McCune, Cherokee • MISSOURI: Mindenmines, Nashville, Kenoma, Golden City, Lockwood, Greenfield, Everton, Pennsboro, Ash Grove, Springfield, Williard, Walnut Grove, Glidewell, Fordland, Seymour, Mansfield, Norwood, Mountain Grove, Pine Crest, Mountain View, Birch Tree, Bartlett, Winna, Fremont, Van Buren, Chicopee, Williamsville, Hendrickson, Asherville, Wappapello, Puxico, Acornridge, Aguilla, Salcedo, Sikeston, Miner, Bertrand, Charleston, Anniston, Wyatt • KENTUCKY: Bardwell, Arlington, Fancy Farm, Mayfield, Brewers, Dexter, Fairdealing, Golden Pond, Cadiz, Caledonia, Hopkinsville, Mewstead, Pembroke, Elkton, Trenton, Daysville, Olmstead, Middleton, Franklin, Mount Aerial, Chapel Hill, Petroleum, Holland, Scottsville, Flippin, Mud Lick, Grandview, Thompkinsville, Judio, Littrell, Kettle, Mount Pisgah, Co-Operative, Pine Knot, Whitley City, Hollyhill, Mountain Ash, Gatliff, Middlesboro, Harrogate • TENNESSEE: Kyle's Ford, Okolona, Mount Carmel, Church Hill, Kingsport, Blountville, Avoca, Bluff City, Sadie, Buladeen,

Shouns, Mountain City • NORTH CAROLINA: Creston, Clifton, Warrensville, Jefferson, Index, Laurel Springs, McGrady, Traphill, Austin, Elkin, Jonesville, Boonville, Smithtown, Flint Hill, Pfafftown, Enon, Lewsville, Winston-Salem, Union Cross, Jamestown, High Point, Archdale, Climax, Pleasant Gardens, Julian, Liberty, Pittsboro, Bynum, New Hill, Holly Springs, Fuquay-Varina, Willow Springs, Smithfield, Four Oaks, Goldsboro, Seymour Johnson Air Force Base, Seven Springs, Rivermont, Wise Forks, Trenton, Rhems, Pollocksville, Riverdale, Croatan, Hewelock, Newport, Morehead City, Otway, Beaufort, Parkers Island, (Shackleford Banks), (Cape Lookout).

TEAPOT: TURK

Detonation Date: 7 Mar 1955 • *Detonation Time:* 5:20 A.M. • *Area:* 2 • *Sponsor:* Livermore Laboratory • *Yield:* 43 kt • *Radiation Level at Ground Zero:* 1,000 R/hr • *Height of Burst:* 500 ft • *Cloud Top Height:* 44,700 ft

40,000-Foot Trajectory: NEVADA: (Mormon Peak) • UTAH: (Snow Canyon), St. George, Washington, Rockville, Kanab, (Vermillion Cliffs), Glen Canyon, Navajo Indian Reservation, (Monument Valley), Mexican Hat • COLORADO: Ute Mountain Indian Reservation, Red Mesa, Southern Ute Indian Reservation, Tiffany, Allison, Arboles, Juanita, Chrome, Ortiz • NEW MEXICO: Chama, San Miguel, Las Pinos, Amalia, Costilla, (Ortiz Peak), Capulin, Grenville, (Mount Dora), Clayton • TEXAS: Texline, Stratford, McKibben, Notla, Glazier, Canadian • OKLAHOMA: Durham, Crawford, Roll, Thomas, Geary, Calumet, El Reno, Yukon, Bethany, Oklahoma City, Midwest City, Woods, Dale, Shawnee, Little, Butner, Wetumka, Vernon, Indianola, Russellville, Quinton, Lewisville, Kinta, Wells, Wister, Poteau, Howe, Monroe • ARKANSAS: Midland, Hartford, Waldron, Harvey, Gravelly, Story, Buckville, Jessieville, Owensville, (Hot Springs National Park), Benton, Redfield, Wright, Sherrill, Altheimer, Lodge Corner, DeWitt, DeLuce, Crumrod, Snow Lake • MISSISSIPPI: Perthshire, Deeson, Shelby, Drew, Minter City, Philipp, La Flora, Duck Hill, Lodi, Tomnolen, Reform, Sturgis, Brooksville, Macon, Prairie Point • ALABAMA: Dancy, Clinton, Stewart, Akron, Havana, Heiberger, Sprott, Plantersville, Winslow, Autaugaville, Hanter, Montgomery, Pile Road, Mathews, Fitzpatrick, Enon, Three Notch, Springhill • GEORGIA: Troutman, Westran, Bronwood, Oakfield, Ashburn, Sycamore, Mystic, Lax, Upton, Douglas, Bickley, Dixie Union, Blackshear, Nahonta, Atkinson, Brunswick, (St. Simons Island).

TEAPOT: HORNET

Detonation Date: 12 Mar 1955 • *Detonation Time:* 5:20 A.M. • *Area:* 3a • *Sponsor:* Los Alamos • *Yield:* 4 kt • *Radiation Level at Ground Zero:* 2,500 R/hr • *Height of Burst:* 300 ft • *Cloud Top Height:* 37,000 ft

40,000-Foot Trajectory: NEVADA: (Papoose Range), Carp • UTAH: (Snow Canyon), Gunlock, Shivwits, Hurricane, La Verkin, Pintura, (Zion National Park), Glendale, Orderville, Mount Carmel Junction, (Valley of the Gods) • COLORADO: Squaw Point, Pleasant View, Silverton, Olney Springs, Numa, Ordway, Sugar City, Chivington, Sheridan Lake, Towner • KANSAS: Horace, Tribune, Selkirk, Lepti, Marienthal, Modor, Scott City, Manning, Grigston, Dighton, Shields, Utica, Ransom, Brownell, McCracken, Liebenthal, Loretta, Galatia, Susank, Beaver, Dubuque, Ellsworth, Carneiro, Brookville, Salina, Kipp, Abilene, Enterprise, Pear, Skiddy, Alta Vista, Hessdale, Keene, Topeka, Pauline, Big Spring, Williamstown, McLouth, Fairmount, Kansas City • MISSOURI: Kansas City, Raytown, Independence, Blue Springs, Wellington, Mayview, Higginsville, Alma, Mount Leonard, Marshall, Malta Bend, Slater, Forest Green, Roanoke, Mount Airy, Moberly, Middle Grove, Paris, Perry, Center, New London, Saverton • ILLINOIS: New Canton, New Salem, Valley City, Chapin, Literberry, Prentice, Pleasant Plains, Salisbury, Cantrall, Williamsville, Mount Pulaski, Chestnut,

Kenny, Lane, Clinton, Weldon, De Laud, Mansfield, Fisher, Dewey, Rantoul, Ludlow, Clarence, East Lynn, Hoopeston • INDIANA: Ambra, Talbot, Fowler, Reynolds, Norway, Sitka, Royal Center, Lucerne, Metea, Perrysburg, Twelve Mile, Denver, Chili, Roann, Urbana, Andrews, Huntington, Zanesville, Ossian, Poe, Hoagland, Williams, Dixon, Monmouth • OHIO: Dixon, Cavett, Scott, Kalida, Pandora, Benton Ridge, Vanlue, Carey, Tymochtee, Belle Vernon, Sycamore, Benton, Chatfield, Tiro, Ganges, Epworth, Paradise Hill, Ashland, England Station, Rowsburg, New Pittsburg, Wooster, Orrville, Massillon, Perry Heights, Canton, Fairhope, Paris, Bayard, Hanoverton, West Point, Frederickstown • PENNSYLVANIA: Blackhawk, Fallston, East Rochester, Fernway, Wexford, Dorseyville, Oakmart, Plum, Sardis, Export, Delmont, Crabtree, New Derry, Derry, Wilpen, Tire Hill, Paint, Scalp Level, Ogletown, Weyant, Imber, New Enterprise, Riddlesburg, Kearney, Enid, Gracey, Clear Ridge, Fort Littleton, Fennettsburg, Metal, Creenvillage, Arendtsville, Table Rock, New Chester, New Oxford, Abbotstown, Spring Grove, Stoverstown, Rye, Felton, Pleasant Grove, Kyleville, Little Britain, Oxford, Strickersville • DELAWARE: Newark, Christiana, Bear, Red Lion, Delaware City • NEW JERSEY: New Castle, Harrisonville, Pointers, Salem, Renton, Alloway, Aldine, Centerton, Norma, Vineland, East Vineland, Milmay, Dorothy, Bargaintown, West Atlantic City, Atlantic City.

TEAPOT: BEE

Detonation Date: 22 Mar 1955 • *Detonation Time:* 5:05 A.M. • *Area:* 7–1a • *Sponsor:* Los Alamos • *Yield:* 8 kt • *Radiation Level at Ground Zero:* 2,000 R/hr • *Height of Burst:* 500 ft • *Cloud Top Height:* 39,700 ft

18,000-Foot Trajectory: NEVADA: Cottonwood Cove • ARIZONA: Bullhead City, Yucca, Congress, Wickenburg, Sun City, Phoenix, Scottsdale, Mesa, Mammoth, San Manuel, Cochise, Portal • NEW MEXICO: Rodeo, (Alamo Hueco Mountains) • TEXAS: Alpine, Sanderson, Dryden, Loma Alta, Campwood, Hondo, San Antonio, Union Valley, Shiner, Rock Island, Eagle Lake, Houston, Crosby, Shiloh, Devers, Beaumont, Orange • LOUISIANA: Vinton, Sulphur, Lake Charles, Church Point, Grand Coteau, Baton Rouge, Livingston, Hammond, Covington • MISSISSIPPI: Picayune, Caesar, Necaise, Wade, Nurley • ALABAMA: Mobile, Malbais, Robertsdale, Lillian • FLORIDA: Pensacola, Panama City, Highland Park, Chipola Park, Tallahassee, Waukeena, Lamont, Taylor, Jacksonville.

TEAPOT: ESS

Detonation Date: 23 Mar 1955 • *Detonation Time:* 12:30 P.M. • *Area:* T-10a • *Sponsor:* Los Alamos, Department of Defense • *Yield:* 1 kt • *Radiation Level at Ground Zero:* 6,000 R/hr • *Height of Burst:* − 67 ft • *Cloud Top Height:* 12,000 ft

10,000-Foot Trajectory: NEVADA: (Pintwater Range), Mopa, Logandale, Overton, (Virgin Peak) • ARIZONA: (Virgin Mountains), (Mount Trumbull), Supai, (Grand Canyon), Tusayan, Cameron, Gray Mountain, (Painted Desert), (Stephen Butte), White Cone, Steamboat Canyon, Cornfields, Sunrise Springs, Ganada, (Cross Canyon), Fort Defiance, St. Michaels • NEW MEXICO: Fence Lake, Trechado, (Gallinas Mountains), Alamo Navajo Indian Reservation, Polvadera, Lemitar, Florida, (Los Pinos Mountains), (Chupadera Mesa), Claunch, Ancho, (Arroyo Del Macho), (Haystack Mountain), Elkins, Milnesand • TEXAS: Griffith, Lehman, Morton, Pettit, Levelland, Lubbock, Roosevelt, Posey, Cap Rock, Canyon Valley, Kalgary, Jayton, Peacock, Swenson, Old Glory, Aspermont, Rule, Haskell, Woodson, Eliasville, Graford, Mineral Wells, Weatherford, Fort Worth, Grand Prairie, Arlington, Irving, Dallas, Mesquite, Balch Springs, Lawrence, Wills Point, Edgewood, Alba, Quitman, Golden, Forest Hill, Hainesville, Rhonesboro, Grice, Thomas, LaFayett, Lone Star, Daingerfield, Red Hill, Atlanta, Queen City, Cass • ARKANSAS: Brightstar, Fort Lynn, Fouke, Lewisville, Falcon,

Rosston, Waterloo, Childester, Amy, Holly Springs, Ramsey, Ivan, Staves, Randall, Ladd, Moscow, Bayou, Lodge Corner, DeWitt, Ethel, St. Charles, Lambrook, Lake View, Wabash, West Helena, Friars Point • MISSISSIPPI: Hill House, Rena Lara, Sherard Baugh, Farrell, Rudyard, Jonestown, Darling, Curtis Station, Pleasant Grove, Sardis, Harmontown, Looxahoma, Tyro, Thyatyra, Waterford, Lows Hill, Potts Camp, Winborn, Ashland, Peoples, Falkner, Chalybeate, Kossuth, Wenasoga, Corinth, Farmington, Kendrick • TENNESSEE: Michie, Acton, Childers Hill, Nixon, Burnt Church, Houston, Center, Crossroads, Ethridge, Webber City, Waco, Mooresville, Lewisburg, Shelbyville, Manchester, Ragsdale, Viola, Irving College, (Cumberland Plateau), Hitchcox, Mount Crest, Cold Spring, (Walden Ridge), Grandview, Roddy, Rockwood, Kingston, Solway, Ball Camp, Knoxville, Mascot, Blaine, Jefferson City, Shiloh, Talbott, Russellville, Whitesburg, St. Clair, Bailytown, McCloud, Fall Branch, Sullivan Gardens, Colonial Heights, Blountsville, Bristol • VIRGINIA: Bristol, Oscoala, Lodi, Adwolf, Attoway, Crockett, Wytheville, Draper, Graysontown, Christianburg, Alleghany Spring, Bent Mountain, Roanoke, Stewartsville, Bedford, New London, Lynchburg, Spout Spring, Appomattox, Guinea Mills, Macon, Richmond, Old Church, King William, Stevensville, Morattico, Burgess, Fair Port, Lilian, Reedville, (Smith Point).

TEAPOT: APPLE-1

Detonation Date: 29 Mar 1955 • *Detonation Time:* 4:55 A.M. • *Area:* 4 • *Sponsor:* Los Alamos • *Yield:* 14 kt • *Radiation Level at Ground Zero:* 500 R/hr • *Height of Burst:* 500 ft • *Cloud Top Height:* 32,000 ft

10,000-Foot Trajectory: NEVADA: (Papoose Range), (Groom Lake), (Timpahute Range), Lake Valley, Baker • UTAH: Garrison, Grantsville, Salt Lake City, (Antelope Island), (Castle Rock), Tremonton, Newton, Plymouth, Cornish • IDAHO: Snowville, Woodruff, Samaria, Malad City, Virginia, McCammon, Swan Valley, Driggs, Felt, Tetonia • WYOMING: (Mount Moran), (Mount Gancock), (Yellowstone Park: Heart Lake, Yellowstone Lake), Pahaska, (Windy Mountain), (Bear Tooth Pass) • MONTANA: Red Lodge, Washoe, Bearcreek, Bridger, Pryor, Crow Indian Reservation, Hardin, Hathaway, Miles City, Locate, Ismay, Ollie • NORTH DAKOTA: Galva, (Tracy Mountain), Southeart, Dickinson, Marshall, Dodge, Halliday, Twin Buttes, White Shield, Roseglen, Ryder, Douglas, Sawyer, Logan, Surrey, Minot, Norwich, Granville, Towner, Berwick, Barton, Mylo, Agate, Porth, Rocklake, Calvin, Hannah.

TEAPOT: WASP PRIME

Detonation Date: 29 Mar 1955 • *Detonation Time:* 10:00 A.M. • *Area:* T-7-4 • *Sponsor:* Los Alamos • *Yield:* 3 kt • *Radiation Level at Ground Zero:* 10 R/hr • *Height of Burst:* 739 ft • *Cloud Top Height:* 32,000 ft

18,000-Foot Trajectory: NEVADA: (Spotted Range), (Pintwater Range), Elgin • UTAH: Enterprise, Newcastle, Cedar City, Enoch, Summit, Parowan, Paragonah, Circleville, Junction, Greenwich, Fremont, (Thousand Lake Mountain), (San Rafael Knob), Willowblind, Uintah and Quray Indian Reservation, Bonanza • COLORADO: Dinosaur, Blue Mountain • WYOMING: Baggs, (Medicine Bow National Forest), Saratoga, (Medicine Bow Peak), Bosler, Iron Mountain, Meriden, Albin • NEBRASKA: Potter, Sidney, Colton, Sunol, Lodgepole, Chappell, Big Springs, Brule, Ogallala, Keystone, Dunning, Almeria, Taylor, Elyria, Ord, North Loup, Scotia, Cotesfield, Elba, Cushing, Palmer, Archer, Central City, Hordville, Marquette, Polk, Arborville, Benedict, Bradshaw, York, Waco, Utica, Beaver Crossing, Cordova, Crete, Wilber, Kramer, Clatonia, Pickrell, Crab Orchard, Tecumseh, Elk Creek, Howe, Stella, Shubert, Barada • MISSOURI: Corning, Craig, Maitland, Graham, Barnard, Guilford, Skidmore, Arkoe, Conception Junction, Ravenwood, Parnell, Grant City, Sheridan • IOWA: Redding, Delphos, Benton, Mount Ayr, Tingley, Arispe, Talmadge, Lorimore, Barney, East Peru, Hanley, Winterset, Patterson, Des Moines, Bonderant, Clyde, Rhodes, Melbourne, Van Cleve, Haverhill, Marshalltown, Le Grand, Clutier, Elberon, Van Horne, Newhall, Atkins, Covington, Cedar Rapids, Mount Vernon, Tipton, Bennett, New Liberty, Sunbury, Maysville, Walcott, Davenport, Bettendorf • ILLINOIS: Moline, Oak Grove, Arion, Andove, Nekoma, Bishop Hill, Galva, LaFayette, Speer, Edelstein, Chillicothe, Rome, Metamora, Eureka, Hudson, Normal, Holder, Bellflower, Blue Ridge, Urbana, Champaign, Philo, Sidney, Allerton, Sidell, Ridge Farm, Scotland • INDIANA: Cayuga, Lodi, Newport, Annapolis, Marshall, Milligan, Morton, Clinton Falls, Brick Chapel, Fillmore, Stilesville, Hazelwood, Mooresville, Smith Valley, Stones Crossing, Greenwood, Whiteland, Rocklane, Boggstown, Needham, Shelbyville, Waldron, St. Paul, Sandusky, Oldenburg, St. Peters, South Gate, St. Leon, New Trenton, West Harrison, Harrison • OHIO: Harrison, New Baltimore, Miamitown, Groesbeck, Monfort Heights, Brentwood, Deer Park, Montgomery, Madeira, Cincinnati, Norwood, Milford, Owensville, Crosstown, Greenbush, Bulford, Gath, Mowrystown, May Hill, Locust Grove, Mount Joy, Sedan, Fire Brick, Eifort, Blackfork, Gallia, Rodney, Gallipolis • WEST VIRGINIA: Point Pleasant, Mount Alto, Cottageville, Liverpool, Reedy, Mount Zion, Sand Ridge, Copen, Cedarville, Napier, Arlington, Rock Cave, Alton, Cassity, Valley Bend, (Spruce Knob, highest point in West Virginia), Judy Gap, Fort Seybert • VIRGINIA: Broadway, Tenth Legion, Alma, Stanley, Brightwood, Leon, Burr Hill, Todds Tavern, Massaponax, Guinea, Woodford, Sparta, Beulaville, Mangohick, Aglett, Walkerton, King William, Port Richmond, West Point, Barhamsville, Williamsburg, Fort Eustis, Lawson, Rescue, Newport News, Norfolk, Chesapeake, Virginia Beach.

Teapot: Ha

Detonation Date: 6 Apr 1955 • *Detonation Time:* 10:00 A.M. • *Area:* T-5 • *Sponsor:* Department of Defense • *Yield:* 3 kt • *Radiation Level at Ground Zero:* None detected • *Height of Burst:* 32,582 + / − 100 ft • *Cloud Top Height:* 55,000 ft

45,000-Foot Trajectory: NEVADA: (Sheep Range), Mesquite, Bunkerville • ARIZONA: Littlefield, (Mount Bangs), (Kaibab Plateau), (Marble Canyon), Cedar Ridge, (Wildcat Peak), Tonalea, Cow Springs, Chilchinbito, Rough Rock, Many Farms, Tsaile • NEW MEXICO: Sanostee, Toadlena, Newcomb, Burnham, Blanco, Nageezi, Ojito, Gavilan, Llaves, El Rito, Vallecitos, Petaca, La Madera, Taos, Pueblo, Talpa, Arroyo Seca, Angel Fire, (Aqua Fria), (Christo Range), (Philmont Boy Scout Ranch), Cimarron, Miami, Springer, Maxwell, (Laughlin Peak), Grenville, Sierra Grande, Moses • OKLAHOMA: Wheeless, Boise City, Keyes, Tyrone, Lookout, Manchester • KANSAS: Elkard, Liberal, Hardtner, Kiowa, Caldwell, Arkansas City, Silverdale, Maple City, Hewins, Elgin, Chautauqua, Caney, Tyro, Coffeyville, Edna, Chetopa, Melrose, Baxter Springs, Treece, Lowell • MISSOURI: Joplin, Fidelity, Sarcoxie, Wentworth, Pierce City, Freistatt, Verona, Marionville, Aurora, Crane, Hurley, Jamesville, Union City, Highlandville, Chadwick, Garrison, Ava, Squires, Gentryville, Drury, Vanzant, (Cedar Knobs), Pomona, Olden, White Church, Peace Valley, Thomasville, Wilderness, Handy, Eastwood, Grandlin, Poplar Bluff, Ash Hill, Fisk, Dudley, Dexter, Essex, Matthews, Whiting, E. Prairie, Wolf Island • KENTUCKY: Hickman, Moscow, Oakton, Cayce, Crutchfield, Water Valley, Cuba, Tri City, Lynn Grove, Murray, Hamlin, La Fayette, Oak Grove, Henleytown, Tiny Town, Keysburg, Adairville, Prices Mill, Providence, Rapids, New Roe, Adolphus, Akersville, Gamaliel, Hestand, Vernan, Littrell, Albany, Static, Sunnybrook, Mount Pisgah, Co-Operative, Pine Knot, Strunk, Saxton, Pearl, Pruden, Fonde, Edgewood, Middleboro, (Cumberland Gap), Weber City, Morrison City • TENNESSEE: Kingsport, Lynn Garden, Bloomingdale, Orebank, Bristol, Sutherland, Laurel Bloomery • NORTH CAROLINA: Lansing, Grassy Creek, Piney Creek, Twin Oaks, Sparta, Lowgap, Bottom, Mount Airy, Bannertown, Francisco, Lawsonville, Sandy Ridge, Stoneville, Eden, Ruffin, Pelham, Yancyville, Concord, Leasburg, Gentry's Store, Allensville, Stovall, Williamsboro, Middleburg, Manson, Norlina, Macon, Warrenton, Vaughan, Littleton, Sunny Side, Roanoke Rapids, Weldon, Jackson, Conway, Petecasi, Murfreesboro, Winston, Union, Tunis, Cofield, Gatesville, Sandy Cross, Trotville, Hobbsville, Morgan's Corner, Shawboro, Gregory, Belcross, Camden, Currituck, Maple, Barco, Waterlily, Aydlett, Carolla.

TEAPOT: POST

Detonation Date: 9 Apr 1955 • *Detonation Time:* 4:30 A.M. • *Area:* 9c • *Sponsor:* Livermore Laboratory • *Yield:* 2 kt • *Radiation Level at Ground Zero:* 1,000 R/hr • *Height of Burst:* 300 ft • *Cloud Top Height:* 15,500 ft

14,000-Foot Trajectory: NEVADA: Sandy, Goodsprings, Jean, Searchlight, Laughlin • ARIZONA: Kingman, Drake, Flagstaff, Winona, White Cone, Steamboat Canyon, Nazlini • NEW MEXICO: Crystal, Naschitti, Brazos, Ensenada, Tierra Amarilla, Cerro, Questa, Red River, Capulin, Moses • OKLAHOMA: Boise City, Keyes, Eva, Optima, Adams, Beaver, Laverne, Freedom, Cherokee, Vining, Medford • KANSAS: Arkansas City, Cambridge, Grenola, Moline, Fredonia, Thayer, St. Paul, Girard, Frontenac • MISSOURI: Lamar, Dadeville, Eudora, Elkland, Grovespring, Success, Oscar, Centerville, Lesterville, Cobalt City, Patton, Sedgewickville, Daisy, New Wells, Pocahontas • ILLINOIS: Alto Pass, Carbondale, Carterville, Energy, Johnston City, Akin, Diamond City, Springerton, Burnt Prairie, Bellmont, St. Francisville • INDIANA: Vincennes, Bicknell, Westphalia, Bloomfield, Bloomington, Unionville, Helmsburg, Spearsville, Marietta, Shelbyville, Rushville, Harrisburg, Richmond • OHIO: Gettysburg, Verona, Nashville, Tipp City, North Hampton, Springfield, Catawba, Tradersville, Columbus, Whitehall, Jacksontown, Gratiot, Hopewell, Zanesville, Opperman, Mount Ephraim, Calais, Ozark, Clarington • WEST VIRGINIA: Wileyville, Fairmont, Newburg, Arthur, Rig, Lost City • VIRGINIA: Edinburg, Mount Jackson, Sperryville, Culpepper, Fredericksburg, Woodford, Bowling Green, Millers Tavern, Dutton.

TEAPOT: MET

Detonation Date: 15 Apr 1955 • *Detonation Time:* 11:15 A.M. • *Area:* Frenchman's Flat • *Sponsor:* Los Alamos, Department of Defense • *Yield:* 22 kt • *Radiation Level at Ground Zero:* 10 R/hr • *Height of Burst:* 400 ft • *Cloud Top Height:* 40,300 ft

40,000-Foot Trajectory: NEVADA: (Pintwater Range), (Pahranagat Range), (Delmar Mountains), Elgin • UTAH: Uvada, (Escalante Desert), Circleville, Junction, Greenwich, Fremont, (San Rafael Knob), (Windowblind Peak), (East Tavaputs Plateau), (Sweetwater Canyon) • COLORADO: (Douglas Pass), Buford, Phippsburg, Oak Creek, (Muddy Pass), Rand, Gould, (Cameron Pass), Poudre Park, Livermore, Wellington, Hereford • NEBRASKA: (Johnson Township, highest point in Nebraska), Kimball, Dix, Potter, Gurley, Oshkosh, Arthur, (Three Mile Lake), Halsey, Purdum, Emmet, O'Neill, Page, Winnetoon, Bazile Mills, Bloomfield, Bow Valley, Hartingen, Obert, Maskell • SOUTH DAKOTA: Vermillion, Burbank, Hub City, Junction City, Big Springs • IOWA: Elk Point, LeMars, Remsen, Peterson, Cornell, Gillett Grove, Ayrshire, Rodman, Whiltemore, Hobarton, Algona, Sexton, Wesley, Hutchins, Britt, Duncan, Miller, Ventura, Clear Lake, Emery, Central Heights, Mason City, Nora Springs, Floyd, Colwell, Alata Vista, Jerico, Little Turkey, Fort Atkinson, Ossian, Frankville, Rossville, Volney, Waukon • WISCONSIN: Prairie du Chien, Wauzeka, Woodman, Ridgeway, Dodgeville, Daleyville, Paoli, Belleville, Edgerton, Indianford, Milton, Lima Center, Burlington, Union Grove, Racine, Kenosha • MICHIGAN: Hagar Shores, Riverside, Milburg, Watervliet, Keeler, Dowagiac, Volina, Wakelee, Vandalia, Jones, Constantine, Mottville • INDIANA: Bristol, Middlebury, Shipshewana, Lagrange, Plato, Stroh, Woodruff, Hudson, Ashley, Hamilton • OHIO: Edgerton, Farmer, Brunersburg, Defiance, Ayersville, New Bavaria, Holgate, Prentiss, Belmore, Townwood, McComb, Findlay, Upper Sandusky, Wyandott, Caledonia, Denmark, Mount Gilead, Pulaskiville, Waterford, Fredericktown, Howard,

Millwood, Newcastle, New Guilford, West Bedford, Cooperdale, New Moscow, Adams Mills, Conesville, Bloomfield, Cambridge, Greenwood, Whigville, Calais, Mittonsburg, Woodsfield, Laings, Round Botton, Hannibal • WEST VIRGINIA: New Martinsville, Porters Falls, Reader, Folsom, Sedalia, Clarksburg, Rangoon, Belington, Elkins, Red Creek, Harmon, Onego, Milam • VIRGINIA: (Shenandoah Mountains), Bergton, Fulks Run, Timberville, Broadway, New Market, Tenth Legion, Alma, Haywood, Brightwood, Madison, Aroda, Rapidan, Paytes, Post Oak, Snell, Thornburg, Milford, Owenton, Stephens Church, Bruington, Truhart, Saluda, Glenns, Hartfield, Hudgins, Diggs, (Chesapeake Bay), Eastville, Cheriton, (Wreck Island), (Cobb Island).

Teapot: Apple-2

Detonation Date: 5 May 1955 • *Detonation Time:* 5:10 A.M. • *Area:* 1 • *Sponsor:* Los Alamos • *Yield:* 29 kt • *Radiation Level at Ground Zero:* 500 R/hr • *Height of Burst:* 500 ft • *Cloud Top Height:* 51,000 ft

30,000-Foot Trajectory: NEVADA: (Shoshone Peak), (Belted Range), (Egan Range), (Snake Range), (Humbolt National Forest) • UTAH: Trout Creek, Faust, Vernon, Fairfield, Oram, Provo, (Daniels Pass), Fruitland, Upalco, Myton, Randlett • COLORADO: Rangely, Rio Blanco, New Castle, Glenwood Springs, Cardiff, Cattle Creek, El Jezebel, Basalt, Snowmass, Woody Creek, Aspen, (Mount Elbert, highest point in Colorado), Twin Lakes, (Weston Pass), Fairplay, Estabrook, Pine, Foxton, South Platte, Leuviers, Littleton, Bennett, Strasburg, Woodrow, Akron, Platner • NEBRASKA: Champion, Wellfleet, Lexington, Overton, Elm Creek, Kearney, Minden, Norman, Bladen, Superior, Hardy • KANSAS: Republic, Rydal, Wayne, Agenda, Clyde, Vining, Clifton, Morganville, Fort Riley, Manhattan, Ogden, Miller, Osage City, Melvern, Agricola, Waverly, Harris, Garnett, Bush City, Blue Mound, Mantey, Harding, Fulton • MISSOURI: Richard, Deerfield, Nevada, Milo, Montevallo, Jerico Springs, Arcola, Dadeville, Walnut Grove, Ash Grove, Williard, Springfield, Nichols, Battlefield, Nixa, Linden, Ozark, Sparta, Chadwick, Bradleyville, Brownbranch, Longrun, Theodosia, Isabella, Howards Ridge • ARKANSAS: Gemalel, Viola, Mitchell, Wiseman, Sidney, Mount Pleasant, Cave City, Saffell, Dowdy, Egypt, Cash, Otwell, Bay, Caraway, Trumann, Keiser, Marie, Driver, Osceola • TENNESSEE: Garland, Covington, Stanton, Hillville, Uptonville, Henderson, Enville, Saltillo, Clifton, Center, Webber City, Campbellsville, Wales, Frankewing, McBurg, Fayetteville, Skinem, Coldwater, Bellview, Lincoln, Elora, Anderson, Richard City, New Hope • ALABAMA: Bryant • GEORGIA: New England, (Lookout Mountain), Chickamauga, Tunnel Hill, Elton, Crandell, Cherry Log, Robertstown, Helen, Batesville, Turnerville, Tallulah Falls • SOUTH CAROLINA: Long Creek, Westminster, Seneca, Clemson, Utica, Central, Pelzer, Woodville, Owings, Gray Court, Cross Anchor, Sedalia, Delta, Whitmire, Tuckertown, Shelton, Salemn Crossroads, White Oak, Winnsboro Mills, Langtown, DeKalb, Lucknow, Una, Lydia, Oats, Florence, Quinby, Peedee, Blue Brick, Marion, Zion, Nichols, Mullins • NORTH CAROLINA: Tabor City, Mollie, Nakina, Cruise Island, Winnabow, Bolivia, Boiling Spring Lakes, Seabreeze, Carolina Beach, Kure Beach.

Teapot: Zucchini

Detonation Date: 15 May 1955 • *Detonation Time:* 5:00 A.M. • *Area:* 7–1a • *Sponsor:* Los Alamos • *Yield:* 28 kt • *Radiation Level at Ground Zero:* 500 R/hr • *Height of Burst:* 500 ft • *Cloud Top Height:* 40,000 ft

40,000-Foot Trajectory: NEVADA: (Delmar Mountains) • UTAH: (Morman Range), Central, New Harmony, Cedar City, Summit, Parowan, Panguitch, Teasdale, Grover, Torrey, Bicknell, (Temple Mountain), Green River, (East Tavaputs Plateau), Bonanza • COLORADO: Dinosaur, (Dinosaur National Monument), Greystone, (Vermillion Bluffs) • WYOMING: Table

Rock, Wamsutter, Red Desert, (Great Divide Basin), (Green Mountains), Jeffrey City, Gas Hills, Moneta, Lyside, Lost Cabin, Hyattsville, Greybull, Shell, (Bald Mountain), Kane, Lovell, (Horseshoe Bend) • MONTANA: (Bighorn Lake), Crow Indian Reservation, Billings, Lockwood, Huntley, Shepherd, Warden, Klein, Roundup, Forestgrove, Hilger, Christina, Suffolk, Iliad, Eagleton, Rocky Boy • MINNESOTA: Greenbush, Strathcona, (Mud Lake), Goodridge, High Landing, Trail, Gully, Lengby, Ebro, Roy Lake, Ponsford, Snellman, Osage, Wolf Lake, Midway, Evergreen, Hillview, Bluffton, Wrightstown, Eagle Bend, Clotho, Little Sauk, Ward Springs, Melrose, Greenwald, St. Martin, Roscoe, Paynesville, Crow River, Grove City, Litchfield, Greenleaf, Corvuso, Cedar Mills, Hutchinson, Stewart, Brownton, Ferando, New Auburn, Winthrop, Gaylord, Norseland, St. Peter, Kasota, Mankato, Eagle Lake, Smiths Mill, St. Clair, Alma City, Waldorf, Matawan, Minnesota Lake, Freeborn, Manchester, Albert Lea, Twin Lakes, Emmons, Glenville • IOWA: Silver Lake, Kensett, Mankey, Rock Falls, Mason City, Nora Springs, Rockford, Marble Rock, Greene, Packard, Clarksville, Shell Rock, Waverly, Finchford, Cedar Falls, Waterloo, Garrison, Van Horne, Newhall, Norway, Walford, East Amana, Amana, Tiffin, Iowa City, Coralville, Hills, Lone Tree, Conesville, Fredonia, Wapello, Toolesboro, Oakville, Northfield Kingston • ILLINOIS: Oquawka, Gulf Port, Media, Bushnell, New Philadelphia, Ipava, Summum, Bath, Chandlerville, Curran, Chatlam, Glenarm, Pawnee, Morrisonville, Wenonah, Nokomis, Ramsey, St. Elmo, Altamont, Edgewood, La Clede, Iola, Louisville, Clay City, Wynoose, Samsville, Bone Gap, Gards Point, Mount Carmel • INDIANA: East Mount Carmel, Johnson, Owensville, Haubstadt, Warrenton, Elberfeld, Daylight, Chandler, Boonville, Pelzer, Yankeetown, Hatfield, Eureka, Richland, Patronville • KENTUCKY: Owensboro, Philpot, Whitesville, Fordsville, Short Creek, Leitchfield, Grayson Springs, Millerstown, Jonesville, Pikes View, Campbellsville, Hatcher, Yuma, Casy Creek, Pellyton, Dunnville, Mintonville, (Daniel Boone National Forest), Lidu, Bush, Bluehole, Ogle, Brightshade, Roark, Chappell, Gilley, Benham • VIRGINIA: Keokee, Big Stone Gap, East Stone Gap, Fort Blackmore, Nickelsville, Collinwood, Benhams • NORTH CAROLINA: Baldwin, Fleetwood, Moravian Falls, Love Valley, Union Grove, Turnersburg, Harmony, Cooleemee, Churchland, Cid, Denton, Farmer, Utah, Seagrove, Highfalls, Parkwood, Spout Springs, Spring Lake, Fayettevile, Vanda, Stedman, Autreyville, Parkersburg, Ingold, Harrells, Penderlea, Watha, Holly Ridge.

PLUMBBOB: BOLTZMANN

Detonation Date: 28 May 1957 • *Detonation Time:* 5:55 A.M. • *Area:* 7c • *Sponsor:* Los Alamos • *Yield:* 12 kt • *Radiation Level at Ground Zero:* 20 R/hr • *Height of Burst:* 500 ft • *Cloud Top Height:* 33,000 ft

10,000-Foot Trajectory: NEVADA: Warm Springs, Manhattan, Luning, Hawthorne, Wellington, Lake Tahoe • CALIFORNIA: Tahoe Pines, (Squaw Valley Ski Area), Placerville, Loomis, Lincoln, Trobridge, Marysville, Yuba City, Hamilton City, Richfield, Red Bluff, Cottonwood, Redding, Weed, Edgewood, Gazelle, Yreka, Hornbrook, Hilt • OREGON: Ashland, Medford, Shady Grove, Drew, Cottage Grove, Springfield, Albany, Salem, Brooks, Newburg, Beaverton, Hillsboro, Burlington, Columbia City, Rainier • WASHINGTON: Longview, Lexington, Ryderwood, Curtis, Chehalis, Fords Prairie, Littlerock, Shelton, Port Angeles.

PLUMBBOB: FRANKLIN

Detonation Date: 2 Jun 1957 • *Detonation Time:* 4:55 A.M. • *Area:* 3 • *Sponsor:* Los Alamos • *Yield:* 140 tons • *Radiation Level at Ground Zero:* 35 R/hr • *Height of Burst:* 300 ft • *Cloud Top Height:* 16,700 ft

16,000-Foot Trajectory: NEVADA: (Belted Range), (Egan Range) • UTAH: (Frisco Peak), Minersville, Enoch, Cedar City, (Zion National Park), Rockville, Hilldale • ARIZONA: Colorado City, (Mount Trumbull), Hualapai Indian Reservation, Nelson, Yucca • CALIFORNIA:

Needles, (Sada Mountains), (Tiefort Mountains), Argos, Borosolvay, Dunmovin, Olancha, Cartago, (Mount Whitney), (Mount Woodworth), (Florence Lake), Mono, Hot Springs, (Ritter Range), (Eagle Peak), (Sweetwater Mountains) • NEVADA: Wellington, Smith, Wabuska, Silver Springs, Fernley, Nixon, (Seven Troughs Range), (Jackson Mountains), (Disaster Peak) • OREGON: (Trout Creek Mountains), Rome, Arock, Danner • IDAHO: Melba, Kuna, Bowmont, Mora, Boise, Idaho City, Stanley, Sunbeam, Bonanza, Challis, May, Leadore, (Continental Divide) • MONTANA: Bell, Lima, (Beaverhead National Forest), Raynolds Pass, West Yellowstone • WYOMING: (Mount Holmes), Canyon, Pelican Cone, (Sleeping Giant Mountain), (Buffalo Bill Dam), Cody, (Elk Butte), Manderson, Ten Sleep, Sussex, (Thunder Basin National Grassland) • NEBRASKA: Chadron, Hay Springs, (Big Hill), Broken Bow, Litchfield, Poole, Wood River, Diniphan, Hansen, Trumbull, Harvard, Saronville, Sutton, Geneva, Milligan, Tobias, Swanton, Plymouth, Beatrice, Filley, Elk Creek, Howe, Stella, Shubert, Barada • MISSOURI: Craig, Corning, Maryville, Skidmore, Arkoe, Conception Junction, Gentry, Bethany, Modena, Spickard, Osgood, Milan, Green Castle, Novenger, Pure Air, Kirksville, Hardland, Edina, Knox City, La Belle, Monticello, Canton • ILLINOIS: Meyer, Mendon, Camp Point, Clayton, Mount Sterling, Ripley, Bluff Spring, Philadelphia, Ashland, Pleasant Plains, Springfield, Riverton, Mechanicsburg, Decatur, Elwin, Mt. Zion, Lake City, Lovington, Arthur, Arcola, Bushton, Kansas, Paris, Grandview, Elbridge, Vermillion, Dennison • INDIANA: St. Mary-of-the-Woods, North Terre Haute, Brazil, Harmony, Reelsville, Manhattan, Belle Union, Crown Center, Hall, Bethany, Waverly, Stones Crossing, New Whiteland, Whiteland, Needam, Shelbyville, Rays Crossing, Blue Ridge, New Salem, Milroy, Richland, Andersonville, Laurel, Blooming Grove, Bath, Mixerville • OHIO: Morning Sun, West Elkton, Greenbush, Franklin, Springboro, Lytle, Ridgeville, Corwin, Kingman, Reeseville, Sabina, Staunton, Good Hope, Austin, Greenland, Andersonvile, Kinnickinnick, South Bloomingville, Hue, Mount Pleasant, Orland, New Plymouth, The Plains, Athens, Canaanville, Stewart, Little Hocking • WEST VIRGINIA: Parkersburg, Cedar Grove, Belmont, Wick Mountain, Alma, Lima, Alvy, Smithfield, Mannington, Arnettsville, Westover, Morgantown, Hazelton • PENNSYLVANIA: Markleysburg, Addison, Springs, West Salisbury, Boynton, Salisbury, Pocahontas, Pleasant Union, Wellersburg, Purcell, Inglesmith, Buck Valley, Plum Rush, Sylven, Claylick, Welsh Run, Shady Grove, Waynesboro, Fountain Dale, Green Mounds, Barlow • MARYLAND: Silver Run, Union Mills, Hampstead, Whitehouse, Butler, Sparks, Sunnybrook, Sweet Air, Perry Hall, White Marsh, Chase, Newtown, Melitota, Chestertown, Barclay, Roberts, Mount Zion, Henderson • DELAWARE: Petersburg, Sandtown, Felton, Masten Corner, Chestnut Knoll, Milford, Lincoln, Milton, Nassau, Harbeson, Angola, Seabreeze, Cottonpatch Hill.

Plumbbob: Wilson

Detonation Date: 18 Jun 1957 • *Detonation Time:* 4:55 A.M. • *Area:* 9a • *Sponsor:* Livermore Laboratory • *Yield:* 10 kt • *Radiation Level at Ground Zero:* 20 R/hr • *Height of Burst:* 500 ft • *Cloud Top Height:* 35,000 ft

10,000-Foot Trajectory: NEVADA: Lathrop Wells, (Funeral Mountains) • CALIFORNIA: (Death Valley), (Last Chance Range) • NEVADA: (Magruder Mountain), Lida, (Montezuma Peak), Tonopah, (Pinion Peak), (Pancake Range), (Mount Hamilton), Steptoe, Tippett • UTAH: Ibapah, (Great Salt Lake Desert), Grantsville, Salt Lake City, Layton, Syracuse, Clearfield, Roy, Ogden, Laketown • WYOMING: Cokeville, Calpert, La Barge, (Continental Peak), (Great Divide Basin), Bairvil, Muddy Gap, (Emigrant Gap), Casper, Clareton, Newcastle, Osage, Four Corners • SOUTH DAKOTA: Cheyenne Crossing, Deadwood, Lead, Sturgis, Stoneville, Faith, Red Elm, Glencross, Trail City, Mobridge, Glenham, Eureka • NORTH DAKOTA: Venturia, Ashley, Fredonia, Jud, Nortonville, Millarton, Montpelier, Ypsilanti, Eckelson, Rogers, Dazey, Sibley, Cooperstown, Sharon, Aneta, Northwood, Kempton, Karimore, Arvilla, Honeyford, Gilby, McKinock, Manvel, Ardoch • MINNESOTA: Oslo, Aluorado, Argyle, Strandquist, Strathcona, Wannaska, Pencer, Roosevelt, Wheelers Point.

PLUMBBOB: PRISCILLA

Detonation Date: 24 Jun 1957 • *Detonation Time:* 6:30 A.M. • *Area:* Frenchman's Flat • *Sponsor:* Los Alamos, Department of Defense • *Yield:* 37 kt • *Radiation Level at Ground Zero:* 500 R/hr • *Height of Burst:* 700 ft • *Cloud Top Height:* 43,000 ft

40,000-Foot Trajectory: NEVADA: Alamo, Ash Springs, Caliente • UTAH: Uvada, Moderna, Beryl, Circleville, Junction, Loa, Lyman, Bicknell, (Canyons National Park), Dead Horse Point, La Sal • COLORADO: Bedrock, Mount Wilson, Lizard Head Pass, San Juan Mountains, Conejos Peak, (Rio Grande National Forest), Ortiz • NEW MEXICO: Los Pinos, Cerro, Valdez, Eagle Nest, Arroyo Ceso, Angel Fire, Black Lake, Ocate, Wagon Mound, Roy, Solano, Mosquero, Galegos • TEXAS: Glenrio, Hereford, Arney, Happy, Tulia, Rock Creek, Silverton, Gasoline, Flomot, White Flat, Paducah, Sneedville, Chalk, Benjamin, Rhineland, Munday, Throckmorton, Woodson, Crystal Falls, Caddo, Frankell, Huckaby, Stephenville, Selden, Duffau, Iredell, Meridian, Cranfill's Gap, Valley Mills, China Spring, Waco, Bellmead, Riesel, Otto, Ben Hur, Groesbeck, Thornton, Oletha, Jewett, Donie, Buffalo, Crockett, Latexo, Kennard, Ratcliff, Clawson, Central, Lufkin, Redland, Etoile, Chireno, Norwood, Penning, San Augustine, Fords, Corner, Sexton • LOUISIANA: Zwole, Natchitoches, Robaline, Natchez, Hazlewood, St. Maurice, Atlanta, Packton, Urania, Kelley, Olla, Clarks, Rosefield, Holum, Grayson, Fort Necessity, Extension, Jigger, Chase, Newlight, Somerset, Afton, Mound • MISSISSIPPI: Edwards, Oakley, Bolton, Raymound Forest, Jackson, Pelhatchie, Morton, Kalem, Forest, Conehatla, Lake, Decatur, Duffee, Collinsville, Susqualena, Martin, Obadiah, Daleville, Lauderdale • ALABAMA: Sumpterville, Epes, Forkland, Greensboro, Heiberger, Stanton, Maplesville, Fairview, Coopers, Verbena, Mountain Creek, Equality, Nixburg, Cottage Grove, Jacksons Gap, Dadeville, Lafayette, Buffalo, Fredonia • GEORGIA: La Grange, Stovall, Greenville, Gay, Woodbury, Molena, Meansville, Zebulon, Aldora, Milner, Barnesville, Forsyth, Juliette, East Juliette, Round Oak, Wayside, Devereaux, Sparta, Calverton, Jewell, Dearing, Boneville, Harlem, Grovetown, Martinez • SOUTH CAROLINA: Augusta, Graniteville, Aiken, Vaucluse, Wagener, New Holland, Thor, Pelion, Gaston, Gadsden, Eastover, Statesburg, Horatio, Dalzell, Oswego, St. Charles, Lynchburg, Atkins, Cartersville, Timmonsville, Florence, Quinby, Peedee, Blue Brick, Sellers, Floyd Dale, Kemper • NORTH CAROLINA: Orrum, Bladenburg, Abbottsburg, Butters, Elizabethtown, Tomahawk, Harrells, Delway, Wallace, Teachey, Rose Hill, Greenovers, Chinquapin, Lyman, Beulaville, Fountain, Catherine Lake, Richlands, Petersburg, Belgrade, Pollocksville, Riverdale, Croatan, Rhems, New Bern, Minnesott Beach, Arapahoe, Olympia, Merritt, Stonewall, Bayboro, Mesic, Florence, Hoboken, Pamlico Point, Bluff Point, New Holland, Gulrock, Rodantha, Waves, Salvo.

PLUMBOB: HOOD

Detonation Date: 5 Jul 1957 • *Detonation Time:* 4:40 A.M. • *Area:* 9a • *Sponsor:* Livermore Laboratory • *Yield:* 74 kt • *Radiation Level at Ground Zero:* 100 R/hr • *Height of Burst:* 1,500 ft • *Cloud Top Height:* 48,000 ft

10,000-Foot Trajectory: NEVADA: (Railroad Valley), Duckwater, Duckwater Indian Reservation, (Butte Mountains), Currie, Wendover • UTAH: (Great Salt Lake Desert), (Dolphin Island), Snowville • IDAHO: Woodruff, Samaria, Dayton, Clifton, Banida, Mink Creek, Bern, Bennington • WYOMING: Smoot, (Salt River Range), Halfway, Merna, (Gannett Peak, highest point in Wyoming: 13,806 feet), (Wind River Range), Burris, Hamilton Dome, Winchester, Worland, (Powder River Pass), Upton, Four Corners • SOUTH DAKOTA: Nemo, Piedmont, Blackhawk, Hereford, Milesville, Hayes, Pierre, Lower Brule Indian Reservation, Crow Creek Indian Reservation, Wessington Springs, Lane, Artesian, Carthage, Roswell, Ramona, Madison, Nunda, Rutland, Ward • MINNESOTA: Verdi, Ruthton, Garvin, Godahl, La Salle, Garden City, Good Thunder, Mapleton, Waldorf, New Richland, Blooming Prairie, Oslo, Hayfield,

High Forest, Stewartville, Chatfield, Peterson, Whalan, Houston, Bratsberg, Brownsville • WISCONSIN: Stoddard, Genoa, Chaseburg, Newry, Westby, Bloomgingdale, Rockton, Valley, Hillsboro, Union Center, Wonewoc, Lake Delton, Wisconsin, Dells, Briggsville, Friesland, Cambria, Fox Lake, Waupun, Brownsville, Knowles, Le Roy, Le Mira, Kewaskum, Random Lake, Belgium, Cedar Grove • MICHIGAN: Roosevelt Park, Norton Shores, Cloverville, Conklin, Alpine, Grand Rapids, Saranac, Portland, Eagle, Grand Lodge, Lansing, Okemos, Haslett, Williamston, Bell Oak, Oak Grove, Fowlerville, Howell, Hartland, Highland, Milford, Walled Lake, Commerce, Farmington Hills, Southfield, Ferndale, Oak Park, Highland Park, Detroit, Grosse Point Woods, (Lake St. Clair) • ONTARIO: Windsor, Tecumseh, Belle River, S. Woodslee, Comber, Wheatley • OHIO: (Hubbard Homestead), Ashtabula, North Kingsville, Bashnell, Kellogsville, Monroe Center • PENNSYLVANIA: Pennside, Springboro, Hickernell, Mosiertown, Saegertown, New Richmond, Blooming Valley, Townville, Troy Center, Gresham, Titusville, E. Titusville, Pleasantville, West Hickory, Starr, Guitonville, Marienville, Roses, Halfton, Portland Mills, Brandy Camp, Toby, Byrnedale, Force, Weedville, Caledonia, Karthaus, Pine Glen, Clarence, Howard, Jacksonville, Nittany, Lamar, Clintondale, Tylerville, Livonia, Hartleton, Millmont, White Springs, Dice, New Berlin, Kratzerville, Shamokin Dam, Sunbury, Selinsgrove, Edgewood, Shamokin, Gowen City, Ranshaw, Kulpmont, Locust Gap, Helfenstein, Gordon, Primrose, Minersvile, Jonestown, Marlin, Pottsville, Mount Carbon, Schuylkill Haven, Adamsdale, Orwigsburg, Deer Lake, Eckville, Port Clinton, Albany, Lenhartsville, Klinesville, Grimville, Maxatawney, Trexlertown, Breinigsville, Alburtis, Mertztown, Macungie, Shimerville, Old Zionsville, Zionsville, Spinnerstown, Milford Square, Rich Hill, Hargersville, Blooming Glen, Dublin, Plumsteadville, Gardenville, Danbord, Fountainville, Mechanicsville, Lahaska, Buckingham, Doylestown, Furlong, Pineville, Penns Park, Washington Crossing, Yardley, Marrisville • NEW JERSEY: Ewing, Trenton, White Horse, Groveville, Creamridge, Hornerstown, Lakehurst, Ridgeway, Pine Lake Park, Toms River, Gilford Park, Pine Beach, Bay Shore, Island Heights, (Pelican Island), Seaside Heights, Seaside Park, South Seaside Park.

PLUMBBOB: DIABLO

Detonation Date: 15 Jul 1957 • *Detonation Time:* 4:30 A.M. • *Area:* 2b • *Sponsor:* Livermore Laboratory • *Yield:* 17 kt • *Radiation Level at Ground Zero:* 200 R/hr • *Height of Burst:* 500 ft • *Cloud Top Height:* 32,000 ft

30,000-Foot Trajectory: NEVADA: Indian Springs, Las Vegas, Overton, Logandale, Mesquite • UTAH: Santa Clara, Pine Valley, New Harmony, Kanarraville, Cedar City, Enoch, Summit, Parowan, Paragonah, Circleville, Junction, Marysvale, Monroe, Annabella, Glenwood, Sigurd, Salina, Price, Helper, Kenilworth, Bridgeland, Roosevelt, Cedarview, Whiterocks, Tridell, Dry Fork, (Mount Lena) • WYOMING: (Richard's Mountain), Red Desert, Creston, Shirley Basin, (Laramie Mountains), Douglas, Orpha, Lance Creek • SOUTH DAKOTA: Pringle, Fairburn, Hermosa, Owanka, Wall, Quinn, Ottumwa, Hayes, Fort Pierre, Pierre, Blunt, Harrold, Holabird, Highmore, Ree Heights, Miller, St. Lawrence, Veyland, Wessington, Bonilla, Hitchcock, Broadland, Carpenter, Willow Lake, Bryant, Vienna, Lake Norden, Hayti, Dempster, Estelline, Toronto, Astoria • MINNESOTA: Hendricks, Wilno, Ivanhoe, Marshall, Lynd, Revere, Lamberton, Sanborn, Comfrey, Sveadahl, Darfur, St. James, Grogan, Lewisville, Winnebago, Huntley, Delavan, Frost, Bricelyn, Kiester • IOWA: Scarville, Lake Mills, Leland, Ventura, Clear Lake, Thornton, Latimer, Iowa Falls, New Providence, St. Anthony, Clemons, Melbourne, Newton, Rasnor, Otley, Flagler, Pershing, Attica, Maysville, Weller, Melrose, Iconium, Mystic, Brazil, Centerville, Numa, Cincinnati • MISSOURI: Hartford, Pure Air, Melrose, Ethel, New Cambria, Kaseyville, Prairie Hill, Salisbury, Forest Green, Glasgow, Lisbon, Boonesboro, Boonville, Pilot Grove, Bellair, Syracuse, Stover, Climax Springs, Urbana, Louisburg, Halfway, Brighton, Pleasant Hope, Glidewell, Springfield, Clever, Aurora, McDowell, Ridgley, Exeter • ARKANSAS: Pea Ridge, Bentonville, Rogers, Highfill, Robinson, Siloam Springs • OKLAHOMA: West Siloam Springs, Kansas, Daks, Leach, Peggs, Yonkers, Wagover, Red Bird, Coweta, Leonard, Mounds, Slick, Beggs, Nuyaka, Henryetta, Pharoah, Vernon, Hanna, Indianola, Krebs, Alderson, Dow, Haileyville, Hartshorne, Daisy, Jumbo, Miller, Farris, Boehler, Sunkist, Cade, Bokchito, Utika, Achille, Hendrix • TEXAS: Denison, Bells, Ida, Tom Bean, Sherman, Gunter, Tioga, Pilot Point, Sanger, Boliver, Krum, Ponder, Argyle, Justin, Roanoke, Bartonville, Grand Prairie, Arlington, Irving, Midlothian, Waxahachie, Maypearl, Italy, Frost, Milford, Martens, Emmett, Irene, Malone, Mount Calm, Axtell, Mart, Riesel, Ben Hur, Otto, Perry, Marlin, Cedar Springs, Rosebud, Baileyville, Burlington, Ben Arnold, Cameron, Minerva, Milano, Rockdale, Tanglewood, Old Dime Box, Lincoln, Dime Box, Hills, Giddings, Winchester, West Point, Plum, Muldoon, High Hill, Engle, Moravia, Breslau, Shiner, Sweet Home, Halletsville, Speaks, Cordele, Louise, Danevang, Bay City.

PLUMBBOB: JOHN

Detonation Date: 19 Jul 1957 • *Detonation Time:* 7:00 A.M. • *Area:* 10 • *Sponsor:* Department of Defense • *Yield:* Approximately 2 kt • *Radiation Level at Ground Zero:* None detected • *Height of Burst:* 20,000 ft • *Cloud Top Height:* 44,000 ft

40,000-Foot Trajectory: NEVADA: Currant, Ruth, Steptoe • UTAH: Wendover, Park Valley, Clear Creek • IDAHO: Naf, Bridge, Sublett, Rockland, American Falls, Pocatello, Chubbock, Blackfoot, Basalt, Shelly, Idaho Falls, Ammon, Lincoln, Ucon, Ririe, Heise, Archer, Rexburg, Teton, Drummond, Marysville, Warm River • WYOMING: (Old Faithful in Yellowstone National Park), (Craig Pass), Canyon, (Dunraven Pass), Tower Junction • MONTANA: (Gallatin National Forest), Limestone, Greycliff, Reedpoint, Rapelje, Belmont, Lavina, Flatwillow, Cat Creek, Mosby, (Fort Peck Lake), Frazier, Fort Peck Indian Reservation, Plentywood, Westby.

PLUMBBOB: KEPLER

Detonation Date: 24 Jul 1957 • *Detonation Time:* 4:50 A.M. • *Area:* 4 • *Sponsor:* Los Alamos • *Yield:* 10 kt • *Radiation Level at Ground Zero:* 100 R/hr • *Height of Burst:* 500 ft • *Cloud Top Height:* 28,000 ft

20,000-Foot Trajectory: NEVADA: (Papoose Range), (Timpahute Range), • UTAH: Garrison, (Cedar Mountains), (Great Salt Lake), Corinne, River City, Honeyville, Garland, Fielding, Newton, Clarkston, Lewiston • IDAHO: Franklin, St. Charles, Paris, Bloomington, Montpelier • WYOMING: Daniel, Pinedale, Crowheart, Wind River Indian Reservation, (Owl Creek Mountains), Thermopolis, East Thermopolis, Lucerne, Kirby, Ten Sheep, (Powder River Pass), Buffalo, Weston, Colony • SOUTH DAKOTA: Hoover, Zeona, Meadow, Bullhead, Walker • NORTH DAKOTA: Fort Yates, Strasburg, Wishek, Lehr, Merricourt, Monango, Crete, Gwinner, Milnor, De Lamere, Wyndmere, Barney, Wahpeton • MINNESOTA: Breckenridge, Everdell, Fergus Falls, Underwood, Urbank, Perkers Prairie, Rose City, Flensburg, Little Falls, Buckman, Ramey, Morrill, Milaca, Grandy, Stanchfield, Stark, Harris • WISCONSIN: Atlas, Trade Lake, Frederic, Clam Falls, Barranett, Haugen, Brill, Mikana, Ladysmith, Jump River, Little Chicago, Wausau, Schofield, Ringle, Hatley, Norrie, Wittenberg, Pella, Caroline, Embarrass, Navarino, Nichols, Briarton, Seymour, DePere, Morrison, Wayside, Reedsville, Whitelaw, Manitowoc • MICHIGAN: Whitehall, Dalton, Casnovia, Harrisburg, Sparta, Belmont, Rockford, Cannonsburg, Lowell, Saramac, Portland, Eagle, Grand Lodge, Lansing, Millett, Dimondale, Golt, Mison, Dansville, Millville, Plainfield, Gregory, Hell, Ann Arbor, Dixboro, Ypsilanti, Carleton, Rockwood, South Rockwood, Newport, Estral Beach • OHIO: Lorain, Sheffield Lake, North Ridgeville, Elyria, Columbia Station, Brunswick, Weymouth, Sharon Center, Norton, Barberton, Liberty, Greensburg, Marshand, North Canton, East Canton, Mapleton, Oneida, Pattersonville, Wattsville, North Canton, East Canton, Mapleton, Oneida, Pattersonville, Wattsville, Bergholz, Richmond, Steubenville, Colliers • WEST VIRGINIA: Follansbee, Wellsburg • PENNSYLVANIA: Penowa, Avella, West Middletown, Washington, Gabby Heights, Vestaburg, LaBelle, Millsboro, East Millsboro, Isabella, Filbert, Hibbs, New Salem, Uledi, Newcomer, Fairchance, Elliotsville • MARYLAND: Asher Glade, Selbysport, Friendville, Accident, Bitlinger, Luke, Bloomington, Westernport, McCoole • WEST VIRGINIA: Keyser, Burlington, Junction, Rio, Wardensville • VIRGINIA: Mount Olive, Maurertown, Detrick, Bentonville, Viewtown, Rixeyville, Brandy Station, Richardsville, Flat Run, Fredericksburg, Four Mile Fork, Guinea, Villboro, Bowling Green, Spark, Millers Tavern, Center Cross, Laneview, Church View, Urbanna, Locust Hill, Hartfield, Dixie, Amburg, Deltaville, Gwynn, Hudgins, Diggs, Eastville, Cheriton, Bay View, (Ship Shoal Island).

PLUMBBOB: OWENS

Detonation Date: 25 Jul 1957 • *Detonation Time:* 6:30 A.M. • *Area:* 9b • *Sponsor:* Livermore Laboratory • *Yield:* 9.7 kt • *Radiation Level at Ground Zero:* 1,000 R/hr • *Height of Burst:* 500 ft • *Cloud Top Height:* 35,000 ft

10,000-Foot Trajectory: NEVADA: Currant, (Pancake Summit), Ruby Valley, Lamoille, (Secret Pass), (Humboldt Range), Wells, Metropolis, Thousand Springs, Contact, Jackpot • IDAHO: Rogerson, Kimberly, Eden, Dietrich, Picabo, Gannett, (Borah Peak, highest point in Idaho), Small • WYOMING: (Yellowstone National Park), West Thumb, Pahaska, (Windy Mountain), (Bear Tooth Pass) • MONTANA: Belfry, St. Xavier, Busby, Lame Deer, Ashland, San Labre Mission, (Custer National Forest) • SOUTH DAKOTA: Camp Crook, Zeona, Maurine, Isabel, Firested, Timber Lake, Wakpale, Mobridge, Herreid, Artas • NORTH DAKOTA: Zeeland, Wishek, Nortonville, Jud, Grand Rapids, La Moure, Verona, Stirum, Gwinner, Cayuga, Sisseton Indian Reservation • SOUTH DAKOTA: Velben, Hammer, Claire City, Sisseton, Peever, Big Stone City • MINNESOTA: Beardsley, (Hartford Beach State Park), Ortonville, Odessa, Louisburg, Milan, Watson, Montevideo, Wegdahl, Granite Falls, North Redwood, Evan, Cobden, Sleepy Eye, Leavenworth, Darfur, Butterfield, Mountain Lake, Bergen, Alpha, Jackson, Petersburg • IOWA: Huntington, Superior, Terril, Dickens, Greenville, Rossio, Peterson, Cherokee, Quimby, Washta, Pierson, Climbing Hill, Sloan • NEBRASKA: Walthill, Pender, Wisner, Clarkson, Schuyler, Columbus, Bellwood, Rising City, Surprise, Cresham, Waco, Lushton, Grafton, Sutton, Ong, Davenport, Ruskin, Hardy • KANSAS: Webber, Lovewell, Formoso, Montrose, Jewell, Randall, Hunter, Ash, Grove, Lucas, (Wilson Lake).

PLUMBBOB: STOKES

Detonation Date: 7 Aug 1957 • *Detonation Time:* 5:25 A.M. • *Area:* 7b • *Sponsor:* Los Alamos • *Yield:* 19 kt • *Radiation Level at Ground Zero:* 50 R/hr • *Height of Burst:* 1,500 ft • *Cloud Top Height:* 37,000 ft

30,000-Foot Trajectory: NEVADA: Ely, Tippett • UTAH: Ibapah, Brigham City, Logan, Pickleville • WYOMING: Geneva, Afton, Bondurant, Dubois, Meeteetse, Lovell, Kane • MONTANA: (Bighorn Canyon), Saint Xavier, (Custer Battlefield), Castle Rock, Hathaway, Fort Keough, Miles City, Wibaux • NORTH DAKOTA: Grassy Butte, Parshall, Makoti, Logan, Granville, Denbigh, Towner, Rugby, Wolford, Bisbee, Egeland, Munich, Langdon, Leroy, Pembina • CANADA: Montreal • NEW YORK: Moopers Forks, West Chazy, Beekmantown, Plattsburgh, Clintonville, Westport, Mineville, Crown Point, Ticonderoga, Putnam Station, Clemons, Whitehall, South Hartford, Cossayuna, Salem, Greenwich, Johnsonville, West Steventown, New Concord, Hillsdale, West Copake, Hope Farm, Wingdale, Holmes, Brewster, Pleasantville, White Plains, New Rochelle, New York City.

PLUMBBOB: SHASTA

Detonation Date: 18 Aug 1957 • *Detonation Time:* 5:00 A.M. • *Area:* 2a • *Sponsor:* Livermore Laboratory • *Yield:* 17 kt • *Radiation Level at Ground Zero:* 500 R/hr • *Height of Burst:* 500 ft • *Cloud Top Height:* 32,000 ft

20,000-Foot Trajectory: NEVADA: (Belted Range), (Reveille Range), (Railroad Valley), (Pancake Range), (Pancake Summit), Cherry Creek, (Becky Peak), (Sugarloaf Peak) • UTAH: (Great Salt Lake), (Promontory Mountains), Corinne, Bear, River City, Wellsville, Deweyville, Logan, Providence, Hyrum, Round Valley, Laketown, (Bear Lake) • WYOMING: (Commissary Ridge), La Barge, Atlantic City, Gas Hills, (Pine Mountain), Bill • SOUTH DAKOTA: Edgemont, Smithwick, Manderson, Porcupine, Wounded Knee, Batesland • NEBRASKA: Merriman, Eli, Rose, Raeville, Petersburg, Creston, Leigh Ames, Fremont, Inglewood, Elk City, Bennington, Omaha • IOWA: Council Bluffs, Mineola, Malvern, Strahan, Imogene, Essex, Norwich, Yorktown, Shambaugh, Braddyville • MISSOURI: Clearmont, Pickering, Ravenwood, Conception, Gentryville, McFall, Pattenburg, Altamont, Gallatin, Breckinridge, Mooresville, Ludlow, Braymer, Coloma, Bogard, Carrollton, Bosworth, Malta Bend, Marshall, Napton, Nelson, Syracuse, Tipton, Fortuna, Latham, High Point, Etterville, Marys Home, Capps, St. Anthony, Iberia, Hancock, Dixon, Devils Elbow, Duke, Flat, Licking, Raymondville, Yukon, Eunice, Summersville, Pine Crest, Mountain View, Teresita, Thomasville, Rover, Alton, Couch, Myrtle • ARKANSAS: Dalton, Noland, Walnut Ridge, Hoxie, Sedgwick, Bono, Harrisburg, Payneway, Twist, Marion, West Memphis • MISSISSIPPI: Glower, Barks, Eudora, Arkabutle, Coldwater, Seratobia, New Town, Looxahoma, Taylor, Springdale, Water Valley, Bunner, Shepherd, Pittsboro, Calhoun City, Slate Spring, Houhenlinden, Maben, Sherwood, Reform, Bradley, Longview, Sturgis, Brooksville, Macon, Shuqualak, Paulette, Binnsville • ALABAMA: Panola, Warsaw, Gainsville, Boligee, Forkland, Prairieville, Gallion, Founsdale, Uniontown, Safford, Alberta, Boykin, Darlington, Rosebud, Oakhill, Pine Apple, Red Level, River Falls, Andalusa, Carolina, Libertyville, Florala • FLORIDA: Paxton (highest point in Florida), Glendale, Ponce de Leon, Live Oak, New Hope, Crystal Lake, Bennett, Wewahitchka, Sumatra, Carrabelle, (Gulf of Mexico), Palm Harbor, Ozona, Tampa, Center, Balm, Fort Lonesome, Fort Green, Wauchula, Zolfo Springs, Lake Placid, Brighton, (Lake Okeechobee), Palm City, Stuart, Jensen Beach, Sewall's Point.

PLUMBBOB: DOPPLER

Detonation Date: 23 Aug 1957 • *Detonation Time:* 5:30 A.M. • *Area:* 7a • *Sponsor:* Los Alamos • *Yield:* 11 kt • *Radiation Level at Ground Zero:* 50 R/hr • *Height of Burst:* 1,500 ft • *Cloud Top Height:* 38,000 ft

40,000-Foot Trajectory: NEVADA: (Papoose Range), (Pahranga Range), Hiko, (Wilson Creek Range) • UTAH: (Indian Peak), (Black Rock Desert), Flowell, Holden, Fayette, Ephraim, Manti, Hiawatha, Price, Wellington, Sunnyside, East Carbon, (Desolation Canyon), (Sweetwater Canyon) • COLORADO: (Douglas Pass), Rio Blanco, Burns, Bond, Green Mountain Camp, Geeny, (Arapahoe National Forest), Black Hawk, Central City, Golden, Arvada, Denver, Englewood, Aurora, Watkins, Bennett, Strasburg, Byers, Deer Trail, Shaw, Seibert, Vona, Stratton, Bethune, Burlington • KANSAS: Kanorado, Brownville, Monument, (Castle Rock), Brownell, McCracken, Hargrave, La Crosse, Bison, Shaffer, Otis, Olmitz, Albert, Heizer, Great Bend, Ellinwood, Silica, Raymond, Alden, Saxman, Sterling, Nickerson, Medora, Hutchinson, Halstead, Furley, Towanda, Haverhill, Leon, Latham, Elk Falls, Elk City, Bolton, Jefferson, Deating, Coffeyville • OKLAHOMA: South Coffeyville, Centralia, Vinita, Ketchum, Jay, Colcord, Siloam Springs, Watts, Ballard • ARKANSAS: Weddington, Farmington, Greenland, Prairie, Brentwood, Winslow, Ozark, Hunt, Atlas, Coal Hill, Midway, (Magazine Mountain, highest point in Arkansas: 2,753 feet), Bellevile, Plainview, Rover,

Mountain Pine, Royal, Lake Hamilton, Bismark, Caddo Valley, Arkadelphia, Curtis, Amy, Chidester, Camden, Buena Vista, Louann, Smackover, Shaler, Newell, Wesson, Junction City • LOUISIANA: Summerfield, Lisbon, Vienna, Ruston, Grambling, Clay, Ausley, Quitman, Hudson, Georgetown, Fishville, Kolin, Echo, Bunkie, Whiteville, Beggs, Washington, Grand Coteau, Carencro, Lafayette, Broussard, Youngsville, Abbevile, Delcambre, Avery Island, (Shell Keys).

The 40,000-foot trajectory passed over the highest point in Arkansas.

PLUMBBOB: FRANKLIN PRIME

Detonation Date: 30 Aug 1957 • *Detonation Time:* 5:40 A.M. • *Area:* 7b • *Sponsor:* Los Alamos • *Yield:* 4.7 kt • *Radiation Level at Ground Zero:* 100 R/hr • *Height of Burst:* 750 ft • *Cloud Top Height:* 32,000 ft

30,000-Foot Trajectory: NEVADA: Ash Springs, Alamo, Hiko, Caliento • UTAH: Deseret, Hinckley, Nephi, Provo, Orem, Hailstone, Lake Town • WYOMING: Cokeville, Bondurant, Valley, (Buffalo Bill Dam), (Bear Tooth Pass) • MONTANA: Red Lodge, Bear Creek, Joliet, Laurel, Billings, Musselshell, Sand Springs, Glasgow, Geltana • NEW YORK: Potsdam, Parishville, Saranac Lake, Whitehall • VERMONT: Poultney, (Green Mountain National Forest), Houghtonville, Cambridgeport, Bellows Falls • NEW HAMPSHIRE: Walpole, Surry, West Peterborough, Noone, Greenville, Mason • MASSACHUSETTS: Woburn, Lexington, Arlington, Medford, Boston, Beechwood, Egypt, Green Garbor, Hyannis Port.

PLUMBBOB: SMOKY

Detonation Date: 31 Aug 1957 • *Detonation Time:* 5:30 A.M. • *Area:* 2c • *Sponsor:* Livermore Laboratory • *Yield:* 44 kt • *Radiation Level at Ground Zero:* 300 R/hr • *Height of Burst:* 700 ft • *Cloud Top Height:* 38,000 ft

10,000-Foot Trajectory: NEVADA: (Shoshone Peak), Beatty, (Funeral Mountains) • CALIFORNIA: (Death Valley), Baker, Kelso, Essex • ARIZONA: Wikieiup, (Snow Mountain), Valentine, Truxton, Peach Springs, Lake Mead, (Hoover Dam) • NEVADA: (Sheep Range), (Timpahute Range), (Grant Range), Preston, Ely, East Ely, (Shell Creek Range), Goshute Indian Reservation • UTAH: Goshute Indian Reservation, (Great Salt Lake Desert), (Cedar Mountains), Grantsville, (Great Salt Lake), (Antelope Island), Brigham City, Wellsville, Logan, Smithfield, Richmond • IDAHO: Weston, Franklin, Whitney, Preston, Benida, Mink Creek, Thatcher, Bench, Grace, Soda Springs, Conda, Freedom • WYOMING: Etna, Freedom, Merna, (Wind River Range), (Wolverine Peak), Fort Washakie, Ethete, Kinnear, Riverton, Moneta, Hiland, Waltman, Powder River, Natrona, Bill • SOUTH DAKOTA: Rockford, Nemo, Piedmont, Elm Springs, Milesville, Hayes, Fort Pierre, Pierre, Crow Creek Indian Reservation, Gann Valley, Crow Lake, Storia, Mitchell, Ethan, Dimrock, Milltown, Menno, Mayfields, Volin, Vermillion, Elk Point, Jefferson, North Sioux City, Sioux City, South Sioux City • IOWA: Bronson, Climbing Hill, Holly Springs, Smithland, Ticonic, Ute, Dunlap, Earling, Westphalia, Marne, Atlantic, Cumberland, Mount Etna, Prescott, Stringtown, Diagonal, Mount Ayr • MISSOURI: Hatfield, Blue Ridge, Gilmar City, Bedford, Avalon, Hale, (Swan Lake), Triplett, Brunswick, Glasgow, Fayette, New Franklin, Rocheport, Wooldridge, Huntsdale, Columbia, Ashland, Holts Summit, Wainwright, Loose Creek, Bland, Bele, Cuba, Steelville, Cherryville, Courtois, Edgehill, (Taum Sauk Mountain, highest point in Missouri), Glover, Sabula, Coldwater, Gipsy, Zalma, Sturdivant, Advance, Painton, Morley, Blodgett, Diehlstadt, Charleston, Wyatt, Wilson City • KENTUCKY: Bardwell, Kirbyton, Fancy Farm, Mayfield, Kirksey, Murray, New Concord • TENNESSEE: Faxon, Waverly, Hurricane Mills, Bold Spring, Spot, Shipps Bend, Centerville, Twomey, Chapel Hill, Mount Pleasant, Culleoka, Mooresville, Lewisburg, Bellfast, Richmond, Booneville, Lynchburg, Winchester, Estill Springs, Decherd, Alto, Sewanee, Monteagle, Sequatchie, Victoria, (Signal Mountain), Ridgeside, McDonald, Waterville, Parksville, Benton, Reliance, Servilla, Cokercreek, (Great Smoky Mountains National Park) • NORTH CAROLINA: Webster, Waynesville, Asheville, Little Switzerland, Celo, Collettsville, Valmead, Kings Creek, Hamptonville, Flint Hill, Rural Hall, Dennis, Reidsville, Ruffin, Pelham, Providence, Blanch, Milton • VIRGINIA: Danville, Turbeville, South Boston, Red Oak, Fairview, Chase City, Dundas, McKenney, DeWitt, Burrowsville, Brandon, Williamsburg, Gloucester, Ware Neck, Gwynn, (Chesapeake Bay), Onancock, Tasley, Mappsville, Chincoteague.

PLUMBBOB: GALILEO

Detonation Date: 2 Sept 1957 • *Detonation Time:* 5:40 A.M. • *Area:* 1 • *Sponsor:* Los Alamos • *Yield:* 11 kt • *Radiation Level at Ground Zero:* 200 R/hr • *Height of Burst:* 500 ft • *Cloud Top Height:* 37,000 ft

40,000-Foot Trajectory: NEVADA: (Pahute Mesa), Ash Springs • UTAH: (Dixie National Forest), Central, New Harmony, Kanarraville, Hatch, Tropic, (Natural Bridges National Monument) • COLORADO: Northdale, Dove Creek, Ophir, Red Mountain, (Spring Creek Pass), (Mesa Peak), Timpas, Toonerville • KANSAS: Dodge City, Windthorst, Preston, Varner, Waterloo, Garden Plain, Wichita, Latham, Howard, Neodesha, Pittsburg • MISSOURI: Mindonmines, Lockwood, Springfield, Cabool, Pine Crest, Garwod, Bell City • KENTUCKY: Cairo, Paducah • ILLINOIS: Unionville, Hamletsburg, New Liberty • KENTUCKY: Smithland, Salem, Shady Grove, Manitou, Livermore, Bedo, Sulphur Springs, Hardin Springs, Stephensburg, Elizabethtown, Frederickstown, Mooresville, Willisburg, Duncan, McAffee, Mayo, Troy, Lexington, Mount Sterling, Morehead, Soldier, Jacobs, Lawton, Grahn, Grayson, Kilgore, Rush • WEST VIRGINIA: Huntington, Milton, Hometown, Goldtown, Kentuck, Speed, Milestone, Glenville, Troy, Westan, Lost Creek, Quiet Dell, Bridgeport, Grafton, McGee, Arthurdale, Morgantown, Hazelton • VIRGINIA: Markleysburg, Addison, Listonburg, St. Paul, Glencoe, Fairhope, Rainsburg, Clearville, Crystal Spring, Harrisonville, Metal, Shippenburg, Walnut Bottom, Mount Holly Springs, Lisburn, Harrisburg, High Springs, Lebanon, Mount Aetna, Trexler, Wanamakers, Jacksonville, Palmerton, Effort, Reeders, Henryville, Milford, Millrift • NEW YORK: Rio, Port Jervis, Slate Hill, Johnson, Ridgebury, New Hampton, Goshen, Blooming Grove, Salisbury Mills, Mountainville, Cornell-on-Hudson, Nelsonville, Kent Cliffs, Lake Carmel, Putnam Lake • CONNECTICUT: New Fairfield, Hawleyville, Southbury, Waterbury, Marion, Plantsville, Kensington, Berlin, Wethersfield, Rocky Hill, Glastonbury, Manchester, South Willington, Westford, North Ashford, Quinebaug • MASSACHUSETTS: Dudley Hill, Dudley, Webster, Manchaug, West Sutton, Sutton, Riverdale, Northbridge, Upton, Milford, Holliston, Sherborn, Harding, Dover, Needham, Dedham, Brookline, Boston, Winthrop.

PLUMBBOB: WHEELER

Detonation Date: 6 Sept 1957 • *Detonation Time:* 5:45 A.M. • *Area:* 9a • *Sponsor:* Livermore Laboratory • *Yield:* 197 tons • *Radiation Level at Ground Zero:* 10 R/hr • *Height of Burst:* 500 ft • *Cloud Top Height:* 17,000 ft

10,000-Foot Trajectory: NEVADA: Goldfield, Hawthorne, Smith, Weed Heights, Reno, Sparks • CALIFORNIA: Twin Bridges, Dardanelle, Mammoth Lakes, Death Valley, Needles • ARIZONA: Drake, Sedonia, Winslow, Holbrook • NEW MEXICO: Fence Lake, Grants, Seyboyeta, Los Alamos, Santa Fe, San Ignacio, Mosquero • TEXAS: Dalhart, Morse (30 miles north of Wheeler, Texas), Higgins • OKLAHOMA: Arnet, Cestos, Longdale, Lacey, Bison, Douglas, Covington, Red Rock, Bowring • KANSAS: Dearing, Mound Valley,

Fort Scott • MISSOURI: Nevada, Walker, Schell City, Rockville, Deepwater, Clinton, Windsor, Green Ridge, Sedalia, Boonville, Clark, Paris, Hannibal • ILLINOIS: Hall, Beverly, Fishhook, Beardstown, Kilbourne, Delavan, Danvers, El Paso, Streator, Lisbon, Plattville, Plainfield, Cicero, Chicago • MICHIGAN: Beechwood, Lamont, Sparta, Pierson, Lakeview, Clare, Gladwin, Selkirk, Lincoln.

PLUMBBOB: COULOMB B

Detonation Date: 6 Sept 1957 • *Detonation Time:* 1:05 P.M. • *Area:* 3g • *Sponsor:* Los Alamos • *Yield:* 0.3 kt • *Radiation Level at Ground Zero:* 100 R/hr • *Height of Burst:* 3 ft • *Cloud Top Height:* 18,000 ft

10,000-Foot Trajectory: NEVADA: (Shoshone Peak), (Sarcobatus Flat) • CALIFORNIA: (Scotty's Castle), Bishop Indian Reservation, Bishop, Chalfant, Benton • NEVADA: (Boundary Peak, highest point in Nevada), Mount Montgomery, Basalt, (Monte Christo Range), Tonopah, (Mud Lake), (Reveille Range), Tempiute, Caliente • ARIZONA: Littlefield, (Mount Delenbaugh), Red Lake, (Humphreys Peak, highest point in Arizona), Winona, Leupp Corner, Winslow, (Painted Desert), (Petrified Forest National Park), Zuni Indian Reservation • NEW MEXICO: Zuni Indian Reservation, Ramah Navajo Indian Reservation, Laguna Indian Reservation, Los Chavez, Dalies, Bosque Farms, Isleta, Tijeras, Edgewood, Moriarty, Clines Corners, Santa Rosa, Puerto De Luna, McAlister, House, Field, Pleasant Hill • TEXAS: Bovina, Rhea, Friona, Black, Summerfield, Hereford, Umbarger, Canyon, Lake Tanglewood, Pullman, Washburn, Panhandle, White Deer, Kings Mill, Pampa, Hoover, Miami, Canadian, Glazier, Higgins • OKLAHOMA: Shattuck, Gage, Fargo, Fort Supply, Camp Houston • KANSAS: Aetna, Medicine Lodge, Zenda, Murdock, Midway, Andale, Bentley, Sedgwick, Elbing, Florence, Cedar Point, Clements, Elmdale, Dunlap, Bushong, Eskridge, Dover, Topeka, Kiro, Meriden, Rock Creek, Valley Falls, Nortonville, Cummings, Atchison, Doniphan, Wathena, Blair • MISSOURI: St. Joseph, Avenue City, Rochester, Union, Star, King City, Gentryville, New Hampton, Bethany, Ridgeway, Blythedale • IOWA: Allerton, Corydon, Bethlehem, Confidence, Melrose, Georgetown, Hiteman, Eddyville, Rose Hill, What Cheer, Keswick, North English, Parnell, Oxford, Homestead, Amana, Swisher, Shueyville, Ely, Martelle, Anamosa, Amber, Scotch Grove, Bernard, St. Donatus • ILLINOIS: Galena, Charles Mound (highest point in Illinois) • WISCONSIN: South Waynbe, Browntown, Monroe, Brodhead, Footville, Janesville, Lima Center, Whitewater, Mukwonago, Big Bend, Franklin, Muskego, Hales Corners, Greenfield, Cudahy, St. Francis, Milwaukee • MICHIGAN: Montague, Hesperia, Aetna, Ramona, White Cloud, Big Rapids, Rodney, Barryton, Sherman City, Brinton, Farwell, Vernon City, Clare, Beaverton, Rhodes, Bentley, Sterling, Maple Ridge, Twining, Turner, National City, Tawas City, East Tawas, Au Sable, Oscoda.

PLUMBBOB: LA PLACE

Detonation Date: 8 Sept 1957 • *Detonation Time:* 6:00 A.M. • *Area:* 7b • *Sponsor:* Los Alamos • *Yield:* 1 kt • *Radiation Level at Ground Zero:* 50 R/hr • *Height of Burst:* 750 ft • *Cloud Top Height:* 20,000 ft

10,000-Foot Trajectory: NEVADA: (Spotted Range), (Sheep Range), (Valley of Fire State Park), Logandale, Overton • ARIZONA: (Virgin Mountains), (Grand Wash Cliffs), (Grand Canyon National Park), Hualiai Indian Reservation, (Trinity Mountain), Ash Fork, (Casner Mountain), Sedonia, (Mogollon Plateau), Holbrook, Woodruff, Zuni Indian Reservation • NEW MEXICO: Zuni Indian Reservation, Ramah Navajo Indian Reservation, Belen, Los Chavez, (Manzano Mountains), (Mosca Peak), Escabosa, Edgewood, Clines Corners, Pastura, Sumner Lake, House, McAlester, Forrest, Grady, Cameron • TEXAS: Vega, Ady, Exell, Masterson, Pringle, Morse, McKibben, Spearman, Waka, Farnsworth, Perryton, Twitchell, Booker •

OKLAHOMA: Clear Lake, Knowles, Gate • KANSAS: Englewood, Sitka, Protection, Coldwater, Wilmore, Belvidere, Croft, Coats, Pratt, Natrona, Preston, Neola, Plevna, Abbyville, Willowbrook, Medora, Hutchinson, Buhler, Elyria, Lehigh, Durham, Pilsen, Lost Springs, Burdick, Delavan, Wilsey, Hessdale, Keene, Williard, Kiro, Topeka, Silver Lake, Elmont, Valley Falls, Half Mound, Nortonville, Cummings, Atchinson, Doniphan, Wathena, Elwood, Blair • MISSOURI: St. Joseph, Nodaway, Amazonia, Savannah, King City, Gentryville, Albany, Martinsville, Brooklyn, Eagleville, Blythdale • IOWA: Davis City, Pleasanton, Woodland, Corydon, Millerton, Melrose, Georgetown, Albia, Avery, Eddyville, Cedar, Wright, Fremont, Delta, Sigourney, South English, Iowa City, Morse, Cedar Bluff, Buchanan, Clarence, Massillon, Lost Nation, Elwood, Maquoketa, Springbrook • ILLINOIS: Savanna Army Depot, Loran, Kent, Pearl City, Freeport, Eleroy, Dakota, Davis, Shirland, Harrison, Rockton, South Beloit • WISCONSIN: Beloit, Clinton, Allen, Darien, Lyons, Springfield, Honey Creek, Rochester, Burlington, Franksville, Wind Point, North Bay • MICHIGAN: Muskegon, Cloverville, Ravenna, Baily, Kent City, Sand Lake, Trufant, Langston, Stanton, Elm Hall, Sumner, Alma, Ithaca, Nelson, Saginaw, Frankentrost, Reese, Richville, Gifford, Akron, Fairgrove, Colling, Cass City, New Greenleaf, Tyro, Parisville, Ruth.

PLUMBBOB: FIZEAU

Detonation Date: 14 Sept 1957 • *Detonation Time:* 9:45 A.M. • *Area:* 3b • *Sponsor:* Los Alamos • *Yield:* 11 kt • *Radiation Level at Ground Zero:* 100 R/hr • *Height of Burst:* 500 ft • *Cloud Top Height:* 40,000 ft

40,000-Foot Trajectory: NEVADA: (Pahute Mesa), Nellis Air Force Range, Tonopah, Luning, Shurz, Yerington, Wabuska, Carson City, Silver City, Glenbrook • CALIFORNIA: Tahoe City, Baxter, Emigrant Gap, Dutch Flat, Grass Valley, Nevada City, Loma Rica, Live Oak, Pennington, Colusa Indian Reservation, Maxwell, Ladoga, Ukiah, Calpella, Navarro, Elk, San Francisco, Alameda, Oakland, Berkeley, Orinda, Danville, Brentwood, Middle River, Byron, Stockton, Holt, French Camp, Farmington, Copperopolis, Tuttletown, Tuolumne, Sonora, (Yosemite National Park), Lee Vining • NEVADA: (Boundary Peak, highest point in Nevada), Montgomery, Coaldale, Tonopah, Warm Springs, Ursine, Pioche • UTAH: Beryl, Land, Parowan, Tropic, Cannonville, Henrieville, Mexican Hat • COLORADO: Ute Mountain Indian Reservation, Marvel, Oxford, Chimney Rock, Pagosa Springs, Capulin, La Jara, Bountiful, Sanford, Lasauses, San Acacio, Viejo San Acacio, San Luis, Gulnare, Ludlow, Hoehne, Villegreen, Kim, Stonington • KANSAS: Richfield, Moscow, Fowler, Minneola, Croft, Coats, St. Leo, Murdock, Cheney, Goddard, Schulte, Wichita, Andover, Augusta, Haverhill, Leon, Climax, Toronto, Batesville, Yates Center, Rose, Piqua, Iola, Gas, LaHarpe, Moran, Bayar, Xenia, Mapleton, Mantey, Harding, Fulton • MISSOURI: Hume, Rich Hill, Prairie City, Ohio, Mount Zion, Warsaw, Whitakerville, Gravois Mills, Eldon, Etterville, Henley, St. Thomas, Westphalia, Mount Sterling, Drake, Stony Hill, Washington, Clover Bottom, Labadie, Pond, Ballwin, Manchester, St. Louis • ILLINOIS: East St. Louis, Collinsville, Edwardsville, Marine, Old Ripley, Pocahontas, Vandalia, Haferstown, Bluff City, Browstown, Altamont, Effingham, Teutopolis, Montrose, Jewett, Hidalgo, Greenup, Casey, Martinsville, Marshall • INDIANA: Prairieton, Terre Haute, Cory, Prairie City, Poland, Cunot, Quincy, Lewisville, Centerton, Brooklyn, Bargersville, Whitelaud, Needham, Shelbyville, Rays Crossing, Manilla, Rushville, Glenwood, Connersville, Alquina, Brownsville, Liberty, Kitchell • OHIO: Sugar Valley, Glenwood, Little Richmond, Trotwood, Northridge, Dayton, Sulpher Grove, Fairborn, Medway, Snyderville, Springfield, Catawba, Tradersvile, Plumwood, Hayden, Linworth, Minerva Park, Croton, Lock, Homer, Millwood, Tiverton, Killbuck, Berlin, Trail, Winesburg, Beech City, Boliver, Howenstein, North Industry, Mapleton, Robertsville, Bayard, New Alexander, New Garden, Guilford, East Fairfield, Signal, East Palestine, Negley • PENNSYLVANIA: New Galilee, Ellwood City, Mount Chestnut, Windward Heights, Chicora, Frogtown, Wattersonville, Tidal, Climax, New Bethlehem, South Bethlehem, Ringgold, Panic, Prescottville, Sandy, Oklahoma, Home Camp, (Moshannon State Forest), Keating, Cooks Run, West Renovo, Haneyville, Waterville, Quiggleville, Warrensville, Muncy Valley, Sonestown, Nordmont, Beaumont, Orange, Upper Exeter, Ransom, Scranton, Mount Cobb, Hamlin, Lakeville, Tafton, Greeley, Shohola, Pond Eddy, Millrift • NEW JERSEY: (High Point, highest point in New Jersey: 1,803 feet) • NEW YORK: Port Jervis, Huguenot, Mechanicstown, Campbell Hall, New Windsor, Beacon, Farmers Mills, Ludingtonville, Patterson, Towners • CONNECTICUT: New Fairfield, Brookfield, Brookfield Center, Roxbury Falls, Woodbury, Middleburg, Waterbury, Woodtick, Southington, Kensington, New Britain, Berlin, East Berlin, Rocky Hill, East Glastonbury, Diamond Lake, Willimantic, North Windham, South Killingly • RHODE ISLAND: Foster, North Scituate, Saundersville, Providence, East Providence • MASSACHUSETTS: Taunton, Raynham Center, North Middleboro, Warrentown, Silver Lake, Kingston, Tinkertown, South Duxbury.

PLUMBBOB: NEWTON

Detonation Date: 16 Sept 1957 • *Detonation Time:* 5:50 A.M. • *Area:* 7b • *Sponsor:* Los Alamos • *Yield:* 12 kt • *Radiation Level at Ground Zero:* 50 R/hr • *Height of Burst:* 1,500 ft • *Cloud Top Height:* 32,000 ft

30,000-Foot Trajectory: NEVADA: (Papoose Lake), (Papoose Range), (Pahranagat Range), Ash Springs, Caliente, Panaca • UTAH: Uvada, Modena, Lund, Minersville, Beaver, (Delano Peak), Loa, Bicknel, Teasdale, Torrey, Cainesville, Hanksville, (Canyonlands National Park), (Lisbon Valley) • COLORADO: Norwood, Ridgeway, (Sheep Mountain), Powderhorn, Doyleville, Sargents, (Ouray Peak), Poncha Pass, Wellsville, Howard, Parkdale, (Royal Gorge), Canon City, Fort Carson, Fountain, Widefield, Ellicott, Yoder, Rush, Hugo, Arriba, Flagler, Hale • KANSAS: St. Francis • NEBRASKA: Benkelman, Danbury, Naponee, Red Cloud, Superior, Hardy, Byron, Chester, Hubbell, Thompson, Steele City, Barneston, DuBois, Falls City, Preston, Rulo • KANSAS: Cedar Bluffs, Lyle, Long Island, Woodruff, Thornburg, Womer, Northbranch, Burr Oak, Webber, Republic, Narka, Mahaska, Hollenberg, Oketo, Summerfield, Bern, Berwick, Reserve, Iowa Sac and Fox Indian Reservation, White Cloud • MISSOURI: Fortescue, Mound City, Maitland, Barnard, Guilford, Stanberry, Conception Junction, Albany, Bethany, Mount Moriah, Modena, Mill Grove, Newtown, Pollock, Lemons, Graysville, Worthington, Downing, Memphis, Arbela, Farmington, Athens • IOWA: Argyle, Summitville, Montrose, New Boston • ILLINOIS: Nauvoo, Fort Madison, Niota, Raritan, Swan Creek, St. Augustine, Rapatee, Yates City, Elmwood, Kickapoo, Alta, Rome, Chillicothe, Washburn, Rutland, Long Point, Manville, Blackstone, Gardner, Braceville, Symerton, Wilton Center, Monee, Chicago Heights • INDIANA: Highland, Griffith, Gary, Lake Station, Ogden Dunes, Burns Harbor, Town of Pines, Trail Creek • MICHIGAN: Bertrand, Eagle Lake, Adamsville, Constantine, Centreville, Nottawa, Colon, Fairfax, Sherwood, Hodunk, Union City, Tekonsha, Homer, Concord, Parma, Jackson, Waterloo, Hamburg, New Hudson, Farmington Hills, Pontiac, Birmingham, Rochester Hills, New Baltimore, Marine City • NEW YORK: Sandy Pond, Ellisburg, Pierrepont Manor, Adams, Lorraine, Worth, Copenhagen, West Carthage, Carthage, Indian River, (Alder Bed Mountain), Sabattis, (Seymour Mountain), Keene Valley, Elizabethtown, Wadhams, Whallonsburg • VERMONT: Westport, Vergennes, Irasville, Waitsfield, Montpelier, Berlin, Barre, Groton, Ryegate • NEW HAMPSHIRE: Lyman, Lisbon, Franconia, Bethlehem, Twin Mountain, Bretton Woods, North Chatham • MAINE: Center, Louell, Waterford, South Paris, Hebron, North Monmouth, Monmouth, Winthrop, Hallowell, Gardinier, Randolph, Coopers Mills, Washington, Northport, Lincolnville, Harborside, Islesboro, Brooksville, Blue Falls, North Sedgwick, Bar Harbor, Corea, Winter Harbor, Petit Manan Pt.

PLUMBBOB: WHITNEY

Detonation Date: 23 Sept 1957 • *Detonation Time:* 5:30 A.M. • *Area:* 2 • *Sponsor:* Livermore Laboratory • *Yield:* 19 kt • *Radiation Level at Ground Zero:* 200 R/hr • *Height of Burst:* 500 ft • *Cloud Top Height:* 30,000 ft

10,000-Foot Trajectory: NEVADA: Warm Springs, Crescent Valley, Carlin, Metropolis, Pequop, Montello • UTAH: (Grouse Creek Mountains), Park Valley • IDAHO: Holbrook, Buist, Arbon, Pocatello, Chubbuck, Riverside, Terreton, Dubois, Spencer, Humphrey • MONTANA: Monida, Sheridan, Twin Bridges, Silver Star, Butte, McQueen, Basin, Rimini, Blossburg, Marysville, Canyon Creek, Choteau, Miller Colony, Bynum, Pendroy, Valier, Ethridge, Sweetgrass.

PLUMBBOB: CHARLESTON

Detonation Date: 28 Sept 1957 • *Detonation Time:* 6:00 A.M. • *Area:* 9a • *Sponsor:* Livermore Laboratory • *Yield:* 12 kt • *Radiation Level at Ground Zero:* 50 R/hr • *Height of Burst:* 1,500 ft • *Cloud Top Height:* 32,000 ft

20,000-Foot Trajectory: NEVADA: (Belted Range), (Revielle Range), (Pancake Range), (Diamond Mountains), Ruby Valley, Wells, (Delano Peak) • IDAHO: Oakley, Marion, Burley, Rupert, Minidoka, Atomic City, Taber, Roberts, Terneton, Hamer, St. Anthony, Island Park • WYOMING: (Yellowstone National Park: Old Faithful), Canyon, Silver Gate • MONTANA: (Granite Peak; highest point in Montana), Alpine, Red Lodge, Luther, Roberts, Franberg, Edgar, Pryor, Crow Indian Reservation, Hardin, Brandenberg, Valborg, Powderville, Ekalaka, Mill Iron • SOUTH DAKOTA: Buffalo, Reva, Sorum, Usta, Red Elm, Dupree, Eagle Butte, Mission Ridge, Blunt, Stephen, Wessington Springs, Letcher, Farmer, Emery, Monroe, Lennox, Worthing, Canton • IOWA: Beloit, Lebanon, Struble, West LeMars, LeMars, Moville, Climbing Hill, Holly Springs, Rodney, Castana, Moorhead, Logan, Neola, McClelland, Treynor, Hastings, Malvern, Randolph, Anderson, Riverton, Hamburg • MISSOURI: Watson • NEBRASKA: Brownville, Nemaha, Verdun, Dawson • KANSAS: Berwick, Sabetha, Kelley, Goff, Corning, Havensville, Onaga, Louisville, Wamego, Wabaunsee, Alta Vista, Council Grove, Strong City, Elmdale, Matfield Green, El Dorado, Haverhill, Douglass, Rock, Akron, Udall, Oxford, Geuda Springs, Ashton • OKLAHOMA: Braman, Billings, Covington, Hayward, Lovell, Crescent, Cashion, Piedmont, El Reno, Union City, Cogar, Dutton, Anadarko, Cyril, Apache, Fletcher, Geronimo, Devol • TEXAS: Burkburnett, Mankins, Dundee, Padgett, Crystal Falls, Breckenridge, Eastland, Rising Star, Brownwood, Trickham, Whon, Fife, Lohn, Pear Valley, London, Junction, Segovia, Barksdale, Camp Wood, (Military Mountain), (Kelly Peak), (Bolling Mountain), (Salmon Peak), (Turkey Mountain), Spofford, (Cline Mountain), Blewett, Dabney, Normandy, Eagle Pass.

PLUMBBOB: MORGAN

Detonation Date: 7 Oct 1957 • *Detonation Time:* 5:00 A.M. • *Area:* 9a • *Sponsor:* Livermore Laboratory • *Yield:* 8 kt • *Radiation Level at Ground Zero:* 100 R/hr • *Height of Burst:* 500 ft • *Cloud Top Height:* 40,000 ft

20,000-Foot Trajectory: NEVADA: (Spotted Range), (Pintwater Range), (Sheep Range), (Mormon Peak) • ARIZONA: Colorado City, Cane Beds, Moccasin, Kaibab Indian Reservation, Fredonia, Page, (Monument Valley), Mexican Water, Teec Nos Pos • UTAH: St. George, Hildale, Kanab, Glen Canyon, (Navajo Mountain), (Rainbow Bridge National Monument), (Monument Valley), Mexican Hat, Ute Mountain Indian Reservation • COLORADO: Ute Mountain Indian Reservation, (Mesa Verde National Park), Hesperus, Durango, Trimble, Hermosa, (Sunlight Peak), Spar City, Wagon Wheel Gap, (Rio Grande National Forest), (Sangre De Cristo Mountains), Lincoln Park, Rockvale, Florence, Canon City, Penrose, Portland, Fort Carson, Fountain, Yoder, Rush, Hugo, Flagler, Seibert, Hale • KANSAS: St. Francis • NEBRASKA: Benkelman, Stratton, Trenton, Stockville, Eustis, Lexington, Miller, Amherst, Pleasanton, Poole, Ravenna, Boelus, Cairo, Chapman, Hordville, Marquette, Polk, Arborville, Gresham, Ulysses, Bee, Dwight, Valparaiso, Agnew, Ceresco, Ashland, Memphis, Gretna, Springfield, Cedar Creek, LaPlatte, Bellevue • IOWA: Mineola, Silver City, Henderson,

Macedonia, Griswold, Lyman, Cumberland, Berea, Fontanelle, How, Arbor Hill, Cumming, Norwalk, West Des Moines, Colfax, Prairie City, Newton, Oakland Acres, Grinnell, Belle Plaine, Luzerne, Blairstown, Norway, Fairfax, Covington, Cedar Rapids, Puralta, Springville, Fairview, Anamosa, Amber, Center Junction, Onslow, Fulton, Andrew, Springbrook, Green Island • ILLINOIS: Savanna, Pearl City, German Valley, Seward, Winnebago, Rockford, Belvidere, Marengo, Union, Crystal Lake, Libertyville, Wauconda, Lake Bluff, Lake Forest, North Chicago • MICHIGAN: Paw Paw Lake, Glendale, Lawrence, Kalamazoo, Westwood, Galesburg, Springfield, Battle Creek, Brownlee Park, Mershall, Devereaux, Jackson, Munith, Stockbridge, Unadilla, Pinckney, Hell, Hamburg, Lakeland, New Hudson, Wixom, Walled Lake, Orchard Lake, Sylvan Lake, Pontiac, Birmingham, Troy, Rochester Hills, Sterling, New Baltimore, Anchorville, Fair Haven, Pearl Beach • NEW YORK: (Lake Ontario), Dexter, Brownville, Watertown, Evans Mills, Philadelphia, Antwerp, Oxbow, Wegatchie, Somerville, Natural Dam, Gouverneur, Richville, DeKalb, Rensselaer Falls, Canton, Morley, Madrid, Chamberlain Corners, Chase Mills, Louisville, Massena, Massena Center, Rooseveltown • VERMONT: Rouses Point, Alburg Springs, Highgate Springs, East Franklin, Rickford, Stevens Mills, Missisquoi, North Troy, Beebe Plain, Rock Island, Derby Line, Norton, Canaan, Beecher Falls • NEW HAMPSHIRE: Pittsburg, (Shatney Mountain), Happy Corner, The Glen, (Deer Mountain), (Salmon Mountain) • MAINE: Coburn Gore, (Kirby Mountain), (Spencer Mountain), (Coburn Mountain), (Indian Pond), (Big Squaw Mountain), (Whitecap Mountain), (Jo-Mary Mountain), Millinocket, East Millinocket, Reed, (Wytopilock Lake), Haynesville, Orient, North Amity.

STORAX: SEDAN

Detonation Date: 6 Jul 1962 • *Detonation Time:* 9:00 A.M. • *Area:* U10h • *Sponsor:* Livermore Laboratory • *Yield:* 110 kt • *Radiation Level at Ground Zero:* 500 R/hr • *Height of Burst:* − 635 ft • *Cloud Top Height:* 16,000 ft

16,000-Foot Trajectory: NEVADA: (Belted Range), (Reveille Range), (Railroad Valley), Duckwater, (Mount Hamilton), (Pancake Summit), (Newark Lake), (Long Valley), (Ruby Lake), (Spruce Mountain), Shafter, (Pilot Peak) • UTAH: (Great Salt Lake Desert), (Hogup Mountains), (Hansels Mountains), (Dolphin Island in Great Salt), Snowville, Portage • IDAHO: Stone, Samaria, Woodruff, Malad City, Oxford, Clifton, Dayton, Banida, Mink Creek, Swan Lake, Liberty, Bern, Bennington, Ovid, Montpelier, Geneva • WYOMING: (Salt River Range), (Commissary Ridge), (Bridger-Teton National Forest), Marbleton, Boulder, Big Sandy, (Wind River Peak), Lander, Hudson, Hiland, Waltman, Powder River, Natrona, (Teapot Dome), Bill, Redbird • SOUTH DAKOTA: Provo, Ardmore, Pine Ridge • NEBRASKA: Eli, Cody, Kilgore, Crookston, Valentine, Sparks, Springview, Winnetoon, Creighton, Marquet, McLean, Randolph, Sholes, Wakefield, Emerso, Winnebago Indian Reservation, Homer, Winnebago • IOWA: Sloan, Rodney, Grant Center, Ticonic, Castana, Ute, Dow City, Earling, Defiance, Kirkman, Red Line, Jacksonville, Kimballton, Elk Horn, Brayton, Lorah, Wiota, Cumberland, Massena, Bridgewater, Williamson, Nevinville, Spaulding, Creston, Afton, Hopeville, Westerville, Leon, Woodland, Lineville • MISSOURI: South Lineville, Ravenna, Lucerne, Newtown, Harris, Milan, New Boston, Ethel, Callao, New Cambria, Bevier, Number Eight, College Mound, Cairo, Moberly, Middle Grove, Centralia, Thompson, Mexico, Auxvasse, Shamrock, Williamsburg, Readsville, Americus, Rhineland, Hermann, Gasconade, New Haven, Stony, Beaufort, Stanton, Richwoods, Fertile, Blackwell, Cadet, Bonne Terre, Desloge, Leadwood, Elvins, Flat River, Farmington, Junction City, Fredericktown, Patton, Scopus, Millersville, Burfordville, Whitewater, Dutchtown, Chaffee, New Hamburg, Benton, Diehlstadt, Charleston • KENTUCKY: Bardwell, Arlington, Milburn, Beulah, Fulgham, Wingo, Cuba, Lynnville, Fairbanks • TENNESSEE: Jones Mill, Paris, India, Springville, Manlyville, Big Sandy, Black Center, Eva, Denver, New Johnsonville, Hustburg, Bakerville, Sycamore Landing, (Tennessee National Wildlife Refuge), Only, Coble.

APPENDIX C

Maps of Fallout Trajectories

Areas of the Continental United States Crossed by More Than One
Nuclear Cloud from Aboveground Detonations.

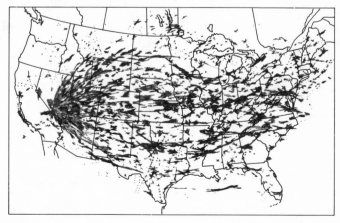

Ranger: Able Jan. 27, 1951 1 kt

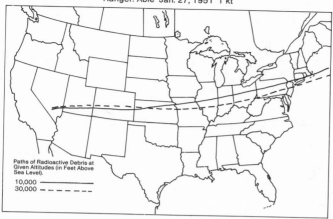

Paths of Radioactive Debris at
Given Altitudes (in Feet Above
Sea Level).

10,000 —————————
30,000 — — — — — —

Ranger: Baker Jan. 28, 1951 8 kt

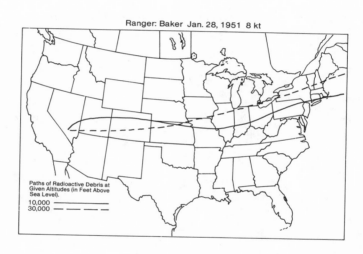

Paths of Radioactive Debris at
Given Altitudes (in Feet Above
Sea Level).

10,000 —————————
30,000 — — — — — —

Ranger: Easy Feb. 1, 1951 8 kt

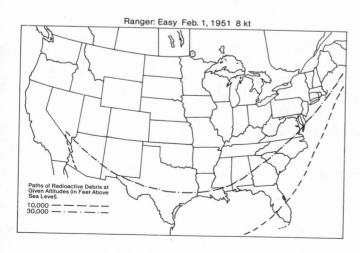

Paths of Radioactive Debris at
Given Altitudes (in Feet Above
Sea Level).

10,000 — — — — — —
30,000 — · — · — · —

445

Ranger: Baker-2 Feb. 2, 1951 8 kt

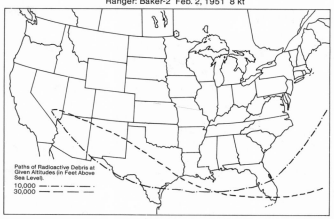

Paths of Radioactive Debris at
Given Altitudes (in Feet Above
Sea Level).
10,000 —·—·—·—·—·
30,000 —— —— —— ——

Ranger: Fox Feb. 6, 1951 22 kt

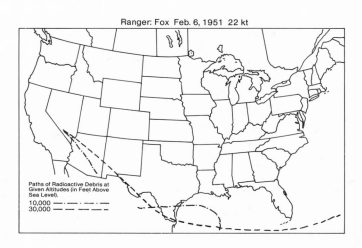

Paths of Radioactive Debris at
Given Altitudes (in Feet Above
Sea Level).
10,000 —·—·—·—·—·
30,000 —— —— —— ——

Buster: Able Oct. 22, 1951 Less than 0.1 kt

Paths of Radioactive Debris at
Given Altitudes (in Feet Above
Sea Level).

8,000 —·—·—·—·—·

446

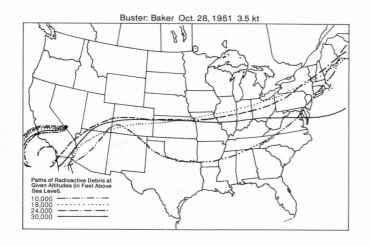

Buster: Baker Oct. 28, 1951 3.5 kt

Paths of Radioactive Debris at Given Altitudes (in Feet Above Sea Level).
10,000
18,000
24,000
30,000

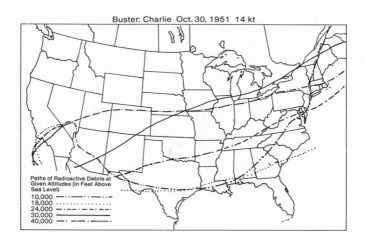

Buster: Charlie Oct. 30, 1951 14 kt

Paths of Radioactive Debris at Given Altitudes (in Feet Above Sea Level).
10,000
18,000
24,000
30,000
40,000

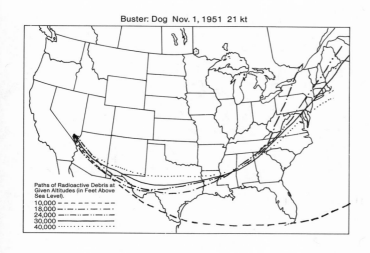

Buster: Dog Nov. 1, 1951 21 kt

Paths of Radioactive Debris at Given Altitudes (in Feet Above Sea Level).
10,000
18,000
24,000
30,000
40,000

447

Buster: Easy Nov. 5, 1951 31 kt

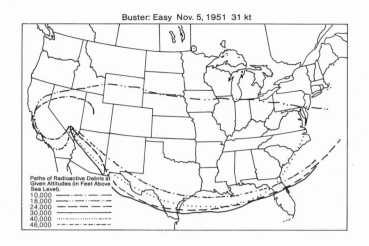

Paths of Radioactive Debris at
Given Altitudes (in Feet Above
Sea Level).
10,000
18,000
24,000
30,000
40,000
46,000

Jangle: Sugar Nov. 19, 1951 1.2 kt

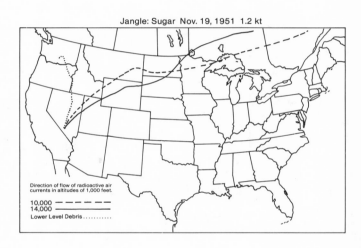

Direction of flow of radioactive air
currents in altitudes of 1,000 feet.

10,000
14,000
Lower Level Debris . . . .

Jangle: Uncle Nov. 29, 1951 1.2 kt

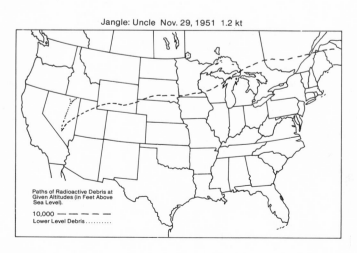

Paths of Radioactive Debris at
Given Altitudes (in Feet Above
Sea Level).

10,000
Lower Level Debris . . . .

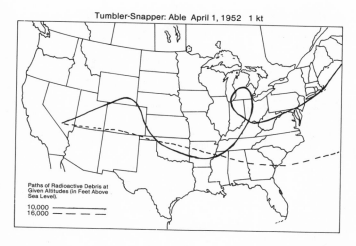

Tumbler-Snapper: Able April 1, 1952   1 kt

Paths of Radioactive Debris at
Given Altitudes (in Feet Above
Sea Level).

10,000 ——————
16,000 — — — —

See Tumbler-Snapper: Baker map on p. 469.

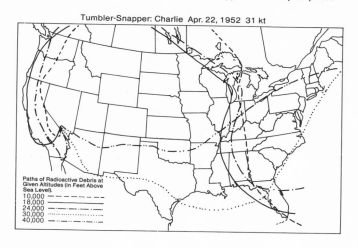

Tumbler-Snapper: Charlie Apr. 22, 1952   31 kt

Paths of Radioactive Debris at
Given Altitudes (in Feet Above
Sea Level).

10,000 — — — — —
18,000 —·—·—·—
24,000 —··—··—··—
30,000 ················
40,000 —···—···—

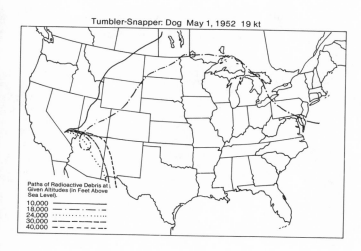

Tumbler-Snapper: Dog May 1, 1952   19 kt

Paths of Radioactive Debris at
Given Altitudes (in Feet Above
Sea Level).

10,000 ——————
18,000 —·—·—·—
24,000 ················
30,000 — — — — —
40,000 — — — — —

449

Tumbler-Snapper: Easy May 7, 1952 12 kt

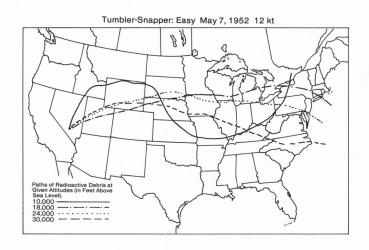

Paths of Radioactive Debris at Given Altitudes (in Feet Above Sea Level).
10,000 ————
18,000 —·—·—·—
24,000 ···········
30,000 —— —— ——

Tumbler-Snapper: Fox May 25, 1952 11 kt

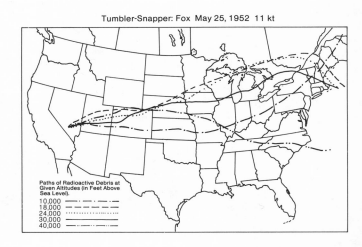

Paths of Radioactive Debris at Given Altitudes (in Feet Above Sea Level).
10,000 —·—·—·—
18,000 — — — —
24,000 ···········
30,000 ————
40,000 —— —— ——

Tumbler-Snapper: George June 1, 1952 15 kt

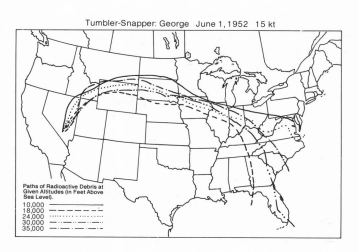

Paths of Radioactive Debris at Given Altitudes (in Feet Above Sea Level).
10,000 ————
18,000 — — — —
24,000 ···········
30,000 —— —— ——
35,000 —·—·—·—

Tumbler-Snapper: How June 5, 1952 14 kt

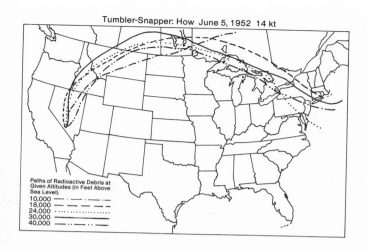

Paths of Radioactive Debris at
Given Altitudes (in Feet Above
Sea Level).
10,000
18,000
24,000
30,000
40,000

Upshot-Knothole: Annie Mar. 17, 1953 16 kt

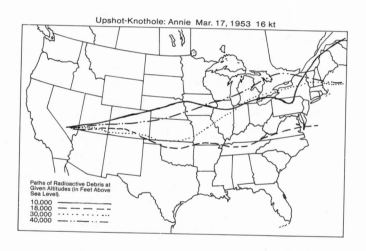

Paths of Radioactive Debris at
Given Altitudes (in Feet Above
Sea Level).
10,000
18,000
30,000
40,000

Upshot-Knothole: Nancy Mar. 24, 1953 24 kt

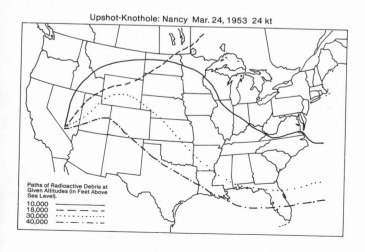

Paths of Radioactive Debris at
Given Altitudes (in Feet Above
Sea Level).
10,000
18,000
30,000
40,000

451

Upshot-Knothole: Ruth Mar. 31, 1953 0.2 kt

Paths of Radioactive Debris at
Given Altitudes (in Feet Above
Sea Level).
10,000 ——————
14,000 — — — — —

Upshot-Knothole: Dixie Apr. 6, 1953 11 kt

Paths of Radioactive Debris at
Given Altitudes (in Feet Above
Sea Level).
30,000 ···················
40,000 — ·· — ·· — ·· — ·

Upshot-Knothole: Ray Apr. 11, 1953 0.2 kt

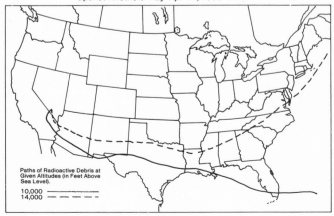

Paths of Radioactive Debris at
Given Altitudes (in Feet Above
Sea Level).
10,000 ——————
14,000 — — — — —

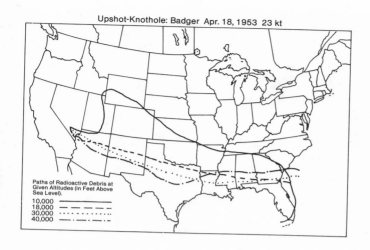

Upshot-Knothole: Badger Apr. 18, 1953 23 kt

Paths of Radioactive Debris at Given Altitudes (in Feet Above Sea Level).
10,000
18,000
30,000
40,000

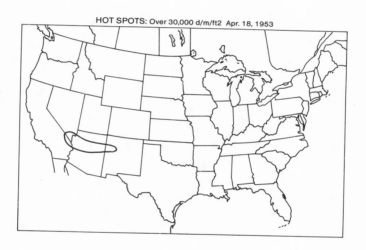

HOT SPOTS: Over 30,000 d/m/ft2 Apr. 18, 1953

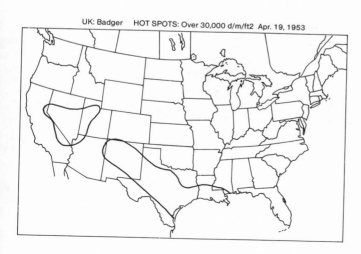

UK: Badger   HOT SPOTS: Over 30,000 d/m/ft2 Apr. 19, 1953

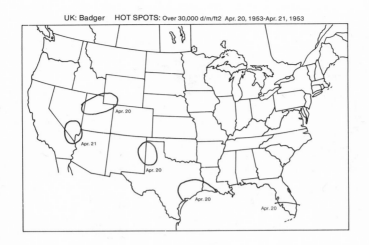

UK: Badger   HOT SPOTS: Over 30,000 d/m/ft2 Apr. 20, 1953-Apr. 21, 1953

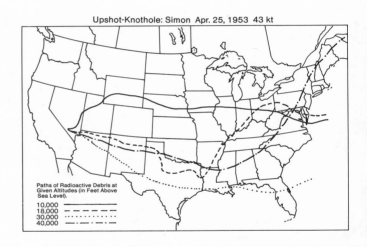

Upshot-Knothole: Simon Apr. 25, 1953 43 kt

Paths of Radioactive Debris at
Given Altitudes (in Feet Above
Sea Level).
10,000 ——————
18,000 — — — — —
30,000 ·············
40,000 —·—·—·—

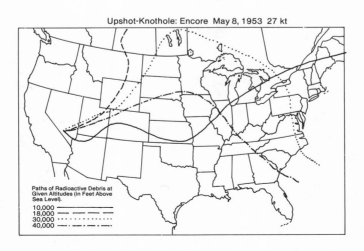

Upshot-Knothole: Encore May 8, 1953 27 kt

Paths of Radioactive Debris at
Given Altitudes (in Feet Above
Sea Level).
10,000 ——————
18,000 — — — — —
30,000 ·············
40,000 —·—·—·—

454

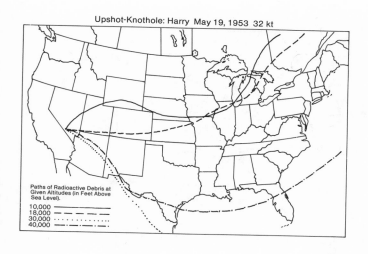

Upshot-Knothole: Harry May 19, 1953 32 kt

Paths of Radioactive Debris at
Given Altitudes (in Feet Above
Sea Level).

10,000 ————————
18,000 — — — —
30,000 ·················
40,000 —·—·—·—·

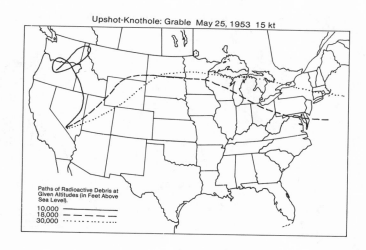

Upshot-Knothole: Grable May 25, 1953 15 kt

Paths of Radioactive Debris at
Given Altitudes (in Feet Above
Sea Level).

10,000 ————————
18,000 — — — —
30,000 ·················

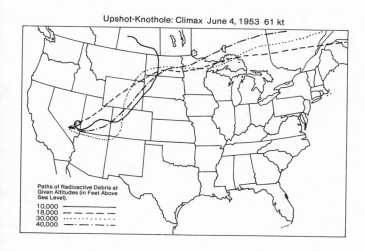

Upshot-Knothole: Climax June 4, 1953 61 kt

Paths of Radioactive Debris at
Given Altitudes (in Feet Above
Sea Level).

10,000 ————————
18,000 — — — —
30,000 ·················
40,000 —·—·—·—·

Teapot: Wasp Feb. 18, 1955 1 kt

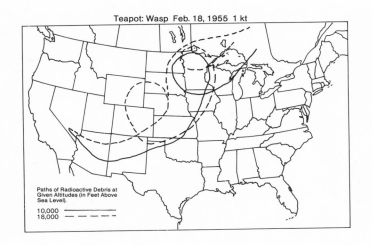

Paths of Radioactive Debris at
Given Altitudes (in Feet Above
Sea Level).

10,000 —————
18,000 — — — —

Teapot: Moth Feb. 22, 1955 2 kt

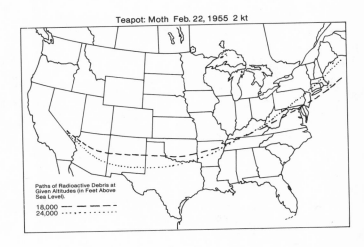

Paths of Radioactive Debris at
Given Altitudes (in Feet Above
Sea Level).

18,000 — — — —
24,000 ············

Teapot: Tesla Mar. 1, 1955 7 kt

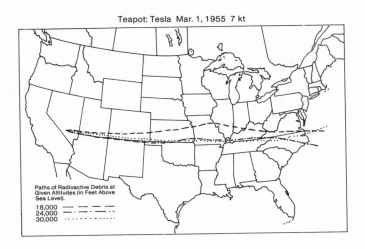

Paths of Radioactive Debris at
Given Altitudes (in Feet Above
Sea Level).

18,000 — — — —
24,000 —·—·—·—
30,000 ············

Teapot: Turk Mar. 7, 1955 43 kt

Paths of Radioactive Debris at
Given Altitudes (in Feet Above
Sea Level).

10,000 ————
18,000 — — —
30,000 ·············
40,000 —·—·—·—

Teapot: Hornet March 12, 1955 4 kt

Paths of Radioactive Debris at
Given Altitudes (in Feet Above
Sea Level).

10,000 ————
18,000 — — —
30,000 ·············
40,000 —·—·—·—

Teapot: Bee Mar. 22, 1955 8 kt

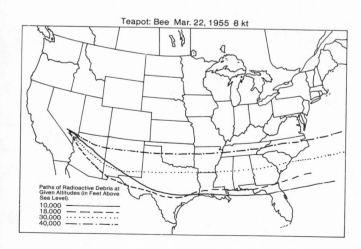

Paths of Radioactive Debris at
Given Altitudes (in Feet Above
Sea Level).

10,000 ————
18,000 — — —
30,000 ·············
40,000 —·—·—·—

457

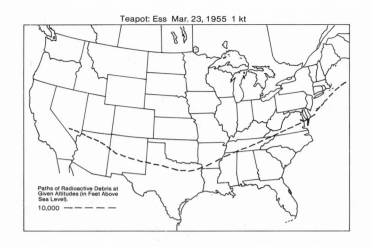

Teapot: Ess Mar. 23, 1955 1 kt

Paths of Radioactive Debris at
Given Altitudes (in Feet Above
Sea Level).

10,000 — — — — —

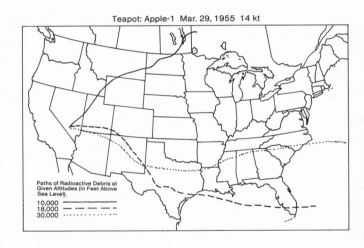

Teapot: Apple-1 Mar. 29, 1955 14 kt

Paths of Radioactive Debris at
Given Altitudes (in Feet Above
Sea Level).

10,000 ————————
18,000 — — — —
30,000 · · · · · · · · · ·

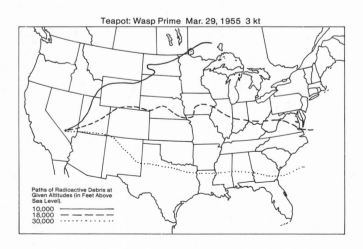

Teapot: Wasp Prime Mar. 29, 1955 3 kt

Paths of Radioactive Debris at
Given Altitudes (in Feet Above
Sea Level).

10,000 — — — —
18,000 — — — —
30,000 · · · · · · · · · ·

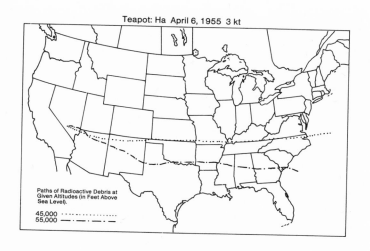

Teapot: Ha April 6, 1955 3 kt

Paths of Radioactive Debris at
Given Altitudes (in Feet Above
Sea Level).

45,000 · · · · · · · · · · · · · · ·
55,000 — · · — · — · · — · —

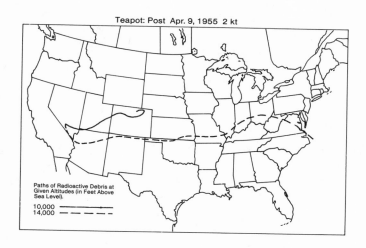

Teapot: Post Apr. 9, 1955 2 kt

Paths of Radioactive Debris at
Given Altitudes (in Feet Above
Sea Level).

10,000 ——————————
14,000 — — — — — —

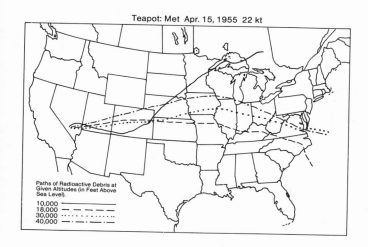

Teapot: Met Apr. 15, 1955 22 kt

Paths of Radioactive Debris at
Given Altitudes (in Feet Above
Sea Level).

10,000 ——————————
18,000 — — — — — —
30,000 · · · · · · · · · · · · · · ·
40,000 — · · — · · — · · —

459

Teapot: Apple-2 May 5, 1955 29 kt

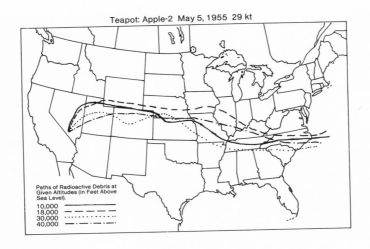

Paths of Radioactive Debris at Given Altitudes (in Feet Above Sea Level).
10,000 ———————
18,000 — — — —
30,000 ·············
40,000 —·—·—·—

Teapot: Zucchini May 15, 1955 28 kt

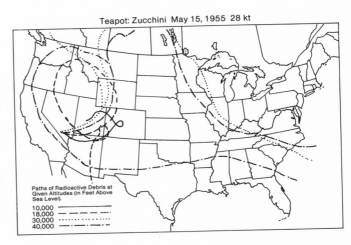

Paths of Radioactive Debris at Given Altitudes (in Feet Above Sea Level).
10,000 ———————
18,000 — — — —
30,000 ·············
40,000 —·—·—·—

Plumbbob: Boltzmann May 28, 1957 12 kt

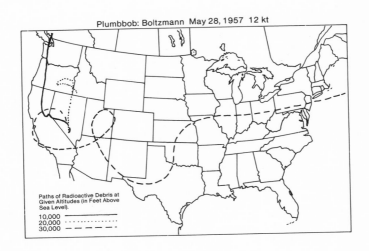

Paths of Radioactive Debris at Given Altitudes (in Feet Above Sea Level).
10,000 ———————
20,000 ·············
30,000 — — — —

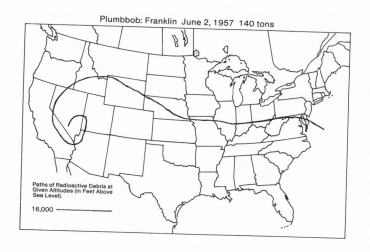

Plumbbob: Franklin June 2, 1957 140 tons

Paths of Radioactive Debris at Given Altitudes (in Feet Above Sea Level).

16,000 ─────────

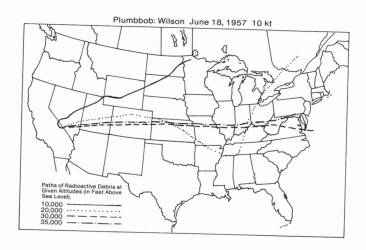

Plumbbob: Wilson June 18, 1957 10 kt

Paths of Radioactive Debris at Given Altitudes (in Feet Above Sea Level).

10,000 ─────────
20,000 ·············
30,000 ─ ─ ─ ─ ─
35,000 ─·─·─·─·─·

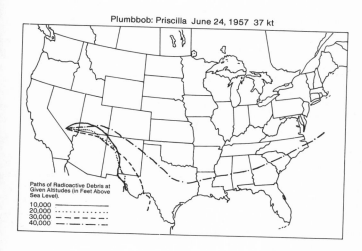

Plumbbob: Priscilla June 24, 1957 37 kt

Paths of Radioactive Debris at Given Altitudes (in Feet Above Sea Level).

10,000 ─────────
20,000 ·············
30,000 ─ ─ ─ ─ ─
40,000 ─·─·─·─·─·

461

Plumbbob: Hood July 5, 1957 74 kt

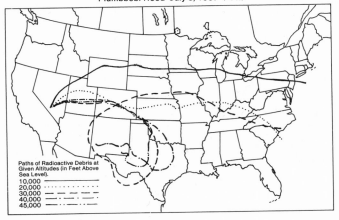

Paths of Radioactive Debris at
Given Altitudes (in Feet Above
Sea Level).

Altitude	Line
10,000	———
20,000	··········
30,000	— — —
40,000	—— —— ——
45,000	—·—·—·—

Plumbbob: Diablo July 15, 1957 11 kt

Paths of Radioactive Debris at
Given Altitudes (in Feet Above
Sea Level).

Altitude	Line
10,000	———
20,000	··········
30,000	— — —

Plumbbob: John July 19, 1957 2 kt

Paths of Radioactive Debris at
Given Altitudes (in Feet Above
Sea Level).

Altitude	Line
40,000	—·—·—·—

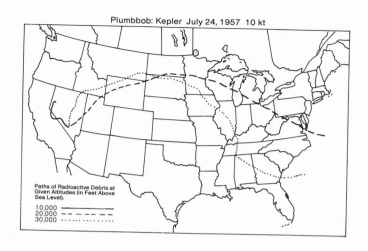

Plumbbob: Kepler July 24, 1957 10 kt

Paths of Radioactive Debris at
Given Altitudes (in Feet Above
Sea Level).
10,000 —————
20,000 — — — —
30,000 ⋯⋯⋯⋯

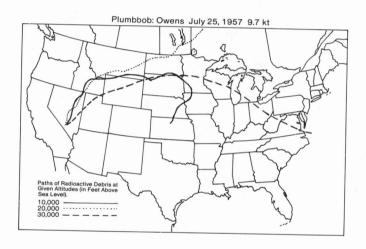

Plumbbob: Owens July 25, 1957 9.7 kt

Paths of Radioactive Debris at
Given Altitudes (in Feet Above
Sea Level).
10,000 —————
20,000 ⋯⋯⋯⋯
30,000 — — — —

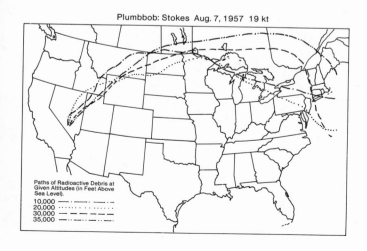

Plumbbob: Stokes Aug. 7, 1957 19 kt

Paths of Radioactive Debris at
Given Altitudes (in Feet Above
Sea Level).
10,000 —·—·—·—·
20,000 ⋯⋯⋯⋯
30,000 — — — —
35,000 —··—··—··—

Plumbbob: Shasta Aug. 18, 1957 17 kt

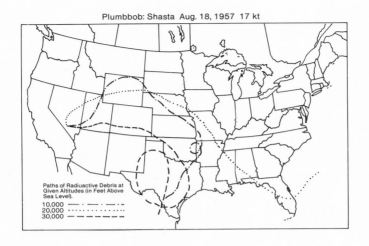

Plumbbob: Doppler Aug. 23, 1957 11 kt

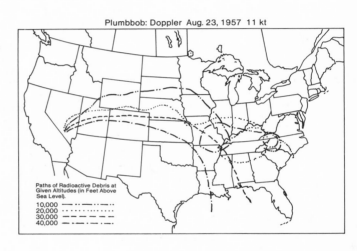

Plumbbob: Franklin Prime Aug. 30, 1957 4.7 kt

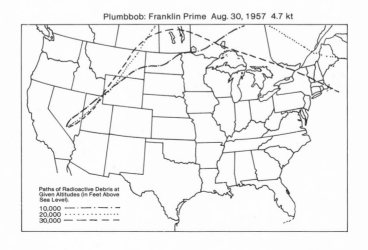

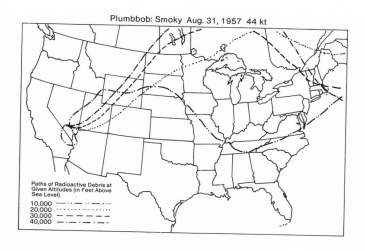

Plumbbob: Smoky Aug. 31, 1957 44 kt

Paths of Radioactive Debris at
Given Altitudes (in Feet Above
Sea Level).

10,000 ——·——·——···
20,000 ················
30,000 ——— ——— ———
40,000 ——·——·——·—·.

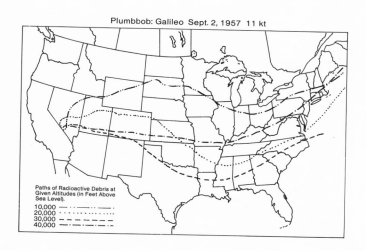

Plumbbob: Galileo Sept. 2, 1957 11 kt

Paths of Radioactive Debris at
Given Altitudes (in Feet Above
Sea Level).

10,000 ——— ——·—— ·
20,000 ················
30,000 ——— ——— ———
40,000 ——·——·——·—·.

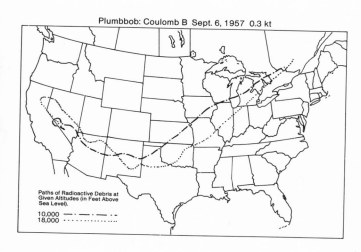

Plumbbob: Coulomb B Sept. 6, 1957 0.3 kt

Paths of Radioactive Debris at
Given Altitudes (in Feet Above
Sea Level).

10,000 ——·——·—— ··
18,000 ················

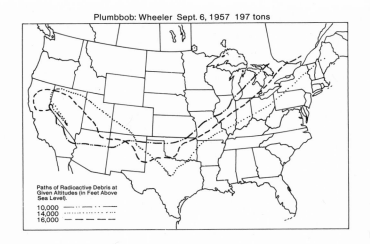

Plumbbob: Wheeler Sept. 6, 1957 197 tons

Paths of Radioactive Debris at
Given Altitudes (in Feet Above
Sea Level).
10,000
14,000
16,000

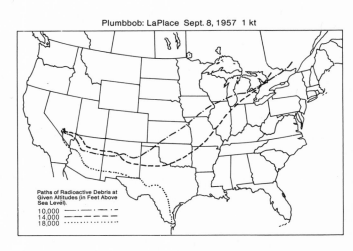

Plumbbob: LaPlace Sept. 8, 1957 1 kt

Paths of Radioactive Debris at
Given Altitudes (in Feet Above
Sea Level).
10,000
14,000
18,000

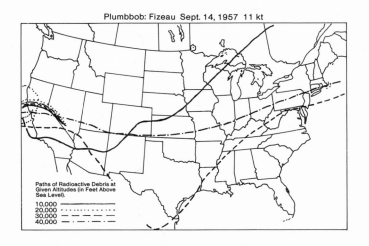

Plumbbob: Fizeau Sept. 14, 1957 11 kt

Paths of Radioactive Debris at
Given Altitudes (in Feet Above
Sea Level).
10,000
20,000
30,000
40,000

466

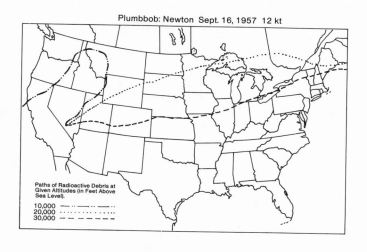

Plumbbob: Newton Sept. 16, 1957 12 kt

Paths of Radioactive Debris at Given Altitudes (in Feet Above Sea Level).

10,000 — · — · · — · ·
20,000 · · · · · · · · · · · ·
30,000 — — — — — —

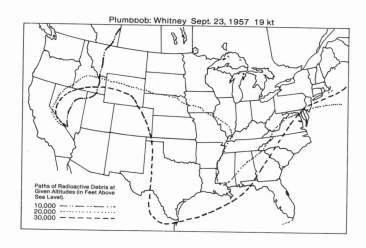

Plumbbob: Whitney Sept. 23, 1957 19 kt

Paths of Radioactive Debris at Given Altitudes (in Feet Above Sea Level).

10,000 — · — · · — · ·
20,000 · · · · · · · · · · · ·
30,000 — — — — — —

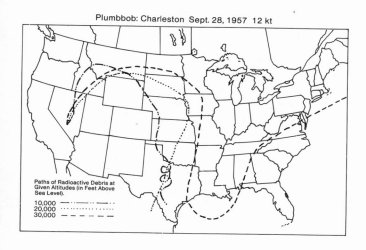

Plumbbob: Charleston Sept. 28, 1957 12 kt

Paths of Radioactive Debris at Given Altitudes (in Feet Above Sea Level).

10,000 — · — · · — · ·
20,000 · · · · · · · · · · · ·
30,000 — — — — — —

467

Plumbbob: Morgan Oct. 7, 1957 8 kt

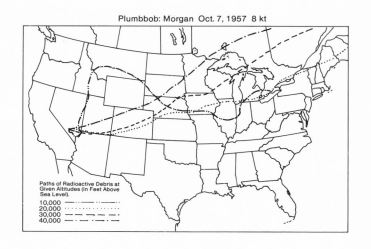

Paths of Radioactive Debris at
Given Altitudes (in Feet Above
Sea Level).

10,000
20,000
30,000
40,000

Nougat: Antler Sept. 15, 1961 2.6 kt 9,000 MSL Trajectory

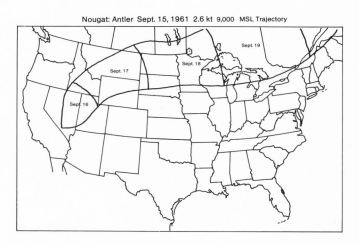

Plowshare Gnome   Dec. 10, 1961   3 kt   Area of Gnome Cloud

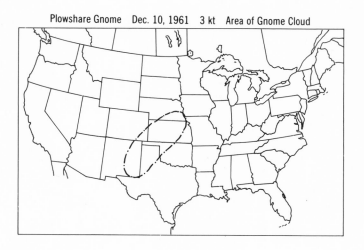

Nougat: Danny Boy Mar. 5, 1962 0.43 kt 10,000 MSL Trajectory

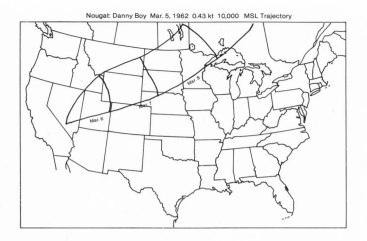

Nougat: Platte Apr. 14, 1962 1.85 kt 13,500 MSL Trajectory

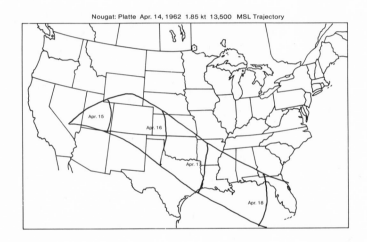

Tumbler-Snapper: Baker Apr. 15, 1952 1 kt

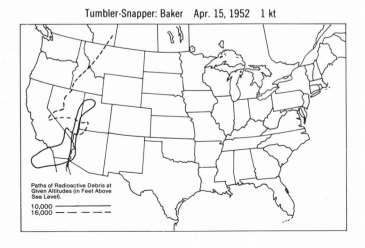

Paths of Radioactive Debris at
Given Altitudes (in Feet Above
Sea Level).

10,000 ——————
16,000 – – – – – –

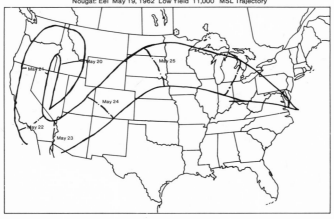

Nougat: Eel May 19, 1962 Low Yield 11,000 MSL Trajectory

Storax: Sedan July 6, 1962 104 kt

Paths of Radioactive Debris at
Given Altitudes (in Feet Above
Sea Level).

10,000 ————— · — · — · —
16,000 ——— — — — —

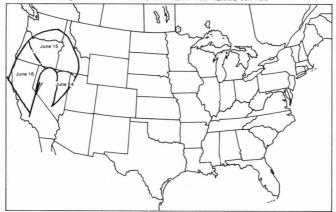

Nougat: Des Moines June 13, 1962 10,000 MSL Trajectory Low Yield

470

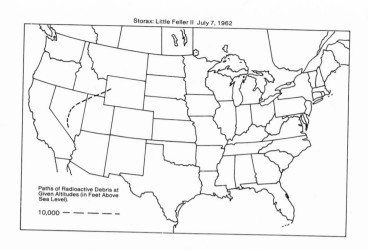

Storax: Little Feller II   July 7, 1962

Paths of Radioactive Debris at
Given Altitudes (in Feet Above
Sea Level).

10,000 — — — — —

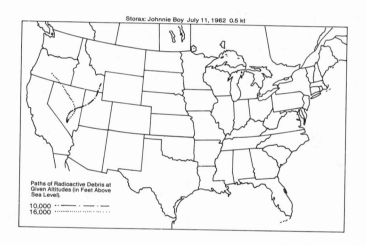

Storax: Johnnie Boy   July 11, 1962   0.5 kt

Paths of Radioactive Debris at
Given Altitudes (in Feet Above
Sea Level).

10,000 ·· —— · —— · ——
16,000 ···························· ··· ····

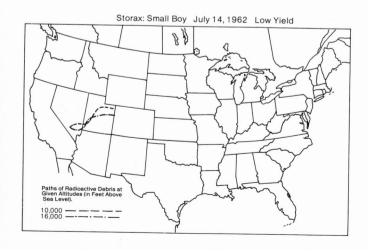

Storax: Small Boy   July 14, 1962   Low Yield

Paths of Radioactive Debris at
Given Altitudes (in Feet Above
Sea Level).

10,000 — — — — —
16,000 —·— ·— ·— ·—

471

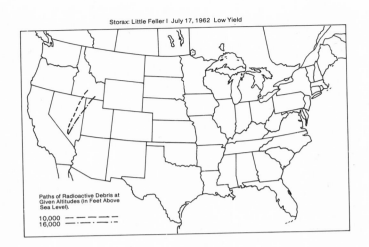

Storax: Little Feller I July 17, 1962 Low Yield

Paths of Radioactive Debris at
Given Altitudes (in Feet Above
Sea Level).

10,000
16,000

472

APPENDIX D

Fallout in Selected Cities from Operations Tumbler-Snapper and Upshot-Knothole*

Fallout: TUMBLER-SNAPPER: ABLE

Location	Activity (d/min/ft²/day)	Precipitation (inches)
1. Concordia, KS	170,000	3
2. Columbia, MO	35,000	2
3. Wichita Falls, TX	14,000	0
4. Jackson, MS	6,800	6
5. Port Arthur, TX	2,000	4

Fallout: TUMBLER-SNAPPER: BAKER

Location	Activity (d/min/ft²/day)	Precipitation (inches)
1. Santa Catalina, CA	23,000	2
2. Mobile, AL	1,800	0
3. Bermuda	380	3

Fallout: TUMBLER-SNAPPER: CHARLIE

Location	Activity (d/min/ft²/day)	Precipitation (inches)
1. Santa Catalina, CA	54,000	0
2. Savannah, GA	51,000	6
3. Montgomery, AL	42,000	4
4. Florence, SC	34,000	4
5. Eureka, CA	25,000	0
6. Tallahassee, FL	18,000	0
7. Richmond, VA	17,000	7
8. Baltimore, MD	16,000	7
9. Harrisburg, PA	13,000	5
10. Medford, OR	6,300	0
11. Jacksonville, FL	3,000	6

*Some cities are listed more than once because measurements were taken on separate days. The cities are listed in descending levels of fallout. The abbreviation "d/min/ft²/day" means "disintegrations/minute/square foot/day."

Fallout: TUMBLER-SNAPPER: DOG

Location	Activity (d/min/ft²/day)	Precipitation (inches)
1. Flagstaff, AZ	5,500	0
2. Atlanta, GA	2,400	0
3. Northhead, WA	370	0

Fallout: TUMBLER-SNAPPER: EASY

Location	Activity (d/min/ft²/day)	Precipitation (inches)
1. Salt Lake City, UT	7,900,000	4
2. Salt Lake City, UT	3,300,000	0
3. Scottsbluff, NE	160,000	4
4. Greenville, SC	42,000	3
5. Birmingham, AL	7,900	2
6. Port Arthur, TX	7,600	0
7. Atlanta, GA	6,500	2
8. Jackson, MS	6,000	0
9. Birmingham, AL	3,900	0
10. Montgomery, AL	3,600	0
11. Lynchburg, WV	3,300	0
12. Tallahassee, FL	3,300	2
13. Mt. Washington, NH	2,700	0
14. Bermuda	1,800	0
15. Del Rio, TX	730	4
16. Binghamton, NY	590	0

Fallout: TUMBLER-SNAPPER: FOX

Location	Activity (d/min/ft²/day)	Precipitation (inches)
1. Grand Junction, CO	350,000	2
2. Goodland, KS	180,000	5
3. St. Cloud, MN	76,000	6
4. Flagstaff, AZ	62,000	2
5. Fargo, ND	14,000	3
6. Albuquerque, NM	11,000	0
7. Tucson, AZ	8,900	0
8. New Orleans, LA	4,400	0
9. Abilene, TX	4,100	0
9. Rochester, NY	4,100	0
10. Del Rio, TX	3,400	0
11. Corpus Christi, TX	3,300	0
12. Goose Bay, Labrador	2,600	2
13. Yuma, AZ	2,200	0
14. Northhead, WA	2,100	5
15. East Port, ME	920	0
16. Goose Bay, Labrador	390	0

Fallout: TUMBLER-S**NAPPER:** G**EORGE**

Location	Activity (d/min/ft²/day)	Precipitation (inches)
1. Pocatello, ID	1,400,000	2
2. Elko, NV	710,000	0
3. Terre Haute, IN	460,000	5
4. Grand Rapids, MI	400,000	6
5. Milwaukee, WI	290,000	5
6. Concordia, KS	280,000	0
7. Norfolk, NE	260,000	3
7. Peoria, IL	260,000	5
8. Des Moines, IA	240,000	5
9. Watertown, NY	170,000	5
10. Tucson, AZ	160,000	3
11. Oswego, NY	140,000	4
11. Rochester, MN	140,000	4
12. Wichita, KS	130,000	7
13. Fort Smith, AZ	110,000	6
14. Fort Wayne, IN	99,000	3
15. Huron, SD	98,000	6
16. Rochester, NY	93,000	3
17. Albuquerque, NM	68,000	6
17. Dansville, NY	68,000	6
18. Medford, OR	61,000	5
19. La Guardia, NY	60,000	6
19. Reno, NV	60,000	0
20. Providence, RI	57,000	4
21. Albany, NY	55,000	4
21. Dunkirk, NY	55,000	3
21. Rapid City, SD	55,000	6
22. Texarkana, AR	52,000	0
23. Reno, NV	47,000	2
24. Rapid City, SD	46,000	0
25. Huron, SD	45,000	0
26. East Boston, MA	43,000	3
27. Spokane, WA	36,000	3
28. Billings, MT	35,000	0
29. Louisville, KY	34,000	4
29. Syracuse, NY	34,000	3
30. Nashville, TN	31,000	5
31. Alpena, MI	29,000	4
32. Eureka, CA	27,000	3
33. Mt. Washington, NH	26,000	2
34. Florence, SC	24,000	0
35. Fresno, CA	23,000	0
35. Wichita Falls, TX	23,000	5
36. Knoxville, TN	22,000	3
36. East Port, ME	22,000	4
37. Bismarck, ND	21,000	3
38. Toledo, OH	20,000	2
38. Youngstown, OH	20,000	3
39. Texarkana, AR	19,000	6
39. Yuma, AZ	19,000	2
40. Columbia, MO	18,000	0
40. Dayton, OH	18,000	6
40. Fresno, CA	18,000	2

Fallout: TUMBLER-SNAPPER: GEORGE
(Cont.)

Location	Activity (d/min/ft²/day)	Precipitation (inches)
41. Abilene, TX	17,000	4
41. Caribou, ME	17,000	0
41. Toledo, OH	17,000	0
41. Lynchburg, WV	17,000	2
41. Wilmington, DE	17,000	4
42. Nashville, TN	15,000	0
43. Caribou, ME	14,000	6
43. Green Bay, WI	14,000	4
44. Norfolk, NE	13,000	0
44. Baltimore, MD	13,000	0
44. Escanana, MI	13,000	3
44. Terre Haute, IN	13,000	0
45. Williston, ND	12,000	0
46. Grand Rapids, MI	11,000	0
47. Dayton, OH	10,000	0
47. Memphis, TN	10,000	4
47. Rock Springs, WY	10,000	0
48. Charlestown, WV	8,400	2
48. St. Cloud, MN	8,400	0
49. Binghamton, NY	8,100	2
50. Scottsbluff, NE	7,800	0
51. Grand Junction, CO	7,400	0
52. Knoxville, TN	6,900	0
53. Green Bay, WI	6,800	0
54. Fort Wayne, IN	6,700	0
55. Peoria, IL	6,400	0
56. Fargo, ND	6,300	4
56. Mobile, AL	6,300	4
57. Buffalo, NY	6,000	0
57. Corpus Christi, TX	6,000	2
57. Des Moines, IA	6,000	0
58. Alpena, MI	5,900	0
59. La Guardia, NY	5,500	0
59. Milwaukee, WI	5,500	0
60. Harrisburg, PA	4,600	0
60. Louisville, KY	4,600	0
61. Charlestown, WV	4,200	0
62. Goodland, KS	4,100	0
62. Memphis, TN	4,100	0
63. Wilmington, DE	3,700	0
64. Richmond, VA	3,200	0
65. Rochester, MN	3,000	0
66. Dansville, NY	2,800	0
66. Fort Smith, AR	2,800	0
66. Marquette, MI	2,800	0
67. Escabana, MI	2,500	0
68. Youngstown, OH	2,400	0
69. Albany, NY	2,100	0
69. East Boston, MA	2,100	0
69. Providence, RI	2,100	0
69. Syracuse, NY	2,100	0
70. Watertown, NY	1,900	0
71. Greenville, SC	1,500	0
72. Oswego, NY	1,400	0
73. Savannah, GA	960	0

Fallout: Tumbler-Snapper: How

Location	Activity (d/min/ft²/day)	Precipitation (inches)
1. Boise, ID	5,900,000	2
2. Great Falls, MT	3,600,000	4
3. Elko, NV	400,000	4
4. Great Falls, MT	190,000	0
5. Pocatello, ID	140,000	0
6. Wichita, KS	85,000	0
7. Billings, MT	69,000	2
8. Sault Ste. Marie, MI	67,000	0
9. Boise, ID	24,000	0
10. Williston, ND	16,000	4
11. Spokane, WA	13,000	0
12. Sault Ste. Marie, MI	12,000	6
13. Marquette, MI	8,100	5
14. Jacksonville, FL	7,800	0
15. Bismarck, ND	7,600	0
16. New Orleans, LA	5,400	5
17. North Bay, Ont.	5,200	3
18. Dunkirk, NY	4,500	0
19. Moosonee, Ont.	1,700	0
20. North Bay, Ont.	1,000	0

Fallout in Selected Cities from Upshot-Knothole

Location	Date in 1953	Activity (d/min/ft²/day)	Precipitation
Shot 1 (Annie)			
1. Knoxville, TN	March 18	1,900,000	yes
2. Ft. Worth–Dallas, TX	March 18	1,000,000	no
3. New York, NY	March 18	900,000	yes
4. Memphis, TN	March 18	630,000	no
5. Philadelphia, PA	March 18	560,000	yes
6. Nashville, TN	March 19	340,000	no
7. Texarkana, AR	March 18	210,000	no
8. Washington, DC	March 18	130,000	yes
9. Baltimore, MD	March 18	96,000	yes
10. Deep River, Ont.	March 18	36,000	yes
11. Ft. Smith, AR	March 17	30,000	yes
10. Atlanta, GA	March 18	13,000	yes
11. Watertown, NY	March 18	12,000	no
12. Lynchburg, VA	March 18	9,600	yes
13. Dunkirk, NY	March 21	2,200	no
Shot 2 (Nancy)			
1. Salt Lake City, UT	March 24	15,000,000	no
2. Casper, WY	March 24	2,100,000	no
2. Ely, NV	March 24	2,100,000	no
3. Williston, ND	March 25	1,000,000	no
4. Rapid City, SD	March 25	680,000	no
5. Mobile, AL	March 26	300,000	no
6. Kansas City, KS	March 26	230,000	no
7. Miami, FL	March 26	150,000	no
8. St. Louis, MO	March 26	120,000	no

Fallout in Selected Cities from UPSHOT-KNOTHOLE
(Cont.)

Location	Date in 1953	Activity (d/min/ft²/day)	Precipitation
9. Monsoonee, Ont.	March 27	100,000	yes
10. Elko, NV	March 24	69,000	no
11. Huron, SD	March 25	63,000	no
12. Fargo, ND	March 26	60,000	no
13. Rock Springs, WY	March 24	60,000	no
14. Des Moines, IA	March 26	28,000	no
15. Montgomery, AL	March 26	21,000	yes
16. Butte, MT	March 25	16,000	yes
17. Green Bay, WI	March 27	5,400	no
18. Port Hardy, B.C.	March 29	1,400	yes

Shot 3 (Ruth)

Location	Date in 1953	Activity (d/min/ft²/day)	Precipitation
1. Phoenix, AZ	April 1	330,000	no
2. Amarillo, TX	April 4	36,000	yes
3. Tucson, AZ	April 2	28,000	no
4. Port Hardy, B.C.	April 8	540	no

Shot 4 (Dixie)

Location	Date in 1953	Activity (d/min/ft²/day)	Precipitation
1. Boston, MA	April 7	5,100,000	yes
2. Jacksonville, FL	April 8	390,000	no
3. Raton, NM	April 6	180,000	yes
4. Wichita, KS	April 6	72,000	yes
5. Boston, MA	April 9	45,000	no

Shot 5 (Ray)

Location	Date in 1953	Activity (d/min/ft²/day)	Precipitation
Yuma, AZ	April 12	450,000	no

Shot 6 (Badger)

Location	Date in 1953	Activity (d/min/ft²/day)	Precipitation
1. Port Arthur, TX	April 19	1,500,000	no
2. Las Vegas, NV	April 18	940,000	no
3. New Orleans, LA	April 19	630,000	no
4. Stephenville, Newfoundland	April 20	530,000	yes
5. Reno, NV	April 19	84,000	yes
6. Corpus Christi, TX	April 19	78,000	no
7. Las Vegas, NV	April 21	33,000	yes
8. San Francisco, CA	April 20	12,000	yes
9. Los Angeles, CA	April 25	11,000	yes
10. Churchill, Manit.	April 24	6,900	yes
11. Del Rio, TX	April 22	5,700	yes
12. Sacramento, CA	April 20	4,500	no
13. Fresno, CA	April 19	2,600	yes
14. Winnemucca, NV	April 20	2,500	no
15. Fresno, CA	April 22	2,100	no
16. Medford, OR	April 25	1,300	yes
17. Los Angeles, CA	April 22	900	no

Shot 7 (Simon)

Location	Date in 1953	Activity (d/min/ft²/day)	Precipitation
1. Albany, NY	April 26	16,000,000	yes
2. Flagstaff, AZ	April 25	3,600,000	no
3. Grand Junction, CO	April 26	2,900,000	no
4. New Haven, CT	April 27	930,000	yes
5. Moncton, N.B.	April 27	780,000	yes

Fallout in Selected Cities from Upshot-Knothole
(Cont.)

Location	Date in 1953	Activity (d/min/ft²/day)	Precipitation
6. Roswell, NM	April 28	780,000	yes
7. Abilene, TX	April 26	360,000	no
8. Seven Islands, P.Q.	April 27	350,000	yes
9. Montreal, P.Q.	April 26	330,000	no
10. Caribou, ME	April 27	250,000	yes
11. Memphis, TN	April 28	240,000	yes
12. Jackson, MS	April 28	210,000	no
13. Colorado Springs, CO	April 27	190,000	no
13. Concordia, KS	April 27	190,000	no
14. Cheyenne, WY	April 26	130,000	no
14. Roswell, NM	April 26	130,000	no
14. St. Louis, MO	April 28	130,000	yes
15. Casper, WY	April 28	120,000	yes
16. Flagstaff, AZ	April 27	110,000	yes
17. Huron, SD	April 28	105,000	yes
17. Rapid City, SD	April 28	105,000	yes
18. East Port, ME	April 27	94,000	yes
19. Louisville, KY	April 27	66,000	yes
20. Fargo, ND	April 29	63,000	yes
21. Port Arthur, TX	April 28	54,000	yes
22. Goodland, KS	April 28	50,000	yes
23. Jackson, MS	April 29	45,000	yes
23. New Orleans, LA	April 29	45,000	yes
24. Nashville, TN	April 29	42,000	yes
25. Scottsbluff, NE	April 27	36,000	no
26. Abilene, TX	April 28	33,000	yes
27. Lynchburg, VA	April 28	29,000	no
28. Ft. Worth–Dallas, TX	April 28	24,000	yes
28. Texarkana, AR	April 28	24,000	yes
28. Washington, DC	April 29	24,000	no
29. Pittsburgh, PA	April 29	16,000	no
30. Reno, NV	April 28	15,000	no
31. Caribou, ME	May 1	9,000	no
32. East Port, ME	May 3	4,200	no
33. Seven Islands, P.Q.	April 29	3,900	no
34. Boise, ID	May 6	3,000	no
35. Fort Simpson, Northwest Territories	May 9	3,000	yes
36. Moncton, N.B.	May 2	2,700	no
37. Phoenix, AZ	April 27	2,600	yes
38. Corpus Christi, TX	April 27	2,200	yes
39. Binghamton, NY	May 3	390	no

Shot 8 (Encore)

Location	Date in 1953	Activity (d/min/ft²/day)	Precipitation
1. Williston, ND	May 8	1,200,000	yes
2. Bermuda	May 11	570,000	yes
3. Billings, MT	May 9	420,000	yes
4. Butte, MT	May 9	90,000	no
5. Regina, Sask.	May 9	60,000	yes
6. Providence, RI	May 11	45,000	no
7. New Haven, CT	May 11	16,000	no
8. San Francisco, CA	May 11	11,000	no
9. Alpena, MI	May 9	3,600	no
10. Prince George, B.C.	May 20	3,000	yes
11. Winnipeg, Manit.	May 8	2,400	no

Fallout in Selected Cities from Upshot-Knothole
(Cont.)

Location	Date in 1953	Activity (d/min/ft²/day)	Precipitation
12. Dansville, NY	May 11	2,000	no
13. Sacramento, CA	May 18	1,300	yes
14. North Bay, Ont.	May 10	720	no
15. Edmonton, Alber.	May 27	150	no
Shot 9 (Harry)			
1. Grand Junction, CO	May 19	11,000,000	yes
2. Albuquerque, NM	May 19	7,800,000	no
3. Raton, NM	May 19	2,000,000	no
4. Amarillo, TX	May 19	1,600,000	no
5. Des Moines, IA	May 20	1,500,000	yes
6. Concordia, KS	May 20	1,100,000	yes
7. Marquette, MI	May 20	940,000	yes
8. Milford, UT	May 19	780,000	yes
9. Goodland, KS	May 20	700,000	no
10. Wichita, KS	May 20	560,000	no
11. Pueblo, CO	May 19	550,000	no
12. Kansas City, KS	May 20	540,000	yes
13. Minneapolis, MN	May 20	480,000	yes
14. Green Bay, WI	May 20	360,000	yes
15. Milwaukee, WI	May 20	240,000	yes
16. Pittsburgh, PA	May 21	190,000	yes
17. Denver, CO	May 21	160,000	no
18. Detroit, MI	May 20	150,000	no
19. Chicago, IL	May 20	140,000	yes
20. Louisville, KY	May 21	130,000	no
21. Detroit, MI	May 21	120,000	yes
21. Ft. Smith, AR	May 20	120,000	no
21. Knoxville, TN	May 22	120,000	no
22. Scottsbluff, NE	May 22	110,000	yes
23. Grand Rapids, MI	May 20	100,000	yes
24. Binghamton, NY	May 22	87,000	yes
25. Atlanta, GA	May 22	81,000	no
25. Charleston, SC	May 22	81,000	no
26. Buffalo, NY	May 21	72,000	yes
22. Salt Lake City, UT	May 19	66,000	yes
28. North Bay, Ont.	May 21	59,000	yes
29. Montgomery, AL	May 21	51,000	no
30. Miami, FL	May 20	48,000	yes
31. Ely, NV	May 23	45,000	yes
32. Dansville, NY	May 21	39,000	yes
32. Del Rio, TX	May 22	39,000	no
33. Montreal, P.Q.	May 22	36,000	yes
34. Syracuse, NY	May 21	24,000	yes
35. Albany, NY	May 21	21,000	no
36. Jacksonville, FL	May 20	14,000	yes
37. Bermuda	May 21	8,400	no
38. Minneapolis, MN	May 23	6,900	no
39. Charleston, SC	May 20	6,000	yes
39. New York, NY	May 23	6,000	no
39. Philadelphia, PA	May 23	6,000	no
40. Marquette, MI	May 22	4,800	no
41. Syracuse, NY	May 23	2,500	no
42. Eureka, CA	May 24	1,300	yes
43. Seattle, WA	May 25	1,200	no

Fallout in Selected Cities from Upshot-Knothole
(Cont.)

Location	Date in 1953	Activity (d/min/ft²/day)	Precipitation
Shot 10 (Grable)			
1. Spokane, WA	May 26	480,000	yes
2. Kalispell, MT	May 26	420,000	yes
3. Boise, ID	May 26	230,000	yes
4. Pocatello, ID	May 26	66,000	no
5. Winnemucca, MV	May 28	63,000	yes
6. Seattle, WA	May 26	48,000	yes
7. Albuquerque, NM	May 27	45,000	yes
7. Milwaukee, WI	May 26	45,000	no
8. Baltimore, MD	May 26	28,000	no
9. Billings, MT	May 31	26,000	no
10. Dunkirk, NY	May 29	25,000	yes
11. Chicago, IL	May 26	19,000	no
11. Edmonton, Alber.	May 26	19,000	yes
11. Elko, NV	May 28	19,000	yes
12. Pocatello, ID	May 27	16,000	yes
13. Helena, MT	May 31	7,200	yes
14. Buffalo, NY	June 5	4,200	no
15. Helena, MT	May 27	3,600	no
16. Grand Rapids, MI	May 28	3,300	no
17. Tucson, AZ	May 27	3,000	yes
18. Spokane, WA	May 28	1,300	no
Shot 11 (Climax)			
1. Rock Springs, WY	June 5	230,000	yes
2. Denver, CO	June 5	180,000	yes
2. Pueblo, CO	June 5	180,000	yes
3. Cheyenne, WY	June 5	160,000	yes
4. Colorado Springs, CO	June 5	84,000	yes
5. Rochester, NY	June 6	57,000	yes
6. Deep River, Ont.	June 7	48,000	no
7. Watertown, NY	June 6	23,000	yes
8. Rochester, NY	June 7	7,200	no
9. Regina, Sask.	June 6	4,200	no

Total Fallout (d/min/ft²) as of June 14, 1953, in the Continental United States by Regions and Bursts, Extrapolated to July 1, 1953
(Excluding the Test Site Area)

Location	Area (%)	Amount	Total (%)
Totals: Bursts 1–10 Total: 278,797			
Washington-Oregon	5.46	3,272	1.17
Montana Idaho Wyoming	10.87	11,087	3.98
North Dakota South Dakota Nebraska	7.44	12,631	4.53

Total Fallout (d/min/ft^2) as of June 14, 1953, in the Continental
United States by Regions and Bursts, Extrapolated to July 1, 1953
(Excluding the Test Site Area)
(Cont.)

Location	Area (%)	Amount	Total (%)
Minnesota Wisconsin	4.64	13,894	4.98
Michigan Indiana Ohio Kentucky	5.83	15,788	5.66
New York Pennsylvania New Jersey	3.40	14,880	5.34
Maine New Hampshire Vermont Massachusetts Rhode Island Connecticut	2.20	10,796	3.87
California	4.25	435	0.16
Nevada Utah Arizona	10.24	18,920	6.79
Colorado New Mexico	7.47	77,217	27.70
Kansas Oklahoma	5.04	23,776	8.53
Iowa Illinois Missouri	6.03	17,778	6.38
Virginia West Virginia Maryland Delaware District of Columbia	2.57	6,888	2.47
Texas	8.85	16,543	5.93
Arkansas Louisiana	3.36	8,951	3.21
Tennessee Alabama Mississippi	4.68	16,703	5.99
North Carolina South Carolina Georgia Florida	6.66	9,238	3.31
Average U.S. exposure:		17,930	

References

Robert J. List, *Radioactive Debris From Operations Tumbler and Snapper*, NYO-4512, U.S. Weather Bureau, February 25, 1953, Table 4.2.

Derived from Robert J. List, *The Transport of Atomic Debris From Upshot-Knothole*, NYO-4602, U.S. Weather Bureau, June 25, 1954, Table 2.2, pp. 8–13.

Notes

Prelude (pp. 1–9)

1. Howard L. Rosenberg, *Atomic Soldiers* (New York: Harper and Row, 1982), pp. 60–61.
2. Ibid.
3. Monitors found 250 milliroentgens outside and 160 milliroentgens inside. New York Times News Service Aug. 12, 1979.
4. Robert List. "Transport of Atomic Debris from Upshot-Knothole," NYO-4602, Weather Bureau, Washington, D.C., June 25, 1954. Memo to William S. Johnson, off-site operations officer, NPO, from R. E. Stafford and E. J. Weathersbee, rad/safe off-site monitors; subject: Special Study Post Shot VII; Apr. 29, 1953.
5. Among areas near the test site receiving fallout from SIMON: St. George, Cedar City, Hurricane, Kanab, Mt. Carmel Junction, Zion National Park, Bryce Canyon National Park, Rainbow Bridge National Monument—all in Utah.
6. List, op. cit., NYO-4602 (R-3.7, May 6, 1953).
7. Ibid., p. 32.
8. Ernest J. Sternglass, *Secret Fallout* (New York: McGraw-Hill, 1981), pp. 1–5, 21. Also: Herbert M. Clark, *Science*, May 7, 1954, pp. 612–622; Herbert M. Clark, et al, *Journal of the American Water Works Association*, November 1954, pp. 1101–1111.
9. List, op. cit., NYO-4602, p. 71. From the official report,

> The 40,000-foot trajectory, which was representative of the movement of the bulk of the mushroom, moved very rapidly to the northeast after passing through a pressure trough in the Mississippi Valley, reaching speeds of over 100 knots. This brought a heavy concentration of debris over Albany, New York, on April 26 at the time a thunderstorm was in progress, resulting in the highest surface activity ever recorded by the monitoring network. On the same day, dry fallout from lower levels resulted in very high activities in Utah, New Mexico [13 million disintegrations/minute/square foot/day at Roswell], and northern Texas. . . . By April 27, most of the central part of the country was covered by the dry fallout and in the extreme northeast considerable activity came down in rain. Debris from this burst covered most of the country east of the Rockies on April 28. . . . [ibid., p. 32]

The Beginning (pp. 11–28)

1. J. K. Wagoner, in his 1979 report "Uranium: the United States experience, a lesson in history" (a report of the Environmental Defense Fund, 1525 18th Street, N.W., Washington,

D.C. 20036), cites a source as early as 1547 indicating the miners had a high frequency of fatal lung disease.

2. Franklin Miller, Jr., *College Physics*, 2nd ed. (New York: Harcourt, Brace and World, 1967), pp. 601–603.
3. Leo Szilard, *His Version of the Facts*, vol. 21, Spencer R. Weart and Gertrude Weiss Szilard, eds. (Cambridge, Mass.: MIT Press, 1978), pp. 16–17.
4. H. G. Wells, *The World Set Free* (New York: Dutton, 1914), p. 152.
5. Peter Wyden, *Day One: Before Hiroshima and After* (New York: Simon and Schuster, 1984), p. 23.
6. Ibid.
7. *The Nation*, Nov. 22, 1945.
8. Wyden, op. cit., p. 32.
9. Ibid., p. 35.
10. The cost for the project would eventually reach $2 billion.
11. That was not the only coincidence. Also mentioned in the story is a scientist named Korzybski who was associated with another specialist, Lentz. Years later, George B. Kistiakowski would be in charge of the high explosive "lens" system for the world's first atomic bomb. A beryllium "target" is involved (beryllium would eventually be used as a neutron reflector in nuclear weapons) and the power plant is located in the American Southwest, not far from the future site of atomic testing. Chicago and Manhattan are mentioned in Robert Heinlein's "Blowups Happen" (published in a Street & Smith magazine in 1940); Chicago would be the home for many of the scientists working to build the first bomb, while the code-name for the operation was, of course, Manhattan.
12. *Los Alamos Science*, Winter-Spring 1983, p. 12.
13. Andrew Cockburn, *The Threat: Inside the Soviet Military Machine* (New York: Random House, 1983), pp. 81–82.
14. It would, however, be far worse for the beleaguered Russians in Leningrad. Food supplies had been cut off and, by Christmas Day 1941, over 3,700 Russians in the city had died of starvation.
15. Wyden, op. cit., p. 85.
16. Simon Goodenough, *War Maps* (London: St. Macdonald and Co. Ltd., 1982), p. 86.
17. Basil Collier, *A Short History of the Second World War* (1967); J. F. C. Fuller, *The Second World War, 1939–1945: A Strategical and Tactical History* (1945); conversations with Dr. Leslie Anders, professor of military history, Central Missouri State University. Also Goodenough, op. cit.
18. Wyden, op. cit., p. 86.
19. Peter Pringle and James Spigelman, *The Nuclear Barons* (New York: Holt, Rinehart and Winston, 1981), p. 69.
20. The Soviets, despite their enormous losses, by the end of 1942 were making twice as many aircraft and four times as many tanks as the Germans. As Soviet defense expert Andrew Cockburn has said, "For the Russian leadership of today, all of whom retain vivid memories of the wartime crisis, there could be no better confirmation of the virtues of putting enormous resources into defense production." (Cockburn, op. cit., pp. 81–82.)
21. Igor Golovin, *I.V. Kurchatov*, and P.N. Astashenkov, *Kurchatov*. The serialization of *I.V. Kurchatov* was published in *Sovietskaya Rossiya* produced by the Joint Publications Research Service, ref. JPRS 37, 804.

Trinity (pp. 29–38)

1. Peter Wyden, *Day One: Before Hiroshima and After* (New York: Simon and Schuster, 1984), p. 106.
2. Ibid., p. 218.
3. Ibid., p. 45.
4. Ibid., p. 99.

5. Ferenc Morton Szasz, *The Day the Sun Rose Twice* (Albuquerque: University of New Mexico Press, 1984), p. 28.
6. Lansing Lamont, *Day of Trinity* (New York: Atheneum, 1965), p. 70.
7. Szasz, op. cit., pp. 40–41.
8. Lamont, op. cit., p. 99.
9. David Irving, *The German Atomic Bomb* (New York: Simon and Schuster, 1967), pp. 279, 282–285, 289–290; referenced in Wyden, op. cit., p. 188.
10. Barton C. Hacker, "Trinity," Chapter 4, "Elements of Controversy: a History of Radiation Safety in the Nuclear Weapons Testing Program (in manuscript). Quoted in Szasz, op. cit. Also: Itinerary of trip made by Colonel Stafford Warren, Captain Whipple, and L. H. Hempelmann on August 12, 1945, Los Alamos report LA–329, available at J. Robert Oppenheimer Laboratory, Los Alamos, N. Mex.
11. Szasz, op. cit., pp. 79–82.
12. Lamont, op. cit., p. 237.
13. Szasz, op. cit., p. 85.
14. Lamont, op. cit., pp. 240–241.
15. Ibid., p. 244.
16. James W. Junetka, *City of Fire: Los Alamos and the Atomic Age, 1943–1945*, rev. ed. (Albuquerque: University of New Mexico Press, 1979), p. 170.
17. Los Alamos report LA–1027 DEL (means "parts deleted") in Szasz, op. cit.
18. Wyden, op. cit., pp. 222–223.
19. References: Martin J. Sherwin, *A World Destroyed* (New York: Knopf, 1975), p. 225; Len Giovannitti, and Fred Freed, *The Decision to Drop the Bomb* (New York: Coward-McCann, 1965), pp. 222–224; Charles L. Mee, *Meeting at Potsdam* (New York: Evans, 1975), p. 222; Robert H. Ferrell, ed., *Off the Record: The Private Papers of Harry S. Truman* (New York: Penguin paperback, 1980), p. 54; David Holloway, *The Soviet Union and the Arms Race* (New Haven: Yale University Press, 1983), pp. 20, 22; Stimson diary, p. 31, July 21, 1945, referenced in Wyden, op. cit., pp. 221–226.

Hiroshima (pp. 39–48)

1. Simon Goodenough, *War Maps* (London: St. Macdonald and Co. Ltd., 1982), pp. 184–185.
2. Wheeler, Keith, *Bombers Over Japan* (Alexandria, Va.: Time-Life 1982), p. 194.
3. Ibid., pp. 135–136.
4. Ibid., p. 180.
5. Ibid., p. 135.
6. Peter Wyden, *Day One: Before Hiroshima and After* (New York: Simon and Schuster, 1984), p. 231.
7. The Allies were in fact planning operations Olympic and Coronet, which would involve invasions of the Japanese mainland. They were scheduled to begin on November 1, 1954, and continue well into 1946.
8. "Neutrality Pact": Keith Wheeler, *The Fall of Japan* (Alexandria, Va.: Time-Life, 1983), p. 98.
9. The "psychological factor" was a touchy subject with many military strategists. In the early days of World War II, during the siege of Britain, the British decried as immoral Germany's bombing of "innocent civilians." They went on to conclude that contrary to lowering morale, such activity actually strengthened the resolve of the populace. This was the accepted official position until it became evident that the Royal Air Force couldn't get any closer to their targets than 5 miles. As a result, innocent *German* civilians began dying in the raids. Churchill, enraged at the RAF's ineptitude, in the fall of 1941 canceled raids into Germany.

   The RAF high command, worried that their infant organization would be swallowed by the British army or navy, launched a political counterattack. Headed by RAF founder

Hugh "Boom" Trenchard, and the chief of air staff Charles "Peter" Portal, the RAF began to lobby for "area bombing"—that is, attacks on civilians as well as military targets. Churchill countered that such activity would strengthen German morale just as it had the British. Wrong, said Portal, and trotted out Frederick Lindemann (later Lord Cherwell), who in turn produced questionable scientific "calculations" that showed the Germans were psychologically more susceptible to "dehousing" than were the English. Churchill relented.

On February 14, 1942, Portal gave the RAF a Valentine's Day present: The new target was civilian morale—that is, civilian targets.

For more detailed information, see Sir Charles Webster and Noble Frankland, *The Strategic Air Offensive Against Germany 1939-46,* vol. 1. (London: H.M.S.O., 1961). The Valentine's Day bombing directive is reproduced on page 323. See also: Peter Pringle and James Spigelman; *The Nuclear Barons* (New York: Holt, Rinehart and Winston, 1981), p. 72.

10. Target Committee, notes on meetings: April 27, May 10, May 11, May 28, 1945. Groves Top Secret Files, Folder 5D, RG 77, National Archives, Washington, D.C.
11. Quoted in Wyden, op. cit., pp. 197–198.
12. Ibid., p. 254 (*New York Times*, Tuesday, Oct. 11, 1955).
13. Gordon Thomas and Max Morgan Witts, *The Enola Gay* (New York: Pocket Books, 1977), p. 335; John Toland, *The Rising Sun* (New York: Bantam, 1971), p. 878; Wyden, op. cit., pp. 244–245.
14. Wyden, op. cit., p. 253; Wheeler, *The Fall of Japan*, pp. 124–125.
15. *Newsweek*, July 29, 1985, p. 36.
16. Wyden, op. cit., p. 302.
17. No one who survived near the epicenter remembered hearing an explosion (Wheeler, *Fall of Japan*, p. 121).
18. The account of conditions at the hypocenter is taken from various eyewitness accounts of aboveground atomic detonations from 1945 to 1947 and from scientific documentation of conditions inside the base surge and stem of an aboveground atomic detonation.
19. On August 16, ten crewmen from the downed B-29 Nip Clipper were taken prisoner and brought to what remained of Hiroshima. There they met the two American POWs, Neal and Brissette. In an interview with Robert Karl Manhoff, published in the *New York Times Magazine*, the co-pilot and bombardier of the Nip Clipper recalled the meeting: "They were in terrible shape. We got to talking with them, and they said that they knew of Americans in the town when the bomb went off, and their statement was that some of them were killed outright, and the two dove into a cesspool. . . . Those two fellows were really dying a very horrible death. You could tell that just by looking at them." The crew members related how their bodies were covered with bruises. (Robert Karl Manhoff, "American Victims of Hiroshima," *New York Times Magazine*, Dec. 2, 1984.)
20. It is possible that, in addition to Neal and Brissette, four others may have survived the initial blast. Rumors circulating among the citizens of Hiroshima concerned two American soldiers who were stoned to death near one of the bridges. It is known that on August 7, at 9:30 A.M., a blond, green-eyed American POW was tied to the Aioi Bridge and killed. Another rumor involved the sighting of an "American dressed only in red and white underwear dying beneath a bridge." For more information regarding the American POWs please see the Gary De Walt film: *Genbaku Shi: Killed by the Atomic Bomb.*
21. One Japanese navy surgeon declared that the bomb was an "electron incendiary bomb." An army weapons specialist concluded the weapon was a "sulphuric acid bomb." (Wyden, op. cit., p. 300.)
22. Wyden, op. cit., p. 296.

Nagasaki (pp. 49–57)

1. Because of the lingering deaths, some thought that the bomb contained a poison gas or deadly bacteria. It was not until after Nagasaki that Japanese scientists became convinced

that the weapons were atomic. (Keith Wheeler, *The Fall of Japan* [Alexandria, Va.: Time-Life, 1983], p. 134.)

2. Ibid., p. 98.
3. Ibid., p. 99.
4. Ibid., p. 100.
5. The photo plane was circling the same general area but at a higher altitude.
6. To fly from Yakushima Island to Kokura, a navigator would have to take into account the magnetic variation from due north, which in Japan is 6 degrees west. They would add this to the true heading, 10 degrees, to arrive at their final compass heading of 16 degrees (assuming no wind).
7. After the drop, Sweeney circled the mushroom cloud for twelve minutes, using up fuel. When they returned to their heading for Okinawa, they had only 300 gallons of gasoline left. As Okinawa came into view, the fuel gauges read empty. At the same time, the right outboard engine died. The landing field at Okinawa was packed with planes. To scatter them, the pilot ordered all the flares fired. There was no time for a traffic pattern; he bounced the plane in and came to a stop 10 feet from the end of the runway—with just 7 gallons of fuel left.
8. Wheeler, *The Fall of Japan*, pp. 100–101.
9. Ibid., p. 142.
10. Ibid., p. 128.
11. The condition of the children indicates that they were at a close proximity to the blast. The weapon was detonated 1,500 feet over the Urakami Valley industrial complex.
12. Wheeler, *Fall of Japan*, pp. 129–131.
13. Information from weather map, 6:00 A.M., August 9, 1945. Chuo Kishodai (Central Meteorological Observatory) Tenkizu (Weather Chart) no. 221, 1945. Also, drawings of the mushroom cloud as viewed from Mt. Unzen (Y. Ishida, "Formation of clouds due to the atomic bomb detonation as observed from Unzen" in CRIABC, vol. 1, 1953, p. 139).
14. NGO International Symposium on the Damage and Aftereffects of the Atomic Bombing, Nagasaki Preparatory Committee and Expert Committee for the Preparation of the Nagasaki Report, 1977b p. 38. Reported in *Hiroshima and Nagasaki: The Physical, Medical and Social Effects of the Atomic Bombings*, The Committee for the Compilation of Materials on Damage Caused by the Atomic Bombs in Hiroshima and Nagasaki. (New York: Basic Books, Harper Colophon Books, 1981.)
15. Still, Komatsu's bone marrow had probably been affected. He would later be diagnosed as having chronic anemia. (Wheeler, *The Fall of Japan*, p. 132.)
16. Keith Wheeler's *The Fall of Japan* (pp. 152–155) gives a more complete account of the discussions and intrigues that involved Japan's final days in the war.
17. Ibid., p. 155.
18. Ibid., p. 156.

Fallout (pp. 58–65)

1. The source of the Iowa River is located near the towns of Hayfield and Miller, both about 21 miles from Minnesota.
2. Promethium is obtained by neutron bombardment of neodymium (Robert C. Weast, Editor in Chief, *Handbook of Chemistry and Physics*, 46th ed. [Cleveland, Ohio: CRC Press, 1966], p. B-130).
3. Note: Cerium-141 is produced by neutron bombardment of cerium-140. It decays with a half-life of $32\frac{1}{2}$ days to lanthanum-141 and promethium-141.
4. J. H. Webb, "The Fogging of Photographic Film by Radioactive Contaminants in Cardboard Packaging Materials," *Physical Review*, vol. 76, Aug. 1, 1949: pp. 375–380. Also: Ferenc Morton Szasz, *The Day the Sun Rose Twice* (Albuquerque, University of New Mexico Press, 1984), p. 135.
5. The ranchers name was Will Wyre. Reported in Szasz, op. cit., pp. 21–33.
6. UCLA-60. Referenced in Szasz, op. cit., pp. 135–136.

7. Howard M. Blakeslee, Associated Press, "Party of Newsmen Inspects Scene Near Alamogordo," *Albuquerque Journal*, Sept. 12, 1945. Reported in Szasz, op. cit.

8. Donald L. Collins, "Pictures from the Past: Journeys into Health Physics in the Manhattan District and Other Diverse Places" in *Health Physics: A Backward Glance*: edited by Ronald L. Kathen and Paul L. Ziemer (New York: Pergamon Press, 1980).

9. K. Shinohara, S. Morita, K. Kora, N. Kawai, and M. Yokota. "Radiation of the ground in Nagasaki city and vicinity. Part II. Radioactivity near the hypocenter," in CRIABC, vol. I. (Science Council of Japan, 1953.) "Genshibakudan Saigai Chosa Gokokushu" (Collections of the Reports on the Investigation of the Atomic Bomb Casualties) (Tokyo: Nihon Gakujutsu Shinkokai). In Japanese.

10. N. Pace, and R. E. Smith, "Measurement of the residual radiation intensity at the sites of the Hiroshima and Nagasaki atomic bombs," Atomic Bomb Casualty Commission TR, pp. 26–59.

    The average chest X-ray delivers between 30 and 50 millirads of energy to the site. Fluoroscopy deposits 10 rads per minute while fluoroscopy in "cine" mode will deliver up to 50 rads per minute.

11. S. Okijima, K. Takeshita, S. Antoku, T. Shiomi, W. J. Russell, S. Fujita, H. Yoshinaga, S. Neriishi, S. Kawamoto, and T. Norimura, "Radioactive fallout effects of the Nagasaki atomic bomb," *Health Physics*, vol. 34, 1978, p. 621.

12. Peter Wyden, *Day One: Before Hiroshima and After* (New York: Simon and Schuster, 1984), p. 326. Also: Joseph Hirshfelder, "The Scientific and Technological Miracle at Los Alamos," in *Reminiscences of Los Alamos 1943–1945* edited by Badash, Hirshfelder, and Broida (Boston: Reidel, 1980), pp. 87–88.

13. T. Kajitani and S. Hatano, "Medical survey on acute effects of atomic bomb in Hiroshima," CRIABC, vol. 1, 1953, p. 522.

14. O. Ichikawa, "Pathological study of atomic bomb diseases in horses," ibid., p. 247. R. Katashima, "Zoological investigation on the effects of the atomic bomb," in *Seishi no Hi—Hiroshima Daigaku Genbaku Hi sai Shi* (Light of Fate—Record of the Hiroshima University A-bomb Disaster), Hiroshima University A-bomb Dead Memorial Functions Committee, ed. Hiroshima Daigaku Genbaku Shibotsusha Irei Gyoji Iinkai, Hiroshima, 1977). F. Maekawa, "Stenographic records of the first Report of the Special Committee for Atomic Bomb Casualties: Biology Section," CRIABC, op. cit., p. 21. K. Okada, "Biological investigation of atomic bomb disasters. Part I. Effect on animals" and "Stenographic records of the first Report of the Special Committee for Atomic Bomb Casualties: Biology Section," ibid., pp. 217 and 42. M. Uda, Y. Sugahara, and I. Kita, "Meteorological conditions related to the atomic bomb explosion in Hiroshima," ibid., p. 98.

15. J. Robert Oppenheimer, cited in *Los Alamos Science* (Fortieth Anniversary issue), vol. 4, Winter/Spring 1983; p. 15.

16. J. Robert Oppenheimer, "Physics in the Contemporary World," *Bulletin of the Atomic Scientists*, vol. 4, 1948, p. 66.

17. Peter Pringle and James Spigelman, *The Nuclear Barons* (New York: Holt, Rinehart and Winston, 1981) p. 60.

18. David Holloway, *Technology, Management and the Soviet Military Establishment* (London: Institute for Strategic Studies, 1971), p. 41.

19. One nuclear administrator, Vassily Emelyanov, later noted, "What would have happened if we hadn't made it then? They would have shot us. Just shot." (Pringle and Spigelmen, op. cit., p. 63.)

20. Zhores Medvedev, *Nuclear Disaster in the Urals* (New York: W. W. Norton, 1979), p. 156.

21. Heinz Barwich, *Der Spiegel*, no. 44, 1965.

22. Igor Golovin, *I. V. Kurchatov A Socialist-Realist Biography of the Soviet Nuclear Scientist* (Moscow: Mir Publishers, 1969). Also translated by Joint Publications Research Service (JPRS 37 1804), Washington, D.C.

23. *The Large Soviet Encyclopedia*, 3rd ed., vol. 23, p. 543. Also: Golovin, op. cit., JPRS 37 1804, p. 17.

24. Information about the area is taken from Medvedev, op. cit.
25. Golovin, op. cit., JPRS 37 1804, p. 22.
26. Arnold Kramish, *Atomic Energy in the Soviet Union* (Stanford, Calif., Stanford University Press, 1959), p. 170. Also: Anonymous, "Soviet Operation of Uranium Mines in Eastern Germany," East European Fund, Mimeographed Series, No. 11, 1952.

Postwar (pp. 66–71)

1. Thomas B. Cochran, William M. Arkin, and Milton M. Hoenig, *Nuclear Weapons Databook*, vol. 1 (Cambridge, Mass.: Ballinger Publishing Co., 1984), p. 32.
2. Howard Morland interview with Vernon Kendrick in Howard Morland, *The Secret That Exploded* (New York: Random House, 1981), pp. 4–6.
3. Roger Rappoport, *The Great American Bomb Machine* (New York: Ballantine, 1971), p. 125.
4. Otto Frisch, *What Little I Remember* (Cambridge: Cambridge University Press, 1979), p. 162. Frisch had leaned over some unshielded U-235 when his body reflected back some neutrons, causing the uranium to go critical. "Actually," he said, "the dose of radiation I had received was quite harmless . . . but if I had hesitated for another two seconds before removing the material or if I hadn't noticed that the signal lamps were no longer flickering, the dose would have been fatal."
5. Rappoport, op. cit., pp. 126–127.
6. Peter Pringle and James Spigelman, in their *The Nuclear Barons* (New York: Holt, Rinehart and Winston, 1981), wrote that the first Soviet test was conducted near the town of Semipalatinsk (p. 69). Strobe Talbott, translator for *Khrushchev Remembers* (Boston: Little Brown, 1971, 1974), claims the first shot was in the Ust-Urt desert (p. 59).
7. Stalin had ordered the designers to copy the plane down to the last nut and bolt, even down to the mysterious hole beneath the left wing. The B-29 had been through a bombing raid over Japan and the hole might have been produced by a shell. Nevertheless, it was included in the design, and all the Tu-4s were made with holes under their left wings.
8. Andrew Cockburn, *The Threat: Inside the Soviet Military Machine* (New York: Random House, 1983) pp. 146–147.
9. Lewis L. Strauss, *Men and Decisions* (Garden City, N.Y.: Doubleday, 1962), pp. 201–202.
10. Norman Moss, *Men Who Play God: The Story of the H-Bomb and How the World Came to Live with It* (New York: Harper and Row, 1968), pp. 24–25.
11. Truman's close scientific advisor, Dr. Vannevar Bush, had just completed a book, *Modern Arms and Free Men*. In it he predicted the Soviets wouldn't have the bomb for ten years. The presses had to be stopped so Bush could modify his prediction.
12. Stanley A. Blumberg, and Gwinn Owens, *Energy and Conflict: The Life and Times of Edward Teller* (New York: G. P. Putnam's Sons, 1976), p. 200.

The Testing Begins (pp. 73–81)

1. The big musical hits of 1946 were "Prisoner of Love" by the singing barber, Perry Como, and "McNamara's Band" by Bing Crosby and The Jesters. Recorded on December 6, 1945, in Los Angeles, "McNamara's Band" eventually became a million seller. (Joseph Murrells, *The Book of Golden Discs* [London: Barrie and Jenkins, 1976] p. 35.)
2. Peter Pringle and James Spigelman, *The Nuclear Barons* (New York: Holt, Rinehart and Winston, 1981), pp. 125–126. In a speech to the United Nations, the French ambassador said: "The goals which the French government has assigned for the research of its scientists and technicians are purely peaceful. It is our hope that all the nations of the world may do the same as swiftly as possible." At the time, the French were beginning work on an atomic bomb. The project would take fourteen years and would culminate in an atomic detonation in the Sahara Desert in 1960. The first British nuclear weapon was detonated in 1952.
3. William D. Leahy, *I Was There* (London: Victor Gollancz, 1950), pp. 502–514.

4. Lewis L. Strauss, *Men and Decisions* (Garden City, N.Y.: Doubleday, 1962), pp. 189–195. Also: Fletcher Knebel and Charles W. Bailey, *No High Ground* (New York: Bantam Books, 1960), p. 181.

5. *Las Vegas Daily Optic*, Sept. 20, 1945, Scrapbook 71, New Mexico State Records Center and Archives, Santa Fe. Reported in Ferenc Morton Szasz, *The Day the Sun Rose Twice* (Albuquerque: University of New Mexico Press, 1984), p. 151.

6. William L. Laurence, "Bikini's King Gets Truman's Thanks," *New York Times*, July 16, 1946.

7. *Atomic Cafe*, a film by Jane Loader (director), Kevin Rafferty, and Pierce Rafferty. The Archives Project.

8. David Lillenthal, *The Atomic Energy Years, 1945–1950* (New York: Harper and Row, 1964), p. 200.

9. Ibid.

10. *El Paso Times*, Aug. 8, 1945.

11. DNA Personnel Review Series: Operation CROSSROADS, fig. 23, p. 90.

12. David Bradley, *No Place to Hide* (Hanover, N.H.: University Press of New England, 1983), pp. 66–68.

13. Corinne Browne and Robert Munroe, *Time Bomb* (New York: Morrow, 1981), p. 63. Note: Though Browne and Munroe mention the USS *Burleson*, the Defense Nuclear Agency Personnel Review of CROSSROADS carries no mention of the ship.

14. Bradley, op. cit., pp. 50–55.

15. Browne and Munroe, op. cit., p. 63.

16. Bradley, op. cit., p. 60.

17. Ibid., p. 70.

18. Browne and Munroe, op. cit., p. 64.

19. Bradley, op. cit., p. 86–87.

20. Defense Nuclear Agency, DNA 6032F, p. 101.

21. Browne and Munroe, op. cit., p. 65.

22. "A-Bomb Creates 'Most Poisonous Fog' in History," *Los Angeles Times*, Aug. 2, 1946.

23. DNA 6032F, p. 101.

24. Browne and Munroe, op. cit., p.66.

25. William Manchester, *The Glory and the Dream* (Boston: Little, Brown, 1974), p. 491.

26. *New York Times*, Mar. 3, 1948.

27. Hiss was accused of passing classified documents to the Soviets in 1938. When pressed to produce evidence, his accuser, Chambers, came up with several documents and strips of microfilm, some of which he hid in a carved-out pumpkin on his farm. In December 1948, Chambers directed federal agents to the pumpkin containing the film. While most of the contents of the microfilm was somewhat mundane, it had been transmitted in Code D, the State Department's most secret code.

28. DNA 6033F, p. 18.

29. Thomas B. Cochran, William M. Arkin, and Milton M. Hoenig, *The Nuclear Weapons Databook*, vol. 1 (Cambridge, Mass.: Ballinger Publishing Co., 1984), p. 9.

30. While the 23-kiloton CROSSROADS shots had been similar in yield to the earlier detonations, two of SANDSTONE's yields almost doubled that. The second test of the series, Yoke, produced a spectacular explosion equivalent to 49,000 tons of TNT.

31. Bernard J. O'Keefe, *Nuclear Hostages* (Boston: Houghton Mifflin, 1983), pp. 148–149.

32. In a confidential memo, Harwell scientist W. G. Marley indicated that the humidity at Wick could damage delicate monitoring equipment. Also, there might be hazards to the locals. The paper was read in March 1985 to the Australia Royal Commission investigating British nuclear tests in Australia between 1952 and 1953.

33. AEC 141/7 Dec. 13, 1950.

34. As it turned out, the nuclear material from Pimlico Sound would probably have traveled northeast to New England.

35. O'Keefe, op. cit., p. 149.

36. "The interlacing fingers of the Las Vegas, Sheep and Desert Ranges of low mountains screen the test site from direct view from any direction." (Gladwin Hill, *New York Times*, Feb. 1, 1951.)

37. Coincidentally, a nearby area slightly northeast of Las Vegas is listed in a 1942 airline route map as the "Valley of Fire." (*Columbia Standard Illustrated World Atlas* [Chicago: Consolidated Book Publishers, Inc. 1942–43], p. 1.)

Ranger (pp. 83–106)

1. *Time*, Feb. 5, 1951.
2. Defense Nuclear Agency, DNA 6022F.
3. On some Ranger shots, the capsule was inserted while in a circular pattern just above the drop zone.
4. Statement of Gloria Gregerson for Citizen's Call on S.1483. The Radiation Exposure Compensation Act of 1982, before the U.S. Senate Committee on Labor and Human Resources in Salt Lake City, Utah, Apr. 8, 1982.
5. Pike was an unusual commissioner in that he stood for less secrecy in the AEC's dealings with the public. Early on, he had experienced run-ins with Lewis Strauss and others because of his views. In 1950, in order to slip Pike's confirmation past Congress, President Truman had to agree to Senator Brien McMahon's request that Pike would not be chairman of the AEC.
6. Clint Mosher, International News Service, "A Frightening White Light, Then Silence, Then Blasts," *Houston Chronicle*, Feb. 2, 1951.
7. Statement of Gloria Gregerson for Citizen's Call on S.1483, op. cit.
8. Ibid.
9. Baker arrived over New York State about 4:00 P.M., January 30, 1951. Harsh upper-air disturbances had stretched the cloud into a long, thin stream. The fallout from the second shot finally ended at 4:00 P.M. the next day.
10. Gladwin Hill, "Third Atom Test Lights Nevada Dawn; Peaks Stand Out In Weird Glare," *New York Times*, Feb. 1, 1951.
11. Mosher, op. cit.
12. "Atom Blast No. 4 Is Biggest So Far," *New York Times*, Feb. 2, 1951.
13. Ibid.
14. "Radiation Higher, Called Harmless," *New York Times*, Feb. 2, 1951.
15. *Houston Chronicle*, Feb. 5, 1951, p. 12.
16. *Atomic Cafe*, a film by Jane Loader (director), Kevin Rafferty, and Pierce Rafferty. The Archives Project.
17. Ibid.
18. International News Service, "Las Vegas Braces for 'Real Humdinger' Bomb Test," *Houston Chronicle*, Feb. 5, 1951.
19. Leonard Slater, *Newsweek*, Feb. 19, 1951, p. 25.
20. The purple that Slater noticed was the result of intense radiation upon the nitrogen and oxygen atoms in the air.
21. Slater, op. cit., p. 25.
22. "Great Blast Ends Atom Series," *New York Times*, Feb. 6, 1951.
23. Associated Press, "Blast Is Felt 300 Miles From Nevada Site," *Houston Chronicle*, p. 1.
24. Slater, op. cit., p. 25.
25. At the time of the explosion, the winds were fluctuating wildly. At the surface, there was a slight breeze from the southeast at 2 mph; 2,000 feet above the ground, the wind had shifted to the east-northeast at 8 mph; while at 3,000, the wind was slightly stronger but from the north. The wind direction seemed to change in a counterclockwise rotation with altitude until it reached 270 degrees (west) at 5,000 feet. A thousand feet higher and the wind was from the northwest again. Before the detonation, no one really knew where the winds would carry Fox.

The Race for the Super (pp. 107-118)

1. Emil Lengyel, *1000 Years of Hungary* (New York: John Day, 1958), p. 227.
2. Absolutely essential to any understanding of Edward Teller's role in history is the authorized biography by Stanley A. Blumberg and Gwinn Owens, *Energy and Conflict: The Life and Times of Edward Teller* (New York: G. P. Putnam's Sons, 1976). The information about Teller's early childhood is taken from this book, pp. 9–20.
3. Though Teller's mother, father, and sister narrowly escaped death, his brother-in-law and childhood best friend, Edward "Suki" Harkanyi, apparently was killed by the Nazis during a final Jewish purge in the last days of World War II. (Blumberg and Owens, op. cit., pp. 25, 168.)
4. Years later, Teller would, in the words of his biographers, "champion a stable and democratic government, based upon a conservative capitalism and protected by a strong military. (Blumberg and Owen, op. cit., p. 23.)
5. Bethe first came up with the proposal in 1939. He theorized that stars produce energy through a complex series of reactions called the "carbon cycle," where "normal" carbon acts as a "proton catcher" to eventually produce a helium atom, two positrons, two gamma rays, two neutrinos, and 24.7 million electron volts of energy per atom. For those interested in the technical aspects of Bethe's carbon cycle, see W. Wallace McCormick, *Fundamentals of College Physics* (New York: Macmillan, 1965), pp. 781–783.
6. Blumby and Owens, op. cit., p. 109. It is not known if the term "thermonuclear" was coined during the meeting.
7. Tritium, an even rarer form of hydrogen, consists of an electron, a proton, and *two* neutrons.
8. Edward Teller, "The Work of Many People," *Science*, vol. 121, February 25, 1955, p. 267.
9. Blumberg and Owens, op. cit., pp. 188–189.
10. Ibid., pp. 190–192. Dr. Manfred Mayer of Johns Hopkins University assisted Teller's biographers, in the translation of Thirring's work. Edward Teller had never read Thirring's book, but later said, "Maybe I should have." When shown a copy of Chapter 42 and asked if Thirring had been correct in his assumptions, Teller's only reply was "Thirring was not a fool."
11. Report from Oak Ridge National Laboratory, dated June 28, 1950: "The separation of the isotopes of lithium by chemical methods has been under investigation at ORNL for approximately nine months."
12. Andrei Sakharov, *Sakharov Speaks* (New York: Knopf, 1974), pp. 6–9.
13. William Manchester, *The Glory and the Dream* (Boston: Little Brown, 1974), pp. 571–572.
14. *New York Times*, Jan. 22, 1950.
15. Manchester, op. cit., p. 572.
16. The Rosenbergs would eventually die in the electric chair. David Greenglass, a worker at Los Alamos who supplied information to the Soviets about the explosive lenses, was sentenced to fifteen years in prison.
17. Harold J. Ness, president, Lithium Company, Newark, N.J. Letter to Carroll L. Tyler, manager, Santa Fe Operations, U.S. Atomic Energy Commission, Los Alamos, New Mexico, February 3, 1950.
18. Blumberg and Owens, op. cit., p. 272.
19. The "problem" has been officially classified and remains so in 1985.
20. Blumberg and Owens, op. cit., p. 280.
21. The conversation was between Teller biographers, Stanley Blumberg and Gwinn Owens, and Major Theodore Walkowicz, who, in 1951, was the executive officer for the Scientific Advisory Group (SAG) of the air force, a unit set up in 1945 by air force chief general H. H. Arnold:

    Walkowicz: "There was a Russian shot fired that we did not understand."
    Question: "You mean an atomic explosion?"

Walkowicz: "Yes, it was a Soviet atomic explosion, and we did the usual thing of collecting air samples. A thing known as AFOAT One was in existence at that time. It flew airplanes all around the periphery of Russia and captured the debris after each one of the shots. These debris samples were analyzed, and from that there were deductions made as to the nature of the Soviet shot."

Question: "Why don't you understand it?"

Walkowicz: "It was understandable only in terms of assuming that there had been a thermonuclear component to it. It wasn't a pure fission shot. There had to be fusion involved in it. . . . I remember [John von Neumann] reporting to the Scientific Advisory Board [nicknamed the "Tree Full of Owls"] . . . and to a lot of air force officers, that there was something chilly and strange in the debris samples. The implication was that it could be understood only in terms of there having been a fusion component in the shot." [Blumberg and Owens, op. cit., pp. 270-273]

22. The fallout analysts knew what to expect from a typical fission shot. A fusion burst would produce a different spectrum of fallout products.

23. Blumberg and Owens, op. cit., pp. 270-273.

24. Thomas B. Cochran, William M. Arkin, Milton M. Hoenig, *The Nuclear Weapons Databook*, vol. 1 (Cambridge, Mass.: Ballinger Publishing Co., 1984), p. 27.

25. The neutron energy curves for a fission weapon all have the same slope—that is, the spectrum does not vary with distance. A thermonuclear reaction produces neutrons in the 8.18 to 15 million electronvolt (MeV) range that predominates at 400 yards, but are barely present at four times that distance. Thus, for a fission reaction, the entire neutron spectrum decreases with increasing distance; for a fusion reaction, the higher energies are attenuated more quickly and the shape of the neutron spectrum changes with distance. See Samuel Glasstone and Philip J. Dolan, *The Effects of Nuclear Weapons* (U.S. Department of Energy, 1977) pp. 366-368.

26. Cochran, Arkin, and Hoenig, op. cit., p. 27.

27. It has not been made public whether liquid deuterium or tritium had been used for the GEORGE shot, but a fair guess would be that it was not. Instead, it was likely that lithium deuteride was one of the additives to the GEORGE device. Lithium had been recognized for quite some time as essential to the thermonuclear bomb. Teller's biographers are vague: "Teller's new theoretical concept was confirmed at the third shot of the GREENHOUSE series. It was the only one designed as a steppingstone to a full-fledged hydrogen bomb. The new concept involved a means of igniting liquid deuterium and tritium in a massive thermonuclear explosion, but it also pointed the way to a compact, deliverable bomb. This would be fueled not with impractical liquid isotopes of hydrogen, which must be refrigerated, but with lithium deuteride. The lithium deuteride version of the hydrogen bomb would have the double advantage of requiring no refrigeration and no expensive tritium." (Blumberg and Owens, op. cit., p. 273.)

28. The official Department of Energy account notes: "According to the published account of one of the leaders in nuclear weapon development of the period GEORGE demonstrated the initiation of a sustained thermonuclear reaction by use of a fission reaction. This led directly to the MIKE operation." (DOE 6034F: GREENHOUSE, p. 21.)

29. DOE 6034F: GREENHOUSE, p. 21.

30. Technically, the "pit" refers to the fissile material plus the tamper/reflector.

31. J. Carson Mark, *The Bulletin of the Atomic Scientists*, Mar. 1983, p. 47.

32. Cochran, Arkin, and Hoenig, op. cit., p. 31.

33. Robert D. Krohn, Technical Information Group, Los Alamos, New Mexico. Letter to Arthur D. Thomas, Classification Officer, Lawrence Livermore Laboratory, Livermore, Calif., Dec. 11, 1974. Reported in Blumberg and Owens, op. cit., pp. 274-275.

34. For those interested, the reaction is as follows:

(a) Li^6 + neutron (from fissioning core)$\rightarrow He^4$ + tritium + 4.8 MeV

(b) Deuterium + tritium→He^4 (3.52 MeV) + neutron (14.07 MeV)

(c) Deuterium + deuterium→Tritium (1.01 MeV) + proton (3.02 MeV)3

or,

→He^3 (0.82 MeV) + neutron (2.45 MeV)

(d) Tritium + tritium→He^4 + 2 neutrons + 11.4 MeV

The result of the reaction is two helium atoms and 22.4 MeV energy. (Cochran, Arkin, and Hoenig, op. cit., pp. 23–27.)

35. Lee Bowen, *A History of the Air Force Atomic Energy Program 1943–1953*, Vol. IV (Washington, D.C.: U.S.A.F. Historical Division), p. 40. Reported in Cochran, Arkin, and Hoenig, op. cit., p. 27.

36. Blumberg and Owens, op. cit., p. 277.

37. *In the Matter of J. Robert Oppenheimer*. Transcript of Hearings Before the Personnel Security Board, Washington, D.C., April 12, 1954, through May 6, 1954 (Washington, D.C.: U.S. Government Printing Office, 1954), p. 305.

38. Blumberg and Owens, op. cit., p. 286.

39. Ibid., p. 288.

40. Ibid., p. 290.

41. Ibid., pp. 292–293.

42. Defense Nuclear Agency, DNA Personnel Review: Operation Ivy, p. 136.

43. Bernard O'Keefe, *Nuclear Hostages* (Boston: Houghton Mifflin, 1983), p. 150.

44. Blumberg and Owens, op. cit., p. 295.

45. O'Keefe, op. cit., p. 151.

46. John McPhee, *The Curve of Binding Energy* (New York: Farrar Strauss & Giroux, 1973), p. 83.

47. Another thing was named for Enrico Fermi, the distance equal to the diameter of one electron: 10^{-13} centimeters is defined as one fermi.

48. McPhee, op. cit., p. 82–83.

49. DNA 6035F, p. 204.

50. Paul Johnson, *Modern Times* (New York: Harper and Row, 1983), p. 455.

51. One even turned up in the U.S. ambassador's house—in the Great Seal of the United States. (Johnson, op. cit., p. 455.)

52. Ronald Hingley, *Joseph Stalin: Man and Legend* (London: 1974), p. 404.

53. T. H. Rigby, *The Stalin Dictatorship: Khrushchev's 'Secret Session' Speech and Other Documents* (Sydney, Australia: 1968), p. 81.

54. Peter Pringle and James Spigelman, *The Nuclear Barons* (New York: Holt, Rinehart and Winston, 1981), p. 144.

55. Robert Payne, *The Rise and Fall of Stalin* (London: 1968), pp. 718–719. Khrushchev later claimed that Beria had actually been shot—or strangled—on June 26, the day of his arrest. His "official" trial and execution came several months later. Soviet historian Roy Medvedev, however, in his book *Khrushchev*, claims that Beria was executed immediately after his trial, in December of that year. (Roy Medvedev, *Khrushchev: A Biography* [Garden City, N.Y.: Doubleday, 1983].)

Buster-Jangle (pp. 119–134)

1. Howard L. Rosenberg. *Atomic Soldiers* (New York: Harper and Row,), p. 34.

2. Ibid.

3. Defense Nuclear Agency, DNA 6022F.

4. Rosenberg, op. cit., p. 37.

5. *New York Times*, May 5, 1951.

6. "New Atom Weapon Hinted By Picture," *New York Times*, July 1, 1951.

7. Harvey Wasserman and Norman Solomon, *Killing Our Own* (Garden City, N.Y.: Doubleday, 1982), p. 69.
8. *New York Times*, Oct. 23, 1951.
9. International News Service, *Houston Chronicle*, Oct. 22, 1951.
10. Gladwin Hill, "Atom Battle Bomb Dims Sun in Nevada," *New York Times*, Oct. 29, 1951.
11. Philip W. Allen and Lester Machta, "Operation BUSTER: Transport of Radioactive Debris from Operations BUSTER and JANGLE, Project 7.1," Armed Forces Special Weapons Project, Washington, D.C., March 15, 1952, WT-308.
12. *Houston Chronicle*, Nov. 2, 1951, p. 10.
13. The following army units participated in the tactical maneuver at shot DOG: First Battalion, 188th Airborne Infantry Regiment, 11 Airborne Division, Camp Campbell, Kentucky; Third Medical Platoon, 188th Airborne Medical Company, Camp Campbell, Kentucky; Platoon, Company A, 127th Engineer Battallion, Camp Campbell, Kentucky; Battery C, 546th Field Artillery Battalion, Fort Lewis, Washington.
14. A car traveling 55 mph can cover 500 yards in 18.6 seconds.
15. Rosenberg, op. cit., pp. 43–45.
16. Recently declassified government documents indicate the base of the mushroom cloud was much higher, at 31,000-feet which would place it at least 19,090 feet above Hill's position.
17. Gladwin Hill, "Huge Blast Marks War Games," *New York Times*, Nov. 1, 1951.
18. The 10,000-foot level moved south, crossing Mexico, then the southern tier of Texas counties: Zapata, Starr, Hidalgo, and Cameron. At the time, the orange and grapefruit crops were being readied for harvest.
19. *Houston Chronicle*, Nov. 6, 1951.
20. Rosenberg, op. cit., p. 48.
21. Allen and Machta, op. cit., p. 71.
22. The experiment conducted by the Naval Ordnance Lab indicated the base surge phenomenon was, in fact, more pronounced with underground shots than with underwater detonations.
23. Allen and Machta, op. cit., p. 108.
24. Ibid., p. 112.
25. Ibid.
26. Ibid., p. 110.
27. Michael Uhl and Tod Ensign, *G.I. Guinea Pigs* (New York: G. P. Putnam's Sons, 1983), p. 63.

Maneuvers

TUMBLER-SNAPPER *(pp. 137–156)*

1. *The Fragrance Reference Guide* New York: Fragrance Foundation, 1979), p. 36.
2. Samuel Glasstone and Phillip J. Dolan, *The Effects of Nuclear Weapons*, 3rd ed. (United States Department of Defense and the United States Department of Energy, 1977), p. 277.
3. Ibid., pp. 289–291. A 20-kiloton shot at 2½ miles would induce a heat load of three calories per square centimeter.
4. Ibid., p. 125.
5. AEC Meeting No. 667, April 1, 1952. Reported in Howard L. Rosenberg, *Atomic Soldiers* (New York: Harper and Row, 1982), p. 50.
6. Letter from AEC chairman Gordon Dean to Brigadier General Herbert Loper, chief, Armed Forces Special Weapons Project, April 2, 1952. Reported in Rosenberg, op. cit.
7. George H. Quester, *Nuclear Diplomacy: The First Twenty-Five Years* (Cambridge, Mass.: Dunellen, 1970), p. 35.
8. Omar Bradley, "This Way Lies Peace," *The Saturday Evening Post*, vol. 227, Oct. 15, 1949, pp. 32–33.

9. Sidney Lens, *The Bomb* (New York: Dutton, 1982), p. 26.

10. Ibid., p. 42.

11. Quester, op. cit., pp. 72–73.

12. Gladwin Hill, "New Atomic Device Set Off in Nevada," *New York Times*, Apr. 1, 1952.

13. United Press, "Atomic Fireball Unfurled From B-29," *New York Times*, Apr. 15, 1952.

14. Ibid.

15. "Huge Atom Blast Is Set for Today," *New York Times*, Apr. 22, 1952.

16. The following units were involved: *Army*: 2nd Battalion, 504th Airborne Infantry Regiment, 82nd Airborne Division, Fort Bragg, North Carolina; Company B, 167th Infantry Regiment, 31st Infantry Division, Camp Atterbury, Indiana; Company C, 135th Infantry Regiment, 47th Infantry Division, Fort Rucker, Alabama; Tank Platoon, 11th Armored Cavalry Regiment, Camp Carson, Colorado; Engineer Platoon, 369th Engineer Amphibious Support Regiment, Fort Worden, Washington; Medical Detachment (augmented), Sixth Army, numerous Sixth Army posts; *Air Force*: 140th Fighter-Bomber Group (Provisional), 140th Fighter-Bomber Wing, Clovis Air Force Base, New Mexico.

17. William Laurence, "Atom Bomb Fired With Troops Near; Chutists Join Test," *New York Times*, Apr. 22, 1952. Additional note: According to legend, AEC construction worker Tom Sherrod took a door from an outdoor privy, painted the words *News Nob* on it in yellow letters, and staked the sign at the site; thus the name. (Rosenberg, op. cit., p. 58.)

18. Hansen Baldwin, "Troops Maneuver After Atom Blast," *New York Times*, Apr. 22, 1952.

19. DNA 6020F, "Operation Tumbler-Snapper," p. 94.

20. The troops were scheduled to begin the jump at 11:15, aiming for an area slightly north-northwest of ground zero.

21. For some reason, some of the paratroopers in one plane jumped six minutes early. As a result, they landed 8 miles from the drop zone. After they hit the ground, the pilot received word that five soldiers had been injured in the jump. At 11:20, the pilot radioed Air Operations Center and requested a helicopter be sent to pick up the injured personnel. A Y-12 helicopter was sent out twenty minutes later. Shortly before noon, the chopper pilot radioed to base that the paratroopers injuries were minor.

22. Baldwin, op. cit.

23. Ibid.

24. Robert J. List, "Radioactive Debris From Operation Tumbler-Snapper," NYO-4512. U.S. Weather Service, Feb. 25, 1953.

25. At 10:00 A.M., Pacific Standard Time, on the same day the Geiger counter at Columbia University began acting up, part of the Charlie cloud was crossing Los Angeles at 18,000 feet. Four days later, at 6:00 A.M., the same cloud drifted over Chicago, then moved south toward Memphis, crossing that city at 9:00 the evening of April 27.

26. The highest pretest activity found on any individual gummed paper was 45/disintegrations/minute/square foot/day. List, op. cit., NYO-4512, p. 12.

27. Baldwin, op. cit.

28. John McPhee, *The Curve of Binding Energy* (New York: Farrar Strauss & Giroux, 1973), p. 115.

29. On May 1, the Dog device was detonated at 8:30 A.M. sharp over Area 7, Target 3 of the Nevada Test Site. Charlie had exploded at such a high altitude that the stalk had not linked up with the mushroom. With Dog, "a gray-black, massive and dense [column] surged up instantly and persisted as a solid 'stalk' for many minutes." The reporters also noted that "the rolling, red-orange fireball following the initial flash was visible for the unusually long period of ten seconds, and the cottony white radioactive cloud that developed soared quickly to four or five miles before it was caught by the wind and attenuated southward." (Gladwin Hill, "Marines Get Taste of Atomic Warfare," *New York Times*, May 1, 1952.)

30. Michael Uhl and Tod Ensign, *G.I. Guinea Pigs* (New York: Putnam, 1983) p. 67.

31. List, op. cit., NYO-4512, p. 34.

32. Ibid., p. 35.

33. List, op. cit., NYO-4512, p. 13.

34. "New Nevada Blast Most Spectacular," *New York Times*, May 26, 1952.

35. List, op. cit., NYO-4512, p. 39.

36. The following units took part in the assault maneuver during TUMBLER-SNAPPER: GEORGE: 23rd Transportation Truck Company, Camp Roberts, California; 31st Transportation Truck Company, Fort Ord, California; Tank Platoon of the First Armored Division, Fort Hood, Texas; 369th Engineer Amphibious Support Regiment, Fort Worden, Washington.

37. McPhee, op. cit., p. 67.

38. As a result of its location at the north end of a series of ridges, fallout occurred at Elko with some regularity. This event would be no different. Amid the 0.08-roentgen/hour readings created by shot GEORGE, a sliver of relatively intense radiation—0.20 roentgens/hour—extended north toward Elko. Other Nevada communities affected included Eureka, Jiggs, Halleck, Wells, North Fork, Tuscarora, and Carlin.

39. List., op. cit., NYO-4512, p. 39.

40. Minutes of the meeting of the Advisory Committee for Biology and Medicine held in St. Louis, Missouri, June 7–9, 1952. (Rosenberg, op. cit., p. 52.)

41. Memorandum to Dr. John C. Bugher, M.C., AEC Division of Biology and Medicine from Captain John T. Hayward, chief, Navy Weapons Research Branch, September 19, 1952. (Rosenberg, op. cit., p. 52.)

42. Memorandum to Brigadier General K. E. Fields, director, AEC Division, of Military Application from George P. Kraker, deputy manager, AEC Santa Fe Operations Office, October 7, 1952. Subject: Reply to Captain Hayward regarding troop participation in atomic tests. (Rosenberg, op. cit., pp. 52–55.)

43. Letter to Brigadier General K. E. Fields, director, AEC Division of Military Application from Major General Herbert Loper, chief, Armed Forces Special Weapons Project, October 15, 1952. (Rosenberg, op. cit., pp. 52–55.)

44. *Troop Participation in Continental Tests*, report by the director, AEC Division of Military Application, December 1952. Quoted in Rosenberg, op. cit., p. 55.

UPSHOT: KNOTHOLE *(pp. 157–187)*

1. Ad in *New York Times*, Mar. 18, 1953.

2. *New York Times*, Mar. 7, 1953.

3. Ibid.

4. About 400 personnel from Indian Springs Air Force Base, Nevada, and over 2,000 from Kirtland Air Force Base, New Mexico, would participate in the Desert Rock V exercise, as well as members of the 4935th Air Base Squadron, the 4901st Support Wing, and the 55th Weather Reconnaissance Squadron. DNA 6015F-6018F.

5. International News, Mar. 17, 1953.

6. "35th Atom Blast Set Off in Nevada," *New York Times*, Mar. 18, 1953.

7. Samuel W. Matthews, "Nevada Learns to Live With the Bomb," *National Geographic Magazine*, June 1953, p. 839.

8. Ibid., p. 842.

9. There, the radiation level was only one roentgen/hour, but at 600 yards it increased to 50 roentgens/hour. At a point 250 yards south of the tower base, the radiation level was a lethal 2,000 roentgens/hour.

10. In Paris, Missouri, the level was just over 300 disintegrations/minute/square foot. That same night, just 240 miles south, the radioactivity jumped to over 30,000 disintegrations/minute/square foot.

11. High activity had also occurred at Knoxville, Tennessee, one day earlier, when levels of 1.9 million and 1.4 million disintegrations/minute/square foot/day were recorded. This was

the second highest activity ever recorded east of the Mississippi River. Meteorologists thought this high reading was associated with thundershowers that occurred as a cold front passed while the 18,000-foot trajectory was in the area. Annie's nuclear cloud moved east for the next three days and, except for the 10,000-foot level, crossed the East Coast by midnight, March 20. At exactly this same time, the 10,000-foot level was crossing over Detroit. This part of the cloud would leave the country three days later, crossing north-northwest through Maine.

12. Sheep and other animals were tethered almost 2 miles from the blast, while an extremely unlucky few would get a close-up view of the 24-kiloton Nancy: a mere 98.4 yards from the tower.

13. The officers who volunteered were: Lieutenant Colonel George S. Parish, army, Madison, Wisconsin; Captain John J. Sutter, air force, Cincinnati, Ohio; Lieutenant Norman H. Magneson, navy, Santa Ana, California; Lieutenant Paul J. Lewis, navy, Crystal Spring, Mississippi; Colonel Max S. George, army, Punxsutawney, Pennsylvania; Commander Robert E. Thomas, Jr., navy, Rockford, Illinois; Commander Frank B. Voris, navy, Stuart, Florida; Captain Robert R. Coller, army, Battle Creek, Michigan; and Lieutenant Colonel Don Davis, army, Shell Beach, California.

14. The trench position was predicted on a given expected yield that in turn would, at a calculated distance, produce no more than 5 roentgens of initial gamma radiation, 10 roentgens of total radiation, 8 pounds per square inch blast effect, and 1 calorie per square centimeter thermal effect. In the calculation, the officers were asked to include any other factors, such as ground shock, cratering, and base surge.

15. At the surface just prior to the burst, the wind had been practically calm at only 2 mph from the north. Three hundred feet above the surface, at the height of the cab, there had been no wind detected at all. Above those levels, the wind was from the southwest, increasing in speed with height.

16. "Nine Officers Brave New Atomic Blast," *New York Times*, Mar. 25, 1953.

17. *Life*, June 1980, p. 36. Reported in Harvey Wasserman and Norman Solomon, *Killing Our Own* (Garden City, N.Y.: Doubleday, 1982), p. 76. Also: John Fuller, *The Day We Bombed Utah* (New York: New American Library 1984).

18. Instruments recorded that the expanding bomb debris and heated air occluded the inner fireball within 7 milliseconds. Eleven milliseconds later, the air had cleared sufficiently to unmask the inner isothermal sphere, the "second maximum." From this data, the scientists concluded that Ruth's yield was decidedly unspectacular, somewhere on the order of 200 tons of TNT, much lower than planned.

19. Monitors entering the area an hour later found radiation levels of 10 milliroentgens/hour at a distance of 600 yards south of ground zero. The on-site radiation contours indicate the cloud traveled south, then east, in the direction of the Nevada/Utah/Airzona junction; however, the actual cloud track was somewhat farther south, over Las Vegas, Prescott and Winslow, Arizona, and Los Alamos, New Mexico. Although monitoring teams were present at all sites where fallout was expected, no significant radiation levels were recorded—except at Phoenix, on April 1, where a level of 330,000 disintegrations/minute/square foot/day was recorded.

20. Instruments indicated the flash was occluded by superheated air and bomb debris at 10 milliseconds and was again completely visible 127 milliseconds later.

21. John McPhee, *The Curve of Binding Energy* (New York: Farrar Strauss & Giroux, 1973), p. 160.

22. At the Las Vegas airport, the shock wave from Dixie was recorded at 7 pounds per square foot.

23. The lower—and slower—levels of the Dixie nuclear cloud passed over Indian Springs and Las Vegas; however, monitors in those areas detected no activity with the clouds passing. In the area surrounding the test site, the only activity from Dixie was, interestingly, at Dixie College, near St. George, Utah. During a rainstorm, the radiation level there was measured

at 0.4 milliroentgens/hour. Dixie's nuclear cloud tracked over Lubbock, Texas, at 30,000 feet at 10:00 P.M. on April 6. Three hours and thirty minutes later, it crossed over Memphis on its way to the North Carolina coast.

24. Charles Panati and Michael Hudson, *The Silent Intruder: Surviving the Radiation Age* (Boston: Houghton Mifflin, 1981), p. 151.

25. In its report, the Weather Bureau indicated that it is probable "even higher activity would have been measured in the Atlantic Ocean 200 to 300 miles east of New York if observations had been available." (Robert J. List, "The Transport of Atomic Debris from Operation Upshot-Knothole" NYO-4602, Weather Bureau, Washington, D.C., June 25, 1954, p. 23.)

26. Ray was detonated at 4:45 A.M. on April 11. The inner fireball was occluded (first minimum) at 18.2 milliseconds. The outer shell of heated air cleared at 162 milliseconds. Scientists declared the yield at only 200 tons of TNT. (DASA 1251, Vol. 1, "Local Fallout from Nuclear Test Detonations," Defense Nuclear Agency, p. 126.)

27. List, op. cit., NYO-4602.

28. The level was found to be 0.02 microcuries per cubic meter. (DASA 1251, Vol. 1, p. 127.)

29. Excerpts from the official report: "The cloud travelled in a west-southwest direction away from [ground zero] at a fair velocity until it reached the neighborhood of Death Valley where its velocity became practically nil until such time as the cloud tracking planes could no longer distinguish it. . . . Readings taken by the on-site monitoring group indicated that the cloud passed to the west of Mercury and of Las Vegas. Slight positive readings [less than 1 milliroentgen/hour] were found at the Control Point, Mercury, Lathrop Wells, and Shoshone, California." (List, op. cit., NYO-4602.)

30. Among areas crossed by the Ray nuclear cloud: *Nevada*: Indian Springs, Lathrop Wells, Scotty's Junction; *California*: Death Valley, Death Valley Junction, Shoshone, Baker, Panamint Springs, Barstow, Victorville.

31. Four major marine units would be involved in the maneuver: Brigade Headquarters; 1st Battalion, 8th Marine Regiment, 2nd Marine Division; 2nd Battalion, 3rd Marine Regiment, 3rd Marine Division; Marine Helicopter Transport Group 16, also called "MAG-HR-16." Together the four units would be known as the "2nd Marine Corps Provisional Atomic Exercise Brigade." Before the maneuver was over, some of the marines would have exceeded the allowable limit of 6.0 roentgens of radiation.

32. Instruments had difficulty recording the first minimum; in the records it occurs anywhere between 5.6 and 17.75 milliseconds. There is no record available for the first maximum. Yield was estimated to be on the order of 23 kilotons, slightly larger than the Nagasaki burst.

33. Prior to the blast, the surface conditions had been relatively calm. At the surface, there had been a wind from the north of 10 mph, which had increased to 14 mph at 300 feet, the height of the device. At 3,500 feet, the wind had shifted to the west and doubled in intensity to 20 mph. Higher still, at 15,500 feet, the wind was from the northwest at a respectable 40 mph. At 25,500 feet, "mushroom height," the wind was still from the northwest at 53 mph. After shot time, these values changed significantly.

34. Appendix 7: "Special Report by Col. W. F. Lantz as an Observer at a Volunteer Position in Desert Rock Five, Marine Exercise" (Quantico, Va.: Marine Corps Educational Center. April 1953), 4 pages.

35. By the time the group had left the trenches, some dosimeters read over 6.0 roentgens and some film badges indicated readings as high as 7.1 roentgens.

36. Monitors riding in the helicopters watched the radiacs closely, calling directions to the pilot to help them avoid patches of hot air. Unfortunately, two of the choppers flew through areas of greater than 50 roentgens/hour before they could take evasive action.

37. "Marines Capture Atomized Region," *New York Times*, Apr. 19, 1953.

38. There was little directional shear in the winds above 10,000 feet, and most of the cloud was carried eastward over the southern states. Though there was almost no precipitation associ-

ated with this burst, considerable fallout occurred over New Mexico, Texas, and Louisiana on April 19 and over southern Florida on April 20.

39. List, op. cit., NYO-4602, p. 27.
40. Monitors found 250 milliroentgens outside and 160 milliroentgens inside, New York Times News Service, Aug. 12, 1979. Reported in Wasserman and Solomon, op. cit., p. 72.
41. Ernest J. Sternglass, *Secret Fallout* (New York: McGraw-Hill, 1981), pp. 1–5. Also: Herbert M. Clark, *Science*, May 7, 1954, pp. 612–622; Herbert M. Clark, et al., *Journal of the American Water Works Association*, November 1954, pp. 1101–1111.
42. Sternglass, op. cit., p. 21.
43. List, op. cit., NYO-4602, p. 32.
44. Howard L. Rosenberg, *Atomic Soldiers* (New York: Harper and Row, 1982), p. 65. See also United Press, *New York Times*, Apr. 29, 1953.
45. List, op. cit., NYO-4602. Memo to William S. Johnson, off-site operations officer, NPO, from R. E. Stafford and E. J. Weathersbee, rad/safe off-site monitors; subject: Special Study Post Shot VII; Apr. 29, 1953.
46. Other animals were used: two F-80 drone jets, each carrying a monkey and some mice, would be flown through the mushroom at 25,000-foot altitude, roughly seven minutes after the detonation. They would suffer severe radiation poisoning and have to be put to death.
47. List, op. cit., NYO-4602 (R-3.7, May 14, 1953).
48. That night, after the cloud had passed, some Casper residents found their way to the Rex Theater to watch a Sterling Hayden war movie, *Flat Top*. Second on the bill was another Sterling Hayden picture, *Kansas Pacific*: "Bullets, dynamite and blood-stained spikes!" At the Rialto, Dana Andrews starred in *Canyon Passage*. The second feature was a Yvonne DeCarlo movie, *Frontier Gal*. At the Skyline Drive-In, James Mason and Ava Gardner starred in *The Loves of Pandora*. The next evening, as fallout covered much of the eastern half of the nation, on "I Love Lucy," Lucy thinks everyone has forgotten her birthday. Instead, they throw her a surprise party. In this episode, Ricky sings the lyrics to "I Love Lucy."
49. Music was provided by a five-piece orchestra from Culver-Stockton College at nearby Canton, Missouri. The band was set up in the middle of the stage surrounded by a picket fence decorated with sweet peas. Near the band was a wishing well. Close to the ceiling, above the stage of the gymnasium, were suspended two large bags of balloons. Around 11:00 that night, the bags burst and everyone ran across the gymnasium floor, grabbing and popping balloons. At some time during the evening, the band was asked to play "Crazy, Man, Crazy," the new hit by Bill Haley and the Comets.
50. "Spread of Radiation Laid to Atomic Tests," *New York Times*, May 15, 1953.
51. Wasserman and Solomon, op. cit., p. 73. Made available to authors through *Citizen's Call*.
52. "Nevada Atom Test Affects Utah Area," *New York Times*, May 20, 1953.
53. Wasserman and Solomon, op. cit., interview with Citizen's Call state director Preston Truman, p. 74.
54. At ground zero an hour after the blast, radiation monitors found only 10 roentgens/hour. However, the 10-roentgens/hour area extended northeast more than 4 miles. Off-site contours suggest that the cloud then turned east and crossed into Utah and Arizona in a band of radiation slightly over 100 miles wide.
55. Wasserman and Solomon, op. cit., p. 74.
56. Ibid.
57. Ibid., pp. 222–223.
58. Three hours after detonation, St. George received radiation levels of 0.8 roentgen/hour. Forty miles east of the Nevada border and 20 miles north of the Arizona border a small area of intense radiation (2 roentgens/hour) was recorded four hours after the burst. At 2:00 on the morning of May 20, radiation monitors found a maximum external gamma level of 0.4 milliroentgens/hour at Albuquerque, and at 5:00 A.M., the level at Grand Junction, Colorado, was 0.6 milliroentgens.

59. Testimony to the Congressional Joint Committee on Atomic Energy, July 1963. Reported in Sternglass, op. cit., p. 56.
60. Fallout, Radiation Standards and Countermeasures, June 1963, Part I. Quoted in Wasserman and Soloman, op. cit., p. 108.
61. List, op. cit., NYO-4602, p. 37.
62. AEC Commissioners' Meeting Minutes, May 22, 1953.
63. Bernard J. O'Keefe, *Nuclear Hostages* (Boston: Houghton Mifflin, 1983), p. 156.
64. Ibid.
65. Ibid., p. 157.
66. "Atom Shell Fired From Gun in Test," *New York Times*, May 26, 1953.
67. Ibid.
68. O'Keefe, op. cit., p. 157.
69. List, op. cit., NYO-4602, p. 40.
70. Butrico's report of the meeting:

> From: Frank A Butrico, Off-Site Rad/Safe Monitor, N.P.G.
>
> To: William S. Johnson, Off-Site Operations Officer, N.P.G.
>
> Subject: DISCUSSION WITH REPRESENTATIVE STRINGFELLOW IN ST. GEORGE, UTAH.
>
> On the evening of May 25, 1953, Mr. Lamb, the chief of police in St. George, informed me that Representative Stringfellow was going to discuss the fallout incident which developed there as a result of firing Shot IX [HARRY] on May 19. He extended an invitation for me to attend in the event some questions were raised regarding the local situation when the fallout occurred.
>
> Although the meeting lasted three hours, only about thirty [30] minutes were devoted to the fallout incident. Representative Stringfellow informed the group of his meeting with the AEC people at Camp Mercury and that from what they told him, there was no cause for alarm over what happened the week before. He was thoroughly convinced that every possible precaution was being taken to avoid over exposing any of the communities around the proving grounds to excessive amount of radiation. He further indicated that the amount of fallout in St. George from [HARRY] was not dangerous and AEC gave him the figures to back their statements. He read these figures to the group and as a comparison, he quoted some levels of these figures to the group as a comparison, he quoted some levels of exposure that might cause radiation illness, which he obtained from someone with AEC [I would guess the advisory panel]. These figures were going to be released to the press and during a radio broadcast from Cedar City the next day.
>
> It might be mentioned that Representative Stringfellow was rather critical of AEC over their "antiquated security measures." As an example, he mentioned the briefings at the proving grounds at which he and other members of Congress were told they could not release any statement to the effect that they had witnessed the explosion of an atomic shell [GRABLE]. To him, this was ridiculous in view of the great amount of publicity being given to the event on both the radio and press.
>
> —Frank A. Butrico, Off-Site Rad/Safe Monitor, Nevada Proving Grounds

71. Gordon Dean, Diary, May 27, 1953. Reported in Wasserman and Solomon, op. cit., p.75.
72. Gladwin Hill, "Mightiest Atom Blast of Tests Unleashed on Nevada Desert," *New York Times*, June 5, 1953.
73. Ibid.
74. An hour after the shot, monitors found 10 roentgens/hour 800 yards from ground zero, about average for an airdropped device. By this time, the cloud was leaning toward the southeast in a "malevolent gray serpentine." (Hill, "Mightiest Atom. . . .") It would eventually turn toward the northeast, crossing Hibbing, Minnesota, on June 6 at Noon.
75. John Fuller, "The Day We Bombed Utah," *Omni*, May 1983, p. 134.
76. Ibid.

77. Ibid.

78. John Fuller, *The Day We Bombed Utah* (New York: New American Library 1984), pp. 78–79.

79. Authors interview with Ken Clark, who had met with his father immediately after the meeting. To his son, Doug Clark had identified Rust as the man who had told him he was "nothing but a dumb farmer." Steven Brower, now a professor at Brigham Young University, had kept notes of the meeting that concurred on the abusive nature of the AEC personnel present. (Author's interview with Doug Clark, May 19, 1985.)

80. The slides were of *one* sheep out of the 4,000 that had died. (Fuller, op. cit., p. 81.)

81. Fuller, op. cit., p. 81.

82. Ibid., p. 134. In one report, a radiation estimate of 10 rads was changed to 5 rads.

83. Ibid., pp. 134–135.

84. The sheepmen asked for $30 a ewe and $15 a lamb. The Bullochs' claim totaled $34,180. (Fuller, op. cit., p. 117.)

85. Ibid.

86. Producer Howard Hughes originally wanted Marlon Brando in the lead role. Others in the cast included William Conrad, Thomas Gomez, John Hoyt, Ted De Corsia, Lee Van Cleef, and Billy Curtis.

87. Fuller, op. cit., p. 54.

88. Harry and Michael Medved, *Hollywood Hall of Shame* (New York: G. P. Putnam's Sons, 1984), pp. 51–52.

89. Ibid.

90. Ibid., p. 51.

91. Producer Hughes, after hearing of the cancer epidemic rumors, was reported to have felt at least partially responsible for the deaths. He subsequently pulled the film from distribution. (Medved and Medved, op. cit., p. 52.)

CASTLE: BRAVO (pp. 188–194)

1. This is speculation based upon the best evidence available; the construction of the hydrogen bomb remains classified. See Howard Moreland, *The Secret That Exploded* (New York: Random House, 1981), p. 278.

2. Bernard J. O'Keefe, *Nuclear Hostages* (Boston: Houghton Mifflin, 1983), p. 162.

3. Ibid., p. 166.

4. Ibid., p. 175.

5. Ralph E. Lapp, "The Voyage of the Lucky Dragon," *Reader's Digest*, May 1958, p. 114.

6. O'Keefe, op. cit., p. 178.

7. Ibid., p. 179–182.

8. Lapp, op. cit., pp. 115–116.

9. A chest X-ray delivers 30 to 50 millirads. One roentgen is equivalent to a deposition of 98 ergs per gram of soft tissue; one rad is equivalent to a deposition of 100 ergs per gram of material. A rem is a rad multiplied by biological quality factors and other modifiers. While the units are not similar, they are roughly equivalent.

10. O'Keefe, op. cit., pp. 184–185.

11. An eyewitness to the blast, Keith Dallman, recalled the event:

> We had to be on the same side of the ship as the shot, and had to fold our arms one on top of the other and place our arms on a railing on the bulkhead facing inboard of the ship and push our eyes into our arms. . . . When the shot went off, I could see bright daylight, just like looking at a lightbulb that was turned on, through both my arms. Then I heard a bang and a short time later felt the shock wave from the shot. Then the ship sailed toward Bikini Atoll island on which the shot went off. There were parts of palm trees floating all over the water. [*Atomic Veteran's Newsletter*, Jan.–Feb. 1985.]

12. O'Keefe, op. cit., pp. 190–192.

13. Ibid., pp. 194–196.
14. Ibid., p. 197.
15. Ibid.
16. Lapp, op. cit., pp. 118–119.
17. Ibid., p. 120.
18. The next major Pacific tests would involve the MK-17, a huge 21-ton device fitted with tiny tail fins and three concentric rings around the nose. It would be dropped from an aircraft on May 20, 1956, during shot CHEROKEE, operation REDWING.

Watching the Bombs Go Off (pp. 195–204)

1. "Sir M. Thomas Sees Atom-Powered Flying Boats as Airlines in 25–50 Years," *New York Times*, Dec. 31, 1954.
2. *New York Times*, May 1, 1954.
3. *New York Times*, Apr. 21, 1954.
4. *New York Times*, May 25, 1954.
5. *New York Times*, Sept. 25, 1954.
6. *New York Times*, Nov. 20 and Dec. 18, 1954.
7. *New York Times*, Jan. 12 and Jan. 30 1955.
8. *New York Times*, Feb. 21, 1955. The cobalt bomb was actually a possibility. It was based on the fact that irradiated cobalt, Co-60, has a half-life of about twenty-five years and is extremely radioactive. By wrapping natural cobalt around a fission device, the resulting detonation would create a cloud of intensely radioactive Co-60.
9. *New York Times*, Feb. 16, 1955.
10. *New York Times*, Feb. 18, 1955.
11. *New York Times*, Feb. 19, 1955.
12. *New York Times*, Mar. 11, 1955.
13. *New York Times*, Mar. 12, 1955.
14. *New York Times*, Mar. 13 and Mar. 14, 1955. Also: Harvey Wasserman and Norman Solomon, *Killing Our Own* (Garden City, N.Y.: Doubleday, 1982), p. 92.
15. Wasserman and Solomon, op. cit., p. 93.
16. H. Peter Metzger, *The Atomic Establishment* (New York: Simon and Schuster, 1972), pp. 97–98.
17. *New York Times*, Apr. 2, 1955.
18. The article was probably prepared around the time of the March 14 AEC meeting in which Libby made his now-famous remark: "People have got to learn to live with the facts of life, and part of the facts of life are fallout."
19. "The Facts About A-Bomb 'Fall-Out,'" *U.S. News & World Report*, Mar. 25, 1955, pp. 21–26.
20. All emotion-charged words such as "fallout," "strontium-90," and "mutations" were enclosed in quotation marks, perhaps reflecting an effort to diminish their validity to the reader.
21. *New York Times*, Apr. 26, 1955.
22. *New York Times*, May 12, 1955.
23. *New York Times*, June 4 and June 7, 1955.
24. *New York Times*, June 11, 1955.
25. *New York Times*, June 14, 1955.
26. Roger Rappoport, *The Great American Bomb Machine* (New York: Ballantine, 1971), pp. 120–121. Curie exposed his arm to a radiation source for one hour. At the site of injury, his skin turned a bright red. Fifty-two days later the area turned gray. It will not be known what effect this had on his longevity; shortly after that, he was hit by a carriage.
27. Ibid., p. 122.

28. Ibid., p. 157.
29. *New York Times*, May 25, 1953.

The Soviets I: Bombs in the Kremlin (pp. 205–208)

1. *Military Thought* (Moscow), November 1966. In another article published three years later, in February 1969, the author said that "Soviet military strategy primarily reflect the political strategy of the Communist Party of the Soviet Union. It is in the interests of political strategy that military strategy makes use of the achievements of scientific-technical progress which materialize in weapons of varying power. Somed of these weapons are capable of doing considerable damage to a continent, others only to individual states. . . . Finally, still others lead to defeat of the enemy's armed forces without doing essential injury to the economy or populace of states whose aggressive rules unleashed the war. . . ." (Sam Cohen, *The Truth About the Neutron Bomb* [New York: William Morrow, 1983], p. 164.)

2. In 1957, at the Second United Nations International Conference on the Peaceful Uses of Atomic Energy, held in Geneva, Artismovich presented a paper describing a method by which deuterium-deuterium and deuterium-tritium reactions may be generated by compressing the material using simple TNT rather than fission devices. His experiments had begun in 1952. (Cohen, op. cit., pp. 160–169.)

3. The GRU supplies cigarette lighters and fountain pens to the bureaucrats who work at headquarters.

4. Viktor Suvorov, *Inside Soviet Military Intelligence* (New York: Macmillan, 1984), pp. 51–52, 113–118.

5. Nikita S. Khrushchev, *Khrushchev Remembers*, vol. 2 (Boston: Little Brown, 1974), pp. 70–71. Also: Andrew Cockburn, *The Threat: Inside the Soviet Military Machine* (New York: Random House, 1983), p. 191.

6. Cockburn, op. cit., p. 276.

7. Ibid.

8. Ibid., p. 91.

Hot Spots (pp. 209–212)

1. Philip W. Allen and Lester Machta, "Operation Buster: Transport of Radioactive Debris from Operations Buster and Jangle" Project 7.1 Armed Forces Special Weapons Project, Washington, D.C., March 15, 1952, WT-308, p. 108.

   List also wrote of a second mechanism for high levels of fallout: "A second potential source of high radioactivity at the ground, one that has received little attention, is a low-level cloud which reaches an inhabited area before adequate dilution takes place. The relatively high activity at Elko, Nevada, following the Surface and Underground bursts illustrates the potential of such low-level transport. If all the active debris were beneath a strong temperature inversion through which little diffusion is possible, one might find surprisingly high values at points remote from the Site. It would be worthwhile to track the lower portions of clouds to ascertain more properly the degree of activity at these elevations."

2. Ibid., p. 109.

3. Robert J. List, "The Transport of Atomic Debris from Operation Upshot-Knothole, NYO-4602, June 25, 1954, pp. 70–71.

4. Ibid., p. 74.

5. Ibid., p. 75.

6. Ibid., pp. 80–81.

TEAPOT (pp. 213–242)

1. The early implosion bombs, such as the ones used at Nagasaki, were extremely inefficient. Perhaps less than 5 percent of the material actually fissioned. The rest of the plutonium was vaporized and scattered with the other parts of the bomb. The use of reflectors and improved tampers helped solve this problem. A dense metal, such as steel, was wrapped

around the nuclear capsule. Acting as a mirror, it reflected back neutrons escaping from the surface of the plutonium sphere, thus creating more energy. The steel covering also acted as a tamper, helping to keep the fissioning plutonium together an extra microsecond or so, increasing the pressure even more before the device blew apart under the million-atmosphere pressure created by the chain reaction.

2. Beryllium is one of the lightest metals known; its use in a weapon would result in a considerable weight reduction. In addition, beryllium atoms, when sprayed with alpha particles, produce neutrons. So, in effect, there would be three potential neutron sources: the polonium-beryllium initiator at the center of the nuclear material, the plutonium, and the reflector.

3. Report: U.S. Marine Corps Report of Exercise Desert Rock IV, 1955, p. vii–2.

4. This exercise assumes the reader is between 5½ and 6 feet tall.

5. Minutes of AEC meeting, March 14, 1955. Quoted in Harvey Wasserman and Norman Solomon, *Killing Our Own* (Garden City, N.Y.: Doubleday, 1982), p. 89.

6. John Fuller, *The Day We Bombed Utah* (New York: New American Library, 1984), pp. 108–116.

7. Paul Jacobs, "Clouds from Nevada," *The Reporter*, May 16, 1957.

8. Ibid., p. 22.

9. In Lexington, those braving the rain that day could have seen a Dean Martin–Jerry Lewis feature at the Capitol: *Three-Ring Circus*. Or they could have visited the Lexington Theater, where Van Heflin and Anne Bancroft were starring in *The Raid*.

10. Experimental in nature, Tesla would apparently be used to determine new material configurations that could result in a more efficient weapon.

11. Thomas H. Saffer and Orville E. Kelly, *Countdown Zero* (New York: G. P. Putnam's Sons, 1983), pp. 228–230.

12. Ibid., p. 231.

13. The soldiers looking up saw the bottom of the mushroom that was 14,279 feet overhead, while the top of the cloud reached 25,979 feet above the desert floor. Though the winds were calm at the surface, at the height of the mushroom the wind was blowing from the southeast at 30 mph. A later examination of the radiation contour at ground zero indicated an initial path northeast, then a turn due east. The movement of the cloud indicated it would pass north of Las Vegas and cross the Nevada border in a band 30 miles wide with the center located about 15 miles north of the Utah-Arizona border.

14. DNA Fact Sheet, Subject TEAPOT series, DNA 6010F–6013F: The men were found to have received radiation exposures of 16.0 and 19.3 roentgens of radiation. They were not allowed in any other radiation areas after that time. Seven other men, four belonging to the Naval Research Lab and three belonging to the Chemical and Radiology Lab, also received exposures exceeding the 3.9 roentgen limit. The highest exposure of the group was 12.3 roentgens.

15. Gladwin Hill, *New York Times*, Mar. 2, 1955.

16. Those with television sets may have been watching Edward Arnold star in the "Climax" episode "South of the Sun."

17. *New York Times*, Mar. 6, 1955.

18. Intercontinental ballistic missile. At the time, the only way to carry a nuclear warhead to the enemy was by strategic bomber.

19. Jacobs, op. cit.

20. Although HORNET was relatively small, only 4 kilotons, its mushroom cloud climbed to 33,000 feet above the desert floor, then, caught in a 50-mph air current, began to move southeast, toward Mt. Turnbull, in Arizona.

21. One hour after detonation, BEE's radiation contour was egg-shaped, pointing due east. Within 300 feet of ground zero, monitors found 2,000 roentgens/hour. At three times that distance, radiation levels were still lethal: 1,250 roentgens/hour.

22. After passing over Las Vegas, the cloud crossed Lake Mead, then into Arizona, moving toward the towns of Chloride, Hackberry, and Kingman.

23. As the nuclear cloud reached the East Coast, people with televisions sets might have been watching such shows as "Public Defender" or "Treasury Men in Action." Both shows that evening, incidentally, featured a young actor named Charles Bronson. One episode was titled "Cornered"; the other, "The Case of the Deadly Dilemma."

24. Produced during 1960–63, the weapon had a plutonium warhead that weighted 58.6 pounds. The device was produced in two different configurations, dubbed M-129 and M-159. In addition to the suitcase charge, the warhead was also used in the "Davy Crockett" atomic rocket. It had a diameter of 11 inches and a length of 25½ inches. (Thomas B. Cochran, William M. Arkin, and Milton M. Hoenig, *Nuclear Weapons Databook*, vol 1 [Cambridge, Mass.: Ballinger Publishing Co., 1984], p. 60. Also: U.S. Army, Nuclear Weapons Maintenance Specialist, Soldiers Manual, FM 9-55G4 [June 1980] pp. 3–86.)

25. ESS was an afternoon shot, detonated at precisely 12:30 P.M. on March 23. Observers watched as tons of Nevada soil was blown skyward by the detonation. The cloud climbed to 7,712 feet, drifted first southeast, then east, passing north of Las Vegas toward the Nevada-Utah-Arizona junction. It crossed the Arizona border approximately nine hours after the shot.

26. At the crater's lip one hour after the shot, the monitors calculated the radiation level to be approximately 6,000 roentgens/hour.

27. The lower levels of the cloud, the 10,000-foot trajectory, traveled north past Ogden, Utah; Billings, Montana; Minot, North Dakota; and Winnipeg, Manitoba. The higher trajectories moved across the southern half of the U.S., crossing Albuquerque and Santa Fe, New Mexico; Dallas–Fort Worth, Texas; Greenville, South Carolina; and Miami, Florida.

28. *New York Times Magazine*, May 26, 1957.

29. *New York Times*, Apr. 4, 1955.

30. 350 millicuries/100 square miles. Robert J. List, "Radioactive Fallout in North America from Operation Teapot," NYO-4696, U.S. Atomic Energy Commission, Washington, D.C., February, 1956.

31. 290 millicuries/100 square miles. Ibid.

32. It had originally been set for April 3, the date of the Strauss speech, but had been rescheduled when the plane that was to have dropped it developed difficulties.

33. The cloud passed at 45,000 feet over the East Coast at 1:00 P.M. on April 7. That evening, Lorne Greene starred in the "Climax" episode, "Private Worlds."

34. POST had originally been scheduled to coincide with the HADR and MET events, but various equipment and weather problems had stretched the schedule somewhat.

35. At ground zero one hour after the detonation, monitors found radiation readings of 1,000 roentgens. Camp Mercury received between 0.02 and 0.08 roentgens/hour.

36. Interestingly, though the path of the fallout cloud was due west, POST produced a hot spot on April 10 that included the eastern half of Nevada, all of Utah, and a large portion of southwestern and central Wyoming. All recording sites within this area registered over 500 millicuries/100 square miles. The day the cloud crossed over Norfolk, Virginia, a band of showers dropped slightly radioactive rain across the Mississippi River valley. The small town of Axis, Alabama, about 10 miles inland from Mobile, received a record 20.33 inches of rain in twenty-four hours. The rain was slightly radioactive; the downpour increased the radioactivity of the area by 58 millicuries/100 square miles.

37. Michael Uhl and Tod Ensign, *G.I. Guinea Pigs* (New York: Putnam, 1983), p. 74.

38. The wind gradient gradually increased with altitude. At the surface a gentle 16-mph breeze from the west barely kicked up the dust; at 36,000 feet, however, the wind roared along at 87 mph. As a result, even as MET's mushroom was still climbing, its stem began to break up at 20,000 feet altitude. The steady westerly winds carried the cloud in an east-northeast direction.

39. The cartoon was "Playful Puss." Those staying home to watch television that night could have seen Bruce Bennett in a "Damon Runyon Theater" episode, "Pick the Winner."

40. That evening, central Missouri received about 320 millicuries/100 square miles of radioactivity. The same day, rain fell in the eastern Great Lakes. Detroit received 2,400

millicuries/100 square miles, while Cleveland received 4,700 millicuries/100 square miles. List, op. cit., NYO-4696.

41. Task Force Razor was composed of the following armored units: 723rd Tank Battalion, Camp Irwin, California; and Company C, 510th Armored Infantry Battalion, 4th Armored Division; Company B, 510th Armored Infantry Battalion, 4th Armored Division; First Platoon, Battery A, 22nd Armored Field Artillery Battalion, 4th Armored Division; First Platoon, Company C, 24th Armored Engineer Battalion, 4th Armored Division; Provisional Aviation Company, First Armored Division, all from Fort Hood, Texas.

42. While it was calm—and hot—on the ground, at 7,000 feet the wind was steady from the southeast at 16 mph. Another 10,000 feet, at "stem level," the wind had shifted toward due north at 36 mph. Still higher, the pattern moved clockwise until at 47,000 feet, the height of the "icecap," the wind was steady toward the northeast.

43. The vehicles used in the maneuver consisted of fifty-five M-48 tanks, two M-41 tanks, five M-74 tank recovery vehicles, one M-75 armored personnel carrier, twenty-five M-59 armored personnel carriers, four M-B2 self-propelled 105mm howitzers, and about 150 wheeled vehicles. After the event, the task force would march overland back to Camp Irwin, where they would participate in a chemical warfare exercise.

44. A standard measure of radiation protection used by the army in 1955 was that one inch of armor is equal to about 6 inches of concrete. Since the fronts of the Patton tanks were plated with 4 inches of steel, it was assumed that the gamma radiation would be attenuated by 1/16. Since other sides of the vehicle were not so well protected, officials estimated that if the tanks crossed areas of 8 roentgens, the personnel inside would receive only one roentgen. After the test, this was revised downward somewhat to a ration of 1 to 12.

45. Anthony Leviero, "Armor Rides Out Shock, Men Safe," *New York Times*, May 5, 1955.

46. Gladwin Hall, "Atom Blast Rocks a Capsule Town," *New York Times*, May 5, 1955.

47. Leviero, op. cit.

48. Hill, op. cit.

49. Uhl and Ensign, op. cit., p. 81

50. The military also discovered that rubber was not particularly affected by radiation.

51. At 3:00 P.M. local time, the cloud crossed into Utah, leaving behind it a band of fallout 90 miles wide. The center of the band was 170 miles north of the Nevada-Utah-Arizona junction. At the center, monitors found 0.02 roentgens/hour at 4:00 P.M. near the towns of Ibapah, Utah, and Callao.

The official report indicates: "Dry fallout at Ely, Nevada, on the day of the burst resulted in the highest activity observed at any station during the test series. On the following day, Colorado experienced its highest activity for this series. . . . The activity in the San Francisco area on the sixth was most probably globe-circling debris from an earlier test [most likely the persistant MET cloud]. Deposition continued to be heavy, both in and out of rain areas, for several days following APPLE-2 over most of the United States east of the test site." (Radioactive Fallout in North America From Operation Teapot," AEC Document 14323.)

52. Less than 120 millicuries/100 square miles radioactivity. (List, op. cit., NYO-4696.)

53. By May 7, all central plains states were receiving radioactivity from the sky. Monitors in Missouri recorded 1,400 millicuries/100 square miles. Monitors in New Mexico and west Texas recorded between 380 and 1600 millicuries/100 square miles. (List, op. cit., NYO-4696.)

54. On May 15, 1955, the top five songs in the nation were: "Ballad of Davy Crockett" by Bill Hayes; "Unchained Melody" by Al Hibbler; "My Babe" by Little Walter; "Cherry Pink and Apple Blossom White" by Perez Prado; and "Don't Be Angry" by Nappy Brown.

55. The ZUCCHINI cloud climbed to 35,755 feet above the desert in just four minutes, half the usual time for a nuclear cloud. Weather Bureau meteorologists initially were relieved; the top of the cloud missed the stratosphere by only 4,000 feet.

56. The radiation band seemed to follow U.S. 15 north past Parowan, Beaver, and Cove Fort, Utah, where monitors found radiation levels about 0.008 roentgens/hour.
57. Up to 1,400 millicuries/100 square miles. At the same time, Kalispell and Libby, Montana, just east of the Bitterroot Mountains, received dry fallout amounting to 360 millicuries/100 square miles. (List, op. cit., NYO-4696.)
58. President Eisenhower authorized approval for the shot on December 9, 1954.
59. The column of water climbed to between 900 and 1,450 feet and was about 3,100 feet in diameter.
60. DNA Personnel Report: WIGWAM.
61. PROJECT 56 involved four safety detonations that took place at the Nevada Test Site between November 1, 1955, and January 18, 1956. All were safety experiments in which nuclear weapons were subjected to explosions, shock, and fire in an attempt to see if the bomb would explode accidentally. Usually in these experiments, the conventional explosive surrounding the core detonates, scattering plutonium particles without producing a measurable yield.

1956: The Year of Fallout (pp. 243–248)

1. Jeffrey D. Merritt, *Day By Day: The Fifties* (New York: Facts On File, 1979), p. 507.
2. At 11:15 P.M. on January 20, 1952, Stevenson called a friend and told him, "This is Adlai, and I've just had the most incredible experience. Would you mind terribly coming down to the hotel for a little talk?" When the friend arrived, Stevenson told him: "I've just come from Blair House, and the President wants me to save the world from Dwight Eisenhower." (*New York Times*, Jan. 24, 1952.)
3. Nixon had made a name for himself during the highly publicized trial in which Whittaker Chambers was found to have been a member of the Communist party. An excellent account of Nixon's role in the affair is found in William Manchester's *The Glory and the Dream* (Boston: Little Brown, 1974), pp. 493–512.
4. John Alsop, brother of columnist Stewart Alsop, came up with the term prior to the 1952 election. He said that "while Stevenson was appealing and appealed strongly to people's minds, Eisenhower, as a man and as a figure, was appealing far more strongly to people's emotions." He told his brother, "sure, all eggheads are for Stevenson, but how many eggheads are there?" (Manchester, op. cit., p. 625.)
5. Manchester, op. cit., p. 648.
6. Merritt, op. cit., p. 491.
7. Ibid., p. 509.
8. Ibid., p. 523
9. Manchester, op. cit., pp. 599–602.
10. Ibid., op. cit., p. 769.
11. *New York Times*, Jan. 20, 1956.
12. *New York Times*, Feb. 27, 1956.
13. *New York Times*, Apr. 21, 1956.
14. *New York Times*, May 29, 1956. General Starbird was wrong about the Albuquerque site also.
15. *New York Times*, June 13, 1956.
16. *New York Times*, June 21, 1956.
17. *New York Times*, July 1, 1956.
18. A close contender for the position of Stevenson's running mate was Massachusetts senator John F. Kennedy. Texas senator Lyndon Johnson had nominated Kennedy by shouting "Texas proudly casts its vote for the fighting sailor who wears the scars of battle!" (Manchester, op. cit., p. 770.)
19. Edward Teller with Allen Brown, *The Legacy of Hiroshima* (Garden City, N.Y.: Doubleday, 1962), p. 68. Also Stanley A. Blumberg and Gwinn Owens, *Energy and Conflict: The Life and Times of Edward Teller* (New York: G. P. Putnam's Sons, 1976), p. 396.

20. *New York Times*, Oct. 16, 1956.
21. *New York Times*, Oct. 17, 1956.
22. For more information see Edwin Kessler, ed., *The Thunderstorm in Human Affairs* (Norman: University of Oklahoma Press, 1981).
23. If the idea never caught on in scientific circles, it subsequently enjoyed a popularity in science fiction B-movies. In 1961, a British film, *The Day the Earth Caught Fire*, was released. It was about nuclear tests knocking the Earth off its axis and toward the sun. One of the stars was Arthur Christiansen, the ex-editor of the *Daily Express*. The 1977 motion picture *Damnation Alley* was based on the same premise.
24. *New York Times*, Oct. 18 and Oct. 20, 1956.
25. *New York Times*, Oct. 20, 1956.
26. Ibid.
27. *New York Times*, Oct. 24, 1956.
28. *New York Times*, Oct. 27, 1956.
29. *New York Times*, Nov. 3, 1956.
30. Merritt, op. cit., p. 613.
31. Author's interview with Martha Bordoli Laird, May 14, 1985.
32. *Life*, June 1980, p. 39.
33. Philip W. Allen and Lester Machta, "Operation Buster: Transport of Radioactive Debris From Operations Buster and Jangle, Project 7.1, Armed Forces Special Weapons Project, Washington, D.C., March 15, 1952, WT-308, pp. 87, 89.

Hot Dust, Hard Rain

PLUMBBOB (pp. 251–293)

1. According to the letter, the AEC wanted to: (1) proof-test a weapon for desired military characteristics before it entered the national stockpile; (2) provide a firm basis for undertaking the extensive engineering and fabrication efforts that must be expended to carry a "breadboard" model to a version satisfactory for stockpile purposes; (3) demonstrate the adequacy, inadequacy, or limitations of current theoretical approaches; (4) explore phenomena that can vitally affect the efficiency and performance of weapons but which are not susceptible to prior theoretical analysis of sufficient certainty. (DNA: PLUMBBOB.)
2. As with other shots, the Cambridge, Massachusetts, engineering firm of Edgerton, Germehausen and Grier, Inc., would be responsible for the timing and firing signals.
3. The military troops participating in the PLUMBBOB series included: an infantry company from the First Battle Group, 12th Infantry Regiment, 4th Infantry Division, Fort Lewis, Washington (also called Task Force Warrior); Fourth Marine Corps Provisional Atomic Exercise Brigade; Provisional Company, 82nd Airborne Infantry Division (to be tested to determine psychological reactions of troops to tactical nuclear warfare); Third Transportation Battalion (provided helicopter support); 506th Pathfinder Unit (assigned to the Third Transportation Battalion; among its responsibilities was radiation safety monitoring).
4. A criterion was established for the positioning of troops at the nuclear events: (1) Overpressure: The troops would not be allowed to wait out a blast if the overpressure exceeded 3 pounds/square inch. (2) Nuclear radiation: 5 rem (roentgen equivalents man) at any one test of which no more than 2 rem is prompt. Also, the whole-body radiation should not exceed 5 rem in any six-month period. The only radiation the AEC considered in this criteria was gamma. Alpha, beta, and neutron radiation was not included—the AEC had not decided on safety criteria for these types of radiation. (3) Thermal radiation: The troops were not to receive more than two-thirds of the heat necessary to produce a first-degree burn on bare skin.

   In order to meet these criteria, the engineers devised a table that would indicate the required distance from ground zero with reference to kiloton yield:

Max. Predicted Yield (Kiloton)	Troops in Open (Yards)	Troops in Trenches (Yards)	Troops in Armored Vehicles (Yards)
0.1	1,700	1,400	1,600
0.5	2,100	1,700	2,000
1	2,300	1,900	2,200
2	2,500	2,100	2,300
4	3,000	2,300	2,600
10	4,000	2,600	2,800
20	5,200	3,100	3,100
30	6,200	3,500	3,500
40	7,000	3,900	3,900
50	7,600	4,200	4,200
60	8,200	4,400	4,400
70	8,700	4,700	4,700
80	9,200	4,900	4,900
90	9,600	5,100	5,100
100	10,200	5,300	5,300

Each serviceman arriving at Camp Desert Rock was to be issued a DuPont dosimeter film packet Type 559. This packet consisted of film covered with three metal filters, one each of aluminum, copper, and laminated tin-lead. The varying density of the filters allowed estimation of both gamma and beta exposures. Over 33,000 film badges would be issued for the Plumbbob series of tests. Less than that number would be recovered and analyzed. (DNA 15.10 6007F.)

5. It was possibly around this time that the weapons designers were working with "dial-a-yield" configurations in which varying amounts of fusion components such as tritium were bled into the pit during arming.

6. In an interview with Ralph Friedman of *The Reporter*, the merchant said, "The (Boltzmann) fallout pattern was supposed to stretch out over the uninhabited area of central Nevada, but it took off, as though it had a mind of its own, and went past Reno and plumb over the mountains and kept on going and dropping radioactive material until it was way over the ocean. Next time it might take a mind to visit Chicago." Actually, the 30,000-feet trajectory almost did just that. (Ralph Friedman, "Next Door to Ground Zero," *The Reporter*, Oct. 19, 1957.)

7. *Life*, vol. 42, no. 23, June 10, 1957, pp. 24–29.

8. Friedman, op. cit., p. 258.

9. "Illness at Birth Seen From Fall-Out," *New York Times*, June 3, 1957, p. 11.

10. *Life*, vol. 42, no. 23, June 10, 1957, pp. 24–29.

11. On the ground directly below where the balloon had been, radiation levels reached over one roentgen/hour. Interestingly, alpha radiation levels were found to be high within a radius of 246 feet of ground zero. Alpha radiation typically comes from the heavier elements, such as uranium and plutonium, weapon components that should have fissioned; the high levels may have meant Lassen was largely fizzle. Because of the high alpha contamination, the ground zero area was closed for thirty-five hours after the shot.

12. *U.S. News & World Report*, June 14, 1957, p. 45.

13. "The Biological Effects of Atomic Radiation," The National Academy of Sciences, report to the public, 1956.

14. DNA 6008F.

15. Thomas H. Saffer and Orville E. Kelly, *Countdown Zero* (New York: G. P. Putnam's Sons, 1982), p. 47.

16. Ibid.

17. Ibid., p. 50.

18. The nuclear cloud crossed directly over Waco before turning northeast, passing over Jackson, Mississippi, and Augusta, Georgia, before leaving the North Carolina coast on June 26.

19. Of the remaining four safety experiments conducted during the PLUMBBOB series, two, PASCAL—A (July 26) and COULOMB B (September 6) would produce a slight nuclear yield. No information has been released to indicate the explosive configuration used in these experiments.

20. Ernest O. Lawrence was head of the Livermore Laboratory at the time, while Teller was its chief scientist. Mark Mills was a special assistant to Teller. In the Blumberg and Owens book, John H. Morse, special assistant to Lewis Strauss recalls the visit from accounts he heard later: "The president seemed really interested in only one thing that they brought up, and that was the possibility of removing the radiation from large weapons; in other words, producing mostly fusion rather than fission reactions. And Dr. Teller made the statement, as he told me, that he thought over a period of time, if they worked hard at it, they could reduce the fission component of nuclear weapons to five percent, a very small proportion. The president was greatly interested in that as a peaceful application of nuclear explosions." (Stanley A. Blumberg and Gwinn Owens, *Energy and Conflict: The Life and Times of Edward Teller* [New York: G. P. Putnam's Sons, 1976], pp. 397–398.)

21. John W. Finney, "U.S. Eliminates 95% of Fallout From The H-Bomb," *New York Times*, June 25, 1957.

22. Gladwin Hill, "Atom Test Rips Blockhouse 14 Miles From Site of Blast," *New York Times*, June 24, 1957.

23. "A Super A-Blast Is Set for July 4," *New York Times*, July 3, 1957.

24. Saffer and Kelly, op. cit., pp. 72–73.

25. Mr. Schofield, startled by the blast wave, strained his neck. A week later the government agreed to pay medical expenses for the injury.

26. Saffer and Kelly, op. cit., pp. 76–77.

27. Coincidentally, HOOD's 30,000-foot and 40,000-foot trajectories passed about 50 miles either side of Fort Hood, Texas.

28. Saffer and Kelly, op. cit., p. 83.

29. The same problem had happened five years before, at shot TUMBLER-SNAPPER: Fox. At that misfire, EG&G engineers Herb Grier and Bernie O'Keefe flipped a coin to see who would disarm the weapon. O'Keefe lost and, along with test director Jack Clark and Los Alamos physicist John Wieneke, had to climb the tower. It was determined that an experiment being performed by another group had malfunctioned and had locked out the firing signal. (Bernard J. O'Keefe, *Nuclear Hostages* [Boston: Houghton Mifflin, 1983], pp. 152–156.)

30. Loudin S. Wainwright, "The Heroic Disarming of Diablo," *Life*, Aug. 1957.

31. Howard L. Rosenberg, *Atomic Soldiers* (New York: Harper and Row, 1982), p. 88.

32. The 20,000-foot trajectory had left the United States at the northern borders of North Dakota and Minnesota. After spending time over Canada, the cloud returned to the country near Cleveland, circling around Cincinnati before tracking southwest over West Virginia, Virginia, and North Carolina.

33. In October of that year, Sputnik made it appear that the Russians didn't really need bombers to deliver their weapons to American soil. But in mid-July 1957, the Genie air-to-air missile seemed like a good idea. Actually, the Sputnik shot was mostly show. The rocket that pushed the satellite into orbit was not particularly useful as an intercontinental ballistic missile.

34. Rosenberg, op. cit., pp. 89–92.

35. *Time*, July 29, 1957, p. 16.

36. At 10:00 that evening, the cloud passed 40,000 feet over the small Montana town of Westby.

37. The two higher trajectories traveled north and east, tracking over such cities as Ogden, Utah, and Pocatello, Idaho, before crossing over the Standing Rock Indian Reservation, Corson County, South Dakota. From there, the 20,000-foot trajectory tracked over such cities as Waterloo and Cedar Rapids, Iowa, Peoria, Illinois, and Evansville, Indiana, before crossing Tennessee, Alabama, and finally, Georgia. The 30,000-foot trajectory took a more northerly track, passing over Green Bay, Wisconsin, Grand Rapids, Michigan, Cleveland, Ohio, Wheeling, West Virginia, and northern Virginia. KEPLER crossed 30,000 feet over the small town of Alma, Georgia, at 3:00 A.M. on July 31, 1957.

38. Back at the test site, gamma intensities of one roentgen/hour were confined to an area slightly less than a mile (4,890 feet) from ground zero.

39. The middle, "stem," trajectory crossed over Montana and North Dakota, leaving the continental United States at 20,000 feet over the small border town of Sarles, North Dakota. The 30,000-foot trajectory crossed over the northern U.S. before turning south, crossing Front Royal, Virginia, at 11:00 the night of July 27. The lowest OWEN's trajectory meandered over northern Utah, Wyoming, South Dakota, Minnesota, and Iowa before turning back west and dissipating over the small town of Corinth, Kansas.

40. "Nuclear Device Exploded Over Desert as Pacifist Group Prays 30 Miles Away," *New York Times*, Aug. 8, 1957.

41. Though there would be no troop maneuvers, over 600 Desert Rock troops would participate in the SHASTA event, either as part of indoctrination and training, or as part of a technical service project. Twenty-one men from the Sierra Ordnance Depot at Fort Huachuca took part in the Sixth Army Radiological Training Project. Thirty-two soldiers from the Army Signal Research and Development Labs at Fort Huachuca and Fort Meade took part in the Cloud-Detection and Tracking project, while the balance, 557 men from various posts took part in project 50.8, "Detection of Atomic Burst and Radioactive Fallout." As part of this project, the men would learn to recognize an atomic detonation.

42. R. Baldwin, *Experiences At Desert Rock VII and VIII* (AO5) AD/AD44 440, Washington, D.C., Human Resources Research Office, March 1958, 91 pages.

43. Gladwin Hill, "55 Miles From The Bomb," *New York Times Magazine*, May 26, 1957, p. 10.

44. Baldwin, op. cit. (A05) AD/A044.

45. As with most balloon shots, DOPPLER produced a circular radioactive area on the desert floor. Within 500 yards of the epicenter, the measured radiation rate was approximately 50 roentgens/hour.

46. The first time at 30,000 feet, the second time at 10,000 feet, and the third time at 20,000 feet.

47. "Small Atomic Blast Is Set Off in Nevada," *New York Times*, Aug. 31, 1957.

48. Leslie J. Freeman, *Nuclear Witnesses* (New York: W.W. Norton, 1981), pp. 183-184.

49. *Wolf Point Herald News*, Aug. 29, 1957. Also: Karen Wyon, Roosevelt County Library, 220 2nd Avenue South, Wolf Point, Montana, 59201; personal correspondence, March 1, 1984.

50. OTI-57-93 Nevada Test Organization, August 24, 1957.

51. Rosenberg, op. cit., p. 92.

52. Ibid., pp. 83-84.

53. Ibid., p. 85.

54. Freeman, op. cit., p. 184. Actually, the drug was probably cysteine. At the time, it was thought that the amino acid cysteine somehow protected the body against the effects of radiation.

55. Rosenberg, op. cit., p. 120-121.

56. Freeman, op. cit., p. 187.

57. Ibid., p. 191.

58. Harvey Wasserman, and Norman Solomon, *Killing Our Own* (Garden City, N.Y.: Doubleday, 1982), p. 94.

59. Ibid., p. 93.

60. Freeman, op. cit., p. 192.

61. Author's interview with Martha Bordoli Laird, May 17, 1985.

62. John Fuller, *The Day We Bombed Utah* (New York: New American Library, 1984), p. 155. The only area not bright red was where her diapers had covered her.

63. *Nashua Telegraph*, Sept. 3, 1957.

64. While SMOKY's debris was crossing over various communities in the first days of September 1957, radio stations were playing David Seville's first song, on the Liberty label, "Gotta Get to Your House." SMOKY was apparently more successful in that particular endeavor; Seville's song only made it to number 77 on the music charts.

65. Jean Arbeiter, *No Matter How Thin You Slice It, It's Still Baloney* (New York: Quill, 1984), p. 48.

66. Rosenberg, op. cit., p. 129.

67. "Troops Carry On After Atomic Blast 2.7 Miles Away," *New York Times*, Sept. 3, 1957.

68. This was about half a mile short of the stratosphere, which, at the time, was hovering $6\frac{1}{2}$ miles above the desert floor. Below 10,000 feet the winds were blowing at less than 10 mph, essentially calm. Even at mushroom height, the sky was remarkably quiet, with a breeze blowing from the north at only 14 mph. As a result, the on-site radiation pattern began to spread out somewhat. At the epicenter, the radiation rate exceeded 200 roentgens/hour. At the troop location, however, the level was something less than 0.01 roentgen/hour.

69. William Manchester, *The Glory and the Dream* (Boston: Little Brown, 1973), p. 816.

70. High-speed photos taken at detonation reveal five taut cables suspended in midair, smoke pouring from ends no longer attached to anything, all pointing toward a brilliant fireball at the center of the scene.

71. Pushed by southeast winds at 29 mph, WHEELER's cloud began a slow trek to the northwest, toward Carson City and Reno. The 10,000- and 14,000-foot levels, apparently impeded by the mountains, then turned back and eventually moved east. The 16,000-foot level crossed over the Sierra Nevadas into California, passing over Lodi, Fairfield, Napa, Redding, and 9,892-foot Eagle Peak before crossing back into Nevada and heading east.

72. At 2:30 A.M. September 11, 1957, the center of the cloud passed 37 miles north of Wheeler, along the border between Lipscomb and Hemphill counties.

73. The nuclear cloud from COULOMB B separated into two segments, one at 10,000 feet, the other at 18,000 feet. Both traveled northwest for a while, then backtracked first to the southeast, then to the northeast.

74. Courtesy Jennie C. Britt, Wheeler Public Library, Wheeler, Texas; personal communication, February 28, 1984.

75. That evening, a Saturday, the television show "Have Gun—Will Travel" began on CBS. The guest was Charles Bronson. The two events are thought to be unrelated.

76. DNA 6001F–6008F.

77. The eighteenth conventional nuclear test scheduled in the PLUMBBOB series, LAPLACE, involved a number of projects; however, Desert Rock personnel took part in only two of them: One, Project 50.3, was an evaluation of the Medium Range Detonation-Detection and Cloud Tracking System. The other, Project 50.8, was entitled, "Detection of an Atomic Burst and Radioactive Fallout." Both projects involved 128 military personnel. The military wanted to know if instruments could be used to detect close-in nuclear explosions. In order to track the clouds, four radar units were set up: one 112 miles southeast of the epicenter, one 56 miles south on Angel's Peak, and two 7.4 miles west of the epicenter. As with other shots, a mobile van was used to obtain, process, and relay weather information. For LAPLACE, it was parked next to the weather station at Camp Mercury.

78. The cloud moved in a wedge across northern Arizona and central New Mexico before splitting up near the Texas border. The 10,000- and 18,000-foot levels moved northeast, while the 14,000-foot level tracked south across central and southern Texas, crossing the citrus-producing area of McAllen-Harlingen-Brownsville at 10:00 P.M. on September 12.

79. "19th Atomic Blast Set Off in Nevada," *New York Times*, Sept. 15, 1957, p. 15.
80. The 30,000-foot level dipped first into Mexico, then tracked back toward the United States, crossing high over the Rio Grande near Brownsville, Texas, at 11:00 P.M. on September 16. It then crossed over the Gulf before reentering Texas south of Port Arthur.
81. "20th Nuclear Device Exploded; Flash Is Seen 350 Miles Away," *New York Times*, Sept. 17, 1957.
82. Eventually, both levels turned northeast, the 30,000-foot level crossing over Baltimore, Maryland, at 7:00 A.M. on September 29 and the 20,000-foot level crossing the same place at 4:00 P.M. on September 30. The lower, 10,000-foot, level moved north from the test site, crossing Pocatello, Idaho, and Butte, Montana, finally crossing into Alberta, Canada, near Milk River.
83. An hour after the detonation, monitors at ground zero found radiation levels of only 50 roentgens/hour. The radiation trailed off rapidly with distance; 500 yards from the epicenter, the level was only 10 roentgens/hour.
84. Strong (44 mph) southerly winds quickly pushed the CHARLESTON cloud north over Idaho, where it turned east and fanned out over the Dakotas before turning south. One day after the detonation, the 30,000-foot level crossed over Iowa Falls, Iowa, at 4:00 P.M. local time, and Marshall, Missouri, six hours later.

    The 20,000-foot level turned south over Lewis, Iowa, then crossed the Missouri River at Brownville, Nebraska, on a path toward Kansas, Oklahoma, and Texas. The 10,000-foot level, meanwhile, was also moving south, caught up in a somewhat turbulent cold front. As a result, between October 1 and October 4, 1957, residents of some central Texas towns had several levels of nuclear debris floating through their skies. The clouds finally parted company just west of Kerrville; the 20,000-foot level traveled south, entering Mexico over Eagle Pass, while the 10,000-foot trajectory dissipated between the towns of Clegg and Annarose in southwestern Live Oak County.
85. Partially because of the cool morning air (45 degrees F), the cloud quickly shot up to 35,786 feet, half a mile into the stratosphere. Westerly winds at 55 mph quickly pushed the cloud east. The top and middle levels of the MORGAN cloud fanned out toward the northeast, while the lower, 10,000-foot, level first crossed over Las Vegas before turning due north. After crossing over Nevada and Idaho, the cloud reached 10,240-foot Fish Peak in Montana and turned east, toward Billings. From there it took a more southeasterly course, passing over Rapid City, South Dakota, then turning due east over Omaha.

    The 20,000-foot level had also tracked toward Omaha, but from the southwest, crossing just south of that city during late rush hour on Monday, October 7. From there, it moved on into Iowa, crossing the town of Corning two hours later. The debris crossed Chicago at 11:00 A.M. on October 9 on its way to a 2:00 P.M. rendezvous with Battle Creek, Michigan, home of Kelloggs Frosted Flakes. Two days after that, on October 11, radioactive material at the 10,000-foot level arrived over Corning, Iowa, crossing from west to east at 4:00 P.M. It would go on to Morning Sun, just north of Burlington, at 5:00 the next morning, then it, too, would head for Battle Creek, crossing that city at 5:00 P.M. the next day.

Hot Dust, Hard Rain (pp. 294–298)

1. PuO_2
2. One-tenth micron in diameter.
3. Edward A. Martell, "Actinides in the Environment and Their Uptake by Man," NCAR-TN/STR 110, National Center for Atmospheric Research, May 1975, p. 15.
4. Under normal atmospheric pressure, but very high temperatures, iron oxide stabilizes in the 3:4 iron to oxygen ratio, which is magnetite (Fe_3O_4). These particles, being large, constituted part of the early, or close-in, fallout.
5. C. E. Adams, N. H. Farlow, W. R. Schell, "The compositions, structures and origins of radioactive fallout particles," *Geochimica et Cosmoshimica Acta*, vol. 18, 1960, pp. 42–56.

6. Ibid. The particles resulting from high air bursts were found to have a specific gravity of 3 to 4 grams/cc.
7. Ibid. The particles resulting from surface and tower bursts were found to have a specific gravity of 1 to 3 grams/cc.
8. Ibid.
9. See chapters on SIMON and DIXIE.
10. Usually the material will leave the stratosphere the first winter or spring season following the burst that placed it there.
11. If the debris is in the troposphere, the time is much shorter; half of the material will have crossred the equator after only ten months. (Samuel Glasstone and Philip J. Dolan, *The Effects of Nuclear Weapons* (U.S. Department of Energy and Department of Defense, 1977), pp. 387–450.
12. John Fuller, *The Day We Bombed Utah* (New York: New American Library, 1984), p. 182.
13. Radiation monitors surveying the areas close the test site occasionally found elongated hot spots across the landscape. These were found to be areas of light rain that moved slowly across the Earth.
14. Glasstone and Dolan, op. cit., p. 419.
15. Author's interview with E. A. Martell, April 1984.
16. Fuller, op. cit., p. 227.
17. Cesium-137 also is sequestered in the liver, muscles, and spleen as well as the lungs and lower gastrointestinal tract. See *Radiological Health Handbook* U.S. Department of Health, Education and Welfare, Public Health Service, January 1970, pp. 205–208.
18. Manganese is a cofactor in the arginase and phosphotransferase enzymes. Iron is used in the cytochromes, peroxidase, catalase, and ferredoxin, and is, of course, found in all red blood cells, while zinc is used as a cofactor for the enzymes alcohol dehydrogenase, carbonic anhydrase, and carboxypeptidase. See Albert L. Lehninger, *Biochemistry: The Molecular Basis of Cell Structure and Function* (New York: Worth Publishers, Inc., 1970), p. 149.
19. Manganese-54 has a half-life of 313 days; it decays to iron-54 by emitting low-energy electrons.
20. Other examples: vitamin B-12 and its derivative, 5-deoxyadenosylcobalamin, is a chemical absolutely necessary in the nutrition not only of man, but of most animals and plants. It is found only in the most minute traces in living tissues and appears to be a product of anerobic bacteria (it is found in great quantities in sewage, manure, and soil). Hidden deep inside the structure of the vitamin B-12 molecule and attached to the four inner nitrogren atoms is a single atom of cobalt. Bacteria manufacturing vitamin B-12 use cobalt where they find it, whether it is the stable variety (cobalt-59) or the exceedingly hot radionuclide cobalt-60 (half-life: 5.2 years). (Lehninger, op. cit., p. 428.)
21. Henry A. Schroeder, *Trace Elements and Man*, (Old Greenwich, Conn.: Devin-Adair, 1973), p. 93.
22. *Radiological Health Handbook*, op. cit., p. 207.
23. Strontium-90 slowly decays to yttrium-90, a carcinogen.
24. Rubidium-86, with a half-life of 18.6 days, decays to strontium-86 by ejecting high-energy beta particles and gamma rays.
25. AEC, Health and Safety Laboratory, Quarterly Summary Report, HASL-142, Jan. 1, 1964, pp. 15–17. Ruthenium-103 has a specific strength of 32,100.28 curies per gram. A curie is equal to 3.7 multiplied by 10^{10} disintegrations per second. The more disintegrations per second, the hotter the material.
26. Ruthenium-193 has a half-life of 39½ days. In its decay, it emits beta particles and gamma rays.
27. Schroeder, op. cit., pp. 7, 149.

Fallout: The Questions (pp. 299–304)

1. Paul Jacobs, "Clouds From Nevada," *The Reporter*, May 16, 1957.

2. Years later, in 1980, Martha Bordoli Laird said that she did not consider her son "a small sacrifice."
3. *Life*, June 1980, p. 38.
4. According to the view held by the National Academy of Sciences in 1957: "Individual persons should not receive a total accumulated dose to the reproductive cells of more than 50 roentgens up to age 30 years, and to more than 50 roentgens additional up to age 40." (*U.S. News & World Report*, June 21, 1957, p. 47.)
5. See Appendix A: Fallout: The Radiation.
6. Ibid.
7. Ibid.
8. The cloud had caused a peculiar "acid-like taste" in the throats of those at the Fallini Ranch. (Jacobs, op. cit., p. 23.)
9. Ibid.
10. The AEC claimed that a film badge had been placed at a site half a mile from the school four days after the series began and that it showed a low radiation dose. (Jacobs, op. cit., p. 23.)
11. Jacobs, op. cit., p. 16.
12. See the chapter "Hot Dust, Hard Rain."
13. "If You're Still Wondering About Fall-Out Danger," *U.S. News & World Report*, June 21, 1957, pp. 46–47.
14. "What the Folks Say in 'Fall-Out City,'" *U.S. News & World Report*, June 28, 1957.
15. Author's interview with M. K. McGregor, M.D., May 21, 1985.
16. Author's interview with Ellis Everett, May 21, 1985.
17. E. B. Lewis, "Leukemia and Ionizing Radiation," *Science*, May 17, 1957, pp. 965–972.
18. Linus Pauling, "How Dangerous Is Radioactive Fallout?" *Foreign Policy Bulletin*, June 15, 1957, p. 149.
19. *Life*, June 1980, p. 36.
20. Ibid.
21. Peter Pringle and James Spigelman, *The Nuclear Barons* (New York: Holt, Rinehart and Winston, 1981), p. 231.

Hardtack I–II (pp. 305–310)

1. On June 3, 1957, just after the Boltzmann test, Pauling issued a statement that there would be 200,00 mentally or physically defective children in each of the next twenty generations as a result of the testing. In addition, Pauling predicted a five- to ten-year life-expectancy drop for a million people because of the fallout. A year later, Pauling claimed that a million would die from leukemia as a direct result of the testing. (*New York Times*, June 3, 1957; Mar. 29, Mar. 31, and Apr. 29, 1958.)
2. *New York Times*, May 28, 1957.
3. *New York Times*, June 4, 1957.
4. *New York Times*, Mar. 26, 1958.
5. *New York Times*, Apr. 30, 1957.
6. *New York Times*, June 6, 1957. Defense Secretary Charles Wilson said that cigarettes are a greater hazard than fallout and stated that scientists "lacked datas and experience" to prove fallout was hazardous.
7. Alice Stewart, Josefine Webb, David Hewitt, "A Survey of Childhood Malignancies," *British Medical Journal*, 1958, pp. 1495–1508. Stewart's 1970 study confirmed her earlier findings. See Alice Stewart and George Kneale, "Radiation Dose Effects in Relation to Obstetric X-Rays and Childhood Cancers," *Lancet, 1970, pp. 1185–1188*.
8. *New York Times*, June 8, 1957.
9. *New York Times*, Apr. 15, 1958. The two-inch column appeared on page 35.
10. Thomas H. Saffer and Orville E. Kelly, *Countdown Zero* (New York: G. P. Putnam's Sons, 1983), pp. 121–122.

11. Ibid., p. 116. A rocket propulsion engineer at the site, Walt Fitzpatrick, recalled that a scientist told him that "they really didn't know what would happen."
12. *Honolulu Star-Bulletin*, Aug. 1, 1958.
13. Samuel Glasstone and Philip J. Dolan, *The Effects of Nuclear Weapons* (U.S. Department of Energy and Department of Defense, 1977), pp. 519–525.
14. AEC, Health and Safety Laboratory, Quarterly Summary Report HASL-142, Jan. 1, 1964, p. 255–256.
15. Glasstone and Dolan, op. cit., p. 77.
16. DASA 1251, pp. 484–489.
17. *New York Times*, Oct. 31, 1958.
18. *New York Times*, Mar. 24, 1959.
19. *New York Times*, Mar. 27, 1959.
20. *New York Times*, Mar. 29 and Apr. 4, 1949.
21. Carl Bernstein and Bob Woodward, *All the President's Men* (New York: Warner Books, 1974), pp. 57–58.
22. Stanley A. Blumberg and Gwinn Owens, *Energy and Conflict: The Life and Times of Edward Teller* (New York: G. P. Putnam's Sons, 1976), pp. 412–413.
23. Edward Teller with Allen Brown, *The Legacy of Hiroshima* (Garden City, N.Y.: Doubleday, 1962), p. 180.
24. Ibid., p. 82.
25. Gerald W. Johnson and Harold Brown, "Non-Military Uses of Nuclear Explosives," *Scientific American*, vol. 199, no. 6, Dec. 1958, pp. 29–35.

Plowshare *(pp. 311–313)*

1. Edward Teller, "We're Going to Work Miracles," *Popular Mechanics*, vol. 113, no. 3, Mar. 1960, p. 97.
2. Arthur Grahame, "A-Test Alaska Threat?," *Outdoor Life*, Jan. 1961.
3. An environmental group, the Greater St. Louis Citizen's Committee for Nuclear Information (CNI) reported that "Alaska officials, some hunting guides, and the people of the two Eskimo villages have expressed concern over the possible effects of the explosion on living conditions." In the report, the CNI quoted an AEC statement: "An experiment would be conducted only after the Commission is assured that public health and safety will be protected." (*Science*, vol. 132, p. 608.)
4. Teller, op. cit., p. 278.
5. *Fallout, Radiation Standards and Countermeasures*, Aug. 1963, Part 2. Quoted in Harvey Wasserman and Norman Solomon, *Killing Our Own* (Garden City, N.Y.: Doubleday, 1982).
6. Wasserman and Solomon, op. cit., p. 122.
7. Raymond E. Brim and Patricia Condon, "Another A-bomb Cover-Up." *Washington Monthly*, Jan. 1981, p. 48.

Accidents

Bombs Over Mars Bluff *(pp. 317–318)*

1. *New York Times*, Mar. 12, 1958.
2. Walter Gregg and his immediate family suffered only cuts and bruises. His niece, Ella Davis, suffered a cut forehead and an injured spleen. All are alive and well in 1985. (Author's interview with Walter Gregg, March 11, 1985.)

Bombs Over Goldsboro *(pp. 319–321)*

1. Those killed were: Major Eugene Shelton, radar operator; Major Eugene Richards, electronics operator; Technical Sargeant Francis Barnish, gunner. According to reports,

Shelton delayed ejection trying to get Richards out of the plane. When Shelton was finally able to bail out, the plane was too close to the ground.

2. *Goldsboro News–Argus*, Jan. 24, 1960. Courtesy Kaye Brimmage, librarian, Wayne County Public Library, Inc., Goldsboro, North Carolina.
3. Ralph Lapp, *Kill and Overkill* (New York: Basic Books, 1962), p. 227.
4. Michael Riordan, ed., *The Day After Midnight: The Effects of Nuclear War* (Palo Alto, Calif.: Cheshire Books, 1982), p. 59.
5. Samuel Glasstone and Philip J. Dolan, *The Effects of Nuclear Weapons* (U.S. Department of Energy and Department of Defense, 1977), p. 181.
6. Operation CASTLE, DNA 6000 Series, p. 236.
7. U.S. Forest Service Pamphlet, 1980. Quoted in Sheila Tobias, Peter Goudinof, Stefan Leader, Shelah Leader, *The Peoples Guide to National Defense* (New York: William Morrow, 1982), p. 65. According to Tobias et al., "One extra pound of air pressure would break windows; five extra pounds per square inch will destroy a house and rupture eardrums, twenty extra pounds per square inch does lung damage, and 35 psi destroys a building built to withstand earthquake." (p. 65.)
8. Since the bombs were parachute-retarded, they must have been either the Mark 36, 39, or B53. While all three designs were megaton-range weapons, the largest-yield warhead ever put into production was the 8,000-pound 9-megaton W53 warhead riding atop the Titan missiles. It is extremely unlikely that a bomber, even the huge B-52G, would carry a bomb with a yield larger than a Titan missile warhead. Further, it is known that the largest nuclear device detonated by the United States was the 15-megaton CASTLE: BRAVO shot. It is doubtful that the military would add to their strategic system any untested nuclear device, particularly one with a yield of 24 megatons.

   (References: Author's correspondence with Richard L. Ray, historian, National Atomic Energy Museum, Department of Energy, Albuquerque Operations Office, Albuquerque, New Mexico, 87115, Apr. 19, 1985; SASC, FY 1983 DOD, Part 7, p. 4172; Thomas B. Cochran, William M. Arkin, and Milton M. Hoenig, *Nuclear Weapons Databook, vol. 1* [Cambridge, Mass.: Ballinger Publishing Co., 1984], p. 38.)
9. The Category C PAL incorporated a single 6-digit coded switch "with limited try"—that is, after a given number of tries (i.e., false numbers) had been entered, the weapon would lock and key components would become unusable. The weapon would then have to be returned to the assembly plant—at a cost of about $50,000.

   (References: SASC, FY 1982 DOE pp. 266–267; *Military Applications of Nuclear Technology* part 1, p. 44ff; ACDA, FY 1979 ACIS [Arms Control and Disarmament Agency; Arms Control Impact Statement], p. 92; ACDA, FY 1978 ACIS, p. 96; ACDA, FY 1979 ACIS, p. 136; Cochran, Arkin, and Hoenig, op. cit., p. 30.)
10. In *Kill and Overkill* (op. cit.), Dr. Lapp cites as his reference "Accidental War: Some Dangers in the 1960's," a study by the Mershon National Security Program group at Ohio State University. He noted that the study was published in the Congressional Record for August 12, 1960, pages 15080–15086. Checking in the Congressional Record, the study was found on pages 16266–16271. The only mention of a specific incident was on page 16268: "On one occasion, in North Carolina, a nuclear weapon was accidentally dropped by a B-47 in flight with a chemical explosion on impact." No mention is made of the 24-megaton Goldsboro incident.

The Soviets II: Chelyabinsk 40 (pp. 322–328)

1. *New York Times*, Apr. 1, 1958.
2. The Russian word for "village" is usually translated as *derevnya*, meaning a small agricultural settlement. The settlements between Sverdlovsk and Chelyabinsk were workers' settlements.

3. This is speculation. By 1957, each settlement supposedly had between 10,000 and 30,000 inhabitants.

4. Peter Pringle and James Spigelman, *The Nuclear Barons* (New York: Holt, Rinehart and Winston, 1981), p. 62.

5. The Soviets added a slightly different mix of ores to their weapons than did the United States. The presence of the short-lived isotope manganese-54 in fallout would indicate its Soviet origin.

6. This equals 1,029 square miles. Description is based on CIA Report 8014401: Kyshtym. All other information from Zhores Medvedev, *Nuclear Disaster in the Urals* (New York: W.W. Norton, 1979.)

7. The dimensions of each room was 91 by 163 by 13 feet.

8. It is uncertain whether the waste materials were placed in containers or in a pit. A CIA letter dated February 4, 1977, seems to indicate the materials were placed in steel containers, then buried. Quoted in Medvedev, op. cit.

9. Near Chelyabinsk-40, just outside the village of Maloyaroslavets, a nuclear research institute had also been built; its name was Maloyaroslavets-2. In 1968, it would be officially renamed Obninsk, for the nearby Ob River.

10. In 1968, Soviet academician A. P. Alexandrov, admitted that "from 1946 to 1948 some of our employees got radiation cataracts of the eyes." (Pringle and Spigelman, op. cit., p. 231.) Since Chelyabinsk-40 was located in the main nuclear production area, it is assumed that the same or similar difficulties occurred there.

11. Arnold Kramish, *Atomic Energy in the Soviet Union* (Stanford, Calif.: Stanford University Press, 1959); also Trud (Moscow), Dec. 19, 1968.

12. This report was received by the CIA; it may have been related to an atomic test that was performed in northern Siberia or Novaya Zemyla in the early sixties. It is believed that the Soviets had built a "doom city" in Siberia, complete with a subway, populated it with goats and other animals, then airdropped a 20-megaton bomb on it. Reportedly, the village was "eliminated" but the subway survived. CIA 00E324/0 1015–77, Jan. 24, 1977.

13. *Washington Post*, Nov. 26, 1977.

14. As a result of the disaster, Professor G. D. Baisogolov, who worked in Chelyabinsk at the time, was presented the Lenin Prize for developing methods of treatment for radiation burns. Baisogolov went on to become the deputy director of the Radiology Institute at Obninsk (originally Maloyaroslavets-2). Another winner of the Lenin Prize was A. I. Burnazian, deputy minister of health, also for developing methods of treatment for radiation burns. (Medvedev, op. cit., p.164.)

15. The government apparently built new homes for the victims at a safer location.

16. Medvedev, op. cit., p. 110.

17. The source of the Techa is Lake Kiziltash, a lake of some 20 square miles, and Lake Ulagach, size unknown. It empties into the Iset River at Dalmatovo. During 1958, the Techa had become highly radioactive.

18. CIA Report on Nuclear Installations in the U.S.S.R., Feb. 1961. Released Jan. 1977. (Medvedev, op. cit., p. 187.)

19. Ibid.

20. The Kyshtym disaster was not the only misfortune to befall the Sverdlovsk-Chelyabinsk area. An accident at the Biological Warfare Research plant in Sverdlovsk in the spring of 1979 resulted in the exposure of 3,000 persons to anthrax. The germs traveled almost due south through the city. Soviet sources said that poison meat caused the problem; however, the people were treated for *respiratory* anthrax, contractable only via gassing.

21. A Bendix Corporation facility, which manufactures an H-bomb component, is located in a Kansas City suburb.

22. Francis Gary Powers with Curt Gentry, *Operation Overflight: The U-2 Pilot Tells His Story for the First Time* (New York: Holt, Rinehart and Winston, 1970).

The Abyss

Khrushchev (pp. 331–332)

1. William Manchester, *The Glory and the Dream* (Boston: Little Brown, 1974), p. 908.

Showdown (pp. 333–335)

1. Congressional Record, Aug. 12, 1960, pp. 16268 and 16270.
2. On the day after the final meeting in Vienna, reporter James Reston watched Kennedy collapse onto a couch and pull his hat down over his eyes. "Pretty rough?" Reston asked. "Roughest thing in my life," Kennedy replied.

   He later told Reston: "I've got two problems. First, to figure out why he did it, and in such a hostile way. And second, to figure out what we can do about it. I think the first part is pretty easy to explain. I think he did it because of the Bay of Pigs. I think he thought anyone who was so young and inexperienced as to get into a mess like that could be taken, and anyone who got into it and didn't see it through, had no guts. So he just beat hell out of me. So I've got a terrible problem. If he thinks I'm inexperienced and have no guts, until we remove those ideas we won't get anywhere with him. So we have to act."

   As for Khrushchev's view of the meeting: "I was genuinely pleased with our meeting in Vienna. Even though we came to no concrete agreement, I could tell that he was interested in finding a peaceful solution to world problems. . . . He was a reasonable man, and I think he knew that he wouldn't be justified in starting a new war over Berlin."

   (References: *New York Times*, June 4, 1961; David Halberstam, *The Best and the Brightest* (New York: Random House, 1972), p. 76; Nikita Khrushchev, *Khrushchev Remembers* [Boston: Little Brown, 1970]; The meeting in Vienna is described in detail in William Manchester, *The Glory and the Dream*, [Boston: Little, Brown, 1974], pp. 909–11.
3. Both Secretary of State Dean Acheson and Vice President Lyndon Baines Johnson suggested to Kennedy that he declare a state of emergency.
4. ANTLER had been fired in a tunnel, but nevertheless showered fallout across the country. Others in the NOUGAT series that traveled cross-country were DANNY BOY (March 5, 1962), PLATTE (March 14, 1962), EEL (May 19, 1962), and DES MOINES (June 13, 1962). Interestingly, DES MOINES never made it to Des Moines, Iowa. It was tracked only as far as Southern California.
5. At the Communist Party Congress on October 17, 1961, Khrushchev said: "The western powers are showing some understanding of the situation and are inclined to seek a solution to the German problem and the issue of West Berlin. . . . If that is so, we shall not insist on signing a peace treaty [with East Germany] absolutely before December 31, 1961." André Fontaine, *History of the Cold War: From the Korean War to the Present* (New York: Pantheon, 1969), pp. 423–425.
6. Fred Kaplan, *The Wizards of Armageddon* (New York: Simon and Schuster, 1982). Also quoted in Andrew Cockburn, *The Threat: Inside the Soviet Military Machine* (New York: Random House, 1983), p. 192.

Novaya Zemlya (pp. 336–342)

1. Robert A. List of the United States Weather Bureau analyzed the weather conditions for the Soviet tests. In an article in *Newsweek* (Sept. 25, 1961), he said: "The southward flow would have carried fallout over Murmansk and Archangel, and possibly all the way to Leningrad. The edges of the pattern could also have hit Finland and northern Norway . . . it was raining in Archangel Thursday morning [September 14]. I'm fairly certain that if there was debris in the air, they got it on the ground."
2. Murmansk is the northernmost metropolis in the world. It is also the largest city inside the Arctic Circle.

3. *Newsweek*, Sept. 25, 1961.

4. *New York Times*, Oct. 26, 1961.

5. *Newsweek*, Sept. 25, 1961.

6. *New York Times*, Oct. 26, 1961.

7. *New York Times*, Oct. 28, 1961.

8. A. D. Sakharov, *O Strane i mire* (My Country and the World) (New York: Khronika, 1976), pp. vii–viii.

9. Ibid.

10. Ibid. In the book *Sakharov Speaks*, the last sentence is translated: "I would be a slob and not Chairman of the Council of Ministers if I listened to the likes of Sakharov." (A.D. Sakharov, *Sakharov Speaks* [London: Collins, 1974], p. 254.)

11. Sakharov, op. cit., p. 254.

12. In their book, Peter Pringle and James Spigelman describe Slavsky: "When an official Soviet work calls Slavsky 'tempermental,' it is easy to believe his detractors who called him an hysteric. He apparently displayed the full range of the worst characteristics of the Red Specialists. He was totally ruthless, would never listen to reasons for delay or failure, and, unlike Vannikov and Zavenyagin, was not respected by either scientists or engineers for his technical knowledge." (Pringle and Spigelman, *The Nuclear Barons* [New York: Holt, Rinehart and Winston, 1981], p. 67.)

13. Sakharov, op. cit., p. 254.

14. *New York Times*, Nov. 1, 1961.

15. *New York Times*, Oct. 31 and Nov. 1, 1961.

16. *New York Times*, Oct. 18, 1961.

17. *New York Times*, Nov. 3, 1961.

18. *New York Times*, Dec. 10, 1961.

19. Those with radiation detected off-site were: ANTLER (September 15, 1961), FEATHER (December 22, 1961), PAMPAS (March 1, 1962), DANNY BOY (March 5, 1962), and PLATTE (April 14, 1962). (*Announced United States Nuclear Tests*, Office of Public Affairs, U.S. Department of Energy, Nevada Operations Office, NVO-209 [Rev 3], January 1983.) PLATTE released the following isotopes: Ru-103, Ru-105, Zr-Nb-95, Ca-141, Ca-144, K-40, I-131, I-133, I-135, and Te-132. "The cloud drifted in a northerly direction." (DASA 1251, p. 534.)

20. DASA 1251, p. 552.

21. Ibid., p. 574.

22. U.S. Army, "Operation and Employment of the DAVY CROCKETT Battlefield Missile," XM-28/29, FM9-111, June 1963. Also: Thomas B. Cochran, William M. Arkin, and Milton M. Hoenig, *Nuclear Weapons Databook*, vol. 1 (Cambridge, Mass.: Ballinger Publishing Co., 1984), p. 33.

Deadly October (pp. 343–350)

1. Zhores Medvedev, p. 186.

2. The surface-to-air missiles were of the variety that shot down Francis Gary Powers in 1960. These missiles are not designed for strategic use; they are generally considered for use as defense only and are not equipped with nuclear warheads.

3. Medvedev, op. cit., p. 184–185.

4. Elie Abel, *The Missile Crisis* (New York and Philadelphia: Lippincott, 1966), p. 29–30.

5. Ibid., pp. 17–32.

6. Robert Kennedy, *Thirteen Days: The Cuban Missile Crisis, October, 1962* (London: Macmillan, 1969), p. 31.

7. Medvedev, op. cit., p. 187.

8. Roger Hilsman, *To Move a Nation* (Garden City, N.Y.: Doubleday, 1967), p. 100.

9. Andrew Cockburn, *The Threat: Inside the Soviet Military Machine* (New York: Random House, 1984), p. 192.

10. Streamlining didn't help matters either. It allowed the rocket to go so fast that a hailstone hitting it would have serious consequences. In his book, Andrew Cockburn tells about a 1972 test of the streamlined Mark 12 warhead when it "ran into a tropical storm and almost disintegrated." (Cockburn, op. cit., p. 211.)

11. The SS-6 was a first-generation Soviet missile. It was replaced in the mid-sixties by the SS-9 and later by the SS-11. All were liquid-fueled. The first Soviet missile using solid fuel was the SS-13. (Cockburn, op. cit., p. 116.)

12. *New York Times*, Oct. 18, 1962.

13. Kennedy, op. cit., p. 36.

14. Abel, op. cit., pp. 76–83.

15. Nikita Khrushchev, *Khrushchev Remembers* (Boston: Little Brown, 1971), p. 496.

16. *New York Times*, Oct. 23, 1962.

17. Ibid.

18. Medvedev, op. cit., p. 188.

19. Arthur M. Schlesinger Jr., *A Thousand Days: John F. Kennedy in the White House* (Boston: Houghton Mifflin, 1965), p. 817, and Medvedev, op. cit., p. 189.

20. *New York Times*, Oct. 24, 1962.

21. *New York Times*, Oct. 25 and Oct. 27, 1962.

22. Kennedy, op. cit., p. 71.

23. Ibid.

24. *New York Times*, Oct. 26, 1962.

25. Medvedev, op. cit., p. 189.

26. *New York Times*, Oct. 27, 1962.

27. Kennedy, op. cit., p. 109.

28. William Manchester, *The Glory and the Dream* (Boston: Little Brown, 1974), pp. 970–971.

29. Kennedy, op. cit., pp. 80–90.

30. *New York Times*, Oct. 28, 1962.

31. Medvedev, op. cit., p. 192.

32. Kennedy, op. cit., pp. 96–97.

33. *Khrushchev Remembers* Edward Crankshaw, London, Andre Deutsch, 1971, p. 496.

34. Medvedev, op. cit., p. 191.

35. *Izvestiya*, Oct. 30, 1962.

36. *New York Times*, Oct. 29, 1962.

37. Abel, op. cit., pp. 180–186.

38. Medvedev, op. cit., p. 192.

The Hot Years (pp. 351–355)

1. They sang "I'm a Ding Dong Daddy From Dumas" and "Side by Side." Six-year-old Donny would appear on the show in December 1963. (Tim Brooks and Earle Marsh, *The Complete Directory to Prime Time Network TV Shows: 1946–Present* [New York: Ballantine, 1979], p. 30.)

2. Half-hour reruns of "Gunsmoke" were seen on Tuesday nights as "Marshall Dillon." The series ran from September 10, 1955, to September 1, 1975, the longest-running series with continuing characters in the history of television (Brooks and Marsh, op. cit., pp. 243–244.)

3. *Time*, Nov. 2, 1962, p. 62.

4. Ibid., pp. 91–94.

5. Ibid., p. 34.

6. *Time*, Nov. 23, 1962, p. 54. McPhee, of course, would later go on to write the excellent *The Curve of Binding Energy*, about nuclear weapons designer Ted Taylor.

7. "Wild Weekend" was in turn based loosely on a 1962 song by Gary "U.S." Bonds, "Seven Day Weekend."

8. AEC, Health and Safety Laboratory, Quarterly Annual Report, HASL-142, Jan. 1, 1984, Fig. 8, p. 184.

9. Among the events in July 1963: On July 8, a Monday, NBC's David Brinkley covered the reunion of the bomber crew that dropped the atomic bomb on Hiroshima. Among the new motion picture releases were Federico Fellini's *8½*, *Hud* starring Paul Newman and Patricia Neal, and *PT 109* with Cliff Robertson as John F. Kennedy. Among the best-selling books in July 1963 were *Shoes of the Fisherman*, *Seven Days in May*, and *Raise High the Roof Beam, Carpenter* by J. D. Salinger. (*Time*, Jul. 12, 1963, p. 4.)

On July 14, 1963, St. Louis radio station KXOK played a new single by Del Shannon, "From Me to You," a song originally recorded by a then-unknown English group called the Beatles. A top-selling album released in the summer was "21 Golden Hits" by Paul Anka, in celebration of his 21st birthday.

On Saturday, July 20, thousands of Americans trekked to Bangor, Maine, to witness the total eclipse of the sun, the first over the United States since 1954. In New York and Chicago, the afternoon sky dimmed noticeably as 88% of the sun's disk was blacked out. In Boston, there was a pronounced twilight. (*Time*, July 19, 1963, p. 52.)

10. HASL-142, Fig. 8, p. 184.

11. HASL-142, Table 1f, p. 167. The low figure for the Pacific Northwest may be partially because the collections began in the middle of the month.

12. HASL-142, Table 1e, p. 165. The April level for manganese-54 in fallout over Pittsburgh was 21.6 and 21.7 millicuries/square mile; for antimony-124, it was 0.25 and 0.35 millicuries/square mile.

13. HASL-142, Table 1d, p. 164. Westwood received 0.056 and 0.148 millicuries of tellurium-204 in March 1963.

14. Irving Sax, *Dangerous Properties of Industrial Materials* (New York: Van Nostrand Reinhold, 1979), p. 1009.

15. HASL-142, p. 162. The level of Fe-55 reached its highest level, 101 millicuries/square mile between March 13 and 15.

16. J. Rivera, "Cs-137 in the 1962 U.S. Wheat Crop," HASL-142, p. 297.

17. HASL-142, Table 3, p. 183. Bakery products (in micro-microcuries/kilogram): New York City (May 1963): 555; Chicago (July 1963): 679; San Francisco (June 1963): 445.

18. *New York Times*, Sept. 20, 1963.

19. William Manchester, *The Glory and the Dream* (Boston: Little Brown, 1974), p. 985.

20. Prior to then, atomic testing—usually underground—had continued at a steady pace, occasionally with major off-site releases. In May 1963, a plutonium-laden cloud from safety shot DOUBLE TRACKS swept over Scotty's Junction, Lathrop Wells, Lida Junction, and Beatty, Nevada. Among those exposed were twenty-two men working at an asphalt batch plant in a desolate area 32 miles north of Beatty. (Roger Rappoport, *The Great American Bomb Machine* [New York: Ballantine, 1971], p. 69.)

21. The French would continue to detonate nuclear devices aboveground as late as 1971; the Chinese as late as 1980.

Confrontation (pp. 357–367)

1. John Fuller, *The Day We Bombed Utah* (New York: New American Library, 1984), pp. 156–157.

2. Ibid., p. 157.

3. Ibid., p. 45. Major Robert Veenstra, veterinarian with the U.S. Navy Radiological Defense Laboratory, had placed a Geiger counter to a sheep's neck and watched the meter go off the scale. "This is hotter," he said, "than a two-dollar pistol."

4. Frank H. Netter, M.D., "Endocrine System and Selected Metabolic Diseases," *CIBA Collection of Medical Illustrations: Vol 4* (Summit, N.J.: CIBA Pharmaceutical Company, 1970), pp. 49, 58–59.

5. C. Donnell Turner and Joseph T. Bagnara, *General Endocrinology,* 5th ed., (Philadelphia: W.B. Saunders, 1971), pp. 182–183.
6. H.E. Stanbury, K. Ohela, and R. Pitt-Rivers, "The metabolism of iodine in 2 goitrous cretins compared with that in 2 patients receiving methiomazole," *Journal of Clinical Endocrinology,* vol. 15, 1955, p. 54.
7. H. Lardy, K. Tomita, F. C. Larson, and E. C. Albright, "The metabolism of thyroid hormones by kidney and the biological activity of the products," *CIBA Found. Colloq. Endocr.,* vol. 10, 1957, p. 156.
8. In sheep, the parathyroids are spatially separated from the thyroid lobes. (Turner and Bagnara, op. cit., p. 241.)
9. Turner and Bagnara, op. cit., p. 256, 260.
10. *New York Times,* Jan. 27, 1960.
11. *New York Times,* Mar. 5, 1960.
12. *New York Times,* May 1, 1957.
13. Linus Pauling, *No More War* (New York: Dodd, Mead, 1958), pp. 74–75.
14. Fuller, op. cit., p. 159.
15. Roger Rappoport, *The Great American Bomb Machine* (New York: Ballantine, 1971), p. 159. (No, it's not a mistake; both Fuller and Rappoport mention Knapp on page 159 of their respective books.)
16. Fuller, op. cit., p. 159.
17. Strontium-90 emits beta radiation with a maximum energy of 0.545 MeV.
18. I-131 decays to Xe-131.
19. I-131 emits beta radiation with a maximum energy of 0.806 MeV. It also emits gamma rays, 82 percent of which have an energy of 0.364 MeV. (*Radiological Health Handbook* [U.S. Department of Health, Education and Welfare, Public Health Services], p. 298.)
20. Other researchers, such as E. B. Lewis, had suggested I-131 was a toxic hazard; the AEC, however, had largely recognized only strontium-90, cesium-137, and plutonium as the primary radiological hazards in fallout. (*New York Times,* June 21, 1959.)
21. Harold Knapp; "The Contribution of Hot Spots and Short-Lived Activities to Radiation Exposure in the U.S. from Nuclear Test Fallout," AEC 1961.
22. Fuller, op. cit., p. 160.
23. Ralph Lapp, *Science,* September 1962.
24. Fuller, op. cit., p. 34.
25. In an agency memo, Butrico noted that "it was just as well . . . I was afraid it would create a disturbance." (*Chicago Tribune,* "Radiation," April 1–5, 1979, p. 9.)
26. Charles L. Dunham, "Draft Document Average and Above Average Doses to the Thyroid of Children in the United States from Radioactive Fallout from Nuclear Weapons Tests," AEC memo, October 24, 1962, files of U.S. House of Representatives Commerce Subcommitteed on Oversight and Investigation.
27. Ibid., p. 162.
28. Harold Knapp, "Observed Relations Between Deposition Level of Fresh Fission Products from Nevada Tests and Resulting Levels of I-131 in Fresh Milk," AEC Report, March 1, 1963, files of U.S. House of Representatives Commerce Subcommittee on Oversight and Investigations.
29. Rappoport, op. cit., p. 160.
30. Ibid.
31. Fuller, op. cit., pp. 162–163.
32. Gordon Dunning to N. H. Woodruff, AEC memo, re: Knapp Paper, files of U.S. House of Representatives Commerce Subcommittee on Oversight and Investigations.
33. John Goffman, quoted in *Nuclear Witnesses: Insiders Speak Out,* Leslie J. Freeman, ed. (New York: W.W. Norton, 1981), pp. 89–90.
34. Rappoport, op. cit., p. 161.

35. Ernest J. Sternglass, "Cancer: Relation of Prenatal Radiation to Development of Disease in Childhood," *Science*, June 7, 1963, pp. 1102–1104.
36. Ernest J. Sternglass, quoted in Freeman, op. cit., p. 59.
37. Ibid., p. 58. As of 1985, there is no evidence that the etiology of Tay-Sachs is related to radiation exposure.
38. Sternglass, *Science*, op. cit., pp. 1102–1104.
39. X-radiation and gamma radiation are both forms of electromagnetic radiation. X-rays originate from within the electron cloud; gamma rays originate from within the nucleus.
40. *Science*, vol. 212, May 22, 1981, pp. 900–903.
41. Fuller, op. cit., p. 170. SEDAN track from DOE Archives.
42. Ibid.
43. Ibid., p. 173.
44. Ibid., p. 174.
45. Ibid., p. 175.
46. Ibid., p. 177.

Deadly Rain (pp. 369–375)

1. Sternglass had locked horns with New York Public Health officials over the matter, arguing that they had improperly compared the Troy-Utica death rates with that of the entire state. He claimed that the entire state had been exposed to the SIMON fallout and was an improper control.
2. Ernest J. Sternglass, *Secret Fallout* (New York: McGraw-Hill, 1981), p. 42.
3. Ibid.
4. Ibid., p. 96.
5. Ernest J. Sternglass, "Infant Mortality and Nuclear Tests," *Bulletin of the Atomic Scientists*, April 1969, p. 19.
6. Sternglass, *Secret Fallout*, op. cit., p. 98.
7. Ibid., p. 112.
8. Ernest J. Sternglass, "The Death of All Children," *Esquire*, September 1969, p. 1a. Interestingly, this article seems to be one that is often missing from libraries. When I checked in December 1983, the article had been removed—torn out—from the September 1969 issue of *Esquire* at both the Boston and the Houston public libraries. An associate informed me that the entire issue had been removed from the public library in Kansas City, Missouri. It apparently is a popular article.
9. Ibid. Sternglass thought strontium-90 was the primary culprit:

   The evidence . . . suggests that radioactive strontium appears to be a far more serious hazard to man through its long-lasting action on the genetic material of the mammalian cell than had been expected on the basis of its well-known tendency to be incorporated into bone. The resultant effect appears to express itself most noticeably in excess fetal and infant mortality rates among the children born two or more years after a nuclear explosion. . . . Strontium-90 takes twenty-eight years to decay to half of its initial activity, long enough for most of it to return to earth well before another generation of children is born.

10. This view was in direct opposition to that held by many federal officials and some academicians; Dr. Edythalena Tompkins, for example, had said that "low levels of radiation are not only harmless, but stimulate the body's natural repair mechanisms." Edythalena Tompkins was the wife of Dr. Paul Tompkins, former head of the Federal Radiation Council. (Howard L. Rosenberg, *Atomic Soldiers*, [New York: Harper and Row, 1982], p. 152.)
11. Shot SCHOONER, fired the year before, had deposited debris all the way to Canada, and a 40-kiloton gas-stimulation experiment, was being readied for Rulison, Colorado, on Sep-

tember 10, 1969. The government, with just cause, was fearful of public antinuclear demonstrations at the RULISON event.

12. Corinne Browne and Robert Munroe, *Time Bomb* (New York: William Morrow, 1981), p. 138.

13. Ibid., pp. 138–139.

14. John W. Gofman, "Irrevy: An Irreverent, Illustrated View of Nuclear Power " (San Francisco: Committee for Nuclear Responsibility, 1979.)

15. Just prior to the *Esquire* article, Gofman and Tamplin had characterized the PLOWSHARE program as "biological insanity." Since the program was the brainchild of Livermore's director, Edward Teller, Gofman and Tamplin were jokingly referred to as "the enemy within."

16. Browne and Munroe, op. cit., p. 139.

17. Ibid.

18. John Gofman, M.D., "Lest We Envy the Dead," *The Nation*, November 15, 1980, pp. 507–509.

19. Browne and Munroe, op. cit., p. 140.

20. Ibid., p. 141.

21. Rappoport, op. cit., p. 134–135. Holifield, to his credit, eventually went on to schedule hearings to study radiation exposure to the uranium miners.

22. Browne and Munroe, op. cit., p. 142.

Evidence (pp. 377–389)

1. Corinne Browne and Robert Munroe, *Time Bomb* (New York: William Morrow, 1981), p. 142.

2. Ibid., p. 143.

3. Ibid.

4. Ibid., p. 144.

5. That did not stop Totter from sniping that he "thought about as much of Gofman's radiation and cancer calculations as he did of his heart-disease work." Gofman later shared the Stouffer Prize for outstanding contributions to research in arteriosclerosis.

6. Browne and Munroe, op. cit., pp. 146–149.

7. Ibid., p. 149.

8. On March 11, 1955, the *Las Vegas Review–Journal* carried a news item: "Use of taller towers from which atomic devices are detonated at the Nevada Test Site introduces an added angle of safety to residents living outside the confines of the Atomic Energy Commission's continental testing ground, nuclear scientists believe."

9. In 1977, ERDA would be taken over by the newly formed Department of Energy.

10. John Fuller, *The Day We Bombed Utah* (New York: New American Library, 1984), pp. 215–216.

11. James W. Linman, *Principles of Hematology* (New York: Macmillan, 1966), p. 336. The text reads:

    Other etiologic factors include *ionizing radiation*, which is clearly leukemogenic in experimental animals and appears to play a role in the pathogenesis of some cases of human leukemia. Strongest support for such a casual relationship is the unequivocal increase in the incidence of leukemia in survivors of the atomic bomb explosions in Nagasaki and Hiroshima, Japan. There is also a definite but less marked increase in the frequency of leukemia in patients of therapeutic doses of radioactive iodine. In addition, the incidence of leukemia in physicians (especially roentgenologists) is greater than in the general population."

12. J. L. Lyon, M. R. Klauber, J. W. Gardner, et al., "Childhood leukemias associated with

fallout from nuclear testing," *New England Journal of Medicine*, vol. 300, Feb. 22, 1979, pp. 397–402.

13. J. L. Lyon (Correspondence), *New England Journal of Medicine*, vol. 300, June 28, 1979, p. 1492.
14. Harold L. Beck and Philip W. Krey, "External Radiation Exposure of the Population of Utah From Nevada Weapons Tests," EML-401. Environmental Measurements Laboratory, Department of Energy, New York, NY 10014.
15. Harold L. Beck and Philip W. Krey "Radiation Exposure in Utah from Nevada Nuclear Tests," *Science*, vol. 220, April 1, 1983, pp. 18–24 (specifically p. 22). Also: Plutonium was now a permanent fixture in the soil of northern Nevada. See also: U.S. Energy Research and Development Administration, "Final Environmental Impact Statement, Nevada Test Site, Nye County, Nevada (Washington, D.C., ERDA, September 1977, pp. 2-88 to 2-91.)
16. Carl J. Johnson, M.D., "Cancer Incidence in an Area of Radioactive Fallout Downwind From the Nevada Test Site," *JAMA*, vol. 251, no. 2, Jan. 13, 1984.
17. "Announced United States Nuclear Tests," NVO-209 Rev. 3, January 1983, DOE.
18. Committee for the Compilation of Materials on Damage Caused by the Atomic Bombs in Hiroshima and Nagasaki, *Hiroshima and Nagasaki: The Physical, Medical, and Social Effects of the Atomic Bombings* (New York: Harper and Row, 1981), p. 30.
19. "New A-Bomb Studies Alter Radiation Estimates," *Science*, vol. 212, May 22, 1980, pp. 900–903.
20. Dean Kaul was with Science Applications, Inc., in Chicago; Jess Marcum was with Research and Development Associates in Santa Monica, California.
21. "New A-bomb Studies," op. cit., p. 901.
22. See Albert L. Lehninger, *Biochemistry: The Molecular Basis of Cell Structure and Function* (New York: Worth Publishers, Inc., 1970), pp. 251–252.
23. Belton A. Burrows and (by invitation) John C. Cardarelli, Eldon A. Boling, and F. M. Sinex, "The Medical Effects of Radioactive Fallout: Role of Stable End Products?" unpublished report. From: the Nuclear Medical Service, Boston Veterans Administration Medical Center; the Nuclear Medicine Section, Evans Memorial Department of Clinical Research and Department of Medicine, University Hospital, Boston University Medical Center; and Department of Biochemistry, Boston University School of Medicine, Boston. Supported by the Evans Medical Foundation, Inc., and the Research Service, Veterans Administration (p. 227).
24. Belton A. Burrows, et al., "The Variability in Fallout Radionuclide Distribution: Potential Radiochemical Damage," *Transactions of the American Clinical and Climatological Association*, vol. 94, 1982, p. 154–160.
25. "Veteran's groups fault cancer deaths study," *Houston Chronicle*, June 4, 1985.
26. Fuller, op. cit., pp. 220–223.
27. Ibid., pp. 229–230.
28. Ibid., p. 164.
29. Ibid., p. 137.

Epilogue: The Last Nuclear Weapon (pp. 391–397)

1. *Time*, May 6, 1985, pp. 74–77.
2. Also contributing: Paul Crutzen of the Max Planck Institute for Chemistry in Mainz, West Germany, and John Birks of the University of Colorado.
3. Carl Sagan, Paul R. Ehrlic, Donald Kennedy, Walter Orr Roberts, et al., *The Cold and the Dark: The World After Nuclear War* (New York: W. W. Norton, 1984).
4. *Los Angeles Examiner*, Mar. 12, 1955, and *Albuquerque Journal*, Mar. 22, 1955.
5. Abraham Kaplan, *The Conduct of Inquiry* San Francisco: Chandler Publishing Co., 1964), p. 218.

Index